MOUS
Essentials

ACCESS 2000

ROBERT FERRETT,
EASTERN MICHIGAN UNIVERSITY

JOHN PRESTON,
EASTERN MICHIGAN UNIVERSITY

SALLY PRESTON,
WASHTENAW COMMUNITY COLLEGE

Prentice
Hall

Upper Saddle River, New Jersey

MOUS Essentials: Access 2000

International Standard Book Number: 0-13-019103-5

Printed in the United States of America

03 02 01 00   4 3 2 1

Interpretation of the printing code: the rightmost double-digit number is the year of the book's printing; the rightmost single-digit number is the number of the book's printing. For example, a printing code of 00-1 shows that the first printing of the book occurred in 2000.

Library of Congress Cataloging-in-Publication Data

Ferrett, Robert.
    MOUS essentials. Access 2000 / Robert L. Ferrett. John Preston, Sally Preston.
        p. cm.
    ISBN 0-13-019103-5
    1. Electronic data processing personnel—Certification. 2. Microsoft software—Examinations—Study guides. 3. Microsoft Access. 4. Database management.
    I. Title: Access 2000. II. Preston, John M. III. Preston, Sally. IV. Title.

    QA76.3 .F47 2000
    005.75'65—dc21

                                                              00-037312

Editor-in-Chief:
Mickey Cox

Acquisitions Editor:
Lucinda Gatch

Assistant Editor:
Jennifer Stagman

Technical Editor:
Lisa Smith

Managing Editor:
Monica Stipanov

Editorial Assistant:
Mary Toepfer

Director of Strategic Marketing:
Nancy Evans

Marketing Manager:
Kris King

AVP/Director of Production & Manufacturing:
Michael Weinstein

Manager, Production:
Gail Steier de Acevedo

Project Manager:
Tim Tate

Manufacturing Buyer:
Natacha St. Hill Moore

Associate Director, Manufacturing:
Vincent Scelta

Book Design:
Louisa Klucznik/Graphic World Inc.

Cover Design:
Pisaza Design Studio, Ltd.

Full Service Composition:
Graphic World Inc.

About the Authors

Robert L. Ferrett is the Director of the Center for Instructional Computing at Eastern Michigan University. His center provides computer training and support to faculty at the university. He has authored or co-authored nearly 40 books on Access, PowerPoint, Excel, Publisher, Word Perfect, and Word, and was the editor of the *1994 ACM SIGUCCS Conference Proceedings*. He is a series editor for the *Learn 97* and *Learn 2000* books. He has been designing, developing, and delivering computer workshops for nearly two decades. He has a BA in Psychology, an MS in Geography, and an MS in Interdisciplinary Technology from Eastern Michigan University. He is ABD in the PhD program in Instructional Technology at Wayne State University.

John Preston is an Associate Professor at Eastern Michigan University in the College of Technology where he teaches microcomputer application courses at the undergraduate and graduate levels. He has been teaching, writing, and designing computer training courses since the advent of PCs, and has authored and co-authored more than three dozen books on Microsoft Word, Excel, Access, Publisher, and PowerPoint. He is a series editor for the Learn 97 and Learn 2000 books. He has received grants from the Detroit Edison Institute and the Department of Energy to develop Web sites for energy education and alternative fuels. He has also developed one of the first Internet-based microcomputer applications courses at an accredited university. He has a BS from the University of Michigan in Physics, Mathematics, and Education, and an MS from Eastern Michigan University in Physics Education. He is ABD in the PhD degree program in Instructional Technology at Wayne State University.

Sally Preston is President of Preston & Associates, a computer software training firm, where she utilizes her extensive business experience as a bank vice president in charge of branch operations along with her skills in training people on new computer systems. She provides corporate training through Preston & Associates and through the Institute for Workforce Development at Washtenaw Community College, where she also teaches computer courses part-time. She has co-authored more than 20 books on Access, Excel, PowerPoint, Publisher, Word Perfect, and Word, including the *Learn 97* and *Learn 2000* series, as well as the *Office 2000 Essentials* and *Access 2000 Essentials* books. She is a series editor for the *Learn 97* and *Learn 2000* books. She has an MBA from Eastern Michigan University.

Acknowledgments

We want to express our appreciation to the entire *MOUS Essentials 2000* team—other authors, editors, production staff, and those in marketing who start and end the process of developing and delivering a quality text. Special thanks go to those with whom we were most involved on a day-to-day basis, **Monica Stipanov, Lucinda Gatch,** and **Tim Tate**. They earned our respect and gratitude for the prompt, professional, and always pleasant way in which they managed the creative process.

Trademark Acknowledgments

All terms mentioned in this book that are known to be trademarks or service marks have been appropriately capitalized. Prentice Hall cannot attest to the accuracy of this information. Use of a term in this book should not be regarded as affecting the validity of any trademark or service mark.

Microsoft is a registered trademark of Microsoft Corporation in the United States and in other countries. Some of the product names and company names used in this book have been used for identification purposes only and may be trademarks or registered trademarks of their respective manufacturers and sellers.

Screens reproduced in the book were created using Collage Plus from Inner Media, Inc., Hollis, NH.

Contents at a Glance

	Introduction	ix
Project 1	Getting Started with Access 2000	1
Project 2	Creating a Database	23
Project 3	Entering and Editing Data	47
Project 4	Querying Your Database	69
Project 5	Creating and Using Forms	101
Project 6	Creating and Printing Reports	127
Project 7	Integrating Access with Other Sources of Data and the Internet	151
Project 8	Making Data Entry Easier and More Accurate	175
Project 9	Managing Data Using Smaller, Related Tables	203
Project 10	Adding Useful Features to Your Forms	233
Project 11	Special Purpose Reports and Advanced Report Procedures	265
Project 12	Automating Your Database with Macros	297
Project 13	Managing Your Databases with Special Action Queries and Database Utilities	323
Project 14	Using Access on the Web and Linking to Other Documents	347
Project 15	Designing a Complex Database	371
Project 16	Making the Input Form More User-Friendly	403
Project 17	Managing Changing Data	431
Project 18	Using Access Tools	457
Project 19	Analyzing and Reporting Data	481
Project 20	Filtering Data in a Linked Table Using Parameters and Form Filters	513
Project 21	Sharing a Database with Others	533
Appendix A	Using the MOUS PinPoint 2000 Training and Testing Software	551
Appendix B	Preparing for MOUS Certification	569
	Glossary	573
	Index	579

Table of Contents

Introduction   **ix**

Project 1   **Getting Started with Access 2000**   **1**

Lesson 1: Copying and Renaming a Database File 2
Lesson 2: Opening a Database and Using the Objects Bar 4
Lesson 3: Opening and Closing Database Objects 6
Lesson 4: Identifying Access Window Elements 8
Lesson 5: Using the Office Assistant and the What's This? Feature 11
Lesson 6: Closing a Database and Exiting Access 15

Project 2   **Creating a Database**   **23**

Lesson 1: Creating a New Database 24
Lesson 2: Creating a New Table Using Design View 26
Lesson 3: Saving a Table Design and Creating a Primary Key 31
Lesson 4: Adding Fields to a Table 33
Lesson 5: Editing Fields 34
Lesson 6: Changing Views and Moving Fields 37
Lesson 7: Deleting Fields 39

Project 3   **Entering and Editing Data**   **47**

Lesson 1: Adding Records 48
Lesson 2: Moving Among Records 50
Lesson 3: Editing Records 52
Lesson 4: Copying, Pasting, and Deleting Record 53
Lesson 5: Adjusting Column Widths and Hiding Columns 56
Lesson 6: Finding Records 58
Lesson 7: Sorting Records 60

Project 4   **Querying your Database**   **69**

Lesson 1: Creating a New Query 70
Lesson 2: Modifying and Sorting a Query 77
Lesson 3: Matching Criteria and Using Multiple Criteria 79
Lesson 4: Using Comparison Operators in a Query 83
Lesson 5: Using Wildcards in a Query 84
Lesson 6: Adding Calculated Fields to a Query 86
Lesson 7: Summarizing Data Using the Total Function 90
Lesson 8: Changing Query Properties 91

Project 5   **Creating and Using Forms**   **101**

Lesson 1: Creating an AutoForm 102
Lesson 2: Entering and Editing Data Using a Form 104
Lesson 3: Saving, Closing, and Opening a Form 106
Lesson 4: Creating a New Form in Design View 107
Lesson 5: Adding Fields to Forms 109
Lesson 6: Moving and Resizing Fields in Forms 111
Lesson 7: Adding a Form Header and Label 114

Project 6   **Creating and Printing Reports**   **127**

Lesson 1: Printing the Table Data 128
Lesson 2: Creating a Report Using the Report Wizard 131
Lesson 3: Printing and Renaming a Report 134
Lesson 4: Modifying a Report Design 136
Lesson 5: Saving the Report with a New Name 140
Lesson 6: Adding Labels to Reports 140

Project 7   **Integrating Access with Other Sources of Data and the Internet**   **151**

Lesson 1: Converting a Database from a Previous Version of Access 152

Lesson 2: Linking an Access Table to a Form Letter in Word 153

Lesson 3: Merging an Access Table with a Form Letter................................156

Lesson 4: Importing a Table from Excel 158

Lesson 5: Saving a Form as a Data Access Page 161

Lesson 6: Using a Browser to Interact with the Database 163

Project 8   **Making Data Entry Easier and More Accurate**   **175**

Lesson 1: Creating Consistent Data Formats 176

Lesson 2: Creating Conditional Formats for Positive, Negative, and Null Values 179

Lesson 3: Changing the Data Input Structure Using Input Masks....................181

Lesson 4: Restricting Entries Using Validation Criteria................................184

Lesson 5: Requiring Entry of Necessary Information 187

Lesson 6: Preventing Duplicate Entries Using Indexed Fields 189

Lesson 7: Creating a Lookup Column to Allow Selection from a List 190

Lesson 8: Entering a Default Value...194

Project 9   **Managing Data Using Smaller, Related Tables**   **203**

Lesson 1: Designing Related Tables to Hold Repetitive Data 204

Lesson 2: Defining the Relationship Between the Tables...............................206

Lesson 3: Printing Table Relationships and Displaying Subdatasheets in Tables 209

Lesson 4: Creating Queries That Draw Data from Both Tables......................212

Lesson 5: Automatically Filling in Data from One of the Joined Tables 216

Lesson 6: Updating Tables by Entering or Deleting Data in the Query 219

Lesson 7: Finding Duplicate Records in an Existing Table 221

Project 10   **Adding Useful Features to Your Forms**   **233**

Lesson 1: Adding Formats in the Form Design View......................................234

Lesson 2: Creating a List Box..238

Lesson 3: Looking Up Valid Entries from a Table or Query Using a Combo Box 241

Lesson 4: Using Information from a Query to Fill in Fields Automatically........243

Lesson 5: Entering the Current Date in a Field Automatically.........................245

Lesson 6: Adding the Current Date and Time to a Form Automatically 247

Lesson 7: Changing the Tab Order...249

Lesson 8: Creating Subforms 251

Lesson 9: Printing the Form for Filing Purpose 254

Project 11   **Special Purpose Reports and Advanced Report Procedures**   **265**

Lesson 1: Creating Labels for Mailings 266

Lesson 2: Creating Calculated Controls in a Report......................................271

Lesson 3: Grouping and Sorting Data in a Report 277

Lesson 4: Keeping Grouped Data Together in Reports 280

Lesson 5: Adding Calculated Controls to Group Headers and Footers 282

Lesson 6: Inserting a Graphic Background by Modifying Report Properties ...285

Project 12   **Automating Your Database with Macros**   **297**

Lesson 1: Creating a Macro to Close a Form 298

Lesson 2: Creating a Macro to Print a Report..299

Lesson 3: Using the Macro Builder to Open a Form in the Read Only Mode 302

Lesson 4: Running a Macro from a Button on a Form 305

Lesson 5: Creating a Switchboard Using the Switchboard Manager...............308

Lesson 6: Creating a Macro to Automatically Launch the Main Switchboard Form 314

Project 13   **Managing Your Databases with Special Action**
Queries and Database Utilities   323
    Lesson 1:   Making Backup Copies of Your Data Using the Export Feature 324
    Lesson 2:   Saving an Access 2000 Database as an Access 97 Database 328
    Lesson 3:   Compacting and Repairing Files for Efficient Storage 329
    Lesson 4:   Creating a Query that Creates an Archive Table 331
    Lesson 5:   Modifying the Archive Setup Query to Delete
               Records from a Table 333
    Lesson 6:   Creating a Query to Append Records to an Archive Table 335
    Lesson 7:   Creating a Macro to Run Two Queries and Attaching
               it to a Switchboard Button 336
    Lesson 8:   Transferring Access Data to Excel 338

Project 14   **Using Access on the Web and Linking**
to Other Documents   347
    Lesson 1:   Adding Hyperlinks from Forms to Word Documents 348
    Lesson 2:   Adding Hyperlinks from Forms to Excel Spreadsheets 354
    Lesson 3:   Saving Database Objects as Static HTML Pages 357
    Lesson 4:   Viewing HTML Pages on a Local Drive Using a Browser 360

Project 15   **Designing a Complex Database**   371
    Lesson 1:   Defining Desired Output 372
    Lesson 2:   Organizing the Fields into Several Tables 374
    Lesson 3:   Relating Tables Using One-to-One and
               One-to-Many Relationships 378
    Lesson 4:   Relating Two Tables Using a Third Table 382
    Lesson 5:   Refining the Design to Eliminate Redundant Fields 384
    Lesson 6:   Creating Queries and Testing the Design 388
    Lesson 7:   Documenting the Design 392

Project 16   **Making the Input Form More User-Friendly**   403
    Lesson 1:   Changing the Color of Text, Backgrounds,
               and Borders Using Buttons 404
    Lesson 2:   Using the Format Painter to Copy Formats Between Controls 407
    Lesson 3:   Formatting More Than One Control at a Time 409
    Lesson 4:   Changing Colors Using Properties 411
    Lesson 5:   Adding Status Bar Instructions in Form View 413
    Lesson 6:   Adding Customized ControlTips to Controls 416
    Lesson 7:   Creating a Custom Toolbar 418
    Lesson 8:   Using the Macro Builder to Attach a Macro to a Form 422

Project 17   **Managing Changing Data**   431
    Lesson 1:   Replacing Data in a Table Using an Update Query 432
    Lesson 2:   Replacing Portions of Fields Using an Update Query 436
    Lesson 3:   Updating Tables Using a Calculated Expression 439
    Lesson 4:   Updating a Table Based on Values in Another Table 442
    Lesson 5:   Updating Linked Tables Automatically 445

Project 18   **Using Access Tools**   457
    Lesson 1:   Customizing Data Entry Using AutoCorrect 458
    Lesson 2:   Analyzing a Table 461
    Lesson 3:   Analyzing Database Performance 465
    Lesson 4:   Updating the Database Using Name AutoCorrect 468
    Lesson 5:   Using Office Links to Analyze Data with Excel 471

Project 19   Analyzing and Reporting Data   481

Lesson 1:   Using the Totals Tool in a Query 482
Lesson 2:   Creating Crosstab Queries Based on Multiple Tables 485
Lesson 3:   Adding a Subform to an Existing Form 487
Lesson 4:   Inserting Subreports into Reports Using the
            Subform/Subreport Wizard 491
Lesson 5:   Creating Charts as Forms Using the Chart Wizard 496

**Project 20   Filtering Data in a Linked Table Using Parameters
and Form Filters   513**

Lesson 1:   Using Data in Another Database 514
Lesson 2:   Selecting Records Using Filter by Selection 518
Lesson 3:   Selecting Records Using Filter by Form 520
Lesson 4:   Using Parameters as Matching Criteria in a Query 522
Lesson 5:   Using Parameters with Comparison Operators in a Query 524
Lesson 6:   Using Parameters with Wildcards as Criteria in a Query 525

Project 21   Sharing a Database with Others   533

Lesson 1:   Assigning a Password to Your Database 534
Lesson 2:   Changing or Removing a Database Password 536
Lesson 3:   Encrypting a Database 537
Lesson 4:   Setting Startup Parameters 539
Lesson 5:   Setting Access Defaults 542

**Appendix A Using the MOUS PinPoint 2000 Training and
Testing Software   551**

            Introduction to PinPoint 2000 552
                The PinPoint 2000 Launcher 552
                Concurrency 552
                Trainer/Evaluation Pairs 552
                Tasks 552
                System Requirements 553
            Running PinPoint 2000 554
Lesson 1:   Installing the Launcher on Your Computer 554
Lesson 2:   Preparing to Run the PinPoint 2000 Launcher 556
Lesson 3:   Starting the PinPoint 2000 Launcher 556
Lesson 4:   Starting PinPoint 2000 Trainers and Evaluations 558
Lesson 5:   Running a Trainer 560
Lesson 6:   Running an Evaluation 563
Lesson 7:   Viewing Reports in the Launcher 564
Lesson 8:   Recovering from a Crash During a Trainer or Evaluation 566
Lesson 9:   Removing PinPoint 2000 567

Appendix B Preparing for MOUS Certification   569

            What This Book Offers 569
            Registering for and Taking the Exam 570

            Glossary   573

            Index   579

Introduction

Essentials courseware from Prentice Hall is anchored in the practical and professional needs of all types of students. Each title in the series reflects a "learning-by-doing" approach that encourages you to grasp application-related concepts as you expand your skills through hands-on tutorials.

The *MOUS Essentials* series has an added focus—preparing you for certification as a Microsoft Office User Specialist. The Specialist designation distinguishes you from your peers as knowledgeable in using Office products, which can also make you more competitive in the job market.

The Specialist program is available for many Office 2000 applications at both Core and Expert User levels. You can learn more about the Specialist program in Appendix B, "Preparing for MOUS Certification," and at the www.mous.net Web site.

How To Use this Book

You have selected a book providing a comprehensive approach to learning Access, with emphasis on skill sets designated by Microsoft as *Core* or *Expert* for purposes of certification as a Microsoft Office User Specialist. Please take a few moments to familiarize yourself with the icons used in this book and its conventions. If you have questions or comments, visit the related Prentice Hall *MOUS Essentials* Web site: www.prenhall.com/mousessentials.

Each *MOUS Essentials* text consists of modular lessons that are built around a series of numbered step-by-step procedures that are clear, concise, and easy to review. Brief explanations are provided at the start of each lesson and, as needed, between steps. Many lessons contain additional notes and tips.

Each *MOUS Essentials* book includes 15-21 projects, two appendixes and a glossary. Each project covers one area (or a few closely related areas) of application functionality, and is divided into lessons related to that topic. For example, a project on querying your database includes lessons on creating a query, modifying and sorting a query, using matching criteria, using comparison operators, using wildcards, creating a calculated field, using the Total function, and changing query properties. Each lesson presents a specific task or a closely related set of tasks in a manageable chunk that's easy to assimilate and retain.

Each element in a *MOUS Essentials* title is designed to maximize your learning experience. Here's a list of the *MOUS Essentials* project elements and a description of how each element can help you:

- **Required MOUS Objectives Table**   These tables are organized into three columns: Objectives, Required Activity for MOUS, and Exam Level. The Objectives column lists the general objectives of the project. The associated MOUS requirements for each objective are listed in the Required Activity for MOUS column. The particular exam levels of those activities—Core or Expert—are listed in the Exam Level column. Look over the objectives and MOUS requirements on the opening page of each project before you begin, and review them after completing the project to identify the main goals for each project.

- **Key Terms**   This book includes useful vocabulary words and definitions specific to the application. Key terms introduced in each project are listed in alphabetical order on the opening page of the project. These key terms then appear in bold italic within the text and are defined during their first occurrence in the project. Definitions of key terms are also included in the glossary.

- **Why Would I Do This?**   You are studying Access to accomplish useful tasks in the real world. This brief section at the beginning of each project tells you why these tasks or procedures are important. What can you do with the knowledge? How can these application features be applied to everyday tasks?

- **Microsoft Office Core Objective Icon**   This icon indicates that a lesson or exercise relates to a specific MOUS Core-level skill. MOUS skills may be covered by a whole lesson or perhaps just a single step within a lesson. They may also be covered in an end-of-project exercise.

- **Microsoft Office Expert Objective Icon**   This icon indicates that a lesson or exercise relates to a specific MOUS Expert-level skill. There may be a mix of Core and Expert objectives within a project. Also, some objectives cover topics included in the both Core and Expert required activities.

- **Lessons**   Most lessons contain one or more tasks that correspond to an objective or MOUS requirement, which are listed on the opening page of the project. A lesson consists of step-by-step tutorials, associated screen captures, and sidebar notes of the types described later.

- **Step-by-Step Tutorial**   The lessons consist of numbered, bolded, step-by-step instructions that show you how to perform the procedures in a clear, concise, and direct manner. These hands-on tutorials, which are the "essentials" of each project, let you "learn by doing." A short paragraph may appear after a step to clarify the results of the step. Screen captures are provided after key steps so that you can compare the results on your monitor. To review the lesson, you can easily scan the bold, numbered steps.

- **Exam Notes**   These sidebars provide information and insights on topics covered in MOUS exams. You can easily recognize them by their distinctive icon. It's well worth the effort to review these crucial notes again after completing a project.

- **Inside Stuff**   Inside Stuff comments provide extra tips, shortcuts, and alternative ways to complete a process, as well as special hints. You may safely ignore these for the moment to focus on the main task at hand, or you may pause to learn and appreciate these tidbits.

- **If You Have Problems...**   These short troubleshooting notes help you antici-pate or solve common problems quickly and effectively. Even if you don't encounter the problem at this time, do make a mental note of it so that you know where to look when you find yourself having difficulties.

- **Summary**   This section provides a brief recap of the activities learned in the project. The summary often includes suggestions for expanding your knowledge.

- **Checking Concepts and Terms**   This section offers optional true/false and multiple choice questions designed to check your comprehension and assess retention. If you need to refresh your memory, the relevant lesson number is provided after each question. For example, [L5] directs you to review Lesson 5 for the answer.

- **Skill Drill**   This section enables you to check your comprehension, evaluate your progress, and practice what you've learned. The exercises in this section mirror and reinforce what you have learned in each project. Generally, the Skill Drill exercises include step-by-step instructions.

- **Challenge**   This section provides exercises that expand on or relate to the skills practiced in the project. Each exercise provides a brief narrative introduction followed by instructions. Although the instructions are usually written in a step-by-step format, the are not as detailed as those in the Skill Drill section. Providing fewer specifics helps you learn to think on your own. A Core or Expert icon will indicate if a MOUS required activity is introduced in a Challenge exercise.

- **Discovery Zone**   These exercises require advanced knowledge of project topics or application of skills from multiple lessons. Additionally, these exercises might require you to research topics in Help or on the Web to complete them. This self-directed method of learning new skills emulates real-world experience. A Core or Expert icon will indicate if a MOUS required activity is introduced in a Discovery Zone exercise.

- **PinPoint Assessment**   Each project ends with a reminder to use the MOUS PinPoint training and testing software to supplement the projects in the book. The software aids you in your preparation for taking and passing the MOUS exams. A thorough explanation of how to use the PinPoint software is provided in Appendix A, "Using the MOUS PinPoint 2000 Training and Testing Software."

Typeface Conventions Used in this Book

We have used the following conventions throughout this book so that certain items stand out from the rest of the text:

- Key terms appear in **_bold italic_** the first time they are defined.
- Monospace type appears frequently and looks `like this`. It is used to indicate 1) text that you are instructed to key in, 2) text that appears on screen as warnings, confirmations, or general information, 3) the name of a file to be used in a lesson or exercise, and 4) text from a dialog box that is referenced within a sentence, when that sentence might appear awkward if the dialog box text were not set off.
- Hotkeys are indicated by underline. Hotkeys are the underlined letters in menus, toolbars, and dialog boxes that activate commands and options, and are a quick way to choose frequently used commands and options. Hot keys look like this: File, Save.

How To Use Student Data Files on the CD-ROM

The CD-ROM accompanying this book contains PinPoint as well as all the data files for you to use as you work through the step-by-step tutorials within projects and the Skill Drill, Challenge, and Discovery Zone exercises provided at the end of each project. The CD contains separate parallel folders for each project.

The names of the student data files correspond to the filenames called for in the textbook. Each filename includes initial letter(s) indicating the application, a dash, two digits indicating the project number, and two digits indicating the file number within the project. For example, the first file used in Access Project 2 is named AC-0201. The third file in Access Project 14 is named AC-1403. The Word document named `ac-stufiles.doc` on the companion Web site (www.prenhall.com/mousessentials) provides a complete listing of data files by project, including the corresponding names used to save each file.

Please refer to the Readme file on the CD for instructions on how to use the CD-ROM.

Supplements

Instuctors get extra support for this text in the following supplements:

- *Instructor's Resource CD-ROM*—The Instructor's Resource CD-ROM includes the entire Instructor's Manual for each application in Microsoft Word format and also contains screen shots that correspond to the solutions for the lessons in the book. A computerized testbank is included to create tests, maintain student records, and to provide online practice testing. Student data files and completed solution files are also on the CD-ROM. PowerPoint slides, which elaborate on each project, are also included.

- *Companion Web Site (www.prenhall.com/mousessentials)*—For both students and instructors, the companion Web site includes all the ancillary material to accompany the MOUS Essentials series. Students can also access the Interactive Study Guide online, allowing them to evaluate their understanding of the key concepts of each application with instant feedback on their results. Instructors will find the data and solution files, Instructor's Manual, and PowerPoint slides for each application.

Microsoft Access 2000 MOUS Core and Expert User Skills

Each MOUS exam involves a list of required tasks you may be asked to perform. This list of possible tasks is categorized by skill area. The following tables list the skill areas and where their required tasks can be found in this book. Table A contains the Core-level tasks. Table B contains the Expert-level tasks.

 **Table A   Microsoft Access 2000 Core MOUS Skills**

Skill Set	Required Activity for MOUS	Project	Lesson(s)	Page(s)
Planning and designing databases	Determine appropriate data inputs for your database	2 15	1 2	24 374
	Determine appropriate data outputs for your database	15	1	372
	Create table structure	2 15	2 2, 5	26 374, 384
	Establish table relationships	15	3	378
Working with Access				
	Use the Office Assistant	1	5	11
	Select an object using the Objects Bar	1	2-3	4, 6
	Print database objects (tables, forms, reports, queries)	4 6 10	8 1 9	91 128 254
	Navigate through records in a table, query, or form	3	2	50
	Create a database (using a Wizard or in Design View)	2	1, Discovery 1	24, 45
Building and modifying tables	Create tables by using the Table Wizard	2	Challenge 2	44
	Set primary keys	2	3	31
	Modify field properties	8	1-2, 5-6, 8	176,179, 187,189,194
	Use multiple data types	2	2, 5	26, 34
	Modify tables using Design View	2	4-7	33, 34, 37, 39
	Use the Lookup Wizard	8	7	190
	Use the Input Mask Wizard	8	3	181
Building and modifying forms	Create a Form with the Form Wizard	5 10	1 4	102 243
	Use the Control Toolbox to add controls	5	5, 7	109,114
	Modify format properties (font, style, font size, color, caption, etc.) of controls	5 16	6 1-4	111 404, 407, 409, 411
	Use form sections (headers, footers, detail)	5	7	114
	Use a Calculated Control on a form	10	Challenge 3	262

Core Level MOUS Skills (continued)

Skill Set	Required Activity for MOUS	Project	Lesson(s)	Page(s)
Viewing and organizing information	Use the Office Clipboard	3	4	53
	Display related records in a subdatasheet	9	3	209
	Create a calculated field	4	6	86
		11	4	280
	Create and modify a multi-table select query	9	4	212
		15	6	388
	Switch between object views	2	6	37
	Enter records using a datasheet	3	1	48
	Enter records using a form	5	2	104
	Delete records from a table	3	4	53
	Find a record	3	6	58
	Sort records	3	7	60
	Apply and remove filters (filter by selection)	20	2	518
	Apply and remove filters (filter by form)	20	3	520
	Specify criteria in a query	4	3-5	79, 83, 84
Defining relationships				
	Establish relationships	9	2	206
	Enforce referential integrity	9	2	206
Producing reports				
	Create a report with the Report Wizard	6	2	131
		11	1	266
	Print database objects (tables, forms, reports, queries)	6	3	134
	Move and resize a control	5	6	111
		6	4	136
	Modify format properties	6	4, 6	136, 140
	Use the Control Toolbox to add controls	6	6	140
	Use report sections (headers, footers, detail)	6	6	140
		11	5	282
	Use a Calculated Control in a report	11	2, 5	271, 282
Integrating with other applications	Import data to a new table	7	4	158
		20	1	514
	Save a table, query, form as a Web page	14	3	357
	Add hyperlinks	14	1	348
Using Access tools				
	Print database relationships	9	3	209
	Backup and restore a database	13	1	324
	Compact and repair a database	13	3	329

Table B   Microsoft Access 2000 Expert MOUS Skills

Skill Set	Required Activity for MOUS	Project	Lesson(s)	Page(s)
Building and modifying tables	Set validation text	8	4	184
	Define data validation criteria	8	4	184
	Modify an input mask	8	Discovery 1	201
	Create and modify Lookup Fields	8	7	190
	Optimize data type usage (double, long, int, byte, etc.)	8	Discovery 2	201
Building and modifying forms	Create a form in Design view	5	4	107
		12	Discovery 2	231
	Insert a graphic on a Form	10	Discovery 2	263
	Modify control properties	10	1-3	234, 238, 241
		16	1-4	404, 407 411, 418
	Customize form sections	10	5-7	245, 247, 249
	Modify form properties	10	1	234
		16	5-7	245, 247, 249
	Use the Subform Control and synchronize forms	10	8	251
		19	3	487
	Create a Switchboard	12	5	308
Refining queries	Apply Filters (filter by form and filter by selection) in a query's recordset	20	2-3	518, 520
	Create a totals query	19	1	482
		4	7	90
	Create a parameter query	20	4-6	522, 524, 525
	Specify criteria in multiple fields	4	3-4	79,83
	Modify query properties	4	6, 8, Discovery 2	86,91,99
	Create an action query (update, delete, insert)	13	4-6	331, 333, 335
		17	1-4	431, 432, 439, 442
	Optimize queries using indexes	8	6	189
	Specify join properties for relationships	15	3	378
Producing reports	Insert a graphic on a report	11	Discovery 2	294
	Modify report properties	11	6	285
	Create a report in Design view	6	Challenge 3	147
	Modify control properties	6	4, 6	136,140
	Set section properties	11	Discovery 2	294
	Use the Subreport Control and synchronize reports	19	4	491

Expert Level MOUS Skills (continued)

Skill Set	Required Activity for MOUS	Project	Lesson(s)	Page(s)
Defining relationships				
	Establish one-to-one relationships	15	3	378
	Establish many-to-many relationships	15	4	382
	Cascade Update and Cascade Delete options	17	5	445
Utilizing Web capabilities				
	Create hyperlinks	14	1-2	348, 354
	Use the Group and Sort features of data access pages	7	6	163
	Create a data access page	7	5	161
Using Access tools				
	Set and modify a database password	21	1-2	534, 536
	Set startup options	21	4-5	539, 542
	Use Add-Ins	18	2-3	461, 465
	Encrypt and decrypt a database	2	1 3	537
	Use simple replication (copy for a mobile user)	13	2	328
	Run macros using controls	12	4	305
	Create a macro using the Macro Builder	12	3	302
		16	8	422
	Convert database to a previous version	13	2	328
Data integration				
	Export database records to Excel	7	4	158
		13	8	338
		18	5	471
	Drag and Drop tables and queries to Excel	7	4	158
	Present information as a chart (MS Graph)	19	5	496
	Link to existing data	20	1	514

Project 1

Getting Started with Access 2000

Key terms introduced in this project include

- database
- Database window
- field
- launch
- object

- Office Assistant
- properties
- query
- read-only
- record

- ScreenTip
- table
- What's This?

Objectives	Required Activity for MOUS	Exam Level
➤ Copy and Rename a Database File		
➤ Open a Database and Use the Objects Bar	Select an Object using the Objects Bar	Core
➤ Open and Close Database Objects	Select an Object using the Objects Bar	Core
➤ Identify Access Window Elements		
➤ Use the Office Assistant and the What's This? Feature	Use the Office Assistant	Core
➤ Close a Database and Exit Access		

Why Would I Do This?

Microsoft Access is a ***database*** program that enables you to store, retrieve, analyze, and print information. Companies use databases for many purposes: for managing customer files, for tracking orders and inventories, and for marketing purposes. An individual might set up a database to track household expenses or manage a list of family, friends, and business addresses. Teachers often set up a database to track student grades and other class information. A database allows the user to access and manage thousands, even millions, of pieces of data in an organized, efficient, and accurate manner.

Tables are the foundation of the database, because they store the data in the database and provide the structure by which it is organized. Each table stores a set of related data. Tables are made up of ***records*** that include related information about one object, person, event, or transaction. Records are displayed in rows. Each category of information in a record is known as a ***field***. Fields are displayed in columns; the field name appears in the database table as a column heading. A table organizes data within a predefined structure.

To make the best use of your time, you will use the databases included with this book. In most instances, you will open and modify these sample files rather than create them from scratch. In this project, you learn how to copy and rename a database file. You also open a database and a database table in Access to get a taste of what databases look like. Finally, you learn how to get help and exit Access.

Lesson I: Copying and Renaming a Database File

A large number of database files are included on your student disk. Because you cannot open the databases on your CD-ROM and make changes, you will need to make copies of each file, place the files on another disk drive, and give each file a new name—one that describes the function of the database.

Because many computer labs do not allow you to save files to the hard drive, it is assumed that you will be saving the files to drive A:. If you are using a hard drive to save your files, you can use the Windows Explorer to copy each file from the CD-ROM to your folder on the hard drive, or you can install the files on your hard drive using the automatic installation program built into the CD-ROM. If you are using a floppy disk, it is important that you follow the procedure starting with Step 8 to remove the ***read-only*** status for each file you copy from the CD-ROM.

To Copy and Rename a Database File

1 **Click the Start button on the taskbar, and select <u>P</u>rograms from the Start menu.**

2 **Find Microsoft Access in the Programs menu, and click it with the left mouse button.**
This ***launches*** (runs) the Access program.

3 **Select <u>O</u>pen an existing file from the Microsoft Access dialog box, and click OK.**
The Open dialog box is displayed.

4 **Place the CD-ROM that came with this book in the proper drive, then click the list arrow at the right end of the Look in text box and select the CD-ROM that contains the project files.**

The files supplied with the book may be on a CD-ROM that would be on drive D: or E: (or some other higher letter), or they may have been placed on a network drive if you are using this book in a classroom setting.

5 **Open the Student folder on the CD-ROM that contains the AC-0101 database file.**

The project databases included with this book are displayed.

6 **Make sure you have an empty disk in drive A:. Click the right mouse button on the AC-0101 file.**

The file may appear as AC-0101.mdb. This is the same file, but your computer has had the file extensions turned on.

 Inside Stuff: Including the .mdb Extension When Renaming a File

The file names for your project files may show this database extension: .mdb. This indicates that if the Hide MS-DOS file extensions option has not been turned on in the Windows Explorer View, Options menu. If the extensions are showing, then the file extension (.mdb) must be included when renaming the file. In the previous example, the new file name would be Address Book.mdb. The rest of the procedure remains the same.

A shortcut menu is displayed (see Figure 1.1).

Figure 1.1
The shortcut menu is opened by clicking the right mouse button on the file name.

File destination

Shortcut menu

7 **Select Send To, and choose 3 1/2 Floppy (A).**

The AC-0101 file is copied to drive A:.

 If You Have Problems...

If you are saving your work to a hard drive, the procedure in steps 6 and 7 won't work. Instead, find the file on the CD-ROM and right-click it. Select Copy from the shortcut menu. Move to your folder on the hard drive, and right-click in an open area. Select Paste from the shortcut menu.

continues ▶

To Copy and Rename a Database File (continued)

8 **Select drive A: from the Look in box, then right-click AC-0101 and select Properties from the shortcut menu.**
Properties are the characteristics of a file or an object in a database. Notice that the Attributes at the bottom of the Properties dialog box say that the file is Read-only. This happens when you copy a file from a read-only storage medium, such as a CD-ROM. You need to change this to Archive before you can make changes to the database.

9 **Click the Archive check box to select it, and then click the Read-only check box to deselect it. Click OK.**

10 **Right-click AC-0101 and select Rename from the shortcut menu.**
The file name is highlighted.

11 **Change the name of the file to Address Book, then press ↵Enter.**
The name of the file is changed (see Figure 1.2). Leave the Open dialog box displayed to continue with the next lesson.

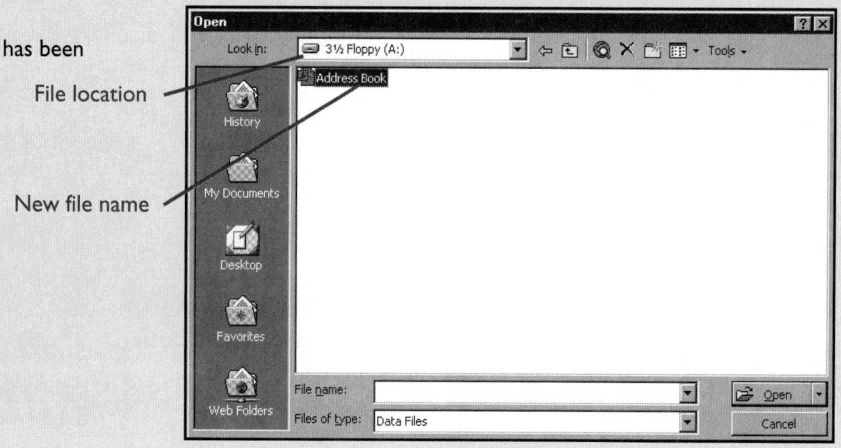

Figure 1.2
The file name has been changed.

File location

New file name

[Open dialog box showing Look in: 3½ Floppy (A:), with "Address Book" file displayed, File name and Files of type: Data Files fields, Open and Cancel buttons, and side panel with History, My Documents, Desktop, Favorites, Web Folders]

 Inside Stuff: **Differences Between Access and Other Office Applications**
In other Microsoft applications such as Word, Excel, or PowerPoint, you may have made copies of files by opening them in the application and then choosing the File menu's Save As option. The Access program uses files differently than most other programs. The Save As menu option saves only what is selected, not the whole database.

Lesson 2: Opening a Database and Using the Objects Bar

Typically, the first thing you do when you launch Access is open an existing database. You can open any database you have created, any database that is included as part of this course, or any database that was included in the Access program.

In this lesson, you open a sample database, called Address Book, which contains the same kind of information you would include in a personal address book. Access can easily manage a database that lists contact information about family members, friends, and associates.

To Open and Close a Database

❶ If the Access program is not already running from the previous lesson, launch Access, click OK, click the list arrow next to the Look in text box, and find the disk drive and folder that contain the Address Book database.

If you left the program running at the end of the previous lesson, the Address Book database will already appear in the Open dialog box.

❷ Click Address Book to select it, then click the Open button to open the database.

The sample Address Book database appears onscreen (see Figure 1.3). The **Database window** lists all the tables in the database. The various database **objects**, such as tables, forms, and reports, are displayed. Object buttons are displayed down the left side of the Database window. Action buttons (Open, Design, and New) are found in the Database window toolbar. You can create or open tables from this window. You can also change the design of existing tables.

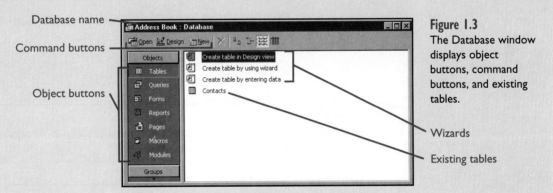

Database name
Command buttons
Object buttons
Wizards
Existing tables

Figure 1.3
The Database window displays object buttons, command buttons, and existing tables.

 Inside Stuff: Adding Wizards to Access

In Figure 1.3, there are three icons in addition to the table. These icons represent wizards that enable you to create tables using three different techniques. If they do not appear on your screen, it means that wizards have not been installed on your computer.

To install the wizards, put the original Office CD-ROM in your computer. Run the setup program, and select the Add or Remove Features option. Click to the left of the Microsoft Access for Windows option, click Typical Wizards, and select Run all from My Computer. Finally, click the Update Now button. You can also install another set of advanced wizards using this same procedure.

❸ Click the Queries object button.

The Queries object button is displayed on the left side of the window, along with the other object buttons. Clicking the button displays the only **query** in this database, named Indiana (see Figure 1.4). A query is used to sort, search, and limit the data to only those records that you need to examine.

continues ▶

To Open and Close a Database   (continued)

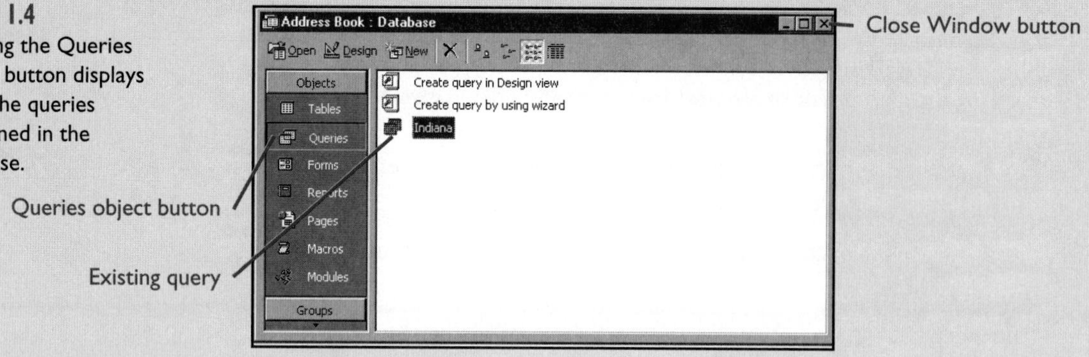

Figure 1.4
Clicking the Queries
object button displays
all of the queries
contained in the
database.

Queries object button

Existing query

Close Window button

④ **Close the database by clicking the Close Window button (the X icon)
on the upper-right corner of the Database window, as shown in Figure
1.4.**
Do not click the Close button on the right edge of the program title bar. The
Database window closes, but the Access program is still running.

If You Have Problems...
If you accidentally close the whole Access program, just launch Access again. You
will not lose any work by making this mistake.

Inside Stuff: Shortcuts to Opening a Database
You can open a database with the commands used in the preceding steps, but two
shortcut methods are also available. You can open a new database by clicking the
<u>N</u>ew button on the Database window toolbar, or by pressing Ctrl + N (holding
down Ctrl and pressing the letter N). You can open an existing database by clicking
the <u>O</u>pen button on the Database window toolbar or by pressing Ctrl + O (holding down Ctrl and pressing the letter O). If you prefer to use the menu, you can
select either <u>N</u>ew or <u>O</u>pen from the <u>F</u>ile menu to create a new database or open
an existing one.

Lesson 3: Opening and Closing Database Objects

Tables are the data storage areas of most databases. Access sets up tables as grids in which
you can enter, edit, and view all the related information in your database. When you want to
work with a table, you first open the database that contains the table, then open the table.

In this lesson, you open a table in the Address Book database that you opened and closed in
Lesson 2.

To Open and Close a Database Table

1 **Click the Open button on the toolbar.**
The Open dialog box is displayed. If necessary, change to the drive or folder containing the database files for this book.

2 **Click Address Book to select it, then click Open.**
Access opens the Address Book database and displays the Database window. It opens to the object window that was in use when the program was closed; in this case, the Queries window.

3 **Click the Tables object button, then select the Contacts table, if necessary (see Figure 1.5).**

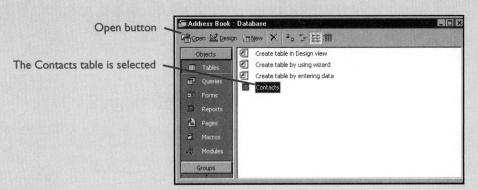

Open button

The Contacts table is selected

Figure 1.5
Click the Open button to open a table.

4 **Click the Open button on the Database window toolbar (refer to Figure 1.5).**
Access displays the Contacts table onscreen. Tables contain a grid of information made up of records and fields. Remember: a record is a row of related data, whereas a field is a column of the same type of data.

Depending on the size of the table window, you may not be able to see all the information in the database table. To display other information, you can scroll through the window using the horizontal and vertical scroll bars (see Figure 1.6).

Fields

Records

Figure 1.6
When you select the name of the table in the Database window and click Open, the table is displayed.

Horizontal scrollbar

Scroll arrow

continues ▶

To Open and Close a Database Table   (continued)

5 **Click the right scroll arrow on the horizontal scrollbar until you scroll to the last field.**
Access displays the information in the ZIP and Phone fields that you may not have been able to see.

6 **Click the left scroll arrow until you scroll back to the first field (First Name).**
You learn more about scrolling through records, entering new records, and sorting records in Project 3, "Entering and Editing Data."

7 **Click the Close button in the upper-right corner of the Contacts table.**
The Database window is still open. Keep the Address Book database open to use in the next lesson.

Lesson 4: Identifying Access Window Elements

The look of the Access window changes, depending on what you are doing with the program. You may recognize many parts of the Access screen as familiar parts of every Windows program—elements such as the Minimize, Maximize/Restore, and Close buttons, as well as the scrollbars.

Other parts of the Access screen offer features that can help you complete your work quickly and efficiently. For example, the menu bar and toolbar are convenient features that you will use in most of the projects in this book.

When you first launch Access, you see only a few items on the menu bar, and most of the buttons on the toolbar are dim (or grayed), which means that they are unavailable. When you open a database, additional menu items appear on the menu bar, and most of the toolbar buttons become available.

As you open and work with individual objects within the database, you see that menu options and toolbar buttons change in relation to the type of object you selected. This lesson explains what you can expect to see in most Access windows.

To Identify Access Window Elements

1 **Look at the elements that appear in the Access window when the Address Book database is open (see Figure 1.7).**
The Address Book Database window should be onscreen from the last lesson, and the Tables object button should be selected. Four key elements appear in the Access window: the title bar at the top of the window, the menu bar below the title bar, the toolbar under the menu bar, and the status bar at the bottom of the window.

Inside Stuff: **Information Available on the Title and Status Bars**
The title bar displays the program name. It also displays the database name and object type when the Database window is maximized. The status bar displays the name of the current object, if any, and several other types of information. The status bar information depends on where you are in the database. If the status bar is not displayed, you can turn it on by selecting Tools, Options from the menu, and then clicking the Status bar check box in the View tab.

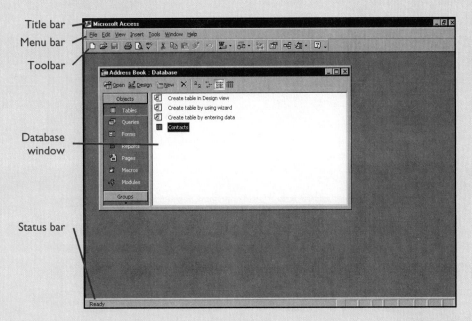

Figure 1.7
Four Access window elements support the Database window.

② **Open the File menu.**
Notice that the commands on this menu option deal with opening, closing, and working with databases. You can use Access menus the same way you use menus in all other Windows applications. If you choose a menu command followed by an ellipsis (...), Access leads you to a dialog box with additional options. Also notice that shortcut keys are displayed to the right of some menu commands, such as Open.

③ **Click on an unused part of the screen outside the File menu.**
This step closes the menu. You can also close the menu by pressing Esc or clicking the File menu option again.

④ **Move the mouse pointer over the button at the far left end of the toolbar.**
Access displays a *ScreenTip*, telling you the name of the button—in this case, New (see Figure 1.8).

Now take a look at how these elements change when a table is open.

⑤ **Select the Contacts table in the Database window, if necessary. Click the Open button.**
Access opens the table in Datasheet view. You could also double-click the table name to open it. The menu bar, toolbar, and status bar change to reflect the tasks you can perform with tables (see Figure 1.9).

continues ▶

To Identify Access Window Elements   (continued)

Figure 1.8
You can use the pointer to determine the name of a particular toolbar button.

Pointer

Button name

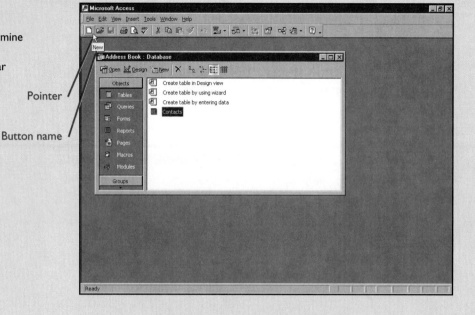

Figure 1.9
The Access window elements change to reflect table-specific tasks.

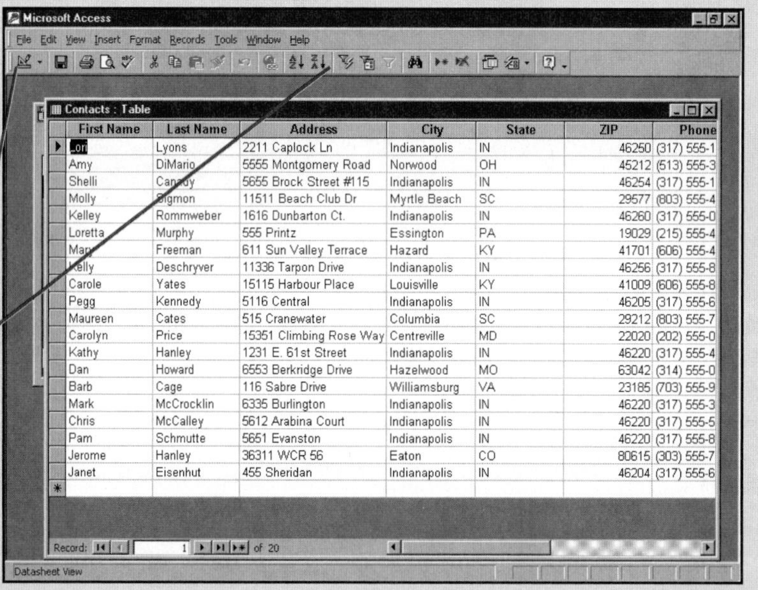

View button

Table Datasheet toolbar

6 **Move the mouse pointer over the View button at the far left of the toolbar.**

The View button may be used to display a list of available views for the table and to switch to another view of the table

7 **Move the pointer over other buttons in the toolbar.**

As you move the pointer over other buttons, read the name that Access provides to get an idea of what each button does. Keep the Contacts table and the Address Book database open for now. At the end of this project, you learn how to close these files and exit Access. In the next lesson, you learn how to use the Access Help system.

Lesson 5: Using the Office Assistant and the What's This? Feature

At some point, you may run into problems as you work with your computer and with software such as Access. If you need a quick solution to a problem with Access, you can use the program's Help feature. The Help system makes it easy to search for information on particular topics. In this lesson, you use the **Office Assistant**, an animated guide that helps you search for help, and the **What's This?** feature, which identifies the features of a single screen element.

The Office Assistant is a flexible help feature included with all Microsoft Office applications. It allows you to ask questions, search for terms, or look at context-sensitive tips.

To Get Help Using the Office Assistant

① **With the Address Book database and Contacts table still open from the preceding lesson, click Help in the menu bar.**

Access displays a drop-down menu of choices. Note that the first item in the Help menu uses the same icon as one of the buttons at the far right of the toolbar. Both of these options launch the Office Assistant. (You can also launch the Office Assistant by pressing F1 at any time.) If the Office Assistant already appears onscreen, all you have to do is click it once to open the Office Assistant window.

② **Click the Microsoft Access Help command.**

Access opens the Office Assistant, as shown in Figure 1.10. The exact location of the Office Assistant will vary.

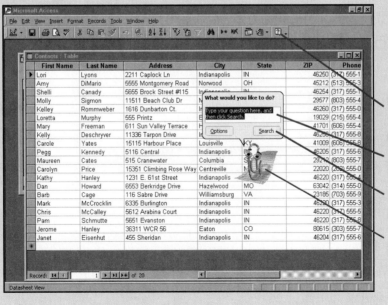

Figure 1.10
The Office Assistant can search for help information that you type as a question.

Microsoft Access Help button

Type the question here

Search button

Clippit

continues ▶

To Get Help Using the Office Assistant   (continued)

 If You Have Problems...
If you get the Microsoft Access Help window instead of the Office Assistant, close the window and choose Help, Show the Office Assistant from the menu.

The animated Office Assistant shown in the figure is called Clippit. You may see one of the other images available for the Office Assistant on your screen.

3 Type How can I get data from an Excel spreadsheet? **in the text box.**

4 Click the Search button.
The program searches through your sentence and looks for keywords. Topics related to your question are listed. If there are too many topics to fit in the window, you may need to click the See more button.

5 Select the topic Import or link data from a spreadsheet.
Access displays the Help window pertaining to this subject (see Figure 1.11). The Help window takes up the right third of the screen, whereas the Access window is reduced to the left two-thirds of the screen.

Figure 1.11
Access displays the Help topic Import or link data from a spreadsheet.

Help topic

Question to the Office Assistant

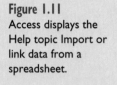
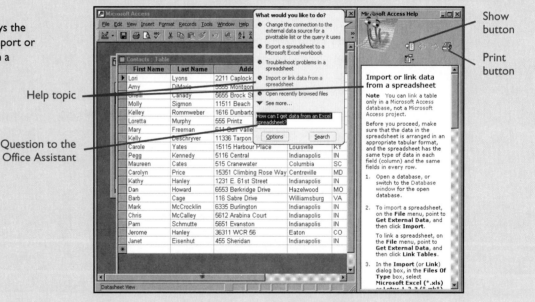

Show button

Print button

You can scroll down the Help window and read about importing and linking data from spreadsheets. You can click any of the words or phrases in blue to get more information. At the end of the Help window are the words "Additional Resources." You can click this text to see related topics, if any are available.

At the top of the Help window are a couple of useful buttons. The first is the Print button, which enables you to print the contents of the help window. The second is the Show button, which enables you to search for help in a more organized way.

6 Click the Show button at the top of the Help window.

Another Help panel takes up the middle third of the screen. Three tabs are available—Contents, Answer Wizard, and Index. You may have to click on the Help window to bring it in front of the Contacts table. You may also need to drag the Office Assistant out of the way.

7 Click the Index tab, if necessary. Type spreadsheet in the Type keywords text box, and click the Search button.

Two boxes show a list of keywords and a list of topics (see Figure 1.12). Information about the highlighted topic is shown in the Help window.

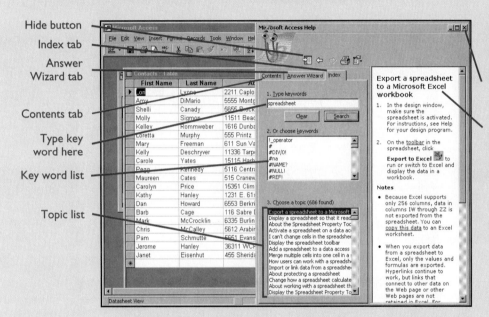

Hide button

Index tab

Answer
Wizard tab

Contents tab

Type key
word here

Key word list

Topic list

Figure 1.12
The index enables you to search key words.

Close button

Help on highlighted topic

8 Click the Hide button to close the center panel.

The middle panel is closed.

9 Click the Close button in the upper-right corner of the Help window.

The Help window closes and the Access window expands to fill the screen. The Office Assistant remains onscreen.

10 Right-click the Office Assistant, and select Hide from the shortcut menu.

This closes the Office Assistant.

 Inside Stuff: **Learn More Access from Help**

The topic that you found when asking your question says that you can import or link data from a spreadsheet. Before you even click this option, the Help menu has already helped you in two important ways. First, you now know that there is help available on the topic. Second, and much more importantly, you know that getting data from an outside source is called importing or linking. Using the Help menus frequently will help you develop your Access vocabulary, which will in turn assist you in finding help!

You can get helpful descriptions of different buttons, menu items, or screen objects by using the What's This? option. In the following section, you learn how to use this feature.

To Get Help Using the What's This? Feature

1 **Click Help in the menu bar.**

2 **Click the What's This? option.**
The pointer changes to include a large question mark.

3 **Click the Find button on the toolbar.**
A window opens that describes this feature in greater detail (see Figure 1.13).

Figure 1.13
The What's This? feature displays a description of the button or menu selection.

Find button

Button description

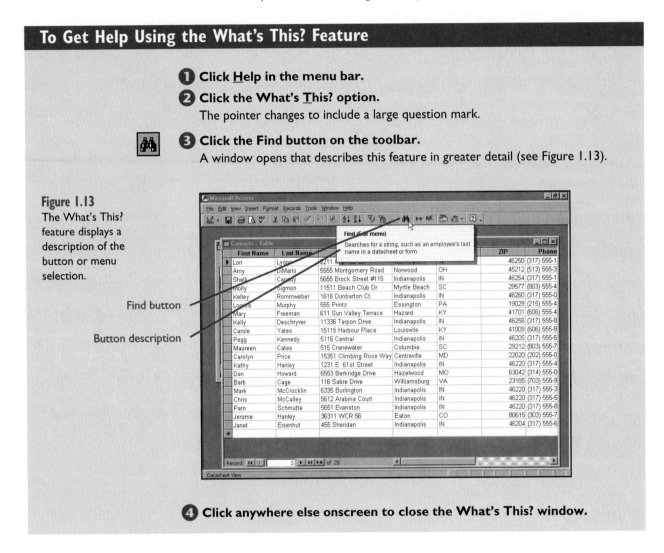

4 **Click anywhere else onscreen to close the What's This? window.**

 Inside Stuff: More Ways to Get Help
Several other options that exist for getting help are available from the Help menu. When you clicked the Show button, you used the Index to search through the Help topics alphabetically by key word. You can also search by topic using the list of topics in the Contents section, or use the Answer Wizard in much the same way as you use the Office Assistant.

Most of your questions about the basic operation of Access can be answered using one of these methods. If you do not find what you need in the help topics supplied with the program, you can select Office on the Web to connect to Microsoft's support Web page on the Internet.

X *If You Have Problems...*
To save space, some people delete help files or don't install them in the first place. If you get a message stating that the help file can't be found, use your original CD-ROM and add the help files.

Lesson 6: Closing a Database and Exiting Access

When you have finished working with Access, you should close all open database objects and exit the program. If you turn off your computer without closing Access or if you lose power, you will probably be able to retrieve most of your data, but some of the recent changes you have made, particularly changes to the structure of a form or report, may be lost. You should get in the habit of saving formatting changes and closing the database before you close Access.

In this project, you close the Address Book database, exit Access, and shut down your computer.

To Close a Database and Exit Access

1 **Click the Close button on the Contacts table window.**
This closes the Contacts table.

2 **Click the Close button on the Address Book Database window.**
This closes the Database window and leaves you with the main Access window open.

 Inside Stuff: **Access Prompts You to Save Your Work**
When you close a database object after having made structural changes, the program will automatically ask you if you want to save your work if you haven't already done so.

3 **Click the Close button for the Access program.**
Access is closed, and you are returned to the Windows desktop. Here you can launch another program or shut down Windows. If you want to work on the exercises at the end of the chapter at this time, do not close Access or exit Windows until you are done using the computer.

4 **To exit Windows and shut down the computer, click the Start button.**

5 **Click the Sh_ut Down option, then click _Yes to confirm that you want to shut down.**
Windows checks your programs and files to be sure that they are closed and saved properly, and then shuts down.

6 **When the message It is now safe to turn off your computer appears onscreen, turn off the power to the computer and monitor.**
Some computers with power management shut themselves down without this message appearing. If this is the case, you may have to turn off your monitor, but will not have to turn off the power to the computer.

If you are finished with your session at the computer, continue with the "Checking Concepts and Terms" section of this project.

Summary

In this project, you were introduced to some of the fundamental Access procedures and components. You learned how to copy a file from your CD-ROM to a floppy disk and then how to rename the file. You opened and closed a database, and a table in a database. You identified some of the Access window elements, and found out how to use various help features to identify everything from buttons to concepts and procedures. Finally, you exited Access and closed Windows.

You can extend your grasp of Access by looking a little more closely at the Access Database window. Move the pointer over buttons and look at the ScreenTips that pop up. See if you can guess what each of the buttons might do. Use What's This? on those that you can't figure out. Don't worry if some of the terms are unfamiliar to you—you'll be adding many of them to your Access repertoire throughout this book.

Checking Concepts and Terms

True/False

For each of the following, check *T* or *F* to indicate whether the statement is true or false.

__T __F **1.** If you click a file name in the Open dialog box using the right mouse button, a shortcut menu will give you the option to rename the file. [L1]

__T __F **2.** The toolbar and menu bar always remain the same in Access, no matter what window you are working in. [L4]

__T __F **3.** Access includes a feature that can answer questions written in the form of sentences. [L5]

__T __F **4.** It's OK to turn off the computer when Access is still running. [L6]

__T __F **5.** To close an Access database but leave the Access program running, click the Close button in the title bar of the Access window. [L6]

Multiple Choice

Circle the letter of the correct answer for each of the following questions.

1. Which of the following is not a type of object that you can display by clicking an object button in the Database window? [L2]

a. form

b. table

c. report

d. spreadsheet

2. How do you display the name of a toolbar button? [L4]

a. Place the mouse pointer on the button.

b. Click the toolbar button.

c. Point to the toolbar button and click the right mouse button.

d. Hold down Ctrl and click the toolbar button.

3. What does a table consist of? [L3]

    a. rows called records and columns called fields

    b. free-form information about each database item

    c. rows called fields and columns called records

    d. queries, reports, forms, and other database objects

4. What does it mean when the mouse pointer has a question mark attached to it? [L5]

    a. Access has detected an error and is helping you find it.

    b. You have activated the What's This? feature.

    c. The database you've loaded is missing a major component.

    d. You have activated a query or a module.

5. What happens when you close a database object after having made structural changes? [L6]

    a. The program will always ask you to save your changes.

    b. You lose your changes if you forgot to save them.

    c. The program will automatically ask you if you want to save your work if you have made unsaved structural changes.

    d. Nothing.

Screen ID

Label each element of the Access screen shown in Figure 1.14.

Figure 1.14

A. Table name

B. Open button

C. Table object button

D. ScreenTip

E. Title bar

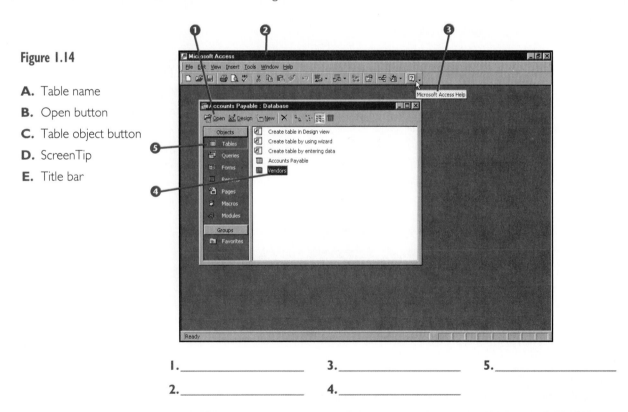

1._____   3._____   5._____

2._____   4._____

Skill Drill

Skill Drill exercises reinforce project skills. Each skill reinforced is the same, or nearly the same, as a skill presented in the project. Each exercise includes a brief narrative introduction, followed by detailed instructions in a step-by-step format.

1. Opening a Database on the CD-ROM

You have always been interested in a number of places and have wanted to visit them. One place that you've found interesting is Alaska. Over the years, you've gathered data on the state, such as pictures, geographic sites, and area attractions. You have finally decided to organize this data by using a database you were given that contains some geographic information. In this exercise you will open the database on the CD-ROM without copying it to another disk drive.

To examine a database of information on Alaska:

1. Launch Access.
2. From the Open dialog box, find the AC-0102 file.
3. Select **AC-0102** and click the <u>O</u>pen button. Notice that a dialog box appears, telling you that you can't make changes to this database because it is read-only.

4. Click OK to open the database in read-only mode.
5. Click the Close Database button in the Database window title bar to close the database. This will leave Access open for the next exercise.

2. Opening and Closing a Database Using the Menu

So far, you have opened your database files by using the dialog box that is displayed when you launch Access, and by clicking the Open button on the toolbar. Some people prefer to use menus. Try using the menus occasionally throughout this book. You may find that you actually prefer this method.

To open and close a database using the menus:

1. Choose <u>F</u>ile, <u>O</u>pen from the menu bar at the top of the screen. The same dialog box is displayed as the one you saw when you clicked the Open button in Lesson 3.
2. Find AC-0102 on the CD-ROM that contains the project files.
3. Make sure you have an empty disk in drive A:. Click the right mouse button on the AC-0102 file, select Send <u>T</u>o, and send the file to drive A:.
4. Move to drive A: and select AC-0102.

5. Right-click the file name and select Properties from the shortcut menu. Deselect <u>R</u>ead-only and select Ar<u>c</u>hive from the Attributes area. Click OK.
6. Right-click the file and select Rena<u>m</u>e from the shortcut menu.
7. Change the name of the file to **Alaska Information**, then click the <u>O</u>pen button to open the database.
8. Choose <u>F</u>ile, <u>C</u>lose from the menu.

3. Getting Help Using the Function Key

In Lesson 5 you learned how to click the Microsoft Access Help button and how to use the What's <u>T</u>his? option from the <u>H</u>elp menu. There is another way to get help, and with this method you don't need to take your hand away from the keyboard to grab the mouse. (Of course, you don't have to move your hand to get to the mouse if you are using a laptop computer either!)

To get help without moving your hands off the keyboard:

1. Open the **Alaska Information** file you created in the previous exercise. Use whichever method you prefer. If you didn't do the previous exercise, open the **Address Book** database you created in this project.
2. Press (F1) on the top row of your keyboard. Notice that the Office Assistant appears, ready for a search.

3. Ask the Office Assistant **How do I get online help?** and click the <u>S</u>earch button in the Office Assistant window.
4. Change online to **on line**. Do the help topics change, or is the Office Assistant "smart" enough to figure out what you mean either way?

5. Press ⎋Esc on the top row of your keyboard. Notice that the search box disappears, but the Office Assistant remains onscreen.

6. Close the Alaska Information or Address Book database, but leave Access open if you are going to continue the Challenge exercises. If not, click the Close button to close Access.

Challenge

Challenge exercises expand on or are somewhat related to skills practiced in the project. Each exercise provides a brief narrative introduction followed by instructions in a numbered step format that are not as detailed as those in the Skill Drill section.

I. Finding Out What's New in This Version of Access

If you have used earlier versions of Access, the following exercise will give you an idea of the improvements to this new version. If you have not used Access before, you will get an idea of some of the features of the database.

To find out what's new in Access:

I. Choose Help from the menu bar.

2. Click Microsoft Access Help.

3. Type How do I design a table? in the Office Assistant text box and click the Search button in the Office Assistant window.

4. Select What's new about Microsoft Access 2000 from the list of topics. Select Working with data and database design. Look at the somewhat limited results.

5. Click the Show button at the top of the Help window.

6. Click the Contents tab to view a list of contents.

7. Scroll down to Creating and Designing Tables in the Contents window and click the plus sign to the left of the topic. A list of related topics is displayed.

8. Scroll down to get an idea of the topics that are available. Click one that interests you and examine the Help window.

9. When you are through, click the Close button to close the Help window. Right-click the Office Assistant and choose Hide from the shortcut menu.

2. Taking Control of the Office Assistant

Do you like Clippit? He's kind of cute, at least the first few times you see him. However, some people get tired of "cute" rather quickly, and would just as soon use the menu or the Microsoft Access Help button to get help when needed, and not have a paper clip lurking on the edges of the screen. You have complete control over Clippit!

To take charge of Clippit:

I. Activate the Office Assistant, if necessary. Clippit should appear onscreen, although you might see another Office Assistant character.

2. Click the Office Assistant Options button and go to the Gallery tab in the Office Assistant dialog box. Scroll through the assistants using the Back and Next buttons to see if there is one you like better. If you find one, click OK to activate it. If there are no more assistants available, it means they were not installed.

3. Go back to the Office Assistant dialog box and select the Options tab. Browse through your options. There is one option that is very appealing if you find the Office Assistant annoying . . . the Use the Office Assistant check box at the top of the dialog box. If you turn off the check mark and click OK, Clippit will fade away, not to be seen again until you turn him back on using Help, Show the Office Assistant. Close the Office Assistant dialog box.

4. Choose Help, Hide the Office Assistant. This is another way to close the Office Assistant.

3. Using the Index to Find Help

To get to the Index feature, you will need to open the Help window. If the Office Assistant is active, you will need to type in a question, then choose an option to get to this window, even though the question may have nothing to do with what you want to look up. One way to get to the Index (and Contents) tab more quickly is to turn off the Office Assistant.

To use the Help index:

1. Click the Microsoft Access Help button on the toolbar, if necessary.

2. Click the Options button in the Office Assistant. Click the Use the Office Assistant check box to deselect it, then click OK.

3. Click the Microsoft Access Help button on the toolbar, and then click the Show button, if necessary.

4. Click the Index tab. Type **Table** in the Type keywords text box.

5. Click the Search button. In the Choose a topic area, click Ways to customize a table. Click the graphic to display the help screen. Click the numbers at the bottom left-hand corner of the screen and read the help information.

6. When you are finished, close the Ways to Customize a Table window.

7. Close the Help window, then close Access.

Discovery Zone

Discovery Zone exercises help you gain advanced knowledge of project topics and application of skills. These exercises focus on enhancing your problem-solving skills. Numbered steps are not provided, but you are given hints, reminders, screen shots, and references to help you reach your goal for each exercise.

I. Sending a Database to the Desktop as a Shortcut

In many cases, the same database will be used over and over. For example, an inventory database for a small business might be opened many times every day. The same machine, however, might also be used for typing letters, doing budgets and payroll, and any other office task that might come up. It is time-consuming to open Access, then search one or more hard disks or network drives for a database. It would be great if you could place an icon on your desktop with the name of the database underneath it. That way you could simply double-click the icon to launch Access and load the database at the same time.

Goal: Figure out how to create a shortcut on your computer desktop.

Use the program's Help features to figure out how to place a shortcut of the Alaska Information database on your desktop. Since this is your first Discovery Zone exercise, you'll get three hints:

> *Hint #1:* The procedure involves a shortcut menu.

> *Hint #2:* You have seen the procedure on the way to learning something else. If all else fails, review what you have done in this project that involves shortcut menus.

> *Hint #3:* If you are working in a lab with security software, this may not work. It will depend on the level of security set by the lab administrator.

2. Finding Online Help from Microsoft

Throughout this project you have used several methods of getting help. You have used the Office Assistant, the What's This? button, the Index, and the Contents tab. These are all help features included with the program. If you have access to the World Wide Web, you will be able to get much more detailed help.

Goal: Explore Microsoft's Office on the <u>W</u>eb online help.

Check with your instructor, and if it is possible, use the <u>H</u>elp menu to go to the online help available from Microsoft. Choose to look at Access help and see what help is available on designing tables. Explore the various categories of help available here.

PinPoint Assessment

You have completed the project and its associated lessons, and have had an opportunity to assess your skills through the end-of-project questions and exercises. Now use the PinPoint software Evaluation Mode to further assess your comprehension of the specific exam activities you have just learned. You can also use the PinPoint Trainer Mode and the Show Me tutorials to practice these exam activities.

Creating a Database

Key terms introduced in this project include

- data type
- Datasheet view
- Design view
- index
- Object Linking and Embedding (OLE)
- primary key
- relationship
- row selector
- undo

Objectives	Required Activity for MOUS	Exam Level
➤ Create a New Database	Create a database	Core
➤ Create a New Table Using Design View	Determine appropriate data inputs for your database; Create table structure; Use multiple data types	Core
➤ Save a Table Design and Create a Primary Key	Set primary keys	Core
➤ Add Fields to a Table	Modify tables using Design View	Core
➤ Edit Fields	Use multiple data types; Modify tables using Design View	Core
➤ Change Views and Move Fields	Modify tables using Design View; Switch between object Views	Core
➤ Delete Fields	Modify tables using Design View	Core
➤ Add a Table to an Existing Database Using a Wizard	Create tables by using the Table Wizard	Core
➤ Create a Database Using a Database Wizard	Create a database using a Wizard	Core

Why Would I Do This?

With Access, you can set up databases to perform a wide variety of tasks. For example, you may want a database (like the one you create in this project) to keep track of staff training for your company. Or perhaps you need a database to keep track of inventory, vendors, and customers for your business. You can set up various databases to store different sets of related information, and you can create as many databases as you need.

Each database consists of a number of related objects, each created to perform a specific task or function. Think of the database as the shell that holds together all the related objects. The fundamental type of object in an Access database is a table. You use tables to store data and organize the information into a usable structure. You can also create other objects, such as forms and queries. You learn about these other database objects later in this book.

Before you begin creating a database you need to know how you will use the information it contains. You should consider what kinds of information you might need to include in a printed report or what information you want to see if you looked at a single record on the screen. For example, if you want to print a list of employee names that is sorted by employee seniority, you need to have a field that indicates the date they were hired. Likewise, if you need to send letters to a group of customers, you might want to include a title field for Mr., Ms., Dr., etc. When you design a table, you need to determine what fields will be included. A field is a category of information, and it should be broken down to the smallest unit that you might need to sort on or search by.

The objects in an Access database interact with each other, and it is hard to design one part until you know what the other parts can do. You will have a much better idea of what fields to include in a table once you have learned how to create queries, forms, and reports.

In this project, you learn how to create a database and table from scratch. You also learn how to edit the basic structure of the table.

In most of this project, you work with the **Design view** of the table, which is the view used to create or change the structure of a table. Later, you look at the **Datasheet view**, which is the view used to look at the records in a table. Most objects in Access have these two views; one is used to design or edit the structure of the object, and the other is used to look at the records.

Lesson 1: Creating a New Database

It is important to understand the difference between the database and the tables within a database. Remember that the table is the object in which you actually store and define the structure for your data, and the database is the shell that houses all of the related tables and other objects. In your Address Book database in Project 1, "Getting Started with Access 2000," you had a table for contacts that included the name, address and phone numbers for people you need to contact. If these are business customers, you may need to keep track of calls that you make to your customers and record any action that is required. To do this you would create another table where you could record dates, events, and conversations. In your work, you may also need another table to keep track of the orders you place for your customers, so you can follow-up as appropriate. All of these tables would be part of the same database.

Before you can begin to create tables, however, you must first create the database. To do that, you open Access and direct the computer where you want the database to be stored and then give it a filename. This is the filename that will be used to whenever you want to open that particular database.

In this exercise, you create a new database to keep track of the personal computer software training received by your staff. You will start with a blank database, which gives you much more control over the database design.

To Create a New Database

❶ Launch Access, then click the Blank Access Database option and click OK.

Access displays the File New Database dialog box. Access suggests a default name (such as db1 or db2) for the new database; however, you can assign a more descriptive name here. You can also tell Access where you want to store the database.

❷ In the File name text box, type Training.

This is the name you want to use for the new database. After you name the database the first time, you won't have to do it again. As you add or edit records, Access updates the database automatically. As you add new objects, however, you must save each of them. When you add a table, for example, you must save it. Access then updates the database to incorporate this new database object.

❸ Click the list arrow next to the Save in box and select your drive or folder.

Access suggests a default drive and folder for saving the new database. Select drive A: unless otherwise instructed (see Figure 2.1).

Select a drive and folder

Create button

Type a filename

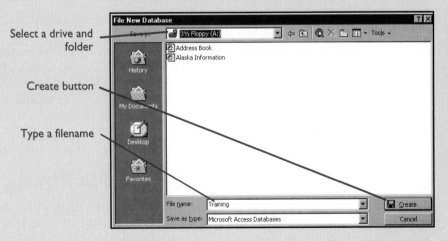

Figure 2.1
Use the File New Database dialog box to assign a name to your database.

❹ Click the Create button.

Access opens the Database window for your new database (see Figure 2.2). The name of the database is displayed in the title bar of the Database window. Notice that there are no tables shown because you have not created any database objects (yet). Three methods of creating new tables are displayed. Keep the Training database open to use in the next lesson. In that lesson, you learn how to add a new table to the database.

continues ▶

To Create a New Database (continued)

Figure 2.2
The name you assign to your database is displayed in the title bar of the Database window.

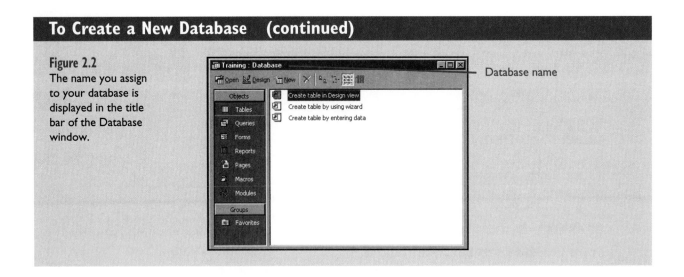

Database name

 Exam Note: **Other Ways to Create a New Database**
There is usually more than one way to perform each function in Access. For example, to create a new database, you can press Ctrl + N, select New from the File menu, or click the New button on the toolbar. You can also create databases using the Database Wizard that provides a choice of several pre-designed databases. Once you have selected the type of database you want to create, the wizard guides you through selecting the tables and fields you want to include.

 Inside Stuff: **Creating Smaller Databases**
It's tempting to create one big database that includes multiple tables to meet many different needs, but it is better idea to create smaller databases, each of which is dedicated to a particular function. Doing so makes managing and using each database much easier. You can relate these smaller databases to one another later, if necessary.

 ## Lesson 2: Creating a New Table Using Design View

After you create your database, you add tables to it to store your information. A database is built on one or more tables, each of which holds a distinct set of information. The table defines the structure of the data—what pieces of data you enter and in what order. You should spend some time planning the structure of your tables. How many fields do you need? What kind of data will be entered in each field? Who will be using the database and how will they be using the information? If necessary, you can add fields later if you need them, but it is very important to map out the fundamental structure of the tables before you get started.

Building a database without a plan is like building a house without a blueprint. The more work you invest in the initial design, the less time you spend in patchwork repairs later. Design your table structures first so that you can immediately put the database to work with confidence.

When you create a new table, you can add any fields you want. Remember that the table consists of records (one set of information—such as the name, address, and phone number for one person) and fields. Fields are the individual pieces of information that together make up a record; for example, an address is a field. To add a field, you type a field name and then select a ***data type***, which defines the kind of information you can enter into that field. Table 2.1 explains the various data types you can use. You can also type a description for the field and set field properties. You learn how to set field properties later in this book.

Table 2.1   *Data Types and What They Mean*

Data Type	Explanation
Text	The default data type. You can enter up to 255 numbers or letters.
Memo	This type of field is useful when you want to include sentences or paragraphs in the field—for example, a long product description. This type of field is not limited by size.
Number	You can enter only numbers.
Date/Time	You can enter only dates or times.
Currency	You can enter numbers. Access formats the entry as currency. If you type 12.5, for example, Access displays it as $12.50.
AutoNumber	Access enters a value that is incremented automatically with each new record added to a table.
Yes/No	A Yes/No field type limits your data to one of two conditions. You can enter only Yes or No, True or False, or On or Off. For example, you may have a Sent Christmas Card field in your address database that would work best as a Yes/No field.
OLE Object	You can insert ***Object Linking and Embedding (OLE)*** objects, which are things such as pictures or charts created in another application package.
Hyperlink	A field that allows you to enter active Web addresses.
Lookup Wizard	A field that looks up data from another source.

In this lesson, you create a table containing fields for first names, last names, and department names.

To Create a New Table Using Design View

❶ With the Tables object button selected in the Training Database window, click the *New* button.
Access displays the New Table dialog box (see Figure 2.3). You can choose between two views of a table, or you can launch one of three wizards to create a new table. The wizards walk you through the process of setting up a table, bringing in a table from another source, or linking the database to another data source without actually moving the information into the database.

 Exam Note: Another Way to Create a New Table
You could also create a new table by double-clicking Create table in the Design view option in the Database window.

continues ▶

To Create a New Table Using Design View   (continued)

Figure 2.3
The New Table dialog box offers five choices for creating a database.

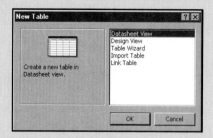

❷ Select Design View and click OK.
The table is displayed in Design view with the default name of Table1 (see Figure 2.4). This is the view that is used to design, edit, and create a table. The new table, as you can see, contains no fields. To add fields to the table, you must first enter the field names, data types, and descriptions. The blinking insertion point is displayed in the first row of the Field Name column. Here you type the first field name.

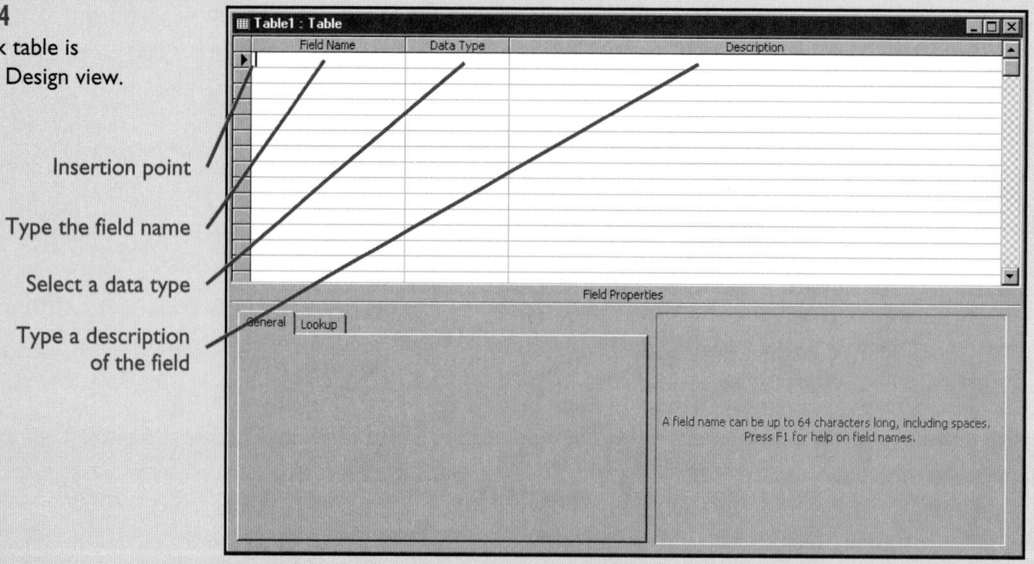

Figure 2.4
The blank table is shown in Design view.

Insertion point

Type the field name

Select a data type

Type a description of the field

A field name can be up to 64 characters long, including spaces. Press F1 for help on field names.

❸ Type First Name and press ⏎Enter.
Access enters the field name for the first field. In the lower half of the window, Access displays the field properties you can set (see Figure 2.5). Access moves the insertion point to the Data Type column so that you can choose the type of data you want the field to contain. The most common data type is Text, which is the default. You can click the down arrow (which is displayed when you move to the Data Type column) to display a drop-down list of data types. Text will be accepted for the First Name field.

❹ Press ⏎Enter.
The Text data type is accepted, and Access moves the insertion point to the Description column.

Text data is displayed

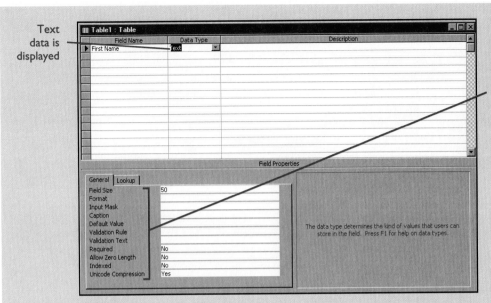

Figure 2.5
Each field has properties you can set.

Field properties for selected field

 Type First name of staff member **and press** ⏎Enter.

Access enters the field description and moves the insertion point to the next row (see Figure 2.6).

> ✍ **Exam Note: Where the Description Field is Shown**
> In Project 1, you looked at records in the Datasheet view of a table. If you include a description for a field, it is displayed in the status bar when you are in Datasheet view. When you place the insertion point in a field, the description information appears in the status bar, providing the user with a more complete description of the purpose of the field.

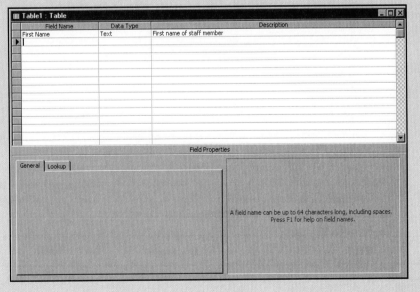

Figure 2.6
The first field of the Table1 table has been created.

6 **Type** Last Name **and press** ⏎Enter **twice.**

This enters the name for the field, accepts the default Text as the data type, and moves the insertion point to the Description column.

continues ▶

To Create a New Table Using Design View (continued)

7 **Type** Last name of staff member **and press** ⏎Enter.

As before, Access enters the field description for this second field and moves the insertion point to the next row so that you can add another field. Adding a field description is optional.

8 **Type** Department **and press** ⏎Enter **twice.**

Again, this step enters the field name, accepts Text as the data type, and moves the insertion point to the Description column.

9 **Type** Staff member's department **and press** ⏎Enter.

This is the description for the third field of your table (see Figure 2.7). By adding these fields to the database table, you have taken the first steps toward creating a database to track staff training. Keep both this table and the Training database open. You learn how to save the table in the next lesson.

Figure 2.7
The Design view of the database table contains three fields.

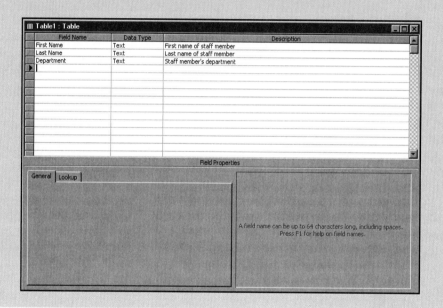

 Exam Note: **Rules for Field Names and Using Table Design View**

You can create a field name using up to 64 characters. Try to use names that are short but meaningful (long names often make the columns wider than the data). You can use any combination of letters, numbers, spaces, and characters, with a few exceptions: periods (.), exclamation points (!), single quotation marks ('), and brackets ([ ]) cannot appear anywhere in the name. Spaces are allowed, but not as the first character of the field name.

You can also use the Tab⇆ key in place of the ⏎Enter key when adding fields, accepting the displayed data types, and entering descriptions in the table Design view.

Lesson 3: Saving a Table Design and Creating a Primary Key

The first time you save the table's design, you are prompted to assign a name. After you save and name the table the first time, it takes only a moment to save changes whenever necessary. If you make changes to the design, such as adding new fields, you must save the changes.

In addition to saving new tables, you should assign or create a ***primary key*** field for each table in your database. Each record's primary key field contains a value that uniquely identifies it; no two records can have the same value in their primary key field. Examples of good primary key fields are things like Social Security Numbers, student ID numbers, or automobile part numbers. You can use this feature to your advantage when you need to establish a ***relationship*** between one table and another. A relationship connects a field in one table to a field in a second table. Relationships allow you to draw information from more than one table at a time for queries, forms or reports. This topic will be discussed in much more detail later in this book.

Assigning a primary key also ensures that you won't enter the same information for the primary key field more than once in a table (because it won't accept a duplicate entry). Because Access automatically builds an ***index*** for primary keys, it can easily search for information and sort tables based on the primary key field. An index is a location guide built by Access for all primary key fields that helps speed up searching and sorting for that field. Indexes can also be created for other fields, as long as they are not OLE or Memo fields.

If you have a unique field, such as an ID number in your table, you can use that as the primary key field. Or you can have Access create a simple counter field.

In this lesson, you have Access create a counter field to use as the primary key field because you cannot ensure that fields such as First Name, Last Name, and Department will contain unique information.

To Save a Table Design and Create a Primary Key

❶ In the `Training` database, with Table1 open, click the Save button on the toolbar.
You could also open the File menu and choose the Save command. The Save As dialog box opens and prompts you to name the table (see Figure 2.8). As you can see, the default name that Access provides doesn't tell you much, so you want to provide a more descriptive name.

Type the table name —

Figure 2.8
You name the table the first time you save it.

❷ Type `PC Software` and click OK.
This is the name you want to assign to the table for this example. The next time you see the list of tables in the Database window, this name will be displayed. The size of a table name isn't limited to eight characters. You can use up to 64 characters, including spaces.

continues ▶

To Save a Table Design and Create a Primary Key (continued)

Access displays a reminder that no primary key has been defined (see Figure 2.9). You are not required to use a primary key, but it is a good idea to include one. An easy way to create a primary key field is to have Access create a counter field that automatically assigns a different number to each record in your table.

Figure 2.9
A dialog box warns you that you haven't defined a primary key.

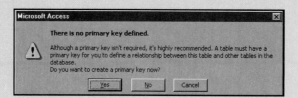

 Inside Stuff: Warning messages
If Help is active on your screen, then messages will display using the Office Assistant Help icon message box, rather than the generic one shown in Figure 2.9.

3 Click the Yes button.
Access saves the table and adds a counter field named ID with an AutoNumber data type. This is now the primary key field. Access automatically places sequential numbers in this field as you add new records. Your table Design view should look like the one shown in Figure 2.10. Notice the key symbol in the *row selector* for the ID field. The key indicates that the ID field is the primary key field for this table.

Figure 2.10
The key symbol indicates the field designated as the primary key.

Primary key field indicator

Primary key field

AutoNumber data type

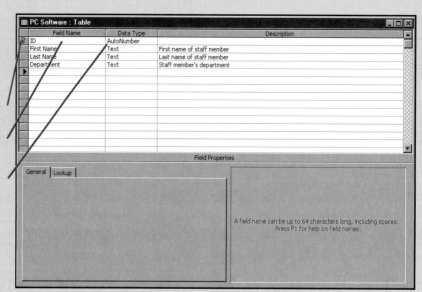

  Exam Note: Defining a New Primary Key
To make another field in the database the primary key, click the row selector for the field you want, then click the Primary Key button on the toolbar. You can also open the Edit menu and choose the Primary Key command. The primary key field is indicated by the key symbol in the row selector.

To save a table quickly, press Ctrl + S.

Lesson 4: Adding Fields to a Table

What happens if you decide you want to track more information than you included in your original PC Software table? You can add new fields to store this additional data. Keep in mind, however, that if you have already added records to the table, any new fields in those existing records will be empty until you type information into them. Other database objects such as queries, forms, or reports that are based on the table will not be automatically updated to include the new fields. Since you have not yet created any other database objects that use this table, this is a good time to make changes.

In this lesson, you add seven new fields to your PC Software table—one for training expense, one for employee number, one for employee's supervisor, and one each for four of the Microsoft Office software applications. Try adding these fields now.

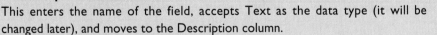

To Add Fields to a Table

1 **With the PC Software table of the Training database still displayed in Design view, position the insertion point in the Field Name box under Department.**

This is the row in which you want to enter the first new field name. The row selector arrow should be displayed next to this row (see Figure 2.11).

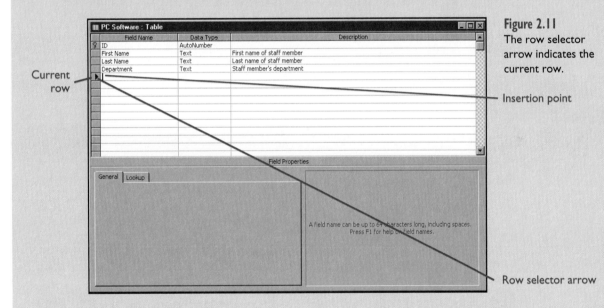

Figure 2.11
The row selector arrow indicates the current row.

2 **Click the Maximize button to maximize the Design view window. Type Cost and press ⏎Enter twice.**

This enters the name of the field, accepts Text as the data type (it will be changed later), and moves to the Description column.

3 **Type Cost of training and press ⏎Enter.**

This is the description for the new field. When you press ⏎Enter, Access moves the insertion point to the next row.

continues ▶

To Add Fields to a Table (continued)

④ Type Employee Number **and press** ⬇.

By pressing ⬇ you enter a name for this field, accept Text as the data type, and skip the Description column. Again, the insertion point is in position to add a new field to the table.

⑤ Type Supervisor **and press** ↵Enter **three times.**

Once again, you have added another new field to the table, accepting Text as the data type, skipping the description, and moving to the next row.

⑥ Type Word **and press** ↵Enter **three times. Use the same procedure to enter fields for** Excel, PowerPoint, **and** Access.

You have now added seven additional fields to the table. Your table should look similar to the one in Figure 2.12, although you may have to scroll up or down to see all of the fields.

Figure 2.12
You have added seven new fields to the PC Software table.

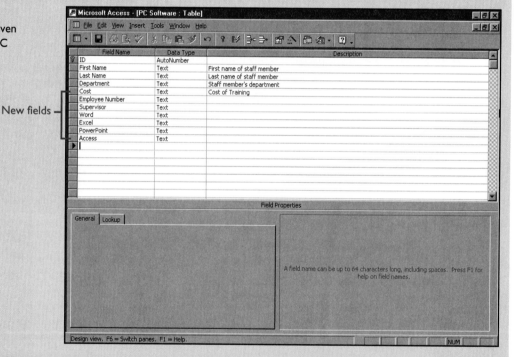

New fields

 ⑦ Click the Save button to save your work and leave both the PC Software table and the Training **database open.**

In the next lesson, you learn another way to alter the structure of your PC Software table.

 ## Lesson 5: Editing Fields

As you create your database, you may want to modify the structure. For example, you may want to change field names, choose a different data type, or edit (or add) descriptions. You make these changes in Design view. Remember, the Design view is used to design, edit, and change the structure of the table.

It is a simple and straight-forward process to make changes to a table prior to entering data. However, changes made after records have been entered may have an effect on the data. For example, if you type text into a field and then change that field to a Yes/No field, you might encounter problems. Access prompts you to let you know when changes in the field type are made and when they might result in a loss of data. Be sure that you want to make the change before you confirm it.

In this lesson, you edit the name of a field, add a description, and change a field type.

To Edit Fields

❶ In the Design view of the PC Software table, position the pointer on the word Cost (the fourth field name) and double-click.
This selects the word you want to change (see Figure 2.13). You may have to scroll up to see this field.

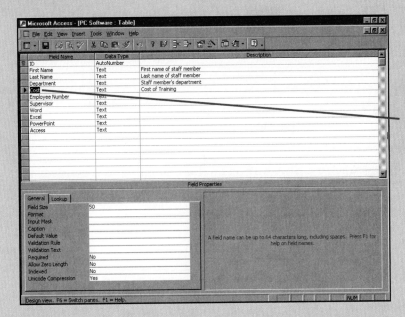

Figure 2.13
To change a field name, you first select it.

Selected field name

❷ Type Training Expense and press ⏎Enter.
The existing highlighted text is replaced with the new text and the insertion point moves to Data Type. Notice that a list arrow is displayed in the Data Type column, which indicates a list of data type options is available.

❸ Click the list arrow.
A list of choices is displayed (see Figure 2.14).

❹ Click Currency from the list.
You have changed the data type to a type that is more appropriate for the information in this field. All data in this field is now displayed with a dollar sign, commas (if needed), and two decimal places.

❺ Click in the Description column for the Supervisor field.
After moving the insertion point to this field, you can add a description.

continues ▶

To Edit Fields (continued)

Figure 2.14
When you click the list arrow in the Data Type column, a list of data types is displayed.

List of available data types —

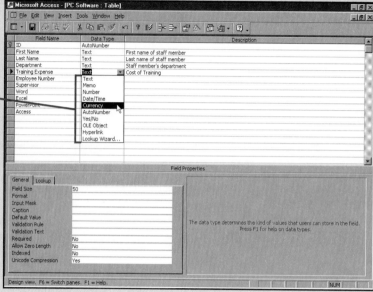

⑥ **Type** Reporting Supervisor.
The description that you enter provides information about what is stored in this field.

 ⑦ **Click the Save button on the toolbar to save your work.**
Leave both the PC Software table and the Training database open. In the next lesson, you learn how to move fields from one location in the table to another.

 Exam Note: Quicker Selection of Data Type
If you know the name of the data type you want to enter in the Data Type column, you don't have to use the mouse to open the drop-down list. Instead, if the Data Type is highlighted, you can type the first letter of the data type you want. Access fills in the rest of the characters for you. By typing the letter c, for example, Access fills in Currency.

 Inside Stuff: Changing a Field Name
If you already have data in your table, changing the field name or description will not have any effect on the data in the table. However, changing the field name may have an unintended effect on any forms, queries, or reports that refer to the field name. Depending on how your Access program is configured, you may have to manually change the references to reflect the new name. Otherwise, these database objects will no longer work as they did before.

Lesson 6: Changing Views and Moving Fields

In addition to changing the name and data type of a field, you can change the order in which the fields are displayed in your database. When you enter records, you may want the fields in a different order. In the PC Software table, for example, you may find it easier to enter the employee's number immediately after you enter the employee's name. You may also want to move the ID (counter) field to the end because you never have to enter anything in this field.

In this lesson, you first look at the table in Datasheet view—the view that displays the records. You then change back to Design view to rearrange the fields.

To Change Views and Move Fields

1 **Click the View button on the toolbar to change from Design view to Datasheet view.**

If you have not saved your changes to the table, Access will prompt you to save them. This changes your view of the database to Datasheet view (see Figure 2.15). Datasheet view is the view you use to enter, sort, and edit the records in the database.

X ***If You Have Problems...***
If the Table Design toolbar is not showing, choose <u>V</u>iew, <u>T</u>oolbars, Table Design from the menu.

Notice that the View button looks different in Datasheet view than it did in Design view. The icon on the View button indicates the view that will be displayed when you click it.

The datasheet you see is blank, except for the field names, because you haven't added any records yet. You learn how to work with records in Project 3. In Datasheet view, you cannot make any changes to the structure of the table, although you make changes to the layout of the datasheet such as changing the column widths.

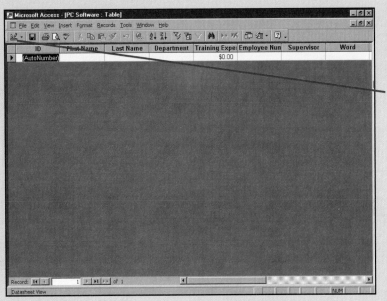

Figure 2.15
The PC Software table is displayed in Datasheet view.

View button icon changes

continues ▶

To Change Views and Move Fields (continued)

2 Click the View button on the toolbar.

This returns you to Design view so that you can make changes to the structure of the table.

3 Click the row selector for the Employee Number field.

This step selects the field you want to move. Notice that the entire row is highlighted (see Figure 2.16). You move this field so that it immediately follows the Last Name field.

Figure 2.16
Click the row selector to select the row you want to move.

Row selector for
Employee Number field

Selected row

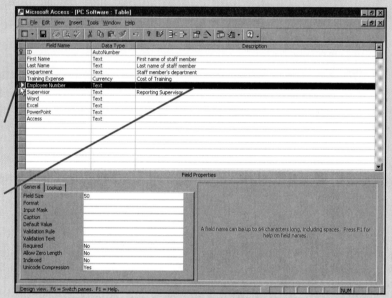

4 Click the row selector again and hold down the left mouse button. Drag the row to its new position under Last Name and release the mouse button.

As you drag, a small gray box is displayed under the mouse pointer, along with a horizontal line showing where the row will be placed. When you release the mouse button, Access places the row in its new spot (see Figure 2.17).

 If You Have Problems...

If the field that you move is displayed in the wrong place after you drag and drop it, don't worry. Just move the field again.

If you see a double-headed arrow as you try to position the mouse, the mouse pointer isn't in the correct spot. If the double-headed arrow is displayed, Access thinks that you want to resize the row height or the Design view window.

 If, when you drag, you accidentally resize rather than move your row, click the **Undo** button (or open the Edit menu and choose the Undo command). The Undo command reverses your most recent action, such as moving a row. Only the most recent change can be undone in Access.

If your window is too small to see all of the rows, maximize the window by clicking on the Maximize button in the upper-right corner of the table window.

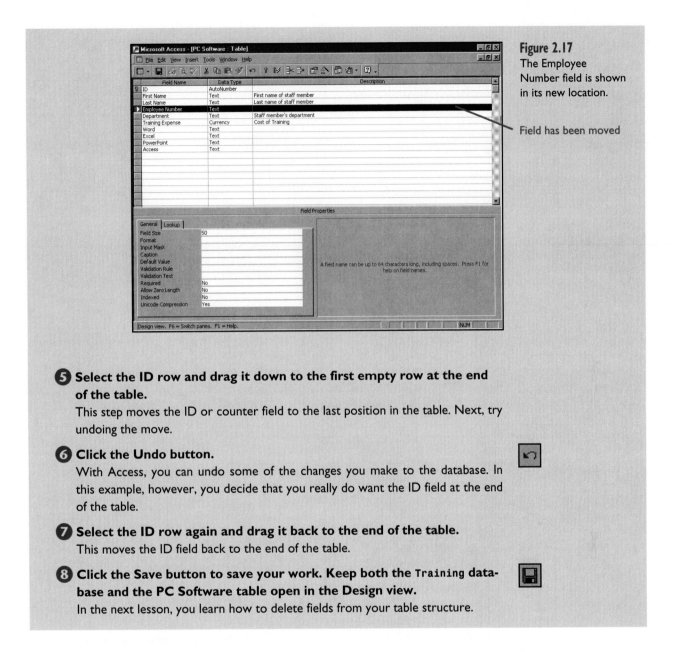

Figure 2.17
The Employee Number field is shown in its new location.

Field has been moved

5 **Select the ID row and drag it down to the first empty row at the end of the table.**
This step moves the ID or counter field to the last position in the table. Next, try undoing the move.

6 **Click the Undo button.**
With Access, you can undo some of the changes you make to the database. In this example, however, you decide that you really do want the ID field at the end of the table.

7 **Select the ID row again and drag it back to the end of the table.**
This moves the ID field back to the end of the table.

8 **Click the Save button to save your work. Keep both the `Training` database and the PC Software table open in the Design view.**
In the next lesson, you learn how to delete fields from your table structure.

Lesson 7: Deleting Fields

Another significant change that you can make to the structure of your PC Software table is to remove fields you no longer need. Suppose that you decide you don't really need a field for the supervisor. Instead of having it take up space in the table design, you can delete the field.

Keep in mind that deleting a field from your table also deletes all the data in that field. Because this may not be what you intended, Access displays a warning that asks you to confirm the change. Read the warning carefully and be sure that you want to delete all the data before you delete the field. If you have already created other database objects such as forms or reports that use this field, they will have to be revised individually.

To Delete a Field

1 **In the Design view of the PC Software table, click the row selector for the Supervisor field.**

The entire Supervisor row is highlighted, indicating that the Supervisor field is selected. This is the field you want to delete.

2 **Click the Delete Rows button to delete the row from your table.**

Access removes the field from the database table and deletes any data that was in that field (see Figure 2.18). If you had entered any data into this field in the Datasheet view, Access would warn you that the data would be lost.

Figure 2.18
The Supervisor field
has been deleted.

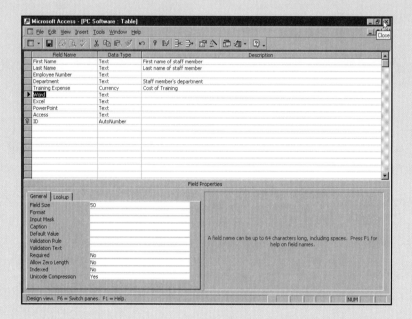

3 **Click the Save button to save your changes.**

4 **Close the PC Software table by clicking the Close Window button in the upper-right corner of the table window.**

5 **Close the Training database by clicking the Close Window button in the upper-right corner of the Database window.**

If you are finished with your session at the computer, click the Close button in the upper-right corner of the Access window. Otherwise, continue with the Checking Concepts and Terms section.

Summary

In this project you were introduced to some of the steps required to create a new database. You created your first database, table, and primary key field. You saved the new table, then went back into Design view to modify the structure of the table, adding, editing, moving, and deleting fields.

To expand your knowledge of the table creation process, use the Office Assistant to get more information about the different data types and in what situations each might be used. There is a link to a summary of field data types near the bottom of the Help window. Click this link (it will be in blue) and look at the expanded data type definitions. Click the double arrow to get more information on defining the Number data type.

Checking Concepts and Terms

True/False

For each of the following, check *T* or *F* to indicate whether the statement is true or false.

__T __F **1.** You can include only eight characters in a table name. [L3]

__T __F **2.** The most common data type is Text, the default. [L2]

__T __F **3.** In Design view, you can move a field by dragging the field name up or down the field list. [L6]

__T __F **4.** After you save your table structure, you cannot edit or change it. [L4]

__T __F **5.** When planning a database you should gather information from the people who will use the database to make sure you understand their needs. [L2]

Multiple Choice

Circle the letter of the correct answer for each of the following questions.

1. Which of the following is the way you can create a new database? [L1]

a. Open the <u>F</u>ile menu and choose the <u>N</u>ew command.

b. Click the New button on the toolbar.

c. Press Ctrl + N.

d. all of the above

2. Which of the following is not a valid data type? [L2]

a. Currency

b. Alpha-numeric

c. Yes/No

d. Text

3. How do you select a data type in the data type column of the table Design view? [L5]

a. Open the Edit menu and choose the type you want.

b. Click the Data Type button on the toolbar.

c. Select the data type from the list.

d. Press Ctrl + D.

4. What is the purpose of the Description entered in table Design view? [L2]

a. It appears in the status bar in the Datasheet view to provide the user with more information when entering data into a field.

b. It appears as a pop-up label when you place the mouse pointer on the field in Datasheet view.

c. Access uses it to automatically test the data you enter into the field.

d. It serves no purpose at all.

5. In Design view, how can you tell that a field is the primary key? [L3]

a. The status bar displays text when you have the field selected.

b. there is not way to tell in Design view.

c. The field name is underlined.

d. The key symbol appears on the row selector button next to the field name.

Screen ID

Label each element of the Access screen shown in Figure 2.19.

Figure 2.19

A. Primary key field

B. Used to set the primary key

C. Used to delete a field

D. Changes view to the datasheet

E. Row selector indicator

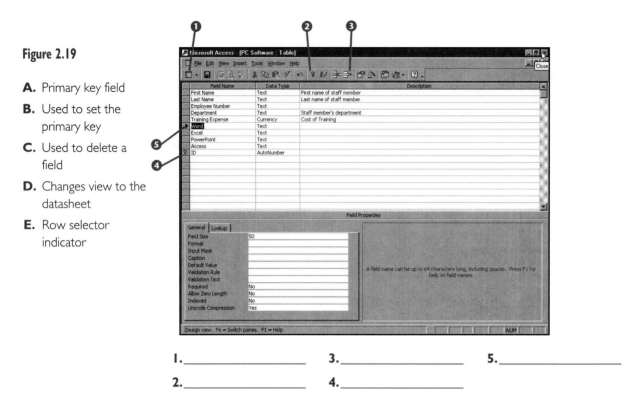

1._____   3._____   5._____

2._____   4._____

Skill Drill

Skill Drill exercises reinforce project skills. Each skill reinforced is the same, or nearly the same, as a skill presented in the project. Each exercise includes a brief narrative introduction, followed by detailed instructions in a step-by-step format.

1. Keeping Track of Your Books

You are an avid reader and have been collecting books for years. You've also borrowed books from the library over the years, and sometimes you can't remember whether you own the book or not. To make matters worse, you read a lot of mysteries, and you sometimes pick up a book and can't remember whether you've read it. You decide it is time to create a database to keep track of your collection.

To create a database to track your book collection:

1. Launch Access and select the <u>B</u>lank Database option.

2. Type `Book Collection` in the File <u>n</u>ame text box.

3. Use the Save <u>i</u>n box to select the drive or folder you want to save your database in, then click the <u>C</u>reate button.

4. Click the <u>N</u>ew button and select Design view to create a new table.

5. Type `Author Last Name` in the Field Name column, accept Text as the Data Type, and type `Last name of the author` in the Description column.

6. Add the following fields. Make them all Text fields, and add a short description in the Description column for each field.

   `Author First Name`

   `Book`

   `Year Published`

   `Type of Book`

   `Publisher`

   `Pages`

7. Click the Save button and name the table `Books`.

8. Click <u>Y</u>es to let Access insert a primary key field.

9. Close the table, but leave the database open if you intend to do the next exercise.

2. Adding and Deleting Fields

After some thought, you decide that you would like to make some changes to your database. You find that you are spending far more time typing than you'd like, and the name of the publisher is the culprit. You can't imagine a need for this field in the future, so you decide to eliminate it. You also realize that you should have included a field for whether or not you have read the book. Skip the first step if you did the previous exercise.

To modify the Books table:

1. Copy the **AC—201** database file from you CD-ROM to your A: drive or other location. Remove the read-only property and rename the database **Book Collection**. Open the database.

2. Make sure the Books table is highlighted and click the Design button to go to the Design view of your table.

3. Place the insertion point in the first empty row in the list of fields.

4. Type **Read?** in the Field Name column.

5. Choose Text as the Data Type.

6. Type **Enter Yes or No only!** in the Description column.

7. Click the row selector in the Publisher field.

8. Click the Delete Rows button to remove the field.

9. Click the Save button to save your changes to the structure of the table.

10. Leave the database open if you intend to do the next exercise.

3. Editing the Data Type of Fields and Moving Fields

Two of the fields, Pages and Year Published, are always going to be numbers. You decide that it would be a good idea to change the data type. You also decide that you'd like the Pages field to follow the Book field. Skip the first step if you did the previous exercise.

To change data type and rearrange fields in your Books table, follow these steps:

1. Copy the **AC—201** database file from you CD-ROM to your A: drive or other location. Remove the read-only property and rename the database **Book Collection**. Open the database.

2. Open the Books table in Design view and click the Data Type column of the Year Published field.

3. Click the list arrow to display the drop-down menu.

4. Select Number from the list.

5. Highlight the data type in the Data Type column of the Pages field.

6. Type the letter **n** to change the data type to Number.

7. Click the row selector of the Pages field.

8. Click the row selector of the Pages field again, and drag the field up between the Book field and the Year Published field.

9. Click the View button to change to Datasheet view.

10. Click <u>Y</u>es to save your changes.

11. Check the order of the fields in Datasheet view to make sure the Pages field is in the right place.

12. Close the database, and close Access unless you are going to continue with the Challenge section.

Challenge

Challenge exercises expand on or are somewhat related to skills practiced in the project. Each exercise provides a brief narrative introduction followed by instructions in a numbered step format that are not as detailed as those in the Skill Drill section.

I. Adding a Table to an Existing Database by Entering Data

There are several ways to create a table—one is by entering data that Access then inter-prets, assigning data types to each field. In this Challenge exercise, you use the datasheet view to add a table to your Alaska database. The table you will add contains information about the wildlife you have seen in your travels.

To create a table using the Datasheet view:

1. Copy AC-0202 to drive A: (or other location). Remove the read-only status and re-name the file Alaska Environment.

2. Open the Alaska Environment database and double-click on Create table by enter-ing data.

3. Enter Black Bear, Garbage Dump, Seward, 1995 in the first four fields.

4. Click the View button and name the table Wildlife I Have Seen. Do not add a pri-mary key field.

5. In Design view, name the four fields Animal, Surroundings, Location, and Year. Accept the data types that have been assigned by Access.

6. Close the table and save your changes.

7. Leave the database open if you intend to do the next exercise.

2. Adding a Table to an Existing Database Using a Wizard

So far you have used the Design view, and the Datasheet view to create new tables. You can also create a table by using the Table Wizard. Wizards are tools that guide you through the necessary steps in a procedure. In this Challenge exercise you learn how to create a table using the Table Wizard. You create a table for the plants you have seen in Alaska. Skip the first step if you did the previous exercise.

To create a table using the Table Wizard:

1. Copy AC-0202 to drive A: (or other location). Remove the read-only status and re-name the file Alaska Environment. Open the database.

2. Double-click on Create table by using wizard.

3. Choose the Personal category and select Plants from the Sample Tables options.

4. For fields, choose CommonName, Genus, Species, LightPreference, TempPreference, Photograph, and Notes.

5. Click next and name your table Plants I Have Seen. Have the program set a pri-mary key.

6. Do not relate this table to any other table.

7. Choose to enter information directly into the table.

8. Enter Dandelion as the Common Name and type Seen all over the place for the Notes field. Leave all of the other fields blank.

9. Close the table. Leave the database open if you intend to do the next exercise.

3. Adding a Primary Key Field to an Existing Table

If you do not set a primary key at the time you create a table, you can always return to the design of the table and add a primary key. Two of your three tables in the Alaska database now have primary key fields, and you have decided that maybe the third one should too.

To add a primary key to an existing table:

I. Copy `AC-0203` to drive A: (or other location). Remove the read-only status and re-name the file **Alaska Environment2**. Open the database.

2. Select the **Wildlife I Have Seen** table and open it in Design view.

3. Add a new field called **ID**.

4. Make the data type of new field AutoNumber.

5. Click the Primary Key button.

6. Close the table and save your changes. Close the database.

Discovery Zone

Discovery Zone exercises help you gain advanced knowledge of project topics and application of skills. These exercises focus on enhancing your problem-solving skills. Numbered steps are not provided, but you are given hints, reminders, screen shots, and references to help you reach your goal for each exercise.

I. Creating a Database Using a Database Wizard

Access has many wizard programs to help you create objects in a database. There are also ten database wizards that can be used to create an entire database structure. You can create the basic structure of a database using a wizard, and then modify it as needed to fit the specific needs of your particular database. These can also be useful tools for understanding how a database can be constructed and the various relationships that may need to be used between tables in a database.

Goal: Create a database using one of the database wizard programs.

Launch Access and choose the <u>A</u>ccess database wizards, pages, and projects option. Select the Contact Management database wizard, or another database of your choice. Follow the instructions in the wizard. Examine the list of the tables and the related lists of field names for each table.

The database will open to a Main Switchboard screen that enables you to move between the various objects created for the database. To view the Database window, click the maximize button on the small title bar for the database that is displayed in the lower left corner of the Access window. Examine the list of tables that have been created. Look at the design view of several of the tables to see how they have been structured. Close the database when you are done.

2. Creating a Primary Key Field Using More Than One Field

Sometimes you want to use information in your database for your primary key field, but no one field is unique. Access offers you a way to use more than one field in combination as a primary key.

Goal: Create a primary key using two fields.

Use the Geography table in the Alaska database (`AC-0202` file on your CD-ROM) and create a primary key field out of the Latitude and Longitude fields. (Two places might have the same latitude or the same longitude, but no two places have both the same latitude and longitude.)

Hint: Use Ctrl to select more than one field at a time.

PinPoint Assessment

You have completed the project and its associated lessons, and have had an opportunity to assess your skills through the end-of-project questions and exercises. Now use the PinPoint software Evaluation Mode to further assess your comprehension of the specific exam activities you have just learned. You can also use the PinPoint Trainer Mode and the Show Me tutorials to practice these exam activities.

Entering and Editing Data

Key terms introduced in this project include

- Clipboard
- current record indicator
- Office Clipboard
- pencil icon
- record selector

Objectives	Required Activity for MOUS	Exam Level
➤ Add Records	Enter records using a datasheet	Core
➤ Move Among Records	Navigate through records in a table, query, or form	Core
➤ Edit Records		
➤ Copy, Paste, and Delete Records	Delete records from a table	Core
	Use the Office Clipboard	Core
➤ Adjust Column Widths and Hide Columns		
➤ Find Records	Find a record	Core
➤ Sort Records	Sort records	Core

Why Would I Do This?

After you create a database and table, you want to be able to put them to work. For your database to be useful, you must enter data into the table (or tables). For example, you can keep track of your business contacts by entering their names, addresses, and phone numbers into the Contacts table of the Address Book database you worked with in Project 1. You can use the Training database you created in Project 2 to keep track of training that your staff receives by entering information about the employees and the training they have received into the PC Software table. As you learned in Project 1, the set of information you enter for each row in a table is called a record.

One reason databases are so useful is that you can work with and modify the records after you enter them. With a paper filing system, you have to cross out, erase, or redo a record when the information changes. With database software, however, you can easily change a record in the table to correct a mistake or to update the information. You can delete records you no longer need, search for a particular record, and sort the records—all quickly and with little effort on your part.

In this project, you learn how to add records to your table, move around in the records within the table, and edit and delete records. You also learn how to search for a particular record and sort your records according to a system that you determine.

 ## Lesson 1: Adding Records

As you recall from Project 2, you worked in Design view when you set up your table structure. In the Design view, you can make changes to the fields in the table—change a field name, add a field, change the data type, and so on. Then, when you want to work with the data in the table, you switch to the Datasheet view. In this view, you can add records or edit them.

In this lesson, you open a database, Employee Training, which matches your database and your PC Software table from Project 2. You switch to Datasheet view, then add records to the database.

To Add Records

① **Launch Access. Click OK to Open an existing file.**
Make sure you have a diskette in drive A.

② **Find the AC-0301 file on your CD-ROM, right-click on it, and send it to the floppy drive. Change the Look in box to drive A and rename the file Employee Training. Remove the read-only status and open the new database.**
The database should open to the Tables object button, and a PC Software table should be listed.

 ③ **Select the PC Software table, then click the Open button to open the PC Software table in the Datasheet view.**
In this project, you use the Training database you created in Project 2. (Employee Training is a completed version of your work from Project 2.) The PC Software table should be displayed onscreen in Datasheet view. Each of the field names appears along the top of the window. At this point, the table consists of only one row, and it is blank. The insertion point is in the first field, and you see a small, black arrow next to the first field. This arrow indicates the current record (see Figure 3.1).

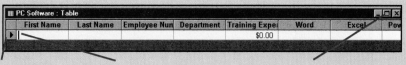

Current record indicator   Insertion point   Maximize button

Figure 3.1
A blank database table
in the Datasheet view.

4 **Maximize the Table window, then type Chantele and press ↵Enter.**
As you type, Access displays a pencil icon in the *record selector*, which is the gray area to the left of the record. You can also use Tab↔ in place of ↵Enter when adding data to the table.

5 **Type Auterman and press ↵Enter.**
The staff member's name is entered, and the insertion point moves to the Employee Number field.

6 **Type 77171 and press ↵Enter.**
The employee number is entered, and the insertion point moves to the Department field.

7 **Type Accounting and press ↵Enter.**
The department is entered, and the insertion point moves to the Training Expense field.

8 **Type 300.00 and press ↵Enter.**
The expense for training this employee is entered, and the insertion point moves to the four fields for specific software training. Notice that Access formats the entry as Currency because in Project 2 you set the data type to Currency after you created this field.

9 **Type 3 and press ↵Enter, 1 and press ↵Enter, 0 and press ↵Enter, and finally 1 and press ↵Enter.**
The level of classes taken are recorded in the four application fields. When you press ↵Enter the last time, Access moves to the counter field, which has a value that was automatically entered when you started entering data in the first field.

10 **Press ↵Enter.**
Access saves the record and moves to the next row so that you can add another record (see Figure 3.2). Whenever you move the insertion point off of the record you are editing, Access immediately saves the record or any changes you have made to the record.

11 **Use the following list of data to add more records to the database table. (The following items are separated by commas only to display the numerous fields in the space available. Do not type in the commas. Press ↵Enter instead of a comma.)**
Chang,Sun,66242,Human Resources,0,0,0,0,0

Jane,Boxer,66264,Purchasing,450,1,2,1,3

Robert,Bauer,66395,Purchasing,0,0,0,0,0

Peter,Bullard,66556,Marketing,250,1,1,3,0

James,Baird,66567,Accounting,300,0,3,1,1

Wayne,Wheaton,66564,Human Resources,150,1,0,2,0

Chris,Hart,77909,Marketing,250,1,0,3,1

continues ▶

To Add Records (continued)

Figure 3.2
Access moves to the next row so that you can add another record.

Record

New row

Insertion point

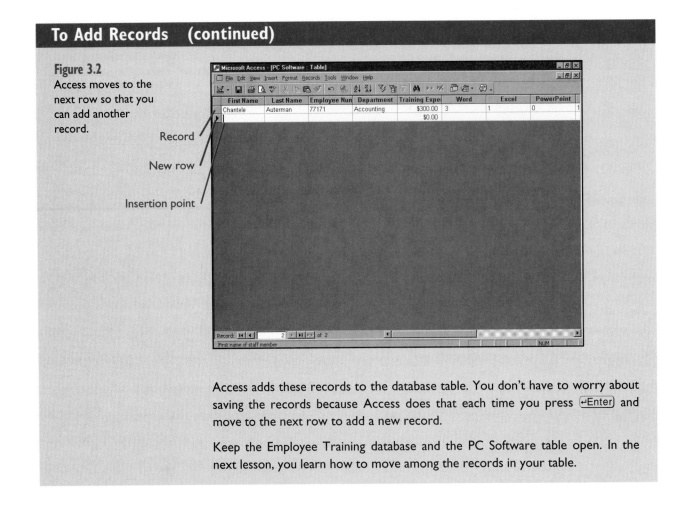

Access adds these records to the database table. You don't have to worry about saving the records because Access does that each time you press ↵Enter and move to the next row to add a new record.

Keep the Employee Training database and the PC Software table open. In the next lesson, you learn how to move among the records in your table.

 Exam Note: Automatic Dollar Signs
You do not need to enter the dollar sign ($) into a currency field. The program will add it automatically. Adding the dollar sign does not hurt anything, but if you learn to leave it off, it will save you a great deal of time if you have to enter large amounts of data. Also, if a dollar amount is a whole number, the program adds the .00 automatically, even if you don't type it.

 ## Lesson 2: Moving Among Records

You have seen that Access displays an arrow next to the current row. When you want to change a record, such as edit a field to change or update its information, you must first move to the row containing the record that you want to change. You can tell what row you have moved to because a black triangular arrow, called the **current record indicator**, is displayed in the record selector box to the left of the current row.

There are several ways to move among the records. If you can see the record you want on-screen, you can simply click it to select it. If you have numerous records in your table, how-ever, you may have to scroll through the records until you can get to the one you want.

To move to a particular record, you can use the vertical scrollbar, the navigation buttons dis-played along the bottom of the window, or the arrow keys on the keyboard. Table 3.1 ex-plains how these navigation buttons and keys work.

Table 3.1   Moving Among Records with the Navigation Buttons and Keys

To Move To	Buttons	Keyboard
First record in table	`◄│`	`Ctrl` + `Home`
Previous record in table	`◄`	`↑`
Next record in table	`►`	`↓`
Last record in table	`│►`	`Ctrl` + `End`
New record at end of table	`►*`	`Ctrl` + `+`

In this lesson, you move among the records in your table by using each of these navigational methods.

To Move Among Records

❶ With the PC Software table of the Employee Training database open, move the mouse pointer to the record selector at the left of the Wayne Wheaton record and click.
The record is selected (see Figure 3.3).

Record selector buttons

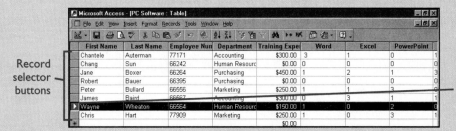

Figure 3.3
Clicking the button to the left of the record selects the record.

Current record indicator

❷ Press `Ctrl` + `Home`. The selection moves to the first record in the database table. Notice the current record indicator arrow to the left of the active record.

❸ Press `↓`.
This action selects the next record in the table.

❹ Click the Last Record navigation button.   `│►`
The selection moves to the last record in the table.

❺ Click the Previous Record button.   `◄`
The selection moves to the previous record in the table.

❻ Click the First Record button.   `◄│`
Access moves to the first record in the table.

❼ Click the New Record button.   `►*`
The selection moves to the next empty record.

Now that you know how to move among the records in your table, the next lesson shows you how to make changes to the records. Keep the Employee Training database and the PC Software table open as you continue with Lesson 3.

 If You Have Problems...

If you click on a particular field in the table and enter the editing mode, the Ctrl + Home and Ctrl + End commands only move to the beginning and end of the current field. These commands move to the beginning and end of the table if a field or record is selected.

Lesson 3: Editing Records

As you work with the data in the database table, you find that you need to make changes from time to time. In your PC Software table, for example, you might want to correct a typing mistake or change other information. You can update or correct any of the records in your table while you are in Datasheet view.

The first step in making any change is to move to the record that you want to change. Next, you have to move to the field that you want to edit. To move among fields using the mouse, click in the field to which you want to move. When you click, Access places the insertion point in the field and does not select the entire text in that field.

You can also use the keys listed in Table 3.2 to move among fields. When you use these keys, Access moves to the specified field and selects all the text in that field.

Table 3.2   Moving Among Fields with the Keyboard

To Move To	Press
Next field	Tab↹ or →
Previous field	⬆Shift + Tab↹ or ←
First field in record	Home
Last field in record	End

After you are in a field, you can add to the current entry, edit the current entry, or delete the current entry.

To Edit Records

❶ With the PC Software table of the Employee Training database open, click after the word Marketing in the Department column of the record for Peter Bullard.
The insertion point is placed where you are going to add new text in the field.

❷ Type a comma (,), press Spacebar, and type Corporate.
As you start typing, notice that Access displays a **pencil icon** in the record selector next to the record. This icon reminds you that you are editing the record and that the change has not yet been saved (see Figure 3.4).

❸ Press ⬆ twice.
This moves the selection to the Department field in the record for Jane Boxer. When you move the selection to another record, Access automatically updates the record you just changed.

The text in that field is selected, as shown in Figure 3.5. Anything you type replaces the selected text.

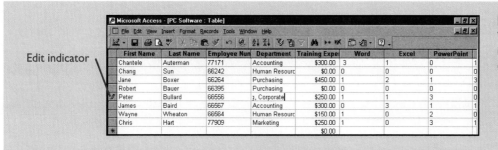

Figure 3.4
The pencil icon indicates that you are editing a field.

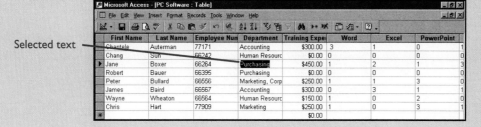

Figure 3.5
Typing replaces the selected text.

④ Type Accounting.
The record has been updated for this employee who has been transferred to a new department.

⑤ Press ⊡.
Access updates the record you just edited and moves to the next record.

Keep the Employee Training database and the PC Software table open. In Lesson 4, you learn how to insert new records and delete records you no longer need.

X **If You Have Problems...**
If you make a change by mistake, you can undo it by clicking the Undo button immediately, or by opening the Edit menu and choosing the Undo command. If you are editing a field and decide you don't want to save your edits, press Esc to ignore your changes.

 Exam Note: Saving a Record
You can also save the change you make by pressing ⧵Shift + ⏎Enter while still on the record you are editing. To save a record using the menu, choose the Records, Save Record command.

Lesson 4: Copying, Pasting, and Deleting Records

When you first create your database table, you can't always predict exactly what information you want to include in it. As you use your database, you will most likely want to insert new records or delete outdated records.

With Access, you don't have to add all your records at one time. You can add a new record to the end of the table at any time. If you want to enter several records containing similar data, you can enter the data for one record, copy that record, paste the new record into your table, and then edit the data in the new record.

You can delete a record by removing the row from the database table. In this lesson, you insert new records and delete a record you no longer need.

To Copy, Paste, and Delete Records

① **With the PC Software table of the Employee Training database open, click in the First Name field of the row marked by an asterisk (see Figure 3.6).**

The insertion point is placed in the First Name field of the empty record where the new record will be added. The current record indicator arrow replaces the asterisk.

Figure 3.6
New records are inserted at the bottom of the table.

Current record indicator

First Name	Last Name	Employee Num	Department	Training Expe	Word	Excel	PowerPoint
Chantele	Auterman	77171	Accounting	$300.00	3	1	0	1
Chang	Sun	66242	Human Resourc	$0.00	0	0	0	0
Jane	Boxer	66264	Accounting	$450.00	1	2	1	3
Robert	Bauer	66395	Purchasing	$0.00	0	0	0	0
Peter	Bullard	66556	Marketing, Corp	$250.00	1	1	3	0
James	Baird	66567	Accounting	$300.00	0	3	1	1
Wayne	Wheaton	66564	Human Resourc	$150.00	1	0	2	0
Chris	Hart	77909	Marketing	$250.00	1	0	3	1
				$0.00				

② **Type the following data for your new record, pressing ↵Enter after each entry. After the last entry, press ↵Enter twice.**

William, Evich, 77517, Accounting, 300, 0, 3, 0, 2

Access adds the new employee record to the end of your table. You can also copy a record and add the copy so that you have two versions of the same record. You may want to do this if you have two or more similar records. This might be appropriate for an inventory database of computer hardware. To practice this skill, you can copy the record you just added.

 Inside Stuff: **Change Key Field Values when Copying Files**
If you copy a record, you should make sure that fields that require unique values are changed before you try to select another record. The Employee Number field is not changed because it will be deleted in the next lesson but it is an example of the type of field that should be changed if you were using this method to reduce the amount of typing that you must do.

③ **To copy the new record, click the record selector next to the record for William Evich to select the entire row.**
Access highlights the entire row.

④ **Click the Copy button.**
Onscreen, you won't notice anything different after you copy the record. At this point, you have just placed a copy of the selected record into the *Clipboard*, which is a temporary storage location for whatever you have copied or cut from your document. Next, you paste the copy of the record into your table.

5 **Click the record selector to highlight the empty record at the end of the table, then click the Paste button.**

Access adds, or appends, the record to the end of the table. Now that you have the basic data in place, you can make any changes necessary for this particular record. Rather than edit this duplicate record just now, you are going to use it to practice deleting a record.

6 **Click the record selector next to the new record you just pasted.**

The record you just pasted is selected. You can also select the record by opening the Edit menu and choosing Select Record when the insertion point is anywhere in the record.

7 **Click the Delete Record button.**

Access wants to be sure that you intended to delete the record, so you are prompted to confirm the deletion (see Figure 3.7). You cannot undo record deletions, so make sure you have selected the correct record before you proceed.

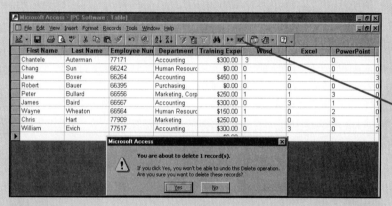

Figure 3.7
Access prompts you to confirm the deletion.

Delete Record button

8 **Click the Yes button.**

Access deletes the record and saves the changes to the database table.

Keep the PC Software table open. In Lesson 5, you learn how to change the width of the columns in your table and how to hide and unhide columns.

Inside stuff: Copying Fields; Deleting and Adding Records

In addition to copying entire records, you can also copy the contents of a field from one record and paste it into another. If you want to enter another record for someone from the Marketing Department, for example, you can copy Marketing from the Department field in another record and paste it in the new record.

To copy an entry, move to the appropriate field and select the text you want to copy by dragging across it. Then click the Copy button. Select the location where you want to place the copied text and click the Paste button. Access pastes the selected text into the selected location.

You can also use shortcut keys: Ctrl + C for Copy and Ctrl + V for Paste.

To delete a record, you can select the record and press Del or place the insertion point anywhere in the record and choose Delete Record from the Edit menu.

To add a new record you can click the New Record button on the toolbar.

Inside Stuff: **Using the Office Clipboard**

If you have several items that you want to copy and then past into another location or into another Office program, you can save time by using the **Office Clipboard**. The Office clipboard is similar to the Windows clipboard but it can hold up to 12 items from any of the Office programs. To copy several items into the Office clipboard, use the <u>V</u>iew, <u>T</u>oolbars, Clipboard commands to display the Clipboard toolbar. Select the item, then click the copy button on the Clipboard toolbar. Select and copy several items to the Office clipboard. To paste from the clipboard, place the insertion point then click on the item you want to paste on the Clipboard toolbar. To learn more about the Office clipboard, search the <u>H</u>elp menu for help on "Collect and paste multiple items."

Lesson 5: Adjusting Column Widths and Hiding Columns

By default, Access displays all the columns in your table with the same width. You can change the column width, making some columns wider so that you can see the entire entry, and making other columns narrower so that they don't take up as much space. The easiest way to adjust the column width is to use the mouse, but they can also be adjusted using F<u>o</u>rmat, <u>C</u>olumn Width from the menu.

In addition to changing the column width, you can also hide columns that you don't want displayed, such as the ID field, which is automatically updated by the program. Adjusting the column width does not change the field size.

To Adjust Column Widths and Hide Columns

❶ **With the PC Software table of the Employee Training database open, place the mouse pointer on the line between the First Name and Last Name field selectors.**

The mouse pointer changes to a thick vertical bar with arrows on either side (see Figure 3.8). This pointer indicates that you can now move the column borders.

Figure 3.8
The appearance of the mouse pointer changes when you are preparing to resize a column.

Mouse pointer

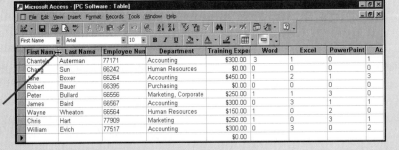

❷ **Press and hold down the mouse button and drag to the left until you think the column is narrow enough and you can still see all the entries in the column. Release the mouse button.**

The new width is set. As you drag to the left, you make the column narrower. Notice that you can see the border of the column move as you drag. Don't worry if you cover up part of the field name.

If You Have Problems...

If you don't see the thick bar with the arrows, you don't have the pointer in the correct spot. Be sure that you are within the gray area of the field selectors and that your pointer is sitting directly on the border separating the two columns.

3 **Move the mouse pointer to the border between the Department and Training Expense columns and then double-click the mouse button.**

Double-clicking is a shortcut method that automatically adjusts the column to fit the longest entry currently displayed onscreen in that column. This often creates a problem when you use long field names, because double-clicking widens the column to show the whole field name if it is the longest entry in the column.

4 **Use the horizontal scrollbar to view the Word, Excel, PowerPoint, and Access fields. Drag across the field selectors for the Word, Excel, PowerPoint, and Access fields.**

When you drag across the headings, you select all four columns (see Figure 3.9). You can then adjust the width of the six columns at one time.

Employee Num	Department	Training Expe	Word	Excel	PowerPoint	Access	ID
77171	Accounting	$300.00	3	1	0	1	
66242	Human Resources	$0.00	0	0	0	0	
66264	Accounting	$450.00	1	2	1	3	
66395	Purchasing	$0.00	0	0	0	0	
66556	Marketing, Corporate	$250.00	1	1	3	0	
66567	Accounting	$300.00	0	3	1	1	
66564	Human Resources	$150.00	1	0	2	0	
77909	Marketing	$250.00	1	0	3	1	
77517	Accounting	$300.00	0	3	0	2	
*		$0.00					(AutoNumbe

Figure 3.9
You can select several columns and resize them together.

5 **Drag the border on the right of the PowerPoint column so that it is just big enough to display the PowerPoint field name.**

Notice that dragging one of the borders resizes all six columns.

6 **Click anywhere in the table to deselect the columns.**

7 **Scroll to the left and click in the field selector of the Employee Number field.**

Now that you have selected this column, you can practice hiding it.

8 **Open the Format menu and choose the Hide Columns command.**

Access hides the column you selected.

9 **Open the Format menu and choose the Unhide Columns command to unhide the column.**

Access displays the Unhide Columns dialog box (see Figure 3.10). If the column has a check mark next to its name, the column is displayed. If there is no check mark, the column is hidden.

10 **Click the Employee Number checkbox, then click the Close button.**

Access closes the Unhide Columns dialog box. The Employee Number column reappears on the screen.

Save your work and keep the PC Software table open. In Lesson 6, you search for specific records in your database.

continues ▶

To Adjust Column Widths and Hide Columns (continued)

Figure 3.10
Use the Unhide Columns dialog box to unhide a column.

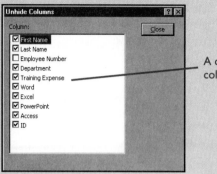

A check mark indicates that the column is displayed

 Inside Stuff: **Other Ways to Adjust and Hide Columns**

You can use the menus to adjust the column width. Move the insertion point to the column you want to adjust. Then open the Format menu and choose the Column Width command. Type a new value (the width of the column in points) and click the OK button.

You can also hide multiple columns by first selecting them and then selecting the Hide Columns command from the Format menu. In addition, you can use the Unhide Columns dialog box to hide columns. In the list displayed in the dialog box, click on the checkbox next to a column to deselect it. This hides the column.

 ## Lesson 6: Finding Records

In a table with many records and many fields, it may be time-consuming to scroll through the records and fields to find a particular record. Instead, you can search for a specific field entry in order to find and move quickly to a record.

For example, if you want to find the Wayne Wheaton record, you can search for *Wheaton*. It is always faster to select the field you want to use for your search and then search just that field, but you can also search for text in any field in the table. In this lesson, you find a record by first searching a single field and then by searching all fields.

To Find a Record

1 With the PC Software table of the Employee Training database open, click in the Last Name field.

It doesn't matter in which row you click. Clicking anywhere in the field tells Access that you want to search for a particular record using the Last Name field only. The field with the insertion point is searched by default.

 2 Click the Find button.

Access displays the Find and Replace dialog box (see Figure 3.11). Here you tell Access what you want to find and where you want to look.

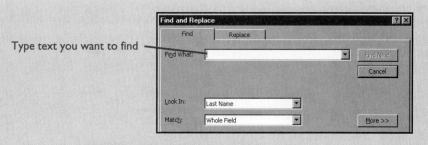

Figure 3.11
You use the Find and Replace dialog box to prepare for your search.

Type text you want to find

❸ Type Wheaton, then click the Find Next button.
Access moves to the first match, and the dialog box remains open. You can continue to search by clicking the Find Next button until you find the record you want.

If you can't see the match because the dialog box is in the way, move the dialog box by dragging its title bar.

❹ Drag across the text in the Find What text box to select it, then type Resources.
This is the next entry you want to find.

❺ Click the list arrow in the Look In drop-down list box and select PC Software: Table.
Instead of restricting the search to just the current field, you are now telling Access to look in all fields.

❻ Click the list arrow in the Match drop-down list box and select Any Part of Field.
The text you want to find (*Resources*) won't be the entire entry; it is only part of the field. For this reason, you have to tell Access to match any part of the field. Figure 3.12 shows the options you have requested for this search.

What to find

What fields to look in

What to match

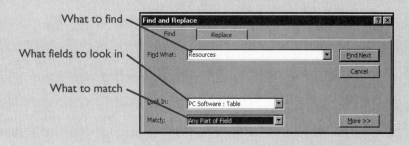

Figure 3.12
You can change your search options in the Find and Replace dialog box.

❼ Click the Find Next button.
Access moves to the first occurrence and highlights Resources in the Department field in the record for Wayne Wheaton. Notice that the search starts from the currently selected record.

❽ Click the Find Next button.
Access moves to the next occurrence and highlights Resources in the Department field in the record for Chang Sun (see Figure 3.13).

❾ Click the Cancel button.
The Cancel button closes the Find and Replace dialog box. The last record found remains selected.

continues ▶

To Find a Record (continued)

Figure 3.13
The Find feature can find information in any part of a field.

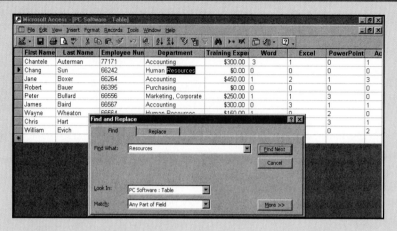

Save your work and keep the PC Software table open. In Lesson 7, you learn how to sort the records in your table.

 Inside Stuff: Searching Before the Current Record

If you see a message telling you that Access has reached the end of the records and asking whether you want to start searching from the beginning, click the Yes button. By default, Access searches from the current record down through the database. The record you want may be located before the current one.

If you see another message telling you that Access reached the end of the records, Access did not find a match. Try the search again. Be sure that you typed the entry correctly. You may need to change some of the options.

 ## Lesson 7: Sorting Records

Access displays the records in your table in an order determined by the primary key. You learned how to create a primary key in Project 2. If your table has no primary key, Access displays the records in the order in which they were entered.

If you use a primary key, Access sorts the entries alphabetically or numerically based on the entries in that field. (If a counter field is your primary key, your records will be displayed in the order in which they were entered.) Fortunately, however, you aren't restricted to displaying your data only in the order determined by your primary key. With Access, you can sort the display by using any of the fields in the database table. You can also sort the display using multiple, adjacent fields.

In this lesson, you first sort your data on the Last Name field. You will then use the toolbar to sort on the Employee Number field.

To Sort Records

1 **With the PC Software table of the `Employee Training` database open, click in the Last Name field.**

Clicking in this field tells Access that you want to base your sort on the Last Name field.

2 **Click the Sort Ascending button.**

Access sorts the records in ascending alphabetical order (A to Z) based on the entries in the Last Name field (see Figure 3.14).

Sort Descending

Sort Ascending

Sorted field

First Name	Last Name	Employee Num	Department	Training Expe	Word	Excel	PowerPoint	Ac
Chantele	Auterman	77171	Accounting	$300.00	3	1	0	1
James	Baird	66567	Accounting	$300.00	0	3	1	1
Robert	Bauer	66395	Purchasing	$0.00	0	0	0	0
Jane	Boxer	66264	Accounting	$450.00	1	2	1	3
Peter	Bullard	66556	Marketing, Corporate	$250.00	1	1	3	0
William	Evich	77517	Accounting	$300.00	0	3	0	2
Chris	Hart	77909	Marketing	$250.00	1	0	3	1
Chang	Sun	66242	Human Resources	$0.00	0	0	0	0
Wayne	Wheaton	66564	Human Resources	$150.00	1	0	2	0
*				$0.00				

Figure 3.14
The result of an ascending sort based on the Last Name field.

3 **Click in the Employee Number field.**

Clicking in this field tells Access that you now want to base your sort on the Employee Number field.

4 **Click the Sort Ascending button on the toolbar.**

Access sorts the table by using the entries in the Employee Number field. Keep in mind that the sort order displayed onscreen does not affect the order in which the records are actually stored.

5 **Close the PC Software table.**

A dialog box asks if you want to save your changes, which in this case were the changes in sort order.

6 **Click the Yes button.**

If you have completed your session on the computer, exit Access and Windows before turning off the computer. Otherwise, continue with the Checking Concepts and Terms section.

Inside Stuff: **Another Way to Sort Records**

You can also use the Records, Sort command from the menu and select the Sort Ascending or Sort Descending option. As with the buttons, you must first have the insertion point in the field you want to sort.

Exam Note: **Sorting by Multiple Fields**

To sort by multiple, adjacent fields (for example, last name, then first name) select the field name for the first sort, hold down the ⁤Shift key and select the second field to sort (the second field must be adjacent and to the right of the first field). You can also click in the first field selector and drag to the right to select the second field. Click the Sort Ascending or Sort Descending button to perform the sort.

When you have completed a sort, if you want to return records to their original order, choose Records from the menu and click Remove Filter/Sort.

If the fields you want to sort upon are not in the proper order (for example, your database Employee Training displays the first name field followed by the last name field) you can move the fields in Design view prior to the sort. By moving the field so that the last name column appears first in your table, with the first name field as the next field immediately to the right, you can sort the table by last name, then by first name. You can also move a field by selecting it, then clicking on the field name and dragging the field to the desired location.

Summary

In this project you worked with records in a table. You added, edited, inserted, and deleted records, and learned how to move around quickly in a table. You also used two of the more important features of a database—finding and sorting records. You also adjusted the widths of the columns to make the table more readable and learned to hide columns without deleting the field.

You can extend your knowledge of tables by asking the Office Assistant how to design a table. There are several topics available about table design, and some of the basic design concepts are discussed in the topics on creating a table.

Checking Concepts and Terms

True/False

For each of the following, check *T* or *F* to indicate whether the statement is true or false.

__T __F   **1.** When the pencil icon appears in the record selector, it reminds you that the record is being edited and the change has not been saved. [L3]

__T __F   **2.** When you add a new record it is added to the end of a table. [L1]

__T __F   **3.** You can undo record deletions. [L4]

__T __F   **4.** When using the Find and Replace dialog box, the default choice is to search in the field where the insertion point is located. [L6]

__T __F   **5.** You can hide only one column at a time. [L5]

Multiple Choice

Circle the letter of the correct answer for each of the following questions.

I. If you want Access to search all fields in the table, which option do you select in the Find and Replace dialog box? [L6]

   a. Current Field

   b. Match Case

   c. Search Fields As Formatted

   d. none of the above

2. Access automatically saves the data you enter to disk when you do which of the following? [L3]

   a. Press ⭡Shift + ↵Enter.

   b. Leave the field in which you entered the data.

   c. Choose Save Record from the Record menu.

   d. all of the above

3. To hide a column, you should do which of the following? [L5]

   a. Select the column and press Alt + H.

   b. Select the column and double-click the right column separator on the border.

   c. Place the insertion point in the column and select Hide Columns from the Format menu.

   d. Place the insertion point in the column and select AutoHide from the Format menu.

4. Access identifies the record you are editing by which of the following? [L3]

   a. the arrow on the record selector

   b. the asterisk on the record selector

   c. the key symbol on the record selector

   d. the pencil icon on the record selector

5. What does the New Record button look like? [L2]

   a. an arrow pointing to an asterisk

   b. a folder with an arrow on it

   c. a folder with a star on it

   d. an arrow pointing to a line

Screen ID

Label each element of the Access screen shown in Figure 3.15.

Figure 3.15

A. First Record button

B. Sort Ascending button

C. Editing record indicator

D. New record indicator

E. Delete Record button

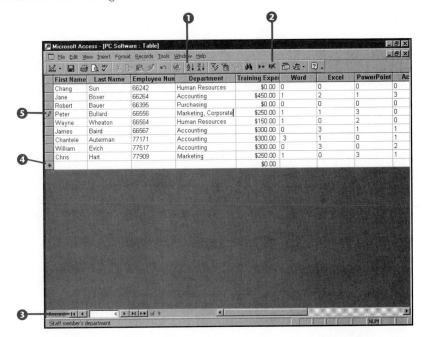

1._____

2._____

3._____

4._____

5._____

Skill Drill

Skill Drill exercises reinforce project skills. Each skill reinforced is the same, or nearly the same, as a skill presented in the project. Each exercise includes a brief narrative introduction, followed by detailed instructions in a step-by-step format.

You are working for a company that does research for other companies. Your current project is to conduct a survey for a cable TV company to find out how subscribers feel about five of the channels offered in their basic cable package. You are just starting out and testing your survey with a small number of families. You have set up a preliminary survey and are recording the results in an Access database.

1. Adding Records

You have decided you need ten families for your trial run, so you will need to add two more families to your survey.

To add records:

1. Find the **AC-0302** database file on your CD-ROM, send it to drive A, and name it **Television Survey**. Remove the read-only status and open the **Questionnaire** table.

2. Click the View button to switch to Design view and read the Description column to see what each of the categories mean. Click the View button again to return to Datasheet view.

3. In Datasheet view, click the New Record button. Use either the one on the toolbar or the one included with the navigation buttons

4. Enter the following information into the Questionnaire table. (*Note:* You can enter checks in the checkboxes by clicking on them with the mouse button or pressing Spacebar.)

Adults	Children	Use	Hours	#1	#2	#3	Doing	Comments
4	0	N	8	DISCOVERY	CNN	SCIFI	Great	I
I	2	Y		DISNEY	SCIFI		Good	More cartoons!!!

5. Close the table but leave the database open.

2. Editing Records

While looking over the paper survey forms you have received, you find that you made a couple of mistakes entering the data.

To edit records:

1. Open the **Questionnaire** table in the Television Survey database. Make sure you are in Datasheet view.

2. Move down to the 8th record (the one that has only CNN in the favorite channel fields).

3. Highlight CNN and type **TNT**.

4. Move to the Improve field and type **No opinion**.

5. Leave the table open for the next exercise.

3. Inserting and Deleting Records

After discussing your sample data with a representative from the cable company, you find that they feel that every household must have at least one of the five channels being tested in their list of favorites. This means that you have one record that needs to be deleted, and you need to find another one to take its place.

To insert and delete records in a table:

1. Click the record selector next to the record with no favorite channels listed. This should be the fourth record.

2. Press [Del] to remove the record.

3. Click the New Record button.

4. Add the following information:

Adults	Children	Use	Hours	#1	#2	#3	Doing	Comments
2	2	Y	2	TNT	CNN	DISCOVERY	Good	Would like more news & nature shows

5. Close the table and the database.

Challenge

Challenge exercises expand on or are somewhat related to skills presented in the lessons. Each exercise provides a brief narrative introduction followed by instructions in a numbered step format that are not as detailed as those in the Skill Drill section.

The table you will be working with in the Challenge section is a list of your CDs in a database called CD Collection. This table has fields for the artist, title, year, label, serial number, and category.

I. Freezing Columns

You have to use the horizontal scrollbar to scroll back and forth to look at all of the fields for a record. When you scroll to the right, the name of the artist disappears from view. You would like to keep the name of the artist and title onscreen at all times.

To freeze columns:

1. Copy the AC-0303 database file to drive A and rename it CD Collection.

2. Remove the read-only status and open the CD Collection table in Datasheet view.

3. Select both the Artist/Group and the CD Title fields.

4. Choose Format, Freeze Columns from the menu.

5. Scroll to the right to make sure the first two columns don't move off the screen.

6. Close the table and save your changes.

2. Finding and Replacing Data

When you show a friend a printout of your CD collection, she points out that you misspelled the name of classical composer Gustav Holst, which you spelled "Holzt." You can scan the entire 371 records and try to make sure you find all of the misspelled words, or you can use the Find and Replace feature to do the hard work for you. You decide to try the latter choice.

To find and replace data:

1. Open the CD Collection table in Datasheet view.

2. Highlight the CD Title column.

3. Choose Edit, Replace from the menu.

4. Type Holzt in the Find What box and Holst in the Replace With box. Make sure that you match any part of the field and look in only the CD Title field.

5. Click Find Next to find the first instance of the misspelled word. Replace it with the correct spelling. You will not be able to undo this action.

6. Click Replace <u>A</u>ll to find the rest of the misspelled words.

7. Close the table and save your changes, if necessary.

3. Formatting Text in a Table

You have seen text formatting on text in word processing programs and spreadsheets, and you wonder if the same thing can be done with text in Access.

To format text in a table:

1. Open the **CD Collection** table in Datasheet view.

2. Use the Access help or online help to find out how to turn on the formatting toolbar in the Datasheet view.

3. Change the background color to a pale blue (or other light background color of your choice).

4. Change the text to a very dark blue (or other dark font color of your choice).

5. Highlight any CD title and click the Italic button. Notice that all of the text in the datasheet is italicized. When you format anything in a datasheet, everything else in the datasheet is formatted the same way.

6. Close the table and save your changes.

Discovery Zone

Discovery Zone exercises help you gain advanced knowledge of project topics and application of skills. These exercises focus on enhancing your problem-solving skills. Numbered steps are not provided, but you are given hints, reminders, screen shots, and references to help you reach your goal for each exercise.

1. Sending a Database to the Desktop as a Shortcut

You frequently buy CDs, and you find that you are opening this database several times a week. It would be a good idea to place an icon representing the database right on your desktop. That way, you will be able to boot your computer and double-click on the CD Collection icon to move directly to the database, saving several steps!

Goal: Create, test, and delete a desktop shortcut to a specific database.

Create a desktop shortcut for your CD Collection database, test it, then delete it from your desktop.

Hint: There are two ways to do this, one within Access and one using Windows. Try to figure out both of them.

2. Using Access Tools

Access has all sorts of tools available to help you enter data more quickly and proof information when you are finished. The most commonly-used tool is the spelling checker, which can be very important to people who are weak in this area. A second, lesser-known tool can be of at least as much help. This is the AutoCorrect feature.

Goal: Use the spelling checker to check spelling and add words to the dictionary, and the AutoCorrect tool to simplify the entry of long text entries.

The spelling checker:

■ Find two ways to activate the spelling checker.

■ Check the spelling of several words in the CD Title column.

- Add one of the words to your dictionary.

The AutoCorrect tool:

- Have the program automatically capitalize the first letter of a sentence if it is not turned on.
- Turn on the feature that changes the second letter of two capital letters to lower case, then make an exception for **CD**.
- Create a shortcut that allows you to type **ASMF** and have it replace those letters with **Academy of St. Martins on the Field (Sir Neville Marriner)**.
- Test the three features you just worked with.

Hint: Look at some of the other tools available for use with your table.

PinPoint Assessment

You have completed the project and the associated lessons, and have had an opportunity to assess your skills through end-of-project questions and exercises. Now use the PinPoint software evaluation mode to assess your comprehension of the specific exam tasks you have just learned. You can also use the PinPoint Trainer Mode and the Show Me tutorials to practice these specific exam tasks.

Project 4

Querying Your Database

Key terms introduced in this project include

- calculated field
- column selector
- comparison operators
- criteria
- criterion
- design grid
- dynaset
- expression
- field list
- Null
- select query
- wildcard

Objectives	Required Activity for MOUS	Exam Level
➤ Create a New Query		
➤ Modify and Sort a Query		
➤ Match Criteria and Use Multiple Criteria	Specify criteria in a query	Core
	Specify criteria in multiple fields	Expert
➤ Use Comparison Operators in a Query	Specify criteria in a query	Core
	Specify criteria in multiple fields	Expert
➤ Use Wildcards in a Query	Specify criteria in a query	Core
➤ Create a Calculated Field in a Query	Create a calculated field	Core
	Modify query properties	Expert
➤ Summarize Data Using the Total Function	Create a totals query	Expert
➤ Change Query Properties	Modify query properties	Expert
	Print database objects	Core
➤ Understand Query Properties and Use Caption Properties	Modify query properties	Expert

Why Would I Do This?

The primary reason you spend time entering all of your data into a database is so you can easily find and work with the information. In your address book database, for example, you may want to display all of your contacts in Indiana. To do so, you would create a query. A query asks a question of the database, such as, "Which records have IN as the state?" and then pulls those records from the database into a subset of records. The subset is called a **dynaset**. You can then work with (or print) just those records selected by your query.

You can also create queries that display all of the records but only show selected fields. For example, you can display only the Last Name and Employee Number fields in the Employee Training database. You can create a query that searches for values in one field, such as the Indiana example just given, but displays only selected fields in the result. You can also create more complex queries. For example, you can query your Employee Training database to display all staff members who have received training in either Microsoft Excel or PowerPoint. Queries are created and saved so they can be used over and over.

In addition to restricting the fields and records that are displayed, queries can be used to calculate values. You can create new fields to calculate values based on other fields in your table, such as the value of your inventory. You can also use the Totals function to aggregate values such as the sum of expenses spent by each department or division in a company.

In this project, you learn how to create a query, select the fields you want to display, and sort using a query. You work with a number of tools that are helpful in restricting the records to just those that you want to see. You also learn how to create a calculated field in a query, use the totals function, and change query properties.

Lesson 1: Creating a New Query

Queries are used to sort, search, and limit the data displayed. A query can be based on one or more tables or queries.

Like a table, you can create a query using the Query Design window, and then view the results of your query by changing to the datasheet view. To start, you click the Queries Object button to view the query list in your database. After you have created a query, it will be shown on this list in the Database window.

Throughout this project, you work with the data in the PC Software table of your Employee Training database. The PC Software table that you use in this project includes the records you entered in Project 3, as well as some additional records. Some other modifications have been made to the table, such as changes to data types and field names. To create a query you choose the design method, add the table (or tables), and select the fields.

To Start a New Query

1 Launch Access. Click OK to Open an existing file.
Make sure you have a diskette in drive A:.

2 Find the AC-0401 file on your CD-ROM, right-click on it, and send it to the floppy drive. Move to drive A:, remove the read-only status, and rename the file Updated Employee Training. Open the new database.
The database opens and displays the Tables objects, The PC Software table is listed.

❸ Click the Queries object button.

The Queries list displays no queries because you have not yet created and saved any queries (see Figure 4.1).

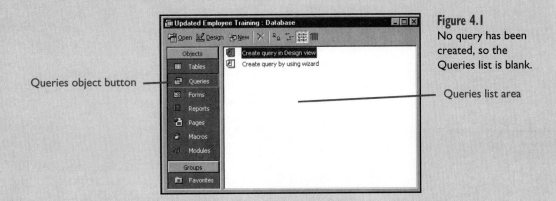

Queries object button

Queries list area

Figure 4.1
No query has been created, so the Queries list is blank.

❹ Click the New button.

The New Query dialog box is displayed (see Figure 4.2). You can use one of the Query Wizards to create a query. This method works best for specific kinds of queries, such as finding duplicate records. None of the wizards are appropriate for the query you want to create for this example, so use the more general Design View method.

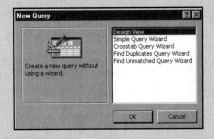

Figure 4.2
Choose the method you want to use to create a new query.

❺ Click Design View and then click OK.

The Show Table dialog box is displayed (see Figure 4.3). Here you select the tables or queries you want to use in your query. For complex queries, you can pull information from more than one table. (You learn how to work with multiple tables later in this book.) For this example, you use just one—the PC Software table.

Table available in database

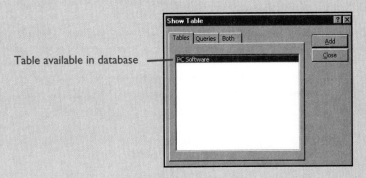

Figure 4.3
Select the table you want to use from the dialog box.

continues ▶

To Start a New Query (continued)

⑥ **The PC Software table is already selected, so click the Add button.**
This step selects the table you want to use. The dialog box remains open so that you can add other tables if necessary.

⑦ **Click the Close button on the Show Table dialog box.**
Access closes the Show Table dialog box and displays the Select Query window (see Figure 4.4).

Figure 4.4
Use the Select Query window to create a new query.

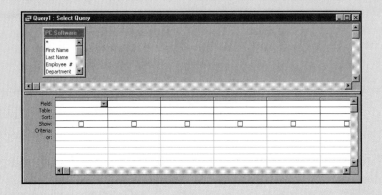

![X] **If You Have Problems...**
If you accidentally add a table more than once, simply click on the extra field list box and press `Del`.

  Exam Note: **If You Need to Open the Show Table Dialog Box**
If the Show Table dialog box is not displayed, or if you close it before you intended, you can open it by clicking the Show Table button on the toolbar.

After you open a new query and select a table, you see a window divided into two panes. The top half of the Query Design window displays a box, known as a ***field list*** box, that contains a list of the fields from the table you selected. Notice that the primary key field appears in bold type. You select the fields you want to include in your query from the field list. You can include as many fields as you want in the query, but you must include at least one. In the lower half of the query window, you see the ***design grid*** with rows labeled Field, Table, Sort, Show, Criteria, and Or. All the columns are blank. The design grid controls which fields are included in your query. The simplest type of query, and the one you will probably use most often, is the ***select query***, which displays data that meet conditions you set.

Next you select the fields you want to include in your query. You can use one of several methods to add fields to your query.

To Choose Fields for a Query

① **Double-click the Last Name field in the field list in the top half of the Select Query window.**

This step places the field name in the first field box in the design grid, and the table name shows in the Table row (see Figure 4.5). Notice that a check mark appears in the check box of the Show row, indicating that this field will be displayed in the query.

 Inside Stuff: Use a Field but Do Not Display It
There are occasions when you may want to use a field but not display its contents. In that case, you would click on the **Show** box to deselect it.

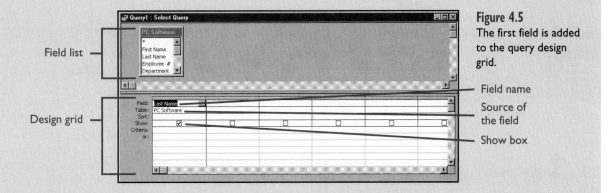

Figure 4.5
The first field is added to the query design grid.

Field list

Design grid

Field name

Source of the field

Show box

2 **Double-click Department in the field list box to add it to the design grid.**
Department is added to the second field box. Next you will add several fields at once.

3 **Scroll down in the Field list box until you see the last field in the box. Click Excel in the field list box, hold down ⬆Shift and click Access.**
Access highlights the two fields you selected, and any field(s) between those two fields (see Figure 4.6). Now you can point to any one of the highlighted fields and click and drag the group of fields to the next available field box in the design grid.

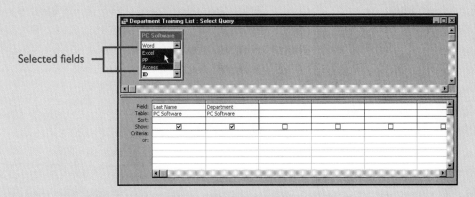

Selected fields

Figure 4.6
Adjacent fields can be selected as a group to add to the design grid.

4 **Point to the selected fields and click and drag to the first empty field box in the design grid.**
You see a stack of fields in the field box as shown in Figure 4.7. When you release the mouse button, the three fields are added to the next three available field boxes in the design gird.

continues ▶

To Choose Fields for a Query   (continued)

Figure 4.7
Several fields can be
added at once to the
design grid.

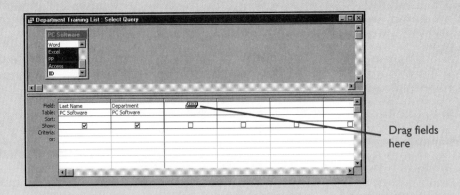

Drag fields
here

✍ **Exam Note: Adding Several Fields at Once**
In addition to adding groups of fields that are contiguous, you can also select fields that aren't listed next to each other. Click the first field you
want to select. Then hold down Ctrl and click the next field you want to
select. Continue holding Ctrl while you click each subsequent field. After
you have selected all the fields you want, release the control key, point to
any one of the selected fields, then click and drag them to the design grid
and place them in the first empty space in the Field row. This will add all
of the selected fields to the query.

⑤ After you release the mouse, click the View button on the toolbar.
This displays the records in Datasheet view, using the fields you selected in the
query (see Figure 4.8). Notice that the title bar displays Select Query to remind
you that you are viewing a dynaset, not the actual table. The difference between
a table and a dynaset is that the table consists of all of the records with all of the
fields; the dynaset consists of a subset of the records.

Figure 4.8
In Datasheet view, you
can see that the query
now includes five
fields.

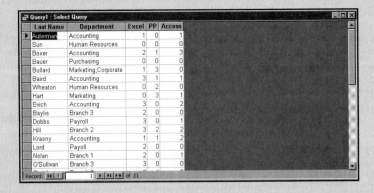

⑥ Click the View button on the toolbar.
The View button now has a different icon. This step returns you to the Design
view for the query. Keep the query window open in this view. Next you learn
how to name and save the query.

Exam Note: **Running a Query**

When you switch from Design view to Datasheet view, you are actually running your query. Instead of switching views, you can open the Query menu and select the Run command or click the Run button on the toolbar.

Inside Stuff: **Other Ways to Add Fields to a Query**

You can also add fields to the design grid by clicking and dragging the field name from the field list box to the field row, typing the field name in the field row, or clicking the list arrow in a field box and selecting a field from the list that is displayed.

As with any object you add to a database, you must save and name the object if you want to keep it. When you save a query, you save the structure of the query, not the dynaset. The dynaset is the result of running the query, which can be different each time it is run because it is based on the current data in your table. If the records in the table have changed, the resulting dynaset will reflect those changes.

The first time you save a query, you are prompted to give it a name. After that, you can save changes to the query without retyping the name. You can open the File menu and choose the Save command, or you can click the Save button on the toolbar. You can also close the query window, at which point the program will ask if you want to save the query.

To Save the Query

1 **Click the Save button on the toolbar**

The Save As dialog box is displayed with the name Query1 (see Figure 4.9). Access suggests Query1 as a default name, but as you can see, it isn't very descriptive.

Figure 4.9
Replace the default name with a more descriptive name for the query.

2 **Type** `Department Training List`.

This is the name you want to assign the query. You can type up to 64 characters, including numbers, letters, spaces, and special characters.

 If You Have Problems...

If Access will not accept your file name, it means that you have used one of the forbidden characters—a period (.), an exclamation point (!), an accent ('), or square bracket ([]). Also, you cannot include leading spaces in the query name. If you use a restricted character in a file name, a message box appears telling you that the name you entered is unacceptable. You can click OK and rename the file, or click the Help button for further information.

continues ▶

To Save the Query (continued)

Inside Stuff: **Changing a Query Name**
If you don't like the name you used—for example, suppose that you accepted the default Query1 name—you can change the name. In the Database window, right-click on the query name and choose Rename from the shortcut menu. Type a new name then press ⏎Enter to accept the it.

❸ **Click the OK button.**
Access saves the query and the database. The name of the query is displayed in the title bar of the query window and also in the list of Queries in the Database window.

Inside Stuff: **Accepting the Default Choice in a Dialog Box**
When you are given choices in a dialog box, one of the buttons will have a dark border. This is the default choice and may be activated by pressing ⏎Enter. If your fingers are already on the keyboard after typing data, it is faster to press ⏎Enter than to reach for the mouse. Be sure to check the default choice before pressing ⏎Enter to make certain it is the action you want to take.

 ❹ **Click the Close Window button in the upper-right corner of the query window.**
Access closes the query window. The Department Training List query is displayed in the Database window (see Figure 4.10).

Figure 4.10
The new query is listed in the Database window.

❺ **Click Department Training List on the Queries page and click the Open button.**
This reopens the query. The query is now displayed in Datasheet view, instead of Design view. Keep the Department Training List query open; you use it in the next lesson.

Inside Stuff: **Closing or Saving a Query**
When you save a new query, you can also choose File, Save from the menu, or press Ctrl + S.

You don't have to save the query, however, if you're sure you won't use it again. Just close the query window without saving. When Access prompts you to save, click the No button.

Lesson 2: Modifying and Sorting a Query

The way your query results are arranged depends on two factors. First, the order in which the fields are displayed is determined by the order in which you add them to the Field row in the design grid. If you don't like the order, you can rearrange the fields into a different order.

Second, the primary key determines the default order in which the records are displayed. You can change the query's sort order by using the Sort row in the design grid.

To Modify and Sort a Query

1 **Click the View button to return to the Design view of the Department Training List; then click the column selector above the Department field.**

When the pointer is on the *column selector* (the thin gray bar just above the field names), you see a black downward arrow for the mouse pointer. When you click the mouse button, the entire column is selected (see Figure 4.11). After you select a column, you can move it or delete it.

2 **With the Department column selected, point to the column selector again, click and drag the Department column until it is the first column in the design grid.**

A dotted box is displayed as part of the pointer to signify that you are dragging the column (see Figure 4.11). A dark vertical line also is displayed to indicate the insertion point for the selected column. When you release the mouse button, Access rearranges the columns in the new order.

Column movement pointer

Dark line indicates new column location

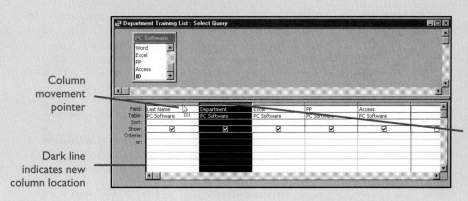

Figure 4.11
The pointer changes when you move a column in the design grid.

Column selector bar

3 **Click in the Sort row of the Department field.**

In this example, you want to sort the query by Department. When you click in the Sort box, Access displays a list arrow.

4 **Click the list arrow.**

Access displays a drop-down list of sort choices (see Figure 4.12).

5 **Click Ascending.**

This selects the sort order (A to Z) you want to use for the Department field. You can check the query by changing to Datasheet view.

continues ▶

To Modify and Sort a Query   (continued)

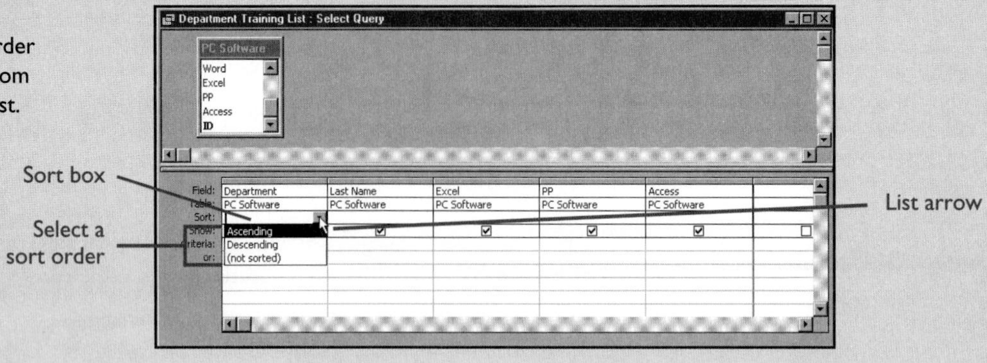

Figure 4.12
Choose a sort order
for your query from
the drop-down list.

6 Click the View button on the toolbar.
You can see the results of your query in the Datasheet view, as shown in
Figure 4.13.

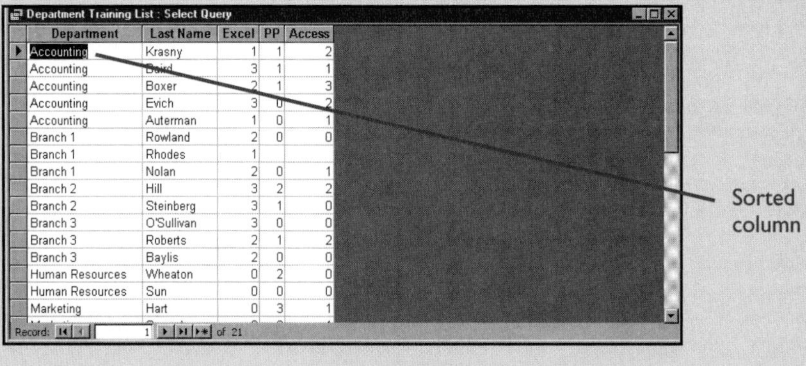

Figure 4.13
In Datasheet view, you
can see that the query
is now sorted by de-
partment.

7 Click the View button on the toolbar again.
The query is once again displayed in Design view.

8 Click the Save button on the toolbar.
This saves the changes you made to the query. Keep the Department Training
List query open in Design view as you continue with the next lesson.

Exam Note: **Sorting on Multiple Fields**
You can sort on multiple fields in a query by selecting a sort order on more than
one field. If more than one field is sorted, Access begins on the left side of the design grid. Make sure that you place the field you want sorted first to the left of
other sorted fields. For example, if you want to sort by region, then by division, the
region field would need to be to the left of division in the query design. The fields
do not have to be adjacent to each other.

Lesson 3: Matching Criteria and Using Multiple Criteria

So far, the query you have created displays all of the records contained in the PC Software table, but only shows the fields you selected. You can also use a query to display only certain records—records that match certain **criteria**. Criteria are a set of conditions that limit the records included in a query. A single condition is called a **criterion**.

You can match a single criterion, such as who has received training in Excel, or you can match multiple criteria, such as staff members in the Marketing or Human Resources departments who have received training in Access or Excel. In this lesson, you begin using combinations of criteria to restrict the records displayed.

To Match Criteria on One Field

1 **In the Design view of the Department Training List query, click the Criteria box in the Department column.**

The insertion point is moved to this location of the design grid. Here you can type the value that you want to match.

2 **Type Human Resources and press ⏎Enter).**

Access automatically adds quotation marks around the criterion that has been entered (see Figure 4.14). However, in some cases, such as when entering values that contain any punctuation marks, you must type the quotation marks.

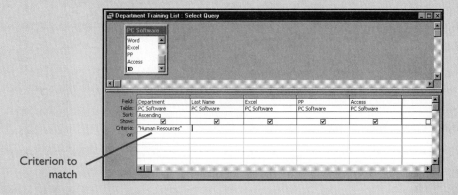

Criterion to match

Figure 4.14
Enter the criterion you want to match.

3 **Click the View button.**

You see the results of the query. Notice that the dynaset now includes only the staff members in the Human Resources Department (see Figure 4.15).

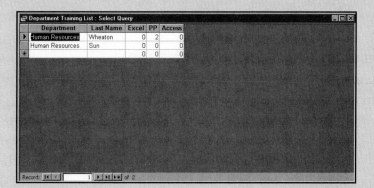

Figure 4.15
The query now lists the people in Human Resources.

continues ▶

To Match Criteria on One Field (continued)

4 **Click the View button again.**
This returns you to the design grid so you can make a change to the query.

5 **Move to the box immediately below the Criteria box where you previously typed Human Resources. This is the or row. Click this box.**

 If You Have Problems...
If the window for the dialog box is not large enough to display more than one line of criteria, the window may scroll the list automatically. This results in some of the criteria disappearing from view. Maximize this window before proceeding, if necessary.

If you want to match more than one condition, you can use this row to specify the second value. For this example, you might want to specify staff members in Human Resources or Accounting who have received training.

6 **Type Accounting and press ⏎Enter.**
When the entry you want to match is one word and contains no punctuation, as in this example, you don't have to type quotation marks. Access adds them automatically.

7 **Click the View button.**
You see the results of the query. Notice that the dynaset now includes trained staff members from Human Resources and Accounting (see Figure 4.16).

Figure 4.16
The query now lists all of the people in Human Resources and Accounting.

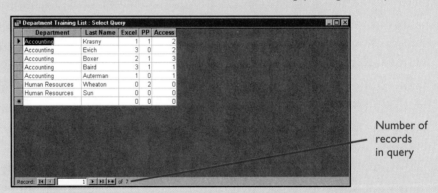

Number of records in query

8 **Choose File, Save As from the menu and type HR and Accounting, then close the query**
This saves the query with a new name, and preserves the Department Training List query.

 Exam Note: **Resolving Query Errors**
If you see a blank dynaset when you switch to Datasheet view, it means that Access found no matching records. Be sure that you typed the value you are trying to match exactly as you entered it in the database table. For example, you can't type "Humans Resources" to match "Human Resources." Check your typing and try again.

If, when you are entering text into the Criteria rows to make a match, Access displays a syntax error message, it means that you did not type the entry in the correct format. Remember that if the text entry contains punctuation, you must supply quotation marks.

You can also restrict records by specifying criteria on more that one field. You can use a combination of the Criteria row and the **or** row to achieve the desired results. For instance, you may want to know who has received the advanced training in Excel and in Access; or you may want to know who in the accounting or the marketing department has been trained to use PowerPoint. In the next example you use criteria for more than one field.

To Match Criteria on Multiple Fields

1 **Click New on the Query page of the Updated Employee Training Database.**
The New Query dialog box opens.

2 **Select Design View from the New Query dialog box and click OK.**
The query design grid opens with the Show Table dialog box displayed on top.

3 **Add the PC Software table to the Query Design view and close the Show Table dialog box.**

 Exam Note: **Using the New Objects Button**
You can also start a new query by using the New Objects button. If you are on the tables object list, click the table you want to use, then click the list arrow next to the New Objects button. Select Query from the drop-down list and choose Design View from the New Query dialog box. The query window opens with the field list of the selected table already displayed. This method pre-selects the object the query is to be based on, and shortens the starting process of a query by two steps.

---

4 **Add the First Name, Last Name, Department, Access, and Excel fields to the design grid.**
Five fields are added to the design grid.

5 **On the Criteria row under Department type** `Accounting`.
The first criterion is added.

6 **On the Criteria row under Access type 3 and press ⏎Enter.**
A second criterion is added to a different field. Notice that since this field is a Number data type field, quotations are not used around the criteria. Your query design should look like the one in Figure 4.17. When you add criteria on the same row for two or more fields it creates an And condition. For a record to be included in the results it must match both criteria.

Criteria added ——

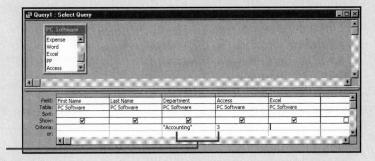

Figure 4.17
The query design shows five fields with criteria for two of the fields.

continues ▶

To Match Criteria on Multiple Fields (continued)

7 **Click the View button to see the results of the query.**

The results show that one person, Jane Boxer in the Accounting Department, has received training in all three Access classes.

8 **Return to the Design view and type 3 on the or line under the Excel field.**

9 **Switch to the Datasheet view to see the results.**

This time you see the person in Accounting who has received training in 3 Access classes, and all of the people who have received training in 3 Excel classes (see Figure 4.18). In this example you have an And condition between the criteria for the Accounting and Access fields and an Or condition for the Excel field criteria.

You decide you want to focus on just the people in the Accounting department.

Figure 4.18
Seven people have received training in three classes in Access or in Excel.

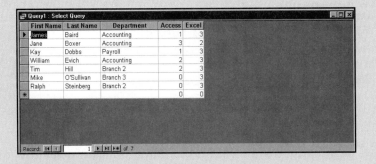

 If You Have Problems...

If you do not see any results make sure you entered the **3** for Excel on the or row under Excel and not on the Criteria row.

10 **Change to the Design view and type Accounting on the or row under the department field. Return to the Datasheet view to see the results.**

The query displays the names of the three people in the Accounting department who have received the highest level training in Access or in Excel (see Figure 4.19). To show only the people from the Accounting department, Accounting has to be specified on both the Criteria row and the or row.

Figure 4.19
The names of the people in the Accounting department with the most training in Access or Excel are displayed.

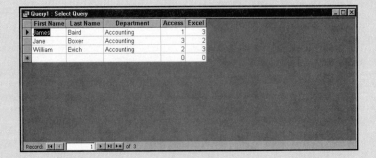

11 **Click the Save button and name the query Accounting Access or Excel Experts. Close the query.**

Leave the database open for the next lesson.

Inside Stuff: Checking the Results of Your Query
As you create a query it is a good idea to frequently check the results of your query by changing to the Datasheet view to see if the query is doing what you expect. You can use the View button or the Run button to move quickly to the datasheet, and then click on the View button again to return to the Design view.

Exam Note: Using And and Or Operators
When you specify criteria in more than one field, Access combines them using the And or the Or operators you have specified. And conditions further restrict the records displayed, while Or conditions expand the number of records displayed. Each row following the or row in the design grid is another or row that can be used to expand the search for matching records. In mathematical terms, the And and Or operators are known as logical operators. For more information about using criteria on multiple fields, look for the help topic: About using criteria in queries or advanced filters to retrieve certain records.

Lesson 4: Using Comparison Operators in a Query

When you add criteria to a query you are creating an **expression** that is used to search for data. An expression is a combination of field names and operators that produce a result, such as setting limits, performing calculations, or displaying built-in functions. You can include expressions in queries, and other Access objects.

In the previous lesson you used the logical **And** and **Or** operators. **Comparison operators** are used to compare values to see if a field contains values that are greater than, equal to, or less than another value. You can also search for values that are between two other values. Comparison operators are useful if you need to print a report that is based on a range of dates, or you want to look at values that exceed a certain amount. Sometimes data needs to be analyzed for exceptions. Comparison criteria can be used to display those values that do not match given criteria. The comparison operators include:

Greater than	>
Less than	<
Greater than or equal to	>=
Less than or equal to	<=
Not equal	<>

You can also use the Between...And operator to help search for a range of values such as the beginning and ending date of a calendar quarter.

In the training database, the entries for the software training represent not only a level of training, but also the number of classes that have been passed for each software. The data type has been changed from Text to Number to make it possible to do a greater variety of comparisons.

Next, you use comparison operators to find the staff members who have received training in both Word and PowerPoint.

To Use Comparison Operators in a Query

1 Click **N**ew in the query page, choose **Design view**, add the **PC Software table, and close the Show Table dialog box.**
The Query Design view shows the PC Software field list.

2 Add the **First Name, Last Name, Word, and PP fields to the design grid.**
The fields you want in your query are added to the design grid.

3 In the Criteria row under Word, type **>0.**
This action restricts the records to only those staff members who have receive some level of training on Word.

4 Press `Tab↹` and type **>0 on the Criteria row under the PP field.**
This action restricts the records to only those staff members who have receive some level of training on PowerPoint. Because the criteria are on the same row, records that are displayed must fit both conditions. Your query design should look like the one in Figure 4.20.

Figure 4.20
Comparison operators are used to show anyone who has received some level of training in both Word and PowerPoint.

Comparison criteria ———

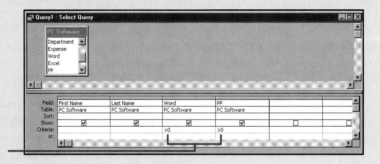

5 Click the Run button to see the results of the query.
Six records are displayed showing the staff members who have been trained in both Word and PowerPoint (see Figure 4.21.)

Figure 4.21
Comparison criteria are used to locate a range of values.

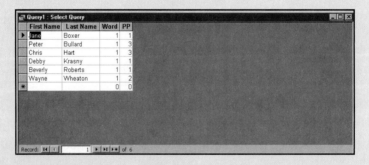

6 Click the Save button and name this query Word and PP Training. **Close the query.**
Leave the database open for the next lesson.

 ## Lesson 5: Using Wildcards in a Query

When you use criteria in a query, Access assumes that you want to match the value that has been entered. Sometimes, however, you may not know exactly how a name or value has been entered. For example if you want to find someone in a database with the first name of Jenny, you may not know how that name is spelled or how it has been entered. It might be Jennifer, Jenny, Jennie, or some other version of the name. You can search for a partial match by using a **wildcard**. A wildcard is a symbol that is used to help search for unspecified data. Sometimes it may simply be easier to search by entering a partial value rather than many specific values that are similar but not identical. For example, in the training database there are several branches. If you wanted to look for the training that has taken place for branch staff members, you could use a wildcard to find all the branches rather than having to specify each branch individually. This is another example where using a wildcard can be valuable. There are a number of different wildcards that can be used in Access, but for the purpose of this exercise you use the asterisk, which works like a universal wildcard.

To Use Wildcards in a Query

① **Click New, select Design View, add the PC Software table to the query, and close the Show Table dialog box.**

② **Add First Name, Last Name, and Department to the design grid.**

③ **On the Criteria row under Department type Branch* and press ⏎Enter.** When you press ⏎Enter, the word Like is added and Branch is surrounded by quotation marks as shown in Figure 4.22. In most cases the program adds these notations automatically because it recognizes the asterisk as a wildcard and knows that you want to search for records that begin with Branch.

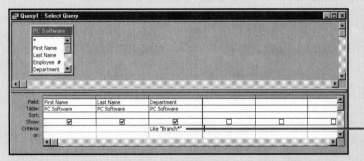

Figure 4.22
A wildcard can be used as part of a criteria expression to widen a search.

Criteria with a wildcard

④ **Run the query to see the results.**
Eight staff members in the branches are in the training database as shown in Figure 4.23.

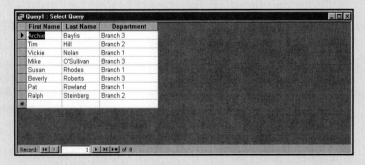

Figure 4.23
Wildcards help locate records when the data may vary.

⑤ **Save the query and name it Branch Training List, then close the query.**
Leave the database open for the next lesson.

> **Inside Stuff: Other Wildcards**
> Like in poker, a wildcard can stand for anything. In the case of the asterisk, it can also stand for any number of characters. You can use the asterisk in front of an expression to search for everything that ends in a particular letter, word or phrase. You can also use single or several question marks, where each question mark represents one alpha character. For instance, m?n, might find min, men, man, whereas m??d might find mind, mood, maid, mend. To learn more about using wildcards Open the Office Assistant, type wildcards and choose the topic: About using wildcard characters to search for partial or matching values.

  # Lesson 6: Adding Calculated Fields to a Query

When designing a database one of the questions you need to answer is what fields should be included and what fields can be calculated based on other fields. Queries can be used to create **calculated fields**, which are fields that display the result of an expression rather than displaying stored values. For example, in a database that includes a field for Parts on Hand, and another field for Cost per Part, you can calculate the value of the parts by multiplying the Parts on Hand field by the Cost per Part field. This would result in a new field that you could name Cost of Parts on Hand. Another example would be if the selling price for parts is set at a specific percent over cost. You could calculate the price by multiplying the cost field by the up-charge factor to derive the price to the customer. Using calculated fields saves space in the overall structure of the database and enables you to keep up with changing values and quantities.

Calculations in Access use the same math symbols that are used in Excel: ⊞ for addition, ⊟ for subtraction, ✻ for multiplication, and ⧄ for division. Each field name used in a calculation is placed inside square brackets—[ ]. In the training database, the levels that have been used for the software classes also reflect the number of classes that a staff member has completed for each application. You determine the total number of classes for each student and then the average cost per class.

 ### To Create a Calculated Field in a Query

❶ Click **New**, choose Design View, and add the **PC Training table to the query design, then close the Show Table dialog box.**

❷ Add the **Last Name field to the design grid.**

❸ **Right-click in the empty Field box next to Last Name.**
When you right-click the mouse, a context sensitive shortcut menu opens and displays several options (see Figure 4.24). You start in an empty field box because you are going to create a new field, which needs to be placed in the field row.

❹ Select **Zoom from the short cut menu.**

The Zoom dialog box opens. You open the Zoom dialog box so it is easier to see the expression you are going to type. You could type the expression directly in the field box, but this way it is easier to spot any errors.

❺ Type: **Number of Classes:[Access]+[Excel]+[Word]+[PP].**

Number of Classes is the title of the new field you are creating. The title of the field must be followed by a colon to identify it as the field title. It shows in the

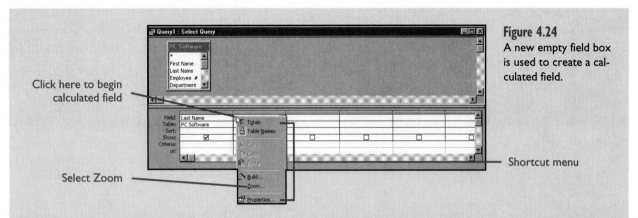

Figure 4.24
A new empty field box is used to create a calculated field.

Click here to begin calculated field

Select Zoom

Shortcut menu

column heading when you view the query and may be used on other calculated fields. Each field name used in the calculation is surrounded by its own pair of square brackets. The addition symbol is placed between the field names—outside the square brackets. Your calculation should look like the one in Figure 4.25.

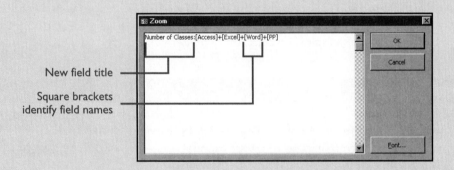

Figure 4.25
The Zoom dialog box helps you see the calculation as you write it.

New field title

Square brackets identify field names

 Inside Stuff: **Other Ways to Open the Zoom Dialog Box**
You can also open the Zoom dialog box by pressing ⬆Shift + F2.

 Exam Note: **Using the Equal Sign**
When you write a calculation in an Access query, you do not start with an equal sign like you do in Excel. However, if you create a calculated expression in a form or a report, the calculation does begin with an equal sign.

6 **Click OK to close the Zoom dialog box, then switch to the datasheet to view the results of the query.**

Your query results should look like the one in Figure 4.26.

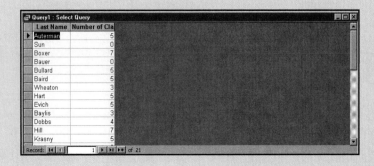

Figure 4.26
The query displays the calculated field for Number of Classes.

continues ▶

To Create a Calculated Field in a Query (continued)

 If You Have Problems...
If you make an error in typing the formula, known as a syntax error, Access will display an error message. A common mistake is to use parenthesis or curly brackets instead of square brackets. If you get this error, click OK on the error message box, and go back to the formula and correct it. Another common mistake is to mistype a field name. The field name must match exactly the name that is in the table or Access will not recognize the field. When this happens, an Enter Parameter Value box displays when you run the query. To fix this, click cancel on the Parameter Value box and review the formula to check for mistyped field names.

Sometimes when you create a calculated field you need to change the format of the field to currency, or to a specific number of decimals. Next, you create a new field to calculate the average expense per class for each staff member. The results will not show as a dollar value until you change the field properties to currency. Properties are used to determine and control the characteristics of fields and objects in Access.

To Change the Field Properties of a Query

1 Return to the Design view. Right-click in the next blank field and choose **Z**oom from the shortcut menu.

2 Type `Average Expense per Class:[Expense]/[Number of Classes]`, then click **OK** to close the Zoom dialog box, and press ↵Enter to set the new field.

This formula calculates the average cost per class by dividing training expense by the calculated field you previously created.

3 Run the query to see the results.

Notice that the new field needs to be formatted so that it displays as currency. Also, the calculation for Sun and Bauer show an error because they have not attended any classes and the program is trying to divide by zero (see Figure 4.27).

Figure 4.27
The new calculated field needs to be formatted.

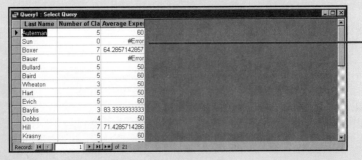

Error displays when a calculation tries to divide by zero

4 Return to the Design view. Right-click on the Average Expense per Class field and choose **P**roperties from the shortcut menu.

A Field Properties box opens. Each field in a query has a properties sheet that can be used to change field properties or create a lookup list. Just like there are properties that are associated with fields in tables, you can also make changes to field properties in a query. (You learn more about table properties in Project 8.) In this case, we want to change the format for the Average Expense Field to currency.

⊠ If You Have Problems...
If the property box that opens is titled Query Properties, it is not the right property sheet. Close the property sheet and try again. You must press ⏎Enter after creating a calculated field to record the new field, before you can open its property sheet.

5 **Click on the Format line, click the list arrow and select Currency from the drop down list.**

Currency is automatically displayed with two decimal places, unless you specify the number of decimals on the Decimal Places line in the Field Properties box (see Figure 4.28).

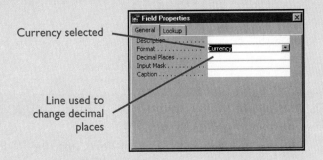

Figure 4.28
Property sheets in queries are used to change the format properties of fields, or to change other query properties.

6 **Close the Property Sheet and then type >0 on the criteria line under the Number of Classes field.**

This prevents the program from trying to calculate values when Number of Classes is zero.

7 **Run the query to see the final results (see Figure 4.29).**

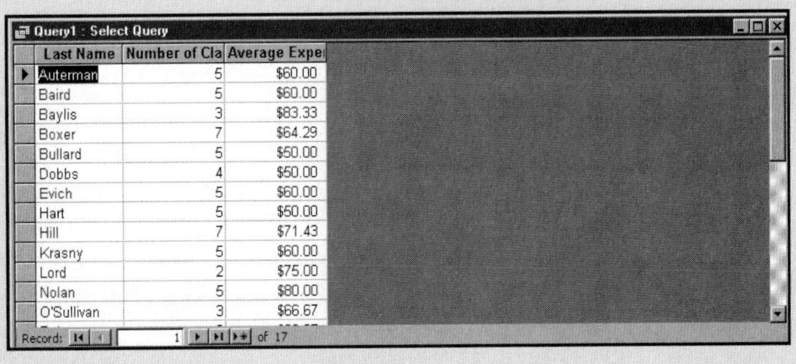

Figure 4.29
The query shows the total number of classes and the average cost per class for each staff member.

8 **Save the query and name it Average Cost per Class, then close the query.**

Leave the database file open for the next lesson.

> **Exam Note: Null Values in Calculations**
>
> A **Null** value is a field that is empty, which is not the same as an entry of zero. If you have records with Null values (empty fields), that record won't be included in the calculation, even though it may have values in other fields that are included in the calculation. For more information, look at the Help topic titled: Understanding how Null values affect numeric calculations.

> **Inside Stuff: Copying and Opening a Query**
>
> If you want to create a similar query, it may be faster to copy an existing query and modify the copy. You can make a copy of a query in the Database window by selecting the query, clicking the Copy button, and then clicking the Paste button. A Paste As dialog box opens so you can give the copy a new name.

 ## Lesson 7: Summarizing Data Using the Total Function

Another type of calculation you can perform using a query is to summarize data by using the Total function. With this tool you can group data and find the sum, average, minimum, or maximum, or calculate basic statistical values. It is important that you only include the fields that you want to use as part of the calculation whenever you use the Total function, otherwise the results could be meaningless.

In this lesson you create a query to calculate the sum of the training expense by department.

To Summarize Data Using the Total Function

1 Click on **New, select Design View, add the PC Software table to the query and close the Show Table dialog box.**

2 Add **Department and Expense to the design grid.**

Two fields are used in this query.

 3 Click the **Totals button on the toolbar.**

A new row titled Total is added to the design grid. The default value that shows on the Total row for both fields is Group By. You want to group by department and then choose sum for the Expense field.

4 Click the **Total row under Expense and click the list arrow. Point to Sum on the list.**

There are several summary functions that can be used. The data will be summarized for each group of values in your query, in this case, for each department (see Figure 4.30).

5 Click **Sum to select it as the type of calculation to be performed on this field.**

The query will sum the Expense field by department.

6 Run the **query to see the results as shown in Figure 4.31.**

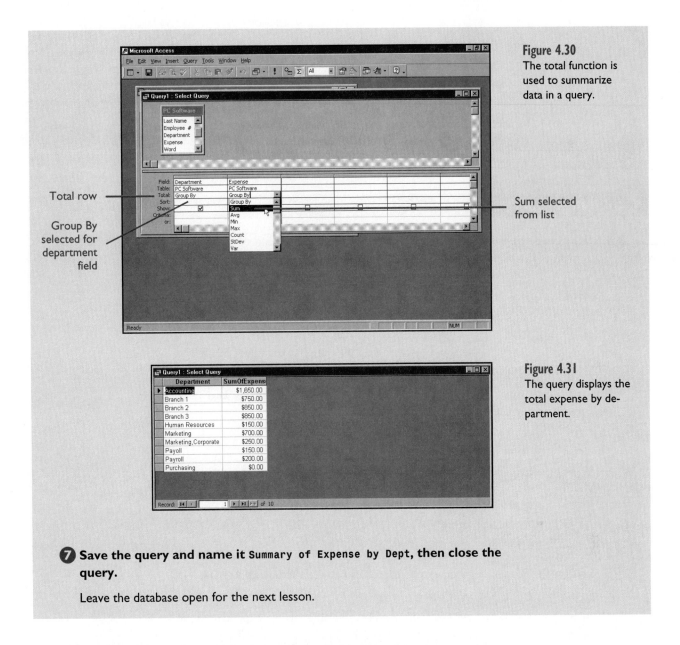

Figure 4.30
The total function is used to summarize data in a query.

Total row ⟶

Group By selected for department field

Sum selected from list

Figure 4.31
The query displays the total expense by department.

 Save the query and name it Summary of Expense by Dept, then close the query.

Leave the database open for the next lesson.

Exam Note: **Counting Fields Versus Grouping Fields**
If you wanted to know how many people were included in each of the departments, you could include a non-numeric field, such as name, and change the function on the Total row under that field to Count. This would count the number of names that occur in each group. If you include a non-numeric field, however, it is important that it is used as a counter, unless it is a field that can be grouped. If you include name, and do not change the function from Group by, Access will group by the name field. Assuming that everyone has a different name you would end up with groups of one, and would not have sums by departments, but have a sum for each name.

Lesson 8: Changing Query Properties

In Lesson 6 you learned how to create a calculated field and change the field properties for the new field you created. There are also query properties that affect the entire query rather than just one field. Two of the more common properties than can be used, are changing the unique values property to "Yes" to display duplicate values only once, or using top values to display just those records that are at the top or bottom of a sorted list. Displaying top values are useful when you have a large database and want to produce a report that will show only the best or worst values in a list.

In this lesson, you use the query properties to display the staff members with the highest training expense to date.

To Change Query Properties

1 **Click _New_, select Design View, add the PC Software table to the query, and close the Show Table dialog box.**

2 **Add First Name, Last Name, and Expense to the design grid.**

3 **Click the Sort box under Expense, click the list arrow and choose Descending.**

Sorting in descending order on a numeric field puts the highest values at the top of the list of expenses.

4 **Right-click in the open gray area in the top half of the window and choose Properties from the shortcut menu.**

The Query Properties box opens.

 If You Have Problems...
Make sure that property box title is Query Properties and not Field Properties. If the title says Field Properties, then a particular field was selected when you chose properties. Click in the open gray area of the query window to change the property sheet to the Query Properties.

5 **Click on the Top Values row, and click the list arrow. Select 5 from the list as shown in Figure 4.32.**

This will limit the list to the five staff members with the highest expenditure for training.

Figure 4.32
The Query Properties dialog box is used to restrict the results to the top five values.

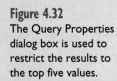
Change Top Values to 5

List arrow

Exam Note: **Other Query Properties**

There are many query properties that can be changed using the Query Properties dialog box. To change a particular property, you open the Query Properties dialog box, click in the box next to the particular property, and select one of the options from the drop down list, or type in the command needed to change the property.

To find out what a particular property does, click in the box next to the property name and press F1. This activates Help and displays information about that particular property. To practice for the MOUS test, checkout the properties for Recordset Type, Unique Values, and Run Permissions.

6 **Close the Query Properties box and run the query to see the results (see Figure 4.33).**

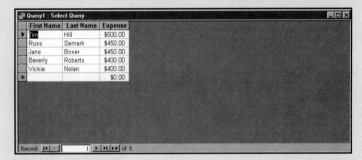

Figure 4.33
The query displays the five staff members who have incurred the highest expense for training.

7 **Save the query as Top Spenders.**

8 **Click the Print button to print the results of the query.**

The results of the query are printed.

9 **Close the query and close the database.**

Close Access unless you are going to work on the exercises that follow.

 Exam Note: **Opening the Properties Dialog Box**

You can also open the Properties dialog box by clicking the Properties button on the toolbar. The Properties dialog box will display the properties of the currently selected field. If no field is selected, the box will display the properties of the entire query.

 Inside Stuff: **More About Printing a Query**

You can preview how a query will look when it is printed by clicking the Print Preview button on the toolbar. If you want to select the pages you want to print, choose File, Print from the menu, and type the page numbers to print in the Print Range area of the Print dialog box.

Summary

This project focused on using queries to search, sort, and restrict your data. You learned how to add fields to a query design, select a sort pattern, and use criteria to restrict the records to those that met certain conditions. You learned a number of techniques to limit records such as using logical **And** and **Or** operators, comparison operators, and wildcards. You also learned how to create a calculated field, use the totals function, and change field and query properties.

You can expand your understanding of how to use queries by looking at the numerous query topics that are available in Help. Open the contents area and open the book titled Working with Queries. You can expand each of the subtopics and click on the ones that are of interest to you. In particular you might want to explore the topics: Creating and Modifying Queries, or Using Criteria Expressions to Retrieve Data.

Checking Concepts and Terms ✓

True/False

For each of the following, check *T* or *F* to indicate whether the statement is true or false.

__T __F   **1.** You must include at least one field in a query. [L1]

__T __F   **2.** The data for a dynaset is stored on disk separately from its source table. [L1]

__T __F   **3.** The Total button is used to find summary data that is be based on groups. [L7]

__T __F   **4.** If you see a blank dynaset when you run a query, Access found no matching records. [L3]

__T __F   **5.** When you write a calculation in a query you use parenthesis ( ) to identify field names. [L6]

Multiple Choice

Circle the letter of the correct answer for each of the following questions.

1. Which of the following will add a field to the query design grid? [L1]
   a. Double-click the field name in the field list.
   b. Use the drop-down list in the Field row of the design grid.
   c. Drag the field name from the field list to the design grid.
   d. all of the above

2. Which of the following is not a way to run a query when you are working in the Query Design view? [L1]
   a. Click the Run button.
   b. Click the Go button.
   c. Open the Query menu and choose the Run command.
   d. Open the View menu and choose the Datasheet view command.

3. How would you write the criterion to search for values that exceed 2000? [L4]
   a. <2000
   b. <=2000
   c. >2000
   d. >=2000

4. How would you write the criterion to search for all the records of last names that end in son? [L5]
   a. *son
   b. son*
   c. >son
   d. ?son

5. Which is the correct formula to calculate the total cost of inventory for a Cost field and a Quantity field? [L6]
   a. Total Cost:[Cost]*[Quantity]
   b. Total Cost:(Cost)*(Quantity)
   c. Total Cost:[Cost*Quantity]
   d. Total Cost (Cost+Quantity)

Screen ID

Label each element of the Access screen shown in Figure 4.34.

Figure 4.34

A. Used to see the query results

B. Show check box

C. Field list

D. Sort order

E. Criteria

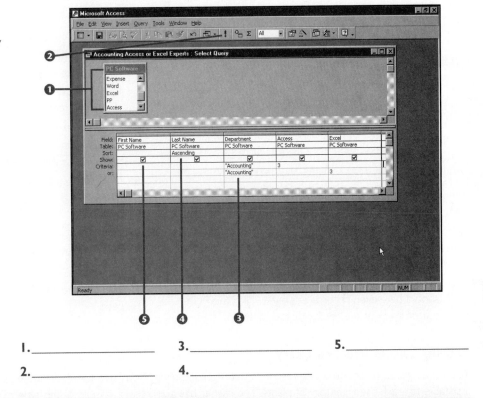

1._____ 3._____ 5._____

2._____ 4._____

Skill Drill

Skill Drill exercises reinforce project skills. Each skill reinforced is the same, or nearly the same, as a skill presented in the project. Each exercise includes a brief narrative introduction, followed by detailed instructions in a step-by-step format.

You have created a database and table to store the information on your vast collection of history books. They are divided into four categories: United States, Ancient, World, and England & Empire. There are fields for Author, Title, Year (either written or published), Pages, and Category. You can create queries to answer a number of questions about this database.

1. Creating a Simple Query

First, you create a query that displays the books printed prior to 1900.

To create a simple query:

1. Find the **AC-0402** database file on your CD-ROM, copy it to drive A:, remove the read-only property and rename the file **History Books**.

2. Open the database and select and open the **History Books** table. Look at the fields to familiarize yourself with the content of the database. Click the Close button to close the table.

3. Click the Queries object button and click <u>N</u>ew to create a new query.

4. Choose Design View and click <u>A</u>dd to add the History Books table. <u>C</u>lose the Show Table dialog box.

5. Add the following fields to the query design grid: **Author**, **Title**, **Year**, and **Category**.

6. Sort the query in ascending order by year.

7. In the criteria box for Year type **<1900** to show all the books printed prior to 1900.

8. View the results of the query. Click the Print button to print the query results. There should be 52 records included.

9. Close the query and save it as **Oldest History Books**.

10. Leave the database open if you intend to do the next exercise.

2. Creating a Query that Uses Multiple Criteria

In the History Books database, you have decided that you would like to see a list of the most comprehensive books you have in the category of ancient history. You decide one way to approach this question is to look for the largest books in that category. You can skip the first step if you did the previous exercise.

To create a query that uses multiple criteria:

1. Find the `AC-0402` database file on your CD-ROM, copy it to drive A:, remove the read-only property and rename the file `History Books`.

2. Open the History Books database and click the Queries object button, click New, select Design View, and add the History Books table to the query.

3. Add `Author`, `Title`, `Pages` and `Category` to the design grid.

4. Type `>=500` in the criteria box under the Pages field, and `Ancient` in the criteria box under Category.

5. Click the Show button for the Category field to hide the field in this query.

6. Click the View button to see the results. There should be eleven records displayed. Click the Print button to print the results of your query.

7. In addition to books classified as Ancient, you want to see the books for World history. Return to the Design view and type `World` on the Or line under the Category field. View the query. The query should show 282 records.

8. Return to the Design view and add criteria to this query to limit the world history books to those that have 500 or more pages.

9. Click in the Show check box for the category field so this field shows, and sort in ascending order by category.

10. View the query and print your results. There should be 65 records displayed.

11. Save the query as `Large Ancient and World History Books`. Close the query and close the database.

3. Using Calculations in a Query

You have agreed to create a database for a local garden shop. You have just started the database and have created the first table to track the inventory of plants. The owner has given you a sample of the type of plant information that needs to be maintained. One of the questions she wants to be able to answer is what is the value of the inventory on hand. The owner would also like to be able to track the cost of the inventory by plant category. To do this you want to test two queries, one to calculate the unit cost times the quantity, the other to summarize the value on hand by category.

To Use Calculations in a Query:

1. Find the `AC-0403` database file on your CD-ROM, copy it to drive A:, remove the read-only property and rename the file `Eve's Garden`. Open the database, open the `Plant Inventory` table and look at the fields, then close the table.

2. Click the Queries object button. Click New, select Design View, and add the `Plant Inventory` table.

3. Add all the fields except the Catalog ID field

4. In the next empty field box, type: `Cost of Inventory:[Unit Cost]*[Quantity]` and press ⏎Enter). Use the Zoom dialog box, if you prefer to help you see what you are typing.

5. Run the query. Click the Print button to print the results. (The cost of inventory for the first record, Begonia, is $10,800.)

6. Save the query with the name `Cost of Inventory`.

7. Return to the Design view. Point to the column selector for Common Name. Click and drag to the right to select the Common Name, Unit Cost, and Quantity fields. Press Del) to remove these three fields from the design grid.

8. Click the Totals button. On the Total line in the design grid, select Count for `Botanical Name`, and Sum for `Cost of Inventory`. Leave Group By for the Category field. This will group the data by category, count the number of names, and sum the inventory by category.

9. Run the query, five groups will be displayed. Choose File, Save As and name this query `Inventory Cost by Category`.

10. Click the Print button to print the query. Then close the query and close the database.

Challenge

Challenge exercises expand on or are somewhat related to skills presented in the lessons. Each exercise provides a brief narrative introduction followed by instructions in a numbered step format that are not as detailed as those in the Skill Drill section.

The database you use for the first two Challenge exercises is the database of history books that was used in the Skill Drill section.

1. Limiting Records by Looking for Words Anywhere in a Text Field

A friend needs to do some research on Native Americans and knows you have an extensive collection of books. You offer to search your books to see if there is anything that would be useful.

To limit records by searching for words anywhere in a text field:

1. Open the `History Books` database from the Skill Drill exercises. If you did not complete those exercises then find the `AC-0402` database file on your CD-ROM, copy it to drive A:, remove the read-only property and rename the file `History Books`.

2. Create a query that will locate all of the books about Native Americans.

3. Include in the query the `Title`, `Author`, `Year`, and `Pages` fields. Sort in descending order by year to get the most recently published books listed first.

   Hint: Many of the book titles use the word Indian(s) somewhere in the title, therefore, you need to use a wildcard at the beginning and end of the key words for which you are searching.

4. Save the query and name it `Native Americans`. (You should find 20 books.) Print the query results, then close it.

5. Leave the database open if you plan to do the next Challenge exercise.

2. Using the Between...And Operator to Find a Range of Dates

You have learned how to use comparison operators to find values greater than or less than a specified amount. You can also use the Between...And operator to look for a range of values or dates. In this challenge exercise you want to locate all of the books you have that were published between World War I and World War II.

To Use the Between...And Operator to Find a Range of Dates:

1. Open the `History Books` database or find the `AC-0402` database file on your CD-ROM, copy it to drive A:, remove the read-only property and rename the file `History Books`.

2. Create a query that displays the Author and Title of all the books published between World War I and World War II. Use the Between . . . And operator in your criteria expression.

   Hint: World War I ended in 1918 and World War II began for the US in 1941. Your query should include books published between 1919 and 1940. Both 1919 and 1940 should be included.

3. Sort on the Year field in ascending order.

4. Run the query to make sure only the books from 1919 to 1940 are included. (*Hint:* There should be a total of 59 books when you successfully set up the query.)

5. Save the query as `Books Published between the Wars` and print the results. Close the query and the database.

3. Using a Calculated Field to Determine a Price

Sometimes you may need increase or decrease a field by a specific amount or by a particular percent. For example, in a employee benefits table, there may be periodic increases in the cost of benefits to employees. Calculated fields are not limited to the product of two existing fields.

To use a calculated field to determine a price:

1. Open the `Eve's Garden` database or find the `AC-0403` database file on your CD-ROM, copy it to drive A:, remove the read-only property and rename the file `Eve's Garden`.

2. Create a calculated field to determine the price of bulbs. The owner of the business indicated that bulbs are priced at 110% above cost.

   Hint: Multiply 1.1 times the unit price, then add it to the unit price to set the price at 110% above the unit price. When you have successfully created the query, it will display nine records and, the price for N. 'DayDream' will be $0.42.

3. Use the property sheet to format the new price field to currency, and select **3** as the number of decimal places to display.

4. Save the query as `Price of Bulbs` and print the results. Close the query and close the database.

Discovery Zone

Discovery Zone exercises help you gain advanced knowledge of project topics and application of skills. These exercises focus on enhancing your problem-solving skills. Numbered steps are not provided, but you are given hints, reminders, screen shots, and references to help you reach your goal for each exercise.

1. Using the Asterisk from the Field List

In a field list box, an asterisk appears at the top of the list. This can be used to include all of the fields in a query. Look in Help for information about using the asterisk from the table field list box to include all the fields in a query. There are two methods that can be used to do this. Then create a query that uses the asterisk method and sort the query on one field.

Goal: Create a query that displays all fields without adding each field individually, and then have it sort on one field.

Open the `History Books` database or find the `AC-0402` file and send it to the A: drive, remove the read-only property and rename it `History Books`. Sort the new query in ascending order by Title. Print the first page of the query. Save the query as `Title Sort`.

   Hint #1: At most, two field boxes are used in the design grid.

   Hint #2: The title should only show once.

   Hint #3: Use the Print dialog box and specify the pages to print in the Print Range area.

Go to the History Books table design and add a new field named `Publisher`. Save the table, but do not add any data. Run the query again. If you created the query correctly, the new Publisher field displays in the query results. Print the first page of the query after the table has been modified. Close the query and leave the database open if you intend to do the next exercise.

2. Understanding Query Properties and Using Caption Properties

Queries have properties just like tables. You have seen the format property and the top values property in previous examples. You can learn more about properties from the Help menu, or you can open the properties sheet in a query, click on one of the property lines, and press F1.

Goal: Add a caption to a field in a query.

Use the **History Books** database or find the **AC-0402** file and send it to the A: drive, remove the read-only property and rename it **History Books**. Create a query that includes Author and Title. Use help to learn about the caption property. Change the caption for the title field to **Title of Book**. Print the first page of the query results. Do not save the query. This change does not affect the table.

PinPoint Assessment

You have completed the project and the associated lessons, and have had an opportunity to assess your skills through end-of-project questions and exercises. Now use the PinPoint software evaluation mode to assess your comprehension of the specific exam tasks you have just learned. You can also use the PinPoint Trainer Mode and the Show Me tutorials to practice these specific exam tasks.

Creating and Using Forms

Key terms introduced in this project include

- AutoForm
- control
- field label
- field text box
- form
- form detail
- form footer
- form header
- label
- selection handles
- tab order

Objectives	Required Activity for MOUS	Exam Level
➤ Create an AutoForm	Create a form with the Form Wizard	Core
➤ Enter and Edit Data Using a Form	Enter records using a form	Core
➤ Save, Close, and Open a Form		
➤ Create a New Form in Design View	Create a form in Design view	Expert
➤ Add Fields to Forms	Use the Control Toolbox to add controls	Core
➤ Move and Resize Fields in Forms	Modify Format Properties (font, style, font size, color, caption, etc.) of controls	Core
	Move and resize a control	Core
➤ Add a Form Header and Label	Use the Control Toolbox to add controls	Core
	Use form sections (headers, footers, detail)	Core

Why Would I Do This?

When you enter records in a table, each record is displayed in a row, and all records are displayed. If the table has many fields, you may not be able to see all of the fields in the table onscreen, and you might find it difficult to find the record you want with all the records displayed. A **form** is used to display one record at a time, and you may place the fields anywhere on the screen. Even if a record has many fields, you may be able to see them all on one screen. You can move the fields around and add text to the form so that it resembles paper forms that are already in use. It is often easier for people to transfer data from paper forms to a form on the screen that looks the same.

Using a form offers the following advantages:

- You can select the fields you want to include in the form, and you can arrange them in the order you want
- You can display only one record at a time, which makes it easier to concentrate on that record
- You can make the form more graphically appealing

Access provides an **AutoForm** that you can create quickly without a great deal of work. The AutoForm is a wizard that sets up an input screen that includes all of the fields in the table. If this form isn't what you need, you can also create a form from scratch. In this project, you use both methods to create forms.

Lesson 1: Creating an AutoForm

If you want a simple form that lists each field in a single column and displays one record at a time, you can use one of the Access Form Wizards to create an AutoForm. The Form Wizards look at the structure of your database table and then create a form automatically. You simply choose the commands to start the Wizards.

To Create an AutoForm

❶ Launch Access. Click OK to open an existing file.
Make sure you have a disk in drive A:.

❷ Find the AC-0501 file on your CD-ROM, right-click on it, and send it to the floppy drive. Go to drive A:, remove the read-only status, and re-name the file New Address List. Open the new database.
In this project, you use a version of the Address database you worked with in Project 1, "Getting Started with Access." You should see the Database window, listing the Contacts table.

❸ Click the Forms object button.
No forms are listed, because you haven't yet created and saved any (see Figure 5.1).

❹ Click the New button.
The New Form dialog box is displayed. First, you have to select a table to use with the form. Then you must decide whether you want to use one of the Form Wizards or start with a blank form.

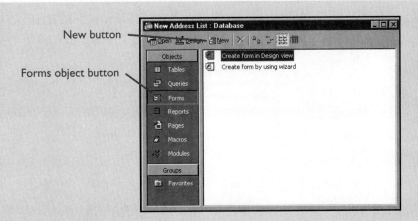

Figure 5.1
No forms are listed, because you have not yet created any.

New button

Forms object button

5 **Click the down arrow in the box labeled Choose the table or query where the object's data comes from.**

You see a list of the tables and queries available in the database (see Figure 5.2). You can base a form on either a query or a table. You must select the Contacts table, even though it is the only table or query available.

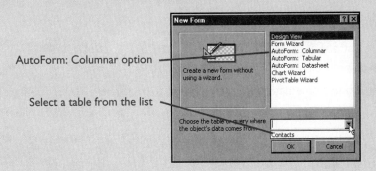

Figure 5.2
From the drop-down list, choose the table or query on which you want to base the form.

AutoForm: Columnar option

Select a table from the list

6 **Click Contacts.**

This step selects the table you want to use.

7 **Click the AutoForm: Columnar option, and then click OK.**

The Form Wizard creates the form. This step may take several seconds. After the AutoForm is built, Access displays the table's first record. Notice that the fields are displayed in a column in the form. Your screen may not have the same background settings. The navigation buttons are displayed at the bottom of the form to enable you to move through the records (see Figure 5.3). Keep this form onscreen as you continue to the next lesson, where you learn more about the navigation buttons.

continues ▶

To Create an AutoForm (continued)

Figure 5.3
An AutoForm containing all fields is displayed in a single column.

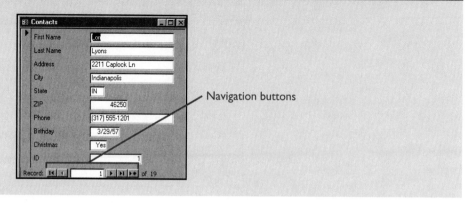

Navigation buttons

Exam Note: **Other Ways to Create a New Form**

You can also create a new form by clicking the drop-down arrow to the right of the New Object button on the toolbar in the Database window. When you are in the table Datasheet view, you can click the New Object list button and select either the <u>F</u>orm button or the AutoF<u>o</u>rm button to create a new form.

 ## Lesson 2: Entering and Editing Data Using a Form

Forms often make it easier to enter and edit data. Before you save the form, you may want to try some data entry to be sure that you like the structure of the form. If you don't like how the form is set up, you can change it or create a new one, as you learn later in this project.

You can use the same tools to enter, find, sort, and display records in a form that you use in a table. In this lesson, you add and edit a record using a form.

To Enter and Edit Data Using a Form

 ① **The AutoForm based on the Contacts table should still be on your screen from the previous lesson. Click either one of the New Record buttons.** New Record buttons are located both on the toolbar and with the navigation buttons on the bottom of the form window. This step adds a new record, and a blank form is displayed (see Figure 5.4).

Figure 5.4
The new form is ready to have information added.

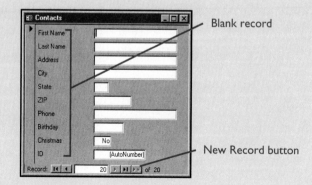

Blank record

New Record button

2 **Type the following data, pressing** Tab⇄ **after each entry to move to the next field:**

```
Janet
Eisenhut
455 Sheridan
Indianapolis
IN
46204
(317) 555-6588
3/29/60
Yes
```

Notice that when you type the phone number, Access automatically provides parentheses around the area code, moves you over so that you can type the exchange, and provides a hyphen after the exchange.

You may have to scroll down to see all the fields in the form. When you reach the last field—the ID field—you do not have to enter a value, because it is a counter field. Also, remember that when you move to another record, Access automatically saves the record you just entered. Keep in mind that the record is saved in the underlying Contacts table. You don't have to worry about updating the table separately.

3 **Click the First Record button.**
This moves you to the first record in the table.

4 **Click the Next Record button to scroll through the records until you see the record for Shelli Canady.**
This is the record you want to edit. Notice that the Birthday field is blank. If the field contained data, you would highlight the field and type over the existing information.

> **X** *If You Have Problems...*
> If you can't find the record that you want to edit by scrolling, you can open the Edit menu and use the Find command. (Refer to Project 3, "Entering and Editing Data," for more information on searching records.)

5 **Click in the Birthday field.**
This action moves the insertion point to the field you want to edit.

6 **Type 11/4/65.**
This enters a birthday for Shelli.

7 **Click the First Record button.**
The form returns to the first record and saves the change to the record you just edited. Keep the form open on your screen as you continue to the next lesson.

 Exam Note: **Undoing Editing Changes**
 If you make an editing change and want to undo it, open the Edit menu and choose the Undo command, or press the Undo button. This will undo your last change.

> ***Inside Stuff:*** **Keyboard Navigation**
> Besides using the navigation buttons, you can use the keyboard to move among records and fields. Press Tab↹ or ↓ or → to move to the next field; ⬆Shift + Tab↹ or ↑ or ← to move to the previous field; PgUp to scroll to the previous record; and PgDn to scroll to the next record. Ctrl + Home will move the insertion point to the first field in the first record, and Ctrl + End will move the insertion point to the last field in the last record.

Lesson 3: Saving, Closing, and Opening a Form

If you use the form and like how it is organized, you can save it so that you can use it again later. If you try to close the form without saving, Access reminds you. You don't have to save the form; you should save it only if you intend to use it again. If you accidentally close the form without saving it, you can simply re-create it (follow the steps in Lesson 1 of this project).

As with the other objects you have created, you are prompted to type a name the first time you save the form. You can type up to 64 characters, including spaces. After you have saved the form, you can close it and open it again when you want to use it.

To Save, Close, and Open a Form

💾

1 The AutoForm **that uses the Contacts table should still be open on your screen. Click the Save button.**
The Save As dialog box is displayed (see Figure 5.5). The default name, Contacts, is the name of the table on which the form is based.

Figure 5.5
Give the form a name before you save it.

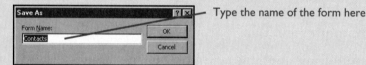

Type the name of the form here

2 **Type** Contacts AutoForm, **then click OK.**
Access saves the form.

3 **Click the Close button in the upper-right corner of the form window to close the form.**
The form window closes, and you see the Database window again. Notice that your new form is now included in the Forms list (see Figure 5.6).

Figure 5.6
The name of your form now appears in the Forms list.

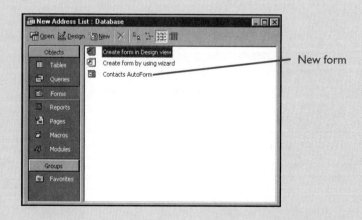

New form

4 Double-click `Contacts AutoForm` **to open it.**
Access displays the first record in the table on which the form is based. You can add, modify, or delete records. As you move from field to field, Access automatically saves any changes you make.

5 Click the Close button.
Access closes the form. Keep the New Address List database open and continue to the next lesson.

Inside Stuff: **Other Ways to Save a Form**
You can choose <u>F</u>ile, <u>S</u>ave from the menu or press Ctrl + S to save the form instead of using the Save button.

Lesson 4: Creating a New Form in Design View

Sometimes the Form Wizards do not create exactly the form you want. When that happens, you can start from a blank form and create one that better suits your needs. The form can include any text, fields, and other **controls** you want to incorporate. Controls are any objects selected from the Toolbox, such as text boxes, check boxes, or option buttons.

A form consists of several different elements. Each part of the form is called a section. The main, or **form detail**, section is the area in which records are displayed. You can also add **form headers** (top of form) or **form footers** (bottom of form). Anything you include in the section will be displayed onscreen in Form view when you use the form. You can also add page headers and page footers, which are not visible onscreen in Form view but will appear if you print the form.

The rest of this project covers some of the common features you can use when you create a form from scratch. Keep in mind, however, that Access offers other form features, such as drop-down lists, groups of option buttons, graphic objects, and much more.

In this lesson, you create a new, blank form.

To Create a New Form in Design View

1 In the New Address List Database window, click the Forms object button (if necessary); then click the <u>N</u>ew button.
The New Form dialog box is displayed. Before you choose whether you want to use the Form Wizard or start with a blank form, you should select the table you want to use for the form.

2 Click the down arrow in the drop-down list in the New Form dialog box, and select the Contacts table.

3 Select the Design View option from the top of the list, and click OK.
The form is displayed in Design view. To work on a blank form, it is useful to have the rulers turned on, and the field list and Toolbox windows open. If they were used the last time the program was in the form Design view, they will be displayed. Examine your screen and compare it to Figure 5.7. Perform the following steps as needed.

continues ▶

To Create a New Form in Design View   (continued)

 4 **If the list of fields does not appear onscreen, click the Field List button on the Form Design toolbar.**

 5 **If the Toolbox does not appear onscreen, click the Toolbox button.**
The Toolbox is displayed in the size, shape, and location it was last used on your computer. It may even be docked along the bottom, top, or side of the screen.

6 **If the ruler does not appear onscreen, choose View, Ruler from the menu bar.**
The Design view should now include the ruler, Toolbox, and field list.

7 **Drag the Toolbox and field list to the right of the Form Design window, as shown.**
The blank form is displayed with the rulers, field list, and Toolbox (see Figure 5.7). Keep this blank form open on your screen. In the next lesson, you learn how to add fields to a form.

Figure 5.7
The blank form should display the field list and the Toolbox.

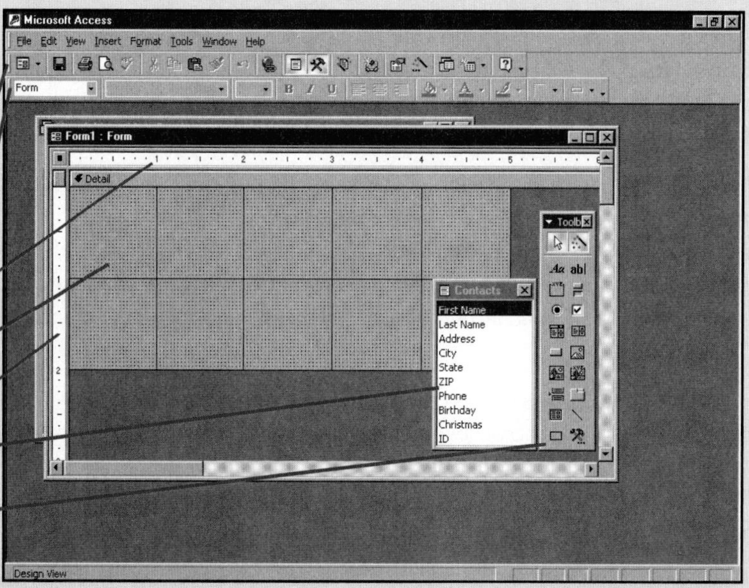

Form Design toolbar

Formatting (Form/ Report) toolbar

Horizontal ruler

Form Detail section

Vertical ruler

Field list

Toolbox

 Exam Note: Controls Tied to the Table Fields
Some controls are bound to the fields in the table. For example, if you create a text box for a field and enter data in the field in the form, the field in the table is updated. Other controls are not tied to the table but, instead, are saved with the form. For example, you may want to add a descriptive title to the form. This type of text is called a *label* and is not bound to the underlying table.

Lesson 5: Adding Fields to Forms

You decided it would be a good idea to send birthday greetings to your customers to help maintain good relations. You added a birthday field to your Contacts table, but you have entered only the birthdays of contacts who are your customers. To make sure that birthday greetings are sent to your customers, you want to create a simple form that lists just the person's name and his or her birthday. This form will include three fields—Last Name, First Name, and Birthday—and will also include a label in the form's header.

When you want to set up or change the structure of a form, you must use Design view. Access includes the following items to help you design the form:

- Toolbar. Use the toolbar to access some form design commands. You can click the Save button to save the form, the View button to view the form, and so on.

- Toolbox. Use the Toolbox to add items, such as labels or images, to the form. As with the toolbar, ScreenTips are available with these buttons. The Toolbox may not be displayed when you create a new form. If it is not, click the Toolbox button to display it.

- Field list. Use the field list to add fields to the form. The field list may not be displayed when you create a new form. If it is not, click the Field List button in the toolbar.

- Rulers. Use the rulers to help position controls on the form.

In this lesson, you use the field list to add fields to the form. The new, blank form you are creating for the Contacts table should still be on your screen from the preceding lesson. Try adding fields to the form now.

To Add Fields to Forms

1 **Click and drag the First Name field from the field list to the Detail section of the form.**
As you drag, your pointer becomes a small, boxed field name. You can use this to help place the field onscreen. The *field text box*, which holds a place for the contents of the field you have selected, is placed where you release the box.

2 **Release the mouse button and drop the field at approximately the 1 inch mark on the horizontal ruler, and down about 1/4 inch from the top of the detail area.**
This places the field text box and *field label*, which is the field name, on the form (see Figure 5.8). The label box will be placed to the left of the text box, so you need to leave space for it.

 If You Have Problems...
If you see only one field box when you drag the field from the field list, you may have placed the field too far to the left (beyond the 1-inch horizontal mark, for example), or the field text box and field label may be on top of one another. You have to move or resize the field so that you can see both the field label and the field text box. You will learn how to move a field in the next lesson.

You can delete the field and start again if you run into problems. To delete a field, click it to select it and then press [Del]. This will remove the field from the form, but it will not delete the field or its contents from the table.

continues ▶

To Add Fields to Forms (continued)

Figure 5.8
You add a field to the form by dragging it from the field list.

Field label

Field text box

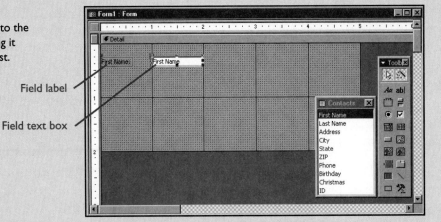

❸ **Drag the Last Name field to the form; place this field below the First Name field at the same horizontal location (the 1 inch mark) and about 1/4 inch below the First Name field.**
This step adds a second field to the form. As you drag and drop the field, try to align the field with the field above it. Make sure that you leave enough room between the two fields—don't drop the fields on top of one another.

❹ **Drag the Birthday field to the form. Place this field 1/4 inch below the Last Name field (also at the 1 inch horizontal mark).**
Your form now includes three fields (see Figure 5.9). You can save and name the form so that these changes won't be lost.

Figure 5.9
The new form contains three fields.

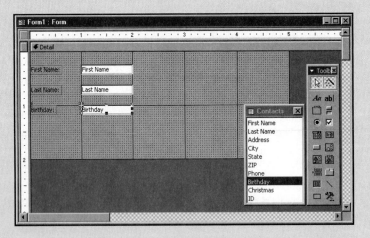

❺ **Click the Save button.**
The Save As dialog box is displayed.

❻ **Type** Birthdays **and click OK.**
Access saves the form and returns to Design view. You can continue building the form, or you can display it.

7 **Click the View button on the toolbar.**
The form is displayed as it will appear when you use it (see Figure 5.10). You can see whether you need to make any adjustments, such as adding a label or resizing the fields. Keep the Birthdays form open, and continue with the next lesson.

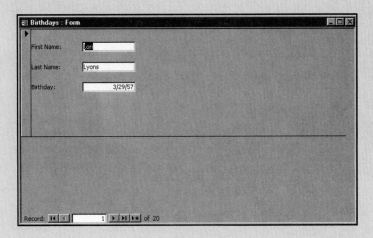

Figure 5.10
Your new form is displayed in Form view.

 Exam Note: Modifying Forms
To modify an existing form, click its name in the Database window; then click the Design command button. Alternatively, you can open the form and then change to Design View by clicking the View button.

Lesson 6: Moving and Resizing Fields in Forms

When you create your form, you may find it difficult to get the fields in the right place the first time. That's OK; you can move or resize the fields after you have added them to the form. You can drag and place them visually, using the ruler as a guide. Otherwise you can have Access align the fields with an underlying grid—making them an equal distance apart.

In this lesson, you move the Birthday field up next to the First Name field.

To Move and Resize Fields in Forms

1 **In the Birthdays form, click the View button to return to Design view.**
To make changes to the form design, you must return to Design view. You cannot make changes in Form view.

2 **If the Birthday field is not selected, click the field text box.**
Selection handles appear around the borders (see Figure 5.11). Selection handles are small squares that appear at the corners and on the sides of boxes. They can be used to change the size of the box. Notice that both the field label and the field text box are selected, because these two items are attached. However, handles only appear all the way around the object on which you clicked. The other one (in this case, the field label) has one large handle in the upper-left corner. Most of the time you want to keep the two together, such as when you want to move them.

continues ▶

To Move and Resize Fields in Forms   (continued)

Figure 5.11
You must click a field to select it before you can move it.

Selection handles

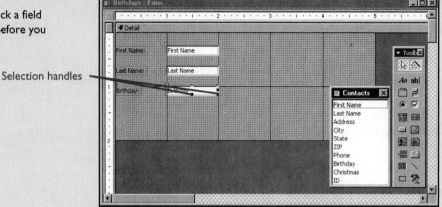

❸ **Place the mouse pointer on one of the borders of the Birthday field text box, but not on one of the handles.**

When the pointer is in the correct spot, it should resemble a small hand (see Figure 5.12). If you see arrows rather than the hand, the pointer isn't in the correct spot. Move it around until you see the hand.

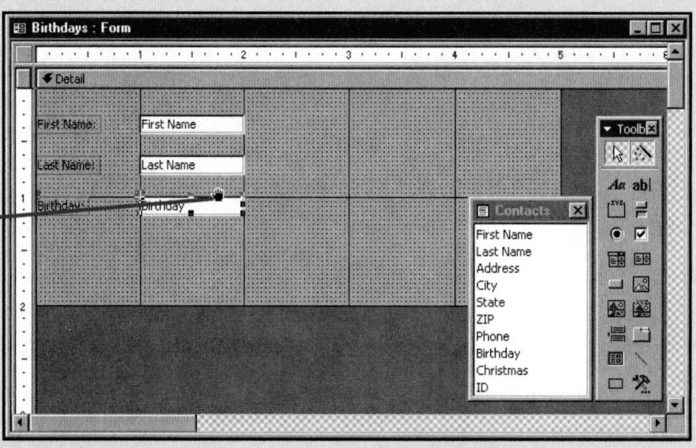

Figure 5.12
To move the field, the pointer must look like a hand.

The pointer appears as a hand

❹ **Drag the Birthday field up next to the First Name field and place it so that the left edge of the Birthday field label is at approximately the 2-1/2 inch mark on the horizontal ruler.**

Notice as you drag that you can see the outline of both the field label and the field text box. When you release the mouse button, Access moves the field up next to the First Name field. (You may need to drag the field list box out of the way so that you can see where you are positioning the Birthday field.)

❺ **Move the pointer to the right side of the Birthday field text box and place it on the center handle. The pointer turns into a two-headed arrow (see Figure 5.13).**

The birthday field is longer than necessary, so you are going to change the size to approximately 1/2 inch wide.

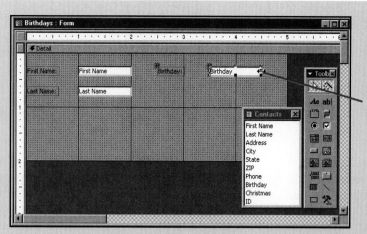

Figure 5.13
Use the selection handles to resize a field.

The pointer appears as a two-headed arrow

6 **Make the field smaller by dragging the right side of the field to the left. Stop at the 4 inch mark on the horizontal ruler so that the field is about 1/2 inch wide.**
The Birthday field is now about the right size to contain a date.

7 **Click the View button to return to Form view to verify that the date will fit in the new box.**

8 **Click the Save button.**

This step saves the form with the changes you just made. Keep the Birthdays form open. In the next lesson, you add a form header to the form.

 If You Have Problems...
If you see arrows in the form and begin to drag, you will resize the field. If you resize by accident, click the Undo button to undo the change.

When you want to move a field, be sure to place the pointer on the edge of the field and wait until it changes to a hand. Don't place the pointer on one of the selection handles.

 Inside Stuff: Moving the Label Box or Text Box Independently
If you want to move the label box separately from the text box, point to the larger square in the upper-left corner of the label box. When the pointer turns into a pointing finger, you can click and drag the label box to a new location. The text box can move independently from the label box by using the same technique. Point to the larger box in the upper-left corner of the text box until the pointer turns into a pointing finger, then click and drag the text box to the desired location.

 Exam Note: Changing Tab Order
When you enter data into a form, the insertion point jumps from one box to the next each time you press Tab↹ or ↵Enter. This is called the **tab order**. When you move fields around in a form, you may need to change the tab order. In Design view, select View, Tab Order from the menu and a list of fields will be displayed. Click once on the field to select the one that you want to move, then click and drag it to the desired position on the list. You can also click the Auto Order button, which often (but not always) sets the tab order the way you want it.

Lesson 7: Adding a Form Header and Label

The final step for this form is to add a form header that will appear at the top of the form and to include a label showing the name of the form. Form headers show up at the top of every form. Form footers are similar to form headers, but they appear at the bottom of every form.

In this lesson, you first add a new section to the form—the Form Header section—and then you add a label to the form. In addition to adding the label, you can change the font and font size of the text so that the form label stands out.

To Add a Form Header and Label

1 **Click the View button to return to the Design view of the Birthday form.**

2 **Choose View, Form Header/Footer from the menu.**
Access adds two sections to the form, a Form Header section and a Form Footer section (see Figure 5.14). You want to include the form label in the header, but the section is too small. Therefore, you need to adjust the size of the section.

Figure 5.14
Form Header and Form Footer sections can be added to the form.

Form Header section

Drag edge to resize

Form Footer section

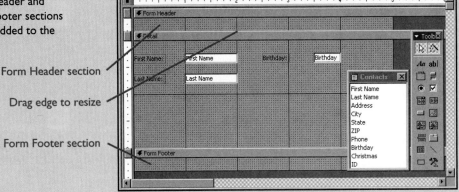

3 **Place the mouse pointer on the bottom edge of the Form Header section (the top edge of the Detail section bar).**
The pointer should change to display a thick horizontal bar with a two-sided arrow crossbar (see Figure 5.15). This pointer shape indicates that you are about to resize this section.

4 **Drag down until the Form Header is about an inch tall.**
You can use the rulers along the left edge of the form's Design view to gauge the size of the section. Don't worry if the size isn't exact. Now that the header is a little bigger, you can add a label to the form.

5 **Click the Label button in the Toolbox.**
The Label button has an uppercase and lowercase "A" on it. Remember that you can place your pointer on a button to see its name.

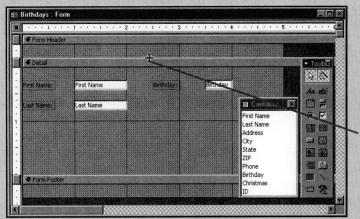

Figure 5.15
The two-sided arrow pointer indicates that you are about to resize the Form Header section.

The pointer appears as a two-headed arrow

6 **Position the crosshairs of the pointer near the upper-left corner of the Form Header section. Drag to the right and down to draw a box. Make the box approximately 2 inches wide and 1/2 inch tall.**

The pointer should appear as a small crosshair with an "A" underneath while you are positioning it (see Figure 5.16). When you release the mouse button, you see a label box with the insertion point inside.

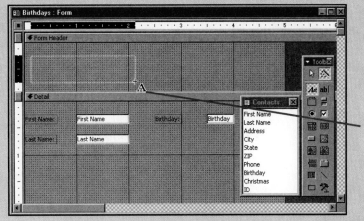

Figure 5.16
The Label pointer is used to place and size the label box.

The Label pointer

> **X** *If You Have Problems...*
> If you make the label box too small, you can always resize it. Click the box to select it, and then place the pointer on one of the selection handles and drag to resize.

7 **Type Birthdays!**

This is the text you want to include as the label. As you can see, the text is fairly small, but you can change it.

8 **Click outside the new label box to end the text-editing mode.**

9 **Click inside the box to select it.**

Notice that the formatting toolbar displays the font and font size in the Font and Font Size drop-down lists. You can use these lists to change the font and the font size (see Figure 5.17).

continues ▶

To Add a Form Header and Label   (continued)

Figure 5.17
You can change the font and font size of a label using the Formatting toolbar.

Font list box

Font Size list box

Selected label

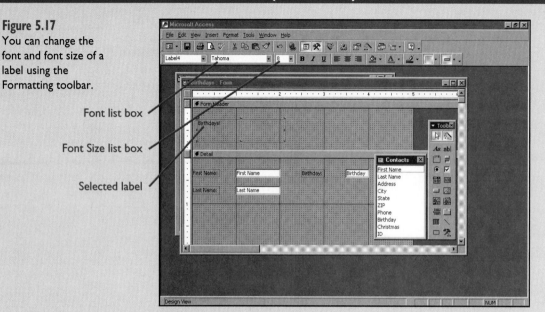

⑩ Click the down arrow next to the Font Size box. Click 24.
This changes the font in the label box to 24-point type. You don't have to change the actual font, but you can make the text bold.

⑪ Click the Bold button on the toolbar.
Access makes the text bold.

⑫ Click the Save button on the toolbar.
The form is saved with the changes you have made.

⑬ Click the View button on the toolbar.
This switches you to Form view so that you can see the form you just created (see Figure 5.18).

Figure 5.18
The Form view shows the results of your design changes.

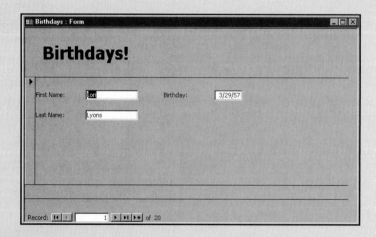

⑭ Close the Birthdays form and then close the New Address List database.
In Project 6, "Creating and Printing Reports," you use a different database to create a report.

Exam Note: Printing Forms and Selected Records

The purpose of creating forms is to make it easy for users to input and read data onscreen. Should you need to print a form, you can view it first by clicking the Print Preview button. If you click the Print button, all records in the database will be printed in a continuous form. If you want to print one record per page, click the Page Break button in the Toolbox and drag the small Page Break symbol onto the form just below the last field.

If you want to print a selected record, move to that record and select <u>F</u>ile, <u>P</u>rint to see the print menu. Choose the Selected <u>R</u>ecord(s) option button on the Print menu. Choosing this option prints only the current record.

If you have completed your session on the computer, exit Access before you turn off the computer. Otherwise, continue with the "Checking Concepts and Terms" section of this project.

Summary

This project focused on the use of the various form features built into Access. You learned how to create an AutoForm from a table, and how to create a new form in Design view. You entered and edited information in a form and modified the form structure by adding fields, moving and resizing fields, and adding form headers and labels.

To enhance your ability to create effective forms, look for help on adding page headers and footers. Pay particular attention to the procedure for adding current information, such as the date, time, or page numbers to headers and footers.

Checking Concepts and Terms

True/False

For each of the following, check *T* or *F* to indicate whether the statement is true or false.

__T __F **1.** AutoForm creates a form containing all the fields in your table. [L1]

__T __F **2.** When you use a form to enter data, that data is saved in the form. You also have to update the table. [L2]

__T __F **3.** To delete a field from a form in form Design view, click once on the field to select it and then press Del. [L5]

__T __F **4.** If you accidentally close a form without saving it, you can simply click the Undo button to restore the form. [L3]

__T __F **5.** When a field text box is selected, its associated label is also selected. [L6]

Multiple Choice

Circle the letter of the correct answer for each of the following questions.

1. How do you create a new record using a form? [L2]

   a. Scroll to the last record and then edit it.

   b. Edit the first record displayed.

   c. Click the New Object button on the toolbar.

   d. Click the New Record button on the Navigation bar and enter data into the empty form.

2. Which type of section includes the record information? [L4]

   a. Detail

   b. Page Header

   c. Page Footer

   d. Form Header

3. What should the pointer look like to move a field? [L6]

   a. a hand

   b. a white cross

   c. a two-headed arrow

   d. a crosshair

4. To save data to the table after you have entered several records using a form, you must do which of the following? [L2]

   a. Choose Save from the File menu.

   b. Choose Update from the File menu.

   c. Click the Save button on the toolbar.

   d. none of the above (because data is saved automatically)

5. Which of the following is a fast way to create a form based on the current table? [L1]

   a. Use the QuickForm.

   b. Use an AutoForm.

   c. Open a blank form and drag the fields onto it from the field list window.

   d. Click NewForm on the Toolbox.

Screen ID

Label each element of the Access screen shown in Figure 5.19.

Figure 5.19

A. Label pointer

B. Field text box

C. Label button

D. Toolbox button

E. Field label

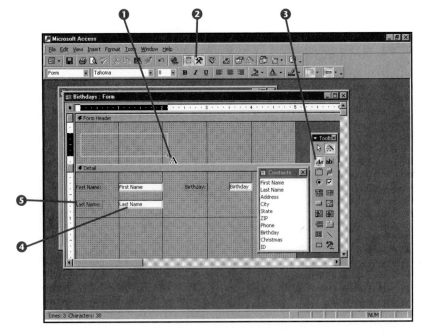

1._____   3._____   5._____

2._____   4._____

Skill Drill

Skill Drill exercises reinforce project skills. Each skill reinforced is the same, or nearly the same, as a skill presented in the project. Each exercise includes a brief narrative introduction, followed by detailed instructions in a step-by-step format.

The database you will be using for these exercises contains two tables, one with information about short story books, and the other with information about the authors of these books.

1. Creating an AutoForm for Entering Information

Entering the data into the Book information table is not easy, since the fields scroll off the screen to the right. It would be a good idea to create a form to make data entry easier. You decide to use the AutoForm feature to create the new form, then enter information on a new book to try it out.

To create an AutoForm and enter information:

1. Find the `AC-0502` database file on your CD-ROM, send it to drive A:, remove the read-only status, and rename it **Short Story Books**. Select and Open the Book information table and look at the fields. Click the Close Window button to close the table.

2. Click the Forms object button and click New to create a new query.

3. Select the Book information table from the drop-down list.

4. Select the AutoForm: Columnar wizard and click OK.

5. Click the Save button and save the form as **Book information data input**.

6. Click the New Record button on the toolbar.

7. Press Enter to skip the BookID field, which is entered automatically.

8. Enter **Rinehart, Mary Roberts** in the Author field.

9. Enter **Affinities and Other Stories** in the Title field.

10. Enter **1920** for the Year field, **282** for the Page field, and **George H. Doran** for the Publisher field.

11. Close the form.

2. Editing Data in the Form

You just found out that the date of publication for Auld Licht Idylls, by J. M. Barrie (also the author of the children's classic Peter Pan) was written in 1888. You need to go into your form and change this information. Skip the first three steps if you did the previous exercise.

To edit data in the form:

1. Find the `AC-0502` database file on your CD-ROM, send it to drive A:, remove the read-only status, and rename it **Short Story Books**.

2. Click the Forms object button and click New to create a new query. Select the Book information table from the drop-down list.

3. Select the AutoForm: Columnar Wizard and click OK. Click the Save button and save the form as **Book information data input**.

4. Place the insertion point in the Title field and click the Find button.

5. Type **Auld** in the Find What drop-down list box. Change the Match drop-down list box to Any Part of Field, if necessary.

6. Click Find Next. Close the Find and Replace dialog box.

7. Type **1888** in the Year field.

8. Close the Book information form.

3. Creating a New Form in Design View

Now that you've created a form for the Book information table, you find that you also need one for the Author information table. You decide to use the form Design view to create this form. Skip the first step if you did either of the first two exercises.

To create a new form in Design view:

1. Find the AC-0502 database file on your CD-ROM, send it to drive A:, remove the read-only status, and rename it **Short Story Books**.

2. Click the Forms object button and click <u>N</u>ew to create a new form.

3. Select the Author information table from the drop-down list.

4. Select Design view and click OK.

5. Click the Toolbox and field list buttons if they are not turned on. Select <u>V</u>iew, <u>R</u>uler to turn the rulers on, if necessary.

6. Drag the Author field onto the form about 0.25 inches down and 0.75 inches to the right of the left edge.

7. Drag the DOB field to the 3 inch mark and line it up to the right of the Author field.

8. Place the Birth City, State, and Birth Country fields under the Author field, about 0.25 inches apart. Use the hand pointer to adjust the field locations, if necessary. Your form design should look like Figure 5.20.

Figure 5.20
Five fields have been added to a form in Design view.

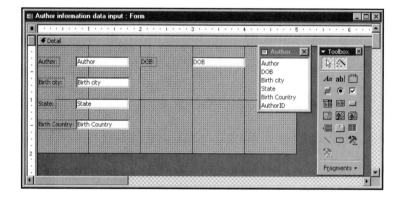

9. Click the Save button and save the form as **Author information data input**.

10. Click the View button to see your form.

11. Close the form, then close the Short Story Books database.

Challenge 💡

Challenge exercises expand on or are somewhat related to skills presented in the lessons. Each exercise provides a brief narrative introduction followed by instructions in a numbered step or bullet list format that are not as detailed as those in the Skill Drill section.

The database you will be using for the Challenge section is the same database of short story books and authors you used in the Skill Drill section. The Book information data input form has been modified. Before you start the Challenge exercises, spend a little time looking at the form in Form view, then look at it in Design view. Notice how it has been laid out, and how some of the field labels have been deleted and replaced by other labels.

1. Adding Information to the Form Header or Footer

You have decided to make your Book information data input form more user-friendly. Since you expect to frequently print out single forms, you would also like to make the forms more informative. It would be a good idea to add the current date to the form header and page numbers to the page footer.

To add information to a form header and footer:

1. Copy the AC-0503 database file to drive A:, remove the read-only status, and rename it Revised Short Story Books.

2. Open the database and open the Book information data input form in Form view. Maximize the form window and examine the form layout.

3. Move to form Design view and examine the layout of the form.

4. Use the Insert menu to place the date (in the 12/31/00 format) and the time (in the 11:59 PM format) in the form.

5. Click the View button. If the date and time are not in the upper-left corner of the form header, return to Design view and move them to that location.

6. Return to form Design view. Use the Insert menu to place the page number (in the Page N of M format). Place the page number at the bottom of the page and center align it.

7. Notice that the program has added Page Header and Page Footer sections, and the page number is in the Page Footer section. If the page number is in the page header instead of the page footer, delete it and insert the page number again, making sure you have selected the correct options in the Page Numbers dialog box.

8. Click the View button to look at the page number. Notice that the page number does not appear. Use your help menu to find out why it does not show up here, and what possible use this feature might have.

9. Close the form and save your changes.

2. Customizing the Look of the Form

You would like to make some changes to the overall form design. You decide to try to change the background color of the Detail area and give the field labels and field text boxes a special effect.

To customize the look of a form:

1. Copy the AC-0504 database file to drive A:, remove the read-only status, and rename it Final Short Story Books. This is a modified version of the database used in the previous exercise.

2. Open the Book information data input form in Design view. The form Design window may be very small, so you will need to maximize the form window.

3. Find the Fill/Back Color button and change the background color of all of the form sections to a pale blue.

4. Select all of the field labels and field text boxes. (Hint: You can move the pointer to the vertical ruler near the top of the Detail area. It changes to a right arrow. Click and drag down to below the last row of fields and release the mouse button. All of the field labels and field text boxes are selected.)

5. Use the right mouse button on any one of the selected field labels or field text boxes. Find the option that will allow you to customize these boxes and select Sunken.

6. Click the View button to see how your changes look on the form. Your form should look like Figure 5.21

Figure 5.21
The background color
and the look of the
labels and text boxes
have been changed.

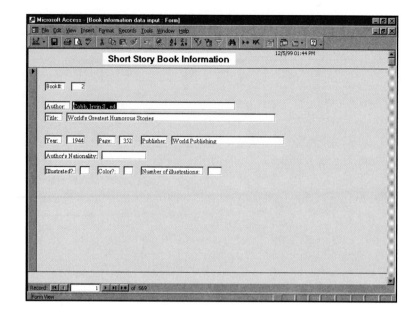

7. Close the form and save your changes.

3. Inserting a Page Break and Printing a Form

The forms will print continuously if you don't add an artificial page break in form Design view.
If you did the previous exercise, you can skip the first step.

To insert a page break and print a form:

1. Copy the AC-0504 database file to drive A:, remove the read-only status, and rename
   it **Final Short Story Books**.

2. Open the Book information data input form in form Design view. Maximize the form
   window.

3. Click the Print Preview button to see what a printout would look like. Notice that
   there are multiple forms on each page, and a lot of blank space in each form. Close the
   Print Preview window.

4. Pull the page footer up so that it is about 0.25 inches below the last row of fields in the
   Detail area.

5. Find and click the Page Break button on the Toolbox. Move the new pointer and click
   at the bottom of the Detail section.

6. Click the Print Preview button to see the results of inserting an artificial page break.
   Use the navigation buttons to scroll through a few records. Close the Print Preview
   window.

7. Click the View button to move to Form view.

8. Choose File, Print from the menu. Make sure the correct printer is selected and the
   printer is turned on.

9. Choose the Selected Record(s) option to print only the current record, then click OK.

10. Close the form and save your changes. Close the Final Short Story Books database.

Discovery Zone

Discovery Zone exercises help you gain advanced knowledge of project topics and application of skills. These exercises focus on enhancing your problem-solving skills. Numbered steps are not provided, but you are given hints, reminders, screen shots, or references to help you reach your goal for each exercise.

I. Adding a Drop-Down List to a Field in a Form

In many cases you will have fields in tables that have a limited number of possible entries. Examples of these would be a field that asks for the name of a state or a department in a company. Access has a feature that enables you to create a drop-down menu that you can use to select from a list of choices. These drop-down menus are called combo boxes.

Goal: Create a combo box in the Publisher field that enables you to select from a list of the most common publishers.

Use the `AC-0505` file to create a new database called **Short Story Books with a Combo Box** on your disk (check to make sure you have enough room on the disk). Use help from your computer or online help to understand how combo boxes are set up. Then go to the Book information data input form Design view and change the Publisher field text box to a combo box. Include the following publishers in the list:

    Century

    Colliers

    Dodd, Mead

    Grosset & Dunlap

    Harpers

    Scribner's

Hint #1: A shortcut menu option will help determine the type of field text box.

Hint #2: The Properties box for the Publisher field text box will be used to determine where the information for the combo box comes from. You can create a table to use as the source, or you can type the value list in another box in the Properties box.

Hint #3: A Value List is usually best when there are only a few items, while a table is best for a larger number of items.

Hint #4: There is an alternative way to create a combo box using a wizard in table Design view.

Your combo box should look like Figure 5.22.

Figure 5.22
A combo box has been added to the form.

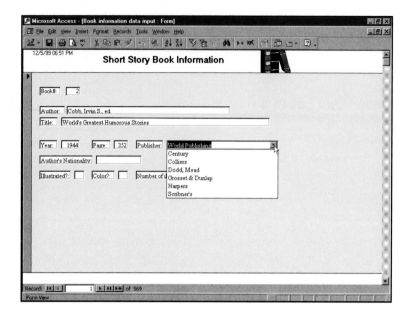

2. Using Multiple Pages with Tabs on a Form

When there are a large number of fields in a table, or the table can be easily divided into more than one category, Access includes a feature that enables you to divide a form into pages. These pages have tabs at the top, and all you have to do to move between pages is to click on a tab.

Goal: Create two tabbed pages on a form based on a table showing the number of cars and trucks by location in the United States.

Use the `AC-0506` file to create a new database called **US Motor Vehicle Statistics** on your disk. Use a new disk, if necessary. Use help from your computer or online to understand how tab control works. Create the new form in Design view and save it as **US Cars and Trucks**. Your form should have the following:

- Two pages, with the tabs labeled **Cars** and **Trucks**.
- The Location, Privately Owned Cars, and Publicly Owned Cars fields on the Cars tab.
- The Location, Privately Owned Trucks, and Publicly Owned Trucks fields on the Trucks tab.
- The numeric fields with commas and no decimal places.
- Identical field labels for both occurrences of the Location field.

Hint #1: This is much easier than it sounds! Look in the Toolbox to get started.

Hint #2: Most of your time will be spent resizing the field labels and the field text boxes and lining them up.

Your tabbed form should look like Figure 5.23.

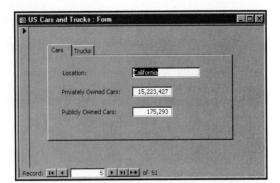

Figure 5.23
The US Cars and
Trucks form now has
two tabs.

PinPoint Assessment

You have completed the project and the associated lessons, and have had an opportunity to assess your skills through end-of-project questions and exercises. Now use the PinPoint software evaluation mode to assess your comprehension of the specific exam tasks you have just learned. You can also use the PinPoint Trainer Mode and the Show Me tutorials to practice these specific exam tasks.

Creating and Printing Reports

Key terms introduced in this project include

- AutoReport
- landscape orientation
- portrait orientation
- report

Objectives	Required Activity for MOUS	Exam Level
➤ Print the Table Data	Print database objects (tables, forms, reports, queries)	Core
➤ Create a Report Using the Report Wizards	Create a report with the Report Wizard	Core
➤ Print and Rename a Report	Print database objects (tables, forms, reports, queries)	Core
➤ Modify a Report Design	Move and resize a control	Core
	Modify format properties	Expert
➤ Save a Report with a New Name	Create a report in Design View	Expert
	Modify control properties	
➤ Add Labels to Reports	Use the Control Toolbox to add controls	Core
	Use report sections (headers, footers, detail)	Core
	Modify control properties	Expert

Why Would I Do This?

There are several ways to display information in your database. One way is to print a form, or print copies of tables or queries. But these printouts are limited in format and flexibility. To produce flexible printouts from tables or queries, you need to learn how to use **reports**. Reports are database objects that are designed to print and summarize selected fields. They are divided into sections that can contain controls, labels, formulas, and even images. In this project, you learn the fundamental tasks involved in creating, modifying, saving, and printing a simple report.

Before you create a report, think about why you need the printed data. Do you want to check the entries to make sure they are correct? Do you need an address list or phone list? Do you need to pass the information along to someone else? If so, what information does that person need and in what order? If you spend a few moments determining the purpose of the report, you can design a report that truly meets your needs.

Access provides many tools for creating a report: you can create an **AutoReport**, use the Report Wizards to create other common report types (single-column report, mailing labels, and so on), or create a blank report that you add information to later. You can also change the layout of an existing report design and add report labels to help make the report more self-explanatory. This project shows you how to use the report tools included with Access.

Lesson 1: Printing the Table Data

If all you need is a printout of a table or query, it is faster to simply print the table without using a report. For example, you may want to print the data in a table so that you can check the accuracy of the records. In this case, you don't have to create a report.

To Print the Table Data

❶ Launch Access. Click OK to Open an existing file.
Make sure you have a disk in drive A:.

❷ Find the AC-0601 file on your CD-ROM, right click on it, and send it to the floppy drive. Move to drive A: and rename the file Softball Team. Remove the read-only property and open the new database.
The Softball Team database includes a table of team members and a table of game information. After you open the Softball database, you should see the two tables displayed in the Tables list. In this project, you work with the Team table.

❸ Click the Team table to select it. Click the Open button to open the Team table. Maximize the Table window.
This table is opened in Datasheet view. You may want to scroll through the table to see how it is set up. The table includes fields for the first and last name of each player, along with his or her position, phone number, address, and dues. You can print this information; but before you print, preview the printout so that you have some idea of what the printed list will look like.

❹ Click the Print Preview button.
A preview of the printed list is displayed (see Figure 6.1). The structure of the printout is fairly simple; each record is displayed as a row in a grid. The navigation button that enables you to scroll to the next page is active, which indicates that the printout will be more than one page. This means that all of the table columns will not fit on one page width when the report is printed.

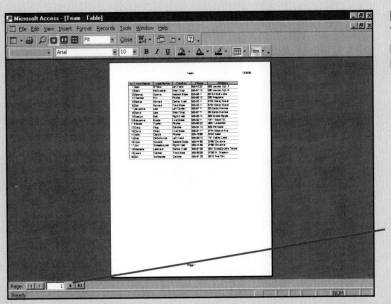

Figure 6.1
The table may be previewed before printing.

Active Next Page button

5 **Click the Next Page button, which is the same as the Next Record button in a form or table.**
This step displays the second page of the printout, which shows the remaining column. If the table is too wide by just a few columns you can still get the table on one page by changing the orientation of the page so that Access prints across the long edge of the page, rather than down the page. Using this *landscape orientation*, you can fit more columns across the page.

6 **Click the Previous Page button to return to the first page of the report. Choose File, Page Setup from the menu.**
The Page Setup dialog box lists options for setting margins and page layouts.

7 **Make sure the margins are all 1 inch, then click the Page tab to display the page orientation (see Figure 6.2).**

Margins tab

Page tab

Orientation options

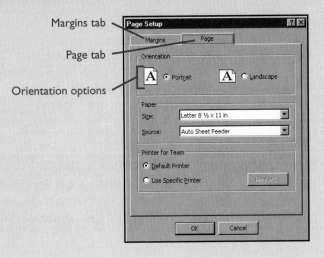

Figure 6.2
Use the Page Setup dialog box to change the page orientation.

continues ▶

To Print the Table Data (continued)

8 **In the Orientation area, click the Landscape option button and then click OK.**

This step changes the orientation of the page to landscape, which is the horizontal orientation of a page. The standard vertical positioning of a page is called *portrait orientation*. Now when you print the report, all the columns fit on a single page.

9 **From the File menu, choose Print.**

The Print dialog box is displayed (Figure 6.3). Here you can control which pages are printed, how many copies are printed, and select other options. The default settings work fine for this one-page printout.

Figure 6.3
Use the Print dialog box to choose the pages you want to print and the number of copies.

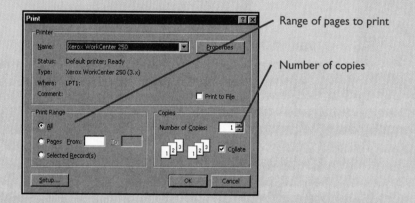

Range of pages to print

Number of copies

10 **Click OK.**

Access prints the table data. If you don't have access to a printer, click Cancel.

11 **Click the Close Window button.**

This step closes the Preview window and also closes the table. Leave the Softball Team database open for the next lesson.

 Inside Stuff: **Previewing the Printout**
You don't have to preview the printout, but previewing is a good idea. You can print directly from Datasheet view. Simply click the Print button on the toolbar or open the File menu and choose the Print command. Access then prints the table. The keyboard shortcut for the Print command is Ctrl + P.

 Inside Stuff: **Fitting Data on the Page**
If the data doesn't quite fit on the page, there are several things you can do to make them fit. You can reduce the width of the columns. If this cuts off some of the data, you can reduce the font size by using Format, Font from the menu.

Lesson 2: Creating a Report Using the Report Wizard

Simple table printouts are limited in what they can do. Access provides several reporting options to make it easy to create more sophisticated reports. Using the New Report feature, you can create the reports described in Table 6.1.

Table 6.1   Common Report Creation Options

Type of New Report	Description
Design View	Opens a design window where you can add fields or text. This option does not use the wizards.
Report Wizard	Guides you through the process of creating a report. The Report Wizard has several options for layout and grouping of data.
AutoReport: Columnar	Places all the fields in a table in a single-column report.
AutoReport: Tabular	Places all the fields of the table in a row-and-column format similar to the layout of a spreadsheet.
Chart Wizard	Guides you through the process of selecting fields that you want to summarize in a graphical form. The Chart Wizard enables you to choose from several chart types, such as pie, line, and bar.
Label Wizard	Enables you to set up and print mailing labels in more than 100 different label styles.

A Report Wizard leads you step by step through the process of creating a report, asking you which fields to include in the report, which sort order to use, what title to print, and so on. After you make your selections, the Wizard creates the report.

In this lesson, you create a columnar report for your Team table in the Softball database. This report works well as an address list.

To Create a Report Using the Report Wizard

① Click the Reports object button.
No reports are listed, since you haven't created any at this point (see Figure 6.4).

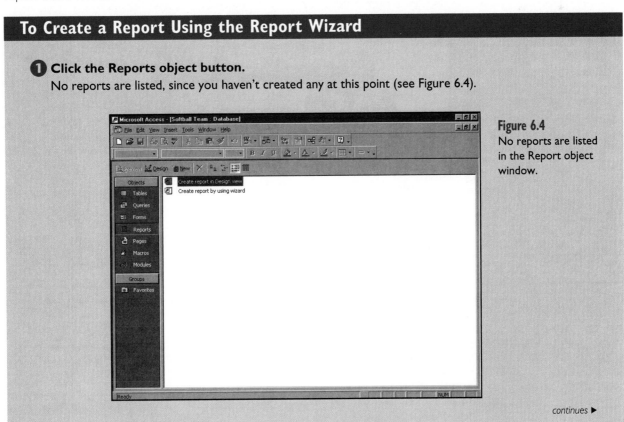

Figure 6.4
No reports are listed in the Report object window.

continues ▶

To Create a Report Using the Report Wizard (continued)

2 **Click the New button.**
The New Report dialog box is displayed (see Figure 6.5). You will need to select the method of creating the report and the table or query on which you want to base the report. This is exactly the same procedure you used to create a form.

Figure 6.5
You choose the method you want to use to create a new report and the table or query on which to base the report.

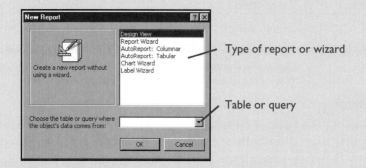

Type of report or wizard

Table or query

3 **Select Report Wizard and click the down arrow next to the Tables/Queries box. Choose the Team table. Click OK.**
The first Report Wizard dialog box is displayed.

4 **In the Available Fields list, click the First Name field. Then click the Add button.**
The Wizard removes the field from the Available Fields list and places the field in the Selected Fields list (see Figure 6.6). The fields will appear in the report in the order you select them. The First Name field, for example, will be the first field listed in the current report.

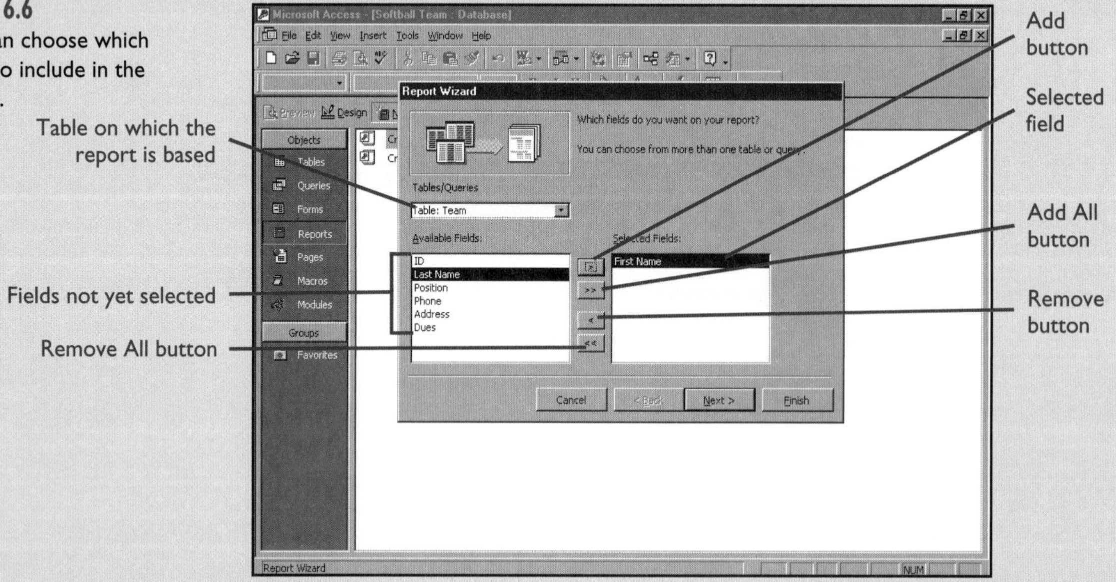

Figure 6.6
You can choose which fields to include in the report.

Table on which the report is based

Fields not yet selected

Remove All button

Add button

Selected field

Add All button

Remove button

5 **Highlight and add the Last Name, Address, and Phone fields to the Selected Fields list.**
Your report now includes four fields. That is all the fields you want to include for this lesson.

6 **Click the <u>N</u>ext button.**

The second Report Wizard dialog box is displayed. You could use this step to group similar records together, such as grouping the team by position played. In this example, we have not included any fields that need to be listed together as a group.

7 **Click <u>N</u>ext again.**

The third Report Wizard dialog box enables you to sort the data on one or more fields. Sorting a name field in ascending order produces a list in alphabetical order.

8 **Click the down arrow next to the first sort selection to reveal the available fields. Select Last Name to sort on. Click <u>N</u>ext.**

The fourth Report Wizard dialog box enables you to select the layout, orientation, and fit (see Figure 6.7).

Orientation buttons

Fit-to-page check box

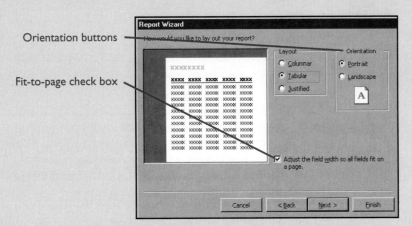

Figure 6.7
Select the layout and orientation options.

9 **Select a <u>C</u>olumnar layout, <u>P</u>ortrait orientation, and the check box labeled Adjust the field <u>w</u>idth so all fields fit on a page. Click the <u>N</u>ext button.**

The fifth Report Wizard is displayed. In this dialog box, you select a report style.

10 **Select the Corporate style report and click the <u>N</u>ext button.**

The final Report Wizard dialog box is displayed. In this screen, you enter the title for the report. By default, the Wizard uses the table name as the title, unless you change it.

 If You Have Problems...

If you make a mistake or change your mind about an option anywhere in the Wizard, you can back up by clicking the <u>B</u>ack button in the Wizard dialog box.

11 **Type Team Addresses and Phone Numbers to change the title of the report, then click the <u>F</u>inish button.**

A preview of the report is displayed (see Figure 6.8) showing the title you entered. You can print, zoom, and save the report, as you learn in the next lesson. Keep the report open for the next lesson, where you print and rename a report.

continues ▶

To Create a Report Using the Report Wizard (continued)

Figure 6.8
The columnar report
can be reviewed
onscreen.

The report name is used as
the default label

Page navigation buttons

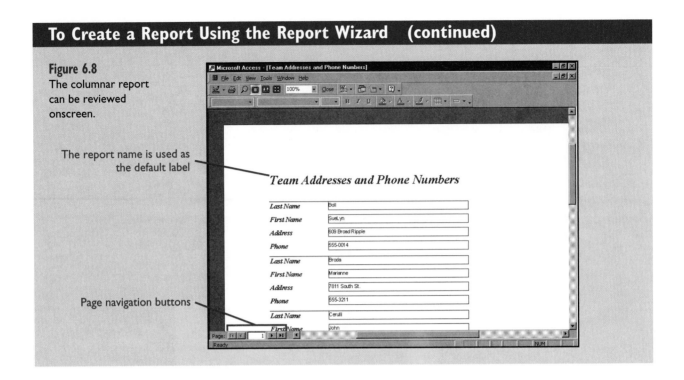

 Exam Note: Using AutoReport Wizard
In Project 5, "Creating and Using Forms," you used the Form Wizard to quickly create an AutoForm. You can also create an AutoReport using the Report Wizards. An AutoReport includes all the fields from the table in the report. The report is in either a one-column or tabular format with as many records on the page as possible. The report also includes a header with the table name and current date, and a footer with the page number. To create this type of report from the Reports page, choose one of the two AutoReport options in the New Report dialog box.

 ## Lesson 3: Printing and Renaming a Report

The next step is to print your report. However, before you print, it's always a good idea to preview the report. In the Print Preview mode, you can use the navigation buttons to check for unexpected additional pages, check the font, the font size, and the actual data in the report. Then, if you click the Zoom button on the toolbar, you can view the entire report to determine, generally, how the printed report will look on the page. If you do not like how the report is set up, you can make changes before you print it. This strategy can save you some time and paper.

You can also rename a report in the Database window to ensure that it's not confused with other database objects with the same name.

To Print and Rename a Report

❶ **With the Preview window still active, click the pointer anywhere on the report.**
Access displays a full-page view of the report, so that you can see the entire page (see Figure 6.9).

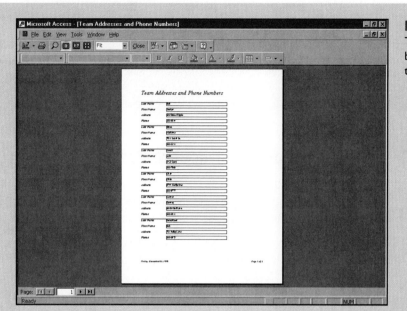

Figure 6.9
The full-page view can
be used to preview
the report.

② **Click on the report again.**

Access zooms in so that you can read the text of the report. It will center on the spot you clicked, so you may need to use the scroll bars to get back to the section you want to see. Now you are ready to print. If you do not have access to a printer, skip the next step.

 If You Have Problems...

This report is three pages long. If you are restricted to printing one page, select File, Print from the menu, then choose to print from pages 1 to 1 in the Print Range section.

Reports are not interactive like forms, queries, or tables. Instead of an Open button, they have a Preview button that allows you to see how the printout will appear. If you want to change a report, you can make changes in the Design view or you can delete the report and generate a new one using the wizard.

③ **Click the Print button on the toolbar.**
Access prints the report.

④ **Click the Close button on the toolbar to close the Preview window.**
The program returns to the report Design view.

⑤ **Click the Close Window button to close the report.**
The new report is shown in the Database window under the Reports list. You may decide that the name you gave the report could be improved.

⑥ **Right-click on the Team Addresses and Phone Numbers report and select Rename from the shortcut menu.**
The name changes to edit mode, in which it can be changed.

⑦ **Type the name Team Roster.**

continues ▶

To Print and Rename a Report (continued)

⑧ Press ↵Enter or click outside the name box to save the change.
The report name is now Team Roster. Keep the database open for the next lesson, in which you modify a report design.

  # Lesson 4: Modifying a Report Design

Once you have created a report, you may decide you want to modify it. The finished report may not be exactly what you intended. Rather than start over with a wizard or a blank form, you can modify the report design so that the report includes the information you want.

When you look through the report Design view, you will notice some unusual-looking things in the page footer. These are expressions, which are predefined formulas that perform calculations, display built-in functions, or set limits.

Suppose that you need a phone list in addition to the team roster. You can modify the Roster report to create this new report. Start by deleting the Address field, which you don't need in your phone list. Then add the position field so you have a list that includes the name, phone number, and position played by each member of the team.

To Modify a Report Design

① Select the Team Roster report and open it in Design view.
The report is displayed in Design view (see Figure 6.10). This view is similar to the Design view you used when you created a form. The same tools are available onscreen. You can use the ruler to place items on the report, the toolbox to add controls, and the field list to add fields.

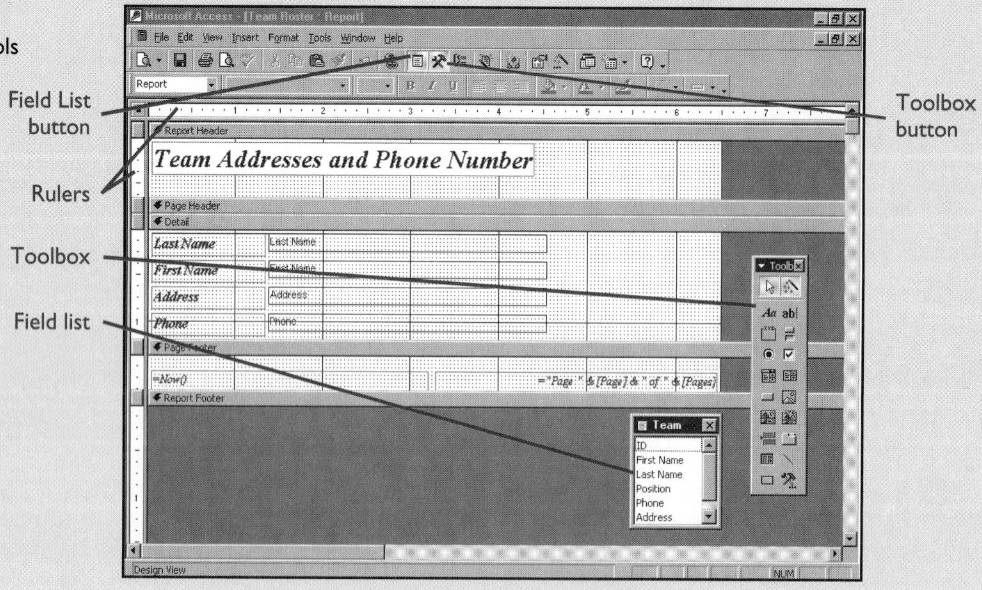

Figure 6.10
In Design mode, tools are available to help you modify your report.

If You Have Problems...
If the toolbox does not show on your screen, click the Toolbox button to open it. If the field list box does not show, click the Field List button to open it. Click and drag the title bar of each box to move it to a location that does not obscure the report design, as shown in Figure 6.11.

2 **Locate the Page Footer Section of the report.**
Notice that the report includes a page footer with the date and page number. The expression **=NOW()** inserts the current date (see Figure 6.11). An expression is similar to a function in spreadsheet software. Access provides many expressions that you can include in your report.

The expression **="Page" & [Page] & "Of" & [Pages]** on the right side of the page footer prints the current page and the total number of pages. Remember that you placed this expression in the form in Project 5.

The Detail section includes four fields: First Name, Last Name, Address, and Phone.

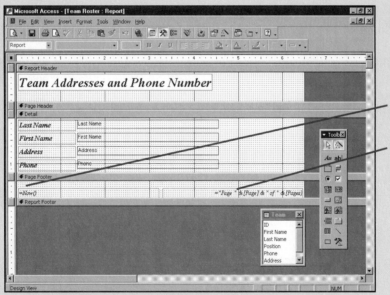

Figure 6.11
Expressions add calculations or functions to a report.

Date expression

Page number expression

3 **Click the Address field text box to select it.**
The field label is on the left, and the field text box is on the right. If you click on the Address field text box, handles will appear at the sides and corners of the field text box and in the upper left corner of the field label box.

4 **Press Del.**
Access removes the field and its label from the report. Now you have a gap between two of the fields. To fix this gap, you can move the Phone field up.

5 **Click the Phone field to select it. Position the pointer on the boundary of the field so that it turns into an open hand.**
When the pointer is an open hand, you can click and drag the control to another location.

continues ▶

To Modify a Report Design   (continued)

6 **Drag the Phone field so that it is directly under the First Name field.**
The Phone field is now moved up closer to First Name. Now you will add the position field to the report.

7 **In the field list box, click the Position field and drag it to the detail section of the report, directly below the Phone field text box, and release the mouse.**
The pointer turns into a small field box when you are dragging the field onto the report. As soon as you release the mouse, the field text box is positioned under the Phone text box and the field label for the new field is added to the left of the field (see Figure 6.12). Next you need to format the new field to match the ones on the report.

Figure 6.12
Fields can be added to a report using the field list.

New field ————

Field list ————

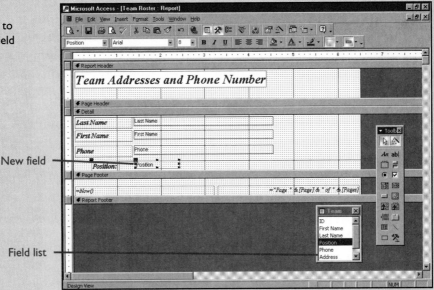

X *If You Have Problems...*
The label is placed to the left of the text box when you drag the Position field onto the report. If the text box is too close to the left edge of the report, the label will appear on top of the text box. If this occurs, you can drag the field to the right or click the Undo button and try again.

---

8 **Point to the Phone field text box above the new Position text box. Hold down ⬆Shift and click. The Phone and Position boxes should both be selected.**

9 **Choose Format, Size, To Widest to match the length of the two boxes.**

10 **Choose Format, Size, To Tallest to match the height of the two boxes.**

11 **Choose Format, Align, Left to match the alignment of the two boxes.**

12 **Click in an unused space in the Detail area to deselect the boxes.**

13 **Select the field label box for Position. Grab the center handle on the left edge of the field label box and drag to the left until it is lined up with the left edge of the Phone field label box.**

14 **Click the Print Preview button on the toolbar.**

The new field should now match the other boxes in size and alignment. However the other field text boxes have a border. Next you add the border to the Position text box.

15 **Click the View button to return to Design view, then click the Position field text box to select it.**

16 **Click the down arrow to the right of the Line/Border Width button on the Formatting toolbar (see Figure 6.13).**

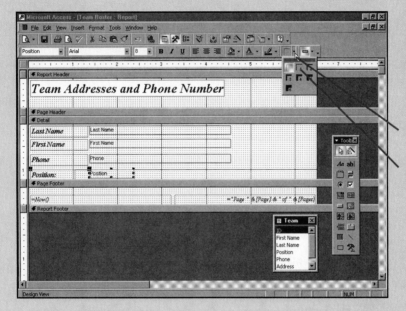

Figure 6.13
The Line/Border Width button is used to add a border or to change the color of a border to a selected control.

Down arrow on Line/Border button

Line/Border Width Option #1

 If You Have Problems...
If the Line/Border button is gray, you may have clicked on the Position label box instead of the text box. Clicking the label box that was already selected puts you into editing mode and places the insertion point inside the label box. The Line/Border option is not available in editing mode so it is inactive.

17 **Select border option #1. Click the Save button to save your changes. Keep this report open for the next lesson.**

 Exam Note: **Modifying Reports Created by Wizards**
The Report Wizards are used to give you all of the necessary elements of a report, and to place these elements in their proper locations. The wizards will save you time, but will seldom provide finished reports. You will almost always need to modify field lengths, add or format labels, modify the spacing between fields, and change locations of some of the elements. If you are asked to create a report using a wizard, make sure you use the Print Preview feature to scan through the data and look for fields that may have been cut off and need to be modified.

Lesson 5: Saving the Report with a New Name

As you modify a report, you may decide that you want to keep the original report as well as your modified version. If this is the case, you can save the modified report with a new name. Doing so enables you to use both reports.

In addition to saving the report with a new name, you should change the report header so that it reflects the purpose of the new report.

To Save the Report with a New Name

1 With the Roster report still onscreen, choose File, Save As from the menu.
The Save As dialog box is displayed with the original name listed (see Figure 6.14).

Figure 6.14
When you choose Save As/Export, Access displays the original name in the New Name box.

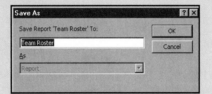

2 Type Phone List and then click OK.
The report is saved with a new name.

3 Click the label box in the Report Header section.
Here you want to replace the existing text with a more descriptive title.

4 Drag across the existing text to select it; then type Phone List.
The new text replaces the selected text.

 5 Click the Save button
This step saves your changes to the Phone List report by writing over the report with that name. Keep the Phone List report open and continue to the next lesson, in which you learn to add labels to a report.

 Inside Stuff: **Another Way to Copy a Report**
You can also create a duplicate report from the Database window. With the Reports tab selected, right-click on the report name and select Copy from the shortcut menu. Right-click again in an open area of the window and select Paste from the shortcut menu. Give the duplicate report a new name when prompted.

  ## Lesson 6: Adding Labels to Reports

When you create a report using a wizard, the labels tend to be short and non-descriptive. Once you have modified the report, as you did in Lesson 4, you will often find that additional labels are necessary to explain exactly what is on the report. Access gives you an easy way to add labels to either the report header or the page header. Labels added to the report header will show up on the first page of the report, while labels added to the page header area will appear on the top of every page.

In this lesson, you add the team name to the page header area.

To Add Labels to a Report

1 **With the `Phone List` report open in the Design view, point to the top edge of the Detail section divider. When the mouse pointer changes to a two-headed arrow click and drag down to make the page header area about 1/2 inch high.**
You will use this space to place the new text label.

2 **Click the Label button in the Toolbox.**
When you move the pointer over an open area of the design window, the pointer turns into a large *A* with a crosshair attached.

3 **Click at the upper left corner in the Page Header section and drag down and to the right until you have a text box about 2 inches wide and 1/4 inch high.**
This label box is for you to enter text (see Figure 6.15).

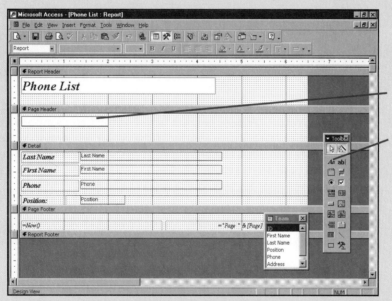

Figure 6.15
The Label button in the Toolbox enables you to add new labels.

Label box

Label button

4 **Type `The Oakville Tigers` in the label box.**
If the label box is too small for the text, you can select the box and resize it to fit.

5 **Click in an open area of the page header.**
This will turn off the text edit.

6 **Click the Print Preview button.**
The original title and the new title you just added are displayed at the top of the report (see Figure 6.16).

7 **Click the Close button on the Print Preview toolbar.**

8 **Click the Save button, then close the report and close the database.**

continues ▶

To Add Labels to a Report (continued)

Figure 6.16
The new label appears at the top of every page of the report.

Label in Page Header section

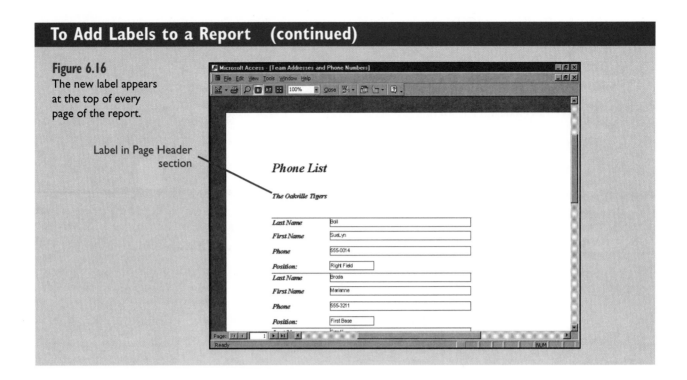

> ![Exam Note icon] **Exam Note: Where Header and Footer Labels Appear**
> Remember, labels that are placed in the report header area will only appear on the first page, and labels that are placed in the report footer area will only appear on the last page of the report. Labels added to the page header and page footer areas will appear on every page of the report.

If you have completed your session on the computer, exit Access and Windows before you turn off the computer. Otherwise, continue with the Checking Concepts and Terms section of this project.

Summary

The main output component of Access is the report. Although you can print a table, as you did in this project, reports are designed to be printed for presentation to others. In this project you created a report using the Report Wizard. You printed the report and renamed it after it had been created. You then learn some of the techniques that can be used to modify a report including how to add and resize fields. After modifying a report you saved it with a new name using the save as command. Finally you used the label tool to add a label to the report.

There are several different report styles and options that can be used as you saw when you used the Report Wizard. To expand your knowledge, create a report and explore the different options that are displayed in the Wizard to see the alternatives that are offered. Use Help and read the topic: Reports: What they are and how they work. Also review the topic: Print a report. Continue with the exercises at the end of this project to practice creating reports.

Checking Concepts and Terms ✓

True/False

For each of the following, check *T* or *F* to indicate whether the statement is true or false.

__T __F **1.** To print table data, you have to use a Report Wizard. You can't just print directly from the table. [L1]

__T __F **2.** You can modify the report layout in Print Preview mode. [L4]

__T __F **3.** To rename a report in the Database window, click once on the report name and type the new name. [L3]

__T __F **4.** To add a label to a report you use the Label tool on the Toolbox. [L6]

__T __F **5.** If the data in a report is too wide to fit in portrait orientation, it may fit in landscape orientation. [L3]

Multiple Choice

Circle the letter of the correct answer for each of the following questions.

1. To change the orientation of the report, which command do you use under the File menu? [L1]

a. Print Setup

b. Print Orientation

c. Page Setup

d. Printer Setup

2. If you make a mistake and want to go to the previous screen in a wizard, which button do you use? [L2]

a. Next

b. Back

c. Previous

d. Go Back

3. How do you delete a control from a report? [L4]

a. Click it and press (Del).

b. Drag it off the report.

c. Double-click it and press (Del).

d. Press (Backspace).

4. To make a group of text boxes the same dimension from top to bottom, select Format, Size, then which command? [L4]

a. Tallest

b. Highest

c. Height, Tallest

d. Largest

5. An AutoReport includes which of the following? [L2]

a. all non-automatic fields in the table

b. all fields in the database

c. the fields you designate in the third dialog box

d. all fields in the source table

Screen ID

Label each element of the Access screen shown in Figure 6.17.

Figure 6.17

A. Toolbox button

B. Field text box

C. Field List button

D. Field label

E. Field list box

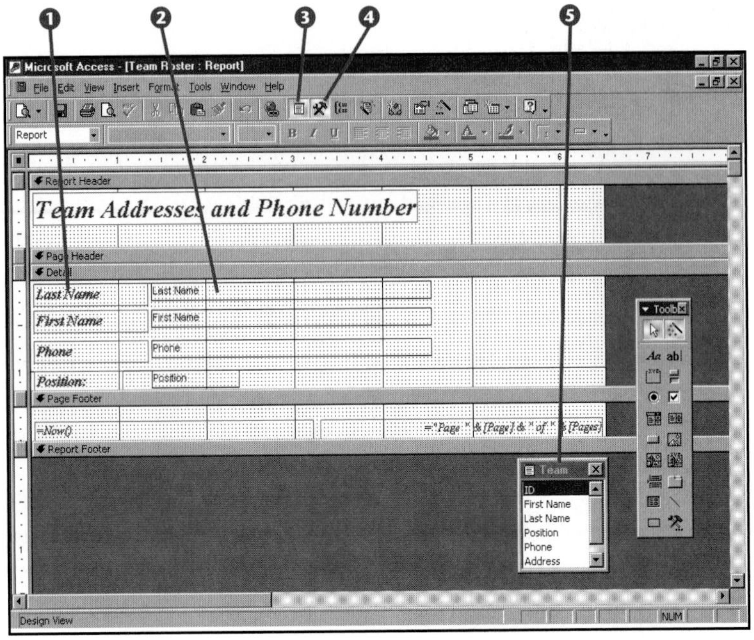

1._____ 3._____ 5._____

2._____ 4._____

Skill Drill

Skill Drill exercises reinforce project skills. Each skill reinforced is the same, or nearly the same, as a skill presented in the project. Each exercise includes a brief narrative introduction, followed by detailed instructions in a step-by-step format.

The database you use for these exercises contains tornado data for the state of Arizona. These records cover a 45-year time span, and include all of the confirmed sightings during that period. The records are an abbreviated form of records produced by the National Oceanic and Atmospheric Administration (NOAA). The fields included in this sample table include the year, date, time of day, number of people killed, number of people injured, a damage scale, the county, and the Fscale (a measure of tornado intensity). Many of the fields are blank because there were no casualties or damage, or because the Fscale was not recorded.

1. Printing Data from a Table

You just want a quick printout of the tornadoes in Arizona over the past 45 years. The layout is not important, and since there are not a lot of fields, you decide to print out the information directly from the table.

To print data from a table:

1. Find the `AC-0602` database file on your CD-ROM, send it to drive A, and name it `Arizona Tornadoes`. Remove the read-only property and open the database. Select and <u>O</u>pen the Arizona Tornadoes table and examine the fields. Notice that the records are displayed in chronological order.

2. Click the Print Preview button to make sure the fields will fit across the page in the portrait orientation.

3. Click the View button to return to Datasheet view.

4. Select <u>F</u>ile, <u>P</u>rint from the menu.

5. Print only the second page (print pages from 2 to 2).

6. Close the table.

7. Leave the database open if you intend to do the next exercise.

2. Creating a Report Using the Report Wizard and Changing the Margins

Printing directly from the table allowed you to quickly scan the data, but did not give you any real control over the final product. You decide to use the Report Wizard to build a more useful, attractive report. Skip the first step if you did the previous exercise.

To create a report using the Report Wizard:

1. Find the `AC-0602` database file on your CD-ROM, send it to drive A, and name it `Arizona Tornadoes`. Remove the read-only property and open the database. Select and <u>O</u>pen the Arizona Tornadoes table and examine the fields.

2. Click the Reports object button.

3. Click the <u>N</u>ew button.

4. Select the Arizona Tornadoes table and choose the Report Wizard.

5. Select all of the fields.

6. Group on the County field.

7. Sort on the Year field first, then the Date field second.

8. Choose the Bloc<u>k</u> layout.

9. Select the Soft Gray style.

10. Maximize the Print Preview window. Click on the preview window to see the whole page. Notice that the report is centered. You intend to punch holes in the left margin and place this report in a binder. It would be better if the left margin were wider than the right margin.

11. Select <u>F</u>ile, Page Set<u>u</u>p from the menu.

12. Change the <u>L</u>eft margin to 1.25 inches and the <u>R</u>ight margin to 0.75 inches.

13. Select <u>F</u>ile, <u>P</u>rint from the menu.

14. Print only page 1. Leave the report open if you intend to do the next exercise.

3. Modifying a Report

The form you created using the Wizard looks pretty good, but the title is not terribly descriptive. You decide to add the period of time covered by the report. If you did exercises 1 or 2, skip the first step.

To modify a report:

1. Find the `AC-0603` database file on your CD-ROM, send it to drive A, and name it `Arizona Tornadoes`, if necessary. Remove the read-only property and open the database. Select and <u>P</u>review the Arizona Tornadoes report.

2. Click the View button to move to the report Design view.

3. Click once on the title in the report header to select it.

4. Grab the center handle on the right edge of the title and drag it to the 6 inch mark. (If your rulers are not turned on, choose <u>V</u>iew, <u>R</u>uler from the menu.)

5. Modify the title so it reads `Arizona Tornadoes, 1951-1995`.

6. Click the View button to see your changes.

7. Close the report and save your changes. Close the database.

Challenge

Challenge exercises expand on or are somewhat related to skills presented in the lessons. Each exercise provides a brief narrative introduction followed by instructions in a numbered step or bullet list format that are not as detailed as those in the Skill Drill section.

The database you will be using for the Challenge section is the same one you used in the Skill Drill section, including the changes you made.

1. Summarizing Data in a Report

As you create reports in the future, you will often want to summarize the data grouped on a field. Access enables you to print all of the data along with summaries, or just the summaries themselves. In this exercise you will create a report that summarizes tornado data by county.

To summarize data in a report:

1. Copy the AC-0604 database file to drive A and rename it **Arizona Tornadoes 2**. Remove the read-only property and open the database.

2. Create a new report based on the Arizona Tornadoes table using the Report Wizard.

3. Select all of the fields and group by county. Don't sort the records, but click the Summary Options button on the sorting page of the Wizard.

4. In the Summary Options dialog box, choose to Sum the Killed and Injured fields, and Avg (average) the Damage and FScale fields.

5. In the same dialog box, choose to display the Summary Only.

6. Use an Outline 2 layout and the Portrait orientation. Select the Bold style.

7. Name the new report **County Summaries**. Notice that some of the categories are empty, and some are shown with seven decimal places. A part of the first page is shown in Figure 6.18.

Figure 6.18
The Arizona tornado records are summarized by county.

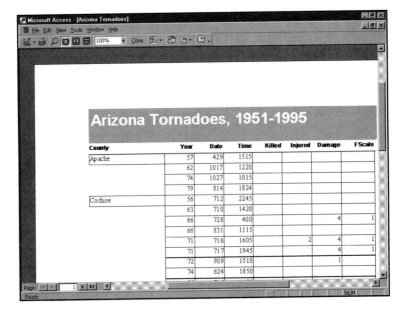

8. Leave the report open if you intend to do the next exercise. Otherwise, close the report and the database.

2. Formatting the Numbers on Reports

The number of decimal places in the Damage and FScale fields are inconsistent. You would like to fix them so that both fields display the results to one decimal place. If you did the previous exercise, you may skip the first step.

To format the numbers in a report:

1. Copy the AC-0605 database file to drive A and rename it Arizona Tornadoes 2, if necessary. Remove the read-only property and open the database. Open the County Summaries report in Design view.

2. In Design view, select both the Damage and the FScale text boxes in which the average is computed. They are in the County Footer area.

3. Click the Properties button in the Report Design toolbar.

4. Use the Help menu to figure out how to set the numbers to a fixed format, and the decimal places to 1.

5. Click the View button to make sure you set both formatting options.

6. Close the report and save your changes. Leave the database open if you plan to do the next exercise.

3. Creating a Report in Design View and Modifying the Format of the Report

You can create a report without using the Report Wizard by starting with an empty report in the Design view. You can change the report properties to indicate what table or query is used as the record source and then drag fields from the Field List box onto the report design. You can apply filters, sort records, and choose formatting options from the Properties box. In this exercise you will create a report to list the tornadoes that injured someone. You will create the report in the design view and use the Properties box, List box, and Toolbox to place the fields and labels, and set the properties of the report.

You may skip the first step if you did the first Challenge exercise.

To create a report in Design view:

1. Copy the AC-0605 database file to drive A and rename it Arizona Tornadoes 2, if necessary. Remove the read-only property and open the database.

2. Click the Reports object button, if necessary and double click Create report in Design view. Maximize the report window.

3. Open the Properties dialog box, if necessary. Choose the Data tab and click the Record Source box. Click the down arrow next to the Record Source box and select Arizona Tornadoes.

4. Click the Filter box and type Injured>0. Click the Filter On box. Click the down arrow next to it and click Yes to turn on the filter.

5. Click the Order By box and type Injured. Change the Order By On box to Yes, if necessary.

6. Click the Format tab on the Report properties box. Click the Caption box and type Injuries in Arizona.

7. Open the field list box, if necessary. Drag the County, Year, Date, Killed, and Injured fields into the Detail area of the report. Close the List box.

8. Resize and rearrange the text and label boxes in the detail area as shown in Figure 6.19.

9. Click and drag the bottom edge of the Detail area upward to reduce its size (see Figure 6.19).

10. Open the Toolbox, if necessary. Click the Label box button and drag a label box in the Page Header area. Type `Tornadoes that Caused Injury`.

11. Click outside the label box. Click on the label box to select it again. Change the font size to 12 and increase the size of the label box and Page Header area (see Figure 6.19).

Figure 6.19
This report is created in Design view.

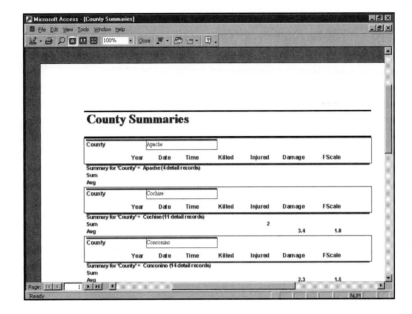

12. Save the report as `Injuries`.

13. Preview the report and confirm that the records displayed are only those that show the number of injuries to be greater than zero and the records are sorted by the number of injuries.

14. Return to the Design view and close the report. Close the database.

Discovery Zone

Discovery Zone exercises help you gain advanced knowledge of project topics and application of skills. These exercises focus on enhancing your problem-solving skills. Numbered steps are not provided, but you are given hints, reminders, screen shots, and references to help you reach your goal for each exercise.

1. Changing the Grouping of Report Data and Keeping the Groups Together

When you finally get your report finished, you may decide that you want to change its focus. You might also consider copying and pasting the report to save the work of creating another one. You can then use this copy to display the data in a different manner. For example, in the Arizona Tornadoes, 1951-1995 report you grouped the data on the County field and sorted on the Year and Date fields. Suppose you also wanted to be able to examine the data by year, and you wanted to make sure the tornadoes of one year did not overlap from one page to the next.

Goal: Change the grouping field in an existing report to keep the tornadoes data grouped together by year and start a new page for each year.

Use the AC-0606 file to create a new database called **Arizona Tornadoes by Year** on your disk. Remove the read-only property and open the database. Use Help from your computer or online to understand how to change the grouped field and how to keep the data together for each of the grouped items. You will modify the Arizona Tornadoes report. To modify this report you should:

- Swap the location of the County field and the Year field in the detail section and swap the labels in the page header.

- Change the grouping to the Year field, rather than the County field.

  Hint: There is a button on the Report Design toolbar that will lead you to a way to make several of the changes.

- Change the sort field to the Date field in ascending order.

- Change the character formatting of the Year field to bold and remove the bold formatting from the County field.

- Have the county name show in every record, but the year be displayed only when it changes (that is, each year should be displayed only once).

  Hint: You can eliminate duplicate years in the Properties box.

Your report should look like Figure 6.20.

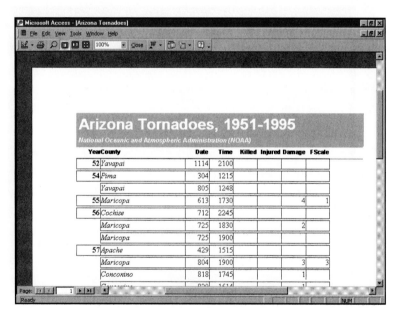

Figure 6.20

- Close the report and the database.

2. Creating Mailing Labels Using the Label Wizard

If you are creating a database for a business, church, or organization, one of the most commonly-used reports will be used to create mailing labels. Mailing labels are usually printed on special sheets that contain ready-to-use labels in various sizes. The Avery company specializes in making labels that fit every need, from folder labels to name tags. Each of the different types of label has its own "Avery number." When you set up your mailing label, you will need to know which Avery label you are using. The Wizard asks for the Avery number, then automatically sets the page up for you.

Goal: Create a report using the Label Wizard that will generate mailing labels from a table of addresses.

Use the **AC-0607** file to create a new database called **Address Labels** on your disk. Remove the read-only property and open the database. Read through the Access help on mailing labels to understand how the Wizard works. Also, carefully read the help provided on each of the Wizard screens. Use the following guidelines:

- The report should use Avery #5160, sheet feed labels. This label uses English measurements.
- The font should be Arial, 10 point.
- The first row should contain the First Name and Last Name fields with a space between them.
- The second row of the labels should contain the Address field.
- The third row of the labels should contain the City field, followed by a comma and a space, then the State field, a space, and finally the ZIP field.
- Sort the labels by Last Name.
- Name your report **Contact Mailing Labels**.

Preview the page, then print the labels.

Your report should look like Figure 6.21.

Figure 6.21

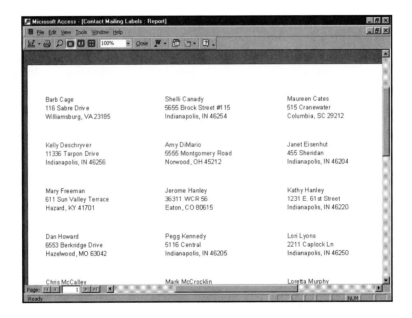

PinPoint Assessment

You have completed this project and its associated lessons, and have had an opportunity to assess your skills through the end-of-project questions and exercises. Now use the PinPoint software Evaluation Mode to further assess your comprehension of the specific exam activities you have just learned. You can also use the PinPoint Trainer Mode and the Show Me tutorials to practice these exam activities.

Integrating Access with Other Sources of Data and the Internet

Key terms introduced in this project include

- browser
- data access page

- delimiters
- mail merge

Objectives	Required Activity for MOUS	Exam Level
➤ Convert a Database from a Previous Version of Access		
➤ Link an Access Table to a Form Letter in Word		
➤ Merge an Access Table with a Form Letter		
➤ Import a Table from Excel	Import Data to a New Table	Core
	Export Database Records to Excel	Expert
	Drag and Drop Tables and Queries to Excel	Expert
➤ Save a Form as a Data Access Page	Create a Data Access Page	Expert
➤ Use a Browser to Interact with the Database	Use the Group and Sort Features of Data Access Pages	Expert

Why Would I Do This?

The data in a database may come from another source—another database, a spreadsheet, or even the Internet. The files you interact with may be on your computer or on a computer anywhere in the world. The tornado information that you used in an earlier project, for example, was obtained over the Internet from the U.S. Storm Data Center. You can also use the power of Access in combination with Microsoft Word to produce form letters that can send data to people individually.

The reports, queries, and forms you create may need to be seen by others. Access is capable of placing information on the World Wide Web so that it can be accessed from anywhere in the world.

Lesson 1: Converting a Database from a Previous Version of Access

Access has changed its basic file structure to conform to an international standard that supports several languages. Databases stored using previous versions of Access will be converted automatically to the new version. Older versions of Access cannot read this data structure and there is no program provided at this time to convert entire Access 2000 databases into older versions of Access (with the exception of Access 97).

In this lesson, you convert a database from the Access 97 format to Access 2000 format.

To Convert a Database from a Previous Version of Access

1 **Launch Access. Click OK to** <u>O</u>**pen an existing file.**
Make sure you have a disk in drive A:.

2 **Find and select the** `AC-0701` **file on your CD-ROM. Click** <u>O</u>**pen.**
The Convert/Open Database window is displayed (see Figure 7.1).

Figure 7.1
The Convert/Open Database window enables you to convert databases created in older versions of Access.

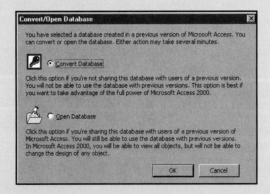

3 **Select the** <u>C</u>**onvert Database option button and click OK.**
The Convert Database Into window is displayed.

4 **Choose 3 1/2 Floppy (A:) in the Save** <u>i</u>**n drop-down list box. Change the name to** `Associates` **in the File** <u>n</u>**ame text box.**
The window should look like Figure 7.2.

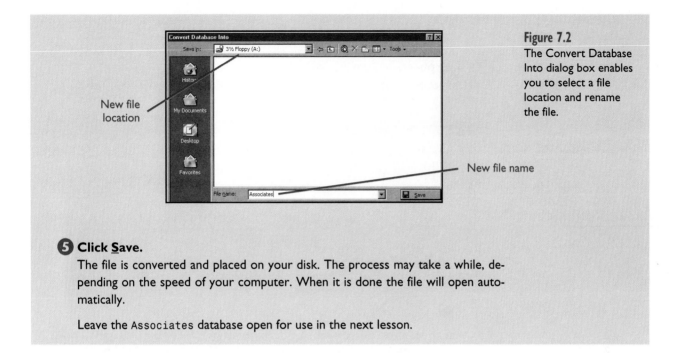

Figure 7.2
The Convert Database Into dialog box enables you to select a file location and rename the file.

New file location

New file name

⑤ Click Save.

The file is converted and placed on your disk. The process may take a while, depending on the speed of your computer. When it is done the file will open automatically.

Leave the `Associates` database open for use in the next lesson.

Exam Note: **Opening the Older Database Without Converting**

The Convert/Open Database window also enables you to use the database without updating it to Access 2000. If you want to open the database without converting it, choose the Open Database option button. This is particularly important if you are sharing the database with someone who is still using an older version of the program. The limitation is that you cannot change the design of any of the objects in the database using Access 2000 until the database has been converted to this version. If you need to make structural changes, it will have to be done by the person using the older version.

Lesson 2: Linking an Access Table to a Form Letter in Word

Databases that contain names and addresses can be merged with Microsoft Word documents to create a series of documents in which each document contains data that is unique to that individual. This feature is known as ***mail merge***. We have all received mail that has a label attached with our names and addresses on it, and most of us have received letters that have our names, birthdays, addresses, or phone numbers embedded in the text. These are examples of how an organization can communicate with its members. Such mailings are not limited to the postal service—you can also create mailings that use fax or email.

In this lesson, you create a letter to notify your business associates that you are moving and will have a new address and phone number.

To Link an Access Table to a Form Letter in Word

① If it is not already highlighted, select the Addresses table in the Database window. Click the list arrow to the right of the OfficeLinks button on the Standard toolbar.
A list of links to other Microsoft Office programs is displayed.

continues ▶

To Link an Access Table to a Form Letter in Word (continued)

2 **Select Merge It with MS Word.**

The Microsoft Word Mail Merge Wizard dialog box is displayed (see Figure 7.3).

Figure 7.3
The Microsoft Word
Mail Merge Wizard di-
alog box enables you
to link to an existing
document or create a
new one.

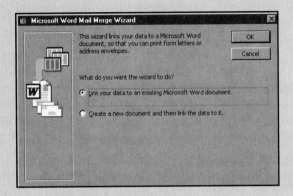

3 **Click the option button labeled Create a new document and then link the data to it. Click OK.**

Microsoft Word is launched and a new document opens. Notice that the Mail Merge toolbar is displayed (see Figure 7.4). If the Word window does not appear, use the taskbar to bring it to the front of the Access window.

Figure 7.4
A new Microsoft
Word document
opens with the Mail
Merge toolbar dis-
played.

The Mail
Merge toolbar

New document

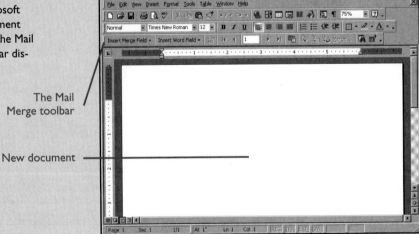

✗ **If You Have Problems...**
The Mail Merge toolbar should open. It may be above or below the formatting or standard toolbar. If it does not open, you can open it by choosing View, Toolbars from the menu and then clicking Mail Merge to open
the toolbar.

4 **Maximize the Word window, change the zoom to 100% and set the font size to 12, if necessary.**

5 Type today's date (the name of the month, the date, and the year) in the first line and press ⏎Enter twice.

Notice that when you begin typing the date, Word automatically suggests the month, then the date. You can press ⏎Enter to accept the month, then press Spacebar. Press ⏎Enter again when today's date appears and the date will be completed for you. Press ⏎Enter twice more to move the insertion point down two lines.

6 Click the Insert Merge Field button on the Mail Merge toolbar.

A list of fields from the Addresses table in the Associates database is displayed. You select one field at a time from this list to create the inside address for a letter.

7 Click FirstName. Press Spacebar.

The name of the field is placed in the document, and is followed by a space.

8 Click the Insert Merge Field button again and click LastName.

The LastName field is placed after the FirstName field.

9 Press ⏎Enter to move to the next line of the address. Refer to the Figure 7.5 to create the rest of the document.

Type your name in the last line rather than <your name>. Be sure to include the comma after the City field and spaces as appropriate. If the Office Assistant opens, just click Cancel to close it.

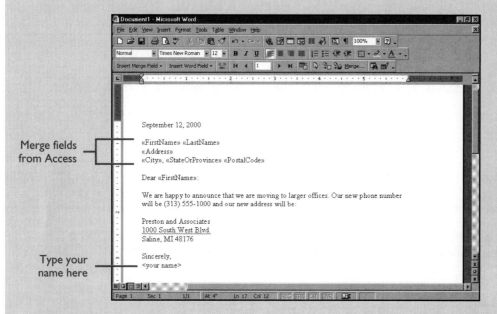

Merge fields from Access

Type your name here

Figure 7.5
The word document has been set up to use the Mail Merge feature.

✗ If You Have Problems...

The font size on your letter may revert to 10 point or whatever default font is set for your computer. If this happens, don't worry about it. The goal of this lesson is to show you how to merge a database file with a word document and the formatting of the letter is not critical to this purpose.

continues ▶

To Link an Access Table to a Form Letter in Word (continued)

⑩ Click the Save button.
The Save As dialog box is displayed.

⑪ Type Associates in the File name text box and use the Save in drop-down list box to select the disk drive and folder that you are using for your files.

⑫ Click Save.
The document is saved as Associates for later use. Leave the Associates document and database open for use in the next lesson.

Exam Note: **Using the Mail Merge Feature with a Query**
You can also use the mail merge feature with a query. This is useful when you need to include a calculated field in the letter, restrict the mailing to clients who meet a certain criteria, or use fields from more than one table.

Inside Stuff: **Naming an Access Database to Match a Word Document**
Microsoft Word documents are automatically saved with a file extension of .doc and Access databases are saved with an .mdb extension. You can use the same name for the Word document and the Access database because they will have different extensions, even though the extensions may not appear onscreen.

Lesson 3: Merging an Access Table with a Form Letter

Once you have linked the database field names into a Word document, you can create a series of documents which each contain the data from a record in the database table. This process creates a file of the merged, personalized letters. You can print a few of the letters to ensure that they do not contain errors before you send the rest of them to the printer.

In this lesson, you merge the database file into the letter and print two of the documents.

To Merge an Access Table with a Form Letter

❶ With the Associates document and database open, click the View Merged Data button on the Mail Merge toolbar in Word.
The data from the first record in the Addresses table is inserted into the document (see Figure 7.6).

❷ Click the Next Record button.
The data from the second record is displayed. Notice that the address of the first person takes two lines, while the second person's address takes only one line. Word adjusts for multiple line addresses and for empty fields.

❸ Click the Merge button on the Mail Merge toolbar.
The ScreenTip for this button displays Start Mail Merge. When you click it the Merge dialog box is displayed.

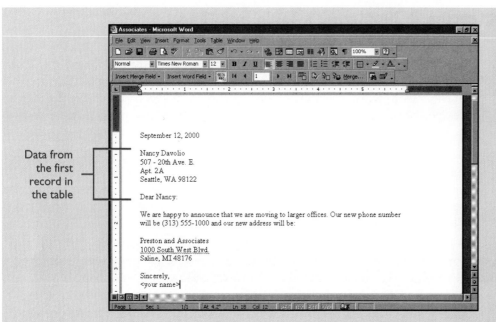

Figure 7.6
The Word document displays the data from the first record in the table.

Data from the first record in the table

September 12, 2000

Nancy Davolio
507 - 20th Ave. E.
Apt. 2A
Seattle, WA 98122

Dear Nancy:

We are happy to announce that we are moving to larger offices. Our new phone number will be (313) 555-1000 and our new address will be:

Preston and Associates
1000 South West Blvd.
Saline, MI 48176

Sincerely,
<your name>

4 **Click the list arrow next to the Merge to drop-down list box.**

Notice that you can send this letter electronically by email as well as by traditional postal service (see Figure 7.7). If your system is set up to use fax, it will also be displayed as an option.

Optional document destinations

Figure 7.7
The Mail Merge document can be sent by fax or to email addresses.

5 **Select Printer. Click the From text box in the Records to be merged section and type 1. Type 2 in the To text box.**

6 **Click the Merge button to print the letters to the first two people in the Addresses table.**

The Print dialog box is displayed.

7 **Click OK.**

The first two letters are printed.

8 **Close the Associates Word document.**

Save any changes when prompted. Close Microsoft Word. Leave the Associates database open for use in the next lesson.

Exam Note: **Starting the Mail Merge Process in Word**

The mail merge process can start with Word rather than Access. You can open Word, use the mail merge procedures for Word to create a document, and then tie it to the Access database that contains the records of the names and addresses for your letter.

 **Lesson 4: Importing a Table from Excel**

Excel has some database management features, such as the capability to sort and filter data. Therefore, many people use Excel as a simple database management program. Often, however, the amount of data that needs to be maintained becomes too cumbersome to work with effectively in Excel. When this happens, you need to import data that is stored in an Excel spreadsheet and use it with an Access database. When you import data, the rows of data are treated as records and are copied into Access. Each column of information in Excel is identified as a field in Access.

In this lesson, you import an Excel spreadsheet that contains budget information for the U.S. government into the Associates database that is open from the previous lesson. The Associates database is being used for convenience—the information being imported in the this lesson is not related to the Addresses table in the database.

To Import a Table from Excel

1 **Launch Excel and open AC-0702 from the CD. Scroll down the rows and examine the data.**
Notice that each row is a record of a type of government expense. The column headings will become field names (see Figure 7.8).

Figure 7.8
The Excel column headings will become Access field names.

Column headings

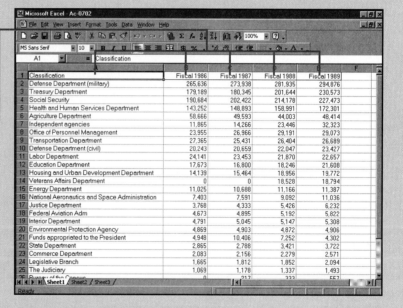

2 **Close the file and close Excel.**
Switch to Access and the Associates database.

3 **Choose File, Get External Data, Import.**
The Import dialog box is displayed.

4 **Click the list arrow next to the Files of type drop-down list box and select Microsoft Excel. Locate and select the AC-0702 Excel file on the CD.**
Your Import dialog box should look like Figure 7.9.

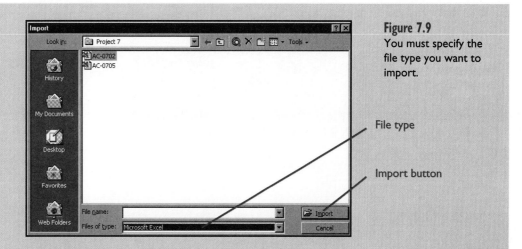

Figure 7.9
You must specify the file type you want to import.

File type

Import button

5 Click the Import button.
The Import Spreadsheet Wizard dialog box is displayed. Make sure the Show Worksheets option button is selected and that Sheet1 is highlighted. Notice that the column headings in the first row are displayed as data (see Figure 7.10).

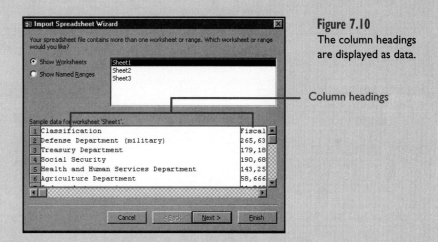

Figure 7.10
The column headings are displayed as data.

Column headings

6 Click Next. Click the check box next to First Row Contains Column Headings, if necessary.
The row that contains the words Classification and Fiscal is converted to headers, which appear as field names in the database table (see Figure 7.11).

7 Click Next. Make sure that the In a New Table option button is selected.

8 Click Next.
Do not add indexes to any of the fields.

9 Click Next. Select Let Access add Primary Key, if it is not already selected.
In this case, there are no unique fields so you can let Access add a field that gives each row a unique number.

continues ▶

To Import a Table from Excel   (continued)

Figure 7.11
The column headings
become field names in
the table.

Check here to
change the first row
into field names

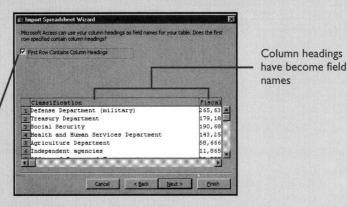

Column headings
have become field
names

⑩ **Click Next. Type** Government Expenses **in the Import to Table text box.**

⑪ **Click Finish. Click OK when Access prompts that the import is finished.**
The Government Expenses data is added to the database as a new table.

⑫ **Click the Open button in the Database window.**
The Government Expenses table is displayed (see Figure 7.12).

Figure 7.12
The Excel worksheet
has been imported as
an Access table.

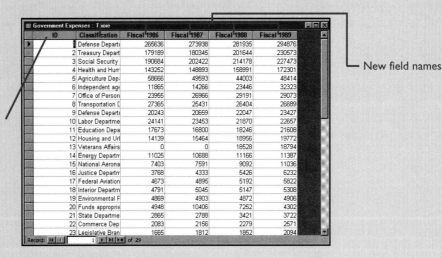

New field names

Primary key field

⑬ **Close the table.**
This table is now available for use. Leave the Associates database open for the
next lesson.

 Inside Stuff: **Preparing to Import a Spreadsheet**
A spreadsheet must be set up like a database table if you are going to import it
successfully. Check to make sure that the Excel data is arranged in rows and
columns where each column is a field and each row is a record. If necessary, copy
the data to a new spreadsheet. Remove blank rows or rows that contain decorative
characters such as long rows of dashes set up to look like a line.

Exam Note: **Moving an Access Table or Query to Excel**
The transfer of data between Access and Excel can go both ways. You can copy table or query data, then paste it into an Excel worksheet. You can also open both an Access and an Excel window, then drag the table or query name from the Database window onto a worksheet. The entire contents of the table or query are transferred to the worksheet. You then need to select the whole worksheet, choose Format, Cells, Alignment from the menu, and turn off the Wrap Text option.

Lesson 5: Saving a Form as a Data Access Page

Access 2000 is capable of saving forms as interactive Web pages. To save an interactive Web page, you save your object as a ***data access page***, which is a special type of Web page that has been designed for viewing and working with data from the Internet. You can place a database on a Web server and interact with it using an interactive Web page. To view an interactive Web page, you must have a browser that supports this feature, such as Internet Explorer 5.0.

In this lesson, you create a Web page that will enable your sales people to look up contact information.

To Save a Form as a Data Access Page

1 **In the** `Associates` **Database window, click the Pages object button and then click New.**
The New Data Access Page window is displayed.

2 **Select Page Wizard, choose the Addresses table as the data source, then click OK.**
The first page of the Page Wizard is displayed.

3 **Use the Add button to select the following fields: FirstName, LastName, Address, City, EmailAddress, HomePhone, WorkPhone, WorkExtension, and FaxNumber.**
Your dialog box should look like Figure 7.13.

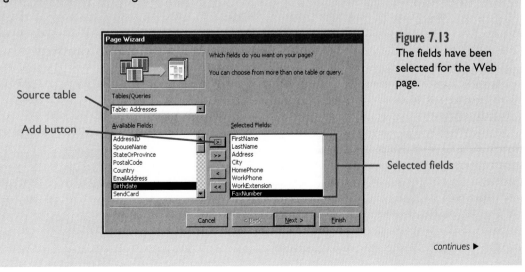

Figure 7.13
The fields have been selected for the Web page.

continues ▶

To Save a Form as a Data Access Page (continued)

④ Click Next.

The second Page Wizard dialog box is displayed. Do not use the grouping option at this time.

⑤ Click Next.

The third Page Wizard dialog box is displayed (see Figure 7.14). This page is used to sort the records.

Figure 7.14
The third Page Wizard dialog box enables you to sort the records.

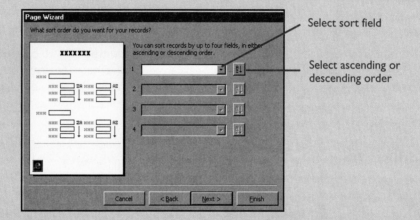

Select sort field

Select ascending or descending order

⑥ Click the list arrow next to the first sorting box and select LastName. Click Next.

The fourth Page Wizard dialog box is displayed, asking you for a title for the page.

⑦ Type the title Contact Information and click Finish.

The Contact Information data access page is created by the wizard. It is opened in Design view.

⑧ Click in the Click here and type title text area and type Business Contacts.

You may have to scroll up to see the title area. You can also type introductory text above the data area (see Figure 7.15).

Figure 7.15
The Design view of the Page window enables you to add titles and supplementary text to the page.

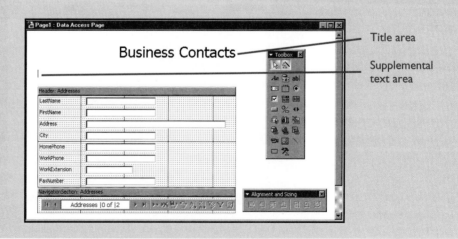

Title area

Supplemental text area

9 **Click the View button to switch to Page view. Maximize the window.**
The title is displayed at the top of the page and the first record is shown. A set of navigation buttons is displayed below the data (see Figure 7.16).

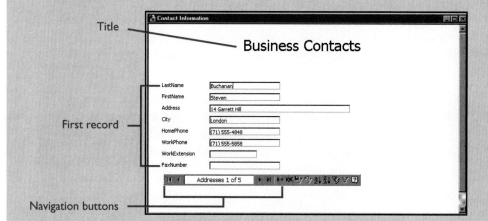

Title
First record
Navigation buttons

Figure 7.16
The Web page is previewed in Page view.

10 **Use the navigation buttons at the bottom of the page to scroll through the records.**

11 **Close the page and choose Yes to save the changes.**
The Save As Data Access Page dialog box is displayed.

12 **Type Contact Access Page in the File name text box. Click Save to save the data access page.**
Make sure the Save in box displays the location of your database. In addition to saving this in the database, the page is also saved separately with an .htm extension in the same location as your database. In this case, the file name is Contact Access Page.htm.

13 **Close the Associates database and close Access.**
In the next lesson you view the data access page as you would on the Internet.

 Exam Note: Saving Data Access Pages
When you create a data access page it is saved as a separate file that can be viewed like a Web page on the Internet. Microsoft Access automatically creates a shortcut to the file, which is what you see in the Database window. The process of creating a data access page is similar to creating forms or reports; however, there can be several different ways a page can be used. The design of the page is influenced by its ultimate purpose. For more information about designing a data access page, open Help and review the topic Data access pages: What they are and how they work.

Lesson 6: Using a Browser to Interact with the Database

If the database table and a related interactive Web page are placed on a Web server (or in a shared folder on a local area network), then others can use the database with a Web browser. A **browser**, such as Internet Explorer or Netscape Communicator, is a program that enables you to view Web pages on the Internet. When you interact with the table on the Web, you can browse through the data. You can also sort and filter the data using any field, and you can even change the data.

In this lesson, you use Internet Explorer to interact with the database on your disk as if it were placed on a Web server.

To Use a Browser to Interact with the Database

❶ Launch Internet Explorer.
You must have Internet Explorer 5.0 or greater to run the Web page you created in Lesson 5. You do not need to connect to the Web, so click Cancel to work off line.

❷ Click in the Address box and type the disk location and name of your Web page, (for example, a:\Contact Access Page.htm), then press ⏎Enter).
As you type, the program automatically starts to search for the file. You may see a list of files displayed that have been previously accessed by your computer. The arrow at the end of the address box opens and closes this list.

The browser displays the page and a toolbar (see Figure 7.17).

Figure 7.17
The Web page is previewed in Internet Explorer.

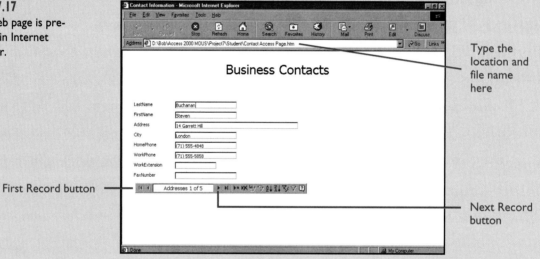

Type the location and file name here

First Record button

Next Record button

 If You Have Problems . . .
If you have saved your file to a folder, the folder may open and icons for the various files will be displayed. Click the file with the Explorer icon and the name Contacts Access Page.htm to view your data access page.

---

 ❸ Click the Next Record navigation button to scroll through the records.

 ❹ Click the First Record navigation button at the far left of the navigation bar to return to the first record.
Notice that the area codes for the two phone numbers are incorrect.

❺ Edit these two phone numbers to change the area code to (717).

❻ Click in the LastName field, then click the Sort Descending button.
Scroll through the records using the navigation buttons. Notice the records are displayed in reverse alphabetical order by last name.

7 **Close the browser.**

Notice that the Access program was not running during this lesson.

8 **Launch Access and open the Associates database.**

9 **Click the Tables object button, open the Addresses table, and scroll to the right until you can see both telephone numbers.**

Both area codes that you changed in the Web page are changed in the database table (see Figure 7.18).

The area codes have been changed —

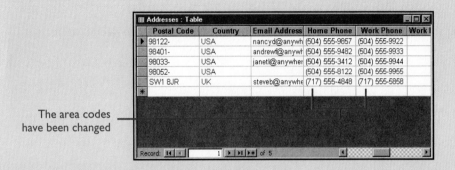

Figure 7.18
The area codes that were changed on the Web page are also changed in the table.

10 **Close the table and close the database.**

If you have completed your session on the computer, exit Access and Windows before you turn off the computer. Otherwise, continue with the Checking Concepts and Terms section of this project.

 Inside Stuff: **Entering Addresses in Internet Explorer**

When you are typing the address in Internet Explorer, once it has determined that you are typing a drive name, it will offer you a drop-down menu. For example, after you type A:\ (if your page was saved on drive A), a drop-down menu is displayed, showing all of the files available on that drive.

Summary

In this project you were introduced to some of the tools and techniques that enable you to work with information from other sources and to publish Access files for use as Web pages. Specifically you learned to convert an existing Access database to the current version, Access 2000. You also imported data from an Excel spreadsheet into Access. You then created a data access page and viewed it using a Web browser.

To learn more about the capability of Access to import data from other sources, go to Help and look at the topic "Data sources Microsoft Access can import or link." Also, examine the topic "Data access pages: What are they and how do they work." This will expand your knowledge about design considerations when you want to make your database accessible using a Web browser.

Checking Concepts and Terms ✓

True/False

For each of the following, check *T* or *F* to indicate whether the statement is true or false.

__T __F   **1.** One reason to view your merged document before printing is to ensure that the document looks the way you intended. [L3]

__T __F   **2.** The Merge function in Access adjusts for multiple address lines and empty fields when it prints a merged document. [L3]

__T __F   **3.** When importing a spreadsheet file into Access, it is important that the first row of the spreadsheet is set up with field names, and each subsequent row is a record. [L4]

__T __F   **4.** If you want to use an Access 2000 database on a computer that has Access 97, you can use the Save As option on the File menu to convert the database. [L1]

__T __F   **5.** You can sort the data in a Web page in ascending or descending order. [L6]

Multiple Choice

Circle the letter of the correct answer for each of the following questions.

1. What can you do with a database created using an older version of Access? [L1]

   a. Enter data with Access 2000 but not change any objects.

   b. Convert it to Access 2000.

   c. Share the database with people using different versions of Access.

   d. All of the above.

2. How do you set up a Microsoft Word mail merge document while you are using Access? [L2]

   a. Click the MailMerge button on the toolbar.

   b. Select the appropriate table, click the OfficeLinks button, and choose Merge It with MS Word.

   c. Select the appropriate table, open MS Word, and choose Link to Access from the Tools menu.

   d. Open the appropriate table, click the OfficeLinks button, and choose Merge It with MS Word.

3. When you import data from Excel into Access how does Access interpret the data? [L4]

   a. Rows of data are interpreted as records and columns are interpreted as fields.

   b. Columns of data are interpreted as records and rows are interpreted as fields.

   c. Access does not make any assumptions and asks you to identify the records.

   d. You enter the names of the fields in the Import Wizard.

4. What is the command used to import data? [L4]

   a. Choose File, Get External Data, Import from the menu.

   b. Click the Import button.

   c. Choose Insert, Data, Import from the menu.

   d. none of the above

5. How do you begin the process to create a page from your database that can be viewed on the Web? [L5]

   a. Click the Create Web page button on the toolbar.

   b. Click the Pages object button and select New.

   c. Select the object you want to use and choose File, Save as, Web page from the menu.

   d. Select the object you want to use and click Officelinks, Publish as Web page from the menu.

Screen ID

Label each element of the Access screen shown in Figure 7.19.

Figure 7.19

A. Returns to first record on Web page

B. Sort Descending button

C. Displays next record on Web page

D. Location of Web page on your disk

E. Data access page title

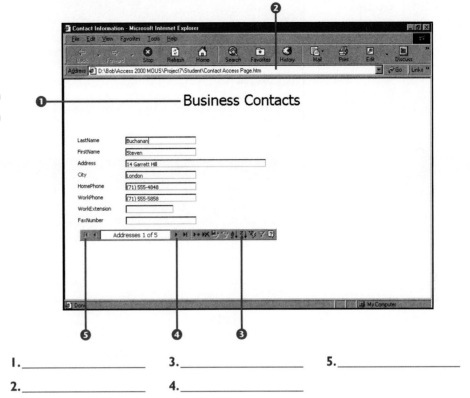

1._____   3._____   5._____

2._____   4._____

Skill Drill

Skill Drill exercises reinforce project skills. Each skill reinforced is the same, or nearly the same, as a skill presented in the project. Each exercise includes a brief narrative introduction, followed by detailed instructions in a step-by-step format.

1. Creating and Printing a Memo Using Mail Merge

Your company is going to have a summer picnic. You have already invited all of your employees, but you decide it would also be a nice gesture to invite your business contacts. You use a new version of the Associates database you worked with throughout this project to create a quick memo to send to the people in the Addresses table.

To create and print a memo using mail merge:

1. Find the AC-0703 database file on your CD-ROM, send it to drive A:, remove the read-only status, and name it Associates-Revised. You may need to use a new disk. Select the Addresses table, if necessary.

2. Edit the Addresses table and enter a guest in the empty spouse field. Close the table.

3. Click the OfficeLinks button and select Merge It with MS Word. Create a new document in Word and click Open.

4. Create a mail merge memo announcing a company picnic. Invite each person by name, and also invite their spouse by name. Use Figure 7.20 as a guide.

Figure 7.20
Your document should include fields for your contact's first and last name, and his or her spouse's name.

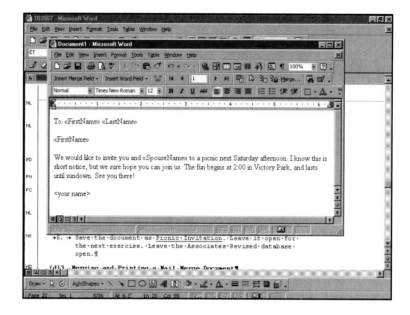

5. Use your name at the bottom of each letter where it says <your name>.

6. Click the View Merged Data button to test your mail merge document. Scroll through the records to make sure the **and guest** edit flows smoothly.

7. Save the document as **Picnic Invitation**.

8. Choose File, Print from the menu. Print the letters for records 1 and 5. To do this in one step, type **1,5** in the Pages box and then click OK.

9. Leave the **Picnic Invitation** document and the **Associates-Revised** database open for the next exercise.

2. Importing a Table from Excel

Your company's sales are based on population growth, so you would like to have some population forecasts available to make long-range sales projections. One of the marketing people has put the information into an Excel worksheet. You want to move it into your Associates database. If you did the previous exercise, skip the first step.

To import a table from Excel:

1. Find the **AC-0703** database file on your CD-ROM, send it to drive A:, remove the read-only status, and name it **Associates-Revised**. You may need to use a new disk..

2. Choose File, Get External Data, Import from the menu.

3. Specify Microsoft Excel in the Files of type box.

4. Find and select the **AC-0704** Excel file, and then click the Import button.

5. Specify that the first row contains column headings, then choose to place the data in a new table.

6. Do not add an index, but select the **Choose my own primary key** option button and select the Year column as the primary key.

7. Name the table **Population Projection**, and then click Finish.

8. Open the table and review it to make sure it translated properly.

9. Print the table and then close it.

10. Keep the **Associates-Revised** database open for the next exercise.

3. Creating and Testing a Data Page for Use on the Web

You want to put the government budget information on a Web page. The first step is to create the data page and decide what information you want to include. The second is to try out your page using a browser. If you did either of the first two exercises, skip the first step.

To create and test a data page for use on the Web:

1. Find the `AC-0703` database file on your CD-ROM, send it to drive A:, remove the read-only status, and name it `Associates-Revised`. You may need to use a new disk.

2. In the `Associates-Revised` Database window, click the Pages object button and click New.

3. Select Page Wizard and choose the Government Expenses table.

4. Select the Classification, Fiscal 1987, Fiscal 1988, and Fiscal 1989 fields. You will not use the ID and Fiscal 1986 fields.

5. Do not group the data, but sort by Classification.

6. Call the data page `Government Budget`.

7. Add a title called `U.S. Government Budget`.

8. Close the Data Access Page design window. When prompted, save the page with the name `Government Expenses`, and then close the Associates-Revised database.

9. Launch Internet Explorer, and enter the location and name of the Government Expenses.htm file you just created. (If you have trouble locating the file, use File, Open, Browse and locate the file in the Microsoft Internet Explorer window.)

10. Open the `Government Expenses` file and use the navigation buttons to scroll through the records. Think about what you might do to improve the quality of this page.

11. Close the Internet Explorer.

Challenge

Challenge exercises expand on or are somewhat related to skills presented in the lessons. Each exercise provides a brief narrative introduction followed by instructions in a numbered step or bullet list format that are not as detailed as those in the Skill Drill section.

1. Opening and Adding Data to an Older Version of Access

You and your sister have been collecting CDs for years, and entering the information into a database. She has a computer that uses Access 97, while you have upgraded to Access 2000. You still want to keep up the database, so you have to open the old version without converting it. You would also like to add another field to help keep track of who owns which CD.

To open and add data to an older version of Access:

1. Copy the `AC-0705` file to drive A:, remove the read-only status, and change the name to `CD Collection`. You may need to use a new disk.

2. Open the `CD Collection` database. When prompted, choose the Open Database option, not the Convert Database option.

3. Open the CD Collection table and add the following record:

> Rollins, Sonny
>
> Saxophone Colossus
>
> 1956
>
> Prestige
>
> OJCCD-291-2
>
> Jazz/Big Band

4. Go to the table Design view and scroll to the first empty field.

5. Add a field called `Whose?` and make it a text field.

6. Click the View button to switch back to the datasheet. What happens? Why?

7. Close the table without saving the changes and close the CD Collection database.

2. Importing Tables Stored in dBASE III and Text Formats

A common database for personal computers in the 1980s was dBASE III. Many database records from that period (especially from the U.S. government) are stored in that format, as are many data sources on the Web. Data is also frequently found in text files in which the fields are separated by tabs, commas, spaces, or some other character. These data separators are known as **delimiters**. If fields are separated by tabs, for example, the file is referred to as tab-delimited. Access can import such files using the Import wizard.

In this exercise, you import data from a 1987 dBASE III+ database that shows statistics about retail establishments and their employees in Michigan by postal code. (Sales and Payroll figures are in 1000s.) You then import hardware data stored in a text file.

To import a table from an old dBASEIII+ database:

1. Create a new database on drive A: and call it `Importing Data`. You may need to use a new disk.

2. Choose File, Get External Data, Import from the menu.

3. Specify that you are looking for dBASE III file types and select the file, `AC-0706.dbf`.

4. Close the Import dialog box. Rename the new table `Retail Statistics`. If you do not remember how to do this, use Help.

5. Open the `Retail Statistics` table. Click the record selector to the left of the first record. (⬆Shift)+click the record selector for the tenth record (zip code is 48009) to select the first ten records.

6. Choose File, Print, Selected Records(s) to print the first ten records.

7. Close the table.

8. Follow the above procedure to import the `AC-0707` file. The file type is Text Files.

9. Follow the Import Text Wizard instructions. Make sure you specify that the first row contains the field names. Accept all of the default settings.

10. Name the new table `Plumbing`. Open the table and take a look at it. Print the table.

11. Close the Plumbing table and close the database.

3. Creating and Using a Data Access Page Based on a Query

You can base a data access page on a query as well as a table. This gives you the ability to use query features, such as critera, to restrict the information you place on the Web. In the following exercise, you use the CD collection information that you worked with in the first exercise in the Challenge section.

To create and use a data access page based on a query:

1. Copy the `AC-0708` database onto drive A: and rename it `New CD Collection`. You may need to use a new disk.

2. Create a new query based on the CD Collection table. Include all of the fields. Set the criteria so that the query only shows classical CDs and call the query `Classical CDs`.

3. Create a new data access page based on the Classical CDs query. Do not group or sort.

4. Add a title that says `Classical CDs`. Save the data access page with the name `Classical CD Collection`.

5. Add `From the collection of <your name>` as body text (type in your name for <your name>).

6. Use the available help to figure out how to add a clip art image to the page. Find an appropriate image and resize it to about 1 inch high. Place it to the left of the title.

7. Close the page and save your changes as `Classical CDs`.

8. Go to the Windows Explorer or My Computer and look at the file you just saved. There should be a new folder that contains a copy of the image you placed in the page. This folder needs to be kept with the page file.

9. Open the Classical CDs page in the browser. Click in the Artist/Group field.

10. Click on the Sort Ascending button on the toolbar at the bottom of the screen. The records are sorted in ascending order by the Artist/Group field.

11. Scroll to the first recording on the RCA label.

12. Click the Filter by Selection button that is near the right end of the toolbar at the bottom of the screen. The middle of the navigation buttons should display 1 of 10. This indicates that there are 10 CDs in the database that were recorded on the RCA label. Scroll through a few records to make sure that the filter worked.

13. Click the Remove Filter button to turn the filter off. All 132 records should be listed in the navigation bar as shown in Figure 7.21.

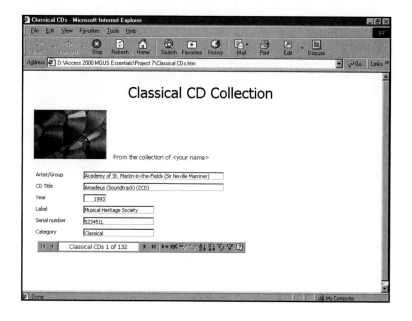

Figure 7.21
You can sort and filter records on a data access page viewed with a browser.

14. Close your browser.

Discovery Zone

Discovery Zone exercises help you gain advanced knowledge of project topics and application of skills. These exercises focus on enhancing your problem-solving skills. Numbered steps are not provided, but you are given hints, reminders, screen shots, and references to help you reach your goal for each exercise.

1. Copying Part of a Table to a Word Document

A convenient way to transfer data from a database table to a document is a simple copy and paste. This results in creating a table in Word that can be formatted in a variety of styles. Try this procedure with the data from the Addresses table in the Associates database that you worked with earlier in this project.

Goal: Copy columns of data from an Access table to a table in Word.

An associate has requested a list of names and addresses from you. Launch Word, and write a short note to your coworker that tells him or her that this is the list of names that was requested. Make sure you include your name at the end of your brief note.

Open the **AC-0703** database as **Associates3** on drive A: (you may need to use a new disk) and use the Addresses table. You need to include first and last names and home and work phone numbers in your memo. To copy these fields to Word, they need to be next to each other so they can be copied as a group. (*Hint:* Do not make this a permanent change to the structure of the table, move the fields in the datasheet view.)

Select and copy the First Name, Last Name, Home Phone, and Work Phone fields, then switch to Word and paste them. Format the table by choosing T<u>a</u>ble, Table <u>A</u>utoFormat from the menu. Choose a format that you like. (*Hint:* Be sure to select the column headings when you are selecting the information to copy.)

Print the document and save it as **Associates3**. Close the Word document and the database.

2. Updating a Table by Pasting Cells from a Spreadsheet

You may want to send a table of data to someone who has Excel, but not Access. To do this you can export the data to Excel.

Goal: Export a table to Excel, make changes to it in Excel, then paste the new cells back into the Access table.

Open the **AC-0703** database as **Associates4** on drive A: (you may need to use a new disk) and use the Addresses table. To ensure that you maintain the original data intact, you want to make a copy of the table and export the copy to Excel. Make a copy of the Addresses table and name the copy **Address Updates**. (*Hint:* right click on the table and use the shortcut menus.)

Export the table to Excel. Use whichever export method you prefer (export, drag-and-drop, or copy-and-paste). Name it **Address Updates**.

Launch Excel and open the **Addresses Updates** file. Scroll to the right and add short comments to the Notes field in the Excel worksheet. Don't be concerned about the width of the columns or the content of the notes. Save the Excel file as **Associates4**.

Now you want to transfer this new information back to the original Access table. Copy the updated cells in the Excel sheet (do not include the heading). Open the **Addresses** table in Access. Click the Notes column selector and paste the entries from the Excel sheet. The information that was entered in Excel is now entered in the original Access table. Close the database, close Excel.

PinPoint Assessment

You have completed this project and its associated lessons, and have had an opportunity to assess your skills through the end-of-project questions and exercises. Now use the PinPoint software Evaluation Mode to further assess your comprehension of the specific exam activities you have just learned. You can also use the PinPoint Trainer Mode and the Show Me tutorials to practice these exam activities.

Project 8

Making Data Entry Easier and More Accurate

Key terms introduced in this project include

- default value
- Expression Builder
- format

- indexed field
- input mask
- placeholder

- validation rule
- validation text

Objectives	Required Activity for MOUS	Exam Level
➤ Create Consistent Data Formats	Modify field properties	Core
➤ Create Conditional Formats for Positive, Negative, and Null Values	Modify field properties	Core
➤ Change the Data Input Structure Using Input Masks	Use the Input Mask Wizard	Core
➤ Restrict Entry Using Validation Criteria	Define data validation criteria, set validation text	Expert
➤ Require Entry of Necessary Information	Modify field properties	Core
➤ Prevent Duplicate Entries Using Indexed Fields	Modify field properties	Core Expert
➤ Create a Lookup Column to Allow Selection from a List	Use the Lookup Wizard	Core
➤ Modify a Lookup Field	Create and modify Lookup Fields	Expert
➤ Enter a Default Value	Modify field properties	Core
➤ Modify an Input Mask	Modify an input mask	Expert
➤ Optimize data type usage	Optimize data type usage (double, long, int, byte, etc.)	Expert

Why Would I Do This?

I t is important that your data is stored and presented in a consistent **format**. Format refers to the way text or numbers are displayed. If some phone numbers are entered as (XXX) XXX-XXXX and some as 1-XXX-XXX-XXXX, it may be difficult to sort or extract the data. If one person designs and enters all of the data, you may be able to get consistent input, but if that person is on vacation or out because of illness, your database could be filled with useless data by someone unfamiliar with your methods.

You may want your database to call attention to negative numbers or to suppress zeros in empty numeric fields. You learn how to use conditional formats to accomplish these goals.

To save time, you can create a list of possible entries. This enables you to pick an entry from a list rather than enter it from the keyboard.

It is also important to guard against common errors. You can check an entry against a set of rules to see if the entry is within allowable limits or matches a list of possible values. You may want to require that all records contain certain fields to guard against duplicate entries.

In this project, you learn how to control the format of your data, check entries against a set of rules, and prevent duplicate entries. The database that you are modifying is designed to track the training employees have received on computer software packages.

Lesson 1: Creating Consistent Data Formats

There are many occasions when you want your data to be displayed in a specific format. For example, you might want to have text displayed in uppercase letters, or you might want dates to appear in a consistent format. Using a drop-down menu can activate some of these formats, while others require that you enter a symbol in a special format box.

In the following procedure you learn how to change the appearance of two of the fields in the Software Training table. You change the format of the Last Name field to display all of the names in uppercase letters, and modify the date format in the Date Hired field.

To Create a Consistent Data Format

1 **Launch Access. Click OK to Open an existing file.**
The Open dialog box is displayed. Make sure you have a diskette in drive A.

2 **Use the Look in box to locate the AC-0801 file on your CD-ROM, right click on it, and use the Send To option to send it to the floppy drive. Select drive A, right-click on the file name, and select Properties from the shortcut menu. Select Archive and de-select Read-only from the Attributes section.**

3 **Right-click on the file name, and select Rename from the shortcut menu. Rename the file PC Training, then open the database.**
The Database window should now be open to the Tables object button (see Figure 8.1).

4 **Click the Tables object button, if necessary, then select the Software Training table and click the Open button to view the data.**
Notice that the data contained in the Last Name field is a mix of upper- and lowercase letters, and the Date Hired field is displayed in the mm/dd/yy format.

5 **Click the View button on the toolbar to switch to Design view.**
The Table Design view is displayed (see Figure 8.2).

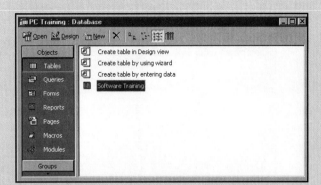

Figure 8.1
The Database window displays the Tables area of the PC Training database.

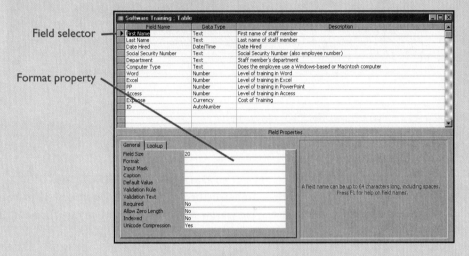

Figure 8.2
The Design view of the Software Training table includes detailed field information.

Field selector

Format property

---

6 **Click anywhere in the Last Name field to select it.**
The Field Properties section in the bottom half of the window changes to display the properties of the Last Name field.

7 **Click in the Format property box in the Field Properties section.**

8 **Type the "greater than" symbol, >, as the Format property.**
The "greater than" symbol tells the program to display all text in the field as uppercase. The "less than" symbol, <, displays all of the text in a field in lowercase. When no entry is made in the Format property box, text is displayed as entered.

9 **Click the View button on the toolbar to switch to Datasheet view.**
Click Yes.
Whenever you make changes in field structures, the program asks you if you want to save your changes. Click Yes whenever this message is displayed. Notice that all of the last names in the Last Name field are now displayed in capital letters.

10 **Click the View button to return to Design view, then click anywhere in the Date Hired field.**

11 **Select the Format property box, then click the drop-down arrow.**
The date Format drop-down list is displayed (see Figure 8.3). Notice that a format can be selected for dates and times, or the General Date can be used to display both date and time.

continues ▶

To Create a Consistent Data Format (continued)

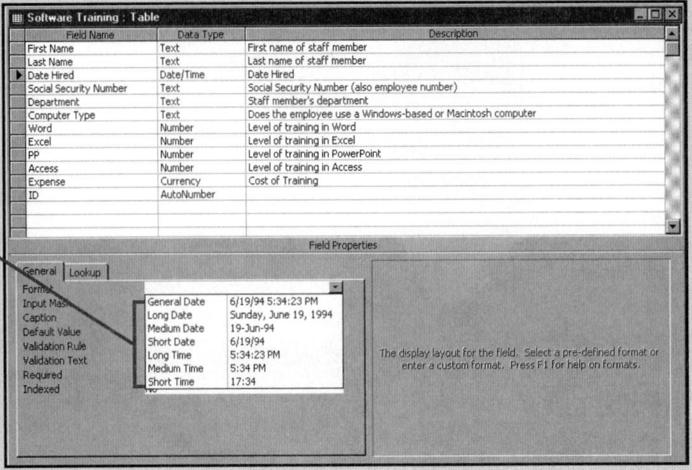

Figure 8.3
The date Format
drop-down list
includes several unique
date and time formats.

Date and time formats

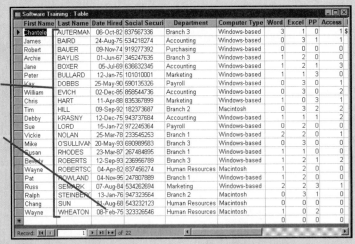

12 **Select the Medium Date format.**
Each format refers to the relative length of the date entries as they appear in the database.

 13 **Click the View button to return to Datasheet view. Click Yes.**
Once again, you have changed the structure of the Table, so you need to save your changes. The Date Hired field is now displayed in the dd-mm-yy format (see Figure 8.4).

Figure 8.4
The Software Training
table shows the
changes in format.

Last names are all capitalized

Date format has
been changed

Keep the **PC Training** database open for the next lesson.

ℹ **Inside Stuff: How Formatted Data is Saved**
The Format property does not change the contents of the table, just how the data is presented. For example, the last names are still saved on your disk as you originally typed them.

Exam Note: **Getting Help on Formatting Fields**

There are many more options available for formatting fields. You can click in any of the Field Properties boxes, then press (F1) to get help on options for every data type.

Lesson 2: Creating Conditional Formats for Positive, Negative, and Null Values

There are more complex procedures available to format fields than those shown in Lesson I. These require a succession of components containing instructions separated by semicolons. Each component represents a specific data format for a certain condition.

Conditional formats are particularly useful for dates and numbers. For example, you could set up a conditional format to display positive numbers with black text, negative numbers in red, and zeros or blanks when no data is entered in the field (a null value). In this lesson, you set up the expense field to leave cells blank when you choose not to enter a number.

To Create a Conditional Format

1 In the PC Training **database, click the View button on the toolbar to switch to Design view of the Software Training table.**

2 **Click anywhere in the Expense field to select it.**

The Expense field is already formatted as Currency. Unfortunately, this displays fields with no entries as $0.00.

3 **Click in the Format box in the Field Properties area.**

4 **Select the Currency format and delete it.**

When formatting numeric fields (such as Number and Currency), the various components are separated by semicolons (;). The first component is always the format of a positive number, while the second is the format of a negative number. The third component tells the program how to display null values.

5 **Enter the following in the Format property box, exactly as shown:**
$#,##0.00;$#,##0.00[Red];#

The first component tells the program to display a dollar sign followed by the number for a positive number. The pound signs (#) to the right of the dollar sign tell the program to place a number there if one has been entered. If there is less than a thousand, a zero will not be forced in that location, and the comma will be dropped. If a number under $1 is entered, a zero is displayed in the first position to the left of the decimal.

Sometimes you want to force a leading zero to identify decimal numbers that may be less than one. There is less possibility of overlooking the decimal point or confusing it with a period if it follows a zero, 0.25, than if it does not, .25

The second component uses the same format but displays negative numbers in red. This is indicated by typing in the word Red surrounded by square brackets (not parentheses). The third component contains a pound sign (#), which tells the program to leave the field blank if no number is typed in.

The properties area should look like Figure 8.5.

continues ▶

To Create a Conditional Format (continued)

Figure 8.5
The property you entered for the Expenses field is displayed in the Format property box.

New currency format

Field Name	Data Type	Description
First Name	Text	First name of staff member
Last Name	Text	Last name of staff member
Date Hired	Date/Time	Date Hired
Social Security Number	Text	Social Security Number (also employee number)
Department	Text	Staff member's department
Computer Type	Text	Does the employee use a Windows-based or Macintosh computer
Word	Number	Level of training in Word
Excel	Number	Level of training in Excel
PP	Number	Level of training in PowerPoint
Access	Number	Level of training in Access
▶ Expense	Currency	Cost of Training
ID	AutoNumber	

Field Properties

General | Lookup

Format	$#,##0.00;$#,##0.00[Red];#
Decimal Places	Auto
Input Mask	
Caption	
Default Value	0
Validation Rule	
Validation Text	
Required	No
Indexed	No

The display layout for the field. Select a pre-defined format or enter a custom format. Press F1 for help on formats.

6 **Click the View button on the toolbar to switch views to Datasheet view. Click Yes.**
Click Yes when prompted to save your changes to the table.

7 **Scroll to the right and notice that the records that had no entries for the Expense field now display a blank instead of $0 (See Figure 8.6).**
Keep the PC Training database open for the next lesson.

Figure 8.6
The Software Training table shows a blank rather than a zero.

A blank replaces a zero

Software Training : Table

Date Hired	Social Securi	Department	Computer Type	Word	Excel	PP	Access	Expense	ID
06-Oct-82	837567336	Branch 3	Windows-based	3	1	0	1	$1,300.00	1
24-Aug-75	534218274	Accounting	Windows-based	0	3	1	1	$300.00	6
09-Nov-74	919277392	Purchasing	Windows-based	0	0	0	0		4
01-Jun-67	345247635	Branch 3	Windows-based	1	3	0	0	$250.00	11
05-Jul-69	636632345	Accounting	Windows-based	1	2	1	3	$450.00	3
12-Jan-75	101010001	Marketing	Windows-based	1	1	3	0	$250.00	5
25-May-90	590135326	Payroll	Windows-based	0	3	0	1	$200.00	12
02-Dec-85	855544736	Accounting	Windows-based	0	3	0	2	$300.00	9
11-Apr-88	835367899	Marketing	Windows-based	1	0	3	1	$250.00	8
09-Sep-92	182373687	Branch 2	Macintosh	0	3	2	2	$500.00	13
12-Dec-75	943737684	Accounting	Windows-based	1	1	1	2	$300.00	14
15-Jan-72	972545364	Payroll	Windows-based	0	2	0	0	$150.00	15
25-Mar-78	233545253	Branch 1	Windows-based	2	2	0	1	$400.00	16
20-May-93	690989583	Branch 3	Windows-based	0	3	0	0	$200.00	17
23-Mar-87	267484895	Branch 1	Windows-based	1	1	0	0	$100.00	22
12-Sep-93	236956789	Branch 3	Windows-based	1	2	1	2	$400.00	21
04-Apr-82	837456274	Human Resources	Macintosh	1	2	0	0	$250.00	23
04-Nov-95	247807889	Branch 1	Windows-based	1	2	0	0	$250.00	20
07-Aug-84	534262694	Marketing	Windows-based	2	2	3	1	$450.00	19
13-Jan-76	947323564	Branch 2	Macintosh	0	3	1	0	$350.00	18
21-Aug-68	543232123	Human Resources	Macintosh	0	0	0	0		2
08-Feb-75	323326546	Human Resources	Macintosh	1	0	2	0	$150.00	7
*				0	0	0	0		ber)

Record: ◄◄ ◄ 1 ► ►► ►* of 22

Inside Stuff: Getting Help with Conditional Formats
The first few times you use conditional formats, you will probably need to use Help. The quickest way to get the right kind of help is to go to Design view, select the field you want to format, place the insertion point in the Format properties box, and press F1. This will take you directly to format help.

Lesson 3: Changing the Data Input Structure Using Input Masks

Input masks are data formats that make data entry more meaningful. They can be used to make certain types of data such as telephone numbers and Social Security numbers easy to enter. Input masks can be entered in the Input Mask properties box. They can also be added using the Input Mask Wizard.

In this lesson, you add an input mask to the Social Security Number field to divide the number into the familiar XXX-XX-XXXX format. Input masks can control the format of the data as it is stored in the table.

To Change the Data Input Structure Using an Input Mask

1 In the PC Training **database, click the View button on the toolbar to switch to Design view of the Software Training table.**

2 **Click anywhere in the Social Security Number field to select it.**

The Social Security numbers in this database have been entered as text. Because all Social Security numbers contain three blocks of numbers of 3, 2, and 4 digits, it would make data entry easier if the field was also set up in this format.

3 **Click the Input Mask box in the Field Properties area.**

A Build button (the one with three dots) is displayed on the right-hand side of the Input Mask box (see Figure 8.7).

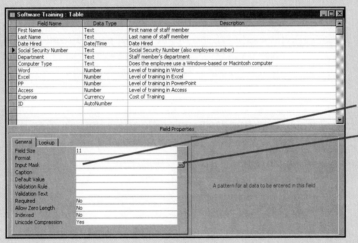

Figure 8.7
Use the Input Mask property box Build button to start the Input Mask Wizard.

Input Mask box

Build button

4 **Click the Build button.**

Before the Wizard opens, a dialog box is displayed telling you that you must first save the table. The first dialog box of the Input Mask Wizard is displayed, showing several of the preset masks (see Figure 8.8). The Input Mask Wizard is used to control the formatting for Text and Date fields only. You can also set an Input Mask manually for Number or Currency fields.

continues ▶

To Change the Data Input Structure Using an Input Mask (continued)

Figure 8.8
The first Input Mask Wizard dialog box asks how you want your data to look.

Social Security Number mask

Try It box

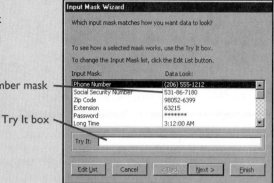

✖ If You Have Problems...

You may get a message that Microsoft Access can't start this Wizard. This means that the Input Mask Wizard has not been installed on your machine. If this is the case, click Yes to install it. A dialog box will ask for the first Microsoft Office installation CD. Place the CD in your CD drive and click OK. Select Add or Remove Features from the installation window. Expand the Microsoft Access for Windows button and click the drop-down arrow for Typical Wizards. Choose whether you want to run the Wizard from the hard disk or the CD, and whether you want to install just the feature you need (in this case the Input Mask Wizard) or all of the typical wizards. Click Update Now to complete the installation.

It is not absolutely necessary to use the Input Mask Wizard. If you know the expression you want to use, you can type it directly into the Input Mask property box. Look at the examples of the input masks in the following section and enter the expression directly into the Input Mask property box.

5 Select the Social Security Number option, then click in the Try It area to see the format that appears in the field.

6 Click the Next button.
The second Input Mask Wizard dialog box is displayed (see Figure 8.9). The basic format is shown, and you are asked if you are satisfied with the format and the *placeholders* used to reserve spaces for the data. In this example, you accept the default settings.

Figure 8.9
The second Input Mask Wizard dialog box enables you to modify the selected input mask.

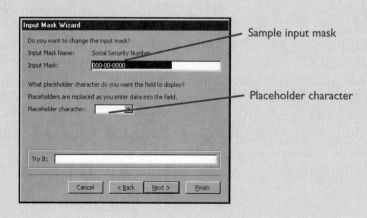

Sample input mask

Placeholder character

7 **Click the Next button.**

The third Input Mask Wizard dialog box is displayed (see Figure 8.10). This dialog box asks whether the program should save the characters, in this case dashes, used to separate the three parts of the Social Security number. The dashes will be displayed in forms and reports that use this field but they will not be part of the actual data stored in each field. If you export the data to another program, the dashes will not be there. The default choice does not save the extra characters.

Save without the symbols option

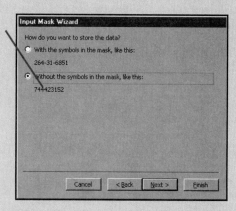

Figure 8.10
The third Input Mask Wizard dialog box asks you how you want to store the data.

8 **Click the Next button to accept the default.**

The fourth Input Mask Wizard dialog box is displayed. This dialog box tells you that you have completed the Wizard.

9 **Click the Finish button to complete the Input Mask Wizard.**

The Input Mask property box contains the following:

000-00-0000;;_

The Input Mask contains three components, which are separated by semicolons. The first component shows the input format. The next component has nothing in it, which indicates that there is no special format for an empty field. The third component has an underscore to indicate that the placeholder for the field is an underscore.

10 **Click the View button on the toolbar to switch to Datasheet view. Click Yes.**

Notice that the Social Security numbers are now in the familiar format (see Figure 8.11).

11 **Click on the New Record button and add another record to see how the data is entered into the field. Use your own name and make up the rest of the information.**

Do not use a Social Security number that is a duplicate of a number in the table. You learn how to automatically guard against this type of error in Lesson 6.

Keep the PC Training database open for the next lesson.

continues ▶

To Change the Data Input Structure Using an Input Mask   (continued)

Figure 8.11
The Input Mask for the
Social Security
Number field has been
added.

Social Security Number
with input mask

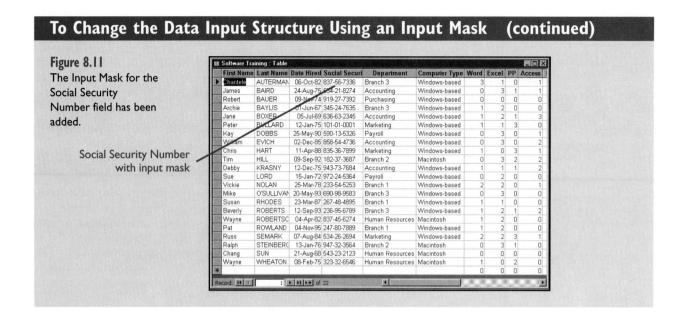

Inside Stuff: Input Mask Limitations
Adding an Input Mask puts certain limitations on data entry. If you have placeholders for nine characters, you need to enter all nine. If you enter eight or fewer characters, you get an error message, and you are not able to move out of the field until you correct the problem. If you do not have all of the characters to enter, don't put any of them in, but press (Esc) to leave the field blank for now.

Lesson 4: Restricting Entry Using Validation Criteria

The data entered in some fields in a database needs to be restricted in some way. For example, a field set up for coded data might only use zeros and ones, while a text field might be used to enter only two possible values. Several fields in the PC Training table fit this category. The Computer Type field has only two possible answers: Windows-based or Macintosh. The four software fields, Word, Excel, PowerPoint, and Access, use only four numbers (0, 1, 2, and 3).

Access gives you the option of restricting the information that will be accepted into a field. This is done by constructing a **validation rule**, which is an expression that the program compares entered data against to see if it is acceptable. If the data is not acceptable, **validation text** can be displayed to explain the reason the data is not acceptable.

Validation rules are used for two purposes: to make sure the user does not enter incorrect data, and to help avoid typographical errors. In this lesson you use the **Expression Builder** to build a validation rule for the four software fields. You also create validation text to be used as an error message for incorrect data entry.

To Restrict Entry Using Validation Criteria

1 In the `PC Training` database, click the View button on the toolbar to switch to the Design view of the Software Training table.

2 Click anywhere in the Word field to select it, then click the Validation Rule box in the Field Properties area.

Notice that a Build button (containing three dots) is displayed to the right of the Validation Rule property box.

3 Click the Build button on the right side of the Validation Rule box.

The Expression Builder dialog box is displayed (see Figure 8.12). You now build a Function, which is the default.

Expression Builder window

Or button

Equal sign button

Functions is the default option

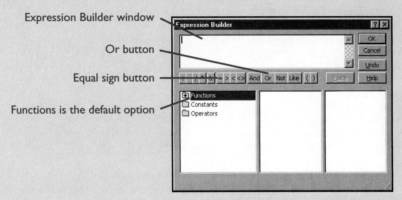

Figure 8.12
Use the Expression Builder dialog box to build a function in a Validation Rule.

4 Click the button with the = (equal sign) to begin building the expression.

The equal sign is displayed in the upper left corner of the Expression Builder window.

5 Type in the number 0 (zero).

6 Click the Or button.

7 Follow this procedure until your expression says:

`= 0 Or 1 Or 2 Or 3`

The Expression Builder window should look like Figure 8.13.

Validation rule

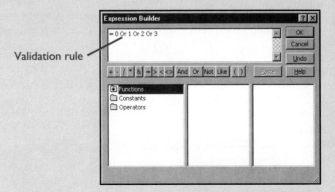

Figure 8.13
The Expression Builder window now contains a validation rule.

8 Click OK, then place the insertion point in the Validation Text box of the Field Properties area.

continues ▶

To Restrict Entry Using Validation Criteria   (continued)

9 **Type the following in the Validation Text property box:** `That is not a valid option. Please enter the number 0, 1, 2, or 3.`

You should now have entries in both the Validation Rule box and the Validation Text box (see Figure 8.14).

Figure 8.14
The Field Properties area should now contain both a validation rule and validation text.

Selected field

Validation rule

Validation text

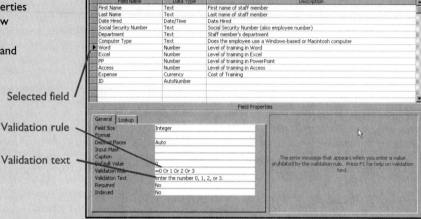

10 **Repeat steps 2 through 9 for the other three software fields (Excel, PowerPoint, and Access).**

To save time and effort, you can use the Copy and Paste commands with Field Properties. Highlight the Validation Rule text in the Word property box, and click the Copy button. Then select the Excel field, click the Validation Rule property box, and click the Paste button. Do this to the other two fields (PowerPoint and Access), then go back and repeat the procedure with the Validation Text property boxes.

11 **Click the View button on the toolbar to switch to Datasheet view. Click Yes.**

As usual when you change the structure of the table, you will be prompted to save your changes. This time, however, an additional dialog box is displayed (see Figure 8.15). This dialog box warns you that `Data integrity rules have been changed; Existing data may not be valid for the new rules.` Whenever a validation rule is added or modified, this warning is displayed. It is important that you are familiar with the content of your data so you can assess whether the data in the table violates the new rule that has just been added. In this case, the data will cause no problem.

Figure 8.15
A message is displayed that notifies you that data integrity rules have been changed.

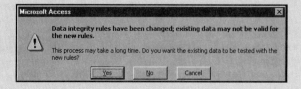

12 **Click Yes. The program tests your fields to find any conflicting data.**

If data integrity is violated, you receive an additional warning box telling you that data has been detected that violates the rules, but the program does not specifically identify the data. You then need to create a query to search for the data that was outside of the rules and change that data, if appropriate.

13 **Attempt to enter the number 5 in one of the software fields and press ⏎Enter to move to the next field.**

Notice how the message you typed in the Validation Text property box is displayed in the error message box (see Figure 8.16).

Invalid number

Validation text

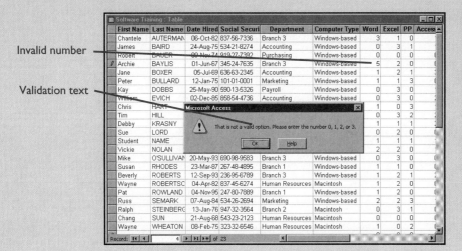

Figure 8.16
The Validation Rule text is displayed when an incorrect number is entered.

14 **Click OK in the error message box, then press Esc to return the field to its original number.**

Keep the PC Training database open for the next lesson.

 Inside Stuff: **Testing Structural Changes on a Backup File**

It is a good idea to test your changes on a backup file before you make major changes to your table structure. If you change the structure of a table on the only file you have, and choose yes when it checks for data integrity, it is always possible that some data could be lost. By testing the structure change on a back-up file, you can thoroughly test the change without having to worry that you are going to incorrectly change the "real" data.

Lesson 5: Requiring Entry of Necessary Information

There are times when you want to force the user to fill in a field. Access enables you to require data in a field. Required responses can be added to all field types except the AutoNumber fields, which are used when sequential numbering is required.

In this lesson, you require that data be entered into the Last Name field.

To Require Entry of Necessary Information

1 **In the** `PC Training` **database, click the View button on the toolbar to switch to Design view, then click the Last Name field to select it.**
You may have to scroll up to find the Last Name field.

2 **Click the Required box in the Field Properties area.**

3 **Click the drop-down arrow to reveal the choices.**
The screen should look like Figure 8.17.

Figure 8.17
The Required property box has two options.

Drop-down arrow

Required property box

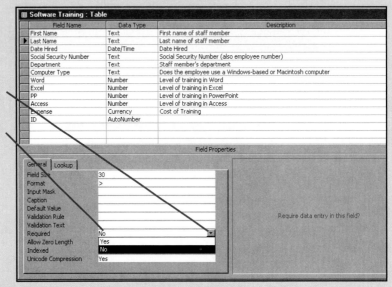

4 **Select Yes to make an entry into this field required.**

5 **Click the View button on the toolbar to switch to Datasheet view. Click** **Y**es **when prompted to save your changes to the table. Click** **Y**es **to acknowledge the warning.**
You are warned about changes to the data integrity rules as you were when you changed the Validation Rule in Lesson 5.

X *If You Have Problems...*
If you entered any records without a last name, you get another warning box that tells you `Existing data violates the new setting for the 'Required' property for the field 'Last Name'`. Choose **Y**es to continue testing with the new setting.

6 **Scroll down to the bottom of the table and enter a new record, but leave the Last Name field blank.**
The program enables you to continue entering data to the end of the record. However, when you press after the last field, another dialog box is displayed (see Figure 8.18), warning you that the Last Name field cannot contain a Null value.

Figure 8.18
The Null value warning is displayed if you try to skip the Last Name field.

7 **Click OK.**

8 **Press** Esc **to back out of the entry.**
Keep the PC Training database open for the next lesson.

Lesson 6: Preventing Duplicate Entries Using Indexed Fields

It is possible in Access to create an *indexed field*. This acts like an index in a book; it speeds up searching and sorting for that field. Indexes can be created for all but Memo, Hyperlink, or OLE fields. Indexed fields can also be set up to prevent duplicate entries in a field. If a field has been designated as the primary key field, it is automatically indexed, with no duplicate entries allowed. Other fields can also be indexed and set to disallow duplicate entries.

In this lesson, you index the Social Security Number field and prevent duplicate entries, because all Social Security numbers should be unique.

To Prevent Duplicate Entries Using Indexed Fields

1 **In the** PC Training **database, click the View button on the toolbar to switch to Design view of the Software Training table.**

2 **Click anywhere in the Social Security Number field to select it, then click the Indexed property box.**
A drop-down arrow is displayed at the right-hand side of the property box.

3 **Click the drop down arrow and select Yes (No Duplicates) from the drop-down menu.**
The Social Security Number properties area should look like Figure 8.19.

Selected field

Drop-down arrow

Indexed property box

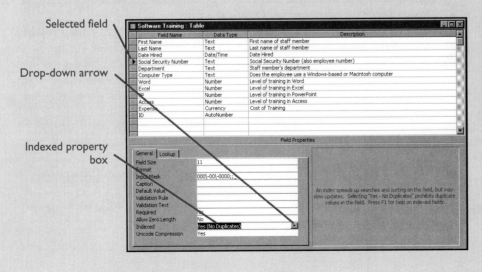

Figure 8.19
The Social Security Number Field Properties area now shows "Yes (No Duplicates)" in the Indexed property box.

continues ▶

To Prevent Duplicate Entries Using Indexed Fields (continued)

4 Click the **View** button on the toolbar to switch to Datasheet view. Click <u>Y</u>es.

5 Scroll down to the bottom of the table.

6 Add a new record, but this time enter a Social Security number from a previous record.

When you try to complete the record, an error message is displayed (see Figure 8.20). Notice that the error message tells you that you have entered a duplicate value in an index, primary key, or relationship, but does not tell you in which field the error occurred. This can be a big problem in a database with a lot of indexed fields.

Figure 8.20

The Duplicate Value error message is displayed when you enter a Social Security number that is already used in the database.

Duplicate Social Security Numbers

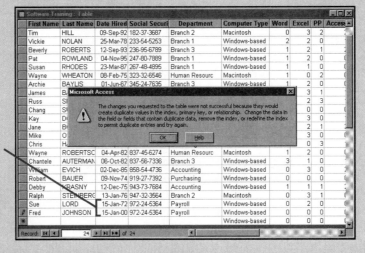

7 Click **OK** in the warning box.

8 Press Esc to back out of the entry.

Keep the PC Training database open for the next lesson.

> *Inside Stuff:* **Searching for Duplicate Entries**
>
> One way to search for a duplicate entry is to use the Find button on the toolbar. Enter the number or word that caused a problem and search for each occurrence of it. Because the error message does not identify which field contains the duplicate entry, you may need to look at the design of the table to determine which fields are indexed or which field is the primary key. Search for duplicate values in these fields.

Lesson 7: Creating a Lookup Column to Allow Selection from a List

There are times when you will have a field that has several common entries. This is particularly true of fields designed for such things as city or state names, job titles, and military ranks.

Access contains a Lookup Wizard in the Data Type column in the Table Design view. This enables you to either enter the common items, or have the program make up a list from a field in another table. Having pre-typed choices available makes data entry far easier, and also prevents the user from making typographical errors. When entering data, if the value you need is not on the list, you can type it in the field.

In this lesson, you add a Lookup list for the Department field. The Lookup Wizard walks you through the steps of creating the data list, and you end up with a drop-down box containing all of the department names in the database.

To Create a Lookup Column to Allow Selection from a List

1 **In the PC Training database, click the View button on the toolbar to switch views to Design view of the Software Training table.**

2 **Click on the Data Type box of the Department field.**
A drop-down arrow is displayed on the right-hand side of the box.

3 **Click the arrow in the Department Data Type box.**
A drop-down menu is displayed (see Figure 8.21). The various data types are shown in this box. At the bottom of the box is the Lookup Wizard choice.

Drop-down arrow

Lookup Wizard option

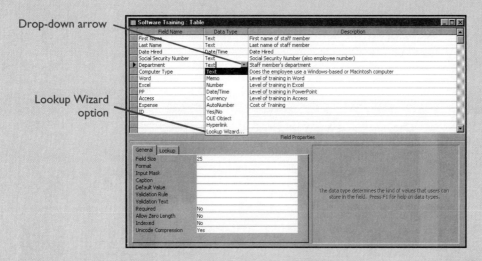

Figure 8.21
The Lookup Wizard option is displayed at the bottom of the drop-down list.

4 **Select Lookup Wizard from the drop-down box.**
The first Lookup Wizard dialog box is displayed (see Figure 8.22).

Choose to type in your own values

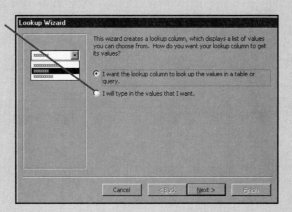

Figure 8.22
The first Lookup Wizard dialog box asks how you want your lookup column to get its values.

continues ▶

To Create a Lookup Column to Allow Selection from a List   (continued)

5 **Choose the second option to type in the values you want, then click Next.**
The second Lookup Wizard dialog box is displayed.

6 **Accept the default number of columns, then type in the departments listed below in the box labeled Col1:**
Do not press ⏎Enter after each entry. This takes you to the next dialog box. Use the ↓ or Tab⇄ key to move down. If you accidentally move to the next dialog box before you finish entering the department names, click Back to return to the data entry area.

Accounting

Branch 1

Branch 2

Branch 3

Human Resources

Marketing

Payroll

As you enter the seven department names (see Figure 8.23), the first one may scroll off the screen. If you need to move up to edit an entry that has scrolled off the screen, use the ↑ key.

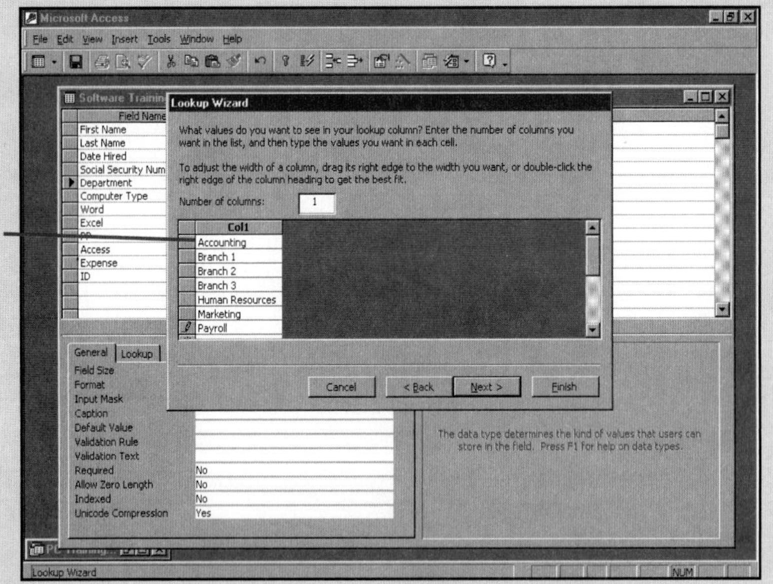

Figure 8.23
Use the second
Lookup Wizard dialog
box to enter the
lookup column values.

Type values here ⸺

7 **Click Next to move to the third Lookup Wizard dialog box.**
This dialog box asks what you want to name your lookup column (see Figure 8.24).

8 **Type Department, as the lookup column name, if necessary, then click Finish.**

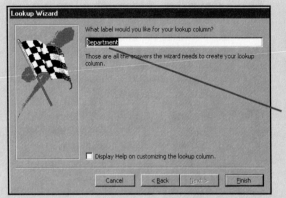

Figure 8.24
The final Wizard dialog box enables you to name the lookup column.

Default name

9 **Click the View button on the toolbar to switch views to Datasheet view. Click Yes.**

10 **Scroll down to the bottom of the table and enter a new record.**

When you get to the Department field, notice that a drop-down arrow is displayed.

11 **Click the arrow to display the drop-down box you just created, then select one of the departments.**

You have now created a time-saving feature for your table (see Figure 8.25).

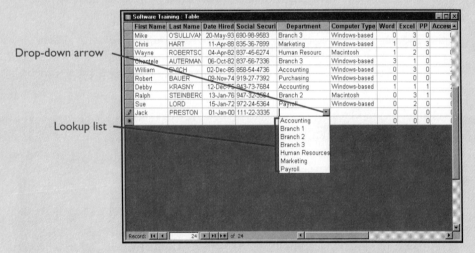

Figure 8.25
The Lookup Wizard creates a drop-down box for the Department field.

Drop-down arrow

Lookup list

12 **Press Esc to back out of the entry.**

Keep the PC Training database open for the next lesson.

Inside Stuff: Effects of Format Changes in a Table

The changes made to the text and number formatting in table design carry over to new forms and reports that are based on this table. Some of the changes such as required fields, validation rules, and default values also show up in existing forms. It is always best to have the table structure complete before creating other objects to ensure that all of the formatting characteristics flow from the table to the objects based on that table. If you make changes to the table structure after other objects have been created, you can add those same formatting characteristics directly to the design of the forms, reports, or queries.

Exam Note: **Modifying a Lookup Field**
If you want to change the value list, open the table in Design view and select the field that uses the lookup feature. In the field properties area, click on the Lookup tab to display the lookup properties. The list of values is displayed in the Row Source box where it may be modified.

 Exam Note: **Features That Improve Data Accuracy**
All of the topics in this project were performed and tested in the table view. By changing the text and number formatting in table design, the formatting carries over to new forms and reports. All of the following features help improve accuracy in forms, tables, and reports:

- consistent data formats
- conditional formats
- input masks
- validation criteria
- required fields
- prevention of duplication

 # Lesson 8: Entering a Default Value

Some fields may have many possible entries but one value is more common than others. You can save time and reduce errors by providing this entry automatically.

In the following procedure you learn how to provide a ***default value***. A default value appears in a field of a new record automatically. The person who enters a new record can change it if necessary, but they also have the option of accepting it by pressing (Tab↹) or (↵Enter).

To Enter a Default Value

 ❶ Click the View button to switch to Design view.
The Design view of the Software Training table is displayed.

❷ Click on the Computer Type field name to select it and display its field properties.
Most organizations use one type of computer with a few exceptions. If most of the computers are Windows-based, it would save a lot of typing to fill that field in automatically for each new record and change it for the exceptions.

❸ Click the Default value box and type Windows-based**.**
The Database window should now be open to the Tables object button (see Figure 8.26).

 ❹ Click the View button to switch to the Datasheet view. Click Yes to save the change.

❺ Scroll to the bottom of the table if necessary and locate the new record row.
Notice that the computer type is already filled in for the next new record (see Figure 8.27).

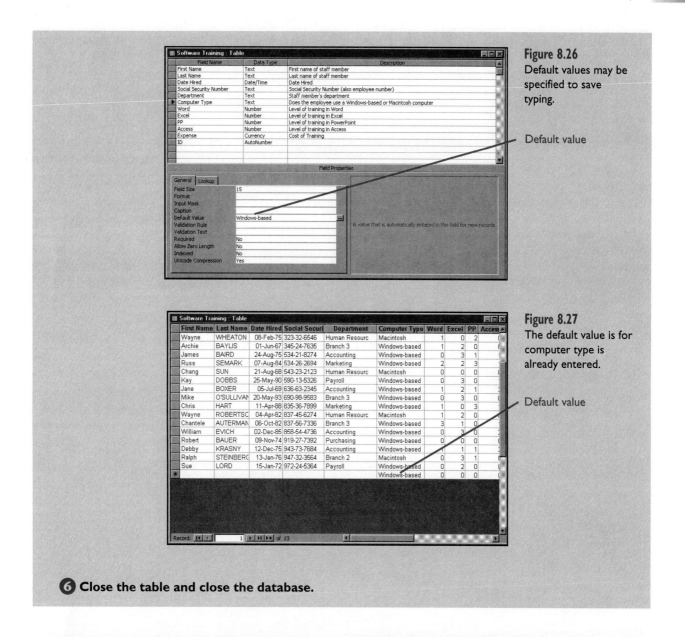

Figure 8.26
Default values may be specified to save typing.

Default value

Figure 8.27
The default value is for computer type is already entered.

Default value

6 **Close the table and close the database.**

Summary

In this project you were introduced to some of the techniques used to refine and control data entry. You learned how to make field entries appear as all upper- or lowercase letters, and how to make data look different depending on the data characteristics. You also set up input masks to assist with entry of consistently formatted data. You learned how to set conditions for accepting data entry, how to require the entry of data in a field, how to provide default values, and how to avoid duplicate entries by indexing a field. You also learned how to create a lookup list to make data entry quicker and more accurate.

You can learn more about taking control of data entry in Access by looking a little more closely at some of the other options available in input masks, conditional and data formatting, and validation criteria in Microsoft help. The best way to do this is to go to the help index and explore the topic. Create a new database and try out these features.

Checking Concepts and Terms

True/False

For each of the following statements, check *T* or *F* to indicate whether the statement is true or false.

__T __F   **1.** When you change the display format of a field in an existing table, the data already stored on your disk is changed also. [L1]

__T __F   **2.** If you want to show negative numbers in red text, you would create a conditional format. [L2]

__T __F   **3.** You must use the Input Mask Wizard to enter an input mask. [L3]

__T __F   **4.** Text you enter into the Validation Text property box will appear in an error message dialog box if the Validation Rule is violated. [L4]

__T __F   **5.** Default values appear in new records without being typed. [L5]

Multiple Choice

Circle the letter of the correct answer for each of the following questions.

1. In a conditional format, what punctuation is used to separate components? [L2]

   a. commas

   b. semicolons

   c. colons

   d. quotation marks

2. The Input Mask Wizard creates formats for what type of fields? [L3]

   a. all types of fields

   b. all types of fields except OLE

   c. text fields only

   d. text and date fields only

3. If you enter duplicate information in a field where duplicates are not allowed, how do you back out of that entry? [L6]

   a. Press Del key.

   b. You can't delete the record.

   c. Press Esc.

   d. Press ↵Enter and go on.

4. What is one way to speed up searching and sorting on a field? [L6]

   a. Prevent duplicate entries in the field.

   b. Make it a required field.

   c. Index it.

   d. Make the data format consistent.

5. How is Validation Text used? [L4]

   a. to explain to the person entering data the reason why the data entered is not acceptable

   b. to verify that only valid data is entered

   c. to validate text fields only

   d. to intimidate the user for making a mistake

Screen ID

Label each element of the Access screen shown in Figure 8.28.

Figure 8.28

A. Build button

B. Controls the display of numeric data

C. Special format for a negative number

D. Text displayed for invalid entries

E. Validation condition

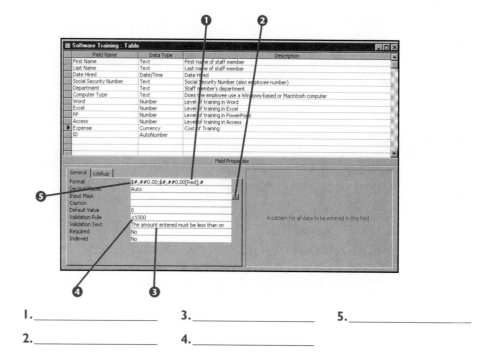

1._____   3._____   5._____

2._____   4._____

Skill Drill

Skill Drill exercises reinforce project skills. Each skill reinforced is the same, or nearly the same, as a skill presented in the project. Each exercise includes a brief narrative introduction, followed by detailed instructions in a step-by-step format.

The database you will use in the Skill Drill exercises contains information about a company's computers. It consists of two tables—one with information about the characteristics of the computers and one with information about the vendors who sold you the computers.

1. Creating a Consistent Data Format

The first thing you want to do is set the computer processor type to all capital letters.

To change the format of text in a field:

1. Find the **AC-802** file on your CD-ROM, right click on it, and send it to the floppy drive. Move to drive A, remove the read-only status, and rename the file **Computer Inventory**.

2. Open the **Computer Inventory** database, then open the **PC Hardware** table in Design view.

3. Place the insertion point anywhere in the Processor field.

4. Click in the Format box in the Field Properties area.

5. Type in a greater than (>) symbol.

6. Click the View button to move to Datasheet view. Save your changes when prompted.

7. Widen the Processor column so you can read the data.

8. Close the table. Because you changed the structure of the table (column width) you will be prompted to save your changes.

9. Leave the database open if you intend to do the next exercise.

2. Adding an Input Mask to a Text Field

The Phone Number field in the Vendors table has a text data type. You will want to add an input mask to this field. This will prompt the user to enter an area code for the number. Skip the first step if you did the previous exercise.

To add an input mask for a telephone number:

1. Find the `AC-0802` file on your CD-ROM, right click on it, and send it to the floppy drive. Move to drive A, remove the read-only status, and rename the file `Computer Inventory`.

2. With the `Computer Inventory` database open, select the Vendors table.

3. Open the `Vendors` table in Design view.

4. Click anywhere in the Phone Number field.

5. Click in the Input Mask box in the Field Properties area.

6. Click the Build button to start the Input Mask Wizard.

7. Select the Phone Number option and click Next.

8. Accept the default input mask, placeholder, and method of saving, and click Next when necessary.

9. Click Finish to complete the input mask.

10. Click the View button to switch to Datasheet view. Save your changes.

11. Make sure your phone numbers are in the proper format, then close the table. Leave the database open if you intend to do the next exercise.

3. Adding a Lookup Column

One of the fields in the PC Hardware table is the name of the vendor that sold you the computers. You have deals with three vendors—Acme Computer, General Comp, and Wilson Electric. Because all of your computers will come from one of these three companies, you can add a drop-down box to the field using the Lookup Wizard. Skip the first step if you did either of the previous two exercises.

To add a lookup column to a field:

1. Find the `AC-0802` file on your CD-ROM, right click on it, and send it to the floppy drive. Move to drive A, remove the read-only status, and rename the file `Computer Inventory`. Open the database.

2. Open the `PC Hardware` table in Design view.

3. Click in the Data Type column of the Vendor field.

4. Click the drop-down arrow in the Data Type box and select Lookup Wizard from the data type menu.

5. Choose to type in the values yourself.

6. Accept the default of one column, then type in `Acme Computer`. Use (Tab⇆) or (↓) to move from one field to the next. (If you accidentally press (↵Enter), click the Back button in the dialog box.) Enter `General Comp`, and `Wilson Electric` in the next two boxes then click Next.

7. Accept `Vendor` as the name of the label.

8. Click the View button to switch to Datasheet view. Save your changes when prompted.

9. Move to the Vendor field and click anywhere in the column. Click the down arrow to see if your lookup column is working.

10. Close the table and the database.

Challenge

Challenge exercises expand on or are somewhat related to skills practiced in the project. Each exercise provides a brief narrative introduction followed by instructions in a numbered step format that are not as detailed as those in the Skill Drill section.

The database you will be using for the Challenge section is for a small online chess club (that started out as a chess-by-mail club). There are yearly dues that help pay for space on a file server where games can be played and saved. Like most clubs, some members have paid in advance, and some are behind in their dues. The database currently contains only one table—a membership list for which you are responsible. You decide that if you have to take care of the list, you might as well set it up the way you want it!

1. Placing Default Text Using a Custom Format

If your computer is set up to operate in the United States, the currency format uses the dollar sign. You decide to experiment with switching to the new European currency standard, the Euro, to make your club seem more open to players from Europe.

To place default text in empty fields using a custom format:

1. Copy the file **AC-0803** from your CD-ROM, place it on your floppy drive, and rename it **Chess Club**. Deselect the Read-only attribute.

2. Open the database and open the **Membership Information** table in Design view. Select the Dues field and click on the down-arrow next to the Format box in the Field Properties section of the window.

3. Change the format to Euro.

4. Click the View button to switch to the Datasheet view. Save the changes to the table.

5. Scroll to the right, if necessary, and view the Dues table. The program does not convert U.S. dollars into equivalent Euro dollars, it just replaces the dollar sign with the Euro symbol.

6. Close the table. Leave the database open if you plan to do the next exercise.

2. Creating a Two-Column Lookup Column

You want to save the State field in the standard two-character format, but you sometimes have trouble remembering what code is used for what state. You decide to add a lookup column that contains both the two-character state code and the full state name. Right now, you have members from Colorado, Georgia, Indiana, and Michigan. You are also pretty sure a person from Missouri will be joining soon. Skip the first step if you did the previous exercise.

To create a two-column lookup column:

1. Copy the file **AC-0803** from your CD-ROM, place it on your floppy drive, and rename it **Chess Club**. Deselect the Read-only attribute. Open the database.

2. Select the Design view of the Member Information table and select the State field's data type.

3. Click the down arrow on the data type box for the State field and choose the Lookup Wizard.

4. Indicate that you want to type in the values, but change the number of columns to **2**.

5. Enter the following information in the columns:

Col1	Col2
CO	Colorado
GA	Georgia
IN	Indiana
MI	Michigan
MO	Missouri

6. Double-click on the line between the Col1 and Col2 column headings to reduce the width of the Col1 column.

7. Choose to store the value from Col1 in your table and accept the default name.

8. Switch to Datasheet view and add another member. Use the lookup column for the State field. The membership information should read: **9998765, Ms., Hawken, Charity, S., 1885 Burtchville Rd.,** [leave Address2 blank], **Jeddo, MO, 63460, (573) 555-1234, 25, 9/9/99, 47.** Notice that the two-character code and the state name both appear, but only the code is entered into the table.

9. Leave the table open in Design view if you plan to do the next exercise.

3. Indexing Multiple Fields

You can create indexes for more than one field in a table. You can also create an index that is based on multiple fields. Because you are anticipating a lot more members in the future, you want to create an index on the Last Name and First Name fields so that the program will sort on these fields faster. Skip the first step if you did either of the previous exercises.

To index multiple fields:

1. Copy the file **AC-0803** from your CD-ROM, place it on your floppy drive, and rename it **Chess Club**. Deselect the Read-only attribute. Open the database.

2. With the Chess Club database open, open the **Member Information** table in Design view.

3. Click the Indexes button on the toolbar. The Indexes dialog box shows two current indexes.

4. Type **Name** in the first available Index Name box.

5. Select the Last Name field from the drop-down box in the Field Name column.

6. Move down one row and select the First Name field from the drop-down box in the Field Name column. Leave the Index Name box blank in this row.

7. Close the Indexes dialog box. The multiple-field index will make little difference with only a few fields, but will improve sorting speed when you work with tables with a lot of records. Close the table and the database.

Discovery Zone

Discovery Zone exercises help you gain advanced knowledge of project topics and application of skills. These exercises focus on enhancing your problem-solving skills. Numbered steps are not provided, but you are given hints, reminders, screen shots, and references to help you reach your goal for each exercise.

The database you use in this Discovery Zone is a slightly modified version of the Chess Club database you used in the Challenge section.

1. Modifying an Input Mask

The Member ID# is set up with last two digits of the year the member joined, followed by a randomly generated five-digit number. You would like to create an input mask that would separate the first two digits from the last five digits with a dash.

Copy the file `AC-0804` from your CD-ROM, place it on your floppy drive, and rename it `Chess Club 2`. De-select the Read-only attribute.

Goal: Create a custom input mask that results in a Member ID # with the following format: **ID 92-23434** (this is the Member ID # for the first record in the table). The input mask should:

- start each Member ID # with the following characters: `ID`.
- use a dash to separate the first two digits (the year) from the last five digits.
- make all seven digits required entries.
- use the underscore as a placeholder.
- do not store the literal characters (for example, the dash) in the table.

Hint #1: All of the information you need is in the Input Mask help section.

Hint #2: You need three sections for this input mask.

 Exam Note: Modifying an Input Mask
If you want to change an input mask, open the table in Design view and select the field that uses the input mask. In the field properties area, click on the General tab to display the lookup properties. The input mask is displayed in the Input Mask box where it may be modified.

2. Optimizing Data Type Usage

Databases can be quite large and take up a lot of storage space. You can use this storage space more efficiently if you choose the data types correctly for fields that store numbers.

Goal: Review the data types in the Michigan Tornadoes table and determine which fields could be stored more efficiently.

Copy the file `AC-0805` from your CD-ROM, place it on your floppy drive, and rename it `Michigan Tornadoes`. De-select the Read-only attribute and open the database. Open the `Michigan Tornadoes` table in Design view. Notice that all the fields with the Number data type use the Double field size.

Launch Access Help and search for help on the topic, FieldSize Property. Observe that the Double option uses 8 bytes of memory to store each number. This setting can store negative numbers, fractions, and very large numbers but is not necessary to store the data in this table. Observe the data in the Michigan Tornadoes table and determine which fields could be stored using the Byte or Integer setting without damaging the data stored in the field.

Hint: Sort each prospective field using the Sort Descending and Sort Ascending buttons to determine the maximum and minimum values in each field.

Change the data type of as many fields as you can from Double to Byte or Integer without losing any data. Close the table and save the changes. You will be warned that data may be lost but a second warning will occur if records are encountered that will be damaged.

The size of the database will not decrease until it is compacted. You learn how to do this in Project 13, "Managing Your Databases with Special Action Queries and Database Utilities."

PinPoint Assessment

You have completed this project and the associated lessons, and have had an opportunity to assess your skills through end-of-project questions and exercises. Now use the PinPoint software evaluation mode to assess your comprehension of the specific exam tasks you have just learned. You can also use the PinPoint Trainer Mode and the Show Me tutorials to practice these specific exam tasks.

Project 9

Managing Data Using Smaller, Related Tables

Key terms introduced in this project include

- cascade
- combo box
- enforce referential integrity

- expand indicator
- Find Duplicates Query Wizard
- Find Unmatched Query Wizard

- foreign key
- one-to-many
- subdatasheet

Objectives	Required Activity for MOUS	Exam Level
➤ Design Related Tables to Hold Repetitive Data		
➤ Define the Relationship Between the Tables	Establish relationships	Core
	Enforce referential integrity	Core
➤ Print Table Relationships and Display Subdatasheets in Tables	Print Database Relationships	Expert
	Display related records in a subdatasheet	Core
➤ Create Queries That Draw Data from Both Tables	Create and modify a multi-table select query	Core
➤ Automatically Fill in Data from One of the Joined Tables		
➤ Update Tables by Entering or Deleting Data in the Query		
➤ Find Duplicate Records in an Existing Table		

Why Would I Do This?

The advantage of using a relational database such as Microsoft Access is the capability to use several tables with related information, and to pull that information together from those tables through the use of related fields. This helps you manage your data more effectively by avoiding data redundancy, thereby reducing the risk of errors, and minimizing the size of the database.

Rather than using one large table, you separate your data into smaller, single-purpose tables. You create relationships between the tables by joining a primary key from one table to the same data field in a second table. Then you can recombine the data as needed by creating queries that draw data from the tables.

Forms or reports can then be based on queries that use more than one table, combining the desired information to get the results you need. If a form is based on a query that is, in turn, based on more than one table, it is possible to have the program automatically fill in some of the needed information on the form. It is also possible to add new data to the tables by entering it into the query.

Lesson I: Designing Related Tables to Hold Repetitive Data

In this lesson, you see how two tables are designed to store related data and how to use them to minimize duplicate data entry. The database used in the lessons of this project is a modified version of the Computer Inventory database you worked on in the Skill Drill section of Project 8, "Making Data Entry Easier and More Accurate."

To Design Related Tables to Hold Repetitive Data

❶ **Find the** AC-0901 **file on your CD-ROM, right click on it, and send it to the floppy drive. (Make sure you begin with an empty disk for this project.) Move to drive A:, right-click on the file name, select Properties from the shortcut menu and de-select Read-only.**

❷ **Right-click on the file name and select Rename from the shortcut menu. Rename the file** Computer Inventory 2. **Click OK, then open the database.**
The Database window should now be open to the Tables area (see Figure 9.1).

Figure 9.1
The Computer Inventory 2 database includes the PC Hardware and Vendors tables.

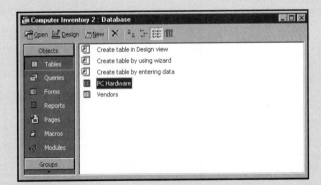

❸ **Click the** Vendors **table to select it, then click Open.**
You could also double-click the Vendors table to open it. This table contains data that is necessary to contact the vendor by mail or by phone. Notice that each vendor's name only appears one time.

4 Click the View button to switch to Design view.

The Name of Vendor field is the primary key field in this table (see Figure 9.2).

Primary key indicator

Primary key field

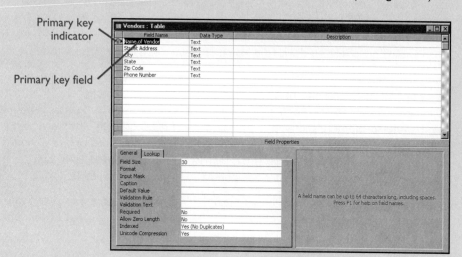

Figure 9.2
The Vendors table displays a primary key field in Design view.

5 Close the Vendors table so you can look at the PC Hardware table.

6 Click the PC Hardware table to select it, then click Open.

The PC Hardware table is displayed in the Datasheet view.

7 Scroll the table to the right to display the Vendor field.

8 Click anywhere in the Vendor field, then click the arrow on the right side of the Field box.

Notice that the Lookup Wizard has been used to attach a lookup box to the Name of Vendor field (see Figure 9.3). This lookup box, also referred to as a **combo box**, uses the contents of the Name of Vendor field in the Vendors table to form its list. A combo box is a combination of a text box and a list box. You can either type in a new vendor, or select one from the list. Selecting a name from the list ensures that there will be an exact match. Notice that the same vendor's name can appear more than once in this table.

Lookup box showing contents of the Name of Vendor field

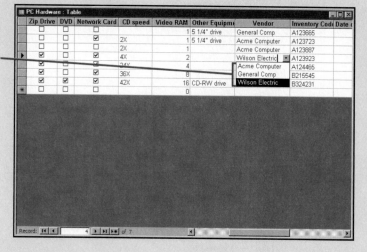

Figure 9.3
The Name of Vendor field of the PC Hardware table contains a lookup box.

9 Close the table.

Keep the database open for the next lesson.

Lesson 2: Defining the Relationship Between the Tables

Whenever the same information is repeated in numerous records it is more efficient to create two tables and join them with a single field. In the Computer Inventory database, the name of the vendor is used to link the two tables. When the user enters the name of the vendor in a record in the PC Hardware table, all of the data for that vendor can be viewed when a relationship is created with the Name of Vendor field in the Vendor table.

To create a relationship between two tables, the fields that are joined must have the same data type, but do not have to have the same name. If they are Number fields, they must also have the same Field Size property setting. The most common type of database relationship is called a **one-to-many** relationship, which is a type of relationship in which a record in one table may be related to more than one record in a second table. This occurs when the field on the one side of the relationship is the primary key. In the related table, that same data may appear many times because it is not a primary key in the second table.

In the following lesson, you learn how to join the Vendors table to the PC Hardware table using a one-to-many relationship between the Name of Vendor field in the Vendors table and the Vendor field in the PC Hardware table.

To Define the Relationship Between the Tables

 1 **With the Computer Inventory 2 database open, click the Relationships button.**
The Relationships window is displayed in the background, with a Show Table dialog box in the foreground (see Figure 9.4). The Relationships window enables you to create and edit relationships between tables.

Figure 9.4
The Vendors table and PC Hardware table are available from the Show Table dialog box.

Available tables

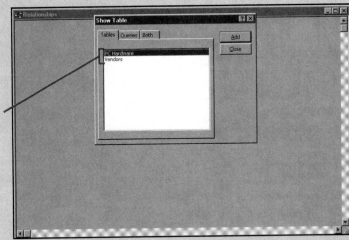

 ☒ **If You Have Problems...**
If the Show Table dialog box is not shown, click the Show Table button on the toolbar.

2 **Click the Add button to add the PC Hardware table to the Relationships window.**
The PC Hardware list box is displayed in the Relationships window.

3 **Select the Vendors table and click the Add button to add the Vendors table to the Relationships window. Click the Close button to close the Show Table dialog box.**

Field list boxes for both tables are displayed in the Relationships window.

4 **Move the mouse pointer to the bottom of the PC Hardware field list box until it changes to a two-headed arrow. Click and drag down until all of the fields are visible. Do the same for the Vendor field list box.**

Notice that the Name of Vendor field in the Vendors table is indicated in bold-face type. This is because it is the primary key field in the Vendors table. The corresponding field in the PC Hardware table, Vendor, is not in boldface type because a vendor can appear many times in the PC Hardware table. When the tables are linked, the corresponding field in another table is identified as the *foreign key*. The foreign key is on the many side of a one-to-many relationship. It is important that you know which field from which table is identified in this manner (see Figure 9.5).

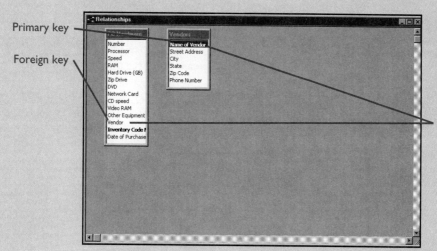

Primary key

Foreign key

Figure 9.5
The Name of Vendor field in the Vendors table corresponds to the Vendor field in the PC Hardware table.

Corresponding fields

5 **Click the Name of Vendor field name in the Vendors list to select it.**

6 **Click and drag this field name to the corresponding field, Vendor, in the PC Hardware field list, then release the mouse.**

The Edit Relationships dialog box is displayed showing the selected fields from both tables (see Figure 9.6). Notice that the table on the right is identified as the related table. Also notice that the Relationship type box identifies this as a one-to-many relationship. Once this relationship is created, you are able to create queries that draw from both tables.

 If You Have Problems...

If you release the mouse pointer when it is on top of another field, that field name will appear in the Related Table/Query side of the Edit Relationships dialog box. Click cancel and try again. It is important that you release the mouse pointer when it is pointing at the matching field, or the relationship will be meaningless.

continues ▶

To Define the Relationship Between the Tables   (continued)

Figure 9.6
The Edit Relationships
dialog box shows that
the two tables are
ready to be joined.

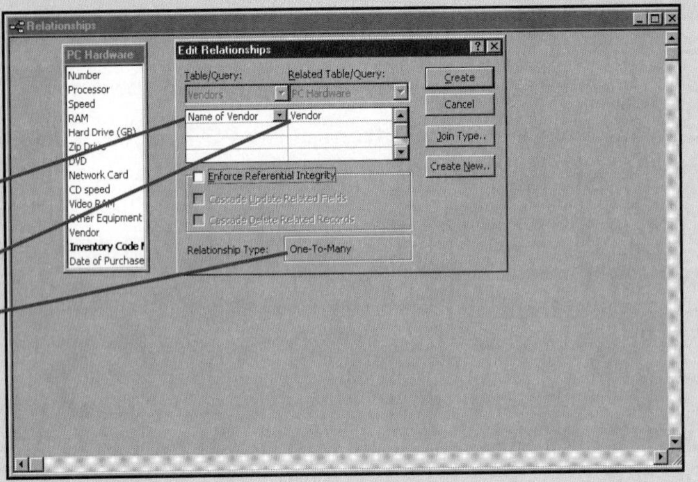

Field from Vendor table

Field from PC Hardware
table

Type of relationship

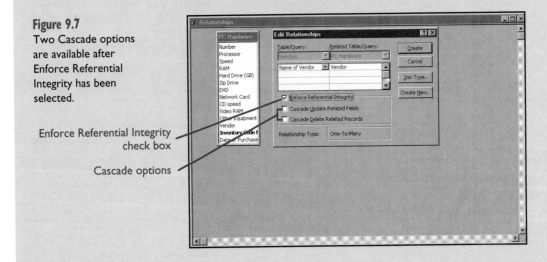

7 **Select the Enforce Referential Integrity text box.**
Enforcing referential integrity prevents the user from entering a record in the PC Hardware table that does not have a corresponding entry in the Vendors table (see Figure 9.7). Likewise, you cannot delete a record in the Vendors table as long as it is related to records in the PC Hardware table. Enforcing referential integrity prevents having orphan (unmatched) records in the many table.

Figure 9.7
Two Cascade options
are available after
Enforce Referential
Integrity has been
selected.

Enforce Referential Integrity
check box

Cascade options

When this box is checked you also have two other options, that enable you to *cascade* changes; that is, to change a field in one table and automatically update related fields. Do not select either of them for this lesson.

Exam Note: Using Cascade Updates and Deletes
When you select the Enforce Referential Integrity option, two other options become available. If you select Cascade Update Related Fields in the second Relationships dialog box, changes in the Vendor table are automatically transferred to the PC Hardware table. For example, if the General Comp company changes its name to Allied Computers, all occurrences of its name would be changed in the PC Hardware table as well. Similarly, if you select Cascade Delete Related Records, deleting a vendor name from the Vendors table would delete all related records from the PC Hardware table.

These two features should be used sparingly and only after careful consideration. Review the information in Help before you select either one of these options to ensure that you understand the impact to your database relationships.

8 Click Create to establish the relationship.
The Relationships box appears with a new line displaying the one-to-many relationship (see Figure 9.8). The "one" field is labeled 1, while the "many" field is indicated by an infinity symbol (∞).

"One" field indicator ———

Relationship line ———

"Many" field
indicator ———

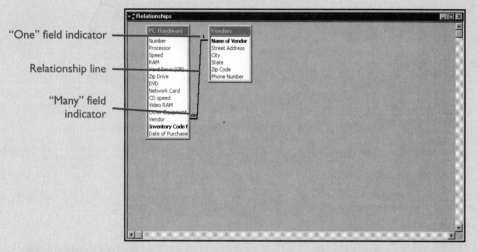

Figure 9.8
A one-to-many
relationship has been
created.

9 Close the Relationships box and click Yes to save the changes made to the layout of the relationships.
Leave the database open for the next lesson

 Inside Stuff: Adding Tables to the Relationships Window
You can also add tables to the Relationships window by double-clicking the table name. If you accidentally add a table twice, simply click the table name in the Relationships window and press Del to remove it from the window.

Lesson 3: Printing Table Relationships and Displaying Subdatasheets in Tables

Once you have created relationships between your tables, you may want to document it so you can tell at a glance how the tables are related. There is a feature in the Relationships window that enables you to print the relationship. It also creates a report of those relationships that is stored as part of the database. By using this feature, you can quickly open the relationships report to view how the tables or queries are related.

Another feature in Microsoft Access 2000 is the capability to see the related records from a primary field. Once you have created relationships, the primary table displays plus marks to the left of the primary field. When you click on this plus mark, it opens a subdatasheet showing all of the related records from the second table.

In this lesson you learn how to print your relationships and how to display the subdatasheets in a table.

To Print Table Relationships

 1 Click the Relationships button.
The Relationships window opens and shows the one-to-many relationship created between the Vendors table and the PC Hardware table.

2 Choose File, Print Relationships from the menu.
A relationships report is created and opens in Print Preview (see Figure 9.9). Notice that the pointer is shaped like a magnifying glass when it is on the report, which means you can click to zoom in or out on the report.

Figure 9.9

Magnifying pointer

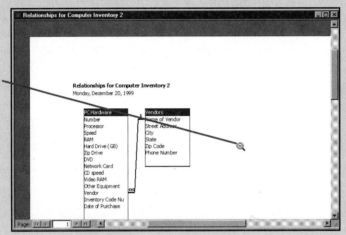

 3 Click the View button.
The view changes to report design view.

 4 Click the Save button and click OK to save the file with the suggested name.

5 Close the Report and close the Relationships window.

6 Click the Reports object button.
The newly created Relationships for Computer Inventory 2 report is listed.

7 Double-click the report name to open it.
The report is displayed onscreen.

 8 Click the Print button to print the report, then close the report.

Exam Note: **Updating the Relationships Report**

If you make changes to the database relationships, the report is not automatically updated. In the Relationships window, choose File, Print Relationships again, to create an up-to-date report showing the changes. Then you can save the new information with the same name as the first report, thus replacing it.

Another tool that is available once you have defined the relationships between your tables, is the capability to display a subdatasheet. A ***subdatasheet*** is a nested datasheet on the one side of the relationship that can be opened to display the related records from a second table.

To Display the Subdatasheet

1 **Click the Tables object button, if necessary, and double-click the Vendors table to open it.**

Notice that there are now pluses to the left of each Vendor record. The plus is called an ***expand indicator***, and means that there is information related to that record in another table, in this case the PC Hardware table. If you click the expand indicator, all of the related information from the PC Hardware table will be displayed in a subdatasheet.

2 **Click the expand indicator on the left side of the Acme Computer record.**

The subdatasheet is displayed, showing the information about all of the computers purchased from that company (see Figure 9.10). The expand indicator for the Acme Computer record has been changed to a minus, showing that the subdatasheet is open for that record.

Click here to close a subdatasheet

Subdatasheet

Click here to open a subdatasheet

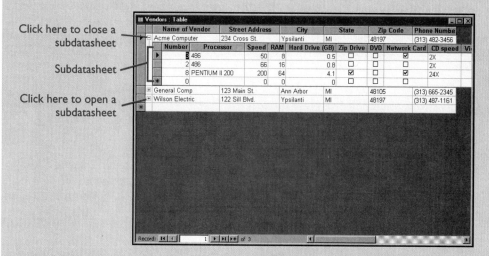

Figure 9.10
A subdatasheet shows related information from another table.

Inside Stuff: **Navigating the Subdatasheets**

When the subdatasheet is displayed, you can use the navigation buttons at the bottom of the table window to move between records and Tab⇄ to move between fields in the subdatasheet. A horizontal scrollbar is displayed so you can scroll to the right as needed to see the other fields in the subdatasheet.

---

continues ▶

To Display the Subdatasheet (continued)

3 Click the minus sign on the left of the Acme Computer field to close the subdatasheet.

4 Click the **Close Window** button to close the table window.
Keep the database open for the next lesson.

 Exam Note: Creating Subdatasheets Directly in a Table
You can create a subdatasheet directly in a table without first creating the relationship in the Relationship window. Open the table in the Datasheet view and choose Insert, Subdatasheet. Select the table you want to insert as a subdatasheet and select the Link Child field and the Link Master field. Then click OK. This will create a relationship and enable you to use a subdatasheet, but it does not enforce referential integrity between the two tables.

 ## Lesson 4: Creating Queries That Draw Data from Both Tables

Queries can be used to look at subsets of data from a single table or from more than one table. Because the query results draw the data from existing tables, they do not take up large amounts of space on your disk. This lets you create as many special-purpose queries as you desire. Queries can also be used as the basis for forms or reports. If a form or report requires data from more than one table, it is often based on a query.

In this lesson, you create a query that includes data from the Vendors table and from the PC Hardware table.

To Create Queries That Draw Data from Both Tables

1 With the `Computer Inventory 2` database open, click the **Queries** object button and click the **New** button.
The New Query dialog box is displayed (see Figure 9.11).

In this example, you design your own query. The other options that appear in the dialog box are Query Wizards that are used for specific purposes. You can click each option and read the explanation on the left side of the dialog box for a brief description of what each wizard will do.

Figure 9.11
Use the New Query dialog box to start a query.

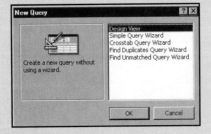

2 Select **Design View** then click **OK.**
The Select Query window opens with the Show Table dialog box in front of it (see Figure 9.12).

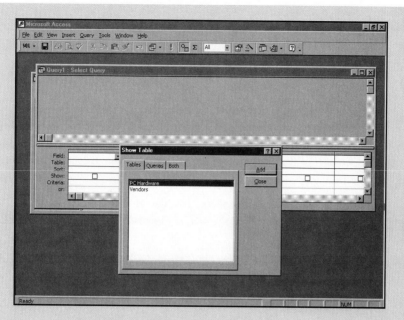

Figure 9.12
The Show Table dialog box opens in front of the Select Query window.

3 **Add both tables to the Select Query window, then close the Show Table dialog box.**

Both tables are added to the Select Query window. The Select Query window becomes active, showing that the Vendors table and the PC Hardware table have been selected for use in this query. The relationship between the tables is also shown, although the Vendor field is hidden for the PC Hardware table.

4 **Click the Maximize button in the upper-right corner of the Select Query window to maximize the window.**

5 **Point your mouse pointer at the thick line dividing the Select Query window into two parts. When the mouse pointer turns into a double-headed black arrow, click and drag the line down to expand the upper portion of the window (see Figure 9.13).**

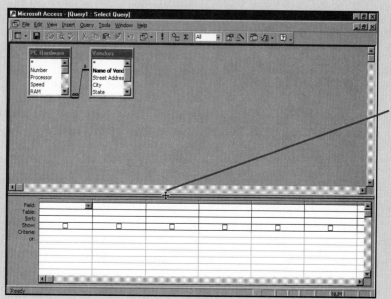

Figure 9.13
The upper portion of the Select Query window has been expanded.

Double-arrow pointer

continues ▶

To Create Queries That Draw Data from Both Tables   (continued)

6 Point to the lower edge of the PC Hardware list box. When the mouse pointer turns into a double-headed arrow, click and drag the lower edge of the box until you can see most of the field names. Do the same for the Vendor list box.

You can move the field list box by clicking in the field list title bar and dragging. You can also drag the right border of each box to the right to adjust the size and position of the boxes so you can see the full length of the field names (see Figure 9.14).

Notice that the Name of Vendor field is the primary key field in the Vendors table, but Vendor is not the primary key field in the PC Hardware table.

Figure 9.14
The Select Query window includes the two expanded field list boxes on which you want to base your query.

Primary key field

Foreign key field

The list box has been widened and lengthened

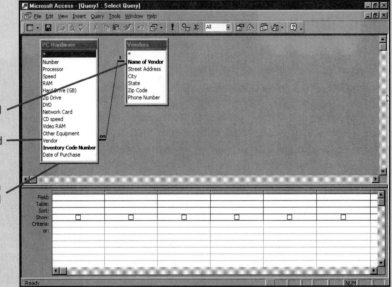

7 Double-click the Vendor field from the PC Hardware list to add it to the first Field box in the query design area.

Notice that the Table box in the query design indicates that this field comes from the PC Hardware table (see Figure 9.15).

The foreign key is used in this case to enable automatic updates. This feature is explained later in this project.

In the next several steps, additional fields are moved to the query design. These fields are being selected so that a maintenance contact list can be created with pertinent information needed to call for repair or maintenance.

8 Double-click the Phone Number field from the Vendors table to add it to the second Field box of the query design.

9 From the PC Hardware list, add the Processor field, the Inventory Code Number field, and the Date of Purchase field.

You may have to scroll down in the PC Hardware list box to find the Date of Purchase field. The final query design should look like Figure 9.16.

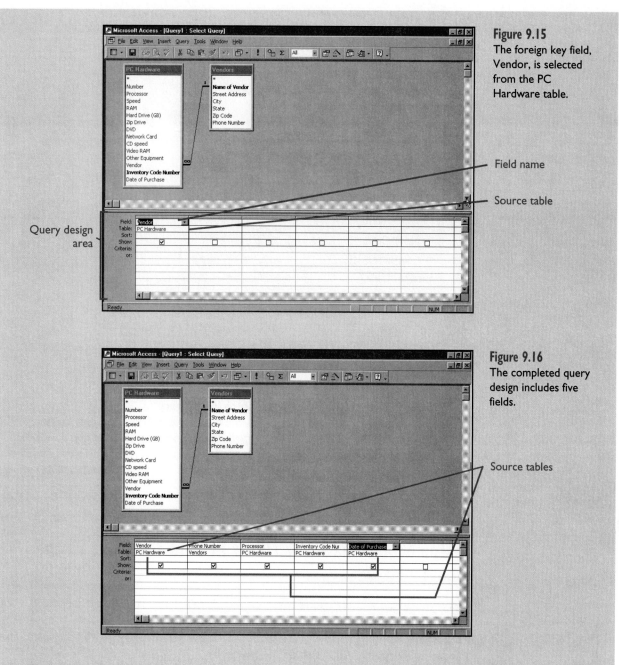

Figure 9.15
The foreign key field, Vendor, is selected from the PC Hardware table.

Field name

Source table

Query design area

Figure 9.16
The completed query design includes five fields.

Source tables

10 **Click the View button to switch to Datasheet view.**
The query displays the combination of data from both tables (see Figure 9.17).

11 **Close the query, and click Yes to save the changes.**

12 **When prompted for a Query Name, type** Vendor Name and Phone Number **for each PC, then click OK.**
Keep the database open for the next lesson.

continues ▶

To Create Queries That Draw Data from Both Tables   (continued)

Figure 9.17
The query results appear when you switch to Datasheet view.

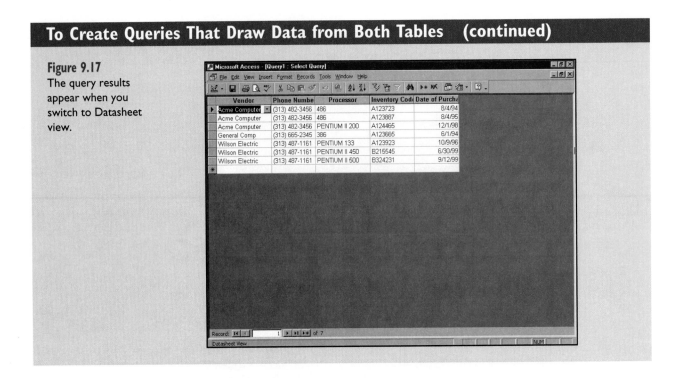

 Exam Note: **Using Multiple Tables in a Query**
You can use any number of tables as the basis for a query. The tables do not need to be related in the Relationships window prior to the creation of the query. You can create a relationship in a query by dragging one matching field to the same field in another table. When you do this, a relationship line is displayed, enabling you to use data from both tables for your query.

Lesson 5: Automatically Filling in Data from One of the Joined Tables

When you create a query that is based on related tables you need to be careful how you deal with the two fields that are used to join the tables. In the Vendors table, the Name of Vendor field was the primary key. The corresponding Vendor field in the PC Hardware table that is used to join the tables is called the foreign key.

When you design a query that draws data from two or more tables, the query automatically fills in data from the primary table if you use the foreign key when designing the query. In the next example, the Vendor field from the PC Hardware table will again be used. This is the foreign key. Information relative to that vendor will be added to the query from the Vendors table. When new data is entered using this query, the fields that have been added from the Vendors table will be automatically filled in once the Vendor field (foreign key) has been entered. This saves time in entering repetitive data and helps to ensure that the information entered is correct.

To Automatically Fill In Fields from One of the Joined Tables

1 In the `Computer Inventory 2` database, click the **Queries** object button, if necessary.

2 Click **New** to design a new query, select **Design** view, and then click **OK**.

3 Add both tables to the query design and close the **Show Table** dialog box.

4 Add the **Vendor** field from the **PC Hardware** list of fields to the first **Field** box in the query design area.

Notice that this field is at the "many" end of the join line, distinguished by the infinity symbol. It is the foreign key.

5 In the **Vendors** list, click **Street Address**, hold down **Shift** and click **Phone number**, then release **Shift**. This selects all of the fields in the **Vendors** table except for **Name of Vendor**. Click and drag the selected fields to the next available field box in the query design area.

The fields are spread across the next five available field boxes. Your query design window should look like Figure 9.18.

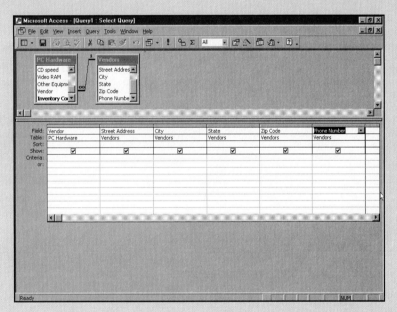

Figure 9.18
The query design window is shown after the vendor information has been added.

6 Add the remaining fields from the **PC Hardware** list by selecting every field except the **Vendor** field, and then click and drag the group of fields to the next open field in the query.

Access will spread out the fields, one to each of the next available Field boxes. Be sure you do not include the Vendor field a second time.

7 Click the **View** button to view the dynaset, then go to the bottom of the list and click in the empty **Vendor** field.

Notice that the Lookup list included in the table design also works in the query.

8 Click the list button to reveal the list of Vendors (see Figure 9.19).

continues ▶

To Automatically Fill In Fields from One of the Joined Tables   (continued)

Figure 9.19
The list of vendors
from the Vendors
table appears in the
query.

List of vendors

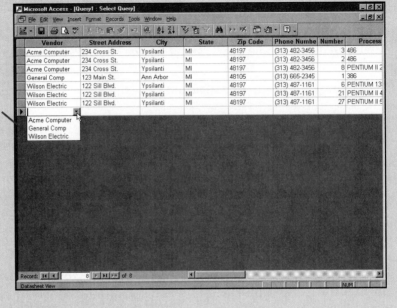

9 **Click Acme Computer to select it.**

Access automatically retrieves the data from the other fields in the Vendors table
that have been included in the query (see Figure 9.20). At this point, you could
scroll to the right and fill in information about a new computer purchase.

Figure 9.20
Data from the vendors
table is automatically
displayed.

Data has been filled
in automatically

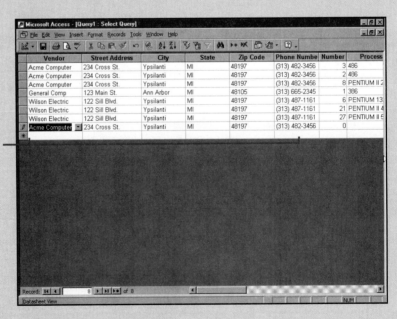

10 **Do not enter a new record at this time. Press** (Esc) **to abort the input
process.**

11 **Close the query, and click Yes to save the changes. When prompted
for a Query Name, type** Vendor and Hardware, **then click OK.**

Keep the database open for the next lesson.

Lesson 6: Updating Tables by Entering or Deleting Data in the Query

Queries can be used to enter data into the tables they are based on. This must be done with care. Once you have established referential integrity between two tables, you cannot add a record in the related table that does not match an existing record in the primary table. In our example, you could not add a new PC in the PC Hardware table and enter a vendor name that was not already in the Vendor Table. If you try to do this, you get an error message. In this lesson you learn some guidelines for successful data entry and how to interpret some of the error messages that you may receive.

To Update Tables by Entering or Deleting Data in the Query

1 **In the** `Computer Inventory 2` **database, select the Vendor and Hardware query and click the <u>O</u>pen button.**

2 **Click the New Record button to add a new record.**

The insertion point is placed in the first field of the empty row.

3 **Click the drop-down button and then select Acme Computer from the drop-down list.**

The remaining fields that are linked to the Vendor table are filled in automatically.

4 **Press** `Tab⇆` **until you get to the Number field.**

Enter the following data in the remaining fields in this record. (Use the mouse to click the check box to indicate the presence of a zip drive, DVD, or network card. You can also press the `Spacebar` to place the (✓) in the box or `Tab⇆` to skip over a box and leave it empty.)

        4
        Pentium II
        450
        64
        8.6
        (✓) for the Zip Drive
        No (✓) for the DVD
        (✓) for the Network Card
        24X
        8
        CD-RW drive
        B763423
        6/25/00

5 **Close the query, click on the Tables object button, select the** `PC Hardware` **table and open it in Datasheet view.**

Notice that the new PC has been entered in the table (see Figure 9.21).

6 **Close the PC Hardware table, click the Queries object button and open the** `Vendor and Hardware` **query in Datasheet view.**

continues ▶

To Update Tables by Entering or Deleting Data in the Query   (continued)

Figure 9.21
The PC Hardware
table includes the new
record for the
Pentium II.

New record

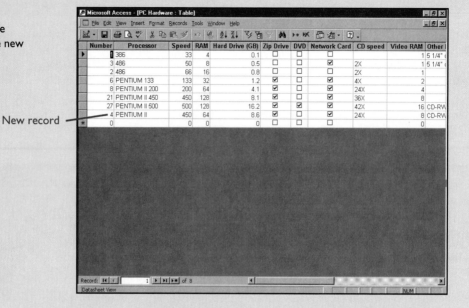

7 **Click the record selector button to select the record for the computer that you just entered.**

Scroll to the right to find the record you just added, because it is not the bottom record anymore (see Figure 9.22). It has been sorted on the foreign key field.

Figure 9.22
Because of automatic
sorting, the record
you just entered is no
longer at the end of
the table.

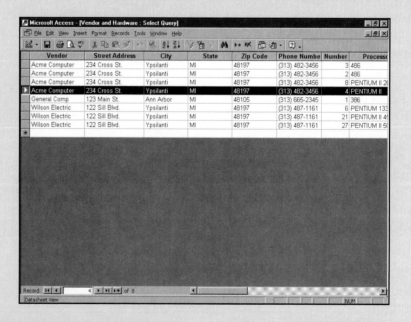

8 **Press Del to delete the record, then click Yes to confirm that you want to delete the record.**

9 **Close the query.**

10 **Click the Tables object button and open the PC Hardware table in the Datasheet view.**

Confirm that the record has been deleted from the table.

11 **Close the table and close the database.**

***Exam Note:*   Changing the Contents of the Foreign Key Field**
You should not try to change the contents of the Vendor field from this query. The Vendor field in this query is the foreign key from the PC Hardware table, not the primary key field from the Vendors table. When you defined the join between these two tables, you specified that referential integrity should be enforced. This meant that there could not be a value in the Vendor field in the PC Hardware table that did not already exist in the Vendors table. Use the list box to select an existing vendor.

***Inside Stuff:*   Dealing with Multiple Primary Keys in a Query**
This query also contains the primary key field from the PC Hardware table, Inventory Code Number. When you use this query to add new records to the PC Hardware table, you must enter a new inventory code number that is not the same as any other code number in the table. If you leave this field empty or enter a duplicate number, you get an error message.

Lesson 7: Finding Duplicate Records in an Existing Table

In some cases, you inherit a table of data from another source where the data entry was not carefully controlled. This table may contain duplicate entries that are difficult to find. Locating duplicates can also be useful when you append two data tables together and are uncertain if there is duplication of some records. Finally, it is useful to look for duplicates when you want to establish a field as the primary key field but are uncertain if there are duplicates in that field.

Fortunately, Access provides a special query that can be used to locate duplicate records. The **Find Duplicates Query Wizard** creates a query that lists the duplicate values in a single table or query.

Another type of error may occur when two related tables have records in one table without corresponding records in the second table. This occurs when referential integrity has not been enforced. The **Find Unmatched Query Wizard** can be used to locate these types of errors. Both of these special purpose queries work in a similar manner. In this lesson, you use the Find Duplicates Query Wizard to locate duplicate entries in a database of economic data. The database used in this lesson was compiled by the government and contains information about the number of service businesses in each zip code area in Michigan. Some duplicate records have been added for this exercise. The database does not have a primary key, but the natural choice is the zip code. When you try to set a primary key, you get an error message that says there is a duplicate value in the primary key, indexed field, or relationship.

You could scroll through the records looking for the duplicate, but there are over 900 records and you do not know how many duplicates there are! This is an instance where you need the Find Duplicates Query Wizard.

To Find Duplicate Records in an Existing Table

1 **Find the AC-0902 file on your CD-ROM, right click on it, and send it to the floppy drive. Move to drive A, remove the read-only property, and rename the file Service Businesses in Michigan-1987.**

2 **Open the database.**

continues ▶

To Find Duplicate Records in an Existing Table (continued)

❸ Click the Queries object button, and then click New.
The New Query dialog box is displayed (see Figure 9.23).

Figure 9.23
The New Query
dialog box enables you
to select the wizard
you want to use.

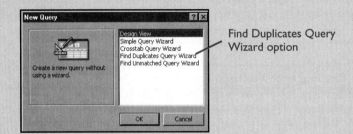

Find Duplicates Query
Wizard option

❹ Select the Find Duplicates Query Wizard, then click OK.
The first Find Duplicates Query Wizard dialog box is displayed (see Figure 9.24).

Figure 9.24
The first Find
Duplicates Query
Wizard dialog box
asks which table or
query you want to
search for duplicates.

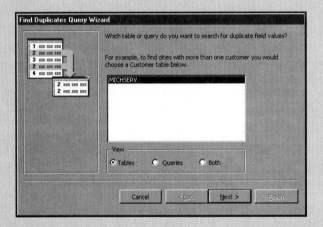

❌ If You Have Problems...
The Find Duplicates Query Wizard may not have been installed on your
machine. If this is the case, either nothing happens, or the program will
prompt you to add the Wizard. Follow the screen instructions to install this
feature. See your instructor or lab administrator if you need assistance.

**❺ Click the Next button to accept the default selection of the
MICHSERV table.**
The second Find Duplicates Query Wizard dialog box is displayed (see Figure
9.25).

**❻ Click the ZIP field to select it, if necessary, then click the Select button
to move the ZIP field into the Duplicate-value fields box. Click Next to
move to the next dialog box.**
The third Find Duplicates Query Wizard dialog box is displayed (see Figure
9.26).

Select button

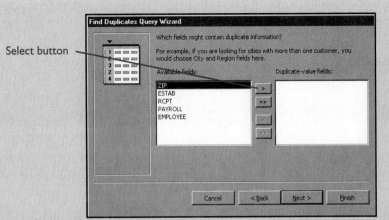

Figure 9.25
The second Find
Duplicates Query
Wizard dialog box
asks which fields might
contain the duplicate
information.

Select All button

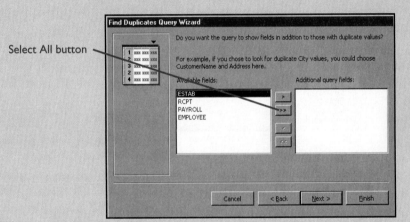

Figure 9.26
Use the third Find
Duplicates Query
Wizard dialog box to
specify other fields you
want to use in the
Find.

**⑦ Click the Select All button to select and move all of the remaining
fields into the Additional Query fields box.**

These additional fields help you to determine how to deal with the duplicate
records when you find them.

⑧ Click the Finish button.

This accepts the default name for the query and displays the final results of your
query (see Figure 9.27). It shows each instance of a duplicate entry in the ZIP
field, and also shows the contents of each of the other four fields.

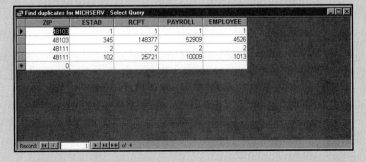

Figure 9.27
The Find duplicates for
MICHSERV: Select
Query found two sets
of duplicate zip code
entries.

When you display the duplicate entries, you need to decide what to do with
them. In this example, the two entries for each of the zip codes might need to be
added together. Let's assume that you do a little research and find that the smaller duplicate entries are errors.

continues ▶

To Find Duplicate Records in an Existing Table   (continued)

9 **Click the record selector to the left of the first record for zip code 48103 (the one that shows 1 in the ESTAB field) and press Del.**
Choose <u>Y</u>es when prompted, to confirm that you want to delete this record.

10 **Delete the next erroneous record (the one that shows 2 in the ESTAB field) for zip code 48111.**

11 **Close the query.**
Access creates a query called Find duplicates for MICHSERV (see Figure 9.28).

Figure 9.28
Access created the query and automatically named it Find duplicates for MICHSERV.

New query

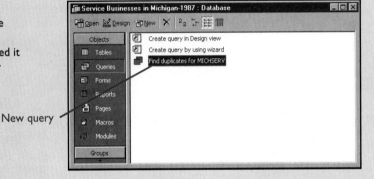

The MICHSERV table can now use the ZIP field as a primary key. (Do not perform that operation at this time.)

12 **Close the database and close Access, unless you want to continue working on the following exercises.**
If you have completed your session on the computer, exit Access and shut down Windows before you turn off the computer. Otherwise, continue with the exercises.

 Inside Stuff: **File Names of Older Databases**
This table was created by the federal government using a database program called dBASE III. Programs that use older operating systems that predate Windows 95 (not including Macintosh computers) were restricted to file names of eight characters or less. Notice how much more descriptive your file name of Service Businesses in Michigan-1987 is compared to MICHSERV.

Summary

In this project you were introduced to some issues involved in managing data. You learned how to join two tables using a one-to-many relationship, and to create queries that draw data from more than one table. You filled in data from several fields in a table by entering just the foreign key field, and you updated the information in tables by entering or deleting data in a query.

You can learn more about managing data by looking through the help on the topics mentioned above. In particular, look at the information about using the Cascade Update and Cascade Delete options in the Relationships window. You learn more about table relationships in Project 15, "Designing a Complex Database."

Checking Concepts and Terms ✓

True/False

For each of the following statements, check *T* or *F* to indicate whether the statement is true or false.

__T __F **1.** To display a subdatasheet you must first create a relationship between the tables using the Relationships window. [L3]

__T __F **2.** When you create a query that automatically fills in fields from table A, you drag the primary key from table A into the query design. [L5]

__T __F **3.** When you create a Find Duplicate query, you need to include enough fields to enable you to decide what to do with the duplicate records. [L7]

__T __F **4.** To create a query based on two tables, both tables must have a field with the same name and data type. [L2]

__T __F **5.** To base a form on more than one table, you can first create a query that is based on those tables and then base your form on the query. [L4]

Multiple Choice

Circle the letter of the correct answer for each of the following questions.

1. In a one-to-many relationship, _____. [L2]

a. the matching field in the many table is the foreign key

b. the matching field in the one table is the foreign key

c. the matching field in the many table is the primary key

d. neither matching field is indexed

2. To create a query that automatically fills in data from one of the joined tables, _____. [L5]

a. use the primary key and the other fields from the same table

b. use the foreign key from the second table and the other fields from the table that has the primary key

c. select a one-to-one join

d. select Automatic Fill from the Tools menu

3. When you choose to enforce referential integrity in a relationship, it means _____. [L2]

a. you cannot enter a record in the many table that does not have a corresponding entry in the one table

b. you cannot delete a record in the one table that has an entry in the many table

c. your data is protected from having orphan records

d. all of the above

4. How do you print your table relationships? [L3]

a. Click New in the Reports object list, and choose Table Relationships Wizard. After the report is created, click Print.

b. In the Relationships window, choose File, Print Relationships. After the report is created, click Print.

c. In the Relationships window, choose New, Create Relationships Report. After the report is created, click Print.

d. In the Relationships window, click the Print button.

5. To create a join between tables click the relationship button, select the tables, then _____. [L2]

a. drag the primary key field from one table to the matching field in the second table and click the create button in the relationship dialog box

b. click the join button to join the two tables, then specify the fields that are to be joined

c. make sure the field names and data types are the same

d. click the join button, match the fields, select enforce referential integrity and save your changes

Screen ID

Label each element of the Access screen shown in Figure 9.29.

Figure 9.29

A. Relationship line

B. Foreign key field

C. Table source

D. Primary key field

E. Many symbol

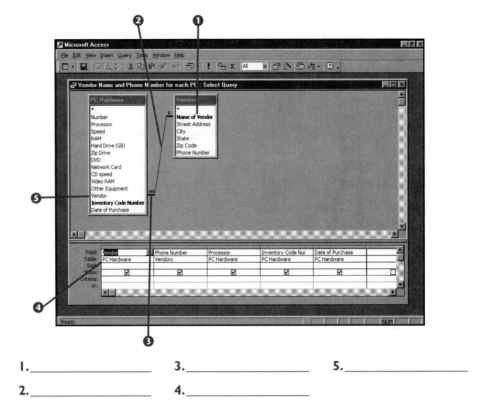

1. _____   3. _____   5. _____

2. _____   4. _____

Skill Drill

Skill Drill exercises reinforce project skills. Each skill reinforced is the same, or nearly the same, as a skill presented in the project. Each exercise includes a brief narrative introduction, followed by detailed instructions in a step-by-step format.

The database you use in the Skill Drill exercises contains information about your book collection and the people you have loaned books to.

1. Enforcing Referential Integrity and Locating Unmatched Records in an Existing Relationship

In this exercise, you have a database that has a table of information about the books in your library and another table that tracks the books others have borrowed from you. Every book that has been borrowed should be listed in the table of books in the library.

When this database was created, referential integrity between the two tables was not enforced, so it is possible that a book was loaned out before it was recorded in the master list of books. In this example you try to enforce referential integrity. After viewing the error message you then use the Unmatched Query Wizard to look for unmatched records between the two tables.

To enforce the referential integrity and locate unmatched records in an existing relationship:

1. Find the `AC-0903` file on your CD-ROM, right click on it, and send it to the floppy drive. Move to drive A, right-click on the filename, open Properties and remove the Read-only attribute. Right-click on the filename again, select Rename, rename the file `Home Library` and open it.

2. Click the Relationships button on the toolbar.

3. Double-click the line that joins the tables to display the Edit Relationships dialog box. Notice that the Enforce Referential Integrity text box was not selected when this relationship was established. There may be unmatched records in the Borrowed table.

4. Select the Enforce Referential Integrity box and click OK. An Error message appears. There are unmatched records in the Borrowed table.

5. Click OK to acknowledge the message, then close the Relationships window.

6. Click the Queries object button and click New to start a new query.

7. Use the Find Unmatched Query Wizard to find the borrowed book that is not listed in the Books table.

8. Select Borrow as the table containing the records you want in the query results.

9. Select Books as the table containing the related records.

10. Accept Book Title as the related field in both tables.

11. Click the Select All button to see all of the fields in the query, then accept the default name.

12. When you have identified the book, enter a new record in the Books table for this book. The author is `Robert Heinlein`, and the name of the book, as you found out in the previous step, is `Notebooks of Lazarus Long`. It is a `Science Fiction` book that was originally published in `1973`. (The type of book is not limited to those in the attached lookup list. You can enter a new type, such as Science Fiction.)

13. Close the Books table. Repeat steps 2 through 4 to enforce referential integrity. This procedure should work now that there are no unmatched records. The relationship line should now show a one-to-many relationships. (Make sure that the Title is an exact match in both tables. It is the joined field.)

14. Close the relationship window and open the `Books` table. Click the expand indicator to the left of the Robert Heinlein book you just added to the field. The subdatasheet displays the name and phone number of the borrower and the date the book was borrowed.

15. Click the expand indicator to close the subdatasheet.

16. Click the expand indicator to the left of the next record (the book by William Coughlin). The subdatasheet is empty, indicating that the book is not on loan. Close the subdatasheet.

17. Close the table, and close the database.

2. Checking for Unmatched Records, Enforcing Referential Integrity, and Printing Table Relationships

A database for a small music retail business keeps a table of music orders and a table of suppliers. Each record in the Orders table has an entry for the supplier that should match an entry in the Suppliers table. In this exercise, you will discover some of the problems involved in enforcing referential integrity. You will discover that some of these problems could have been avoided by careful initial planning!

To Check for unmatched records, enforce referential integrity, and print table relationships :

1. Find the `AC-0904` file on your CD-ROM, right click on it, and send it to the floppy drive. Move to drive A, right-click on the filename, and deselect the read-only attribute. Right-click on the filename again, select Rename, rename the file `Sound Byte Music`, and open the database.

2. Click the Relationships button to determine which fields are linked between the Orders and Suppliers tables.

3. Double-click the link between the two tables. The Edit Relationships dialog box opens. Notice that the Relationship type is listed as Indeterminate. To enforce referential integrity, you need to create a one-to-many relationship between these fields. One way to do this is to make the Record Company field in the Suppliers table a key field (if you are sure there will be no duplicate entries).

4. Click Cancel to close the Edit Relationships dialog box, then close the Relationships window.

5. View the Suppliers table and make sure that there are no duplicates in the Record Company field. Change to Design view, select the Record Company field, then click the Primary Key button. (You can also select Edit, Primary Key from the menu.)

6. Close the table Design view window and save your changes when prompted.

7. Click the Relationships button, then double-click the relationships line. The Edit Relationships dialog box opens again and indicates that the type of relationship is now a one-to-many.

8. Click the Enforce Referential Integrity check box, then click OK. An error message appears that informs you that there are unmatched records. Click OK, then close the Relationships window.

9. Click the Queries object button, then click New to create a new query.

10. Use the Find Unmatched Query Wizard to look for unmatched records in the Orders table that do not have a matching record in the Suppliers table.

11. Compare the name of the supplier in the unmatched order to the Record company name in the Suppliers table to determine why there is no match. Notice that entering the name of the company incorrectly caused a mismatch. The names must match exactly (which is one reason to use a lookup list for this type of field). Open the Orders table and correct that mistake.

12. Click the Relationships button and double-click the relationships line to open the Edit Relationships dialog box.

13. Select Enforce Referential Integrity, then click OK. The relationship should display a 1 at the Supplier Name end of the line and an infinity symbol at the Record Company end. This indicates a successful one-to-many relationship with enforced referential integrity.

14. Choose File, Print Relationships to create a relationships report. Print the report. Save your changes and close the database.

3. Adding a Table, Relating Tables, and Creating a Query Based on Both Tables

The chess club databases you used in Project 8 had a single table design. If you want to track several donations or several months of dues payments, the database needs a second table.

To add a table, relate tables, and create a query based on both tables:

1. Copy the `AC-0905` file to your floppy disk, deselect the read-only status, rename the file `New Chess Club`, and open the database.

2. Open the Member Information table in Design view. The Member ID # field is the primary key field. Remember what the data type is for this field. Close the table.

3. Create a new table to track how much was paid and when. Include a `Member ID #` field, a `Dues` field, and a `Date Paid` field. Make sure the Member ID # field in this table is the same data type as in the other table. Do not designate it as the primary key in this table.

4. Make the Member ID # field a lookup field. Choose to look up the information from the Member information table. Select the Member ID # and last name to display. Make sure to show the key field. Choose Yes when prompted to have the Wizard create a relationship between the two fields. (This is similar to the skill taught in Lesson 7 in Project 8, but in this case you look the information up in another table, rather than typing in the data.)

5. Save the table as `Member Dues`. Close the table and open the Relationships window. Double-click the relationship line to open the Edit Relationships window. Enforce referential integrity.

6. Create a relationship report and print the report. Close the report and save it with the default name when prompted.

7. Create a query that uses both tables. Add Member ID # field from the Member Dues table (foreign key), the first and last name fields from the Member Information table, and the other fields from the Donations table. Save this query as `Names and Dues`.

8. Change to the Datasheet view of the query to enter a new record. Select Jones from the Member ID # drop down list. Notice that the last and first names are filled in. Type `25` in the Dues field and today's date in the Date Paid field.

9. Close the query and close the database.

Challenge

Challenge exercises expand on or are somewhat related to skills presented in the lessons. Each exercise provides a brief narrative introduction followed by instructions in a numbered step format that are not as detailed as those in the Skill Drill section.

1. Establishing Referential Integrity Among Tables

The database used in this exercise contains information about research on the television viewing habits of 20 households. The study focused on six news and education cable channels. This database has four tables and three relationships. The relationships were created without enforcing referential integrity, so there could be orphan records. If you have done all of the exercises in this project thus far, you will need to use a new disk to begin this exercise.

To establish referential integrity among tables:

1. Copy the `AC-0906` file to an empty floppy disk, remove the read-only status, rename the file **Customer Research**, and open the database.

2. Open the Customer Research database. View the relationships. Notice that each of the relationships is between the key field of one table and a non-key field of another table. All three of these relationships should be one-to-many.

3. Double-click on each of the relationship lines and attempt to enforce referential integrity. This is easy to do in two of the three.

4. When you identify which relationship has a problem with unmatched records, close the Relationships window and run an unmatched records query to find the problem. (Warning: It makes a difference which table you pick first when looking for unmatched records. If your first try doesn't find the problem, run the query again but reverse the order of the two tables.)

5. Do not try to fix the problem until you've identified exactly what the problem is. (*Hint:* Look closely at the data in each of the unmatched records queries you ran, then look at the list of participants. The problem is a typographical error that will become apparent as you look at the queries and tables.)

6. You can attempt to fix the problem in either of the related tables, but one of them is an AutoNumber field that can't be changed. Fix the problem, then go back and attempt to enforce referential integrity again. Notice how much easier this would have been if referential integrity had been enforced from the beginning.

2. Enforcing Referential Integrity and Creating One-to-Many Relationships Among Tables

The database used in this exercise contains information about the locations, suppliers, repair, and types of vending machines. The tables in this database were created without concern for data integrity. In this exercise, you establish key fields where appropriate and create one-to-many relationships with referential integrity.

To enforce referential integrity and create a one-to-may relationship among tables:

1. Copy the `AC-0907` file to your floppy disk, change the read-only status to archive, rename the file **Vending Machines**, and open the database.

2. Open the **Vending Machine** database and open the Relationships window. Notice that only one of these tables, Locations, has a primary key. The Name of the supplier should be a unique field in the Suppliers table and the Machine Type field should be the key field in the Machines table.

3. Right-click the Name field in the Suppliers table and select Table <u>D</u>esign from the shortcut menu (this is faster than closing the Relationship and opening up the table.) Make the Name field the primary key field, close the Design view, and save your changes.

4. Use the same procedure to make the Machine Type field the primary key in the Machines table.

5. Double-click the relationship line between the Locations and the Machines table. Try to enforce referential integrity. It will not work. Close the Edit Relationships box and delete the relationship line.

6. Create a new relationship line between the two Machine Type fields, then enforce referential integrity.

7. Remove and replace the other relationships lines and enforce referential integrity. Do these one at a time so you don't forget which fields were related.

8. Create a query that uses fields from the Locations and Machines tables. Name the query `Machines and Sites`.

9. Look at your new query, then close the query and the database.

3. Revising Tables and Relationships in a Database

In this exercise, you remove three redundant fields from one of the tables, enforce referential integrity, and create a query based on three tables.

To revise tables and relationships in a database

1. Locate the `AC-0908` database, copy it to your disk drive, deselect the read-only status, and rename it `Video Store`.

2. Open the `Video Store` database and click the Relationships button to view the relationships between the tables. Maximize the window and expand the field lists so you can see all of the fields.

3. Double-click one of the relationship lines to open the Relationships dialog box. Click the check box to enforce referential integrity. Repeat this process for the other relationship. Close the Relationship window.

4. Open each table and study the fields in each of the three tables. The Video Tapes table has three fields that actually describe the rental activity, and are therefore redundant. Open the `Video Tapes` table and delete the Currently Rented, Current Renter, and Number of Rentals fields.

5. Create a query that uses fields from all three tables. It should at least include the customer's first and last names and phone number, the title of the video rented, and the date rented, date returned, and late fee. Do not include any of the fields that are used to provide links between the tables.

6. Switch to the Datasheet view to test your query. Save the query as `Three Tables`. Close the database.

Discovery Zone

Discovery Zone exercises help you gain advanced knowledge of project topics and application of skills. These exercises focus on enhancing your problem-solving skills. Numbered steps are not provided, but you are given hints, reminders, screen shots, and references to help you reach your goal for each exercise.

The database you use in this exercise deals with short stories from the turn-of-the century (19th to 20th, not 20th to 21st). These are short stories from books of stories by different authors, not books of stories by a single author. There are three tables in the database—one with information about the authors, one with information about the short stories, and one with information about the books. You will need an empty disk to do this exercise.

1. Improving an Existing Database

Copy the file AC-0909 from your CD-ROM to an empty disk in your floppy drive, deselect the read-only attribute, and rename it Short Story Collection.

The three tables in the Short Story Collection database have not had the primary key fields identified, and they are not related. Therefore, orphan records and inconsistent data entry may have occurred and will likely continue to occur unless something is done.

Goal: Identify primary key fields, create relationships, and enforce referential integrity, where possible. (*Note:* Because of the nature of the fields, some relationships can never have referential integrity enforced). In this database you should:

- use the Book Title field as the key field in the Book information table;
- use the Author field as the key field in the Author information table;
- create a relationship between the Book Title field in the Book information table and the Source field in the Short Stories table. You should attempt to enforce referential integrity between the tables;
- create a relationship between the Author field in the Author information table and the Author field in the Short Stories table. You should attempt to enforce referential integrity between the tables.

Hint #1: You need to use a query to check for duplicates before you can identify one of the primary key fields.

Hint #2: You discover one relationship that can never have referential integrity enforced. See if you can figure out which one won't work before you try to set it up.

Leave the database open if you intend to do the next exercise.

2. Adding Information Using Subdatasheets

Subdatasheets are particularly useful when you want to add information to related tables with small numbers of fields. The one-to-many relationship will become much clearer by the time you have finished this exercise, which uses the Short Story Collection database you created in the previous exercise.

This exercise uses the **Short Story Collection** database from Discovery Zone Exercise 1. If you did not do that exercise, open another database where you have created a table relationship and enforced referential integrity. Follow the same procedure and use the subdatasheet to enter two records that are appropriate in the table that is the "many" side of the relationship

Goal: Update records in one table from inside another table using the subdatasheet.

Use the help menu to learn about using subdatasheets. While you are looking through the available help, notice the relationship required between the two fields for this procedure to work. In the Book information table:

- Find the book of Great English Short Stories edited by Christopher Isherwood.
- Add the following stories using the subdatasheet:
    - `Lawrence, D. H. "Blind Man, The" 1922 27 England, My England`
    - `Kipling, Rudyard "Mary Postgate" 1915 22 Diversity of Creatures, A`

Check to make sure the two stories you added in the Book information table have been added to the Short Stories table.

PinPoint Assessment

You have completed this project and the associated lessons, and have had an opportunity to assess your skills through end-of-project questions and exercises. Now use the PinPoint software evaluation mode to assess your comprehension of the specific exam tasks you have just learned. You can also use the PinPoint Trainer Mode and the Show Me tutorials to practice these specific exam tasks.

Project 10

Adding Useful Features to Your Forms

Key terms introduced in this project include

- list box
- subform

Objectives	Required Activity for MOUS	Exam Level
➤ Add Formats in the Form Design View	Modify Control Properties	Expert
	Modify Form Properties	Expert
➤ Create a List Box	Modify Control Properties	Expert
➤ Look Up Valid Entries from a Table or Query Using a Combo Box	Modify Control Properties	Expert
➤ Use Information from Tables to Fill in Fields Automatically	Create a form with the Form Wizard	Core
➤ Enter the Current Date in a Field Automatically	Customize Form Sections	Expert
➤ Add the Current Date and Time to a Form Automatically	Customize Form Sections	Expert
		Expert
➤ Change the Tab Order	Customize Form Sections	
➤ Create Subforms	Use the Subform Control and Synchronize Forms	Expert
➤ Print the Form for Filing Purposes	Print database objects	Core
➤ Add an Image to a Form	Insert a graphic on a form	Expert
➤ Add a Calculated Control in a Form	Use a calculated control on a form	Core

Why Would I Do This?

Consistent data input is one of the primary reasons for using a form. This is particularly true when several people are entering information into the same tables. In Project 8, "Making Data Entry Easier and More Accurate," you looked at ways of creating consistent data input structures, and you learned how to change the look of the data when it is displayed in the datasheet. You can customize the fields in a similar manner on a form.

You also know how to use a default value to avoid unnecessary typing if a field often contains the same data. A default value solves this problem if there is one piece of information that is used in a field the majority of the time. But what if there are five or six items, such as city names, that all occur frequently? The Lookup Wizard helped you build a list that appeared in a drop-down box in Table view. Forms have a similar feature that offers additional options.

Another way to avoid extra typing is to create a form based on more than one table. You can set up the form to look up information from a table and automatically fill in several fields when you enter the information for only one field.

Frequently you will be required to enter the current date (and even time) in a record. There are ways of automating that procedure so that the user does not have to enter anything.

When you enter data, the cursor jumps from one text box to the next when you press Tab. This is called the tab order. If you move the fields around in the form, the tab order may no longer make sense. The tab order in a form can be changed automatically or manually.

Another useful form is the main form/subform. This design places a form within a form and is very useful for displaying a one-to-many relationship between tables. In the main part of the form you see the one side of the relationship, and in the **subform** you see the many related records from the second table. This type of design could be used to display all of the inventory that was purchased from each vendor, or all of the employees that work in each department in a company.

In this project, you learn how to improve data entry speed and accuracy by adding lists and combo boxes. You also add dates that are needed in two different situations. You create a main form/subform and use it to enter new records. Finally, you learn how to print the Form view of a single record. You use modified versions of two of the databases you used in the previous two projects.

Expert Lesson 1: Adding Formats in the Form Design View

When you create a form any input masks, data format expressions, validation rules, and required field properties are brought to the form from the underlying table or tables. You can add additional properties to any field, although you cannot add or change the Required property option in the property boxes.

In the following procedure, you use two formatting techniques to make your data look different. You make the Department name all capital letters, much the same as you did with the Last Name field in Project 8. You then use a standard formatting button to right-align the Social Security Number field.

The database used in this lesson is similar to the one you worked on in Project 8. An extra table and a query have been added for the lessons in this project, and a basic form has been created. A new text field, called City, has also been added. If you are using a floppy disk to store your files, make sure you have enough room to store a new file.

To Add Formats in the Form Design View

1 **Find the AC-1001 file on your CD-ROM, right-click on it, and send it to the floppy drive. Move to drive A: and rename the file Software Training. Remove the read-only property and open the new database.**
This is an expanded version of the Software Training Database you used in Project 8.

2 **Click the Forms object button, if necessary**
Only one form should appear—the PC Training Data Entry Form—and it should be highlighted (see Figure 10.1).

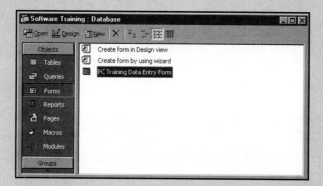

Figure 10.1
One form is listed in the Forms area of the Software Training database.

3 **Click Open to open the form, and then click the Maximize button to open the Form window to its maximum size.**
Your screen should resemble Figure 10.2.

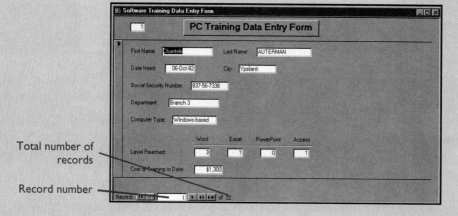

Total number of records

Record number

Figure 10.2
The Software Training Data Entry Form displays the first table record.

4 **Click the View button to switch to Design view.**

> **X** *If You Have Problems...*
> The fields onscreen may be covered by the field list box or the Toolbox. If the field list box is open, click the Close button in the list box title bar to close it. If the Toolbox is in the way, click in the Toolbox title bar and drag it to the right side of the screen.

continues ▶

To Add Formats in the Form Design View (continued)

⑤ Click the Department field text box to select it.
Handles appear around the text box, and a single large handle should appear in the upper-left corner of the label box. Make sure you have selected the Department field text box and not the label box, which is the field name on the left of the text box.

⑥ Click the Properties button on the Form Design toolbar.
The property sheet is divided into five sections. Take a moment to look at each of them by clicking on the five tabs.

Another way to activate the property sheet is to right-click on the field text box and choose <u>P</u>roperties from the shortcut menu.

⑦ Click the Format tab.
Once the Format tab is chosen, the formatting options for the Department field are displayed (see Figure 10.3).

Figure 10.3
The property sheet
shows the Format
options.

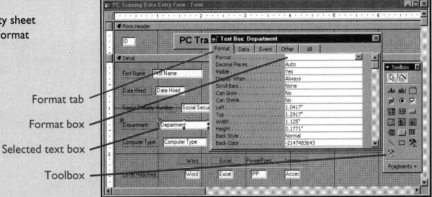

Format tab

Format box

Selected text box

Toolbox

⑧ Type the "greater than" symbol (>) in the Format box.
This is the same procedure you used in Table view in Project 8.

⑨ Click the Close button to close this property sheet.

⑩ Click the View button to return to Form view.
The Department name should now be capitalized, along with the Last Name field, which you formatted in Project 8.

You can also control the alignment of the text within the box.

⑪ Click the View button to move back to Design view.
⑫ Click the Social Security Number field text box to select it.

⑬ Click the Align Right button on the Formatting toolbar.
You have now aligned the Social Security number to the right, the way users expect numbers to be displayed. The reason that this number was aligned left was that it was originally set up as a text field to take advantage of input masking.

You can use any of the Formatting buttons on either the text box or its label. This means that you can display the data using boldface or italics, and you can even change the color of the text.

14 **Click the View button to return to Form view.**

Notice that the Social Security Number field is aligned right (see Figure 10.4).

The Social Security
Number field is
right-aligned

The Department field
is now capitalized

Figure 10.4
The PC Training Data
Entry Form shows the
changes made to the
form.

15 **Click the Close Window button to close the form. Save your changes when prompted.**

16 **Click the Tables object button, and then open the Software Training table.**

Notice that the Department field is not upper case, and the Social Security field is still aligned left (see Figure 10.5).

First Name	Last Name	Date Hired	City	Social Securit	Department	Computer Type	Word	Ex
Chantele	AUTERMAN	06-Oct-82	Ypsilanti	837-56-7336	Branch 3	Windows-based	3	
James	BAIRD	24-Aug-75	Belleville	534-21-8274	Accounting	Windows-based	0	
Robert	BAUER	09-Nov-74	Ann Arbor	919-27-7392	Purchasing	Windows-based	0	
Archie	BAYLIS	01-Jun-67	Ann Arbor	345-24-7635	Branch 3	Windows-based	1	
Jane	BOXER	05-Jul-69	Toledo	636-63-2345	Accounting	Windows-based	1	
Peter	BULLARD	12-Jan-75	Belleville	101-01-0001	Marketing	Windows-based	1	
Kay	DOBBS	25-May-90	Ann Arbor	590-13-5326	Payroll	Windows-based	0	
William	EVICH	02-Dec-85	Ypsilanti	858-54-4736	Accounting	Windows-based	0	
Chris	HART	11-Apr-88	Northville	835-36-7899	Marketing	Windows-based	1	
Tim	HILL	09-Sep-92	Ann Arbor	182-37-3687	Branch 2	Macintosh	0	
Debby	KRASNY	12-Dec-75	Ypsilanti	943-73-7684	Accounting	Windows-based	1	
Sue	LORD	15-Jan-72	Jackson	972-24-5364	Payoll	Windows-based	0	
Vickie	NOLAN	25-Mar-78	Chelsea	233-54-5253	Branch 1	Windows-based	2	
Mike	O'SULLIVAN	20-May-93	Ann Arbor	690-98-9583	Branch 3	Windows-based	0	
Susan	RHODES	23-Mar-87	South Lyon	267-48-4895	Branch 1	Windows-based	1	
Beverly	ROBERTS	12-Sep-93	Plymouth	236-95-6789	Branch 3	Windows-based	1	
Wayne	ROBERTSON	04-Apr-82	Belleville	837-45-6274	Human Resources	Macintosh	1	
Pat	ROWLAND	04-Nov-95	Belleville	247-80-7889	Branch 1	Windows-based	1	
Russ	SEMARK	07-Aug-84	Clinton	534-26-2694	Marketing	Windows-based	2	
Ralph	STEINBERG	13-Jan-76	Monroe	947-32-3564	Branch 2	Macintosh	0	
Chang	SUN	21-Aug-68	Ypsilanti	543-23-2123	Human Resources	Windows-based	0	
Wayne	WHEATON	08-Feb-75	Ann Arbor	323-32-6546	Human Resources	Macintosh	1	

Record: 1 of 22

Figure 10.5
Formatting changes
made in forms do not
affect the formatting of
underlying tables.

Field formatting in
forms has not changed
formatting in tables

17 **Close the table.**

Keep the Software Training database open for the next lesson.

Exam Note: **Formatting Changes in Forms Don't Affect Table Fields**

It is very important to remember that the formatting changes you make go one way but not the other. The changes you make to field properties in Form view do not affect the formatting of the data in the underlying table. If you want to create formats that appear universally throughout the database, make those changes in Table Design view.

Lesson 2: Creating a List Box

Sometimes, when the number of possible values that will go in a field is small, you can put the entire list of values on the screen. This way the user can simply click the correct value for that record. The *list box* is easy to set up and easy to use. The user does not have the option of adding a value that is not on the list, which helps to ensure that correct data is entered.

In the Software Training table there is a field called Computer Type. There are only two values for this field: Windows-based and Macintosh. In this lesson, you create a short list for this field.

To Create a List Box

1 Click the Forms object button, select the PC Training Data Entry Form, and click the Design button.
The form opens in Design view.

2 Right-click on the Computer Type field text box, then move the pointer to Change To in the shortcut menu.
Make sure you click on the Computer Type field text box and not the label box. The Change To submenu is displayed to the right of the shortcut menu (see Figure 10.6).

Figure 10.6
Use the shortcut Change To menu to change the field type to a list box.

Change To option in the shortcut menu

List Box option

Selected field text box

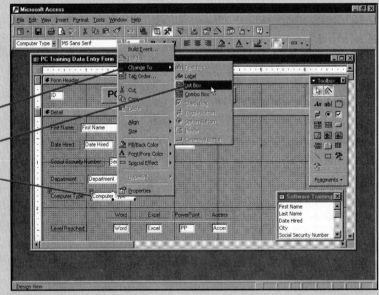

3 Click the List Box option.
The text box for Computer Type appears larger onscreen (see Figure 10.7).

4 Right-click on the new text box, and then select Properties from the shortcut menu.
The List Box property sheet is displayed on the screen.

5 Click the Data tab.

6 Click the Row Source Type option, and then click the drop-down arrow.
The Row Source Type drop-down menu is displayed (see Figure 10.8).

The field box
is enlarged

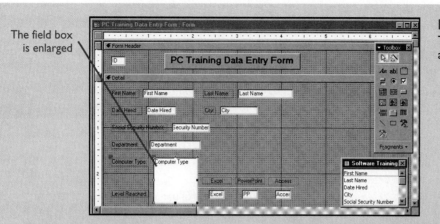

Figure 10.7
The List Box field area
appears on the form.

The Row Source Type
drop-down menu

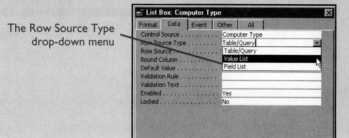

Figure 10.8
The Row Source Type
drop-down menu gives
you three options.

7 **Click Value List from the Row Source Type drop-down box.**

This tells the program to look for the list data in the Row Source box, just below
the Row Source Type box. You type the values into the Row Source box. All values must be separated by semicolons.

The table/query option could be used with a List Box, but for very short lists,
this method is easier.

8 **In the Row Source box, type in the following:**

`Windows-based;Macintosh`

The Data tab in the List Box property sheet should look like Figure 10.9.

The Row Source list

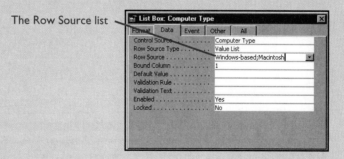

Figure 10.9
The entries have been
entered into the Row
Source box.

9 **Close the List Box property sheet.**

continues ▶

To Create a List Box (continued)

> **Inside Stuff:** **Editing the Entries in a List Box**
> There will be times when you have made a spelling error or want to add another word to the list box. You can edit the list box in Design view by right-clicking on the text box field and choosing <u>P</u>roperties.

10 **Use one of the handles on the bottom of the Computer Type text box to decrease the height of the box to about the height of two lines of text.**

You may have to use the Vertical scrollbar to move down to the bottom of the text box (see Figure 10.10).

Figure 10.10
You can resize the Computer Type text box.

Pointer

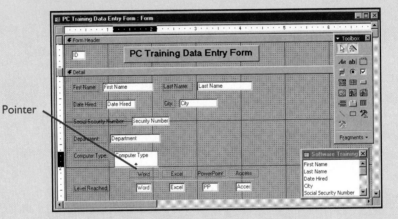

 11 **Click the View button to move to Form view.**

 12 **Scroll through your records using the Next Record button.**
Notice that when you come to a record that contains "Macintosh" for the Computer Type field, the word is highlighted in the list. (Try adding a record to see how this would work if you were entering data, but press ⒺⓈⒸ to back out of the data entry when you get to the last field.)

 13 **Click the Save button to save the changes to the PC Training Data Entry Form.**
Keep the form open for the next lesson.

> **Inside Stuff:** **A Quick Way to Enter List Selections**
> You can type the first letter of a selection in a list. The first word in the list beginning with that letter will be highlighted. When there is only one word beginning with that letter, as there is in this case, you can use this method to select the entry for the field. This is one of the advantages of a list box. A list box remains visible on your screen at all times and is generally best used when the list is short. For further information on how to set up a list box, use the Ⓕ① key or the Office Assistant for help.

Lesson 3: Looking Up Valid Entries from a Table or Query Using a Combo Box

When the number of possible values that will go in a field is small, you can put the entire list of values in a list box, as you did in Lesson 2. If there are many possible entries, you want to use a combo box that can look up values in an existing field, table, or query. With a combo box you also have the option to prevent or allow the user to enter items that are not in the list. You created a combo box in Project 8 by using the Lookup Wizard data type, but you have more control over it if you create the combo box manually.

In this lesson, you create a combo box for the City field, then have the program look up the city names in the City and County Names Query. The query was created to display only the City field, and sorted on the City field. By doing this, the list in the combo box is alphabetized.

To Look Up Valid Entries from a Table or Query Using a Combo Box

① **In the PC Training Data Entry Form, click the View button on the tool-bar to switch to Design view.**

② **Position the pointer on the City field text box, then right-click.**
The shortcut menu is displayed.

③ **From the C̲hange To option in the shortcut menu, choose C̲ombo Box.**
The text box should now have a drop-down arrow on the right edge.

④ **Right-click on the City field text box, choose P̲roperties, and click the Data tab, if necessary.**
The Data properties for the City field are displayed. The default for the Row Source Type should be Table/Query. If it is not, activate the drop-down box for the Row Source Type and change it.

⑤ **Click the Row Source option, then click the drop-down box.**
The Row Source drop-down box should show all of the tables and queries associated with this database (see Figure 10.11). Notice that there are two buttons available on the right side of the Row Source box—a Build button and a drop-down box arrow. Make sure you choose the drop-down arrow.

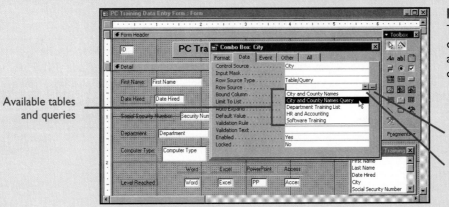

Available tables and queries

Build button

Drop-down arrow

Figure 10.11
The Row Source drop-down list shows all available tables and queries.

⑥ **Choose City and County Names Query from the list.**

continues ▶

To Look Up Valid Entries from a Table or Query Using a ComboBox (continued)

 Exam Note: Other Data Options in the Properties Sheet
You have several other options available in the properties sheet. You can add input masks for text and date fields, set default values, and validate data. You also have the capability to restrict the user to only those items on the list by changing the Limit to List box from No to Yes.

 7 **Close the Combo Box property sheet, then click the View button on the toolbar to switch to Form view.**
Notice that the City field now has a drop-down box attached to it.

8 **Click the drop-down box of the City field.**
A list appears (see Figure 10.12). Notice that there is a vertical scrollbar on the list, indicating that there are more items than are shown onscreen. Scroll down to look at the rest of the items.

Figure 10.12
The combo box for the City field displays a list of cities.

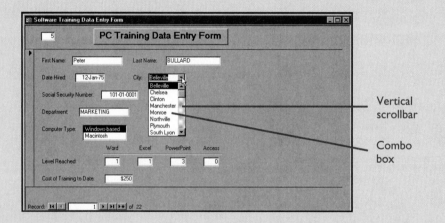

9 **Add a new record to try out your new combo box, but press Esc to back out of the data entry when you get to the last field.**

10 **Close the form, save your changes when prompted, then close the Software Training database.**

 Inside Stuff: A Quick Way to Enter Combo Box Selections
In a list box, you can type in the first letter of a selection in a list. The first word in the list beginning with that letter is highlighted. Using a combo box, however, you can then type in the second letter of the word, and you can get the value you are looking for by typing in enough letters to make your desired value unique.

Lesson 4: Using Information from a Query to Fill in Fields Automatically

In Project 9, "Managing Data Using Smaller, Related Tables," you worked on a database containing two tables: PC Hardware and Vendors. To save a lot of work entering all of the vendor information each time you entered a new record into the query, you used the foreign key field to automatically update the other fields in the Vendors table.

Because most data is entered in the Form view, it is helpful to automatically fill in repetitive data in the same manner you did using queries. In this lesson, you use the Form Wizard to create a form based on the query you built in Project 9.

To Use Information from a Query to Fill in Fields Automatically

1 Find the AC-1002 file on your CD-ROM, right-click on it, and send it to the floppy drive. Move to drive A: and rename the file Computer Inventory-Forms. Remove the read-only property and open the new database.

2 Click **New**, select Form Wizard, and then choose Vendor and Hardware as the query or table to be used as a source for the form.
The New Form dialog box should look like Figure 10.13.

Form Wizard option

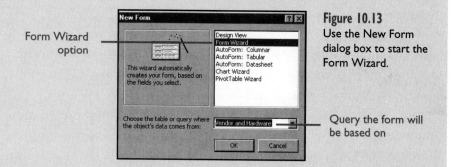

Figure 10.13
Use the New Form dialog box to start the Form Wizard.

Query the form will be based on

3 Click **OK**.
The first Form Wizard dialog box is displayed. It may take several seconds for the Form Wizard dialog box to appear as the program builds the Wizard. You may also experience similar delays between other wizard screens.

4 Click the Select All button to move all of the fields from the **A**vailable Fields window to the **S**elected Fields window.
The fields should all move to the right-hand window (see Figure 10.14).

5 Click **N**ext.
The second Form Wizard dialog box is displayed (see Figure 10.15). This dialog box gives you the option of four layouts for your form. Click each of them. A preview of the formats appears in a window on the left side of the dialog box.

6 Choose **C**olumnar format, then click **N**ext.
The third Form Wizard dialog box is displayed (see Figure 10.16). This dialog box gives you the various style options. Click a few of them to see what styles are available.

continues ▶

To Use Information from a Query to Fill in Fields Automatically (continued)

Figure 10.14
In the first Form Wizard dialog box, select the fields you want to include on your form.

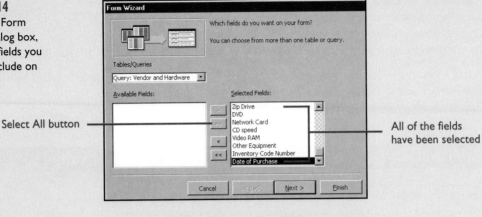

Select All button

All of the fields have been selected

Figure 10.15
Choose a form layout in the second Form Wizard dialog box.

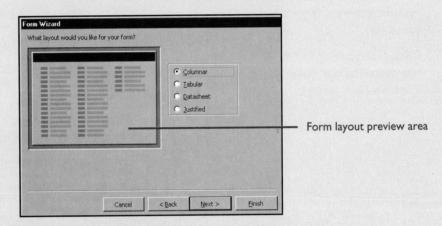

Form layout preview area

Figure 10.16
Choose a style for your form in the third Form Wizard dialog box.

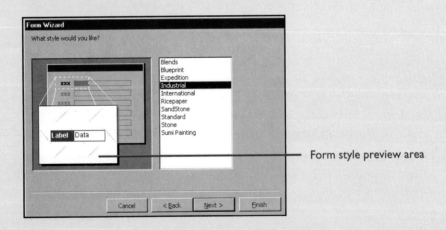

Form style preview area

7 Choose Blends, then click Next.

The fourth (and final) Form Wizard dialog box is displayed (see Figure 10.17). A default name of Vendor and Hardware has been entered in the title box. At this point you have the choice of moving to Form view, or going to Design view to modify the form design. Accept the default name.

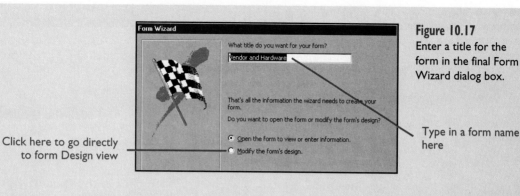

Figure 10.17
Enter a title for the
form in the final Form
Wizard dialog box.

Click here to go directly
to form Design view

Type in a form name
here

8 Click Finish.

The Vendor and Hardware form is created (see Figure 10.18).

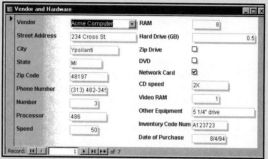

Figure 10.18
The form has been au-
tomatically created by
the Form Wizard.

**9 Click the New Record button and select General Comp from the drop-
down list in the Vendor field.**

Notice that the other fields from the Vendors table are entered automatically.
The default values for several of the fields are also entered.

**10 Press Esc to back out of the data entry, then close the form and close
the database.**

Lesson 5: Entering the Current Date
in a Field Automatically

There are many occasions when a database calls for the current date. This is particularly true
in the business world, where orders are dated as they are received and when they are sent
out.

In the PC Training Data Entry Form of the Software Training database, where Date Hired is
the only date field, let's assume that the vast majority of the personnel files are started on the
day the employee is officially hired. On those occasions when the data is not entered on the
date of hiring, the user has the option of typing in a new date.

In this lesson, you change the default for the Date Hired field to the current date.

To Enter the Current Date In a Field Automatically

1 Open the Software Training database and click the Forms object button, if necessary.
This is the database you used in Lessons 1-3 of this project.

2 Select the PC Training Data Entry Form and click the Design button.

3 Right-click on the Date Hired field text box and choose Properties from the shortcut menu.

4 Click the Data tab, if necessary, then click in the Default Value property box.
A Build button is displayed on the right side of the box (see Figure 10.19).

Figure 10.19
The Default Value box includes a Build button.

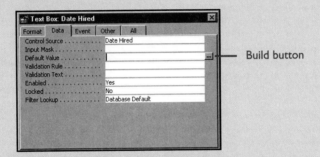

Build button

5 Click the Build button.
An Expression Builder dialog box is displayed.

6 Select Common Expressions from the left column.
A list of common expressions appears in the middle column (see Figure 10.20).

Figure 10.20
The Expression Builder is shown with Common Expressions selected.

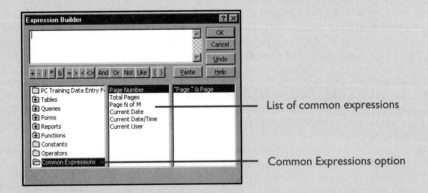

List of common expressions

Common Expressions option

7 Double-click the Current Date option.
Notice that the expression Date() appears in the third column and in the Expression Builder window (see Figure 10.21).

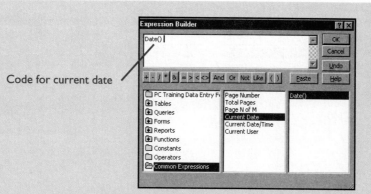

Code for current date

Figure 10.21
The Expression Builder is shown with the Date() expression selected.

 Inside Stuff: Other Uses for the Expression Builder Code
When you get more familiar with Access, you can save yourself time by typing the code directly into the properties box without going to the Expression Builder. You can type the code displayed in the Expression Builder window directly into the Default Value property box.

8 **Click OK, then close the property sheet.**

9 **Click the View button on the toolbar to switch to Form view.**

10 **Click the New Record button.**
Notice that the current date is automatically posted in the Date Hired field.

Keep the `Software Training` database open for the next lesson.

Lesson 6: Adding the Current Date and Time to a Form Automatically

There are times when you want to print out an individual form. It is possible to type in a date or time on the form using the Text tool, but Access gives you a way to add this information automatically. This information, sometimes called a date stamp or a time stamp, is usually placed in the form's header or footer area.

In this lesson, you add a date to the Header area of the PC Training Data Entry Form, then use the same procedure to add the time.

To Add the Current Date and Time to a Form Automatically

1 In the `PC Training Data Entry Form` click the **View** button to switch to **Design view.**

2 From the **Insert** menu, select **Date** and **Time.**
The Date and Time dialog box is displayed (see Figure 10.22). You see your current date and time in the dialog box.

3 **Click the check box next to Include Time to deselect this option.**
The Include Time area should now be grayed out.

continues ▶

To Add the Current Date and Time to a Form Automatically   (continued)

Figure 10.22
Use the Date and
Time dialog box to
add a date and time to
a form.

Include Date check box

Include Time check box

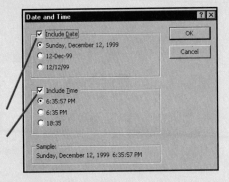

④ **Click the middle option button in the Include Date area.**
The date format is now the same one you used in the Date Hired field.

⑤ **Click OK.**
The date expression is automatically placed in the upper-left corner of the Form Design work area.

⑥ **Drag the date to the upper-right corner of the work area.**
You may have to move the Toolbox to open up the right side of the form.

⑦ **Drag the middle handle on the left side of the date box to reduce the length of the date control box to about 1 1/4 inch.**
Use the horizontal ruler to estimate the width of the date box. The Form work area should now resemble Figure 10.23.

Figure 10.23
The Form window is
shown with a date
added in the Form
Header.

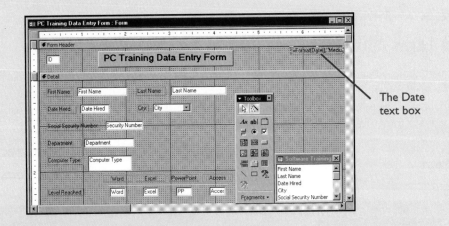

The Date
text box

⑧ **With the date expression still selected, use the Align Right button to align the date to the right.**

⑨ **Follow steps 2-8 to add a right-aligned time stamp just below the date stamp.**
You may have to move the Toolbox to place the time control properly. Use the middle format (2:17 PM). Make sure you deselect Include Date.

⑩ **Click the View button on the toolbar to switch to Form view.**
Notice that the date and time are to the right of the title (see Figure 10.24). If necessary, move back to Design view and adjust the location of the date and time.

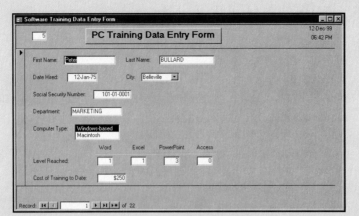

Figure 10.24
The form displays the final location of the date and time.

⓫ **Click the Save button on the toolbar to save your work.**
Keep the `Software Training` database open for the next lesson.

Lesson 7: Changing the Tab Order

When you enter data into the text boxes in a form, the cursor jumps from one text box to the next in a certain sequence. This sequence is called the tab order. In the case of an AutoForm, the tab order is initially determined by the order of fields in the underlying table or query. If you use the Form Wizard to create a form, the original order in which the fields are selected determines the tab order. When you move fields around in the design view, the tab order needs to be adjusted so the cursor moves from field to field in the order in which they are arranged. Fortunately, it is easy to change the tab order to read left-to-right or in columns, depending on how the information flows in your form.

In this lesson, you learn how to change the tab order.

To Change the Tab Order

❶ **In Form view of the `PC Training Data Entry Form`, click on the First Name text box.**

❷ **Press the** Tab⇆ **key repeatedly and watch how the cursor jumps from one text box to another.**
Notice that it skips the City text box and does not return to it until after the Cost of Training to Date box.

❸ **Click the View button to switch to Design view.**

❹ **From the View menu, select Tab Order. Click the Detail option button, if necessary.**
The Tab Order dialog box is displayed with the form fields displayed in the Custom Order list box (see Figure 10.25).

❺ **Scroll to the bottom of the list of field names to show the City field.**
The order of the field names in this dialog box represents the order in which they are selected when you tab through the form.

continues ▶

To Change the Tab Order   (continued)

Figure 10.25
The Tab Order dialog box enables you to change the order of data entry on a form.

Detail option button

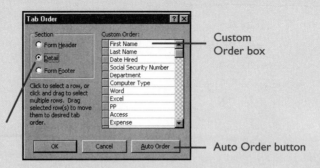

Custom Order box

Auto Order button

6 **Click the Auto Order button.**

This changes the tab order automatically so that the text boxes are selected from left to right and top to bottom, the way you would normally read a page of text.

Notice that the City field has been moved up in the list to follow Date Hired (see Figure 10.26).

Figure 10.26
The tab order is shown after it has been automatically rearranged.

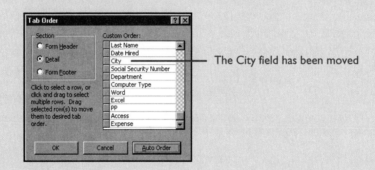

The City field has been moved

7 **Click OK to save the change and close the Tab Order dialog box.**

 8 **Click the View button to switch to Form view.**

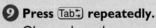 **9** **Press Tab↹ repeatedly.**

Observe how the cursor now jumps from the Date Hired text box to the City text box.

 10 **Click the Save button to save the changes to the form. Close the form and close the database.**

 Exam Note: **Manually Rearranging the Tab Order**

You can rearrange the fields to appear in any order you desire. With the Detail option button selected on the Tab Order dialog box, select a field by clicking on the select box to the left of the field name. Click on the same spot again, hold down the mouse button, and drag the field up or down to a new location.

Lesson 8: Creating Subforms

At times you might want a form that shows the one-to-many relationship between two tables. The main form/subform design is useful for displaying the one side of a relationship in the main part of a form and the related records in a subform. The subform is usually displayed in a datasheet layout. Although these are technically two forms, they can be created together using the Form Wizard.

With this design you can display such datum as all of the employees who work in each department, the furniture and equipment that is assigned to each department, or the clients assigned to each sales representative.

In this lesson, you create a main form/subform that shows all of the computers that were purchased from each vendor in the Computer Inventory-Forms database you worked on earlier in this project. In order to create a form/subform design, a relationship must be established between the two tables. This was done in Project 9, " Managing Data Using Smaller, Related Tables."

To Create a Subform

1 **Open the `Computer Inventory-Forms` database and click on the Forms object button, if necessary. Click the New button to create a new form.**
The New Form dialog box is displayed.

2 **Select the Vendors table from the drop-down list, select the Form Wizard, then click OK.**
The first Form Wizard dialog box is displayed.

3 **Click the Select All button to move all of the fields to the Selected Fields box.**
All of the fields from the Vendors table are included in the main part of the form.

4 **Click the down-arrow at the end of the Tables/Queries drop-down list box and select Table: PC Hardware.**
Once you click on the new table name, the fields for that table are displayed in the Available Fields box (see Figure 10.27).

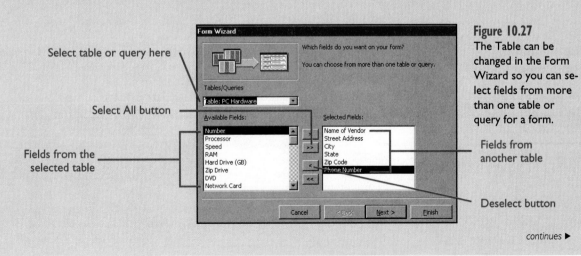

Select table or query here

Select All button

Fields from the selected table

Figure 10.27
The Table can be changed in the Form Wizard so you can select fields from more than one table or query.

Fields from another table

Deselect button

continues ▶

To Create a Subform   (continued)

⑤ Move all of the fields to the Selected Fields box except the Vendor field.

The selected fields from the PC Hardware table area are added to the fields included in the subform (see Figure 10.28).

> **Inside Stuff: A Quick Way to Enter List Selections**
> You can use the Select All arrow to move all of the fields to the Selected Fields box, then highlight the Vendor field from the PC Hardware table and use the Deselect button to move this field back to the Available Fields box.
>
> When there are two fields with the same field name, they are displayed in the Selected Fields box preceded by the name of the table.

Figure 10.28
The fields for the subform are selected from a second table.

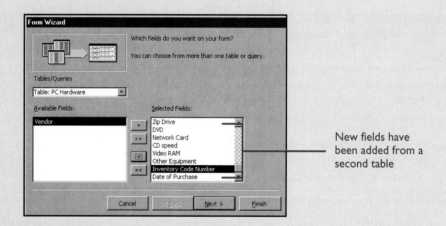

New fields have been added from a second table

⑥ Click Next. The second Form Wizard dialog box asks how you want to view your data.

Because you included the primary key field from the one (Vendors) table, the Vendors fields are displayed at the top of the preview area. Notice the option button for Form with subform(s) is also selected by default (see Figure 10.29). Accept the default settings.

Figure 10.29
The main form shows the vendor information and the subform shows the related records.

Fields from the Vendors table

Fields from the PC Hardware table

Subform option is selected

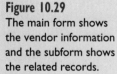

7 **Click Next.**

The next Form Wizard dialog box asks which layout you want for the subform. Accept the default setting of Datasheet.

8 **Click Next to accept the default setting of Datasheet. Choose the Stone style and then click Next.**

The final Form Wizard dialog box is displayed.

9 **Default titles are suggested for the two parts of this form. Accept the suggested titles by clicking the Finish button.**

The form is created and displayed on your screen (Figure 10.30). Notice that the form has two sets of navigation buttons. The navigation buttons at the bottom of the form scroll through the vendors. As the vendor changes, the related records in the datasheet (subform area) change. The navigation buttons in the subform scroll through the PC records that are displayed for each vendor.

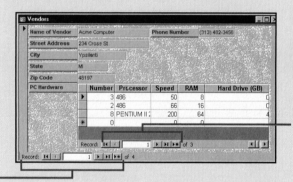

Figure 10.30
The finished main form/subform shows two sets of navigation buttons.

Navigation buttons for the subform

Navigation buttons for the main form

10 **Use the navigation buttons at the bottom of the form to scroll through the list of vendors. Then use the navigation buttons at the bottom of the datasheet to scroll through the PC hardware listed for the Vendor.**

Leave the Vendors form open for use in the next part of this lesson.

 Exam Note: A Quick Way to Enter List Selections

A main form/subform can also be used to edit or add new records to your two tables. You want to make sure that if you use this type of form for adding records, that all of the fields for each of the tables are included. Otherwise, you will end up with records with missing information. For this to work properly, the primary key from the "one" side of the relationship must be included.

Next, you add a record to the main form and to the subform.

To Add Records Using a Main Form/Subform

1 **With the Vendors form open, click on the New Record button in the main form navigation buttons (in the status bar) to move to an empty record.**

continues ▶

To Add Records Using a Main Form/Subform   (continued)

2 **Enter the following vendor information:**

Computer Tyme, 1233 Second Street, Macon, MI 48134, (517) 555-2233

You have added a new vendor to the list of available vendors. Now add a record of hardware purchased from Computer Tyme.

3 **Press** Tab⇄ **to move to the first field for the hardware information and enter the following information.**

1, Pentium II, 500, 128, 19.2, Yes, Yes, Yes, 48X, 32, CD-RW, C112233, 11/10/00

A record for the PC Hardware table has been added (see Figure 10.31).

Figure 10.31
New records can be added using the main form and the subform.

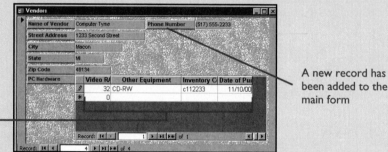

A new record has been added to the main form

A new record has been added to the subform

4 **Close the form and save changes.**
A new Vendors form and a PC Hardware Subform have been added to the list of forms.

5 **Click on the Tables object button and open the** PC Hardware **table.**
Notice the new record that you just added using the main form/subform.

6 **Close the PC Hardware table and open the** Vendors **table.**
Notice that there are now four vendors listed in the table.

7 **Close the table, then close the database.**

 ## Lesson 9: Printing the Form for Filing Purposes

You might want to print the form for an individual record for filing purposes, as a rough draft to check on a particular piece of data, or as a check on the layout when the form is longer than the screen. Although most of the printing in Access is done in reports, some is also done in forms.

In this lesson, you print the information for one of the records in the Software Training database. You then change the background color to try to make the printout more readable.

To Print the Form for Filing Purposes

1 **Open the** Software Training **database, then open the** PC Training Data Entry Form **and maximize the window.**

2 **From the File menu, choose Page Setup.**

The Page Setup dialog box is displayed, with the Margins tab chosen (see Figure 10.32).

Margins tab ————

Print Data Only option ————

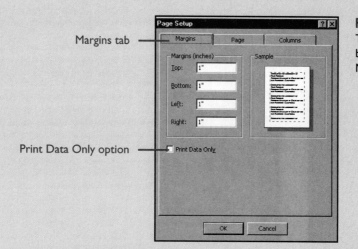

Figure 10.32
The Page Setup dialog box appears with the Margins tab selected.

3 **Change the left and right margins to 0.75 inches.**

To do this, highlight the old margin settings and type the new margins over them.

4 **If the Print Data Only check box is checked, deselect it, then click OK.**

The Print Data Only selection might be used if you are printing a lot of records and have a slow printer, or if you only want to archive the data.

5 **Click the Print Preview button.**

The preview screen shows that the printout is continuous; two complete records are shown, along with most of a third (see Figure 10.33). You can use the pointer, which has changed into a magnifying glass, to zoom in or out on the preview page.

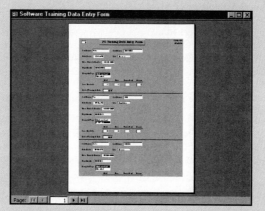

Figure 10.33
The Print Preview screen shows nearly three complete records.

6 **Click the Close button in the toolbar to close the Print Preview window.**

Before you send this form to the printer, there are a few more steps you need to perform.

continues ▶

To Print the Form for Filing Purposes   (continued)

 7 Click the View button on the toolbar to switch to Design view.

8 Right-click the background of the Detail area.
Make sure you do not accidentally click on a text or label box by mistake.

9 Move the pointer to Fill/Back Color in the shortcut menu.
A color palette appears (see Figure 10.34).

Figure 10.34
Use the color palette to choose a background color.

White option

Color palette

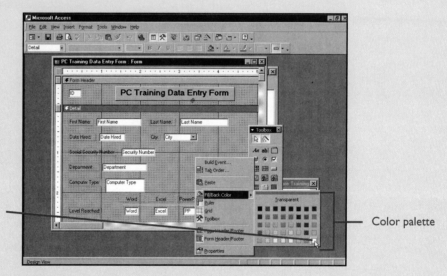

10 Select white, which is located at the lower-right corner of the color palette.
The background color of the Detail section turns white, but the Header and Footer sections remain dark gray.

11 Repeat steps 8-10 for the Header section, then scroll down and do the same for the Footer section.
All three backgrounds are now white. When you print the form, the printer will use less ink.

You are almost ready to print the form, but you need to make sure you only print one form per page.

 12 Click the Toolbox button to open the Toolbox, if necessary. Scroll down so that you can see the Cost of Training to Date field, then click the Page Break button in the Toolbox.

13 Move the cursor just below the Cost of Training to Date field in the Detail area and click the left mouse button. Click in an open area to deselect the page break.
A page break, which is displayed as a series of six dots, is now inserted in that spot (see Figure 10.35). If you want to see what your printout will look like, use the Print Preview as you did in step 5.

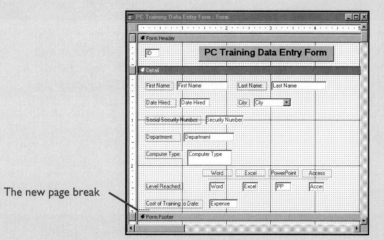

Figure 10.35
A page break can be inserted to print the forms one page at a time.

The new page break

14 **Click the View button on the toolbar to switch to Form view, then go to the File menu and choose Print.**

15 **Click the Selected Record(s) option button in the Print Range area (see Figure 10.36).**

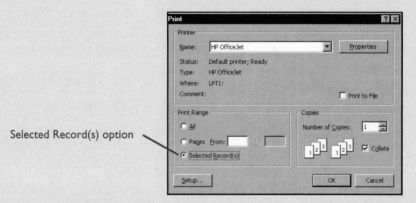

Selected Record(s) option

Figure 10.36
The Print dialog box shows that a selected record has been chosen to print.

16 **Click OK to print the current record.**
This particular form does not have a lot of information on it, but you can see where the capability to print forms could be very helpful.

X *If You Have Problems...*
Depending on the type of printer you have, the Computer Type field may be completely hidden by the highlight, making it appear that the selected value was Macintosh, when it was, in fact, Windows-based. This is one of the drawbacks of using a list box in a form.

17 **Close the PC Training Data Entry Form and save your changes when prompted. Close the database.**
If you have completed your session on the computer, exit Access and shut down the computer. Otherwise, continue with the following exercises.

Summary

In this project you were introduced to many new techniques for improving forms. You learned some procedures that were analogous to procedures that work in tables, such as adding formats, lists, and combo boxes to forms, and filling fields automatically. You created a form/subform that is similar to the datasheet/subdatasheet concept in a table. You added the current date and time to a form header, and changed the order in which data is entered. Finally, you learned how to print a single form.

You can learn more about forms by going to the Help index and typing in `form`. A particularly useful topic is Sections of a form, that describes the uses of the form detail, header, and footer area, and also describes form page headers and page footers.

Checking Concepts and Terms

True/False

For each of the following statements, check *T* or *F* to indicate whether the statement is true or false.

__T __F   **1.** The formatting changes you make in the Form view will also appear in the underlying table. [L1]

__T __F   **2.** A date or time stamp is usually placed in the form Detail section. [L6]

__T __F   **3.** You can set up the form to look up information from a table and automatically fill in several fields when you enter the information for only one field. [L4]

__T __F   **4.** A list box enables users to enter items that are not on the list. [L2]

__T __F   **5.** The Row Source Type property box tells the program where to look for the items in a list or combo box. [L2]

Multiple Choice

Circle the letter of the correct answer for each of the following questions.

1. Automatically adding the current date to a field is done using the _____ in the Default Value area. [L5]

   a. Validation Rule

   b. Expression Builder

   c. Row Source

   d. Input Mask

2. Use the _____ menu to change the background color of a form. [L8]

   a. View

   b. Format

   c. Shortcut

   d. Tools

3. When you want a form to show all of the records in one table that are related to one record in another table on one page, you can create a _____. [L8]

   a. main form/subform

   b. find matched records form

   c. form based on a query

   d. Tabular form

4. A combo box _____. [L3]

   a. appears as a drop-down box

   b. can be overridden by typing in a field that is not available in the combo box

   c. can be set to only accept the fields showing in the combo box

   d. all of the above

5. To change the Tab Order of a form, _____. [L7]

   a. choose F̲ormat, T̲ab Order from the menu

   b. open the detail section property sheet and select T̲ab Order from the Format tab

   c. choose V̲iew, T̲ab Order from the menu

   d. open the detail section property sheet and select Tab Order from the Data tab

Screen ID

Label each element of the Access screen shown in Figure 10.37.

Figure 10.37

A. Tables and queries available for combo box

B. Build button

C. Location of data for combo box

D. List box

E. Page Break button

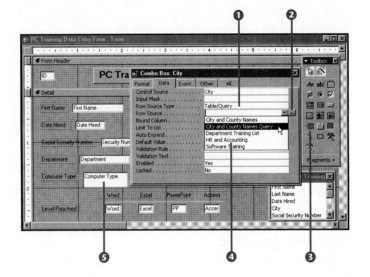

1._____   3._____   5._____

2._____   4._____

Skill Drill

Skill Drill exercises reinforce project skills. Each skill reinforced is the same, or nearly the same, as a skill presented in the project. Each exercise includes a brief narrative introduction, followed by detailed instructions in a step-by-step format.

In this exercise, you have a database that has a table of information about the books in your library, a second table that tracks the books others have borrowed from you, and a third table that lists the various book categories. This is an expanded version of the database you used in the exercises in Project 9. Open the three tables to get a feel for what you'll be working with.

1. Adding a Combo Box to a Form

The Books form contains the six fields from the Books table. There are two fields that could benefit from list or combo boxes. The Book Type field only has three possible answers (hardcover, trade, and paperback). It would be an ideal field for a list box. The Category field has several possible categories, and may also need new ones added in the future. It is an ideal field for a combo box, which is what you will add in this exercise.

To add a combo box to a form:

1. Copy the file AC-1003 from your CD to a new floppy disk. Use the shortcut menu to deselect the read-only status, and rename the copy as My Library. Open the new database.

2. Click the Forms object button, then click Design to move to the Books form Design view.

3. Right-click on the Category field text box and choose Change To, Combo Box.

4. Right-click on the Category text box and select Properties.

5. Click the Data tab and accept Table/Query as the Row Source Type.

6. Click the drop-down arrow on the right of the Row Source box, then select the Book Categories table.

7. Close the Properties box and click the Save button to save your work.

8. Click the View button to switch to Form view.

9. Click the New Record button and enter the following record, using the drop-down box in the Category field to select a category. Notice that the fields do not follow in a logical sequence.

   Green

   Red

   Humor

   Red Green Talks Cars: A Love Story

   Trade

   1997

10. Close the form. Close the database unless you are planning to do one of the following two exercises.

2. Changing the Tab Order

As you entered records in the first exercise, you noticed that the insertion point jumped from field to field in an unusual order. In this exercise, you try a couple of methods to get it operating properly. If you did the first exercise, skip step 1.

To change the tab order:

1. Copy the file AC-1003 from your CD to a new floppy disk. Use the shortcut menu to deselect the read-only status, and rename the copy as My Library. Open the new database. Click the Forms object button.

2. Click Design to switch to the Books form Design view.

3. Select View, Tab Order from the menu.

4. Click the Auto Order button and click OK.

5. Click the View button and press Tab several times. Notice that the tab order now goes from left to right. It would probably be better if the order went down the left column, then to the top of the right column and down.

6. Click the View button to return to Design view. Select View, Tab Order from the menu.

7. Click the row selector for the Author First Name field. Click the row selector again and drag the field up until it is just below the Author Last Name field.

8. Click the Book Title row selector, then click it again and drag the field up just under the Author First Name field. All six fields should now be in the correct order.

9. Close the Tab Order dialog box and click the Save button to save your changes.

10. Click the View button to switch to Form view.

11. Click the New Record button and enter the following record, watching the tab order as you enter the data:

    Davis

    Richard Harding

    King's Jackal, The

    Fiction

    Hardcover

    1903

12. Close the form, but leave the database open if you are going to be doing the next exercise.

3. Creating a Form and Subform

You would like to scroll through your list of books and see the information on the borrower (if the book has been loaned out). To do this, you can create a form with a subform. In this case, the subform will never have more than one record.

To create a form and subform:

1. Click <u>N</u>ew to create a new form. Select Form Wizard and choose Books as the table to retrieve data from.

2. In the first Form Wizard dialog box, select all of the fields from the Books table.

3. Change to the Borrow table, then select all of the fields except the Book Title field.

4. In the second Form Wizard dialog box, choose to view your data by the Books field, and make sure Form with <u>s</u>ubform(s) is selected.

5. Select the Columnar option from the third Form Wizard dialog box, and select the Blends style from the fourth Form Wizard dialog box.

6. Name the Form `Book Information` and the Subform `Borrow Subform`. Click <u>F</u>inish.

7. Use the bottom set of navigation buttons to look at your data. Your form/subform should look like Figure 10.38.

8. Close the form and close the database.

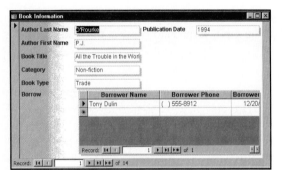

Figure 10.38
The main form shows the name of the book; the subform shows the borrower, if any.

Challenge

Challenge exercises expand on or are somewhat related to skills presented in the lessons. Each exercise provides a brief narrative introduction followed by instructions in a numbered step format that are not as detailed as those in the Skill Drill section.

The database used for the first two Challenge exercises continues with the literary theme used in the Skill Drill exercises. It is the list of short stories that you used in the Discovery Zone section of Project 9. There are three tables—Author Information, Book Information, and Short Stories. Browse through these tables before going on to the exercises. The final exercise uses the training database you opened in Lesson 1.

1. Adding Page Numbers to the Page Footer

If you are going to print out individual records, page numbers are sometimes very helpful. Access enables you to put page numbers in the headers or footers of forms or reports in a variety of formats. The page numbers used with forms do not appear except when the form is printed.

1. Copy the file `AC-1004` from your CD. Use the shortcut menu to deselect the read-only status, and rename the copy as `Short Stories`.

2. Create a tabular AutoForm that contains all of the fields in the Book Information table. Call the form `Book Information`.

3. Move to Design view and maximize the window. Make the page 6 1/2 inches wide, then move the fields and adjust the width of the Editor and Publisher fields and field headings until you are satisfied with the layout. Use the Print Preview button to check your work.

4. Activate the Page Header/Footer from the View menu. Close the page header, but leave the page footer open.

5. Choose Insert, Page Numbers from the menu. Use the Page N of M format, and place it on the right side of the footer.

6. Use Print Preview to check the placement of the page number, then print page 4.

7. Close the form and name it **Book Information**. Leave the database open if you are going to do any of the other Challenge exercises.

2. Adding a Hyperlink to the Form Footer

While entering data in the Book Information table, you decide that you want to have a way to go to the Web and search for information on a book. To do this, it would be a good idea to put a link to your favorite search engine on the Web into the table. (Search engines are programs like Yahoo or AltaVista that allow you to search millions of Web sites for information.)

If you did the first Challenge exercise, use the Short Stories database; otherwise, copy the file **AC-1004** from your CD. Use the shortcut menu to deselect the read-only status, and rename the copy as **Short Stories**. Create a tabular AutoForm that contains all of the fields in the Book Information table. Call the form **Book Information**.

Use the help provided with Access to figure out how to add a hyperlink to a search engine. Use **http://altavista.digital.com** or another favorite search engine of your choice. Have the hyperlinked text shown at the bottom of the screen read "Search for Information." Make sure you put the hyperlink in the right place or it will never be seen while you are entering information!

3. Adding a Calculated Control in a Form

In Project 4 you created a calculated field in a query. You can also create calculated controls in forms and reports. In this exercise, you use the software training database you opened in Lesson 1. The database keeps track of the level each employee has reached for each of the Office applications. The level indicates the number of workshops attended (for example, someone who has reached level 3 in Word has attended all three Word workshops). You add a calculated field to add up the total number of workshops attended by each employee.

1. Copy the file **AC-1001** from your CD. Use the shortcut menu to deselect the read-only status, and rename the copy as **Software Training Totals**.

2. Open the **PC Training Data Entry Form** in Design view.

3. Add a text box to the right of the four boxes that indicate training levels.

4. Right-click the text box and select Properties from the shortcut menu.

5. Select the Data tab and click in the Data Source box.

6. Click the Build button. Type an equals sign in the Expression Builder box.

7. Double-click **Word** from the field list in the middle column, then click the plus sign.

8. Repeat step 7 to add the **Excel**, **PowerPoint**, and **Access** fields, then close the Expression Builder dialog box and close the Properties dialog box.

9. Click the large handle on the upper-left corner of the Label box and move it above the new text box.

10. Change the label to **Totals**.

11. Switch to Form view to make sure your new calculated control works properly. Close the database when you are through.

Discovery Zone

Discovery Zone exercises help you gain advanced knowledge of project topics and application of skills. These exercises focus on enhancing your problem-solving skills. Numbered steps are not provided, but you are given hints, reminders, screen shots, and references to help you reach your goal for each exercise.

1. Drawing Form Data from Three Tables

In earlier exercises, you combined the information from two tables into a form. You are not restricted to two tables, however. In this exercise, you create a form that extracts information from three tables.

Goal: Create a form that draws information from three tables.

Use the **AC-1004** database, remove the read-only status, and name the file **Complete Short Stories**. The form you create should look like Figure 10.39. The fields should be entered in the order in which they are shown, going from top to bottom in the first column, then top to bottom in the second column.

Name the form **Complete Short Story Information** when you are finished.

Hint #1: You need to look at the relationships between the tables and map out which fields should come from which tables.

Hint #2: Review how you drew data from two tables; this procedure is basically the same.

Figure 10.39
Data has been drawn from three joined tables.

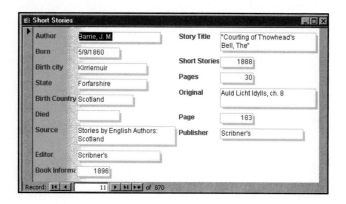

2. Adding an Image to a Form

Although Access is not the easiest Office program to use when it comes to adding images, it is possible to add graphics to forms and reports.

Goal: Add a clip art image to a form.

Use the **AC-1001** database, remove the read-only status, and name the file **Form with an Image**. Add an appropriate image to the PC Training Data Entry Form, such as the one shown in Figure 10.40.

Hint #1: Use ScreenTips to find a Toolbox button that might be helpful.

Hint #2: There are clip art images available, but they cannot be accessed the same way as in other Office programs. You have to find where they are stored, then preview them to find a good one. The file name for the image shown is PE01561.wmf.

Hint #3: When you import the image, it will probably be far too big for the allotted space. There is an image property called Size Mode that will prove very useful!

Figure 10.40
A computer-related
clip art image has been
added to a form.

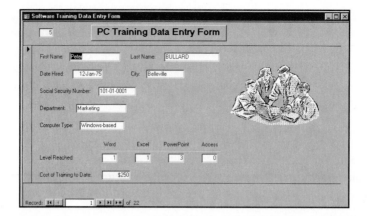

PinPoint Assessment

You have completed this project and its associated lessons, and have had an opportunity to assess your skills through the end-of-project questions and exercises. Now use the PinPoint software Evaluation Mode to further assess your comprehension of the specific exam activities you have just learned. You can also use the PinPoint Trainer Mode and the Show Me tutorials to practice these exam activities.

Project 11

Special Purpose Reports and Advanced Report Procedures

Key terms introduced in this project include

- bitmap format
- sans serif
- section bar
- serif
- unbound object

Objectives	Required Activity for MOUS	Exam Level
➤ Create Labels for Mailings	Create a report with the Report Wizard	Core
➤ Create Calculated Controls in a Report	Use a calculated control in a report	Core
➤ Group and Sort Data in a Report		
➤ Keep Grouped Data Together in Reports		
➤ Add Calculated Controls to Group Headers and Footers	Use report sections	Core
➤ Insert a Graphic Background by Modifying Report Properties	Modify report properties	Expert
	Insert a graphic on a report	Expert
➤ Using the Can Grow Property to Display a Text Field	Set Section Properties	Expert

Why Would I Do This?

If you expect to send mailings to employees, group members, customers, or anyone else in your database, you can produce mailing labels with a special type of report in Access. This label report prints several fields together and includes preformatted layouts that match commercially available adhesive labels.

In many cases, you want to display information in a report that is derived from other fields in a table or query. Access enables you to perform calculations based on existing fields to produce additional columns in your reports. Sometimes the calculations you perform result in the display of error messages—such as when you attempt to divide by zero. You can set conditions so that the text of your choice is displayed when the results of the calculation are not accurate or appropriate.

A report can be made easier to read by grouping data and introducing visual breaks between the groups. You learn how to group and subgroup your data. You can also make sure that related information stays on the same page when you print your report.

You can group data and calculate subtotals. In this project, you learn how to add totals and graphics to report headers and footers. You also learn how to modify properties of the entire report.

Lesson 1: Creating Labels for Mailings

Reports are used to list many records. A mailing label report lists the records in a format that is traditionally used for addressing letters.

In this lesson, you create a report to produce labels that can be attached to envelopes or brochures for mailings. A Label Wizard helps you design your report. Creating labels, even using the Label Wizard, is a process that involves many steps. You will use the database containing the PC Hardware and Vendors tables that you used in the last project. You need an empty, formatted floppy disk for use with the lessons and exercises in this project.

To Create Labels for Mailing

1 Place an empty, formatted disk in drive A. Copy the `AC-1101` file to your disk, remove the read-only status, rename it `Computer Inventory 4`, and open it.
The Database window should open to the Tables area. If it does not, click the Tables object button.

2 In the Computer Inventory 4 database, click the Vendors table to select it, then click <u>O</u>pen.
Notice that this table contains data necessary to contact the vendor by mail or by phone (see Figure 11.1).

Figure 11.1
The Vendors table includes vendor addresses and phone numbers.

Name of Vendor	Street Address	City	State	Zip Code	Phone Number
Acme Computer	234 Cross St.	Ypsilanti	MI	48197	(313) 482-3456
Computer Tyme	1233 Second Street	Macon	MI	48134	(517) 555-2233
General Comp	123 Main St.	Ann Arbor	MI	48105	(313) 665-2345
Wilson Electric	122 Sill Blvd.	Ypsilanti	MI	48197	(313) 487-1161

3 **Close the Vendors table. Click the Reports object button, then click the Ne̲w button.**
The New Report dialog box is displayed.

4 **Click the drop-down button to reveal a list of the tables and queries that are available in this database (see Figure 11.2).**

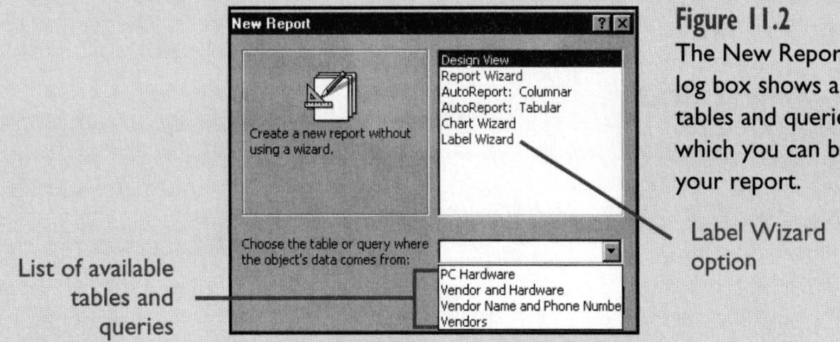

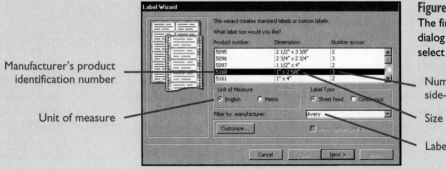

Figure 11.2
The New Report dialog box shows a list of tables and queries on which you can base your report.

Label Wizard option

List of available tables and queries

5 **Click Vendors in the list to select the Vendors table, select Label Wizard from the list of available reports and wizards, then click OK.**
The first Label Wizard dialog box is displayed after a short delay.

6 **Select English as the unit of measurement, and Avery as the manufacturer. Select the Avery number 5160 label.**
This is a form that prints three labels across a single 8.5 inch form (see Figure 11.3). You print these labels on ordinary paper for the purposes of this exercise.

Figure 11.3
The first Label Wizard dialog box is used to select the type of label.

Manufacturer's product identification number

Unit of measure

Number of labels side-by-side

Size of each label

Label manufacturer

7 **Click Ne̲xt.**
The second Label Wizard dialog box is displayed.

8 **Change the font size to 12 and the font name to Arial, if necessary (see Figure 11.4).**
Arial is a plain, easy-to-read font that is appropriate for titles or labels.

continues ▶

To Create Labels for Mailing (continued)

Figure 11.4
In the second Label Wizard dialog box you can select text characteristics.

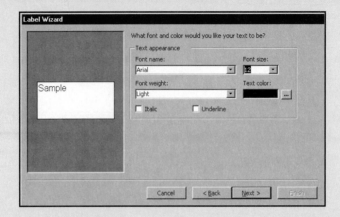

Inside Stuff: Font Selection

The many different typefaces available can be divided into two groups—those with **serifs** and those without serifs, or **sans serif**. Serifs are the horizontal lines at the end of each vertical letter stroke that helped the old-time typesetters line up the letters when they set the type. Today's reading experts find that typefaces with serifs are easier for people to read when the words are arranged in long lines like this paragraph. Sans serif letters are often used for short word groups like titles or labels.

9 Click **N**ext to accept the settings for the font style, size, and weight.

The third Label Wizard dialog box is displayed (see Figure 11.5). This dialog box enables you to construct your labels using existing fields and enter other items you would like to include.

Figure 11.5
You choose what you want to include on the label in the third Label Wizard dialog box.

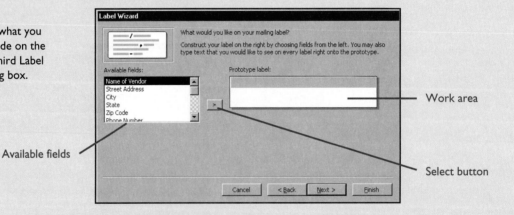

Work area

Available fields

Select button

10 Click the **Select** button to add the **Name of Vendor** field to the Prototype label. Press ↵Enter to move to the next line of the label.

Inside Stuff: Automatic Removal of Blank Lines
When setting up an address database, you often create fields for the person's name, and a field for the company name. When you set up a label, you create four lines—the first line contains the name fields and the second line contains the company field. Some of the entries in the database, however, will not have a company name. Access automatically moves the third and fourth line up so that there is no blank line on the label.

⓫ **Click the Select button to add the Street Address field to the label. Press ⏎Enter to move to the next line of the label.**
If you make a mistake creating the label, you can use the Back button to undo your steps.

 Inside Stuff: Editing in the Prototype Label Box
You can also edit the sample label in the Prototype label box as if it were a normal document. You can add or edit text or punctuation marks, and you can select and delete fields that you have placed there.

⓬ **Click the Select button to add the City field to the label. Type a comma and a space on the keyboard.**

⓭ **Add the State field to the same line of the label. Type in two more spaces from the keyboard and add the Zip Code field.**
You have now set up your mailing label. Curly braces {} surround each field from the Vendors table (see Figure 11.6).

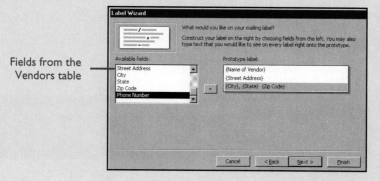

Fields from the Vendors table

Figure 11.6
The Prototype label now includes inserted fields.

⓮ **Click Next.**
The fourth Label Wizard dialog box is displayed. This dialog box enables you to choose the field or fields on which you want to sort. The field you sort on does not have to be one of the fields included in the label.

⓯ **Click the Zip Code field to select it, then click the Select button to add it to the Sort By list.**
Most labels are sorted by Zip Code because of postage savings for mass mailings (see Figure 11.7).

continues ▶

To Create Labels for Mailing (continued)

If you select more than one field the program sorts the records by the first field listed. Then it sorts the records within that grouping by the next field listed. For example, if you had a table with many vendor names and had chosen to sort first by City and then by Name of Vendor, you would get a set of labels for each city. Within each city, the labels would be sorted alphabetically by the name of the vendor.

Figure 11.7
Use the fourth Label Wizard dialog box to choose the sort fields.

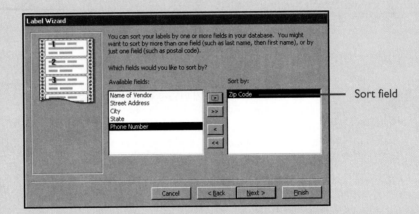

16 **Click Next to move to the last Label Wizard dialog box and change the name of the report to Mailing Labels for Vendors.**
Make certain the option to preview the labels is selected and the Display Help option is not selected. The Display Help option has the same effect as using the Help menu to ask for help about creating reports.

17 **Click the Finish button.**
The report appears in Preview view (see Figure 11.8).

Figure 11.8
After you complete the Label Wizard, a preview of the mailing labels appears.

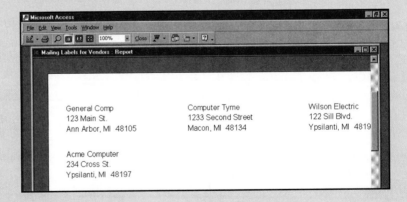

 18 **Click the Print button on the toolbar to print a copy of the labels on a regular sheet of paper.**

19 **Close the report and close the database.**

Inside Stuff: **Printer Requirements**

Some printers require minimum margin settings that are larger than the label settings used in this example. You may get a warning message such as `Some data may
not be displayed`. Proceed to print if you get such messages, and examine the
printout to see if any characters have been left off.

For this project we assume you have a printer that uses separate sheets of paper
rather than the continuous, folded paper that has holes in the sides for a sprocket.
If you have a printer that uses continuous feed paper, you can either select a different label that is about the same size as the one indicated in the lesson or follow the
directions as written and simply preview the labels without sending them to the
printer. Ask your instructor for additional advice about the printing arrangement
that is available with your computer.

 Inside Stuff: **Font Sizes**

The height allowed for each line of print is measured in points. This is an old type-
setter's measurement that goes back to the days of manual printing presses. There
are 72 points to the inch, so 1/4 inch would be 18 points. This is the amount of
space allowed for the line of print and includes enough space above and below the
letters so that the top of the tallest letters do not touch the bottom of the previous lines. The height of the letters also affects their width.

Lesson 2: Creating Calculated Controls in a Report

You may want to display information calculated from data in one of your tables. In this lesson, you learn how to take data from two fields and display the results of dividing the contents of one field by those in another.

First you look at a tabular report that contains the fields you use to calculate the average pay
per employee. You use the Michigan Service Businesses table that you used in Project 9,
"Managing Data Using Smaller, Related Tables."

To Examine the Report That Will Be Modified

1 **Copy the `AC-1102` file to your disk, remove the read-only status, re-
name it `Service Businesses 4`, and open it.**
The Database window should open to the Reports area. If it does not, click the
Reports object button. The Pay per Employee report should be selected.

2 **Click the <u>P</u>review button and maximize the preview window.**
A preview of the report is displayed. The 0 ZIP code in the first row is a code
used by the government to indicate totals for the entire state. Since Access
sorted the report in ZIP code order, this summary line appears at the top of the
report.

3 **Move the mouse pointer onto the report. It becomes a magnifying
glass with a minus sign in it. Click once to decrease the magnification.**
You are able to see the entire first page of the report. Notice that there is room
on the right for an additional column (see Figure 11.9). The magnifying glass
pointer now has a plus in it.

continues ▶

To Examine the Report That Will Be Modified   (continued)

Figure 11.9
The entire first page of the report is displayed in Preview view.

Magnifying glass pointer

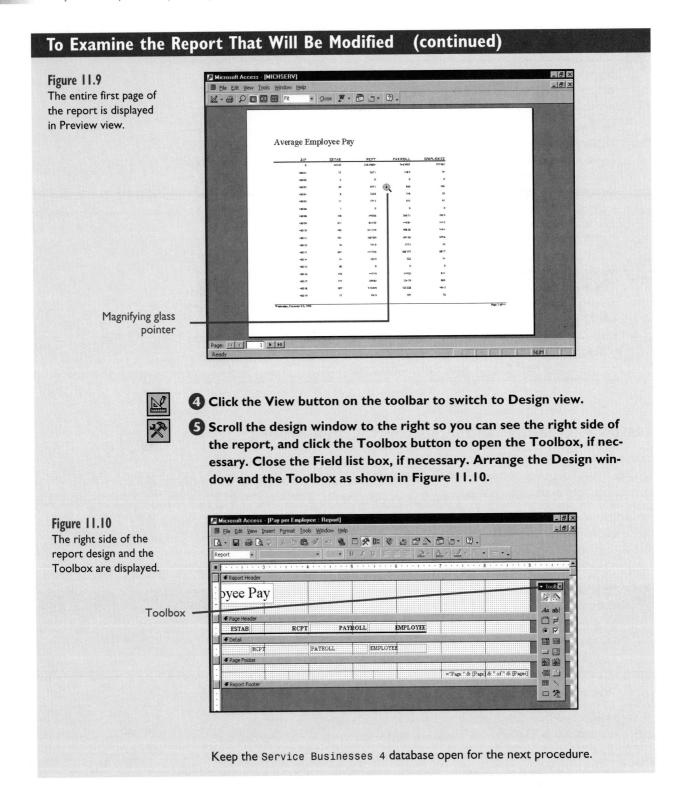

4 **Click the View button on the toolbar to switch to Design view.**

5 **Scroll the design window to the right so you can see the right side of the report, and click the Toolbox button to open the Toolbox, if necessary. Close the Field list box, if necessary. Arrange the Design window and the Toolbox as shown in Figure 11.10.**

Figure 11.10
The right side of the report design and the Toolbox are displayed.

Toolbox

Keep the Service Businesses 4 database open for the next procedure.

You have now set up the report window to add a new field. In this next section, you add a calculated field and a field label to the report.

To Create Calculated Controls in a Report

1 Click the **Text Box** button in the Toolbox. In the detail section of the report design, drag a text box that is approximately the same size as the other text boxes in the detail section (see Figure 11.11).

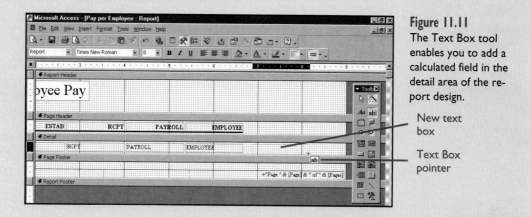

Figure 11.11
The Text Box tool enables you to add a calculated field in the detail area of the report design.

New text box

Text Box pointer

2 Release the mouse button.

When you release the mouse button, an Unbound text box appears along with its label box (see Figure 11.12). An **unbound object** is not connected to an underlying table. The label will probably appear over the top of another field.

> **✖ If You Have Problems...**
>
> When drawing a new text box, it takes some skill to get the box the size you want. You may need to turn the Snap to Grid feature off in the Format menu. If it is not the correct size, press Del and try again. If the size is okay, but the position is not where you want it, point at the text box with your mouse until the pointer turns into a hand, then click and drag the box to a position that is in line with the other boxes.

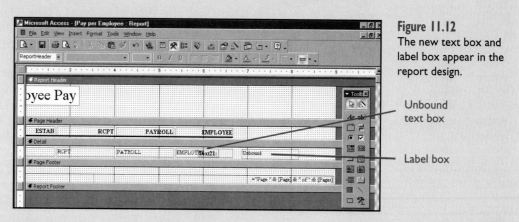

Figure 11.12
The new text box and label box appear in the report design.

Unbound text box

Label box

3 Click an empty part of the report design to deselect the new text box, then click in the unwanted label box to select it. Press Del.

The label box is deleted, but the Unbound text box is unaffected.

continues ▶

To Create Calculated Controls in a Report (continued)

4 Click the new text box, then click the word Unbound.

The word Unbound disappears, and the insertion point is displayed on the left side of the text box (see Figure 11.13).

Figure 11.13
The text box is now ready for formula entry.

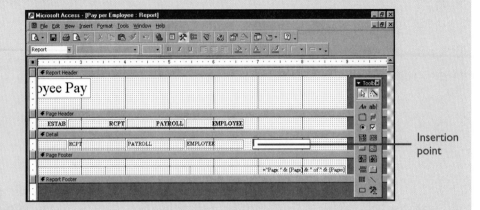

Insertion point

5 Type in the following formula (be sure to use square brackets):
=[PAYROLL]*1000/[EMPLOYEE]

This formula takes the contents of the PAYROLL field (the amount paid to area employees in thousands of dollars), multiplies it by 1,000, then divides by the number of employees in that zip code area.

The principle behind the formulas in calculated fields is the same as that of any formula. Mathematical symbols are used in the same way, but the variable names are simply the field names enclosed in square brackets.

6 Click the Print Preview button to preview the report. Click on the new column to zoom in on it, if necessary, and examine the results of the calculated field.

Many of the values display too many decimal places and some of them display an error message (see Figure 11.14).

Figure 11.14
The Print Preview of the report shows problems with the calculated field.

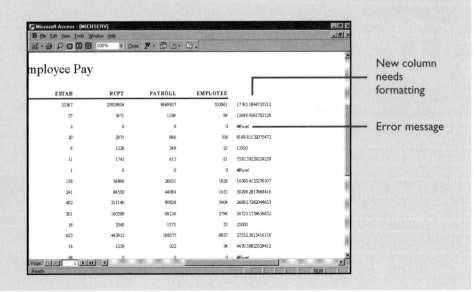

New column needs formatting

Error message

Notice that the average for the first record was approximately $17,765, but the display is showing too many decimal places. Also, there is an error message wherever the number of employees is zero. This error message is displayed when the expression tries to divide by zero.

 If You Have Problems...
If you made a typographical error when typing in the formula, the program will not let you go to the Print Preview window. It will tell you that you made an error, and will even tell you what type of error you made.

7 **Click the Close button on the toolbar to close the report preview.**
Scroll to the right and make sure the calculated text box is still selected.

8 **Click the Properties button on the toolbar to open the Properties dialog box, then select the All tab.**
The calculated field is still selected, even though it may be off screen. The Properties dialog box shows the properties of the selected text box.

9 **Click in the Format box and enter the following format:**
`$#,##0.00`

This displays the number with commas inserted and two decimal places. Remember that the Formats you learned in Project 8, "Making Data Entry Easier and More Accurate," had three parts separated by semicolons. In this case, there are no negative numbers, and the zero values will be handled in another way.

10 **Drag an edge of the properties dialog box to lengthen it. Replace the formula in the Control Source box with the following:**
`=IIF([EMPLOYEE]>0,[PAYROLL]*1000/[EMPLOYEE],"NA")`

This formula uses an IIF function to test for the existence of a number of employees greater than zero. If that condition is true, it uses the same formula we used before. If it is not true, it prints the code NA for Not Applicable. You could have entered this formula directly into the text box the same way you entered the original formula (see Figure 11.15).

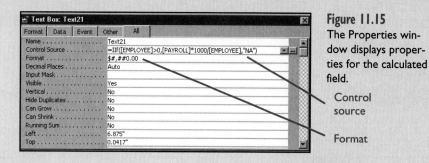

Figure 11.15
The Properties window displays properties for the calculated field.

Control source

Format

11 **Close the Properties dialog box. Click the Label tool in the Toolbox, and drag a box in the Page Header section directly above the calculated field.**
Make the box the same length as the text box below it and the same height as the label boxes to the left.

continues ▶

To Create Calculated Controls in a Report (continued)

⑫ **Enter the label** AVERAGE PAY**, then click outside the label box to deselect it.**

⑬ **Click the new label box to select it, then click the Align Right button on the toolbar.**
The label is right-aligned.

⑭ **Click the dark, horizontal line in the Report Header that underlines the headings to select it.**
You may have to expand the Page Header section to complete this step. The pointer turns into a hand and the end of the line has a handle on it (see Figure 11.16)

Figure 11.16
When you select a line, a handle appears at either end.

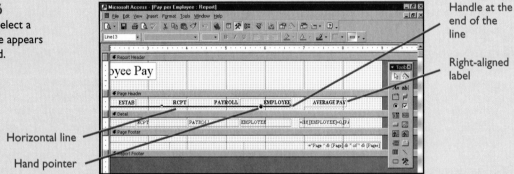

Handle at the end of the line

Right-aligned label

Horizontal line

Hand pointer

⑮ **Move the pointer to the handle at the end of the line and drag it to the right to extend it under the new heading label.**
The dark horizontal line should now extend all the way across the report.

⑯ **Click the Print Preview button to preview the report. Scroll to the right to see the calculated field and its heading (see Figure 11.17).**

Figure 11.17
The calculated field and its heading appear in their final form on the report.

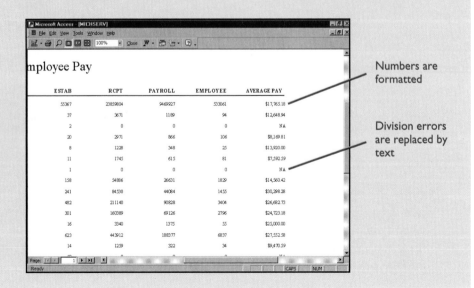

Numbers are formatted

Division errors are replaced by text

⑰ Choose File, Print. In the Print Range area, enter 1 in the From and To boxes, and click OK.
This prints just page 1 of the report.

⑱ Click the Close Window button in the upper-right corner of the Print Preview window and save your changes. Close the database.

Lesson 3: Grouping and Sorting Data in a Report

There are many occasions where it is important to group records to make the report easier to read and understand. You can choose to run the Report Wizard and select grouping levels, then modify the report that the Wizard creates. You can also choose to create your own report, then create the grouping. This gives you the best control over your data.

In this lesson, you learn how to group and sort records. You use a database that lists the orders received by a cleaning supply company, and you set up a report to group all of the orders by customer.

To Group and Sort Data in a Report

❶ Copy the AC-1103 file to your disk, remove the read-only status, rename it Customer Orders 4, and open it.
The Database window should open to the Reports area. If it does not, click the Reports object button. The Orders Grouped by Customer report should be selected.

❷ Click the Preview button and maximize the preview window.
A preview of the report is displayed. The orders are sorted by the ID number (see Figure 11.18). Scroll around the report and look at the fields it contains.

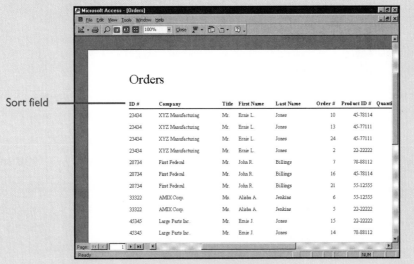

Figure 11.18
The orders are sorted by ID number.

continues ▶

To Group and Sort Data in a Report (continued)

 3 Click the **C**lose button on the toolbar.

This closes the preview and returns you to the Database window with the Reports object button selected.

 4 Click **D**esign, then click the **Sorting and Grouping** button on the toolbar.

The Sorting and Grouping dialog box is displayed (see Figure 11.19).

Figure 11.19
The Sorting and Grouping dialog box is used to sort or group data, or both.

Group Header property

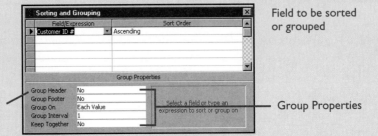

Field to be sorted or grouped

Group Properties

5 Click the down arrow to the right of the first line of the **Field/Expression** box and select **Company**.

Notice that the report is sorted in ascending order on this field.

6 Click the **Group Header** box, then click the down arrow and change this selection to **Yes**.

 7 Click the **Print Preview** button.

The new report is previewed. Notice that the records are now grouped by company, and there is a space above each of the companies (see Figure 11.20). The space was created when you selected a group header. Notice that the records without a company name are shown first when the records are sorted by company.

Figure 11.20
The report is grouped and sorted by company.

Empty field produces spaces

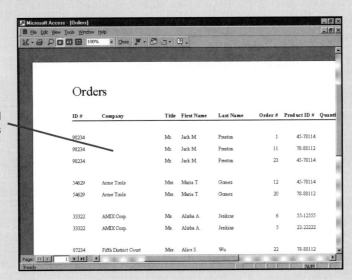

 8 Click the **C**lose button on the toolbar to return to the report design view. Close the Sorting and Grouping dialog box.

Notice that the report design now has a section titled Company Header.

9 **Click the Field List button to open the field list, if it is not already open, then drag the Company field name into the center of the Company Header area.**

Put the new text box toward the middle of the Company Header area, so there will be room to see the text label associated with the text box. The new Company text box has its own label with the word Text plus a number (see Figure 11.21).

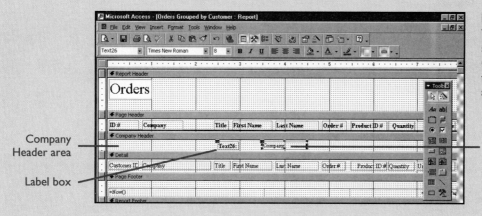

Company Header area

Label box

Text box

Figure 11.21
The Design view is shown with a Company text box in the Company Header area.

10 **Click an empty part of the window to deselect the text box. Click the text box label to select it, then press Del to delete the label.**

The Company text box remains, but without a label.

11 **Click the Print Preview button to preview the report.**

Notice that the headers are too small and not positioned correctly.

12 **Click the Close button on the toolbar to return to Design view, then move the Company text box to the left so it lines up with the left side of the ID # box above and the Customer ID box below.**

13 **Use a handle on the bottom-right of the Company text box to enlarge the box so it is twice as high and about 3 inches long.**

You can drag the bottom downward to enlarge the box, but it will not work if you try to drag the top of the box upward.

14 **Use the Font Size drop-down list on the Formatting toolbar to change the font size to 16 points and click the Bold button to change the typeface to bold (see Figure 11.22).**

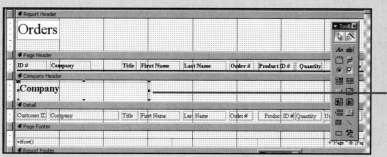

Figure 11.22
The Header text box is shown after it has been enlarged.

The header text box has been enlarged

continues ▶

To Group and Sort Data in a Report   (continued)

15 **Click the Print Preview button to preview the report.**
Notice that the header contains the same information as the Company field (see Figure 11.23).

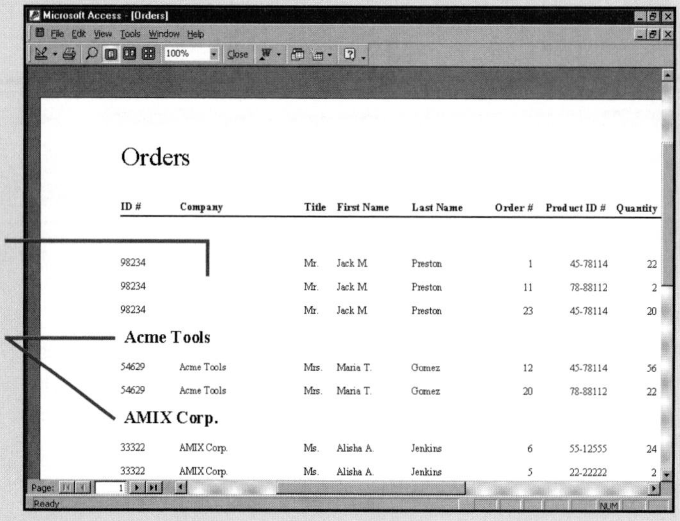

Figure 11.23
The final report is grouped on the Company field and displays headers.

Blank space for records with no company name

Headers

16 **Click the Print button on the toolbar to print the report.**

17 **Close the Print Preview window, close the Design window, and save your changes.**
Keep the Customer Orders 4 database open for the next lesson.

(i) *Inside Stuff:*   **Removing Duplicate Fields**
In this exercise you have a header that duplicates the company name field. It is a good idea to remove the duplicate field from the Detail area.

Lesson 4: Keeping Grouped Data Together in Reports

In most cases grouped data should be kept together on the same printed page. Access gives you the option of starting a new group at the top of the next page instead of splitting the group between pages. This feature works dynamically as you add records to your database.

In this lesson, you designate where to break a page of grouped records.

To Keep Grouped Data Together in Reports

1 **Click the Preview button in the Customer Orders 4 Database window to open the report in Preview view.**

2 **Maximize the preview window, if necessary, then scroll to the bottom of the page.**
Notice that the First Federal heading is detached from its records (see Figure 11.24). You will also often see records from a group split between two pages.

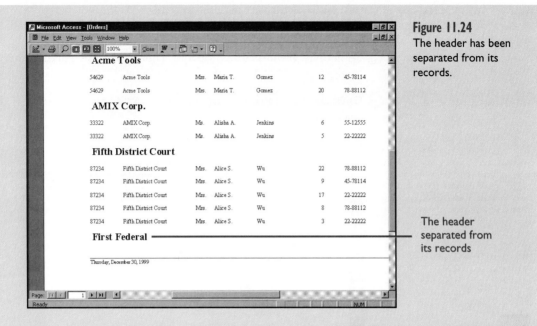

Figure 11.24
The header has been separated from its records.

The header separated from its records

 If You Have Problems...
Your report may not display the First Federal company name on the first page, separated from its records. This is due to the size of the header. Return to Design view and increase or decrease the size of the Company Header (not just the label box) until the preview displays the First Federal header on page I and its related records on page 2.

❸ **Click the Close button on the toolbar.**
This closes the preview and returns you to the Database window with Orders Grouped by Customer selected.

❹ **Click the Design button in the Database window to open the report in Design view.**

❺ **Click the Sorting and Grouping button on the toolbar.**
The Sorting and Grouping dialog box is displayed.

❻ **Click the down arrow in the Keep Together text box in the Grouping Properties area.**
A drop-down list box is displayed (see Figure 11.25).

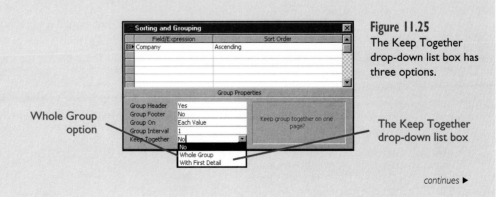

Whole Group option

Figure 11.25
The Keep Together drop-down list box has three options.

The Keep Together drop-down list box

continues ▶

To Keep Grouped Data Together in Reports (continued)

7 Select the **Whole Group** option, then close the **Sorting and Grouping** dialog box.

8 Click the **Print Preview** button and scroll to the bottom of the page, if necessary.

Notice that the page ends at the end of a group (see Figure 11.26).

Figure 11.26
The page breaks at the end of a group.

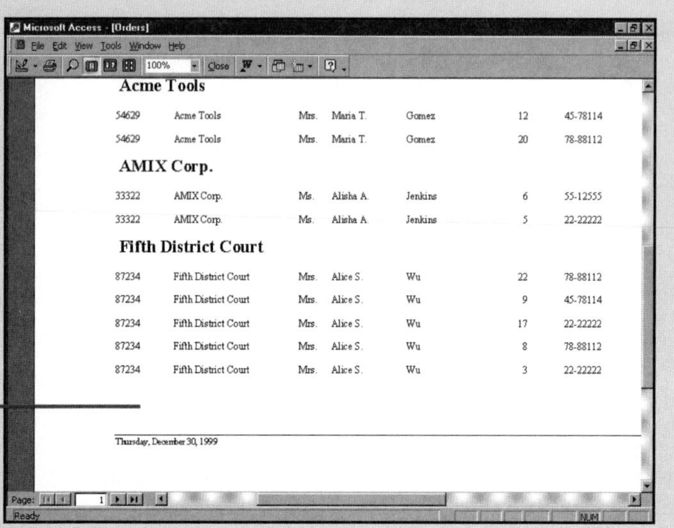

The header is moved to the next page

Acme Tools						
54629	Acme Tools	Mrs.	Maria T.	Gomez	12	45-78114
54629	Acme Tools	Mrs.	Maria T.	Gomez	20	78-88112
AMIX Corp.						
33322	AMIX Corp.	Ms.	Alisha A.	Jenkins	6	55-12555
33322	AMIX Corp.	Ms.	Alisha A.	Jenkins	5	22-22222
Fifth District Court						
87234	Fifth District Court	Mrs.	Alice S.	Wu	22	78-88112
87234	Fifth District Court	Mrs.	Alice S.	Wu	9	45-78114
87234	Fifth District Court	Mrs.	Alice S.	Wu	17	22-22222
87234	Fifth District Court	Mrs.	Alice S.	Wu	8	78-88112
87234	Fifth District Court	Mrs.	Alice S.	Wu	3	22-22222

Thursday, December 30, 1999

9 Click the **Next Page** button and look at the top of page 2 to verify that the page break worked correctly.

10 Click the **Close** button on the toolbar to return to the report Design view. Close the Design view window and save your changes.

Leave the Customer Orders 4 database open for the next lesson.

Lesson 5: Adding Calculated Controls to Group Headers and Footers

If you have a report with grouped records, it is often useful to place calculated information in a header or footer for that group. The values of a number field may be totaled or subtotaled in a footer or header by using a summation expression. If a summation expression is used in a group footer or header, you see the subtotal for that group. Similarly, if the expression is used in a page or report footer or header, you see the total for the page or report respectively.

In this lesson, you add an expression to a group footer to show totals for each group. The same method would work for a group header but is not used here.

To Add a Calculated Control to a Group Footer

1 Click the **D**esign button in the `Customer Orders 4` **Database window to open the Orders Grouped by Customer report in Design view.**

2 Click the Sorting and Grouping button in the toolbar. Choose Yes from the Group Footer drop-down list box.

A Company Footer area is created (see Figure 11.27).

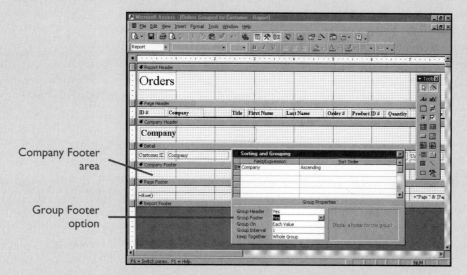

Company Footer area

Group Footer option

Figure 11.27
The Group Footer option has been selected, and a Company Footer area is displayed.

3 Click the Text Box button on the Toolbox. Drag a text box near the right edge of the Company Footer area.

The text box and a label are displayed. Drag the dialog boxes out of the way, if necessary.

4 Click the attached label box to select it. Click it again to turn on the text edit mode. Delete the current label and replace it with the following:

`Customer Total:`

5 Click the text box to select it. Click it a second time to enable the edit mode and enter the following expression:

`=sum([Quantity]*[Unit Price])`

Your screen should look like Figure 11.28.

6 Click in an open area, then click on the text box again to select it. Click the Properties button, then select the Format tab, if necessary.

7 Scroll to the bottom and select Right in the Text Align box.

This should line up the numbers in this field with those in the detail line above if the right edges of both boxes are lined up. If it does not, select the Text Box and adjust the right edge as necessary.

8 While still in the Properties box with the text box selected, scroll up to the Format option.

continues ▶

To Add a Calculated Control to a Group Footer (continued)

Figure 11.28
An expression has been added to the text box and the label has been changed.

New label

New expression

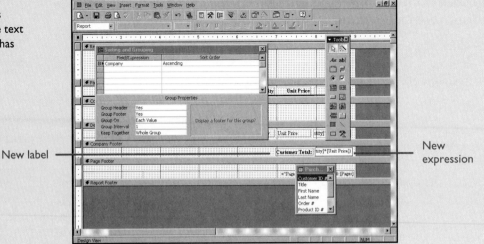

9 **Type $#,##0.00 in the Format box.**
This matches the format of the subtotals with the numbers in the Detail section.

10 **Close the Properties box. With the text box still selected, choose 10 from the Font Size box, and click the Bold button.**
This makes the group totals stand out.

11 **Click the Print Preview button to preview the report. Scroll across the report to reveal the Item Total column.**
Your report preview should look like Figure 11.29. If you need to touch up the formatting, go back to Design view and make your changes.

Figure 11.29
A preview of the final report shows subtotals for each customer.

Group subtotals

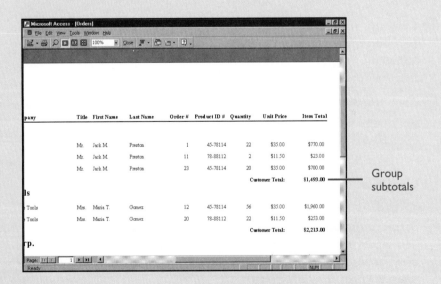

12 **Click the Print button on the toolbar to print the report.**

13 **Close Print Preview, close the report, and save your changes when prompted. Leave the database open for use in the next lesson.**

Exam Note: **Using Expressions**
Standard expressions start with the equal sign. The sum function adds all of the prices for this group. Functions like sum, average, and count are applied according to the section they are in. For example, if the sum function is in a group footer, it sums the field in that group. If the sum function is in a report footer, it sums that field for the entire report. Be careful with the square brackets and parentheses.

Lesson 6: Inserting a Graphic Background by Modifying Report Properties

You can insert a picture into a section of a report using the same methods that work for inserting a graphic on a form. You can also add a graphic background to the report. Access will accept different types of image formats for background images but **bitmap format** works best. Bitmap images are stored by recording individual bits of information for each tiny portion of the screen and occupy much more storage space than other image formats that use file compression methods. Care must be used when choosing a background graphic so that the text is not obscured.

In this lesson, you set the report properties to use a cloud graphic as the background of the first page of a report.

To Insert a Graphic Background by Modifying Report Properties

1 **Open the Orders Grouped by Customer report in Design view, if necessary. Close the Toolbox and the Field List. Click the Properties button on the toolbar to open the Properties dialog box.**
The Properties dialog box displays the properties of the currently selected object.

2 **Click the Report Selector button, if necessary, to select the report and change the title of the properties box to Report.**
You can select the properties of the whole report by clicking the Report Selector button in the upper left corner of Design view (see Figure 11.30).

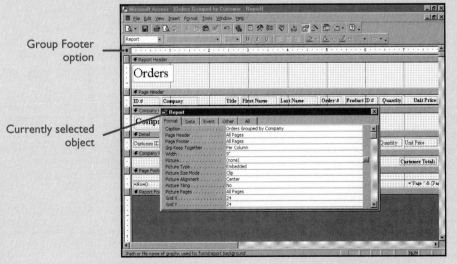

Group Footer option

Currently selected object

Figure 11.30
The report is selected and the Properties dialog box displays the properties of the entire report.

continues ▶

To Insert a Graphic Background by Modifying Report Properties (continued)

3 **Click the Picture box in the Properties dialog box to display a Build button at the right side of the box. Click the Build button.**
The Insert Picture dialog box is displayed.

4 **Locate the Clouds image file in the Student folder on the CD. Select it and click OK.**
The location of the file is displayed in the Picture box. It has a file extension of .bmp to indicate that it is a bitmap file (see Figure 11.31).

Figure 11.31
The bitmap cloud image is selected as a background image for the entire report.

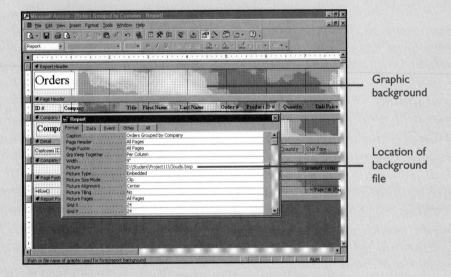

Graphic background

Location of background file

5 **Click the Picture Size Mode box. Click the drop-down arrow at the right of the box and select Stretch from the list of options.**
The stretch option will force the image to fill the entire space available. This option distorts images but the cloud image does not suffer from this distortion due to the undefined shapes of the clouds.

6 **Change the Picture Pages box to First Page, if necessary. Click the Print Preview button to view the report (see Figure 11.32).**

Figure 11.32
The clouds picture fills the background of the report.

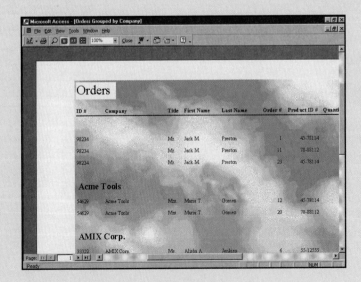

7 **Close the report and save your changes. Close the database.**
If you have completed your session on the computer, exit Access and shut down Windows before you turn off the computer. Otherwise, continue with the Checking Concepts and Terms section.

Summary

In this project you were introduced to many new techniques for improving reports. You created mailing labels from a customer table. You added calculated fields to the records in a report and to group footers. You learned how to group and sort records in a report, and how to break the pages at logical points. You also learned how to change report properties to use a graphic background.

You can learn more about using calculations in reports by going to the Help index and looking for information on expressions. Start with Examples of expressions to see some of the things you can do.

Checking Concepts and Terms ✓

True/False

For each of the following statements, check *T* or *F* to indicate whether the statement is true or false.

__T __F **1.** When field names are used in calculated fields, they must be enclosed by curly braces, {}. [L2]

__T __F **2.** If you put two fields on the same line of a label the program will automatically insert a comma and a space between them. [L1]

__T __F **3.** If you add a text box with a calculated field in the Group Header section of a report, the program automatically adds a label box in the report header using the name of the first field used in the calculation. [L5]

__T __F **4.** You can keep grouped data together on a printed page using the Sorting and Grouping dialog box. [L4]

__T __F **5.** Bitmap images are used for report backgrounds because they take much less storage space than most other image formats. [L6]

Multiple Choice

Circle the letter of the correct answer for each of the following questions.

1. If a report is grouped on a field named Expense, what would the report look like if the following formula were placed in a text box in the Detail section: =[Expense]*.10 [L2]

   a. Ten percent of the total of all the expenses would be displayed in the footer.

   b. Ten percent of the expenses shown in each record would be printed in each record.

   c. The word Expense would be printed in the header of that section.

   d. both a and b but not c

2. If a table contained the field Last Name and the report was grouped on that field, what effect would it have on the report if the following expression were placed in a text box in the Group Header section? [Last Name] [L3]

   a. Each record would start with the last name.

   b. Each group would begin with the last name for that group.

   c. The words "Last Name" would appear at the beginning of each group.

   d. An error message would be displayed because you forgot to start the expression with an equals sign.

3. If a currency value is calculated, it may be displayed with too many decimal places. To control the appearance of the calculated value: [L2]

   a. click the Currency button on the toolbar

   b. choose Format, and Currency from the menu bar

   c. use the following form in the calculated field:

   ="$ "+[expression]

   d. click the Properties button and type in the format you want

4. If you use an operator like IIF in a calculated field, you must: [L2]

   a. begin the calculation with an equal sign, =

   b. place the formula within <>

   c. place the formula within {}

   d. place the formula between three asterisks

5. What is wrong with the following calculated field? =IIF([PAYROLL]<0,0,PAYROLL) [L2]

   a. The IF function is misspelled.

   b. Both zeros should be enclosed by quotation marks.

   c. The field name, PAYROLL, should be enclosed by [].

   d. The field name, PAYROLL, should be enclosed by {}.

Screen ID

Label each element of the Access screen shown in Figure 11.33.

Figure 11.33

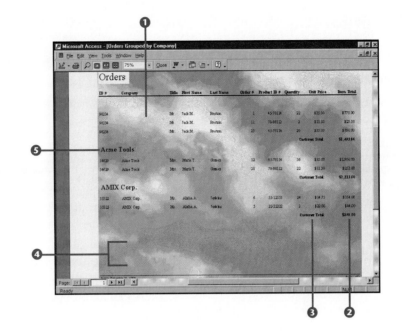

A. Next group forced to page 2

B. Calculation in group footer

C. Missing company name results in blank spaces

D. Label in group footer

E. Text box in group header

1._____   3._____   5._____

2._____   4._____

Skill Drill

Skill Drill exercises reinforce project skills. Each skill reinforced is the same, or nearly the same, as a skill presented in the project. Each exercise includes a brief narrative introduction, followed by detailed instructions in a step-by-step format.

In this exercise, you work with a database you created to track your accounts payable for your plumbing company. You need an empty, formatted disk for these exercises.

1. Creating a Mailing Label Report

The company pays its bills once a month. With the names and addresses of the vendors in the Vendors table, you can make the job a little easier by creating mailing labels.

To create a mailing label report:

1. Copy the file AC-1104 from your CD to an empty, formatted floppy disk. Use the shortcut menu to deselect the read-only status, and rename the copy as **Accounts Payable**.

2. Open the **Accounts Payable** database and click the Reports object button, if necessary.

3. Click the New button in the Reports window. Select the Label Wizard option and choose the Vendors table from the drop-down list box. Click OK.

4. Select the Avery manufacturer. Make sure the units of measure are inches and the Sheet feed option is selected. Select label number 5160 Click Next.

5. Confirm the choice of Arial font and a 12 point font size. Click Next.

6. Click the Select button to select the Vendor field, then press Enter.

7. Select the Street field, then press Enter.

8. Select the City field, then type in a comma and a space. Select the State field, add two spaces, then select the zip field. Click Next.

9. Click the Select button to sort on the Vendor field and click Next.

10. Name your report `Vendor Mailing Labels` and click Finish.

11. Look at your new report, then close the report. If you plan to do the next exercise, leave the `Accounts Payable` database open and skip the first step.

2. Grouping Data in a Report

The Accounts Payable report shows the purchases that your company hasn't paid for yet. It would be a good idea to group the bills together by vendor.

To group data in a report:

1. Copy the file `AC-1104` from your CD-ROM to an empty, formatted floppy disk. Use the shortcut menu to deselect the read-only status, and rename the copy `Accounts Payable`. Open the database.

2. Select the Accounts Payable report and click the Preview button to examine the report and see how it is set up. Click the View button to switch to Design view.

3. Click the Sorting and Grouping button on the toolbar, if necessary, to open the Sorting and Grouping dialog box.

4. Click in the first empty row of the Sorting and Grouping dialog box. Click the arrow and select the Vendor field from the drop-down list box.

5. Change the Group Header property to Yes.

6. Click the View button to switch to Print Preview.

7. Confirm that the labels are sorted and grouped by Vendor.

8. Click the View button to return to Design view.

9. Open the Field List dialog box. Drag the Vendor field to the Vendor Header. Remove the attached label box and move the text box to the left side of the report.

10. Remove the Vendor field from the Detail section and remove the Vendor label from the Page Header.

11. Resize and rearrange the Description, Date, and Cost fields to make the Description field wide enough to display the largest description. Center the Billing text box in the Detail section.

12. Make the Vendor field box in the Vendor Header wider to display the widest vendor name. Change the font of the Vendor text box to Bold, 12 point.

13. Click the Print Preview button to preview the report. See Figure 11.34 to check your work.

14. Close the report and save your work. Close the database.

Figure 11.34
The report is grouped by vendor.

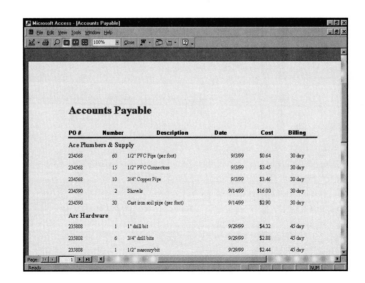

3. Adding Calculated Fields to a Report Detail and Group Footer

You can calculate the total cost for each item by multiplying the number of items purchased by the cost of a single item.

To add calculated fields to report detail:

1. Copy the file **AC-1105** from your CD to your floppy disk. Use the shortcut menu to deselect the read-only status, and rename the copy as **Accounts Payable 2**. Open the database.

2. Select the Accounts Payable report. Click the Design button. Click the Toolbox button, if necessary, to open the Toolbox.

3. Click the Text Box button and draw a box in the Detail area between the Cost field and the Billing field. Delete the label attached to this text box.

4. Click the Label button in the Toolbox and draw a label box in the Page Header area above the Unbound text box. Type **Total Cost** in the box.

5. Click outside the new label box, then click it again and click the Font Size button to change the font size to 9 points. Click the Align Right button to right-align the label.

6. Right-click on the label, choose Properties from the shortcut menu, then scroll down and select Heavy from the Font Weight drop-down list box. Close the Properties box, then make sure all of the page header labels are consistent.

7. Click the Unbound text box and click the Align Right button.

8. Right-click on the box, choose Properties from the shortcut menu, select the Format tab, then click in the Format box. Click the down arrow and select Currency from the drop-down list box.

9. Click the Unbound text box again and type in:

   `=([Number]*[Cost])`

10. Click the Print Preview button to see your new calculated field. Leave the report and the database open to add a calculated field to the group footer.

4. Adding Calculated Controls to a Group Footer

You have taken a plain database report and made it very usable and readable. The last thing you need to do to the report is to add an expression to show how much is owed to each supplier.

To add calculated controls to a group footer:

1. Click the View button to switch to the Design view of the Accounts Payable report.

2. Click the Sorting and Grouping button on the toolbar. Make sure the Vendor field is selected, then choose Yes in the Group Footer box in the Group Properties area. Close the Sorting and Grouping dialog box.

3. Click the Text Box button and draw a box in the Vendor Footer area underneath the Total Cost expression in the Detail section.

4. Click the label box, delete the default label, then type **Total Charges:**.

5. Click the Unbound text box and click the Align Right button and Bold buttons on the toolbar.

6. Right-click on the Unbound box, choose Properties from the shortcut menu, select the Format tab, then click in the Format box. Click the down arrow and select Currency from the drop-down list box.

7. Scroll down to the Font Weight box and select Heavy. Close the Properties box.

8. Click the Unbound text box again and type in:

   `=sum([Number]*[Cost])`

9. Click the Print Preview button to see your new calculated field.

10. Close the report and save your changes when prompted. Close the **Accounts Payable 2** database.

Challenge

Challenge exercises expand on or are somewhat related to skills presented in the lessons. Each exercise provides a brief narrative introduction followed by instructions in a numbered step format that are not as detailed as those in the Skill Drill section.

The database used for the Challenge section is a subset of a historical database. It contains the names of the 123 Haynes Township women who are listed as having had children in the 1900 U.S. Census. The data comes from a transcription by the authors of the 1900 Alcona County, Michigan Census. These records have been filtered from a database containing about 6,000 names. Also, only seven of the more than 30 fields have been included.

1. Grouping Data Using the Report Wizard

1. Copy the file AC-1106 from your CD-ROM. Use the shortcut menu to deselect the read-only status, and rename the copy as Haynes Township 4.

2. Open the 1900 Haynes Township Women with Children table and look at the records. Since you are interested in the place of birth of the women with children, it would make sense to group on the Birth Place field.

3. Use the available help to figure out how to use the Report Wizard to group data on the Birth Place field. Show all of the fields. Sort on the number of children, then the number of children still living. Choose your favorite layout and style, and call the report 1900 Haynes Township Women with Children (see Figure 11.35).

Figure 11.35
The report is grouped by birth place.

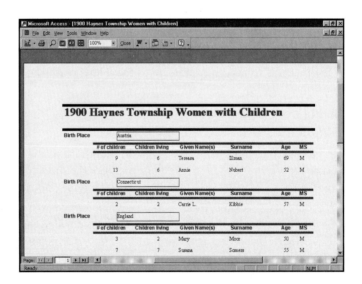

4. Edit the layout so the fields are spaced properly, and the labels are all readable. You may have to shorten the labels to make the report design more attractive. You also want to make the places of birth bold.

5. Close the database. If you plan to do the next exercise, leave Access open.

2. Using the Average Function

You want to compare the number of children in Haynes township by place of birth, and you know that the number of mothers born in each location varies widely. You decide it would be best to use the average number of children born to each woman, the average number of children still living, and the average age of the women.

I. Copy the file AC-1107 from your CD-ROM. Use the shortcut menu to deselect the read-only status, and rename the copy Children.

2. Use the skills you learned in Lesson 5 to insert a place for group subtotals, then use the available help to insert averages for the # of Children, Children Living, and Age fields.

3. Place a label box on the left side of the group footer area and insert the text, Averages:.

4. Format the three averages so that they display one decimal place. The decimal point should be displayed to the right of the numbers in the columns above.

Your report should look like Figure 11.36.

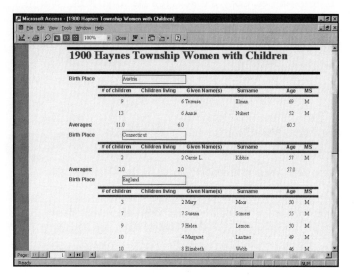

Figure 11.36
The averages are displayed for three fields.

Close the report. If you plan to do the next exercise, leave the database open and skip the first step.

3. Creating a Summary-Only Report

I. Copy the file AC-1107 from your CD-ROM. Use the shortcut menu to deselect the read-only status, and rename the copy Children.

2. Create a new report. Use the Report Wizard and base the report on the 1900 Haynes Township Women with Children table.

3. Select the Age, # of Children, Children Living, and Birth Place fields and group on Birth Place.

4. In the third Report Wizard dialog box, click Summary Options.

5. Select Avg for all three numeric fields, and select the Summary Only option.

6. Choose the Outline 1 layout and the Corporate style. Call your report Averages by Place of Birth.

7. Examine the report in Preview view. Close the report and the database.

Discovery Zone

Discovery Zone exercises help you gain advanced knowledge of project topics and application of skills. These exercises focus on enhancing your problem-solving skills. Numbered steps are not provided, but you are given hints, reminders, screen shots, and references to help you reach your goal for each exercise.

The database you use for these exercises contains tornado data for the state of Arizona. These records cover a 45-year time span, and include all of the confirmed sightings during that period. The records are an abbreviated form of records produced by the National Oceanic and Atmospheric Administration (NOAA). The fields included in this sample table include the year, date, time of day, number of people killed, number of people injured, a damage scale, the county, and the Fscale (a measure of tornado intensity). Many of the fields are blank because there were no casualties or damage, or because the Fscale was not recorded.

1. Grouping on Multiple Fields

In this database, you have data from several different counties and many different years. Some of the years saw multiple tornadoes. Copy the `AC-1108` file to your disk and rename it.

Goal: Create a report using the Report Wizard that groups the data first on the county, then on the year.

The report you create should:

- include all but the Damage field.
- use the County field as the main group field.
- use the Year field as the secondary group field.
- sort the records within the year group in ascending order by the Date field.
- use the Align Left 2 layout in Portrait orientation.
- name the report `Arizona Tornadoes by County and Year` when you are finished.

If you plan to do the next exercise, close the report, leave the `Arizona Tornadoes 4` database open, and skip the first step.

2. Using the Can Grow Property to Display a Text Field

Copy the `AC-1104` file to your disk and rename it `Accounts Payable 3`. Open the report.

Some text fields contain variable amounts of text. When you use one of these fields in a report, you could expand the field horizontally or vertically to fit the largest quantity of text but that would result in a lot of wasted space for most of the other records. You can solve this problem by using the Can Grow property.

Goal: Modify the Accounts Payable report so that the Description and Vendor text boxes will grow vertically when necessary to display the complete text stored in those fields.

The report you create should:

- have a variable size Description field that can grow vertically when necessary to display all of the description.
- have a variable size Vendor field that can grow vertically when necessary to display all of the vendor's name.
- have a variable size Detail section that will accommodate the variable size fields.

Use Help to look up information on the CanGrow property and how it is used with individual fields and with the detail section. Change this property of the Description and Vendor fields in the Accounts Payable report to meet the goal stated above. Click the Detail **Section Bar** (the bar at the top of the Detail section) and observe how the CanGrow property changes automatically from No to Yes in the Detail section. Preview the report to confirm that all the text in these two fields is displayed for each record.

PinPoint Assessment

You have completed this project and the associated lessons, and have had an opportunity to assess your skills through end-of-project questions and exercises. Now use the PinPoint software evaluation mode to assess your comprehension of the specific exam tasks you have just learned. You can also use the PinPoint Trainer Mode and the Show Me tutorials to practice these specific exam tasks.

Project 12

Automating Your Database with Macros

Key terms introduced in this project include

- action
- argument
- macro
- switchboard

Objectives	Required Activity for MOUS	Exam Level
➤ Create a Macro to Close a Form		
➤ Create a Macro to Print a Report		
➤ Use the Macro Builder to Open a Form in the Read Only Mode	Create a macro using the Macro Builder	Expert
➤ Run a Macro from a Button on a Form	Run macros using controls	Expert
➤ Create a Switchboard Using the Switchboard Manager	Create a Switchboard	Expert
➤ Create a Macro to Automatically Launch the Main Switchboard Form		
➤ Using a Blank Form to Create a Switchboard	Create a form in Design View	Expert

Why Would I Do This?

One of the functions computers are best suited for is automating repetitive tasks. Almost any action in Access can be assisted or completely performed by a macro. *Macros* are pre-defined commands that you can invoke and apply to objects in your database. By using macros you can automate a wide range of tasks such as opening and closing forms or reports, printing information, or finding records. Macros help make your database usable by someone else who is not familiar with Access.

You can also create an automated menu, referred to as a **switchboard**, that enables the user to preview and print reports, review table or query contents, enter new records using forms, or close windows. A switchboard gives the user access to information in the database with a simple click of a button. The switchboard is a form that can be designed and created from scratch, or can be created using the Switchboard Manager utility. In either case, the end result is a database that can be used by anyone who can point and click a mouse button.

This chapter covers how to create a macro and how to enter **actions** and **arguments** that control the macro, as well as comments that describe the function of the macro. Actions are Access-defined functions that perform a database task, while arguments are values needed for a macro to perform its function. You learn how to work with the Macro window and toolbar, and how to name, save, and run macros. You can also create macros in a form using the macro builder. This technique is also covered in this project. Finally, you learn how to create a switchboard using the Switchboard Manager and how to have that switchboard open automatically when the database is opened.

Lesson 1: Creating a Macro to Close a Form

It is possible for some macros to perform a generic function, such as closing a form, query, or table. The Close action closes whatever object it is attached to. This macro can be attached to a button that can be used by those who are less familiar with Access. In this lesson, you add this type of macro to the database you have been working on in the previous lessons. Later this macro is added to several forms, so it can be used to close those particular forms.

To Create a Macro to Close a Form

1 Copy the AC-1201 file to your disk, remove the read-only status, and re-name it Customer Orders 5.

2 Open the Customer Orders 5 database, and select the Macros object button.

3 Click the <u>N</u>ew button.
The Macro window opens (see Figure 12.1). The left-hand column is used to specify the action that you want to take. You can choose to list several actions as part of each macro. The right-hand column is used to document the purpose of each action in a macro. In this case only one action will be used.

4 Click the list arrow in the Action box and select Close from the list of actions.
The Action Arguments area becomes available once an action has been selected. The arguments you can use depend on the macro action that has been selected. Normally, you specify an object to which the selected action should apply. In this case, you want the close action to be generic so it can be applied to several forms, so no action arguments are needed.

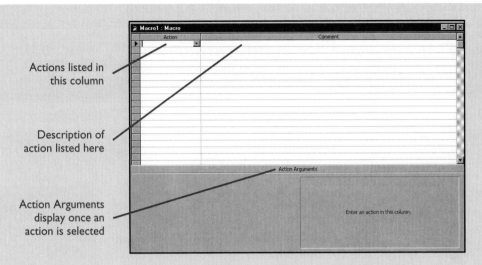

Figure 12.1
The Macro window has three separate areas.

Actions listed in this column

Description of action listed here

Action Arguments display once an action is selected

 Inside Stuff: Creating a Generic Macro
By not specifying a form or report name in the Action Arguments area, you are creating a generic macro that you can use over and over again. You can attach this macro to many buttons throughout your database to close whatever window is active.

⑤ Click the Close button in the upper-right corner of the window and choose <u>Y</u>es to save the macro.

⑥ In the Save As box type Close as the macro name and click OK.
The macro closes and the new macro is shown on the macro list. In Lesson 4 you attach the macro to a form. Keep the Customer Orders 5 database open for the next lesson.

 If You Have Problems...
You can accidentally close the database using the button you created in this lesson. If you double-click the button while you are in the form, or double-click the macro from the Macros window, the database will close. You will not lose any information if this happens, however—just reopen the database.

Lesson 2: Creating a Macro to Print a Report

You can create a macro to perform specific actions that apply to specific objects in a database. In this lesson you create two macros that will print two different reports. The action for each will be the same, but you will specify which report to print and then change the view mode to print, which results in the printing of the specified report.

To Create a Macro to Print a Report

① With the Macros object selected in the Customer Orders 5 database, click the <u>N</u>ew button.
The Macro window is displayed.

continues ▶

To Create a Macro to Print a Report (continued)

2 **Click the drop-down arrow in the first Action box and then scroll down and select the OpenReport option from the list of possible actions (see Figure 12.2).**
OpenReport is a macro instruction that automatically opens the report you select in the following steps. Scroll through the list of actions to see what else is available.

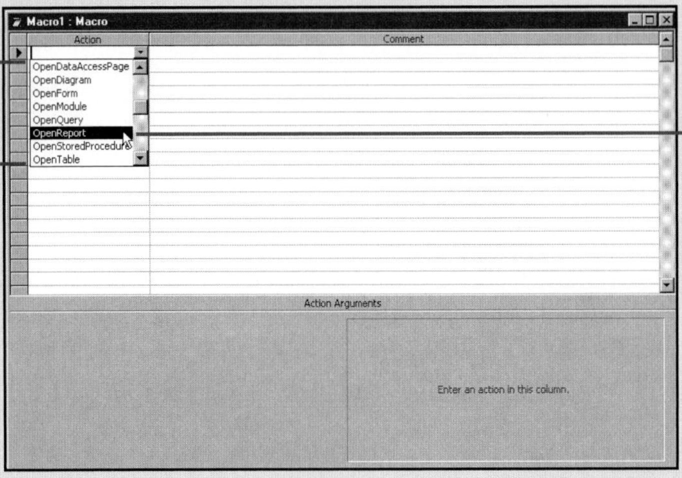

Figure 12.2
The Macro window list box shows a list of available actions.

Action list box

OpenReport action

3 **Press tab to move to the Comment area and type Print Orders Grouped by Customer report.**
This comment serves to document the purpose of the macro action. It is not required for the macro to function, but it is a good database design technique to document each action in a macro so someone else would know what the macro is suppose to do.

4 **Move to the Action Arguments section of the window, and click the Report Name box.**
This box is used to select the report the macro is to print. After you click the box, a list arrow appears at the right side of the box.

5 **Click the list arrow and select Orders Grouped by Customer.**
The Report Name list shows all of the reports in the database (see Figure 12.3).

6 **Click the View box and click the list arrow to see the different views that are available.**
The default view is to print the report. You can, however, also choose to open the report in Print Preview or Design view. Leave the View box as Print

7 **Click the close button in the upper-right corner of the window, and save the macro with the name Print Orders Grouped by Customer Report.**
Macro names should clearly state what the macro does. Later when you want to attach this macro to a button, you will be able to tell what the action of the macro is from its name. (see Figure 12.4).

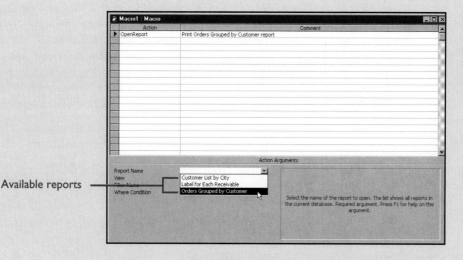

Figure 12.3
The Report Name drop-down box lists all available reports.

Available reports

Figure 12.4
The name you give a macro can be used on a command button.

Run button

New macro

 Inside Stuff: **Renaming the Macro Button**
If you don't like the way the text looks on a macro button, you can change it easily. In Design view, right-click on the button and select Properties from the shortcut menu. Click the Format tab and type the new text in the Caption box.

8 **Select the Print Orders Grouped by Customer Report macro and click the Run button to test the macro.**
The Orders Grouped by Customer report prints. Leave the Customer Orders 5 database open for the next lesson.

 Inside Stuff: **When to Create Macros**
You can create macros at any point while you are developing your database. It is usually best, however, to work on your macros after you have created all of the other database objects.

Exam Note: **A Quick Way to Select an Action in the Macro Window**
A quick way to select an action in the Macro window is to type the first letter of the action that is needed. The list scrolls automatically to the first action that begins with that letter, then you can click the drop-down arrow, if needed, and select the specific action. For example, OpenDataAccessPage is the first action under O and by typing an O in the action box, OpenDataAccessPage is automatically filled in. Pressing ⟨Tab⟩ or ⟨↵Enter⟩ then activates the argument section of the window.

 # Lesson 3: Using the Macro Builder to Open a Form in Read-Only Mode

You can create macros to open a form in edit, add, or read-only mode. Edit mode is the most flexible, enabling the user to view, edit, or add new records. The add mode only allows a user to add new records, but not to look at existing records. If you are setting up a database that will be used primarily for looking up information, you may want to have a form open in read-only mode so the data cannot be changed. This can be done using the Macro window as you did in the previous two examples, or you can use the Macro Builder in the Form Design view to create such an action.

In this lesson you use the Macro Builder to create a macro to open the Customer Information form in read-only mode.

To Use the Macro Builder to Open a Form in Read-Only Mode

1 In the `Customer Orders 5` Database window, click the Forms object button and open the Design view of the `Customer Information` form.
The Form design window is displayed.

2 Maximize the form window. Right-click the Form Selector box in the upper corner of the form where the two rulers meet.
The entire form is selected and a shortcut menu opens as shown in Figure 12.5. Notice that the select object list box now shows Form as the item that is selected.

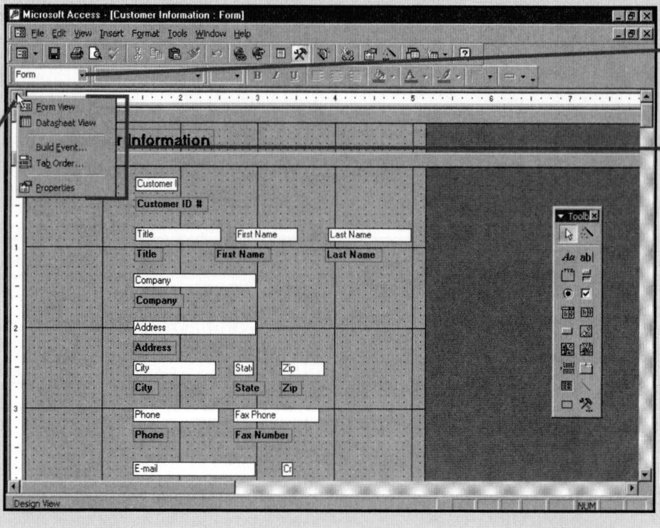

Figure 12.5
A dark square appears in the Form Selector box when the entire form is selected.

Form Selector

Select Object list box

Shortcut menu

3 **Click Build Event from the shortcut menu.**
The Choose Builder dialog box opens.

4 **Choose Macro Builder and click OK**
The Macro window opens and the Save As dialog box is displayed (see Figure 12.6).

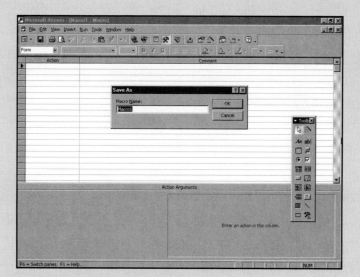

Figure 12.6
Using the Macro Builder opens the Macro window.

5 **Type** `View Customer Information` **and click OK.**
The macro is named first when you use the Macro Builder. Now you design the macro.

6 **In the first box in the Action column choose OpenForm from the Action list.**
The action is selected and the Action Argument area becomes active.

7 **Click in the Form Name box, click the list arrow, then select Customer Information.**
The list disappears and the Customer Information form is displayed in the Form Name box.

8 **In the Data Mode box, click the list arrow to show the list of data entry options, then select Read-Only.**
The Data Mode is now shown as Read-Only (see Figure 12.7).

9 **Click the second box in the action column and type** `m`**.**
Maximize is displayed as the next action in the action column. This will cause the form to maximize and fill the screen when the macro is run.

10 **Click the close button in the upper-right corner of the Macro window and choose Yes when prompted to save the changes.**
You have already named the macro, so it does not display the Save As dialog box again. The Macro window closes and Design view of the form is displayed.

11 **Close the form and save the changes when prompted.**

continues ▶

To Use the Macro Builder to Open a Form in Read-Only Mode (continued)

Figure 12.7
Selecting Read-Only in the Data Mode enables the user to look at the data but not make changes when the form is opened.

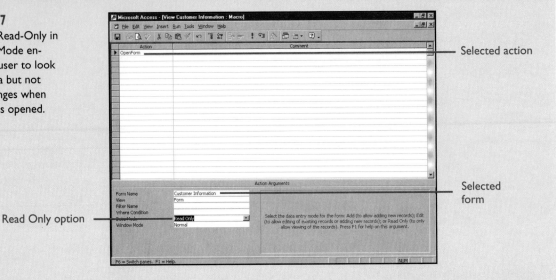

Selected action

Selected form

Read Only option

12 **Click the Macros object button and run the** View Customer Information **macro.**

The Customer Information form opens in Datasheet view and in Read-Only mode (see Figure 12.8). Notice that the Add New button is grayed out both on the toolbar and the navigation bar.

13 **Try to change an existing record.**

Notice that no error message is displayed; Access just does not allow any changes to be made.

Figure 12.8
The form is opened in read-only mode, even though the title bar does not indicate it.

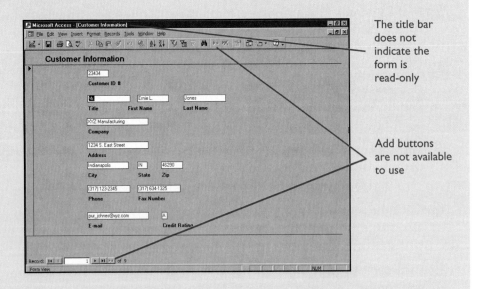

The title bar does not indicate the form is read-only

Add buttons are not available to use

14 **Close the Customer Information form.**

Leave the Customer Orders 5 database open for the next lesson.

Inside Stuff: Testing Your Macros

It is always a good idea to run each macro after it has been created to make sure it works the way you intended. You can run a macro by double-clicking on the macro name. You can also run a macro from the Macro window by clicking the Run button.

Lesson 4: Running a Macro from a Button on a Form

Simple macros can be run from the Database window. They are much more valuable, however, when they are attached to buttons on a form. This process creates the equivalent of a command button on a form that performs the action that has been designated by the macro. A form can contain several different types of command buttons. When you want to create command buttons that are specific to a particular form, it is better to use the Command Wizard in the Form design window toolbox. In this lesson, you add the generic Close macro to several forms. This creates a command button on the form that will be used to close the form.

To Run a Macro from a Button on a Form

1 In the `Customer Orders 5` database, click the **Forms** object button to display the existing forms.

2 Open the `Customer Information` form in **Design** view.

3 Click the **Control Wizards** button in the **Toolbox** to deselect it, if necessary (see Figure 12.9).

Generally the Control Wizards button is pre-selected so that the appropriate wizard opens when you use certain tools in the toolbox. In this example, you create a command button without using the Wizard.

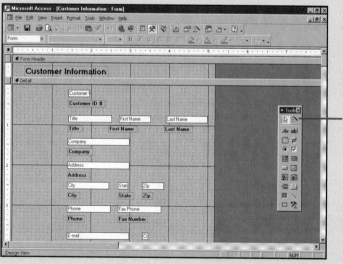

Figure 12.9
A command button will be created without the use of the Wizard.

Control Wizards is deselected

4 Click the **Command** button on the **Toolbox** to select it.

continues ▶

To Run a Macro from a Button on a Form (continued)

5 **Move the pointer to the right side of the Form Header at the 4 inch mark and click (see Figure 12.10).**

A command button is placed in the form header.

Figure 12.10
A command button is placed in the form header.

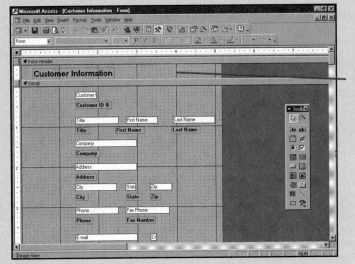

Click here to place the Command button

6 **Right-click the command button and choose Properties from the shortcut menu.**

A property sheet labeled command button is displayed.

7 **Click the Format tab and type Close Form in the Caption box and press ←Enter.**

The caption you type displays on the command button (see Figure 12.11).

Figure 12.11
Use the property sheet to change the caption on the command button.

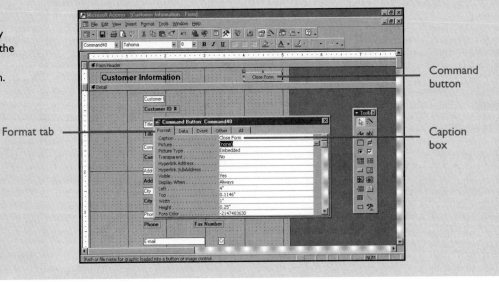

Format tab

Command button

Caption box

8 **Click the Event tab on the Command Button property sheet and click the On Click box.**

A list arrow appears at the end of the On Click box. This box is used to control what happens when you click the command button.

9 **Click the list arrow to display the options available.**

Notice that the options listed are all macros that have been previously created (see Figure 12.12).

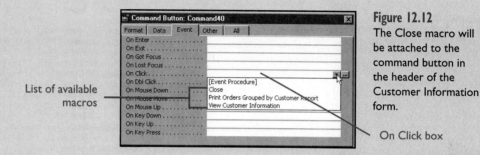

List of available macros

Figure 12.12
The Close macro will be attached to the command button in the header of the Customer Information form.

On Click box

10 **Click Close to select it and then close the property sheet.**

The Close macro is attached to the event that controls what happens when this button is clicked.

11 **Click the View button to change to Form View.**

The new command button is displayed at the top of the form (see Figure 12.13).

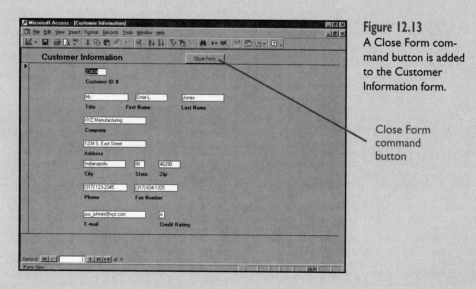

Figure 12.13
A Close Form command button is added to the Customer Information form.

Close Form command button

12 **Click the Close Form button.**

You are prompted to save the form since you have made a change to it. This also tests the Close Form button to make sure that it is functioning correctly.

13 **Choose Yes to save your changes.**

The form closes and the Database window is displayed.

continues ▶

To Run a Macro from a Button on a Form   (continued)

14 Follow steps 4 through 13 to add close buttons to the other two forms in this database (see Figure 12.14).

Figure 12.14
The Close Form command button is displayed on the Orders in Row-and-Column Format form.

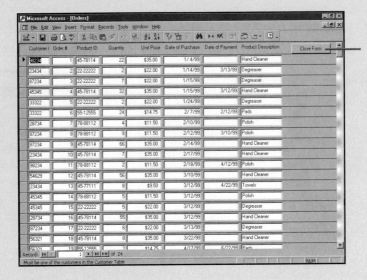

Button created to close the form

Keep the Customer Orders 5 database open for the next lesson.

 Inside Stuff: Placement of Close Button
You can locate a command button anywhere you want on a form—it does not have to be in the form header. It is generally a good idea, however, to place command buttons in the same location on all of your forms to ensure design consistency and ease of use.

Lesson 5: Creating a Switchboard Using the Switchboard Manager

As a database designer, you are often preparing databases for others to use, many of whom have little experience with databases. It is important that they are able to do their jobs quickly and efficiently and it is also important that they do not make changes to the design.

Access provides a feature called a switchboard that is a special purpose form. This form contains buttons that may be used by inexperienced people to open forms for data input, editing, or review as well as printing existing reports.

In this lesson, you learn how to create a switchboard using the Switchboard Manager.

To Create a Switchboard Using the Switchboard Manager

1 **In the `Customer Orders 5` database, choose Tools, Database Utilities, Switchboard Manager from the menu bar.**

Because there is no switchboard to manage yet, the Switchboard Manager message box appears that asks if you would like to create one (see Figure 12.15).

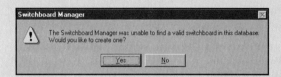

Figure 12.15
The Switchboard manager message box appears if a switchboard does not already exist.

2 **Choose Yes.**

After a brief delay, the Switchboard Manager dialog box appears that displays the default switchboard (see Figure 12.16).

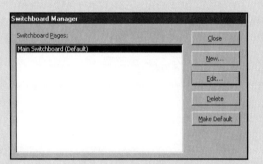

Figure 12.16
The Switchboard Manager dialog box displays the default switchboard option.

3 **Click Edit.**

This enables you to add action buttons to the switchboard. The Edit Switchboard Page dialog box opens so you can edit the Main Switchboard (see Figure 12.17).

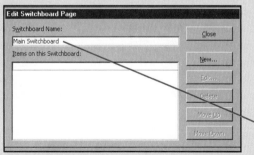

Figure 12.17
The Edit Switchboard Page dialog box can be used to add action buttons to the switchboard.

Switchboard to be edited

4 **Click New.**

This action opens the Edit Switchboard Item dialog box (see Figure 12.18). This box contains a Text box that is used to create a label for the action button. The Command drop-down list is used to select commands to do things like open forms or preview reports.

continues ▶

To Create a Switchboard Using the Switchboard Manager   (continued)

Figure 12.18
The Edit Switchboard
Item dialog box is used
to specify actions.

5 Change the text in the **T**ext box to `Add New Customers`.

6 In the **C**ommand drop-down list, select the **Open Form in Add Mode** option.
The Add Mode enables the user to enter new records but prevents them from viewing existing records. Notice that the title of the third drop-down list box changes depending on your choice in the **C**ommand drop-down list box (see Figure 12.19).

Figure 12.19
The Edit Switchboard
Item dialog box
changes the third
choice in response to
the contents of the
Command drop-down
list box.

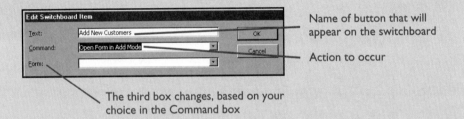

Name of button that will
appear on the switchboard

Action to occur

The third box changes, based on your
choice in the Command box

7 In the **F**orm box, select the **Customer Information** form. Click **OK**.
The Edit Switchboard Page dialog box reappears showing the Add New Customers item on its list of switchboard items (see Figure 12.20).

Figure 12.20
The Edit Switchboard
Page dialog box dis-
plays the item that has
been added to the
switchboard.

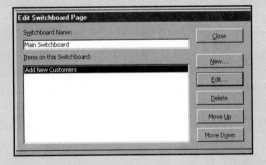

8 Click **N**ew and type `Add New Orders`. Choose the **Open Form in Add Mode** for the **C**ommand Box, and select **Customer Orders** in the **F**orm box.
The next switchboard item is defined as shown in Figure 12.21

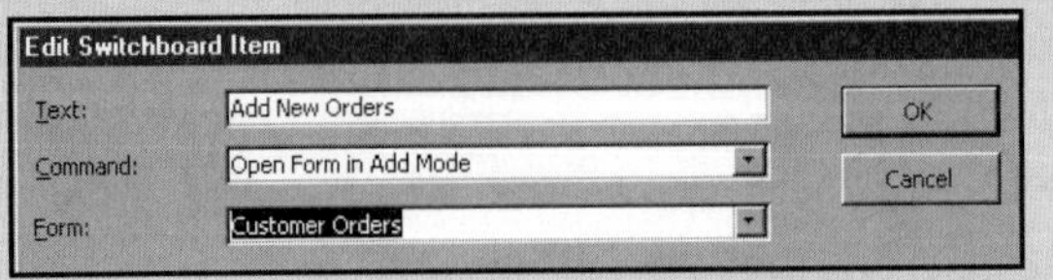

Figure 12.21
The Edit Switchboard
Item dialog box de-
fined to add the next
item.

9 **Click OK. Repeat the process again to add another new item named** `Preview labels for each receivable`. **This time, select the Open Report command and pick the Labels for Each Receivable report.**
The item is defined to open a report (see Figure 12.22).

Box changes to Report to match the command —

Figure 12.22
The Edit Switchboard Item dialog box is set up to open a report.

10 **Click OK.**
The item is added to the list. Leave the `Edit Switchboard Item dialog box` open and continue to the next section.

 Exam Note: **The Switchboard May be Used to Open the Same Form in Three Different Ways**
The same form can be used three different ways and each of them can have its own button on the switchboard. If you open a form in read-only mode, it can only be used to view the records. The add mode displays the form without showing any existing records and is useful for entering new data. The edit mode is the one you have been using and allows the user to make changes, view existing records, and add new records. Add or edit modes are available in the Edit Switchboard Item dialog box. To restrict a form to a read-only mode, you need to create a read-only macro and choose Run Macro as the command in the Edit Switchboard Item dialog box.

This process can be repeated to produce several other switchboard items.

In the next section, you create switchboard items that use the macros that were created earlier in this project. First you add a new item that will open the Customer Information form using the macro that opens this form in read-only mode. Then you add an item that utilizes the Print the Orders Grouped by Customer Report macro.

To Create Switchboard Items That Run Macros

1 **Click <u>N</u>ew and type** `View Customer Information`.
The Edit Switchboard text box is changed.

2 **In the <u>C</u>ommand box select Run Macro from the drop-down list.**
The command reflects the action you want to take.

3 **Click the <u>M</u>acro list arrow and choose View Customer Information.**
The macro you created to open the Customer Information form in read-only mode will be activated when this menu item is selected (see Figure 12.23).

4 **Click OK. Repeat steps 1 through 3 to create another switchboard item that uses the** `Print the Orders Grouped by Customer Report macro`.
The Edit Switchboard Item dialog box should look like the one in Figure 12.24.

continues ▶

To Create Switchboard Items That Run Macros (continued)

Figure 12.23
The Edit Switchboard Item dialog box displays the command and macro that have been chosen.

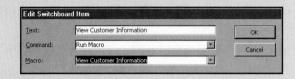

Figure 12.24
The Switchboard item to print a report using a macro is defined.

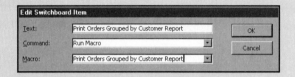

⑤ **Click OK.**
The Edit Switchboard Page shows five items listed (see Figure 12.25).

Figure 12.25
The Main Switchboard contains five items.

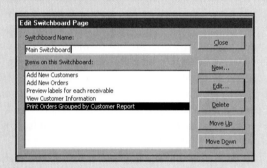

⑥ **Click Close to return to the Switchboard Manager, then click Close again to close the Switchboard Manager dialog box.**

⑦ **Click the Forms object button if necessary.**
The switchboard form is now listed with the rest of the forms in the database.

⑧ **Double-click the Switchboard form to open it.**
The switchboard is displayed with the five items you created listed (see Figure 12.26).

⑨ **Click Add New Customers.**
The Customer Information form opens in add only mode (see Figure 12.27).

⑩ **Click the Close Form button to return to the switchboard.**

⑪ **Test each additional button on the switchboard to make sure it performs as expected.**

⑫ **Close the Switchboard by clicking the Close Window button.**
The Switchboard form closes and the Database window is displayed. Leave the Customer Orders 5 database open for the next lesson.

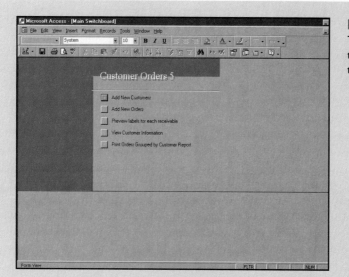

Figure 12.26
The switchboard lists the actions that can be taken.

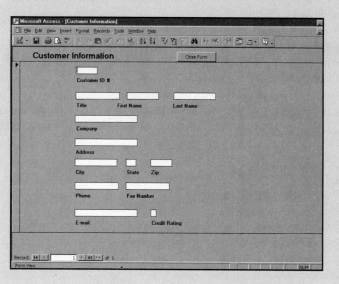

Figure 12.27
The switchboard command opens the form specified.

Inside Stuff: Multi-Tiered Switchboards

If you have more options than will fit on one switchboard or you would like to have multiple levels of switchboards, one of the commands available in the Command box is Go to Switchboard. You can use this to string together several switchboards and to branch from one to another.

Exam Note: Modifying an Existing Switchboard

Once you have created the switchboard, you can modify it by returning to the Switchboard Manager. Choose Tools, Database Utilities, Switchboard Manager, and add or delete items to the switchboard as needed. If you want to modify the design elements in a switchboard, such as the font size or background color, use Form Design view.

If you look at the Tables object list you will notice that a Switchboard Items table has been created. Access creates this table to help manage the form and track the relationship between the items on the switchboard. Do not make any changes to this table.

Lesson 6: Creating a Macro to Automatically Launch the Main Switchboard Form

The Main Switchboard form now performs most of the functions someone would need for everyday use of the database. You could turn the maintenance of the database and production of routine reports over to a staff person who has much less training on Access. It would be convenient if the Main Switchboard form came up automatically whenever this database is opened. Fortunately, there is a special macro name that is reserved for this purpose.

To Create a Macro to Automatically Launch the Main Switchboard Form

1 In the Customer Orders 5 database, click the Macros object button and click the **N**ew button.

2 Select the OpenForm action.

3 Select the form name Switchboard in the Action Arguments area.

4 Click the second Action box and select Maximize from the drop-down list box.
This action maximizes the switchboard form to fill the screen (see Figure 12.28).

Figure 12.28
The Autoexec macro contains two actions.

The macro performs two actions

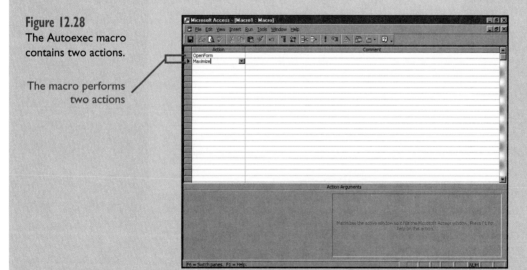

5 Close the macro and name it Autoexec.
Do not include the period. This name means "automatically execute" and is recognized as a macro that is run whenever the database is opened.

6 Close the database.

7 Open the database to test this feature.
The Main Switchboard form appears automatically.

X *If You Have Problems...*
If your switchboard does not open automatically, it almost always means that you have misspelled the word "autoexec." If this is the case, click the Macros object button, right-click on the file name, and select Rename from the shortcut menu. Correct the spelling of the name and try it again.

8 **Close the switchboard form.**

This takes you back to the usual Database window.

9 **Close the database.**

If you have completed your session on the computer, exit Access and shut down Windows before you turn off the computer. Otherwise, continue with the exercises.

Inside Stuff: **Closing Access with a Macro**

You can also create a macro to close the database and Access at the same time. The action for that macro is Quit, with the Save All argument.

Summary

In this project, you created a generic macro that could be used to close any form. You also created a macro to print a report. You learned how to use the Macro Builder in the form design view to create a macro that opens a form in read-only mode. You placed macros on buttons on several forms. Then you used the Switchboard Manager to create a switchboard to act as a menu for your database. Finally, you made the switchboard appear automatically every time you open the database by adding an Autoexec macro.

You can enhance your knowledge of macros by using the available help to examine other types of arguments you can use. You might also find out if there are ways to run macros other than attaching them to buttons.

Checking Concepts and Terms

True/False

For each of the following statements, check *T* or *F* to indicate whether the statement is true or false.

__T __F   **1.** Actions in a macro can be chosen from a drop-down list. [L1]

__T __F   **2.** If you name a macro Autorun, it will run each time the database is opened. [L6]

__T __F   **3.** In the Action box of the Macro window, you can type the first letter of the desired action to quickly scroll to the actions that begin with that letter. [L2]

__T __F   **4.** Each macro can perform only one action. [L3]

__T __F   **5.** A generic close macro does not have to specify an object name. [L1]

Multiple Choice

Circle the letter of the correct answer for each of the following questions.

1. A value needed for a macro to continue its action is called a(n) _____. [Intro]

a. action

b. macro

c. function

d. argument

2. Which of the following data modes would enable the user to enter new records in a form without scrolling to the next empty record? [L5]

a. Read-Only

b. New Record

c. Edit

d. Add

3. You can open a report using a macro in _____ mode. [L2]

a. Preview

b. Edit

c. Add

d. all of the above

4. After a macro has been created, it should be run to _____. [L2]

a. make sure it works as intended

b. set the macro

c. establish a macro program

d. clear the macro path for a new macro

5. When you name a macro, it is best to use a name that _____. [L1]

a. is one word

b. includes the word macro

c. is no longer than 10 letters or spaces

d. would make sense if it was on a button

Screen ID

Label each element of the Access screens shown in Figure 12.29.

Figure 12.29

A. What will display

B. Macro action

C. Data entry/edit option

D. Used to test a macro

E. Type of object affected by macro

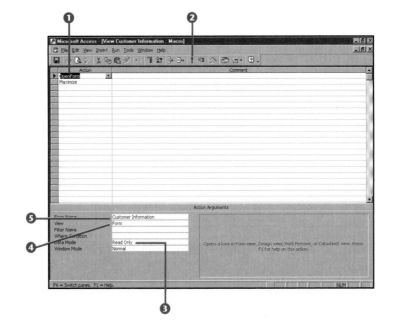

1._____   3._____   5._____

2._____   4._____

Skill Drill

Skill Drill exercises reinforce project skills. Each skill reinforced is the same, or nearly the same, as a skill presented in the project. Each exercise includes a brief narrative introduction, followed by detailed instructions in a step-by-step format.

In these exercises you use the Computer Inventory database you have used in earlier projects. In the Skill Drill section, you will create several macros, put them together in a switchboard, then set up the switchboard to run automatically.

1. Creating Macros Using the Macro Window

Others will use this database and you want to make it as easy as possible for them to work with forms and other objects. In this exercise you create a close button and attach it to forms. Then you create a macro to open a table in read-only view.

To create macros using the Macro window:

1. Copy the file AC-1202 from your CD-ROM to your disk. Use the shortcut menu to deselect the read-only status, and rename the copy as Computer Inventory 5.

2. Click the Macros object button and click New.

3. Select Close from the Action drop-down list box.

4. Close the Macro window and save the macro as Close when prompted.

5. Click New to create another new macro.

6. Choose OpenTable from the Action list. In the comments column, type Open Vendors table in read-only mode.

7. Select the Vendors table from the Table Name list box. Change the Data Mode to Read-Only.

8. Close the macro and save it as View Vendors Table when prompted.

9. Click the Forms object button and open the Vendor and Hardware form in Design view.

10. Move the pointer to the bottom of the Form Footer bar. When it turns into a black two-sided arrow, click and drag down about a 1/2 inch.

11. Deselect the Control Wizards button, if necessary.

12. Click the Command Button and click on the right side of the footer to place a command button in the Form Footer area.

13. Right-click the command button and choose Properties from the shortcut menu.

14. Click the Format tab and type Close Form in the Caption box.

15. Click the Event tab and click the list arrow in the On Click box and choose Close from the list. Save the changes to the form.

16. Repeat steps 9 through 15 to add a Close button to the bottom of the Vendors form.

17. Leave the Computer Inventory 5 database open if you intend to do the next exercise; otherwise close the database.

2. Using the Macro Builder to View Forms

You can also create macros directly in the design view of a form by using the Macro Builder. Next you create a macro to open a form in read-only view using the Macro Builder.

To use the Macro Builder to view a form:

1. If you did the first exercise, skip this step. Otherwise, copy the file AC-1202 from your CD-ROM. Use the shortcut menu to deselect the read only status, and rename the copy as Computer Inventory 5. Open the Computer Inventory 5 database.

2. Click the Forms object button and open the Vendor and Hardware form in Design view.

3. Right-click the Form Selector button and choose Build Event from the shortcut menu.

4. Select the Macro Builder and click OK.

5. Name the macro View Vendor and Hardware Records.

6. Choose OpenForm as the action and select Vendor and Hardware from the Form Name list box. Change the Data Mode box to Read Only.

7. Close the Macro window and save the changes when prompted.

8. Close the Form window and save the changes when prompted.

9. Click the Macros object button and run the View Vendor and Hardware Records macro to test it.

10. Close the Form. Leave the `Computer Inventory 5` database open if you intend to do the next exercise.

3. Creating a Switchboard Using the Switchboard Manager

Next you create a switchboard to be used as a menu for this database so that users can easily access the information they need. In the last part of this exercise you create an Autoexec macro to open the switchboard menu automatically when the database file is opened.

To create a switchboard using the Switchboard Manager:

1. If you did the previous exercise, skip this step. If necessary, copy the file `AC-1202` from your CD-ROM. Use the shortcut menu to deselect the read-only status, and rename the copy as `Computer Inventory 5`. Open the `Computer Inventory 5` database.

2. Choose Tools, Database Utilities, Switchboard Manager from the menu. Click Yes to create a new switchboard.

3. Choose Edit to open the Edit Switchboard dialog box.

4. Click New to add a new item to the switchboard.

5. Type `Add New Vendors` in the Text box.

6. Choose Open Form in Add Mode in the Command list box.

7. Select Vendors from the Form list box and click OK.

8. Repeat steps 4 through 7 to add a new item that will open the Vendor and Hardware form in Add mode. Name it `Add New Hardware`.

9. Repeat steps 4 through 7 to add a new item that will open the Mailing Labels for Vendors Report. Name it `Vendor Mailing Labels`.

10. Repeat steps 4 through 7 to add a new item that will open the Folder Labels by Processor report. Name it `Processor Folder Labels`.

11. If you completed exercise 1 or 2, use the Run Macro command to create switchboard items that use the macros created to open the Vendors table, and/or View the Vendor and Hardware Records.

12. Close the Edit Switchboard Page and close the Switchboard Manager.

13. Click the Forms object button, if necessary. Open the switchboard and test each of the items on the switchboard.

14. Click the Macros object button, if necessary, then click New.

15. Select the OpenForm action.

16. Select Switchboard from the Form Name box in the Action Arguments area.

17. Click in the second action box row and select Maximize as the action.

18. Close the window and save the macro as `Autoexec` when prompted.

19. Close the database, then re-open it. It should run your new switchboard automatically.

20. Close the database. If you are not going to go on to the Challenge exercises, exit Access.

Challenge

Challenge exercises expand on or are somewhat related to skills presented in the lessons. Each exercise provides a brief narrative introduction followed by instructions in a numbered step format that are not as detailed as those in the Skill Drill section.

The database you will use for the Challenge exercises is a slightly modified version of the Computer Inventory 5 database you used in the Skill Drill exercises.

If you completed all of the project lessons and Skill Drill exercises using one disk, you should use a new disk for the Challenge exercises so you do not run out of space. If you are saving files to a hard drive, be aware that the files used for the Challenge exer-cises will use about 1 MB of space.

1. Working with Existing Macros

After you create a macro, you may decide that you need to change it. Just like other objects, you can return to the design of a macro and modify it. You can use one macro as the basis for creating a second macro or delete macros, just like you do other objects. If a macro has been attached to a switchboard or some other form, you will want to remove it from those areas first. In this exercise, you modify an existing macro, then use it as the basis for a new macro, and then you delete a macro.

1. Copy the file AC-1203 from your CD-ROM to a blank disk. Use the shortcut menu to deselect the read-only status, and rename the copy as Computer Inventory 5-2. Open the database.

2. Select the Add a New Vendor macro and click the Design button. Add a Maximize action. Close and save your changes.

3. Select the Add a New Vendor macro and click the Design button. Change the form that is opened to the Vendor and Hardware form. Save it using the Save As dialog box and name it Add New PC Hardware. Close the macro.

4. Select the Preview Folder Labels macro and click the Design button. Add a maximize action and save the changes.

5. Select the Preview Folder Labels macro and click the Design button. Change the report that is opened to the Mailing Labels for Vendors. Change the View to Print. Save the changes as Print Vendor Labels. Close the macro

6. Run the Look at Current PCs macro. You realize that this is a subform and is not very useful.

7. Close the form and delete the macro that opened the form.

8. Leave the Computer Inventory 5-2 database open if you intend to do the next exercise.

2. Adding Command Buttons Using the Command Button Wizard

In this project you learned how to add command buttons to a form by attaching a macro to a button. You can also add a command button to a form by using the Command Button Wizard in Form Design view. To do this, the Control Wizards button needs to be activated. Then you click the Command Button in the toolbox and click on the form. The Command Button Wizard launches and you simply follow the steps in the Wizard to create a command button.

1. If you did the first Challenge exercise, skip this step and use the database file from the previous exercise. Otherwise, copy the file AC-1203 from your CD-ROM. Use the shortcut menu to deselect the read-only status, and rename the copy Computer Inventory 5-2. Open the database.

2. Open the Vendor and Hardware form in Design view. Make sure the Control Wizards button on the toolbox is active.

3. Click the Command button on the toolbox and then click to the right of the Close button in the Form Footer section of the form.

4. On the first page of the Command Button Wizard select Record Navigations from the Categories list, and Goto Next Record from the Actions list. Click Next.

5. On the second page of the Wizard select the Text option button, then click Next.

6. On the third page of the Wizard type Next Record as the name of the button, then click Finish.

7. Repeat this process to add a second button to the Form Footer. Select the Record Operations category and choose the action Add New Record. Choose the Text option and name the button Add Record.

8. Save your changes. Go to the Form view and test the new buttons to make sure they work.

9. Close the form. Leave the `Computer Inventory 5-2` database open if you intend to do the next exercise.

3. Using Multi-Tiered Switchboards

When you create a switchboard using the Switchboard Manager you can create several switchboards. The Main Switchboard can be used as a control center that opens other switchboard menus. Each sub-menu can then be designated for a specific purpose, such as opening forms, previewing reports, or printing reports. Each sub-menu then has a return to Main Switchboard action that enables the user to return to the main menu and select another switchboard page.

1. If you did the first Challenge exercise, skip this step and use the database file from the previous exercise. Otherwise, copy the file `AC-1203` from your CD-ROM. Use the shortcut menu to deselect the read-only status, and rename the copy as `Computer Inventory 5-2`. Open the database.

2. Open the Switchboard Manager and choose Yes to create a new switchboard.

3. Choose New and type `Open Forms`. Repeat this step and create another switchboard page named `View Reports`. Two new switchboard pages are added to the list.

4. Select the Main Switchboard and choose Edit.

5. Choose New, type `Open Forms`, and choose Open Forms from the Switchboard list box. Repeat this step and create a command that goes to the View Reports switchboard. Name it `View Reports`. Now the Main Switchboard has two buttons that open the other switchboards.

6. Close the Edit Switchboard Page dialog box.

7. Choose the Open Forms switchboard and click Edit. Create three new items for this switchboard as listed in Table 12.1.

Table 12.1

Text	Command	Form
Add New Hardware	Open Form In Add Mode	Vendor and Hardware
Add/Edit Vendors	Open Form In Edit Mode	Vendors
Return to Main Switchboard	Go to Switchboard	Main Switchboard

8. Then close the Edit Switchboard Page dialog box.

9. Repeat steps 6 and 8 and create the four items listed in Table 12.2 for the View Reports switchboard.

Table 12.2

Text	Command	Report
View Vendor and Hardware Report	Open Report	Vendor and Hardware
View Folder Labels	Open Report	Folder Labels by Processor
Print Vendor Labels	Run Macro	Print Vendor Labels
Return to Main Switchboard	Go to Switchboard	Main Switchboard

10. Close the Edit Switchboard Page dialog box and close the Switchboard Manager. Open the Switchboard form and test it to make sure all of the links work correctly.

11. Close the Switchboard form and close the database.

Discovery Zone

Discovery Zone exercises help you gain advanced knowledge of project topics and application of skills. These exercises focus on enhancing your problem-solving skills. Numbered steps are not provided, but you are given hints, reminders, screen shots, and references to help you reach your goal for each exercise.

The database you use is a modified version of the Computer Inventory database you have been using in the Skill Drill and Challenge sections.

1. Setting Macro Conditions

Access enables you to set conditions when you write a macro. For example, you can have a report print out just the equipment purchased between two dates, or print just those items that have an entry in a particular field. Use the `AC-1204` database, renamed `Computer Inventory 5-3`.

Goal: Edit the Print Mailing Labels macro to preview only those vendors in Ypsilanti, then add a button to the switchboard.

- Create a macro that views the mailing labels for only those vendors located in `Ypsilanti`.
- Rename the macro `Ypsilanti Mailing Labels`.
- Choose text for the button that indicates the function the macro will perform.

Hint #1: You can find help by clicking in the Where Condition box in the Action Arguments area and pressing F1.

Hint #2: Enter the table name first followed by an exclamation point, then the field name followed by an equals sign. The value you are looking for must be in quotes.

Hint #3: The rules for using a field name in an expression also apply to the table name.

2. Using a Blank Form to Create a Switchboard

Rather than using the Switchboard Manager, you can create a custom designed switchboard by dragging macros onto a blank form. In this exercise, you use the `AC-1203` database to create a switchboard without using the Switchboard Manager. Rename the database `Computer Inventory 5-4`.

Goal: Create a custom designed switchboard form from scratch that resembles the one shown in Figure 12.30.

In this exercise, you should:

- use a blank form design that is not based on any table or query.
- use the Window, Tile Vertically menu option to place the Database window and form design window side-by-side.
- change the Database window to the Macros objects and click and drag all of the macros onto the blank form.
- arrange the buttons as shown in Figure 12.30.
- select the font, font size, and font color that you prefer.

■ add a title to the form and change the color of the background.

■ save the form with the name **Main Menu**.

Close the switchboard and test it to make sure it works properly.

Figure 12.30

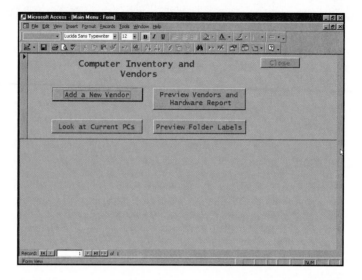

PinPoint Assessment

You have completed the project and its associated lessons, and have had an opportunity to assess your skills through the end-of-project questions and exercises. Now use the PinPoint software Evaluation Mode to further assess your comprehension of the specific exam activities you have just learned. You can also use the PinPoint Trainer Mode and the Show Me tutorials to practice these exam activities.

Managing Your Databases with Special Action Queries and Database Utilities

Key terms introduced in this project include

- archive table
- compact
- MDE file
- text qualifier

Objectives	Required Activity for MOUS	Exam Level
➤ Make Backup Copies of Your Data Using the Export Feature	Backup and restore a database	Core
➤ Back Up and Restore the Entire Database	Backup and restore a database	Core
➤ Save an Access 2000 Database as an Access 97 Database	Convert database to a previous version	Expert
➤ Create a Replica for a Mobile User	Use simple replication (copy for a mobile user)	Expert
➤ Compact and Repair Files for Efficient Storage	Compact and repair a database	Core
➤ Create a Query That Creates an Archive Table	Create an action query (update, delete, insert)	Expert
➤ Modify the Archive Setup Query to Delete Records from a Table	Create an action query (update, delete, insert)	Expert
➤ Create a Query to Append Records to an Archive Table	Create an action query (update, delete, insert)	Expert
➤ Create a Macro to Run Two Queries		
➤ Transfer Access Data to Excel	Export database records to Excel	Expert

Why Would I Do This?

Databases, particularly those used regularly, require some upkeep. This is true of a database for a user on a single machine or for a database used by many people on a network.

One of the first things every database user learns, often the hard way, is to make regular backups of frequently used database files. Accidents do happen, particularly when more than one person uses the database. Files can become damaged, or even be accidentally erased. If you have a regular backup plan, you can minimize the disruption and inconvenience a file problem could cause. There are several ways to backup your data. You can use the copy-and-paste procedure to duplicate the file, or you can export the data in the tables into text files. You might also try backing up your data with either a commercial file backup program or with the Backup program that comes with Windows.

You may also need to share a database with a colleague who is using the previous version of the program, Access 97, also called Access 7.0. Access 2000 enables you to convert a database for use with Access 97.

When you delete and add a lot of records to one or more tables in a database, the database file can become fragmented. This can cause the database to take up more room than necessary on your disk drive and can slow database operations. Access has a feature that loads the database into memory and puts the file back into a single block of information. This speeds up the program and save disk space.

Occasionally databases become corrupted (damaged) and need repair. Sometimes Access detects the damage and prompts you to repair it. Sometimes you can repair the damage even if Access does not automatically recognize that damage has occurred.

Another common problem is the proliferation of records in some tables. When a great deal of data is added to a table, the amount of time needed to do such things as search and sort can increase greatly. In some cases older, "completed" records don't belong in a table. For example, a business that records customer orders in a table might want to remove them when the transaction is completed. Access enables you to move completed records from an active table to an **_archive table_**, which is used to store old, inactive data. You may then delete the records from the original table. Once the queries have been created to archive and delete completed data, you can create a macro and attach it to a button in the switchboard.

Lesson 1: Making Backup Copies of Your Data Using the Export Feature

One method of backing up your information is to export your tables into text files. This method enables you to save the data in your tables without saving the design of your queries, forms, reports, macros, or modules.

There are several benefits to saving your data into text files. First, you reduce the file size by up to 90 percent. Second, you can read this type of text file directly into other databases, spreadsheets, and word processors. Finally, you can give the data set to someone using an earlier version of Access, such as Access 2.0 or Access 95. The other objects, such as reports and forms, will not be saved, but at least the user of an older version of the software can access the data.

In this exercise, you save the data from three tables as text files. The database you will be using is a record of the 807 tornadoes recorded in Michigan over a forty-five year period (1951-1995). The information was compiled from National Oceanic and Atmospheric Administration records.

If you are working on a floppy disk, be sure to start this project with an empty, formatted disk.

To Make Backup Copies of Your Data Using the Export Feature

1 **Copy the AC-1301 file to your disk, remove the read-only status, re-name it Michigan Tornadoes, and open the database.**

2 **If necessary, select the Tables object button and highlight the Michigan table.**

You must use the following procedure for each table you want to back up; Access only backs up the highlighted table.

3 **Choose Export from the File menu. Select the destination for your data file, accept the default File name, and select Text Files from the Save as type drop-down list box.**

The dialog box should look like Figure 13.1.

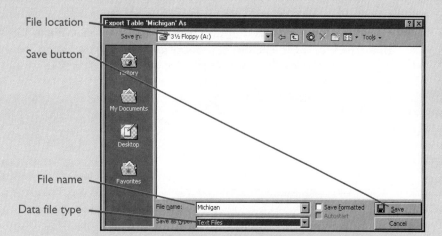

File location

Save button

File name

Data file type

Figure 13.1
The Export Table 'Michigan' As dialog box enables you to choose the data type of the new data file.

4 **Click the Save button in the Export Table dialog box.**

The first Export Text Wizard dialog box is displayed (see Figure 13.2).

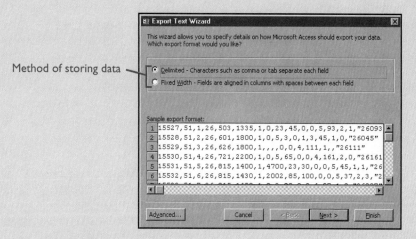

Method of storing data

Figure 13.2
The Export Text Wizard dialog box enables you to choose an export format.

continues ▶

To Make Backup Copies of Your Data Using the Export Feature (continued)

Inside Stuff: **Use of Delimiters Saves Disk Space**
By default, the <u>D</u>elimited option is selected. A delimiter is an ASCII character, such as a tab, comma, semicolon, or space that separates fields in a text file. This means that the contents of each field can be of variable length. The <u>D</u>elimited option saves disk space when the widths of field entries vary.

Inside Stuff: **File Names of Text Files**
The default File name is the same as the table name. When the data is saved as a text file, the program adds a .txt extension, which will help you identify the types of the file on your disk.

⑤ **Make sure the <u>D</u>elimited option is selected, then click <u>N</u>ext. Confirm that Comma is the chosen delimiter and double quotation marks are selected as the Text <u>Q</u>ualifier. Click the <u>I</u>nclude Field Names on First Row check box (see Figure 13.3).**
The type of delimiter used may depend on the application to which you are exporting the file. In this case we will use commas, which are the default choice. The default ***text qualifier*** is quotation marks. This means that every text field entry will be exported surrounded by quotation marks.

Figure 13.3
The second Export Text Wizard dialog box gives you the option of choosing a delimiter and a text qualifier.

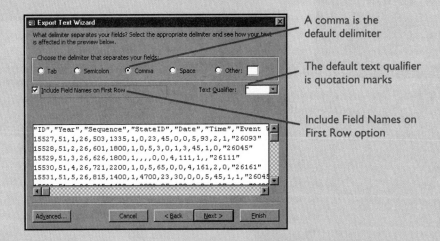

A comma is the default delimiter

The default text qualifier is quotation marks

Include Field Names on First Row option

⑥ **Click <u>N</u>ext.**
The final Export Text Wizard dialog box is displayed (see Figure 13.4). This dialog box enables you to rename the file, if you want. The default name is the same as the table with a .txt extension.

⑦ **Click <u>F</u>inish.**
A message box tells you that the text file was successfully created (see Figure 13.5). It also gives you the name of the file, including the extension.

⑧ **Click OK, and then highlight the County Names table. Repeat steps 3 through 7 to export the data in the County Names table as text.**

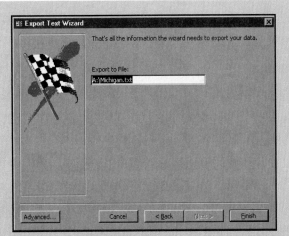

Figure 13.4
The final Export Text Wizard dialog box enables you to rename the file.

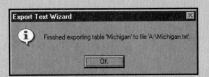

Figure 13.5
A message box tells you that your data has been exported to a text file.

9 **Click OK, and then highlight the State Names table. Repeat steps 3 through 7 to export the data in the State Names table as text.**

10 **Launch the Windows Explorer program and look at the file sizes of the original file and the three table text files.**

Notice that the text files, which contain all of the data in this database, total about 138KB, while the original file is 460KB. (Note: Your numbers may vary depending which version of Windows you are using.)

11 **Double-click the Michigan text file.**

The file opens up in WordPad (see Figure 13.6). Notice that the text field is surrounded by quotation marks, while numbers are not. The field names are displayed in the first row.

Field names

Text qualifiers (quotation marks)

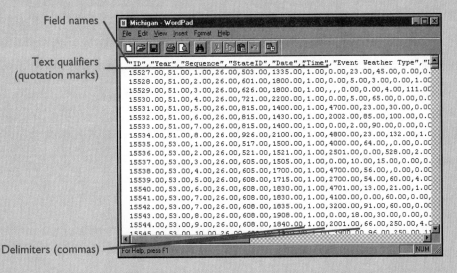

Delimiters (commas)

Figure 13.6
The exported text viewed in WordPad has quotation marks around the text field, with commas separating all fields.

12 **Close the WordPad window and return to the Michigan Tornadoes database. Close the database.**

Exam Note: **Backing Up and Restoring the Entire Database**

In this lesson you backed up only the data. If you want to make backups of your whole database, make sure that the database is not in use by anyone, and use the Windows Explorer (or My Computer) to copy the database and paste it to a floppy disk, zip disk, or network drive. To restore the backup file as the original, copy the backup file and paste it into the folder that contains the original file. Windows Explorer or My Computer will ask if you want to replace the file by the same name that is already in the folder. If you choose to do so, the backup file will replace the file in the folder.

Lesson 2: Saving an Access 2000 Database as an Access 97 Database

You may be working with a colleague who does not have Access 2000, or you may want to take the database home or to a lab that still has Access 97 installed. Access now provides a procedure for converting an Access 2000 database into an Access 97 database. It does not, however, enable you to convert it into any of the earlier versions. The process creates a new file and does not erase the Access 2000 version of the database.

In this lesson, you take a database created in Access 2000 and convert it into an Access 97 file.

To Save an Access 2000 Database as an Access 97 Database

1 **Locate the AC-1302 file and open the database. You do not have to copy the file to your disk or remove the read-only property.**

2 **Choose Tools, Database Utilities, Convert Database, To Prior Access Database Version from the menu.**
The Convert Database Into dialog box is displayed.

3 **Type PC Training-Access 97 in the File name box and select your disk in the Save in box.**

4 **Click the Save button.**
The new file is created on your disk, then you are returned to the original AC-1302 database.

5 **Close the AC-1302 database. Open the PC Training-Access 97 database from your disk.**
Access no longer recognizes the database as an Access 2000 file. Instead, the Convert/Open Database dialog box is displayed (see Figure 13.7).

6 **Click Cancel to leave the database unopened.**

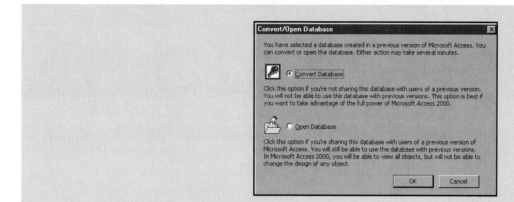

Figure 13.7
Access no longer rec-
ognizes the database
as an Access 2000 file.

> ***Exam Note: Creating a Replica for a Mobile User***
> If your work takes you out of the office but you still need to work with the data-
> base, you can make a replica of the database that can be copied to another com-
> puter such as a laptop. When you return and connect the laptop computer to your
> desktop computer (using a cable or network connection) it is possible to synchro-
> nize the two so that changes made to either version of the database are updated in
> both. To create a replica of a database, open the database and choose <u>T</u>ools,
> Replication, <u>C</u>reate Replica. To find out more about this feature, use the Answer
> Wizard in Access Help and type How do I create a replica of a database?

Lesson 3: Compacting and Repairing Files for Efficient Storage

After you use your database for a while, it is likely that some fragmentation will occur. This
causes the database to use more disk space than necessary and may cause the program to
perform poorly. Access reserves room on the disk for tables, queries, forms, and reports that
have been deleted. In this lesson, you use one of the Access database tools to **compact** and
repair the AC-1302 database, which strips out the extra blank space saved with the database.
While it is compacting the file, Access looks for possible problems and fixes them.

When you delete data or database objects from your hard disk, you create areas of unused
space of varying sizes that are scattered about the disk. The computer's operating system will
try to use these spaces when you add new data. If the new data will not fit into one of the
unused spaces, the system will divide the new data into segments and fit them into the available spaces. When you need to list your database, the computer must hunt all over the disk
to find the segments and reassemble them. Also, when Access deletes objects from a file, it
does not free up the area where the data was stored, but simply marks it as having been
deleted.

To Compact and Repair Files for Efficient Storage

1 **Launch Windows Explorer, if necessary, and check the file size of the AC-1302 database.**
The database should be about 264KB.

2 **Switch to Access. Do not open the database.**

3 **In the Tools menu choose Database Utilities, and then select Compact and Repair Database.**
The Database to Compact From dialog box is displayed. This is the basic Office Find Files dialog box.

4 **Find the AC-1302 database and select it.**

5 **Click the Compact button. Select your disk in the Save in box and type AC-1302 Compacted in the File name box.**
The Compact Database Into dialog box is used to rename the file and save it in a location of your choice (see Figure 13.8).

Figure 13.8
The Compact Database Into dialog box asks you for a new file name.

File name

If You Have Problems...
The Compact and Repair procedure creates a second database file. If you are using a floppy disk that is nearly full, you will get an error message. Remove some of the files from your floppy disk, or use a new one.

6 **Click Save.**
Access compacts the database with the new name. If you try to save the file using the same name, in the same location as the original, a message box appears telling you the file name already exists and asking if you want to replace it. It is a good idea to use a different file name and use the old version as a backup.

7 **Switch to the Windows Explorer and check the new file size.**
The database should now be about 188KB (it may vary slightly). You may have to use the View, Refresh option from the menu to update the display. The compacting procedure reduced the file size by about a third.

Inside Stuff: **Compacting Files to Fit on Floppy Disks**
If you have to transport your database files on floppy disks, this procedure can be extremely helpful. In many cases, you can take a database that is too large for a floppy and reduce it in size so that it will fit. If you have a very large database (up to 5 or 6 megabytes), you can use one of the commercial archiving programs. These reduce file size by up to 80 percent.

Lesson 4: Creating a Query That Creates an Archive Table

Setting up an archive of old records and removing them from the active table is a three-step process and is done with three queries. First, you have to create a query to create an archive table. Then you have to create a query to append records to the archive table in the future. Finally, you need to create a query to remove the archived records from the active table.

The first step in creating an archive system for your database is to create the archive table. This archive table can be created in either the active database or another database. You do this once to create the archive table; then either delete the query or change and rename it (as you do in the next lesson), because running it again will cause Access to write over the old archive table.

To Create a Query That Creates an Archive Table

❶ Copy the AC-1303 file to your disk, remove the read-only status, rename it Customer Orders, and open the database.

❷ Click the Close button to close the switchboard, then click the Queries object button and click New.
The New Query dialog box is displayed.

❸ Select Design View from the New Query dialog box, and then click OK.
The Show Table dialog box is displayed (see Figure 13.9).

Orders table

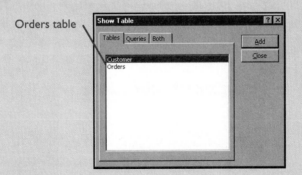

Figure 13.9
The Show Table dialog box lists the tables available for your query.

❹ Select the Orders table, click Add, and then Close the Show Table dialog box.

❺ Select all of the fields and add them to the Field row.

continues ▶

To Create a Query That Creates an Archive Table (continued)

6 **Use the scrollbar to move to the right until you can see the Date of Payment field, then type `>0` in the Date of Payment Criteria box.**
The >0 (greater than zero) identifies those records that have an entry in the Date of Payment field. Those that have been paid will be sent to the archive table. Your Query dialog box should look like Figure 13.10.

Figure 13.10
The Criteria box has been filled in for the Date of Payment field.

Criterion

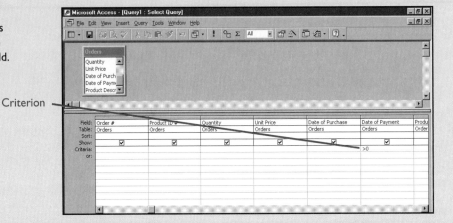

ⓘ *Inside Stuff:* **Problems with the Date Search Expression**
Using >0 in the Criteria box for a date field works well if the dates you are looking for all occur on or after 01/01/1900. If you are working with historical data, you need to know that this procedure will not find any dates before 1900.

---

 7 **Click the arrow on the right of the Query Type button, and then select the Ma̱ke-Table Query option.**
A Make Table dialog box appears, asking you what you want to call the table.

8 **Enter the table name `Completed Orders`.**
Accept the default of C̲urrent Database (see Figure 13.11). If your database is getting too large, you can use the A̲nother Database option in the Make Table dialog box to send the table to another database file.

Figure 13.11
The Make Table dialog box enables you to add the table to the current database or to another database.

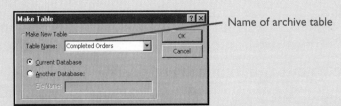

Name of archive table

9 **Click OK, then close the query, save it, and name it `Archive Setup`. Click OK.**
At this point, the query has been designed, but it has not created the table.

🔟 **Select the Archive Setup query and click O̲pen.**
A message box is displayed, warning that you will be modifying data in your table (see Figure 13.12).

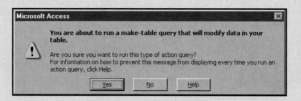

11 **Click Yes.**

Another message box appears, telling you how many records will be added to the new table, and warning you that you will not be able to undo this action (see Figure 13.13).

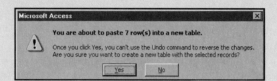

Figure 13.13
The message box warns that you will not be able to undo this action.

This warning is not as dire as it sounds in this instance. If you want to delete the new table, it is easy to do so. This message is more important when you are removing data.

12 **Click Yes. Locate the Completed Orders table and open it. Confirm that it only contains records that have a date of payment. Close the table.**

Notice that only the records that have a date in the Date of Payment field have been copied.

13 **Open the Orders table. Confirm that this table still has the records with no date of payment. Close the Orders table.**

Leave the Customer Orders database open for the next lesson.

 Inside stuff: **Defusing a Potential Make Table Query Problem**

When you have confirmed that the appropriate records have been copied to the archive table, it is a good idea to remove the query that created the table. You can do this by deleting or changing the function of the query. This will ensure that no one will accidentally create a new table that writes over the archive file.

Lesson 5: Modifying the Archive Setup Query to Delete Records from a Table

In the previous lesson, you created a query to archive those records that have an entry in the Date of Payment field. That query is now of no use; in fact, it is dangerous to leave it in your database, especially if more than one person has access to the file.

The Archive Setup query copied records to the Completed Orders table, but did not remove them from the Orders table. In this lesson, you change the function of the query you created in the previous lesson from a Make Table query to a Delete query, which deletes the records that have been archived from the original table.

To Modify the Archive Setup Query to Delete Records from a Table

1 Click the **Queries** object button in the `Customer Orders` database, if necessary, and right-click the **Archive Setup query.**
The shortcut menu is displayed.

2 Choose **Rename**, then type in `Delete Archived Records from the Orders Table.`

3 Click the **Design button.**
The Make Table Query Design window is displayed.

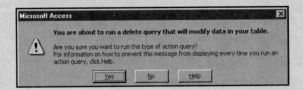

4 Click the arrow on the right of the **Query Type button** and select **Delete Query** from the drop-down list box.

5 Close the query window and save the changes when prompted.
Your Queries window should look like Figure 13.14.

Figure 13.14
The Queries window contains the renamed query.

The new Delete Query ———

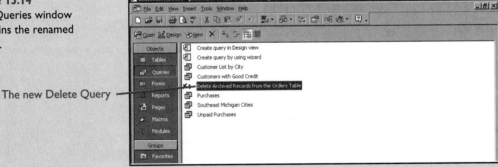

6 Click **Open.**
A message box appears, warning you that you are about to make a change to your table. This message is similar to one you saw in the last lesson (see Figure 13.15).

Figure 13.15
The delete query will remove the records that have a payment date.

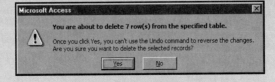

7 Click **Yes.**
Another message box appears, telling you that you are about to delete seven rows and that you will be unable to undo these changes. This message is also similar to one that appeared in the previous lesson (see Figure 13.16).

Figure 13.16
The message box warns that a specific number of rows will be deleted.

8 **Click Yes to delete the records from the Orders table.**

9 **Click the Tables object button, select the Orders table, and click Open.**
Notice that there are only seventeen records in the table now. The other seven have been moved to the Completed Orders table.

10 **Close the table.**
Leave the Customer Orders database open for the next lesson.

Lesson 6: Creating a Query to Append Records to an Archive Table

You have now created an archive table, and built a query to delete records after they have been copied from the Orders table to the archive. The last step is to create a Query you can use on a regular basis to move records from the active table to the archive table you just created.

You can create a new query following the same procedure used in Lesson 4. In this lesson, however, you learn how to save a lot of work by copying the existing query and making one minor modification to it.

To Create a Query to Append Records to an Archive Table

1 **Click the Queries object button in the Customer Orders database and right-click the Delete Archived Records from the Orders Table query.**
A shortcut menu is displayed.

2 **Select Copy from the shortcut menu.**

3 **Right-click on an open spot in the window and select the Paste command.**
The Paste As dialog box is displayed (see Figure 13.17).

Type new query name here

Figure 13.17
The Paste As dialog box enables you to give the new query a name.

4 **Type in the name Append Paid Orders, and then click OK.**
You have copied the Delete Query and renamed it; now all you have to do is change the function of this new query.

5 **Highlight the Append Paid Orders query if necessary, and click Design.**

6 **Click the arrow on the right of the Query Type button and select Append Query.**
An Append dialog box is displayed, asking you which table to send the records to.

7 **Click the drop-down list box in the Table Name box.**
A list of available tables is displayed (see Figure 13.18).

continues ▶

To Create a Query to Append Records to an Archive Table (continued)

Figure 13.18
The Table Name drop-down box displays all available tables.

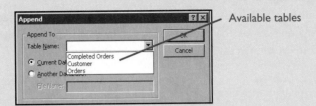

Available tables

8. **Choose the Completed Orders table, click OK, and then close the query. Save your changes when prompted.**

   You are now ready to regularly move paid orders to the archive and delete them from the Orders table.

9. **Click the Tables object button, open the Orders table and add dates to the Date of Payment field for Order # 7 and 12, then close the table.**

10. **Click the Queries object button and open the Append Paid Orders query.**

    This runs the query and appends the records that meet the criteria to the specified table. You will again be warned twice that you are about to make irrevocable changes to your tables.

11. **Open the Delete Archived Records from the Orders Table query to delete the records that meet its criteria.**

    Once again, you are warned twice that you will not be able to undo your changes. Make sure you use the queries in the correct order. If you delete the records first, they will be permanently lost.

12. **Open the Orders table to make sure order numbers 7 and 12 are gone. Close the table.**

13. **Open the Completed Orders table to make sure order numbers 7 and 12 are there. Close the table. Leave the database open for use in the next lesson.**

Lesson 7: Creating a Macro to Run Two Queries and Attaching it to a Switchboard Button

In Lessons 5 and 6 you created queries to append completed records to an archive table, then delete the completed records from the original table. The problem with running these queries is that someone who doesn't understand the program might run them in the wrong order, deleting the completed records before they have been appended to the archive table. You can solve this problem by creating a macro to run the queries in the correct order. You can then attach the macro to a button on your switchboard.

To Create a Macro to Run Two Queries and Attach it to a Switchboard Button

1 **Click the Macros object button and click New.**

2 **Choose Window, Tile Vertically from the menu.**
This option will resize the database object windows and place them side-by-side.

3 **In the Database window, click the Queries object button and drag the Append Paid Orders query to the first Action row in the Macro window. Drag the Delete Archived Records from the Orders Table to the second Action row.**
Your Macro window should look like Figure 13.19. Both actions are the same so you must look at the Query Name in the Action Arguments area to make sure the append query is first and the delete query is second.

Macro window

Selected action

Append Query

Delete Query

Source query for selected action

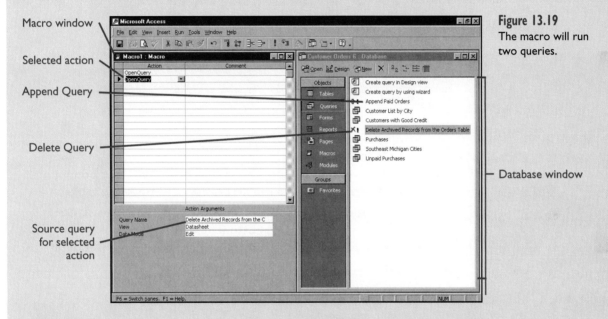

Figure 13.19
The macro will run two queries.

Database window

4 **Close the macro and save it as Update Completed Orders.**

5 **Click the Forms object button, select the Main Switchboard, and click the Design button.**
The Main Switchboard opens in Design view.

6 **Choose Window, Tile Vertically from the menu. Click the Macros object button in the Database window.**

7 **Drag the Update Completed Orders macro to the Main Switchboard. Maximize the Design view of the switchboard form.**

8 **Resize the Update button, move the Close button, and move the Update button to the position the Close button previously occupied.**
The design of the switchboard should look like Figure 13.20.

continues ▶

To Create a Macro to Run Two Queries and Attach it to a Switchboard Button (continued)

Figure 13.20
The macro buttons
are arranged on the
Main Switchboard
form.

New button

Move Close
button here

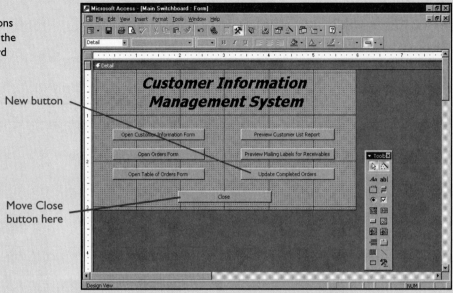

9 **Close the Main Switchboard form and save the changes.**

10 **Click the Tables option button, open the** Orders **table, put a date in the Date of Payment field for the first order, and close the table.**

11 **Click the Forms object button and open the** Main Switchboard. **Click the Update Completed Orders button.**
Notice that you still have to respond to the confirmation dialog boxes.

 Inside Stuff: **Turning Off Confirmation Dialog Boxes**
You can turn off the confirmation dialog boxes by selecting Tools, Options, and clicking the Edit/Find tab. In the Confirm area, you can turn off confirmation on record changes, deletions, and action queries.

12 **Close the switchboard and click the Tables object button. Check the Orders table to verify that order #1 has been deleted. Check the Completed Orders table to verify that order #1 has been appended.**

13 **Close the table. Leave the** Customer Orders **database open for use in the next lesson.**

 Lesson 8: Transferring Access Data to Excel

Access 2000 is not included in some versions of Office 2000. You may need to provide copies of your database tables to others in the form of an Excel workbook.

In this lesson, you export the Orders table to an Excel workbook.

To Transfer Access Data to Excel

1 **Select the Orders table. Choose File, Export from the menu.**
The Export Table 'Orders' To dialog box opens.

2 **Select your disk in the Save in box and select Microsoft Excel 97-2000 in the Save as type box.**
The Convert Database Into dialog box is displayed.

3 **Type PC Training-Access 97 in the File name box and select your disk in the Save in box.**
Your dialog box should display the destination, default file name, and type of file as shown (see Figure 13.21).

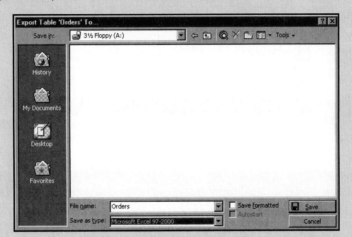

Figure 13.21
The Orders table will be exported to an Excel workbook named Orders.

4 **Click Save.**
The Orders table is exported to your disk as an Excel workbook.

5 **Close the table and the database. Close Access and launch Excel.**

6 **Open the Orders workbook in Excel.**
Confirm that the field names were copied into the first row and the records fill the rows below (see Figure 13.22).

7 **Close the worksheet and close Excel.**

continues ▶

To Transfer Access Data to Excel (continued)

Figure 13.22
The Orders table has
been exported to
Excel.

Field names in first row

Records

Table name becomes the
sheet name

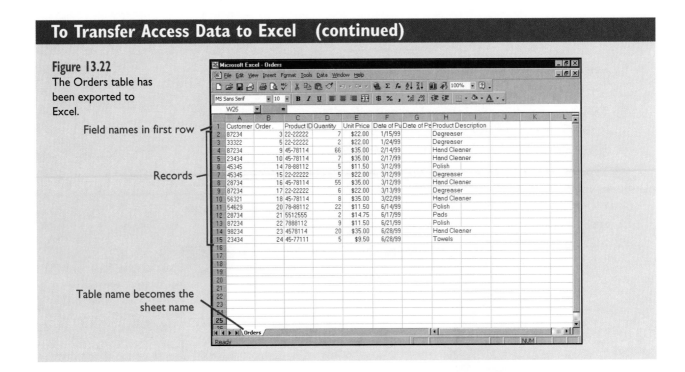

Summary

In this project, you looked at various ways to manage your database. You backed up data from tables to text files, and you converted an Access 2000 database to Access 97. You used Access and Windows tools to compact and repair databases. You learned a three-step procedure for moving completed records to an archive table and automated the procedure by adding a button to a switchboard. Finally, you transferred a table from Access into Excel.

To learn more about Access action queries, go to Help and look at the topic "What is an action query and when would you use one?" You can learn more about Delete, Update, Append, and Make-table action queries.

Checking Concepts and Terms

True/False

For each of the following statements, check *T* or *F* to indicate whether the statement is true or false.

__T __F   **1.** You can save a database created in Access 2000 as an Access 2.0 file. [L2]

__T __F   **2.** A text qualifier is a set of single or double quotation marks that surround text fields in a text file. [L1]

__T __F   **3.** When you compact a database, it is a good idea to write the compacted version over the old version. [L3]

__T __F   **4.** It is a good idea to keep the Make Table Query around in case you need to back up your data again. [L4]

__T __F   **5.** If you use a Delete Query and decide you didn't really want to delete the records, you can recover them by clicking the Undo button. [L5]

Multiple Choice

Circle the letter of the correct answer for each of the following questions.

1. The Export command from the File menu saves _____. [L1]

  a. only the highlighted table

  b. all of the tables in the database

  c. the highlighted table and any associated forms, queries, and reports

  d. all tables, forms, queries, and reports

2. If you enter >0 in a date field's criteria box, you are asking the query to show _____. [L4]

  a. any records containing dates after the current date

  b. any records containing dates before the current date

  c. any records containing dates with only the year entered

  d. all records with any date (after 1900) in that field

3. You can convert Access 2000 databases to _____. [L2]

  a. Access 1 and 2 only

  b. Access 2 only

  c. Access 7 (97) only

  d. all older versions of Access

4. To reduce the size of the database, it is a good idea to use the _____ command occasionally. [L3]

  a. Compact and Repair Database

  b. Compress and Repair Database

  c. Reduce and Repair Database

  d. Pack Database

5. A delimiter is _____. [L1]

  a. a set of quotation marks around text in a text file

  b. ASCII characters such as tabs or spaces used to separate fields in a text file

  c. a restriction as to how long a text file field can be

  d. a fixed-length field size in a text file

Screen ID

Label each element of the Access screen shown in Figure 13.23.

Figure 13.23

A. Delimiter

B. Text qualifier

C. Data record in text format

D. Field names

E. Text editing program

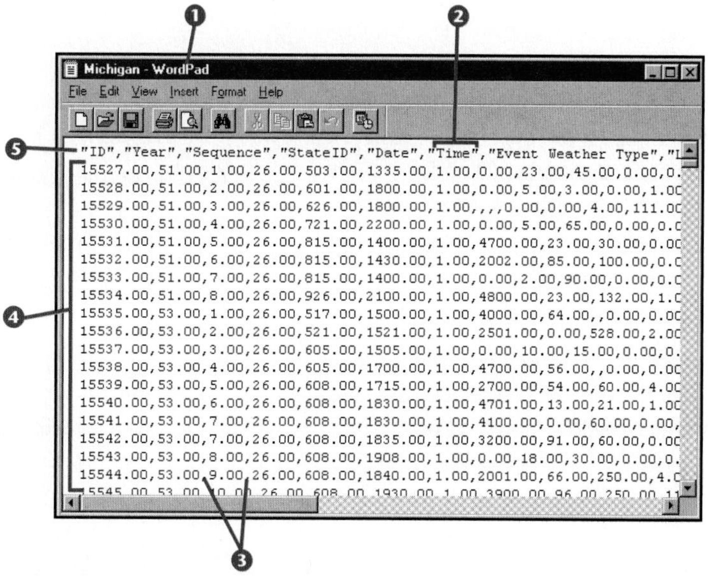

1._____ 3._____ 5._____

2._____ 4._____

Skill Drill

Skill Drill exercises reinforce project skills. Each skill reinforced is the same, or nearly the same, as a skill presented in the project. Each exercise includes a brief narrative introduction, followed by detailed instructions in a step-by-step format.

In these exercises you use two databases that you have seen before. The first is the short story database, and the second is the video store database.

You need an empty, formatted disk to complete these exercises.

1. Compacting and Repairing Files

The Short Stories database on the CD-ROM is 1164 KB. You would like to store it and some other files on a floppy disk, but together they exceed 1400KB, the capacity of the disk. Compact the Short Stories (AC-1304) database that is on the CD-ROM and store the smaller version on your disk.

To compact and repair a file:

1. Put an empty, formatted disk in drive A. Launch Access but do not open a database.

2. Choose Tools, Database Utilities, Compact and Repair Database from the menu.

3. Find the database file AC-1304 in the Student folder on your CD-ROM and select it.

4. Click the Compact button in the Database to Compact From dialog box.

5. Type Short Stories 6 Compacted in the File name box of the Compact Database Into dialog box and select your floppy disk in the Save in box. Click Save.

6. Launch Windows Explorer and locate the file on your disk. Compare the size of the original database to the compacted one. The file size should be reduced from about 1160 KB to 750 KB.

2. Creating a Text File from a Table

The Short Stories table has an extensive list of short stories that you want to send to someone in text format. You need to export the data to a text file. If you did the previous exercise, skip step 1.

To create a data file from a table:

1. Place an empty, formatted disk in drive A. Locate AC-1305 file and copy it to your disk. Rename the file, Short Stories 6 Compacted and remove the read-only property. Open the database.

2. Click the Tables object button, if necessary, and select the Short Stories table.

3. Select File, Export from the menu.

4. Select your disk in the Save in box. Accept the default name, Short Stories, and select Text Files from the Save as type drop-down list box.

5. Click the Save button in the dialog box.

6. Choose Delimited from the first Export Text Wizard dialog box.

7. Choose the Comma as the delimiter, quotation marks as the text qualifier. Also, choose to include the field names in the first row.

8. Click Finish to finish your text file. Close the database.

9. Launch Windows Explorer, find the Short Stories text file, and open it in WordPad or Microsoft Word to make sure the procedure worked. Close the file.

3. Creating a Query That Creates an Archive Table

The three sections in this exercise repeat the archive creation lessons (Lessons 4-6). This time, you deal with a small database of videos rented and returned from a video store. Take a look at the Rental Activity table to get a feel for the table you will be working with

To create a query that creates an archive table:

1. Copy the `AC-1306` file to your disk, remove the read-only status, rename it `Video Store 6`, and open the database.

2. Click the Queries object button, click <u>N</u>ew, and select Design View from the New Query dialog box.

3. Select the Rental Activity table, click <u>A</u>dd, then <u>C</u>lose the Show Table dialog box.

4. Select all of the fields and add them to the Field row.

5. Type `>0` in the Date Returned Criteria box.

6. Click the arrow on the right of the Query Type button, and then select the Ma<u>k</u>e-Table Query option. Call the new table `Returned Videos`.

7. Close the query and name it `Archive Setup`.

8. Select the `Archive Setup` query and click <u>O</u>pen. Click <u>Y</u>es in both dialog boxes.

9. Click the Tables object button and open the `Returned Videos` table. It should contain three records. Close the table. Leave the database open.

4. Creating a Query to Delete Records from a Table

Now that you have created an archive table and moved the completed records to it, it is time to modify the Make-Table Query to delete the completed records in the Rental Activity Table.

To create a query to delete records from a table:

1. Click the Queries object button in the Video Store 6 database and right-click the Archive Setup query.

2. Choose Rena<u>m</u>e, then type in `Delete Archived Records from the Rental Activity Table`.

3. Click the <u>D</u>esign button.

4. Click the arrow on the right of the Query Type button and select <u>D</u>elete Query from the drop-down list box.

5. Close the query window and save the changes when prompted.

6. Click <u>O</u>pen, then click <u>Y</u>es in each of the warning dialog boxes.

7. Click the Tables object button, select the `Rental Activity` table, and click <u>O</u>pen. The three records that had return dates should be deleted. Close the table. Leave the database open.

5. Creating an Append Query

The last step in the process is to create an Append Query to append records to the archive table from the Rental Activity table for videos that have been returned.

To create an append query:

1. Click the Queries object button in the Video Store 6 database and right-click the Delete Archived Records from the Rental Activity Table query.

2. Select <u>C</u>opy from the shortcut menu.

3. Right-click on an open spot in the window and select the <u>P</u>aste command. Type in the name `Append Returned Videos`, and then click OK.

4. Confirm that the Append Returned Videos query is selected, click <u>D</u>esign, then click the arrow on the right of the Query Type button and select Append Query.

5. Click the drop-down list box in the Table <u>N</u>ame box.

6. Choose the Returned Videos table, click OK, and then close the query. Save your changes when prompted.

7. Click the Tables object button, open the Rental Activity table and add a date to the Date Returned field for Video ID 001, then close the table.

8. Click the Queries object button and open the Append Returned Videos query. Answer <u>Y</u>es to both dialog boxes.

9. Open the Delete Archived Records from the Rental Activity Table query to delete the records that meet its criteria. Once again, answer <u>Y</u>es to both dialog boxes.

10. Open the Rental Activity table and the Returned Video table to make sure the video was moved from the active table to the archive table.

11. Close the database.

Challenge 💡

Challenge exercises expand on or are somewhat related to skills presented in the lessons. Each exercise provides a brief narrative introduction followed by instructions in a numbered step format that are not as detailed as those in the Skill Drill section.

The database you use for the Challenge exercises is a slightly modified version of the Customer Orders database you used in this project. In these exercises you transfer data and use a couple of Access utilities to improve the database security.

You need an empty, formatted floppy disk to do the remaining exercises in this lesson.

1. Export a Table in Rich Text Format

In Lesson 1 you created a backup copy of your data in text file format. The file you created was compact but hard to read. Another option is to export a table in rich text format, also known as RTF. This format uses common formatting commands that are widely supported by other programs.

1. Locate the AC-1306 file and open the read-only file.

2. Select the Customer table. Choose <u>F</u>ile, <u>E</u>xport.

3. Accept the default name, Customer, select Rich Text Format in the Save as <u>t</u>ype box. Select your floppy disk in the Save in box. Click <u>S</u>ave.

4. Launch Word and open the Customer document on your floppy disk. Notice that the field names are automatically formatted as column headings.

5. The table may not fit the page. Choose <u>F</u>ile, Page Set<u>u</u>p, Paper <u>S</u>ize, Lands<u>c</u>ape, and click OK. Choose <u>V</u>iew, <u>P</u>rint Layout, if necessary.

6. Click anywhere in the table to place the insertion point in the table. Choose <u>T</u>able, AutoFit, and AutoFit to <u>W</u>indow.

7. Close Word and save your changes. Close the AC-1306 database file.

2. Creating a Text File from a Query

In the first lesson, you backed up your data from a table to a text file. You can use a similar procedure to export the information from two or more tables at the same time by using the <u>E</u>xport command with a Query. The previous exercise worked from a file that had the read-only property turned on. The read-only property must be turned off to export from a query.

1. Locate the AC-1306 file and copy it to your disk. Remove the read-only property and open the file.

2. Click the Query object button and select the Purchases query. This query contains fields from both the Orders and the Customer tables.

3. Choose <u>F</u>ile, <u>E</u>xport from the menu. Use the default **Purchases** file name. Choose Text as a file type.

4. Delimit the data with tabs, and use quotation marks as text qualifiers. Add field names to the data.

5. Check your new text file in WordPad or Microsoft Word. Notice how different a file that contains mainly text looks from those that consist mainly of numbers.

6. Close the text file and the word processing program. Close the database. If you do not plan to do the next exercise, delete the file from your floppy disk to save space. If you plan to complete the next exercise, skip the first step.

3. Sending a Database Object to Another Database

There might be times when you need to develop a database that contains tables that are similar, if not identical, to tables that you have already created. Access enables you to send an entire table to another database, or just the underlying table structure with no data. You can also export other Access database objects, such as queries, forms, and reports to other databases. Because these objects contain no data, you are not given a structure-only option.

In this exercise, you need to use the available help to set up a database with an empty table, a query, a form, and a report.

1. Locate the AC-1306 file and copy it to your disk. Remove the read-only property. Do not open the file at this time.

2. Create a new, blank database and call it Customers. Close the database without creating any tables. Leave Access open.

3. Choose Help, Microsoft Access Help from the menu. Type How do I export tables to another database? and click Search. Choose Export data or database objects to another database or file format. Read the relevant sections on how to export table structure to another database without exporting the actual data. Read the portions about how to export other database objects, such as queries, reports, and forms.

4. Open the file AC-1306 from your floppy disk. Export the Customer table to the Customers database, but without any data. Then send the Customer List by City query, the Customer Information form, and the Customer List by City report to the Customer database.

5. Close the AC-1306 database and open the new Customers database to examine the results of your database object exports. Close the Customers database when you are through. Close the Microsoft Access Help window.

6. Delete the AC-1306 file from your floppy disk.

Discovery Zone

Discovery Zone exercises help you gain advanced knowledge of project topics and application of skills. These exercises focus on enhancing your problem-solving skills. Numbered steps are not provided, but you are given hints, reminders, screen shots, and references to help you reach your goal for each exercise.

1. Creating an MDE File to Protect Your Database Objects from Being Changed

If you have designed a database that you are distributing, you might want to change the file to an **MDE file** format. This enables users to run the database and manipulate data, use forms and queries, and print reports, but stops them from making any changes to the structure of the forms and reports. Also, if you have done any programming in VBA (Visual Basic for Applications), your program code will be unavailable to the user. This procedure works well in some instances, but you must keep an original copy of the database in MDB (normal) format in case you want to make any changes (you cannot make changes in the MDE version either). Make sure you read the help information on MDE files.

Goal: Change an Access database to MDE format.

In this exercise, you should:

- open <u>H</u>elp and read the information on MDE files.
- copy the file `AC-1307` to your floppy disk and remove the read-only property. Rename it `Customers database in MDE format`.
- use the database utilities to make an MDE file out of the `Customers database in MDE format` file. Name the new file `Customers database for distribution`.
- open the `Customers database for distribution` and select a form or report. Notice that the Design button is not functional.
- close the database.
- delete the file `Customers database in MDE format` from your floppy disk to save space.

2. Publish a Report to Word

It is easier to make changes to the format of a report in Microsoft Word than it is to change the layout of text and label boxes in the Design view of a report.

Goal: Publish a report in Word.

In this exercise, you should:

- copy the file `AC-1307` to your floppy disk and remove the read-only property.
- open the `AC-1307` database and preview the Customer List by City report.
- read the Microsoft Access Help on the topics of Office Links and Publish to Microsoft Word.
- publish the report to Word and automatically create the file `Customer List by City` in rich text format (rtf).
- launch Word and open the `Customer List by City` document. Compare the report in Word and the report in Access.
- close the document, the database, Word, and Access. Delete the file AC-1307 from your floppy disk to conserve space.

PinPoint Assessment

You have completed this project and its associated lessons, and have had an opportunity to assess your skills through the end-of-project questions and exercises. Now use the PinPoint software Evaluation Mode to further assess your comprehension of the specific exam activities you have just learned. You can also use the PinPoint Trainer Mode and the Show Me tutorials to practice these exam activities.

Project 14

Using Access on the Web and Linking to Other Documents

Key terms introduced in this project include

- FTP
- HTML
- hyperlink
- Internet
- intranet
- LAN
- static HTML pages
- URL
- Web browser
- World Wide Web

Objectives	Required Activity for MOUS	Exam Level
➤ Add Hyperlinks from Forms to Word Documents	Add hyperlinks	Core
	Create hyperlinks	Expert
➤ Add Hyperlinks from Forms to Excel Spreadsheets	Create hyperlinks	Expert
➤ Save Database Objects as Static HTML Pages	Save a table, query, and form as a web page	Core
➤ View HTML Pages on a Local Drive Using a Browser		

Why Would I Do This?

Internet technology is changing the way people communicate within a company. Many companies are setting up private internets called **intranets**. These intranets use the same **Web browsers** (or simply browsers) that are used on the Internet, but are limited to company networks. For the purpose of brevity, the term "Net" is used in this project to refer to either the Internet or a company intranet.

The advantage of using the Internet or a company intranet to disseminate information is that you retain control of the data. Formerly, you made copies of your data and distributed them to the intended users. This method has two significant drawbacks: 1) the data may become out of date, and 2) some people in the company may need the information, but may not be on the distribution list.

If you publish your data on the Net, anyone may visit the site whenever they need the information, and you can make sure the information is current. Similarly, you can insert links from your forms, documents, worksheets, or presentations to sites provided by others.

  ## Lesson 1: Adding Hyperlinks from Forms to Word Documents

In this lesson, you use two files. The AC-1401 file is a word processing document, and AC-1402 is an Access database. Both are located on your CD-ROM. You create a link from a form in Access to a document written in Word. Access forms can contain **hyperlinks**, also referred to as links, that connect the user directly to documents stored on the user's personal computer, local area network (**LAN**), or the **World Wide Web**. Hyperlinks to other documents can be added to either forms or reports.

The database used in this lesson illustrates the kind of data that a department may keep for tracking purchases of personal computers. The Vendors table contains a list of Vendors that can be used for corporate purchases. In this example, you assume that the purchasing department keeps a current list of approved vendors and makes that list available to other departments as a Word document. The vendor rating can change, and it is important that the user's purchase request reflect the current vendor rating. Access enables you to place a hyperlink in the Vendor Information form that allows you to check the current rating from the Purchasing department document.

To Create a Hyperlink Between an Access Form and a Word Document

1 Find the AC-1401 file on your CD-ROM and open it in Microsoft Word. A list of approved vendors is displayed (see Figure 14.1).

2 Choose **File, Save As**, and save the document to a new disk in drive A: as Approved Vendors.

3 Close the document and close Word.

4 Copy the AC-1402 file to your disk, remove the read-only status, rename it PC Purchases, and open the database.

5 Click the Forms object button to reveal the available forms.

6 Select the **Vendor Information** form and click the **Design** button to reveal the design of the form. Maximize the window for convenient editing (see Figure 14.2).

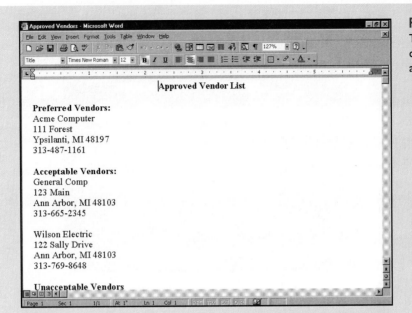

Figure 14.1
The Word document contains a list of approved vendors.

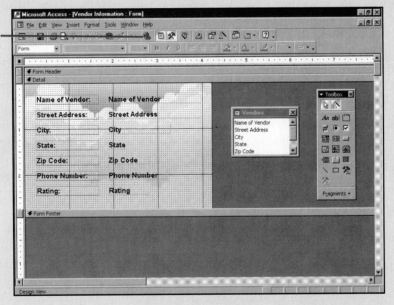

Figure 14.2
Hyperlinks can be placed in a form using Design view.

⑦ Click the Insert Hyperlink button on the toolbar.

The Insert Hyperlink dialog box is displayed (see Figure 14.3). The Inserted Links list will be active (as shown), although the Recent Files list or the Browsed Pages list could be displayed if someone has used one of those options recently.

You can type the path to the file or the **URL** (Uniform Resource Locator) in the `Type the file` or `Web page name` box. A URL is also known as an Internet address. In this example, the file is on a disk, and the File button to the right of the box helps you find the Approved Vendors file that you opened earlier in this lesson.

⑧ Click the File button in the Insert Hyperlink dialog box. Use the buttons on the toolbar of this dialog box to find the Approved Vendor document used in the previous lesson.

continues ▶

To Create a Hyperlink Between an Access Form and a Word Document (continued)

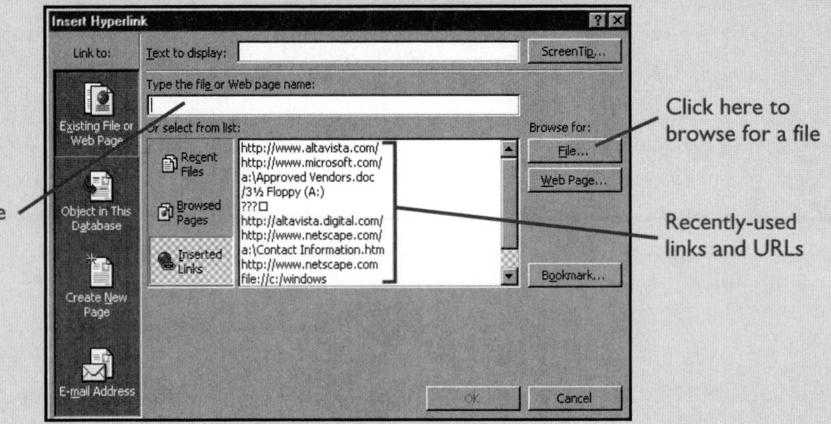

Figure 14.3
The Insert Hyperlink dialog box is used to locate and specify the file to which the hyperlink refers.

The link goes here

Click here to browse for a file

Recently-used links and URLs

9 **Select the Approved Vendors document and click OK.**
The file name and location on the disk is added to the dialog box. Notice that the file name is also displayed in the Text to display box at the top of the Insert Hyperlink dialog box, and that it shows the file extension. This is the text that will be displayed on your form.

10 **Remove the .doc extension from the Text to display text box.**
Your hyperlink now says Approved Vendors instead of Approved Vendors.doc. You still need to remove the file extension from the ScreenTip.

11 **Click the ScreenTip button in the upper-right corner of the Insert Hyperlink dialog box. Type** Order from one of these vendors **in the ScreenTip text box.**
The hyperlink now says Approved Vendors and the ScreenTip gives further instructions (see Figure 14.4).

Figure 14.4
The text for the hyperlink has been changed using the ScreenTip button.

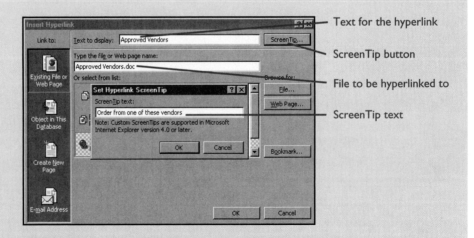

Text for the hyperlink

ScreenTip button

File to be hyperlinked to

ScreenTip text

12 **Click OK to close the Set Hyperlink ScreenTip dialog box, and then click OK again to close the Insert Hyperlink dialog box.**
A link is placed on the form in the upper-left corner (see Figure 14.5).

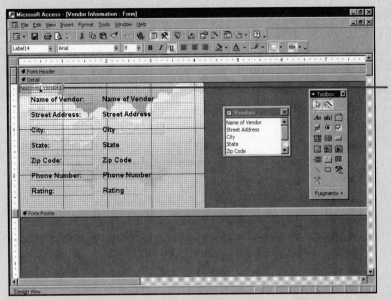

Figure 14.5
A hyperlink is placed in the form design.

A hyperlink has been added

⓭ **Deselect the hyperlink, and then click and drag the hyperlink to a new location to the right of the Rating field.**

You can drag the hyperlink and drop it in the gray area to the right of the current right edge of the form. The form widens to accommodate the hyperlink (see Figure 14.6).

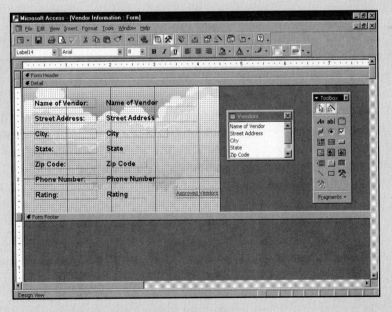

Figure 14.6
The hyperlink can be moved to another location in the form.

 Exam Note: **Formatting the Hyperlink**

You might want to change the format of the hyperlink so that it stands out more. You can use bold or italic, or change the font or font size, but it is recommended that you not change the font color. Blue has become almost universally recognized as the color of a hyperlink, or "hot spot" onscreen.

continues ▶

**To Create a Hyperlink Between an Access Form
and a Word Document (continued)**

14 **Click the View button on the toolbar to change to Form view.**
The hyperlink is displayed on the form in dark blue with underlined text.

15 **Move the pointer to the hyperlink on the form.**
The pointer changes into a small hand, indicating that this text represents a hyperlink. The ScreenTip is also displayed (see Figure 14.7).

Figure 14.7
The pointer turns into
a hand and a
ScreenTip is displayed.

Hyperlink

The hand pointer
indicates a hyperlink

ScreenTip

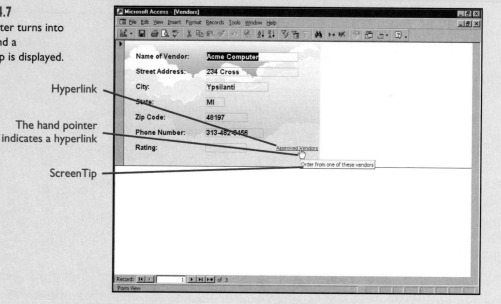

16 **Click the hyperlink in the Approved Vendors document.**
The Word program is launched, if it is not already open, and the Approved Vendors document is opened. The Web toolbar is turned on so you can move back to your original location (see Figure 14.8).

Figure 14.8
The Web toolbar is
automatically turned
on in the hyperlinked
application.

Web toolbar

Navigation buttons

Show Only Web
Toolbar button

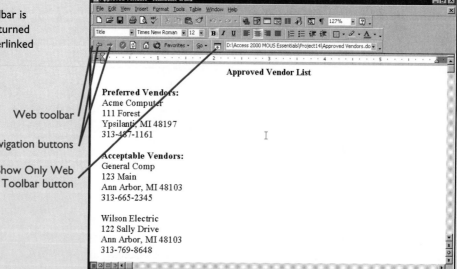

Leave the Approved Vendors document open for use in the next section.

 Inside Stuff: **Displaying Only the Web Toolbar**
You will probably not edit the Word document that you have linked to, so it is often a good idea to close all of the toolbars except the Web toolbar. You can do this easily by clicking the Show Only Web Toolbar button on the Web toolbar. The only time this might be an inconvenience is if you want to copy information from the linked document. If you have turned off all the other toolbars, the Copy and Paste buttons will be hidden, and you will need to use the menu or the keyboard shortcuts to perform these functions.

You can copy information from one file and paste it into another, even if the files were created using different programs. You can also use navigation buttons on the toolbar to quickly jump back and forth between the files once the link is established.

To Copy Information and Move Between Linked Files

In this example, the address of the Acme Computer Company has changed since the last time it was used in the database, as shown in the Approved Vendors document. Because you are updating the database of computer orders for your division, you will want to update the Vendors table of the PC Purchases database.

1 **Select and copy the new address,** `111 Forest`**, into the Approved Vendors document.**

> *If You Have Problems...*
> If the Show Only Web Toolbar button has been clicked, the Copy button will not be available on your toolbar. You can use the menu or keyboard shortcuts to copy the text, or you can click the Show Only Web Toolbar button again to turn on the Standard and Formatting toolbars.

2 **Click the Back button on the Web toolbar.**
This button returns you to the Access Form.

> *If You Have Problems...*
> The Web toolbar should open automatically when you use a hyperlink to move between applications. If for some reason you do not see the Web toolbar, go to <u>V</u>iew, <u>T</u>oolbars and click the Web option to turn on this toolbar. If the Back button does not work, you can still move between applications using the Windows taskbar.

3 **Select the old address for the Acme Computer Company and click the**
Paste button to paste in the new one.

4 **In the Rating box, type** `Preferred` **(see Figure 14.9).**

5 **Click the Forward button on the Web toolbar to return to the**
Approved Vendors document.

continues ▶

To Copy Information and Move Between Linked Files (continued)

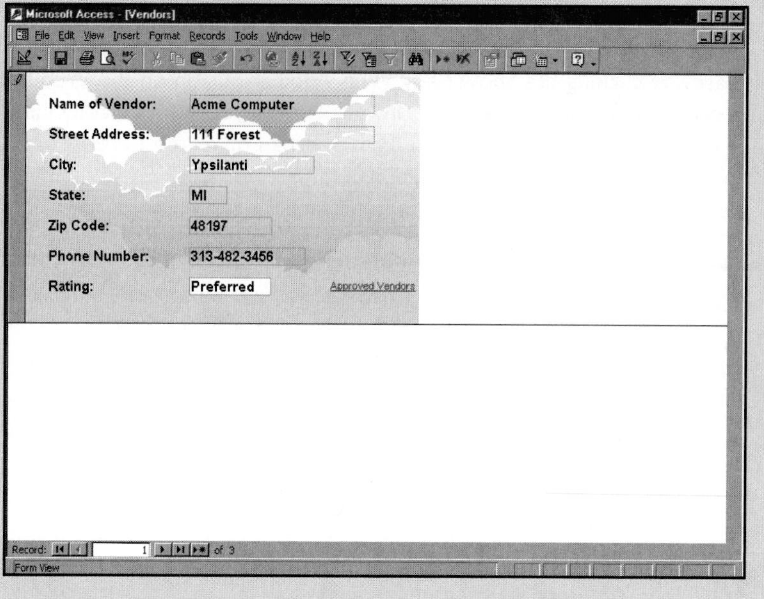
Microsoft Access - [Vendors]
File Edit View Insert Format Records Tools Window Help
Name of Vendor: Acme Computer
Street Address: 111 Forest
City: Ypsilanti
State: MI
Zip Code: 48197
Phone Number: 313-482-3456
Rating: Preferred
Approved Vendors
Record: 1 of 3
Form View

Figure 14.9
The information from the Approved Vendors document has been used to update the Vendors table.

6 Close the document and close Word.
The Vendor Information form should be displayed after you close the Word document. If not, use the taskbar to return to Access.

7 Close the form and save the changes, if necessary.
Leave the `PC Purchases` database open for the next lesson.

Exam Note: **Adding a Hyperlink to an Existing Object**
You can add a hyperlink to an existing label control or picture in a form header or footer. To do this, open the form in Design view and double-click the object. Select the Format tab, click in the Hyperlink Address property box, and click the build button. Type in (or browse for) the address or file name, click OK, and then close the property sheet.

Expert

Lesson 2: Adding Hyperlinks from Forms to Excel Spreadsheets

You can establish links from Access forms to Excel spreadsheets in the same way you linked to a Word document in Lesson 1. In this lesson you connect an Access form to a budget worksheet in an Excel spreadsheet.

To Add a Hyperlink from a Form to an Excel Spreadsheet

❶ Launch Excel and click the Open button. Find the AC-1403 file on your CD-ROM and open it in Microsoft Excel. Save the file on drive A: as Computer Budget.

This will remove the read-only status. This Excel spreadsheet represents the budget for computer purchases for three departments. It consists of a separate sheet for each of three departments—Sales, Marketing, and Engineering, plus a summary sheet showing computer purchases for all three departments.

❷ Close Excel, return to Access, and open the Orders form in Design view. Maximize the window, if necessary.

This form is used to enter computer purchase requests (see Figure 14.10).

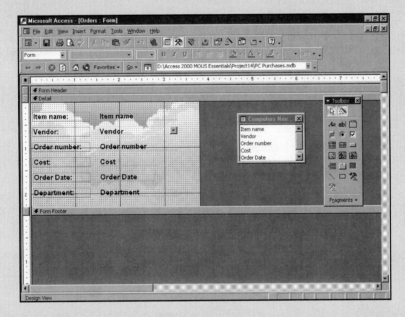

Figure 14.10
Hyperlinks to spreadsheets can be placed in a form in Design view.

❸ Click the Insert Hyperlink button on the toolbar.
The Insert Hyperlink dialog box is displayed.

❹ Click the Browse button and locate the Computer Budget file.

❺ Select Computer Budget and click OK.
The location of the file is entered in the Type the file or Web page name box (see Figure 14.11).

❻ Change the name in the Text to display box to Computer Budget.

❼ Click OK to place the link in the form.
The link is placed in the form in the upper-left corner.

❽ Drag the hyperlink to a position to the right of the Department field (see Figure 14.12).

❾ Click the View button on the toolbar to switch to Form view (see Figure 14.13).

❿ Click the hyperlink to move directly to the budget sheet to see if there is adequate funding for further computer purchases.
The hyperlink launches Excel and opens the spreadsheet (see Figure 14.14).

continues ▶

To Add a Hyperlink from a Form to an Excel Spreadsheet (continued)

Figure 14.11
In the Insert Hyperlink dialog box, enter the name of the spreadsheet and its location using the Browse button.

File to be linked

Figure 14.12
The link to the spreadsheet can be moved anywhere on the form.

New hyperlink

Figure 14.13
The hyperlink is displayed in the form.

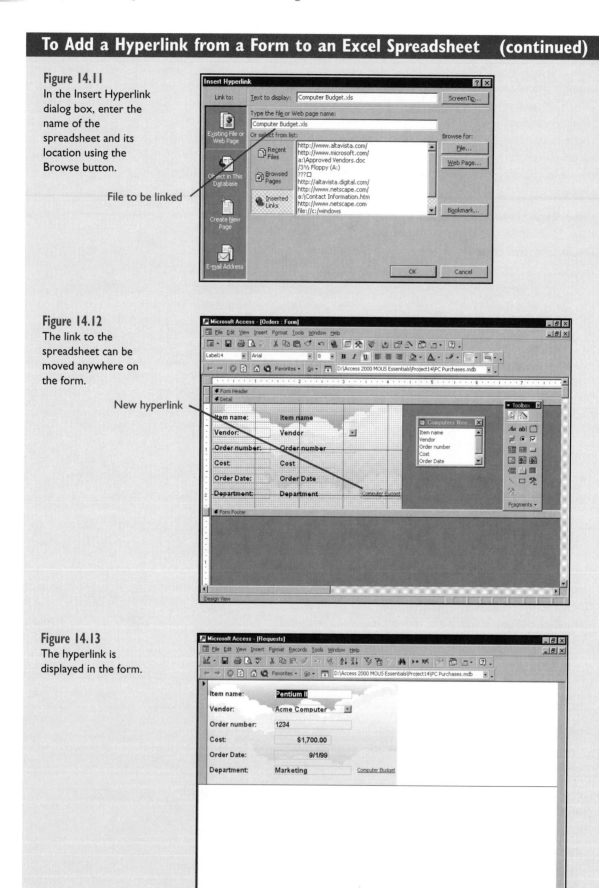

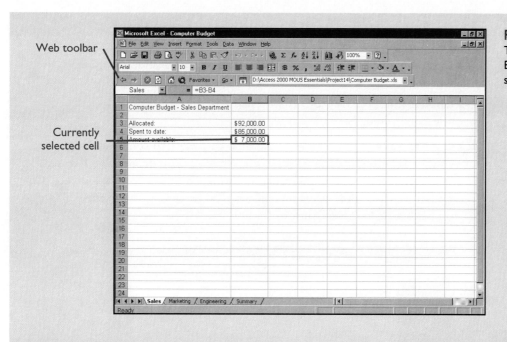

Figure 14.14
The hyperlink launches Excel and opens the spreadsheet.

Web toolbar

Currently selected cell

⑪ **Click the Back button to return to your Access form.**

⑫ **Close the form and save the changes.**
You may want to use the taskbar to return to Excel and close the program.

⑬ **Close the database and close the Excel spreadsheet.**

Lesson 3: Saving Database Objects as Static HTML Pages Core

The World Wide Web is designed to be used by a variety of different computers. They share a common way of sending documents to each other and a common way of viewing those documents. These documents are created with a special set of codes that tell the browser program how to display the text. This set of codes is called **HTML**, the Hypertext Markup Language. It is used to create a basic document that has a limited set of formatting features. Some browsers support additional features that are not common to all browsers. These browsers use additional HTML codes called extensions that handle features such as columns, tables, and animation.

In Project 7, "Integrating Access with Other Sources of Data and the Internet," you created data access pages that enabled the user to interact with the data on the Web. Sometimes you will want to put information on a Web site that can be read, but not manipulated. In this lesson you save a table and a query as **static HTML pages** that may be viewed by an Internet Web browser, but that are not interactive. These pages are also no longer linked to the database from which they were created.

To Save a Table as an HTML Document

① **Copy the AC-1404 file to your disk, remove the read-only status, rename it CD Collection, and open the database.**
This database is a compilation of music CDs, with the name of the artist, the CD title, and other information about each CD.

continues ▶

To Save a Table as an HTML Document (continued)

2 Click the Tables object button, if necessary, and select the CD Collection table.

3 Choose File, Export from the menu.
The Export dialog box is displayed.

4 Use the Save in box to select the disk you want to send the file to, and choose HTML Documents from the Save as type drop-down list.
The default file name is the same as the name of the database object, CD Collection, although it will have a different file extension. The Export Table dialog box should look like Figure 14.15.

Figure 14.15
The Export dialog box enables you to save a database object as an HTML file.

File location

File name

File type

5 Click the Save button.
The program determines a format for the data, then writes all of the data to a text file, with HTML instructions embedded in the document. This enables any browser to read the file and display it in the proper format. You will look at the results of this exercise in the next lesson.

⊠ If You Have Problems...

Many viewers and Internet server computers do not support file names longer than eight characters or file extensions longer than three characters. Access saves the files with a four letter-extension, html. If you view these files directly from your disk in the next lesson with an older browser, they will not link to each other properly.

When Access saves database objects as HTML documents, it adds a sequence number to the name of the file. For example, Form.html becomes Form_1.html. If the name of the table, query, form, or report is longer than six characters, the resulting file name will be longer than eight characters.

To avoid problems with older browsers and Internet servers, make a copy of any of the tables, queries, forms, or reports that will be saved as HTML documents to a name that is six characters or fewer. Export these copies as HTML documents. Once the files have been created, edit the names and change the extensions to .htm rather than .html.

You use the same procedure to save a query in HTML format as you used to save the table. In the following exercise, you follow the same steps you followed above, but with one simple change that significantly alters the look of the Web page.

To Save a Query as an HTML Document

1 **Click the Queries object button and select the `Jazz/Big Band CDs` query.**
This query displays a subset of the CD Collection table.

2 **Click the Open button to open the query.**
Notice that the query has a pale blue background with dark blue, italicized letters (see Figure 14.16).

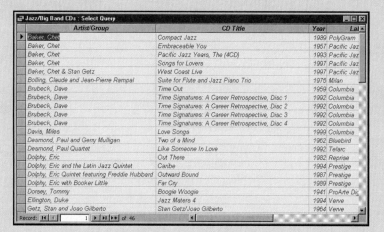

Figure 14.16
The query has had several formatting changes.

3 **Choose File, Export from the menu. Select a file location, choose HTML Documents from the Save as type drop-down list, and accept the default name.**

4 **Click the Save formatted check box.**
The HTML file will now retain the formatting of the original document. The data is saved in table format by default. Your Export dialog box should look like Figure 14.17.

Save All button

Save formatted check box

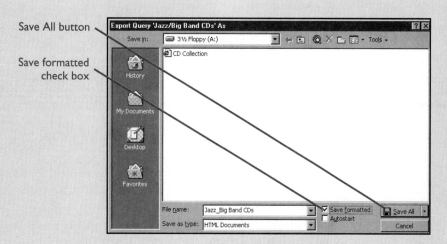

Figure 14.17
The Save formatted option has been selected.

continues ▶

To Save a Query as an HTML Document (continued)

5 **Click the Save All button.**

The HTML Output Options dialog box is displayed (see Figure 14.18). You can use this option if you have design templates you want to use. In this case, skip this step, because you are already using a formatted query.

Figure 14.18
The HTML Output Options dialog box enables you to add a design template if you so desire.

6 **Click OK.**

The HTML file is saved, along with your formatting.

7 **Close the query and close Access.**

You will not need Access to view or edit the HTML files in Lesson 4.

X *If You Have Problems...*

The Select an HTML Template dialog box may not display any HTML templates. To find them, you can use the Advanced search to look for files with .HTM extensions. If Microsoft Office is installed on your hard drive, the HTML files are usually found at C:\Program Files\Microsoft Office\Templates\1033\.

Lesson 4: Viewing HTML Pages on a Local Drive Using a Browser

HTML documents are made to be viewed by a Web browser on the Internet. If you have a browser on your computer, you can open and view the documents created in the previous lesson, even if you are not connected to the net. There are several brands of World Wide Web browsers, but the most popular ones share the features that are used in this lesson. The examples shown use Microsoft's Internet Explorer 5.0 browser, but you should be able to adapt the following commands to most other browsers.

It is common practice to check your HTML documents on your computer before transferring them to the computer that makes them available on the Internet.

In this lesson, you open both of the HTML files you created in Lesson 3, so you can see the difference between the look of the file you saved using the default format and the file you saved with its own formatting.

To View HTML Documents Using a Web Browser

❶ Open the Windows Explorer and select drive A: (or folder in which you placed the HTML files you created in Lesson 3). Click the Details button, if necessary.

If you are using a floppy disk, the Explorer window should look like Figure 14.19. You can identify your default browser by checking the file type.

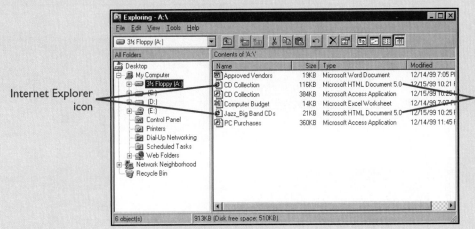

Internet Explorer icon

HTML files

Figure 14.19
The Explorer window identifies the Web browser you are using.

❷ Double-click the CD Collection HTML file. Maximize the window, if necessary.

The CD Collection table is displayed in the default HTML format (see Figure 14.20). The name of the table is automatically used as the page title. If the information is wider than your screen, a horizontal scrollbar will be added.

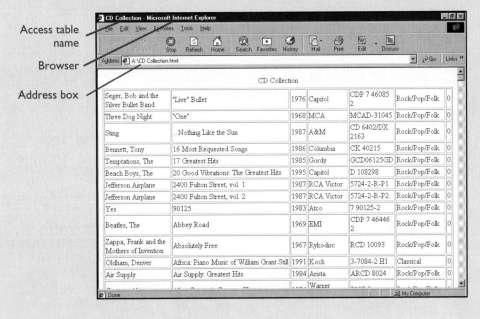

Access table name

Browser

Address box

Figure 14.20
The table is displayed in HTML format.

continues ▶

To View HTML Documents Using a Web Browser (continued)

 If You Have Problems...

If the file type for your HTML files says HTML File in the Windows Explorer, and double-clicking the file name does not result in a table as shown in Figure 14.22, you probably do not have a Web browser installed (or working properly) on your computer. Install (or re-install) a browser, or skip the rest of this lesson.

③ Click the down arrow in the A̲ddress box.
A directory of your computer is displayed (see Figure 14.21). If you were on the Web, you would see URLs instead.

Figure 14.21
The Address box drop-down list displays a directory of your computer.

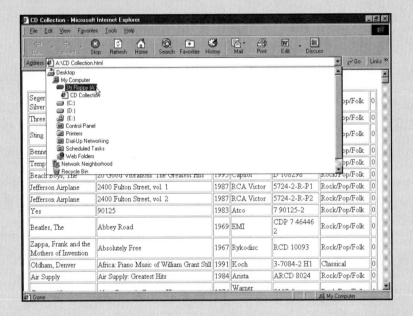

④ Select 3 1/2 Floppy (A:) from the drop-down list.
All of the files on the floppy drive are displayed.

⑤ Double-click the Jazz_Big Band CDs file.
The Internet Explorer opens the Jazz_Big Band CDs file created from the Jazz/Big Band CDs query (see Figure 14.22). The query name is again used as the page title, but the Access query formatting has been transferred to the Web page.

Inside Stuff: Using the Back and Forward Buttons
You can use the Back and Forward buttons to navigate between addresses even though you are not actually online. Notice that the Back button is active, indicating that you can click on it and move back to the previous document. If you click the Back button, you move back to the drive A: screen, then to the CD Collection page. The Forward button becomes active once you click the Back button.

⑥ Try the Back and Forward buttons to move between pages. When you are through, close the browser.

Back button

Forward
button
(inactive)

New address

Query name

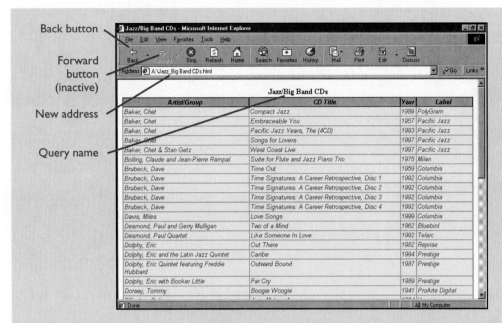

Figure 14.22
The Web page based
on the query has
retained its formatting.

Summary

In this project, you worked with links, both from Access to other programs, and from Access to the Web. You added links from Access forms to a Word document and to an Excel worksheet. You saved a table as an unformatted static HTML page, and a query as a formatted static HTML page. You viewed both of these pages on a browser.

You can enhance your knowledge of HTML by getting one of the many good books on the subject. You can then make and test your changes using the Web browser without ever having to put your pages on a Web server.

Checking Concepts and Terms

True/False

For each of the following statements, check *T* or *F* to indicate whether the statement is true or false.

__T __F **1.** Hyperlinks can only be used to jump to other HTML pages. [L1]

__T __F **2.** Static HTML pages can be viewed but are no longer linked to the database. They can not be used to edit data in the database table. [L3]

__T __F **3.** It is possible to use a browser to check HTML files without connecting to the Internet. [L4]

__T __F **4.** You can choose to save the formatting of a table or query when you create the HTML file. [L3]

__T __F **5.** If you open more than one HTML document in your browser, you can move back and forth between them using the Back and Forward buttons. [L4]

Multiple Choice

Circle the letter of the correct answer for each of the following questions.

1. Once a hyperlink has been used to jump from an Access form to a Word document, how do you return to the Access form? [L1]

  a. Click the Page Up button on the keyboard.

  b. Use the roller button on the mouse.

  c. Click the Back button on the toolbar.

  d. Click the Forward button on the toolbar.

2. To save a static Web page, use the File, _____ option. [L3]

  a. Save As

  b. Save as HTML

  c. Export

  d. Web Page

3. A URL is _____. [L1]

  a. another name for a hyperlink

  b. the link between a form and a Word or Excel document

  c. an HTML instruction

  d. an Internet address

4. When formatting a hyperlink in a form, it is a good idea not to change _____. [L1]

  a. the font size

  b. the font type

  c. the font color

  d. none of the above

5. An advantage of using the Internet or a company intranet to disseminate information in static form is _____. [Intro]

  a. you don't have to worry about updating the information

  b. anyone who wants to can change the information

  c. you retain control of the data

  d. there's no cost involved

Screen ID

Label each element of the Access screen shown in Figure 14.23.

Figure 14.23

A. Click here to browse the Web site to which to link

B. Hyperlink text that appears on the form

C. Document to link to

D. Click here to add pop-up text to the hyperlink on the form

E. Click here to find the document to which to link

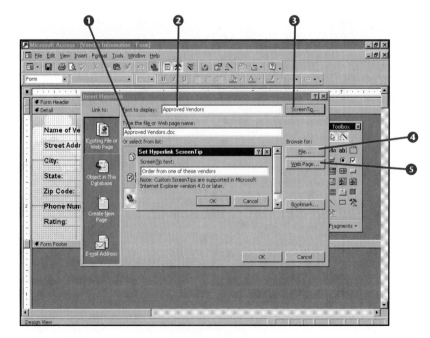

1._____   3._____   5._____

2._____   4._____

Skill Drill exercises reinforce project skills. Each skill reinforced is the same, or nearly the same, as a skill presented in the project. Each exercise includes a brief narrative introduction, followed by detailed instructions in a step-by-step format.

In these exercises, you work with database interactivity using a customer information database. If you are using a disk in drive A:, make sure you have adequate room before you start each exercise.

1. Linking an Access Form to a Word Document

The accounting department has just put out an emergency document on the company Intranet to notify the sales force of new credit ratings for some of the customers. The notice is in Word, and while the new ratings will be added to the database soon, you need to see the new credit ratings immediately to find out if prepayment is necessary for some of the customers whose ratings have dropped.

To link an Access form to a Word document:

1. Copy the AC-1405 file to your disk, remove the read-only status, rename it **Customer Information Management**, and open the database. A switchboard has been added to this database.

2. Copy the AC-1406 Word file to your disk and rename it **New Credit Ratings**.

3. Click the Open Customer Information Form button, then click the View button to switch to Design view.

4. Click the Insert Hyperlink button.

5. Click the File button. Find and select the New Credit Ratings document, then click OK.

6. Remove the .doc extension from the Text to display box.

7. Click the ScreenTip button and type **Make sure you check the new ratings before shipping orders!**

8. Click OK. Move the hyperlink to the right of the first field, then click the View button to switch to Form view. Your form should look like Figure 14.24.

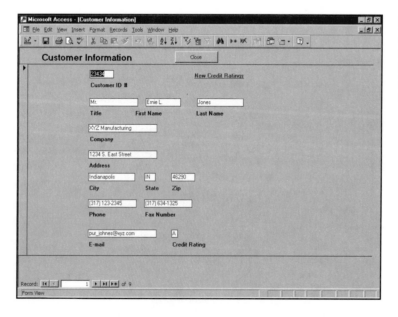

Figure 14.24
A hyperlink has been added to the form, linking the form to a Microsoft Word document.

9. Click the New Credit Ratings button to switch to the Word document. Click the Back button to move back to the Access form.

10. Close the form and save your changes when prompted.

11. Use the taskbar to find and close Word. Leave the **Customer Information Management** database open for the next exercise.

2. Saving an Unformatted Query as an HTML Document

Because the new credit ratings are coming out, the salespeople want to know which of their customers have not paid their bills, and how far behind they are, although this isn't the only factor in determining credit ratings. The Fifth District Court, for example, has not paid for four shipments, but they have never missed a payment, so their rating is high. You decide to post the unpaid bills, again in static form because you don't want anyone changing the data. You will use a query that has received no special formatting. If you did the previous exercise, skip the first step.

To save an unformatted query as an HTML:

1. Copy the AC-1405 file to your disk, remove the read-only status, rename it **Customer Information Management**, and open the database.

2. Click the Close button to close the switchboard. Click the Queries object button, if necessary, and select the Unpaid Purchases query.

3. Choose File, Export from the menu. Select a location for the file using the Save in box, and call the File name **Unpaid Orders**.

4. In the Save as type box, select HTML Documents.

5. Click the Save formatted check box and click the Save button. Ignore the HTML Template option.

6. Open the Windows Explorer, find the Unpaid Orders HTML file, and open the file.

7. Scroll down to see all of the data if necessary.

8. Leave the browser open if you are going to proceed to the next exercise.

3. Saving a Formatted Table as an HTML Document

You want to make a complete list of recent orders available to everyone, but you do not want to give anyone the option of making changes to the data, so you decide to create a static HTML document to place on the net. You have formatted the table to make it look much nicer as a Web page. (*Note:* To change the font, background, and foreground formatting of a table, open the table in Datasheet view, and use the options in the Format menu.) If you did the previous exercise, skip the first step.

To save a formatted table as an HTML document:

1. Copy the AC-1405 file to your disk, remove the read-only status, rename it **Customer Information Management**, and open the database.

2. Click the Close button on the switchboard to move to the Database window.

3. Click the Tables object button, if necessary, and select the Orders table.

4. Choose File, Export from the menu. Select a location for the file using the Save in box, and call the File name **Recent Orders**. Skip the Template dialog box.

5. In the Save as type box, select HTML Documents. Click the Save formatted check box, then click the Save All button.

6. If you did the previous exercise, switch to the browser, use the Address drop-down box, and find and open the Recent Orders file you just created. (If you did not do the previous exercise, Open the Windows Explorer, find the Recent Orders HTML file, and open the file.)

7. Maximize the browser window, if necessary. Use the Back and Forward arrows to move between the unformatted query and the formatted table. Notice what a difference even minor formatting changes can make.

8. Close the browser. Close Access unless you are going to proceed to the Challenge section.

Challenge

Challenge exercises expand on or are somewhat related to skills presented in the lessons. Each exercise provides a brief narrative introduction followed by instructions in a numbered step format that are not as detailed as those in the Skill Drill section.

The database you use for the Challenge exercises is a revised version of the CD Collection database you used earlier in this project. Use a new floppy disk for these exercises.

I. Adding a Hyperlink to a PowerPoint Presentation

In this exercise, you add a hyperlink to a form that opens a PowerPoint presentation.

To add a hyperlink to a form that opens a PowerPoint presentation:

1. Copy the `AC-1407` PowerPoint Show file to your disk and rename it `CD PowerPoint Presentation`.
2. Copy the `AC-1408` file to your disk, remove the read-only status, rename it `Updated CD Collection`, and open the database.
3. Open the `CD Input Form` in Design view and add a hyperlink to the CD PowerPoint Presentation. Use the file name without the extension as the text to display, and add a ScreenTip that says `Click here for instructions`.
4. Move the hyperlink to the right of the Category field. Click the View button, then click the hyperlink. Press (PgDn) to move through the slides.
5. Close the PowerPoint presentation to move back to the Access form. Leave the `Updated CD Collection` database open for the next exercise.

2. Adding a Hyperlink to Connect to a URL

In this exercise you add another hyperlink to the CD Input form, this time to connect the form to a site on the Internet. If you did the previous exercise, skip the first step.

To add a hyperlink to connect to a URL:

1. Copy the `AC-1408` file to your disk, remove the read-only status, rename it `Updated CD Collection`, and open the database.
2. Switch to Design view of the CD Input Form.
3. Click the Hyperlink button. Type the following URL: `http://www.microsoft.com`. *Note:* If you want to use a different URL, please feel free!
4. The hyperlink on the form should read `Go to Microsoft for Help`. Do not add a ScreenTip.
5. Move the hyperlink above the other one. Click the View button and test your new hyperlink. Your form should look like Figure 14.25.

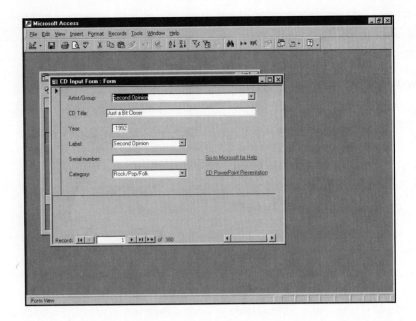

Figure 14.25
A second hyperlink has been added to the form, linking the form to a URL.

6. Close your browser, close the form, and save your changes. Leave the `Updated CD Collection` database open for the next exercise.

3. Creating a One Page HTML Document from a Report

In this exercise you create an HTML document from a one-page report. If you did the previous exercise, skip the first step.

To create a one page HTML document from a report

1. Copy the `AC-1408` file to your disk, remove the read-only status, rename it `Updated CD Collection`, and open the database.

2. Click the Reports object button and select the Country/Western CDs report.

3. Export the report to an HTML file. Skip the template dialog box.

4. View your new Country_Western CDs.html Web page on your Web browser. Notice that the headers and footers are displayed on the Web page.

5. Close your Web browser.

Discovery Zone

Discovery Zone exercises help you gain advanced knowledge of project topics and application of skills. These exercises focus on enhancing your problem-solving skills. Numbered steps are not provided, but you are given hints, reminders, screen shots, and references to help you reach your goal for each exercise.

1. Creating a Multiple Page HTML Document

So far, you have created only HTML documents that are contained in one page. In this exercise, you create an HTML document that consists of several linked pages. You use a database of tornadoes in the state of Arizona.

Goal: Create a multi-page HTML document from a report.

In this exercise, you should:

- move the `AC7-1409` file to your disk and rename it `Arizona Tornadoes Online`;
- save the Arizona Tornadoes report as a multiple-page HTML document;
- test the HTML document and test the links between the pages.

Hint: This is much easier than it sounds. When in doubt, try the procedures you already know.

2. Uploading HTML Files onto a Web Server

Once you have created the Web pages you want, and you have made any editing changes you feel are necessary, you need to get your file(s) onto a Web server (or into a Web Folder) so you can share your pages with the world. Unfortunately, there is no set way to put Web pages on a Web server.

The method you use depends on what type of server you have—Unix, VMS, Windows NT, and so forth. It also depends on what utility programs you use to upload the files. You also need to find out what types of permissions you need to set; that is, who can read the pages and who has the rights to change the pages. Finally, you need to use an **FTP** (File Transfer Protocol) program to transfer the files to the server.

Note: You can also use any number of Web publishing tools, including the Microsoft Web Publishing Wizard, to upload your document(s). This program should be available at C:\Program Files\Web Publish. The file name is Wpwiz. You need all of the information mentioned above to run this program successfully. If you do not have the Microsoft Web Publishing Wizard, you can download it from Microsoft. Go to http://www.microsoft.com and search from there.

Goal: Upload the Arizona Tornadoes pages onto your Web server.

In this exercise, you should:

- create a folder on your server to hold your files.
- transfer the files to your server folder using one of the many FTP programs (WS-FTP LE is available online, and is free to students).
- set the permissions on your server so that people can see your pages, and you can make changes to them.
- find out the URL you need to use to get to your pages.

Hint: Talk to your network administrator if you have never done this before!

PinPoint Assessment

You have completed this project and its associated lessons, and have had an opportunity to assess your skills through the end-of-project questions and exercises. Now use the PinPoint software Evaluation Mode to further assess your comprehension of the specific exam activities you have just learned. You can also use the PinPoint Trainer Mode and the Show Me tutorials to practice these exam activities.

Designing a Complex Database

Key terms introduced in this project include

- equi-join
- first normal form
- fourth normal form
- inner join
- intersection table

- join
- left outer join
- many-to-many
- normalization
- one-to-many

- referential integrity
- right outer join
- third normal form

Objectives	Required Activity for MOUS	Exam Level
➤ Define Desired Output	Determine appropriate data outputs for your database	Core
➤ Organize the Fields into Several Tables	Create table structure	Core
➤ Relate Tables Using One-to-One and One-to-Many Relationships	Establish table relationships	Core Expert
➤ Relate Two Tables Using a Third Table	Establish many-to-many relationships	Expert
➤ Refine the Design to Eliminate Redundant Fields	Create table structure	Core
➤ Create Queries and Test the Design	Create and modify a multi-table select query	Core
➤ Document the Design		

Why Would I Do This?

There is a big difference between creating a database by following directions in a book and designing one yourself. There are errors that are easy to make when you are setting up tables that will not be immediately apparent but will cause major problems later when you try to create reports and analyze data. You may have entered hundreds or thousands of records before you realize that you cannot produce the reports you want, given the table structure that you have.

If you follow a few basic guidelines when creating your tables and setting up the relations between them, you can save yourself a lot of trouble later. Also, if you are working with an existing database that seems to be very difficult to use, you may be able to recognize its design flaws from the things you learn in this project.

This project teaches a method of setting up a database that assumes you have a good idea of the types of reports you want to produce.

Lesson 1: Defining Desired Output

Designing a database takes planning, a knowledge of what the program can do, and its intended use. This design method assumes that you can determine what type of reports are desired, how the forms will be used to look up individual records, what form letters you need to send, and what content should be posted to a Web site. As a person who is familiar with what Access can do, you must talk to the intended users and elicit from them a general description of what the reports, forms, documents, and Web pages must accomplish.

In this project, you use a case study to simulate this process.

The greatest temptation, and your biggest mistake, is to turn on the Access program at this point. If you do, it is likely that you will concentrate on the details before you have a master plan. For that reason, the exercises in the first lesson are done using planning aids, not Access.

In this project, we assume that you are designing a database for a small construction management company. This company has about twenty-five employees whose time is allocated to various projects. Each employee keeps a record of the time they spend on each project. This is done on a paper form that is turned in each week. The manager has come to you with a request that you put these records into a database so that various reports can be generated quickly and easily.

Start by assuming that you have conducted a survey of end-users and managers and compiled a list of fields that would go into a report.

To Define the Desired Output

1 **Launch Microsoft Word.**

2 **Open the file AC-1501 from the student folder on your CD-ROM. This is a sample of a time sheet that each employee fills out each work day (see Figure 15.1).**

3 **Open the file AC-1502 from the Student folder on your CD-ROM. This is a sample of the report that the manager has to prepare each month.**
Do not focus on the layout of the numbers at this point but look at the fields that are used in this report (see Figure 15.2).

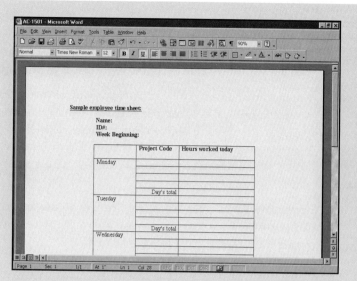

Figure 15.1
Workers fill out a time sheet each day summarizing the time spent on each project.

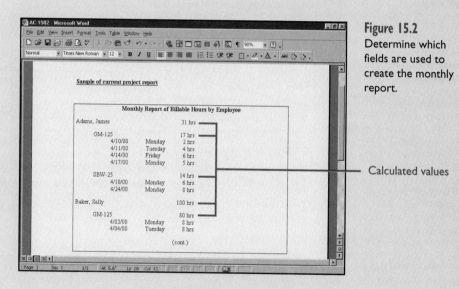

Figure 15.2
Determine which fields are used to create the monthly report.

Calculated values

4 **Open the file AC-1503 from the Student folder on your CD-ROM.**
Based on this information and an interview with the manager and selected end-users, you compile a list of fields and how they will be used. This information is arranged as shown (see figure 15.3).

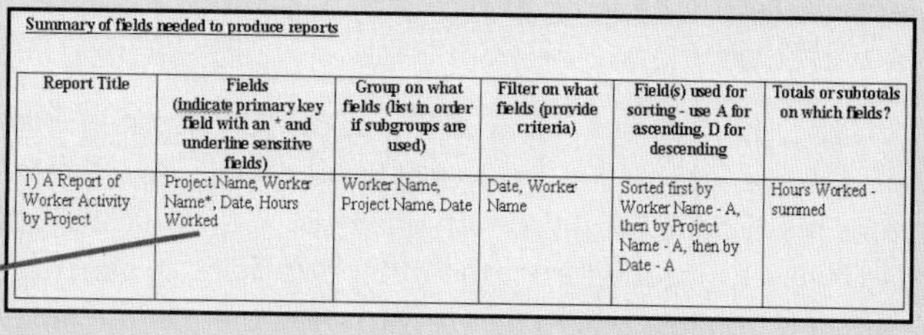

Summary of fields needed to produce reports					
Report Title	Fields (indicate primary key field with an * and underline sensitive fields)	Group on what fields (list in order if subgroups are used)	Filter on what fields (provide criteria)	Field(s) used for sorting - use A for ascending, D for descending	Totals or subtotals on which fields?
1) A Report of Worker Activity by Project	Project Name, Worker Name*, Date, Hours Worked	Worker Name, Project Name, Date	Date, Worker Name	Sorted first by Worker Name - A, then by Project Name - A, then by Date - A	Hours Worked - summed

Asterisk indicates primary key field

Figure 15.3
The fields needed to produce the report are listed along with how they will be used.

It is important to recognize that this process takes several iterations. Do not attempt to get it all right the first time.

continues ▶

To Define the Desired Output   (continued)

5 **Print the file AC-1503. Close all three word documents.**

You use this information about the report fields to plan your database tables.

Another method of getting information out of the database is to view it on-screen. Forms are best for this purpose if you are looking at one record at a time, because they can display a large number of fields on each screen. After further discussion, you identify a list of fields that the manager and end-users would like to see on the screen when they retrieve all the information about one individual.

6 **Open the file AC-1504 from the Student folder on your CD-ROM.**

These are the fields that the manager would like to see onscreen when he or she enters the worker's name (see Figure 15.4).

Figure 15.4
Identify the fields that should be displayed when the user requests information about a worker.

Indicate the key field with an asterisk

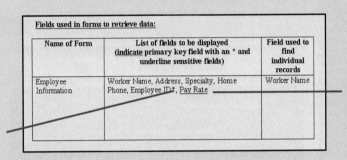

Underline fields that contain sensitive information

7 **Print this page and close the document. Close Word.**

You use these two field lists to design the tables that are used to produce this report and form.

 Lesson 2: Organizing the Fields into Several Tables

The records in a table should be about one thing. Each record should contain data describing one employee, one project, one activity, or one of whatever the table is about. The first step in organizing the fields into tables is to separate them into common groups according to the thing they describe.

Once you have separated the fields into common groups, you examine each field that you have defined to see if it is really two or more pieces of information that should be stored in separate fields. The Worker Name field is a good example. Is that just one field or should it be broken up into two or more fields?

You also check to see if any of the fields are calculated from other fields. For example, you may have a field for Hours Worked and another for Rate of Pay. If so, you do not need to store the product of these two numbers (wages) in the table. The value can be calculated each time it is needed from the other two fields. In general, it is better to calculate numbers each time you need them than it is to store them in the table.

Finally, you look for a field that can be used as the primary key field. It must contain a unique value for each record. If none of the fields qualify, use a counter field for the primary key field.

An examination of the fields listed in the Planning Reports and Planning Forms tables reveals that several of the fields are about employees. Now it is time to launch Access and start designing the tables. The first table you create is the Employee Information table.

Refer to the two field lists you printed in Lesson 1. These fields are used in the following steps. You need an empty, formatted floppy disk for use in this project.

To Organize Fields into Tables

1 **Launch Access. Select the Blank Access Database option, and click OK. Select your floppy disk in drive A and name the database** `Consulting`. **Click the Create button.**
The database is created on your floppy disk in drive A.

2 **Choose the Tables object button, if necessary. Double-click the Create table in Design view option in the Database window.**
The table design view is displayed.

3 **The most obvious field that should go in this table is Worker Name. Enter** `Worker Name` **in the first Field name box.**

4 **Look at the other fields in the report. Decide which ones, if any, directly relate to a worker and add them to the table design.**
If you are not sure, include the field.

5 **Look at the fields needed to produce the form. Decide which fields relate directly to the employee. Add those fields to the table design.**
If you are not sure, include the field. After you have made your selection, refer to Figure 15.5.

Choose appropriate data types.

Figure 15.5
Fields that describe the employee are added to the table.

6 **Revise your list of fields to match those shown in the figure. Close the table. Save the table as** `Employee Information`. **Do not choose a primary key at this time.**

7 **Double-click the Create table in Design view option to create a second table.**
This table is used for the rest of the fields, which have something to do with projects.

8 **Enter the fields related to projects in this table. Make sure that all the fields are used in one table or the other.**
Because this table is about projects, the project name should be unique.

9 **Select the Project Name field and click the Primary Key button (see Figure 15.6).**

continues ▶

To Organize Fields into Tables (continued)

Figure 15.6
Fields that describe the project are used in the Projects table.

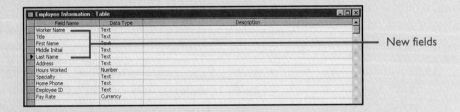

Primary key field

🔟 **Make changes to your table, if necessary, to match the example shown. Close the table and save it as Projects.**
This is not the final configuration of these tables, but it is a good place to start.

It is also necessary to examine each field to determine if it is the smallest practical unit of information. If the field contains two or more individual pieces of information, it is a candidate for further division.

To Make Each Field into the Smallest Practical Unit of Information

① **Select the Employee Information table and click the Design button.**
The Design view is displayed. The employee's name actually consists of several parts—Title, First Name, Middle Initial, and Last Name. The Title field can be used to store titles such as Mr., Mrs., Ms., and Dr. The title and middle initial fields are important if you ever use this information in a form letter.

② **Click in the row below the Worker Name field and click the Insert Rows button four times to insert four new rows. Enter the following field names—Title, First Name, Middle Initial, and Last Name (see Figure 15.7).**
These four text fields replace the Worker Name field.

Figure 15.7
The Worker Name field is divided into four new fields.

New fields

③ **Click anywhere in the Worker Name field and click the Delete Rows button.**

④ **Use this method to replace the Address field with the fields Street Address, City, State, and Postal Code.**

⑤ **Select the Employee ID field and click the Primary Key button (see Figure 15.8).**

⑥ **Close the table and save the changes.**
The smaller units of information provide many more options for sorting, filtering, and grouping the data in reports.

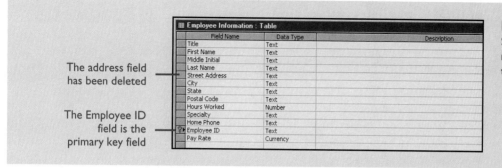

The address field
has been deleted

The Employee ID
field is the
primary key field

Figure 15.8
Smaller units of infor-
mation have replaced
the Address field.

This is a good time to consider security needs. In the last section of the interview, you asked the manager if any of the information is of a sensitive nature and should not be available to most of the people who would use the database. One way to handle this situation is to split a table into two tables—one table that contains the employee information that can be viewed by other employees, and the other table that should not be easily accessible.

To Create a New Table for Sensitive Information

1 **Right-click on the Employee Information table and choose Copy from the shortcut menu.**

2 **Right-click on an empty space in the Database window and select Paste from the shortcut menu.**
The Paste Table As dialog box is displayed.

3 **Enter Private in the Table Name box and select the Structure Only option. Click OK.**
A copy of the table that contains the field names, but no data, is created.

4 **Select the Private table and click the Design button. Delete all of the fields except Employee ID and Pay Rate. Add the fields, Date Hired and Performance Evaluation. Choose Date and Memo as the data types for these two fields.**
The Employee ID field is left because it is the primary key field, not because it is private information. It will be used later to connect this table with the others (see Figure 15.9).

The Employee ID
field will be used to
join tables

Field Name	Data Type	Description
Employee ID	Text	
Pay Rate	Currency	
Date Hired	Date/Time	
Performance Evaluation	Memo	

Figure 15.9
The Private table will
be used to store sensi-
tive information.

5 **Close the table and save the changes.**

6 **Select the Employee Information table and click the Design button.**

7 **Delete the Pay Rate field. Click on the row selector for the Employee ID field. Click and drag the field to the top of the list of fields (see Figure 15.10).**
It helps if the primary key field is listed first. It makes it easier to find if it is al-ways in the same place in the field list.

continues ▶

To Create a New Table for Sensitive Information (continued)

Figure 15.10
The Employee Information table will be used for non-sensitive information only.

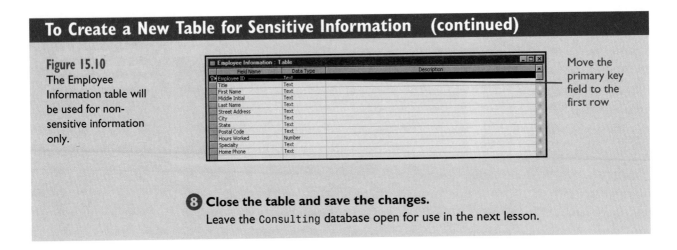

Move the primary key field to the first row

8 **Close the table and save the changes.**
Leave the Consulting database open for use in the next lesson.

 Core Expert **Lesson 3: Relating Tables Using One-to-One and One-to-Many Relationships**

The strength of a relational database such as Access is the capability to divide the data into several specialized tables. If this is done correctly, it minimizes the amount of data that needs to be stored. If you enter a person's address into the database once, there is no need to do it again. Storing each fact only once in a single location makes it much easier to change it.

The challenge to using multiple tables is that each table must be designed correctly and the tables must be linked together according to certain rules.

In this lesson, you establish two kinds of relationships between the tables.

To Link Two Tables Using a One-to-One Relationship

1 **Click the Relationships button. Select the Employee Information table and click the Add button. Repeat this process to add the Private table to the Relationships window, then click Close. Adjust the size of each field list box to display the entire list of names (see Figure 15.11).**
The Relationships window is used to create and view the joins between tables. The primary key field in each table is indicated in boldface type.

Figure 15.11
The Relationships window displays the fields in each table and any relationships.

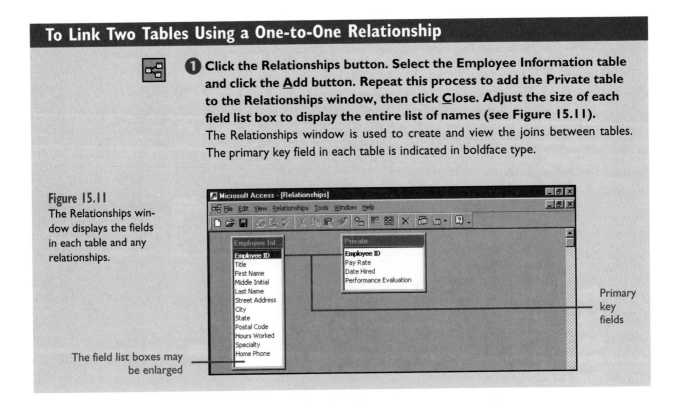

Primary key fields

The field list boxes may be enlarged

2 **Move the pointer onto the Employee ID field in the Employee Information field list. Click and drag the pointer onto the Employee ID field in the Private field list. Release the mouse button and the Edit Relationships dialog box opens.**

The program examines the tables and determines what relationship is possible between the two tables using these two fields. In this case, there is one record per employee. This is an example of a one-to-one relationship (see Figure 15.12).

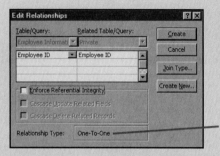

Figure 15.12
The Edit Relationships dialog box displays several relationship options.

There is one record per employee in each table

3 **Click the Join Type button.**

We want to make sure that all the records in the Employee Information table are displayed whether there is a corresponding record in the Private table or not.

> *Inside Stuff:*   **Three Types of Joins**
>
> There are three types of *joins* to handle the situation where one table may have records that do not have a corresponding record in the other table. For example, if temporary employees are listed in the Employee Information table, but nobody bothers to keep sensitive information about them in the Private table, you need to choose join number 2. If you used the first type, the temporary workers would not be included because they do not have matching records in the Private table. An example of a situation in which you might use the third type of join would be if you had some performance evaluation records for employees who were involuntarily out-placed (fired). They would no longer be in the Employee Information table but you would want to keep their performance evaluations. The third join would include all the records in the Private table and any corresponding records in the Employee Information table.

4 **Select option 2 and click OK. Click Create.**

A line between the tables indicates which fields are used to join the tables and the type of join (the arrow points from the table whose records are all included to the table from which only matching records are included.) See Figure 15.13.

5 **Close the Relationships window and save the changes.**

To Link Two Tables Using a One-to-One Relationship (continued)

Figure 15.13
Relationships are represented by join lines.

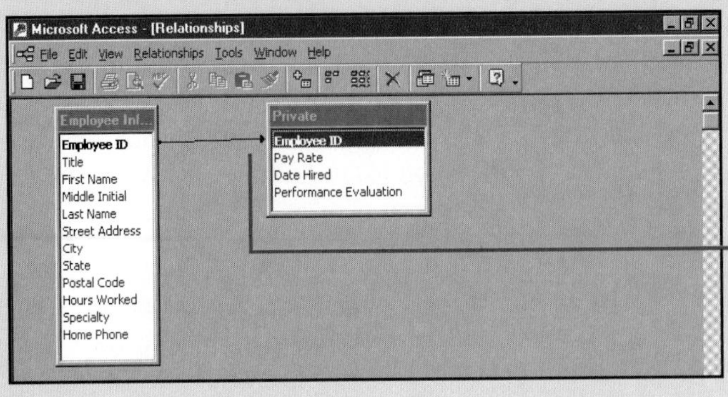

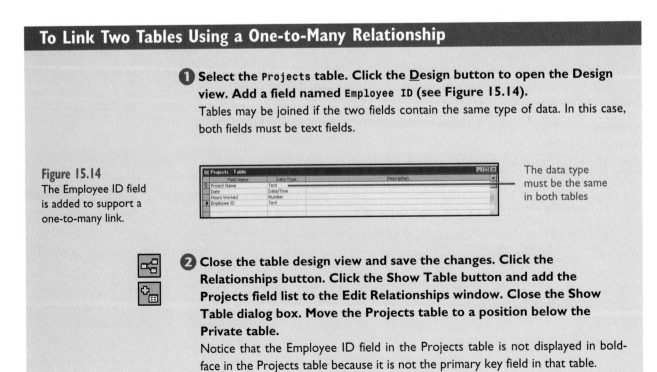

An arrowhead indicates the type of join.

The most common type of relationship is where one record in a table is related to many records in another table. In this example, one person may work on many projects. For each person in the Employee Information table (the "one" side of the relationship), there will be several records (the "many" side) in the Projects table. The way to establish a relationship between the two tables is to connect the primary key of the "one" table to a field in the "many" table that contains the same data.

We can establish this type of relationship between the Employee Information table and the Projects table if we add another field to the Projects table.

In this section, you add a field named Employee ID to the Projects table. This field contains the identification number of the employee who worked on the project. This field can be used to establish a one-to-many relationship.

One-to-many relationships occur between the primary key field in one table and a matching field in another table. The matching field is called the foreign key field.

To Link Two Tables Using a One-to-Many Relationship

1 **Select the `Projects` table. Click the Design button to open the Design view. Add a field named `Employee ID` (see Figure 15.14).**
Tables may be joined if the two fields contain the same type of data. In this case, both fields must be text fields.

Figure 15.14
The Employee ID field is added to support a one-to-many link.

The data type must be the same in both tables

2 **Close the table design view and save the changes. Click the Relationships button. Click the Show Table button and add the Projects field list to the Edit Relationships window. Close the Show Table dialog box. Move the Projects table to a position below the Private table.**
Notice that the Employee ID field in the Projects table is not displayed in boldface in the Projects table because it is not the primary key field in that table.

3 Move the pointer to the Employee ID field in the Employee Information table. Click and drag a join to the Employee ID field in the Projects table.

The Edit Relationships dialog box opens. The program recognizes that one of the fields in the relationship is a primary key field and the other is not. It displays the relationship as one-to-many (see Figure 15.15).

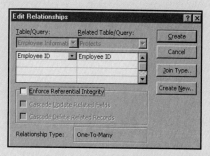

Figure 15.15
The relationship between the Employee Information table and the Projects table is one-to-many.

4 Click the Join Type button.

The three join types are displayed. In this case, we only want to see the records of employees who worked on projects. This is an example of a good time to use the first type of join.

 Inside Stuff: **Names of Joins in a One-to-Many Relationship**

The three types of joins in a one-to-many relationship have their own names. The first type of join that includes only the records that have corresponding records in both tables is called an ***inner join***. It is also referred to as an ***equi-join***. The other two joins assume that the table that uses its primary key field (the "one" table) is on the left and the other table (the "many" table) is on the right. The join that uses all the records from the table on the left (the "one" table) is called a ***left outer join***. The join that uses all the records on the right (the "many" table) is called a ***right outer join***.

These terms make more sense, and are easier to remember, if you envision two circles that overlap. Each circle represents all the items in one table. The overlapping area represents the items that are common to both tables (an inner join). If you want all the items from the left circle and only the items from the right circle that are in the overlapping area, it is a left outer join. If you want all the items in the right circle and only the items from the left circle that are in the overlapping area, it is a right outer join.

---

5 Confirm that option 1 is selected (the inner join) and click OK. Click Create.

A one-to-many relationship is displayed between the two tables.

6 Close the Relationships window and save the changes. Leave the database open for use in the next exercise.

Lesson 4: Relating Two Tables Using a Third Table

Upon further examination, you realize that there is a problem relating the Employee Information and Project tables. Each person's time sheet will list the project name many times. Because the Project Name field is the primary key field, it will not allow duplicate entries. The problem in this case is that there are many employees who work on the same project. This table cannot be used to record the timesheet data.

This is an example of a ***many-to-many*** relationship between Employees and Projects. Access does not have a direct way to join two tables together in a many-to-many relationship. Instead, we create a third table of individual activities, known as an ***intersection table***, that is used as an intermediary. We join the Employee table to it with a one-to-many relationship and then join a new Projects table to it with another one-to-many relationship. The intersection table contains the key fields from the other tables as foreign keys.

In this lesson, you rename the Project table and call it Activity. You use it to record individual activities from the time sheet. You also create a new table named Projects that has general information about the Project. The Projects and Activity tables are joined using the Project Code field.

To Relate Two Tables Using a Third Table

❶ Right-click on the `Projects` **table and choose Rename from the shortcut menu. Change the name to** `Activities`.

 ❷ Click the Design button. Select the Project Name field name. Click the Primary Key button on the toolbar to deselect the field as the primary key. Change the field name from Project Name to `Project Code`.
The Activities table does not have a primary key because all of the fields in it may contain duplicate data.

 ❸ Insert a new row and enter a new field named `Counter`. **Make its Data Type AutoNumber. Make it the primary key field for this table.**
You can use the Employee ID field to join to the Employee Information table and the Project Code field to join to a new table that has general information about the project (see Figure 15.16).

Figure 15.16
The Activities table can be used to join the Employee Information table and the new Projects table.

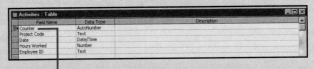

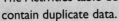
The Counter field is added to act as the primary key

❹ Close the table design and save the changes.

5 **Click the <u>N</u>ew button. Select the Design View option and click OK. Enter the following field names and data types:**

Project Code	Text
Project Name	Text
Description	Text
Start Date	Date/Time
Finish Date	Date/Time
Client Code	Text
Client Name	Text

These fields may be used to describe the project. The Project Code field may be used to join this table to the Activities table.

6 **Select the Project Code field. Click the Primary Key button on the toolbar to mark this field as the Primary Key field.**

The project code will be entered many times in two tables. It is better to use a short code instead of a long name. Your design should look like the example (see Figure 15.17).

The Project Code field will be used to join to the Activities table

Figure 15.17
The new table will be used to store information about the project.

7 **Close the table and name it `Projects`.**
There are now four tables in the database.

8 **Click the Relationships button on the toolbar.**
The Relationships window opens. Notice that you have to reestablish the connections to the Projects table.

9 **Click the Show Table button. Add the Activities table, then close the Show Table window. Adjust the location and size of the tables to resemble the arrangement shown (see Figure 15.18).**

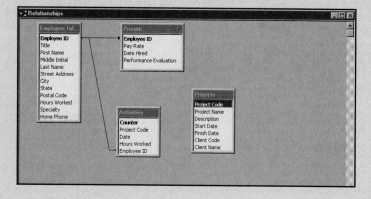

Figure 15.18
The Activities and Projects tables are ready to be joined.

continues ▶

To Relate Two Tables Using a Third Table   (continued)

10 **Right-click on the join line between the Employee Information table and the Activities table and select Edit Relationships from the shortcut menu.**

The Edit Relationships window opens. In the next step we will ensure that an activity can be performed only by an individual who first exists in the Employee Information table.

11 **Select the Enforce Referential Integrity option.**

When you select to enforce *referential integrity*, a matching field is required to exist in the joined table.

> *Exam Note: Attempting to Enter Data without Corresponding Records*
>
> If you attempt to enter an Employee ID number in the Activities table that does not have a corresponding record in the Employee Information table, an error message will be displayed and the entry will not be allowed.

---

12 **Click OK. A one-to-many join line is displayed between the tables.**

13 **Drag a join from the Project Code field in the Projects table to the Project Code field in the Activities table. Select the Enforce Referential Integrity option for this join as well. Click Create.**

The Employee Information table and the Projects table are both joined to the Activities table in one-to-many relationships (see Figure 15.19).

Figure 15.19
A many-to-many relationship can be achieved by using one-to-many relationships with an intermediate table.

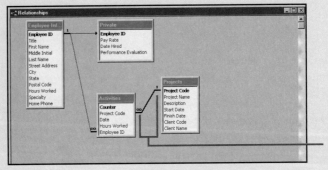

Symbols on the join line indicate a one-to-many relationship with integrity enforced

14 **Close the window and save the changes. Close the database but leave Access open.**

 ## Lesson 5: Refining the Design to Eliminate Redundant Fields

Before you enter data, it is important to make a final check of the design. Database experts have devised standards that you should use to design tables for a relational database. These standards use terms that are familiar to mathematicians. For example, applying one of these standards is called **normalization**. These standards were created to avoid problems when data is inserted or deleted from a table.

You already applied one of the rules when you divided the fields into their smallest practical unit of information. Once this is done, the table is in *first normal form*.

In this lesson, you learn how to evaluate the tables and their relationships to see if they conform to three of these normalization rules plus check for duplication of fields. There are four normal forms that are not included. They are the second normal form, the Boyce-Codd normal form, the fifth normal form, and the domain/key normal form. The second normal form and the Boyce-Codd normal form deal with tables that use two or more fields in combination to form key fields that we have chosen not to cover in this book. The last two types are advanced concepts that are not often used.

The rules that cover most common databases are:

First Normal Form   Each field contains the smallest meaningful unit of information and there are no repeating field names such as project1, project2, project3.

Third Normal Form   Each field in the table that is not a foreign key relates directly to the primary key.

Fourth Normal Form   There are no one-to-many relationships between the primary key field and another field in the same table.

In addition to these rules about individual table design, also make sure that fields that are not primary or foreign keys occur in only one table.

If you have a design that violates any of the first three rules, the solution is to create additional tables and move the problem fields to their own table. If you find the same field in two tables, and it is not being used as a primary or foreign key, remove the field from one of the tables.

At this point in the process, you discover that someone else tried to design a database to manage these projects but did not finish because they could not figure out how to get the reports they wanted. They spent a lot of time trying to get the reports to work, but the problem was really the design of their tables. In the next section, you examine the design that they used.

To Refine the Design and Eliminate Redundant Fields

❶ Click the Open button and locate the AC-1505 database file on the CD-ROM. Open the file directly from the CD.
You do not need to make changes to this database so you can open it in read-only mode.

❷ Click the Relationships button on the toolbar.
The Relationships window opens displaying the fields in the database's two tables and the one-to-many relationship between those tables (see Figure 15.20).

❸ Examine the two tables to see if any of the fields could be reduced to a smaller meaningful unit.
The Employee Name field in the TimeSheet table could be separated into Title, First Name, and Last Name fields (first normal form). The Day's Total and Week's Total may be calculated from the other fields. They should not be in the table at all (third normal form).

continues ▶

To Refine the Design and Eliminate Redundant Fields   (continued)

Figure 15.20
Examine these tables to see if they conform to the rules for table relationships.

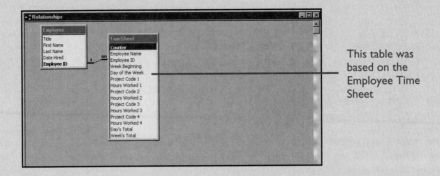

This table was based on the Employee Time Sheet

④ **Examine the TimeSheet table to see if there are repeating field names.**

The project code and hours worked information has been recorded in four different fields (first normal form). One of the reasons that this approach was abandoned was that the designer found out that some of the workers actually did five or six different jobs each day and wrote the work in the margin of the time sheet. The designer would have had to add more fields to the table and all the reports and forms that had already been designed.

⑤ **Examine the TimeSheet table to see if each field in the table (except the foreign key, Employee ID) relates to the primary key field (Counter) and not one of the other fields.**

The counter displays a different number for each row in the time sheet. One row of the time sheet is a day's work on one project. The Week Beginning field and the Day of the Week field have their own one-to-many relationship (third normal form). These two fields should be replaced by a single Date field that relates directly to the project task.

⑥ **Examine the TimeSheet table to see if there are any one-to-many relationships between the primary key (Counter) and any of the other fields.**

The table does not seem to have this problem. The Day's Total and Week's Total fields have a one-to-many relationship to the Counter but in the other direction. They would be removed because of other rule violations anyway.

⑦ **Examine the tables to see if any fields that are not primary or foreign keys are duplicated.**

The Employee Name field in the TimeSheet table contains the same data as the Title, First Name, and Last Name fields in the Employee table. It should be removed. Consider what would happen if an employee changed her or his name. If the name occurs in one location you only have to change it once. In this example, it would need to be changed in every record in the TimeSheet table.

⑧ **Close the Relationships window and close the database. Leave Access open.**

It is no surprise that this project ended in failure. The designer thought that he could just use the fields in the time sheet and then figure out the reports later. The data went in easily, but the reporting proved to be impossibly difficult.

The Consulting database that you have designed does not have as many problems as the database you just examined, but you are not done with the design until you check for these types of problems.

To Check for Design Errors in the Consulting Database

1 **Open the Consulting database and click the Relationships button.**
These tables are in first normal form, but a problem still exists (see Figure 15.21).

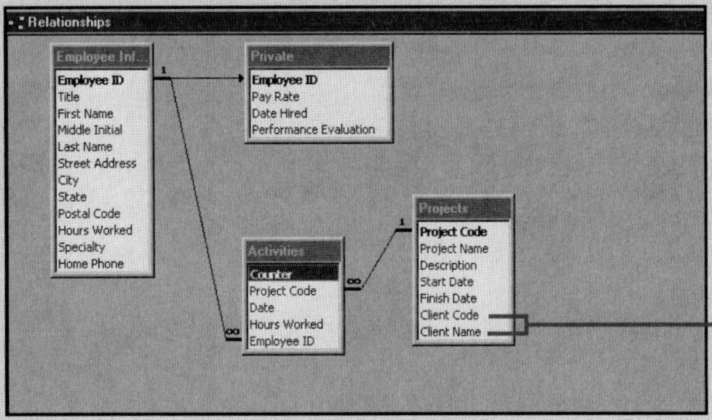

Figure 15.21
Examine these tables to see if they conform to the rules for table relationships.

These fields are related to each other

2 **Examine the tables to see if any of the non-key fields do not provide information about the primary key.**
The Projects table contains two fields, Client Code and Client Name that do not relate directly to the individual project. It would be valuable to know who the client is, but it is not appropriate to have both of these fields in this table. The solution is to create a separate table for Client information.

3 **Close the Relationships window. Click <u>N</u>ew to create a new table, select Design View, and click OK. Add the following text fields: Client Code, Client Name, Phone, Contact Person. Make the Client Code field the primary key. Close the table design and name it Clients.**

4 **Open the Design view of the Projects table. Delete the Client Name field. Close Table Design view and save the changes.**

5 **Click the Relationships button to open the Relationships window. Click the Show Table button and add the Clients table. Create a one-to-many relationship between the Client Code fields in the Clients table and the Projects table. Enforce referential integrity. Adjust the positions of the tables as shown in Figure 15.22).**

6 **Examine the tables to see if there are any examples of a one-to-many relationship between the primary key field and any of the fields in the same table that are not foreign keys.**
None of the tables have this problem.

continues ▶

To Check for Design Errors in the Consulting Database   (continued)

Figure 15.22
These tables are in first, third, and fourth normal forms.

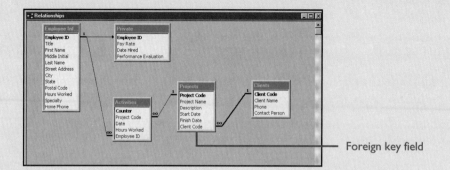

Foreign key field

⑦ **Examine the tables to see if any of the non-key fields are duplicated in more than one table.**
The fields that are used to join the tables are duplicated, but that does not violate this rule. The Phone field in the Clients table and the Home Phone field in the Employee Information table look suspicious, but they contain different information. The Hours Worked field exists in the Employee Information table and the Activities table. One of these fields must be removed.

⑧ **Close the Relationships window and save the changes. Open the Design view of the Employee Information table and delete the Hours Worked field.**
The tables now comply with all the Rules and are in fourth normal form.

⑨ **Close the design window and save the changes. Close the Consulting database. Leave Access open.**

The entire design process to this point could have been done without using a computer, and it may have been faster to do it on paper. Consider all the changes that were made to the table designs. If you had invested time entering data prior to this point, it would have been wasted effort.

 ## Lesson 6: Creating Queries and Testing the Design

The next step is to enter enough data in each table to enable you to test the design and then create the queries that are needed. In general, you want to enter enough records, with enough variety, to test the searching, sorting, filtering, and grouping described in the report and form designs. Then, you create queries that use the same fields that the reports or forms will use and see if you can sort and limit the data in the same way that is required by the report or form.

If your report or form design requires that you restrict the output by specifying criteria, you can test this by creating a query with the fields needed for the report or form.

If no restrictions are specified, you can create the report directly from the tables to test the design. Forms that use fields from several tables are often based on queries. Forms can also incorporate subforms to include fields from additional tables.

To save time, some data has been entered for you in a database on your CD-ROM. Information on the employee's specialty has also been added.

The report description requires that the user be able to restrict the output of the report to one month. If a report or form has such a restriction, create a query that contains the fields used in the report or form and use the criteria boxes in the query design to limit the output as desired.

To Create a Query to Test the Design

1 **Make a copy of the AC-1506 database file from the CD-ROM. Right-click the filename; select Properties from the shortcut menu, and remove the Read-only property. Use the shortcut menu to rename the file Consulting2, and then open the database.**

The name is changed and the Consulting2 database is opened for use. Confirm that you opened Consulting2 and not Consulting.

2 **Click the Queries button in the Objects pane and double-click the Create query in Design view shortcut.**

The Query1: Select Query window opens and the Show Table window opens in front of it.

3 **Add the field lists for the Projects, Activities, and Employee Information tables. Close the Show Table window. Check the report design to confirm that the required fields are present in at least one of these tables.**

The field lists for the three tables are displayed (see Figure 15.23).

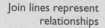
Join lines represent relationships

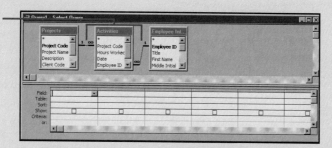

Figure 15.23
These tables contain the fields needed to produce the report.

4 **Refer to the grouping requirements for the report. Add Last Name and First Name to the design grid from the Employee Information table. Add Project Name from the Projects table. Add Date and Hours Worked from the Activities table. Maximize the window, if necessary.**

The fields necessary to create the report have been added to the design grid (see Figure 15.24).

5 **Set the Sort option to Ascending for the Last Name, First Name, Project Name, and Date fields.**

The fields will be sorted from left to right to simulate the sorting required by the report.

6 **To restrict the records to those between two dates, select the Criteria box in the Date column and type Between 4/1/00 and 4/30/00 (see Figure 15.25).**

continues ▶

To Create a Query to Test the Design (continued)

Figure 15.24
The design grid contains the fields needed to produce the report.

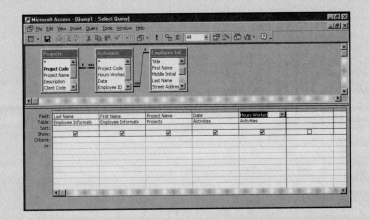

Figure 15.25
The first four fields are sorted and the Date field has a criteria limiting output to dates in April.

The criteria box is not wide enough to display the entire criterion

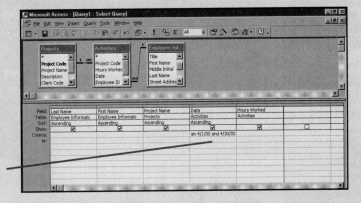

***Inside Stuff:* Using the Zoom Property to Edit Criteria**
The criteria box is too small to view any complex criteria like the one used in this lesson. You can right-click on the criteria box in the query design grid and a shortcut menu opens. Click on <u>Z</u>oom to open the Zoom window. You may use this window to write or edit a criteria that is too long to be displayed in the grid box. You can also open the Zoom window using (⬆Shift) + (F2).

 7 **Click the Run button to view the query in Datasheet view, sorted and limited to the records in April.**
This method of using a criterion will be replaced by a more advanced method, called a parameter query, in a later project. That method enables the user to enter a beginning and ending date each time the query is run.

8 **Close the query and name it** `Employee Projects`. **Leave the** `Consulting2` **database open.**

If a form uses fields from several tables, you can base the form on a query that contains those fields. To test the data to see if you can produce the proper form at a later time, create a query with all of the required fields and then see if you can locate the desired record using a form filter.

To Create a Query to Test a Form

1 **Double-click the Create query in Design view option. Refer to the list of field names that should be in the form. Add the tables that contain those fields. Close the Show Tables window.**
The necessary fields are found in the Employee Information and Private tables.

2 **Select all of the fields in the Employee Information table, then select the Date Hired, Pay Rate, and Performance Evaluation fields from the Private table.**
The Employee ID field does not need to be listed twice.

3 **Click the Run button. Maximize the screen. Scroll across the datasheet to confirm that it can display all the required fields from both tables.**
The fields that were added last are on the right.

4 **Click the Save button. Enter the name Test Form in the Query Name box and click OK.**
The query is saved. It can be used for reports or forms that need to display all of the fields from both tables.

5 **Click the drop-down arrow next to the New Objects button on the toolbar and select AutoForm.**
The fields of the query are placed in a simple form and they are arranged in a single column. This simple form may be modified later or deleted when the testing is finished.

6 **Click the Filter by Form button and click in the Last Name field.**
The form is displayed without data. A drop-down arrow is displayed next to the Last Name field to make it easy to choose from the list of existing names.

7 **Click the drop-down arrow next to the Last Name field and select Adams.**
This name will be used as a criterion for filtering the records displayed in the form.

8 **Click the Apply Filter button.**
All the records matching that criterion are displayed from the Employee Information and Projects tables. This form meets the basic requirements for the form (see Figure 15.26).

9 **Click the Remove Filter button. Click the Save button and save the changes. Close the form and the query. Leave the Consulting2 database open.**

continues ▶

To Create a Query to Test a Form (continued)

Figure 15.26
The form contains all the required information and is searchable by individual name.

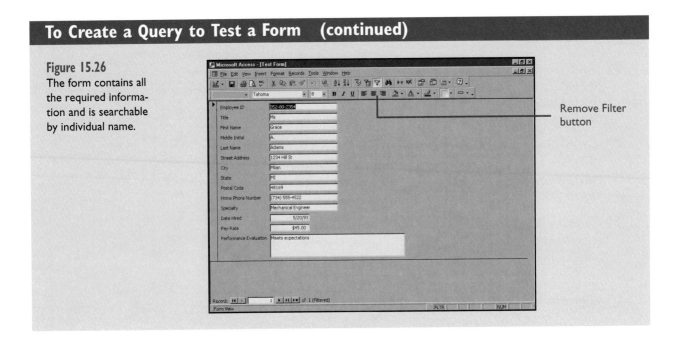

Remove Filter button

Lesson 7: Documenting the Design

The database design is adequate to produce the report and form that are required. It is likely that some additional fields will be required to produce other reports, forms, documents, or Web pages and you may need to add another table or two, but the basic design is sound.

This is a good time to print out the table relationships to document the design of this part of the database.

In this lesson you create a report that displays the table relationships at the time the report was generated. Unlike most other reports, this one does not update automatically when you change the relationships between tables.

To Document the Design

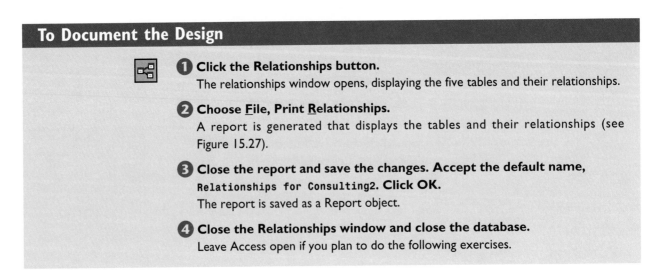

1 **Click the Relationships button.**
The relationships window opens, displaying the five tables and their relationships.

2 **Choose File, Print Relationships.**
A report is generated that displays the tables and their relationships (see Figure 15.27).

3 **Close the report and save the changes. Accept the default name,**
`Relationships for Consulting2`. **Click OK.**
The report is saved as a Report object.

4 **Close the Relationships window and close the database.**
Leave Access open if you plan to do the following exercises.

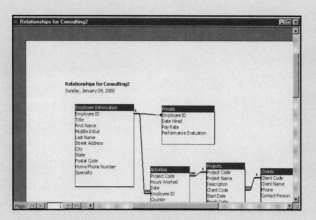

Figures 1.27
A report can be used to document the design of the tables and their relationships.

Summary

Proper design of the tables and the relationships between them is critical to the success of a database. This project uses a method that starts with the desired results and designs the necessary database to produce them. A case study is used to simulate an interview process by which the designer can determine the desired output of the database.

After the interview process determines the characteristics of the desired report and form, you are guided through the process of reorganizing the fields and tables and defining relationships between them so that they conform to rules for proper database design.

When the design is established, a similar database with test data already entered is used to evaluate the design to see if it can produce queries that have the same desired characteristics as the report and form. Once the queries demonstrate that the data can be recalled, as specified, the tables and their relationships are documented for future reference by creating a report that is designed for this purpose.

Checking Concepts and Terms

True/False

For each of the following, check *T* or *F* to indicate whether the statement is true or false.

__T __F **1.** Fields should be grouped into the same table if they all describe one thing, event, or person. [L2]

__T __F **2.** To create a many-to-many relationship between two tables, you drag a join between the primary key fields of each table. [L4]

__T __F **3.** All the fields in a table should describe or relate to the primary key field, not another field in the table. [L5]

__T __F **4.** A one-to-many relationship has a join between the primary key in the "one" table and the foreign key field in the "many" table. [L3]

__T __F **5.** Non-key fields should exist in only one table to avoid duplication. [L5]

Multiple Choice

Circle the letter of the correct answer for each of the following questions.

1. For what purpose are reports used? [L1]

   a. display all the fields, one record at a time

   b. print many records

   c. enter new data into tables

   d. search for data with interactive questions

2. How can forms be used to provide information quickly? [L1]

   a. A form can show all the fields in a record. The user can scroll through the records one at a time using the navigation buttons.

   b. The user can open a form and use the Sort button.

   c. The user can switch from Form view to Datasheet view to see more records at once and then scroll through them.

   d. The user can use the Filter by Form button to enter matching criteria in a blank form then apply the filter.

3. A one-to-many relationship is made between what two fields? [L3]

   a. the primary key field in each table

   b. the primary key in the "one" table and the foreign key in the "many" table

   c. the foreign key in the "one" table and the primary key in the "many" table

   d. the foreign key in each table

4. Two tables can have a many-to-many relationship under what conditions? [L4]

   a. One-to-many relationships are created between each table and a third table where the third table is on the "many" side of both relationships.

   b. The join is created between the primary key fields of each table.

   c. It is impossible.

   d. The join is created between the foreign key fields of each table.

5. Which of the following is not an example of repeating field names that are not in first normal form? [L6]

   a. Project1, Project2, Project3

   b. First Quarter, Second Quarter, Third Quarter, Fourth Quarter

   c. City, State, Postal Code, Phone

   d. Year1, Year2, Year3

Screen ID

Label each element of the Access screen shown in Figure 15.28.

Figure 15.28

A. Show Table button

B. Duplicate non-key fields

C. Field not related to the primary key in that table

D. Primary Key Field

E. Foreign key field

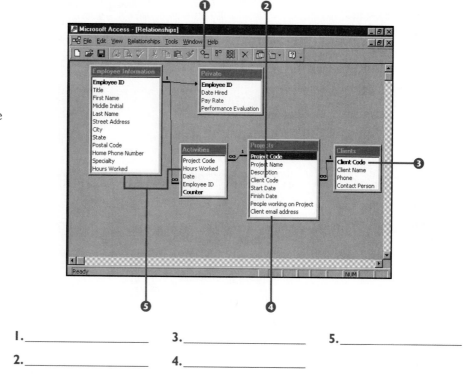

1._____ 3._____ 5._____

2._____ 4._____

Skill Drill

Skill Drill exercises reinforce project skills. Each skill reinforced is the same, or nearly the same, as a skill presented in the project. Each exercise includes a brief narrative introduction, followed by detailed instructions in a step-by-step format.

In the following exercises, you use a database that is essentially the same as the one you just created. (Some records have been changed to make it possible to distinguish the two databases.)

1. Selecting Fields for an Emergency Contact List Report

After your initial interview, the manager sends you a note describing another report that she would like to produce. You need to evaluate this report to see what fields must be added and in which table they belong. The note reads as follows:

The secretary would like a printout that displays a list of employee's names, an emergency contact phone number, the person to contact in case of an emergency, and that person's relationship to the employee. The list should be sorted by the employee's name.

To select fields for an emergency contact list report:

1. Make a copy of the AC-1507 database file from the CD-ROM. Right-click the filename; select Properties from the shortcut menu, and remove the Read-only property. Use the shortcut menu to rename the file Ex1501, and then open the database.

2. Click the Relationships button to view the field lists for the tables.

3. Compare the list of field names that the secretary would like to see in the emergency contact report to the lists of fields that already exist.

4. Determine which fields do not exist in any of the tables.

5. Create a new table named **Emergency Contacts**. Include the Employee ID field as a foreign key and the new fields. Let the program create a primary key when you save the table.

6. Open the Relationships window. Add the Emergency Contacts table and create a one-to-many relationship between the Employee Information table and the Emergency Contacts table. Compare the field lists in your tables with those shown (see Figure 15.29).

7. Close the Relationships window and save your changes. If you plan to do the next exercise, leave the database open and skip the first step.

Hint: Your answers may differ somewhat from those shown. For example, you may use several fields for the Contact Person's name. The definition of "smallest practical unit of information" depends on how the table will be used. If your answers differ from those shown, consider how you would justify your choices.

Figures 15.29
A new table has been added to produce the Emergency Call List report.

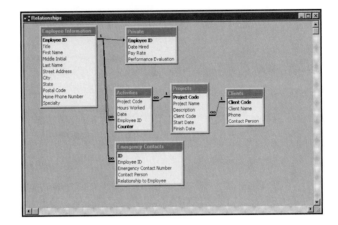

2. Selecting Fields and Modifying the Design to Allow Reporting on Employee Specialty

Another memo arrives on your desk from the manager stating that he or she wants to be able to produce a list of employees that is sorted by their specialty. The list should include their name, specialty, credentials, and the date they were hired. The list should be sub-sorted by date hired within each specialty.

To select fields and modify the design to allow reporting on employee specialty:

1. Launch Access and click the Open button. Locate **AC-1507** on your CD-ROM. Right-click the file and select Send To, 3 1/2 Floppy (A) from the shortcut menu. Change the Look in box to 3 1/2 Floppy (A:). Right-click **AC-1507**, select Properties, and remove the read-only property. Right-click **AC-1507** again and select Rename. Change the name of the file to **Ex1501** and press **↵Enter**. Open the file.

2. Click the Relationships button to view the field lists for the tables.

3. Compare the field names specified in the memo to the lists of fields that already exist.

4. Determine which fields do not exist in any of the tables.

5. Add the field(s) to the Employee Information table.

6. Open the Relationships window. Compare the field lists in your tables with those shown (see Figure 15.30). If you did not do the previous exercise, you will not see the Emergency Contacts table.

7. Close the Relationships window. If you plan to do the next exercise, leave the database open and skip the first step.

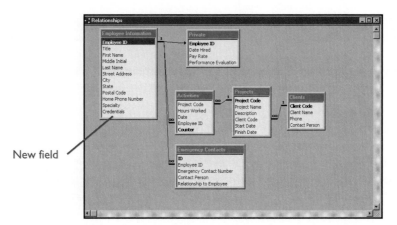

Figures 15.30
The Employee Specialties report can be created by adding one more field to the Employee Information table.

3. Selecting Fields and Modifying the Design to Allow Reporting on Employee Parking

The building manager had lunch with your manager and found out about this project. He would like to have a list of each employee's name and parking permit number so that he can check on cars that are parking in restricted areas. The list should include the employee's name, and parking permit number. The list should be sorted by the parking permit number. A typical number is SC-3459.

To select fields and modify the design to allow reporting on employee parking:

1. Launch Access and click the Open button. Locate **AC-1507** on your CD-ROM. Right-click the file and select Send To, 3 1/2 Floppy (A) from the shortcut menu. Change the Look in box to 3 1/2 Floppy (A:). Right-click **AC-1507**, select Properties, and remove the read-only property. Right-click **AC-1507** again and select Rename. Change the name of the file to **Ex1501** and press ⏎Enter). Open the file.

2. Click the Relationships button to view the field lists for the tables.

3. Determine which fields needed for the parking permit report do not exist in any of the tables.

4. Add the field(s) to the Employee Information table.

5. Open the Relationships window. Compare the field lists in your tables with those shown (see Figure 15.31).

6. Close the Relationships window. Close the database.

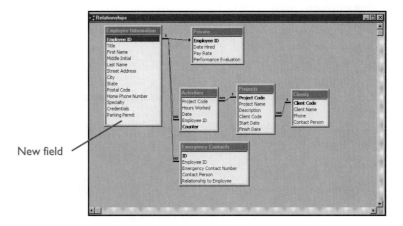

Figures 15.31
Reports on parking permits can be produced by adding one more field

Challenge 💡

Challenge exercises expand on or are somewhat related to skills presented in the lessons. Each exercise provides a brief narrative introduction followed by instructions in a numbered step or bullet list format that are not as detailed as those in the Skill Drill section.

1. Determining if the Design Will Support Summary Reports

The manager sends you another message that describes a report that would be very valuable to her. Each month, she has to submit a report to the owner that shows a list of employees and how many hours each of them spent on projects that could be billed to clients. This report does not show any details other than a list of employees, sorted by last name, the total number of billable hours for each one, and the time period covered by the report. It would be ideal if the secretary could generate that report each month by simply entering the starting and ending date of the month. He or she would like to know if you could do this.

You learn the details of how this type of report is done in a later lesson. Sometimes, you need to decide if something is possible, even if you do not know how to do it yet. At this point, it is enough to know that Access can produce reports that summarize numeric fields using either the Sum, Average, Minimum, or Maximum functions.

To determine if the design will support summary reports:

1. Launch Access and click the Open button. Locate **AC-1508** on your CD-ROM. Right-click the file and select Send To, 3 1/2 Floppy (A) from the shortcut menu. Change the Look in box to 3 1/2 Floppy (A:). Right-click **AC-1508**, select Properties, and remove the read-only property. Right-click **AC-1508** again and select Rename. Change the name of the file to **Ex1502** and press ↵Enter. Open the file.

2. Determine which fields are needed to print and sort the report.

3. Click the Relationships button to view the list of fields and their relationships. Determine which fields should be added to the design, if any, and where they should go. (*Hint*: no new fields are needed.)

4. Determine which field(s) would be summarized (summed in this case).

5. Open the table(s) that contain(s) the field(s) to be summarized. Check the data type to make sure that it is either Number or Currency.

6. If the database contains all the necessary fields and the field that needs to be summarized is a number or currency data type, this report is possible. Write a memo in Word to the manager that explains why this report is possible with the existing database structure or explain what would have to be changed to make it possible. Name the Word file **Memo**.

7. If you plan to do the next exercise, leave the database open and skip the first step.

2. Examining the Design to See if a Form with a Subform Can Be Used Conveniently

The manager calls and tells you that she would like to be able to quickly determine who is working on which project. It would be nice if she could enter the project name and bring up the project name, description, start date, finish date, and percent completed onto the screen and also see a list of the names of people who are working on the project. This is easy if all the fields are contained in two tables that are related by a one-to-many relationship. If the fields are spread out among many tables, it will be more difficult and involve creating queries to bring the data together until you can use a table and a query (or two queries) to create the Form/Subform pair. The purpose of this exercise is to determine if this will be a straightforward problem or a more difficult one.

To examine the design to see if a form with a subform can be used conveniently:

1. Launch Access and click the Open button. Locate AC-1508 on your CD-ROM. Right-click the file and select Send To, 3 1/2 Floppy (A) from the shortcut menu. Change the Look in box to 3 1/2 Floppy (A:). Right-click AC-1508, select Properties, and remove the read-only property. Right-click AC-1508 again and select Rename. Change the name of the file to Ex1502 and press ⏎Enter. Open the file.

2. Open the Relationships window and examine the field lists of tables.

3. Determine if all the fields needed for the project portion of the form exist in the Projects table.

4. Determine if all the fields needed to display the desired Employee information are present in the Employee Information table.

5. Determine if the two tables are joined in a one-to-many relationship. If they are not, a form/subform will not provide the desired results.

6. Write a memo to the manager providing your opinion of whether this form will present a problem to design or if it can be included in the database design without too much additional effort. Name the memo Memo2.

3. Modifying the Design to Create a Report for the Client

The accountant stops by your office to talk about the monthly invoices she has to prepare for each client. To assist in this process, she would like a report that has two levels. The first level would show an alphabetical list of projects. The second level would show a list of people who worked on each project and the total hours they worked.

This level of the report should also look up and display the person's specialty and billing rate. (The client is billed at a set rate per hour for each specialty.) It should then calculate the cost to the customer for that person's time. The report should have a subtotal of the cost per project and a grand total of the cost for the month. You would like to be able to print this report in its entirety or for an individual client and she would like to be able to specify any time period so she can choose between specifying the start and end date for the project or any other range of dates to prepare monthly or annual reports. She provides you with an outline of what the report might look like as shown below:

Project Cost to Client

For the period starting: 4/1/00 and ending: 4/30/00

Client: General Mechanics

Project: Paint Factory – safety inspection and action plan

    Baker   64 hrs   at $95/hr $5760

                      Total $5760

Project: Warehouse renovation

    Adams 2 hrs   at $105/hr $200

    Baker   43 hrs   at $95/hr $3870

                      Total $4070

Total for General Mechanics $9830

To modify the design to create a report for the client:

1. Make a copy of the AC-1508 database file from the CD-ROM. Right-click the file-name; select Properties from the shortcut menu, and remove the Read-only property. Use the shortcut menu to rename the file Ex1502, and then open the database.

2. Determine what fields are needed to produce this report. (*Hint:* The billing rate is not the same as the pay rate in the Private table. It is based on the specialty.)

3. Determine what report values are calculated and which ones are fields.

4. After the previous review, you determine that you need a new table that records billing rates by specialty. Create a new table named Specialty. It will have two fields, Specialty (primary key) and Billing Rate. Enter the following billing rates for the existing specialties as shown below:

Specialty	Billing Rate
Architect	$100
Civil Engineer	$95
Draftsperson	$35
Mechanical Engineer	$105

5. Create a one-to-many relationship between the primary key field of the new Specialty table and the corresponding field in the Employee Information table. Enforce referential integrity (the four specialty names shown above must be spelled exactly as shown or it will not work). See Figure 15.32.

Figure 15.32
The new table will be used to store information about the employee specialty.

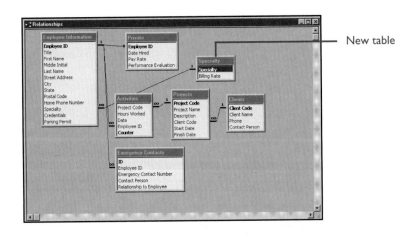

New table

6. Create a query that contains the field that is used to limit the scope of the report by date and the field that is used to limit the report by client. Add the other fields used in the report to the new query.

7. Create a calculated field in the query to determine the product of the hours worked and the billing rate. Use the caption Billed Amount for the field.

8. Use the sorting options in the query design to sort the fields by Client Name, Project Name, Last Name, and Date.

9. Use the criteria option in the Client field to limit the report to Rapid Prototyping Group.

10. Use the Between function in the criteria box for the Date field to limit the report to dates in April, 2000.

11. Test the query to see if it can display the data as specified for the report. You should be able to match the sorting and filtering requirements and display the calculated amount for each worker's billing amount (see Figure 15.33). It is not necessary to calculate the totals and subtotals at this time. They will be added in the final report.

Client Name	Project Name	Last Name	Date	Hours Worked	Specialty	Billing Rate	Billed Amount
Rapid Prototyping Group	Office annex	Adams	4/3/00	1	Mechanical Eng	$105.00	$105.00
Rapid Prototyping Group	Office annex	Adams	4/5/00	3	Mechanical Eng	$105.00	$315.00
Rapid Prototyping Group	Office annex	Adams	4/6/00	4	Mechanical Eng	$105.00	$420.00
Rapid Prototyping Group	Office annex	Adams	4/10/00	1	Mechanical Eng	$105.00	$105.00
Rapid Prototyping Group	Office annex	Adams	4/11/00	1	Mechanical Eng	$105.00	$105.00
Rapid Prototyping Group	Office annex	Adams	4/13/00	1	Mechanical Eng	$105.00	$105.00
Rapid Prototyping Group	Office annex	Adams	4/14/00	2	Mechanical Eng	$105.00	$210.00
Rapid Prototyping Group	Office annex	Adams	4/20/00	5	Mechanical Eng	$105.00	$525.00
Rapid Prototyping Group	Office annex	Adams	4/21/00	5	Mechanical Eng	$105.00	$525.00
Rapid Prototyping Group	Office annex	Adams	4/24/00	6	Mechanical Eng	$105.00	$630.00
Rapid Prototyping Group	Office annex	Adams	4/25/00	5	Mechanical Eng	$105.00	$525.00
Rapid Prototyping Group	Office annex	Adams	4/26/00	4	Mechanical Eng	$105.00	$420.00
Rapid Prototyping Group	Office annex	Adams	4/28/00	5	Mechanical Eng	$105.00	$525.00
Rapid Prototyping Group	Office annex	Baker	4/13/00	4	Civil Engineer	$95.00	$380.00
Rapid Prototyping Group	Office annex	Baker	4/19/00	1	Civil Engineer	$95.00	$95.00
Rapid Prototyping Group	Office annex	Baker	4/21/00	1	Civil Engineer	$95.00	$95.00
Rapid Prototyping Group	Office annex	Baker	4/24/00	1	Civil Engineer	$95.00	$95.00
Rapid Prototyping Group	Office annex	Baker	4/26/00	1	Civil Engineer	$95.00	$95.00
Rapid Prototyping Group	Office annex	Baker	4/28/00	2	Civil Engineer	$95.00	$190.00

Figure 15.33
Use a query to see if the data can be reported as required.

12. Save the query as `Cost to Client`. Close the database.

Discovery Zone

Discovery Zone exercises help you gain advanced knowledge of project topics and application of skills. These exercises focus on enhancing your problem-solving skills. Numbered steps are not provided, but you are given hints, reminders, screen shots, and references to help you reach your goal for each exercise.

These exercises use the same database that was used to do the Skill Drill and Challenge exercises. If you did not do those exercises, follow the instructions in the first Skill Drill exercise to copy the `AC-1505` file, rename it as `Ex0101`, and remove the read-only property.

1. Create a Form Letter and Connect It to a Query in the Company Database

The manager's secretary calls and says that she is supposed to send out a letter to all the employees who are eligible for an increase in benefits. To be eligible, the employee must have worked for the company more than five years. The form letter must include the employee's name, mailing address, a salutation that includes the employee's title (for example, Dear Mr. Jones), and his or her date of employment.

Goal: Create a query that contains the fields necessary for the form letter. Enter a criteria that will limit the records to those whose hiring date is more than five years (1826 days) ago.

You can use the computer's clock to determine today's date and then use that date in a calculation to determine the number of days difference between the value in a date field and the current date.

To create the form letter and it's associated query:

- Create a query that contains the required fields. Be sure to include the Date Hired field from the Private table.
- Sort the records alphabetically by last name and by first name.
- Add a calculated field that subtracts the Date Hired field from the Date().

Hint: For example, if you enter Date()-[Date Hired] in a field box in the query, the program will subtract the Date hired value from today's date. The result is the number of days separating the two dates.

■ Enter a criterion in the calculated field to limit the records to those in which the difference between today's date and the hire date is greater than the number of days in five years (1826).

■ Save the query using the name **Benefits**. Close the query.

■ Merge the query with a Word document that informs the employee that they are eligible for a new benefit. The letter should start with the employee's name, ID number, and mailing address. Insert the date hired somewhere in the body of the letter.

■ Save the letter on the floppy disk. Name it **Benefits Notice**.

2. Learn More About Normalization from the Expert

The seminal work on normalization of databases was written by E. F. Codd in 1970. His paper has been placed on the Internet by the Association of Computing Machinery.

Goal: Gain a historical and professional insight on how database professionals developed the rules for normalizing databases.

To gain a historical and professional insight:

■ Go to `http://wwwacm.org/classics/nov95/toc.html` and read section 3, A Relational View of Data, and Section 4, Normal Form.

■ Write a short paper that expresses Codd's ideas on these two subjects but do it in your own words as if you were trying to explain them to someone else.

PinPoint Assessment

You have completed this project and its associated lessons, and have had an opportunity to assess your skills through the end-of-project questions and exercises. Now use the PinPoint software Evaluation Mode to further assess your comprehension of the specific exam activities you have just learned. You can also use the PinPoint Trainer Mode and the Show Me tutorials to practice these exam activities.

Making the Input Form More User-Friendly

Key terms introduced in this project include

- ControlTip
- Format Painter
- Macro Builder

Objectives	Required Activity for MOUS	Exam Level
➤ Change the Color of Text, Backgrounds, and Borders Using Buttons	Modify Format Properties Modify Control Properties	Core Expert
➤ Use the Format Painter to Copy Formats Between Controls	Modify Format Properties Modify Control Properties	Core Expert
➤ Format More Than One Control at a Time	Modify Format Properties Modify Control Properties	Core Expert
➤ Change Colors Using Properties	Modify Format Properties	Core
➤ Add Status Bar Instructions in Form View	Modify Control Properties Modify Form Properties	Expert Expert
➤ Add Customized ControlTips to Controls	Modify Form Properties	Expert
➤ Create a Custom a Toolbar	Modify Form Properties	Expert
➤ Use the Macro Builder to Attach a Macro to a Form	Create a macro using the Macro Builder	Expert

Why Would I Do This?

Customizing the appearance and functions of Access helps to personalize the database, making it more interesting, informative, and easier to use. Effective use of colors, buttons, and help features can make the difference between a boring database and a professional-looking product.

Most data entry is done in Form view. Changing the text, background, and border colors can improve the look of the form and can also be used to provide important information to the user. You can use colors, for example, to warn the user of required fields. Changing the format or adding new features to each control on a form can be time-consuming. Access has a rapid format feature that can save a great deal of time.

Access gives you the option of adding customized help for the user. You can place instructions on the status bar, and you can even add ControlTips to the controls on a form. You can also improve the functionality of a form by customizing the toolbars. Predefined buttons that are included with Access can be added to any toolbar, and seldom-used buttons can be removed. The order of the buttons can even be rearranged.

Finally, you can use a feature called the Macro Builder to attach a macro to a form when various events occur.

In this project, you learn how to change the appearance of various form controls to give the user more information and to make the database look professional.

Lesson I: Changing the Color of Text, Backgrounds, and Borders Using Buttons

You can make the form easier to read through a restrained use of color. Try not to overdo the use of colors. Too many different colors on a screen can be very distracting, and bright colors with high contrast can be very hard on the eyes. You can also use colors as cues for the user.

In this lesson, you change the colors of the text (foreground), background, and control borders in a form using buttons on the Formatting (Form/Report) toolbar.

To Change the Color of Text, Backgrounds, and Borders Using Buttons

1 Find the AC-1601 database file on your CD-ROM and send it to drive A:. Right click the file name, select **P**roperties from the shortcut menu, and remove the read-only status. Use the shortcut menu to rename the file **Federal Census**, and then open the database.
The Database window should now be open to the Tables area (see Figure 16.1).

2 Click the Forms object button.
The 1900 Alcona County Census form should be highlighted. The table accessed by this form actually contains only the data collected from one township during that census. Because it is a subset of a much larger table, some of the fields may seem unnecessary, and there are empty fields that do contain information in some of the records that have been eliminated in this example.

3 Click the **D**esign button. Maximize the Design window and the Access window, if necessary.
The 1900 Alcona County Census form is ready for design changes.

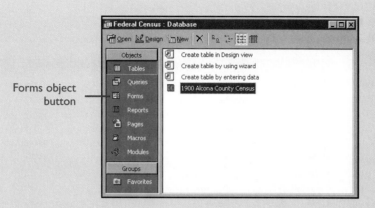

Figure 16.1
The Database window
displays the Tables
area of the Federal
Census database.

4 **Click the title "Alcona County, Michigan: 1900 Federal Census" to select it.**

Handles are displayed around the title (see Figure 16.2).

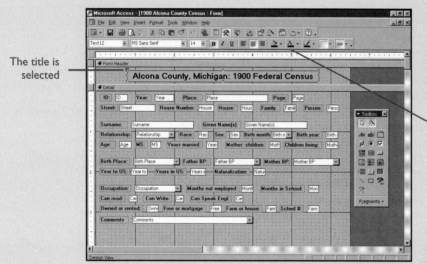

Figure 16.2
The title is in the Form
Header of the form
Design area.

5 **Click the down-arrow on the Font/Fore Color button on the
Formatting (Form/Report) toolbar.**

The Font/Fore Color drop-down palette is displayed. The Font/Fore Color button could, in this case, be called the Text Color button, although it can change
the color of any foreground. The left side of the button shows the current text
color. You use the down arrow to display a menu of optional colors.

6 **Choose a dark blue color (see Figure 16.3) and click it.**

The dark blue color, which appears in the sixth box to the right in the second
row, would be a good choice.

 Inside Stuff: **Default Button Colors**

Notice that the color on the Font/Fore Color button has changed to dark
blue. Once you choose a color for the foreground, background, or lines,
it becomes the default choice for that button on the toolbar. The color of
the button changes to indicate the current default, and you can apply that
color to a selected object by clicking the button without using the drop-
down menu.

continues ▶

To Change the Color of Text, Backgrounds, and Borders Using Buttons   (continued)

Figure 16.3
The Font/Fore Color drop-down palette offers a variety of colors for text.

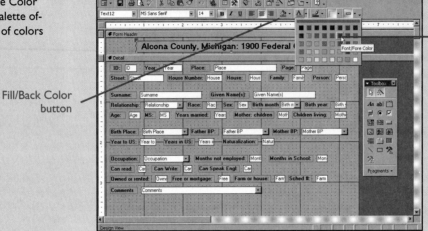

Fill/Back Color button

Dark blue option

 7 Click on the gray background area to the left of the title in the Form Header area. Click the down arrow on the Fill/Back Color button on the Formatting (Form/Report) toolbar.
The Fill/Back Color drop-down palette is displayed.

8 Choose a light blue background.
A background color that goes well with dark blue text is the fifth box to the right in the fourth row. Notice that the background of the title is still gray.

9 Click anywhere on the title to select it.
The title should show a border with handles as it did when selected before.

 10 Click the down-arrow on the Fill/Back Color button and click the **T**ransparent option.
When you want the background of a box to be the same as the background color of the area behind it, you can make the background of the box transparent.

 11 Click the down-arrow on the Line/Border Color button.
A drop-down palette appears. This palette is identical to the one found under the Fill/Back Color button. The most recently used colors are shown at the bottom of the palette (see Figure 16.4).

12 Choose the same shade of blue you selected for the title text from the **Recently Used Colors** area.
You can select the blue color from this area as well as its original location on the menu.

 13 Click the View button on the Form Design toolbar.
This switches from Design view to Form view. Notice the color combination in the Form Header area.

 14 Click the Save button to save your changes, then close the form.
Keep the Federal Census database open for the next lesson.

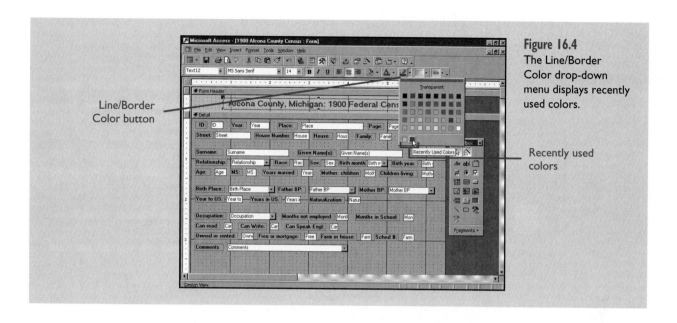

Line/Border
Color button

Figure 16.4
The Line/Border
Color drop-down
menu displays recently
used colors.

Recently used
colors

Lesson 2: Using the Format Painter to Copy Formats Between Controls

You can easily copy formatting from one control to another. The **Format Painter**, on the Form Design toolbar, can be used in several ways to copy formats from one control to one or more other controls.

To Use the Format Painter to Copy Formats Between Individual Controls

1 In the Federal Census database, click the Forms object button, if necessary, and open the 1900 Alcona County Census form in Design view.

2 Click the label for the ID field (ID:) in the Detail section.
Handles should appear around the label control box but not the field text control box (see Figure 16.5). Notice that the ID label is right-aligned.

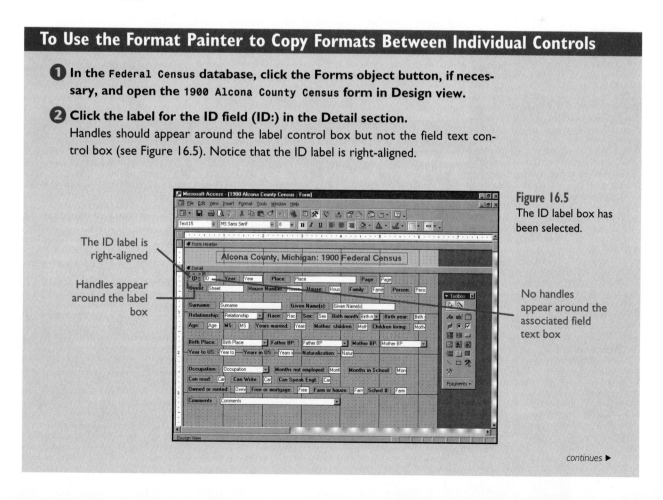

The ID label is
right-aligned

Handles appear
around the label
box

Figure 16.5
The ID label box has
been selected.

No handles
appear around the
associated field
text box

continues ▶

To Use the Format Painter to Copy Formats Between Individual Controls (continued)

❸ Use the Font/Fore Color, Fill/Back Color, and Line/Border Color buttons to change the colors to those you used for the title in Lesson 1.

Just change the ID label box on the left, not the ID field text control box on the right. Click the left side of each formatting button to apply the same colors you used in the previous lesson. If the default color for one of the buttons has been changed, use the drop-down arrow on the right of the button and choose the color the way you did in Lesson 1.

❹ With the ID label box still selected, click the Format Painter button in the Form Design toolbar.

The pointer changes shape, adding a paintbrush to the normal arrow (see Figure 16.6).

Figure 16.6
The Format Painter pointer has a paintbrush added to the arrow.

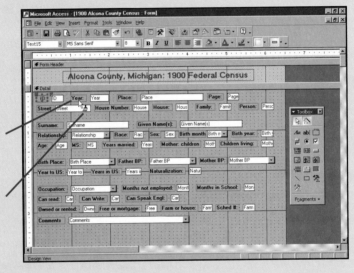

The Year label box

Mouse pointer for the Format Painter

❺ Click the Year label box.

The Fore Color, Back Color, and Border Color now match the ID label. Notice that the pointer no longer has a paintbrush attached.

 Exam Note: Unexpected Consequences of the Format Painter
The Format Painter will also apply the settings for font style, point size, and alignment. Notice that the Year label is now right-aligned. You need to keep an eye on alignment and number formatting to make sure the Format Painter doesn't make unexpected changes in your form!

Also, if you use the Format Painter to copy the format of a label onto a text box, you will not see any immediate problem. However, when you use the form, the text box shows a gray background instead of white when you tab to it to enter data.

❻ With the ID label still selected, double-click the Format Painter button.

Double-clicking locks the button on for repeated use.

7 **Click the label control box for the Place field.**

The Fore Color, Back Color, and Border Color now match the ID field label. Notice that the pointer still has a paintbrush attached. You can continue to paint as many label and field text controls as you want until you click the Format Painter button again to turn it off.

8 **Click the label control box for the Page field.**

Notice that the paintbrush remains with the mouse pointer.

9 **Click the Format Painter button once to turn off the Format Painter.**

Keep the `Federal Census` database open for the next lesson.

Lesson 3: Formatting More Than One Control at a Time

Access provides you with a faster way to change the format of several controls simultaneously. To do this, you need to select a number of controls at the same time.

To Format More Than One Control at a Time

1 **Move the pointer to the vertical ruler, immediately to the left of the ID field.**

The pointer turns into an arrow pointing to the right.

2 **Click and hold down the left mouse button.**

A thin line appears through the first row of controls.

3 **Drag the pointer down until it is to the left of the Age field.**

A thin line should appear through the row of fields that begin with the Age field, and the ruler appears black between the two lines (see Figure 16.7).

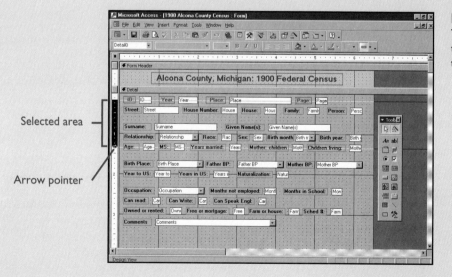

Figure 16.7
The vertical ruler turns black to show the selected area.

4 **Release the left mouse button.**

All of the labels and controls to the right of the dark area of the ruler are selected (see Figure 16.8).

continues ▶

To Format More Than One Control at a Time (continued)

Figure 16.8
Text boxes and label boxes were selected at the same time.

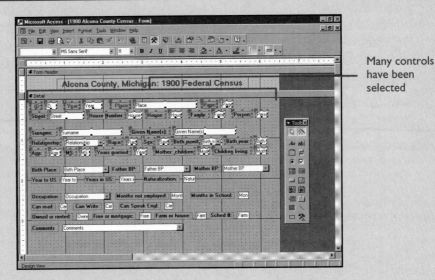

Many controls have been selected

⑤ Use the Font/Fore Color, Fill/Back Color, and Line/Border Color buttons to change the colors to those you used in Lesson 1.
The background, text, and border of the selected labels and controls should be changed. Notice that this method enables you to select the formats separately and does not change the text alignment.

⑥ Repeat steps 1-5 to select the remaining controls in the Detail area of the form and change the colors.

> **✕ If You Have Problems...**
> If you are using a screen with 640x480 resolution, you may not be able to see all of the remaining fields onscreen. Use the vertical scrollbar to scroll down so you can see all the fields that have not been changed.

⑦ Click in a blank area of the Detail section.
The background, text, and border of all the labels and controls should now match the Form Header area.

 ⑧ Use the Fill/Back Color button to change the background of the unused portion of the Detail area to the same light blue you used for the Form Header area.

 ⑨ Click the View button.
Notice the color combination of the form. Also notice that the combo box buttons remain gray and black (or whatever colors were chosen as default colors), as do the perimeter portions of the screen, such as the status bar and the scrollbars (see Figure 16.9).

 ⑩ Click the Save button to save your changes, then close the form.
Keep the Federal Census database open for the next lesson.

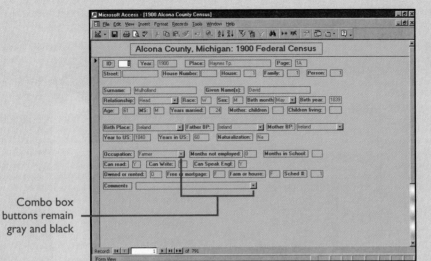

Figure 16.9
The colors of various elements of the form were changed.

Combo box
buttons remain
gray and black

✍️ **Exam Note: Other Shortcuts for Selecting Multiple Controls**
The procedure used in Lesson 3 involves several steps to select all the
components of the Detail area. If you know that all the objects on the
form will be formatted the same way, you can use the Select **A**ll option
from the **E**dit menu. If you are going to format most of the objects the
same way, you can use the Select **A**ll option, then hold ⬆Shift down and
click the ones you don't want to format to deselect them. If you want to
format only a few controls, you can hold down ⬆Shift and click to select
all the controls that you want to format.

Lesson 4: Changing Colors Using Properties

In Lesson 2, you used the buttons on the Form Design toolbar to change the color of the
background, text, and borders. Using the Properties box gives you many more colors and
shades from which to choose. This is especially important if, for example, you are attempting
to make your form colors match your company's colors. Several other formatting options are
available in the Properties box.

In this lesson, you use the Properties box to change the color of the three required fields in
this form. This warns users that these fields are special in some way.

To Change Colors Using Properties

1 Highlight the 1900 Alcona County Census form, click the **D**esign button, and maximize the form, if necessary.

2 Right-click the Surname label control box.
The Surname field is one of the fields you want to identify as required by changing the color.

3 Choose **P**roperties from the shortcut menu and click the Format tab,
if necessary.

continues ▶

To Change Colors Using Properties   (continued)

4 Scroll down until you can click in the Fore Color text box.

The Fore Color is identified by a numeric code (black is 0), and a Build button is displayed on the right side of the Fore Color text box (see Figure 16.10).

Figure 16.10
The Format tab in the Properties box offers a variety of formatting options.

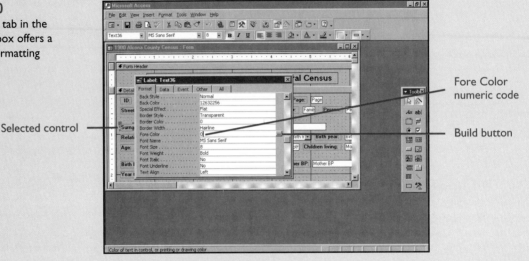

5 Click the Build button.

The Color dialog box is displayed.

6 Click the Define Custom Colors button.

The Color dialog box expands to include a box showing a range of color options. The current color is indicated by an arrow on the right side and by crosshairs at the top edge of the multi-colored box (see Figure 16.11). The look of your color box depends on your computer's display settings.

Figure 16.11
The Color dialog box has been expanded to show custom colors.

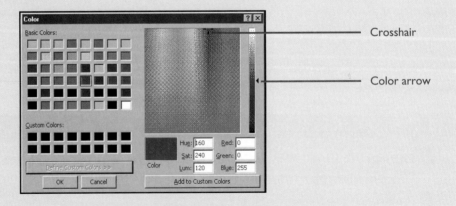

7 Click on a bright red area of the multi-color box and click OK.

8 Close the Properties box.

You have now warned the user that the Surname field is special in some way. (You let them know exactly what is special about it in Lessons 5 and 6). Now copy the format of the Surname label to the other two required fields.

9 **With the Surname label control still selected, double-click the Format Painter button.**

10 **Click the Given Name(s) and Relationship label controls to change the color of the text to match the color of the Surname label.**

11 **Click the Format Painter button again to turn it off.**

12 **Click the View button.**
Notice that the three required fields stand out on the screen (see Figure 16.12).

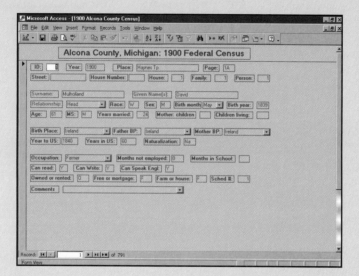

Figure 16.12
Colors have been added to identify special fields.

13 **Click the Save button to save your changes, and then close the form.**
Keep the `Federal Census` database open for the next lesson.

Lesson 5: Adding Status Bar Instructions in Form View

In Lesson 4, you learned how to give the user a visual cue that there was something special about a field. If you want to make the form easy to use, you may also need to give the user help on what to put in the field and provide information on any special characteristics of the field. Access provides several ways to help the user, including printed instructions, status bar messages, and custom ControlTips.

In this lesson, you add help to the status bar. In Lesson 6 you create custom ControlTips.

To Add Status Bar Instructions in Form View

1 **Highlight the `1900 Alcona County Census` form in the Forms window, click the Design button, and maximize the form, if necessary.**

2 **Right-click the Surname text control box.**
Make sure you use the text control box, not the label control box you worked on in Lesson 4. A shortcut menu is displayed.

3 **Choose Properties from the shortcut menu and click the Other tab.**

continues ▶

To Add Status Bar Instructions in Form View (continued)

 Click the Status Bar Text box.

 If You Have Problems...
If you don't see the Status Bar Text box, you probably right-clicked the Surname label control box instead of the Surname field text control box in step 2. Leave the Properties box open and click the Surname field text control box. The Properties box displays the properties of the currently selected object.

 Type the following text:
Enter the person's last name. If unreadable, type a question mark (?); if blank, type "not given".

This is the text that appears in the status bar when the cursor is in the Surname field (see Figure 16.13). The Properties box in Figure 16.13 has been expanded to show the entire label in the Status Bar Text box.

Figure 16.13
Whatever is typed into the Status Bar Text box appears in the status bar.

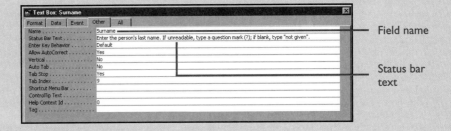

Inside Stuff: Maximum Length of Status Bar Message
When creating a message for the status bar, you want to limit the length of the message so that the entire message is visible on the status bar when that field is selected. Try to keep your message under 75 characters if the database will be used on a machine using 640x480 resolution, and about 120 characters for 800x600 resolution.

 Click the field text box of the Given Name(s) field. Enter the following text in its Status Bar Text box:
Enter the person's given name(s). If unreadable, type a question mark (?); if blank, type "not given".

This message is slightly altered from the text used for the Surname field.

 If You Have Problems...
To see the text box of the Given Name(s) field, you may need to drag the Properties box out of the way. Click on the blue title bar of the Properties box and drag it to another part of your screen so you can select the new control. When you click the Given Name(s) Text box, the title on the Properties box changes to reflect the new field that has been selected. Make sure the title bar says Text box: Given Name(s).

7 **Click the Relationship field text box and place the following text in the Status Bar Text box:**

Enter the person's relationship to the head of household. If unreadable, type ?; if blank, type "not given".

8 **Close the Properties box.**

9 **Click the View button and then click the Relationship text box.**

The message you typed appears in the status bar (see Figure 16.14).

 If You Have Problems...

If the status bar does not appear at the bottom of your screen, choose Tools, Options from the menu. Click the View tab in the Options dialog box, if necessary, and then click the Status Bar check box in the Show area.

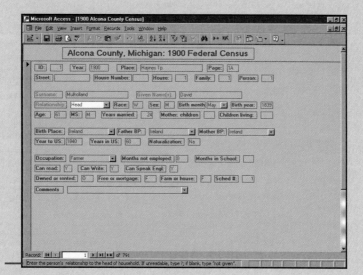

New status bar text ———

Figure 16.14
The status bar displays the message you entered into the Status Bar Text area of the Properties box.

10 **Click the Save button to save your changes, then close the form.**

Keep the Federal Census database open for the next lesson.

 Inside Stuff: Copying and Pasting Status Bar Text

It might seem that the Format Painter could be used to copy status bar text. The Format Painter, however, works on those functions that change the appearance of an object. It does not work on any of the customized features that require that text be entered. If you are entering identical (or similar) text to the status bar for several fields, type the text into a field, highlight it, and then use the copy and paste commands to place the text in the status bar text areas of subsequent fields. (You have to use the keyboard shortcuts or the right mouse shortcut menu to copy and paste because the menu and toolbar versions of copy and paste apply to the selected object, not the boxes in the Properties dialog box.)

Lesson 6: Adding Customized ControlTips to Controls

In Windows, when you move the pointer over a button on a toolbar and leave it there for a short time, a ScreenTip appears telling you what the button does. You can add the same feature to the controls on your forms, which can help make the form easier to use. In a form, these ScreenTips attached to controls are known as **ControlTips**.

In this lesson, you add ControlTips to augment the status bar messages you created in Lesson 5. You also use a ControlTip to tell the user how to change a default value.

To Add Customized ControlTips to Controls

❶ Highlight the `1900 Alcona County Census` **form, click the _D_esign button, and maximize the form, if necessary.**

❷ Right-click the Surname field text control box and choose _P_roperties from the shortcut menu.

❸ Click the Other tab, if necessary, then click the ControlTip Text box.

> **✗** **_If You Have Problems..._**
> There should be 12 Other options. If there are only five, it means you selected the Surname label control box instead of the field text control box.

❹ Type in the following text, adding ⟨⇧Shift⟩+⟨⏎Enter⟩ after each of the first three lines:
```
Do not leave this blank.
Check the status bar on
the bottom of the screen
for further instructions.
```

This is the text that appears in the ControlTip when the pointer is moved over the Surname field. If you don't add the ⟨⇧Shift⟩+⟨⏎Enter⟩ at the end of each line, the ControlTip is displayed as a single line, often disappearing off the edge of the screen. Only the last line entered for the ControlTip is displayed in the ControlTip Text box (see Figure 16.15).

Figure 16.15
The ControlTip Text box appears when the pointer is held over the field in Form view.

Last line of the ControlTip text

❺ Click the Given Name(s) field text box. Locate the ControlTip Text box in the Properties box and enter the same message.

Inside Stuff: **Copying and Pasting ControlTip Text**
Instead of retyping the same text three times, you can copy the text from
the Surname ControlTip text box and paste it into the ControlTip text
boxes for the First Name(s) field. To copy the text, click another box,
then click at the beginning of the ControlTip Text box, hold the mouse
down, and drag to the right and down. This selects all four rows of text.
Press Ctrl+C to copy the text. Move the Properties dialog box until you
can see the Given Names(s) field text control box, click in the ControlTip
Text box, and press Ctrl+V to paste the text. Repeat the procedure for
the Relationship field text control box.

**6 Repeat step 4 to place the identical text in the ControlTip Text box of
the Relationship field text control box.**
In each case, the ControlTip tells the user how to find more information. The
same procedure can be used to give instructions for anticipated problems. In this
database, for example, the Place field has a default value. As the user moves from
township to township, this default value has to be changed.

 Inside Stuff: **Type ControlTip Text into More than One Field
at a Time**
You can change the same property on several controls at the same time.
For example, to add the ControlTip that you entered in this lesson, you
could select the Surname text control box, hold down ↑Shift and click
the other two controls, then open the Properties box. When you type in
the ControlTip text, it is entered into all three controls.

**7 Repeat step 4 for the Place field, but enter the following text in the
ControlTip Text area. Remember to add a ↑Shift+↵Enter after each of
the first four lines:**
```
To change the Place default value, close this form and
click the Tables object button. Select the 1900 Alcona
County Census table and click the Design button. Select
the Place field, then type the new Default Value in the
Field Properties area.
```

There is a limit of 255 characters for a ControlTip message. This message is
close to the maximum size.

8 Close the Properties box.

**9 Click the View button. Click the Surname field and leave the pointer
over the Surname field.**
Look at the ControlTip and the status bar (the cursor is in the Surname field).
These types of messages can be very helpful, especially to a new user (see
Figure 16.16).

10 Click the Save button to save your changes, then close the form.
Keep the Federal Census database open for the next lesson.

continues ▶

To Add Customized ControlTips to Controls   (continued)

Figure 16.16
Status bar and
ControlTip messages
can be of great help to
the new user.

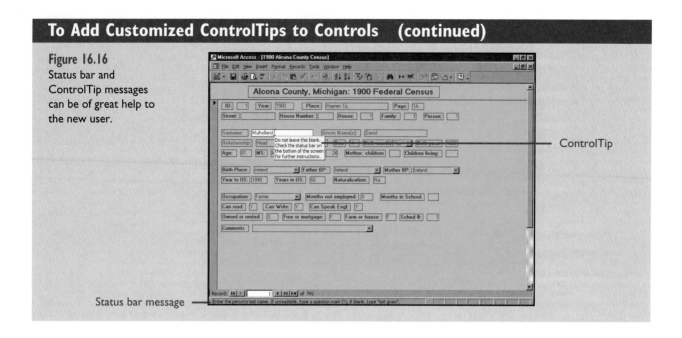

ControlTip

Status bar message

 Exam Note: **ControlTip is Linked to Pointer**
The ControlTip is linked to the pointer, whereas the status bar is linked to the in-
sertion point. If you have the insertion point in one box and point at another, the
ControlTip and the status bar message will not refer to the same field.

 ## Lesson 7: Creating a Custom Toolbar

The toolbars associated with the various components of Access are helpful to both the database designer and the end-user. Although the end-user seldom uses any of the buttons associated with the various design views, there are always tasks that can be performed using
toolbars, such as sorting, filtering, and printing. There are more buttons available than are
shown in the default toolbars. These buttons can be added to toolbars, and unused buttons
can be removed.

In this lesson, you turn on an empty toolbar and add several buttons to it.

To Create a Custom Toolbar

1 **Highlight the** 1900 Alcona County Census **form, click the Open button,
and maximize the form if necessary.**

2 **Right-click the Form View toolbar.**
A shortcut menu is displayed.

3 **Choose Customize from the shortcut menu.**
The Customize dialog box displays tabs for three sections: Toolbars, Commands,
and Options (see Figure 16.17).

4 **Select the Toolbars tab, if necessary. Scroll down the list of toolbars
and click the checkbox for the Utility 1 toolbar.**
This toolbar is normally empty and can be used to create a customized toolbar.
As soon as you check the box, an extra toolbar is added (see Figure 16.18).

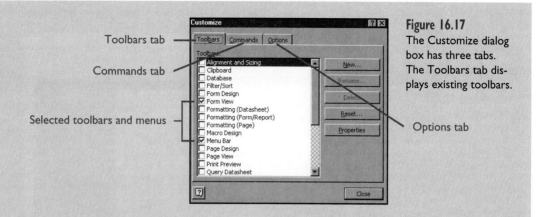

Figure 16.17
The Customize dialog box has three tabs. The Toolbars tab displays existing toolbars.

Toolbars tab

Commands tab

Selected toolbars and menus

Options tab

Figure 16.18
The Utility 1 toolbar is added as soon as its box is checked.

Utility 1 toolbar

⑤ Select the Commands tab in the Customize dialog box.

There are many buttons that can be added to the toolbar. They are grouped by the categories displayed on the left, with the individual buttons shown on the right.

⑥ Click Records in the Categories section.

A list of commands that are useful for dealing with records is displayed.

⑦ Click the Filter Excluding Selection command and drag it up to the new Utility 1 toolbar (see Figure 16.19).

⑧ Release the mouse button.

The command is added to the toolbar. Because this command does not have a button, the text is included on the new button in the toolbar.

> **✕ If You Have Problems...**
>
> To add a new button, you need to drag the button to the beginning of the toolbar at the far-left end where a small box marks the current size of the toolbar. When the button is successfully placed, a large, bold I-bar (**I**) is displayed to show the insertion point.

continues ▶

To Create a Custom Toolbar   (continued)

Figure 16.19
When adding a button to the toolbar, a small button appears to be attached to the pointer arrow.

Insert command pointer

I-bar indicates where the button will go

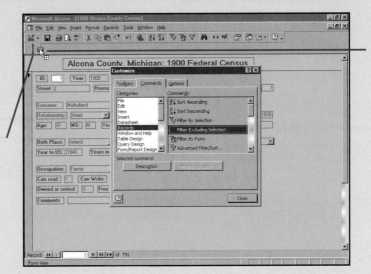

9 Scroll down the list of Records commands to select the command for First. Drag it onto the Utility 1 toolbar to the right of the Filter Excluding Selection button.

10 Add the Previous, Next, and Last buttons to the right of the First button.

You may have to move the Customize dialog box out of the way so you can see your new toolbar, but do not close it. The Customize dialog box must be open for you to customize a toolbar. You now have five buttons on the Utility 1 toolbar. In the next step, you create a separation mark on the toolbar that is useful for visually grouping similar buttons. In this case, the first button is used to manage records, while the next four are navigation buttons that are larger and easier to use than the navigation buttons at the bottom of the window.

11 Click on the First button (the one to the right of the Filter Excluding Selection button) and drag to the right about 1/8 of an inch. Release the mouse button.

This moves the button to the right and inserts a vertical separating bar (see Figure 16.20). The navigation buttons are now grouped together.

 Inside Stuff: **Removing Buttons from a Toolbar**

You will use some of the buttons on the toolbar only rarely. You can easily remove these buttons using the Customize feature you used to add a toolbar and buttons. To remove buttons from a toolbar, right-click on any toolbar and select <u>C</u>ustomize from the shortcut menu. Click on the button you want to remove and drag it below the toolbar. When you release the mouse button, the unwanted button will disappear. (*Note:* You can always return the button to the toolbar; it is not removed permanently.)

12 Close the Customize dialog box. Try the new navigation buttons to make sure they work properly.

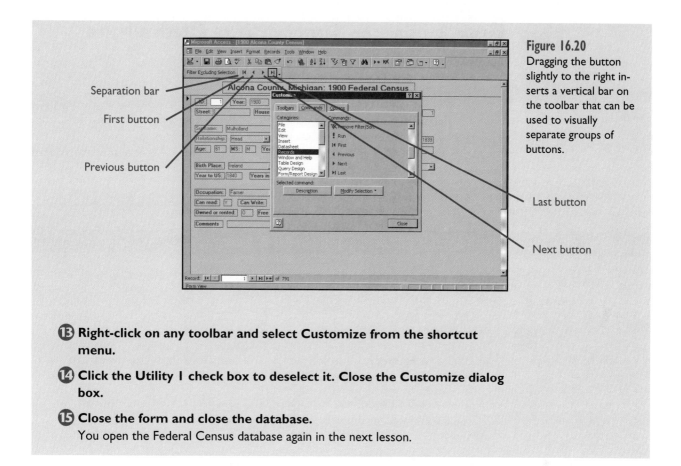

Separation bar

First button

Previous button

Last button

Next button

Figure 16.20
Dragging the button slightly to the right inserts a vertical bar on the toolbar that can be used to visually separate groups of buttons.

13 Right-click on any toolbar and select Customize from the shortcut menu.

14 Click the Utility 1 check box to deselect it. Close the Customize dialog box.

15 Close the form and close the database.
You open the Federal Census database again in the next lesson.

Inside Stuff: **Setting Form Properties**
You can control the level of user access to the form by setting form properties. For example, you can turn many of the screen elements on or off. To do this, double-click the form selector (the little square in the upper-left corner of the Form window). This opens the form property sheet. Select the Format tab, and then turn such things as scroll bars and navigation buttons on or off.

You can also use the same procedure to stop the user from resizing the form window. In the form property sheet, select the Format tab and select one of the Border Style options. The default is Sizable, but you can also choose to have no border on the form, or you can include a thin border, which also enables the user to do everything to the form except resize it.

Exam Note: **Resetting the Toolbars**
The toolbars are part of the Access interface, not one particular database. When you change the toolbars, it affects anyone else who is using the application. Do not change the standard toolbars unless you have the permission of other users or it is your personal machine.

If you are working in a lab environment, you will need to reset any toolbars you have modified to their original condition once you are through with the exercises. To restore the Utility 1 toolbar, right-click on any toolbar, click Customize, highlight the Utility 1 toolbar name, and click the Reset button. Click OK when prompted to reset toolbar.

Lesson 8: Using the Macro Builder to Attach a Macro to a Form

When you opened the 1900 Alcona County Census form for the first time (in Lesson 1), the form window was not maximized. Once you maximize the form, it stays that way until you close the database. Each time you open the database, the form will return to a non-maximized window. You can attach a macro to the form to automatically maximize the form window every time the form is opened. Access even provides a special tool, the ***Macro Builder***, that makes the macro creation process easy.

In this lesson, you attach a macro to a form to maximize the form when it is opened.

To Use the Macro Builder to Attach a Macro to a Form

1 **Open the** Federal Census **database, click the Forms object button, and open the** 1900 Alcona County Census **form.**
Notice that the form window is not maximized.

2 **Click the View button to switch to Design view.**

3 **Click the Properties button on the toolbar and select the Event tab.**
Macros can be attached to nearly all of the events shown.

4 **Click the On Open text box, then click the associated build button.**
The Choose Builder dialog box is displayed (see Figure 16.21).

Figure 16.21
The Choose Builder dialog box enables you to open the Macro Builder.

The On Open event

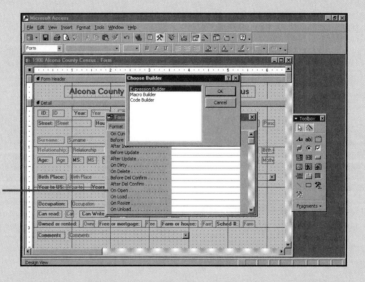

5 **Select Macro Builder and click OK.**
Access asks you to give the macro a name.

6 **Type** 1900 Census Form **in the Save As dialog box and click OK.**
The Macro window is displayed. This is the same window you used to create macros in Project 12, "Using Access Macros."

7 **Click the drop-down arrow in the first row of the Action column and scroll down until you can see the Maximize action.**

Whichever action(s) you choose will be attached to the form properties, and will be executed whenever the selected event, in this case On Open, occurs (see Figure 16.22).

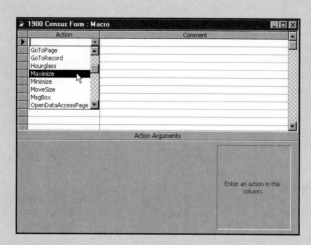

Figure 16.22
The actions you select will be attached to the form properties.

8 **Select the Maximize action, then close the Macro window. Click Yes when prompted to save your changes.**

9 **Close the Properties dialog box.**

10 **Close the form. Click Yes to save your changes.**

The macro is now attached to the form. When you open the form, it should open maximized.

11 **Click Open to open the form.**

Notice that the form is maximized.

12 **Close the form and close the database. Exit Access unless you are going to proceed to the exercises.**

Summary

In this project, you improved the usefulness of a form by changing the formatting of several of the form controls. You also added customized help, and changed the buttons on the toolbar. You created a custom toolbar, and then learned how to use the Macro Builder to create a macro that runs automatically when you open the form.

You can enhance your knowledge of form formatting by right-clicking on the control, opening the control's property sheet, clicking in one of the options, and the pressing F1 to get context-sensitive help.

Checking Concepts and Terms

True/False

For each of the following statements, check *T* or *F* to indicate whether the statement is true or false.

__T __F **1.** Double-clicking the Format Painter button takes you to the Format Painter dialog box. [L2]

__T __F **2.** If you customize a toolbar, the changes only appear when you use the database that was open when the toolbar was customized. [L7]

__T __F **3.** To apply the same format to the entire form you can use the Select Entire Form command under the Format menu. [L3]

__T __F **4.** The first step in creating a macro using the Macro Builder is to click the Macros object button. [L8]

__T __F **5.** To change the Properties box from one control to the next, you must close the first Properties box before you can open the next Properties box. [L4]

Multiple Choice

Circle the letter of the correct answer for each of the following questions.

1. To change the color of text in a form, use the _____ button. [L1]

   a. Fill/Back Color

   b. Line/Border Color

   c. Font/Fore Color

   d. Special Effects

2. To remove a button from a toolbar, go to the Customize dialog box, then _____. [L7]

   a. drag the button below the toolbar and let go

   b. select the button, then press the Del key

   c. select the button, then choose Cut from the Edit menu

   d. click the button with the right mouse button and select Remove from the shortcut menu

3. A ControlTip is activated when you _____. [L6]

   a. place the insertion point in the appropriate control

   b. place the mouse pointer over the appropriate control for a short time

   c. click the field with the left mouse button

   d. click the field with the right mouse button

4. The Fore Color is found on the _____ tab of the Properties box. [L4]

   a. Data

   b. Event

   c. Format

   d. Other

5. To have a ControlTip break over several lines, press _____ to create breaks between the lines of text. [L6]

   a. ⬆Shift+F5

   b. Ctrl+↵Enter

   c. ⬆Shift+↵Enter

   d. Alt+↵Enter

Screen ID

Label each element of the Access screen shown in Figure 16.23.

Figure 16.23

A. Transparent Fill/Back Color

B. Visual cue

C. Status bar message

D. Blue Font/ Fore Color

E. Control Tip

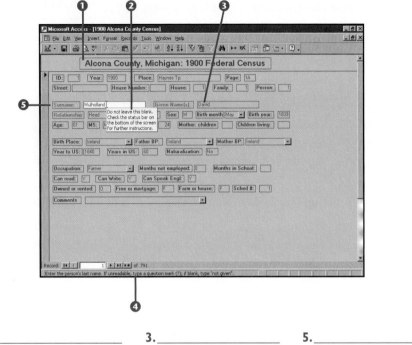

1._____   3._____   5._____

2._____   4._____

Skill Drill

Skill Drill exercises reinforce project skills. Each skill reinforced is the same, or nearly the same, as a skill presented in the project. Each exercise includes a brief narrative introduction, followed by detailed instructions in a step-by-step format.

In these exercises, you work with a database that keeps track of a company's microcomputer purchases and the distributors you buy from.

1. Changing the Color and Background of Controls

In this exercise, you change the color of a form title and change the background to transparent. This will enable the background pattern to show through the title box. Then you select and change the color for all the controls in the Detail section of the form. [L1–3]

To change the color and background of controls:

1. Find the `AC-1602` database file on your CD-ROM; send it to a new disk in drive A:. Right-click on the file name, choose Properties, and turn off read-only status. Right-click on the file name again, choose Rename, and call the file **Computer Inventory**. Open the database.

2. Click the Edit Hardware Information button on the main switchboard. Look at the way the title fill overlaps the background on the left side. Click the View button to switch to Form Design view of the Vendor and Hardware form.

3. Select the title and click the drop-down arrow on the Font/Fore Color button. Select a dark blue color.

4. With the title still selected, select Transparent from the Fill/Back Color button. Click the View button to see your changes.

5. Click the View button to return to Design view.

6. Choose Edit, Select All from the menu to select all of the controls in the form.

7. Hold down ⬆Shift and click the title to deselect it.

8. Click the Font/Fore Color button to change the font color to dark blue for all of the form's controls.

9. With the controls still selected, click the Fill/Back Color button to change the back color to transparent.

10. Click the View button to see your changes. Notice that the check mark boxes are still black, and the Close command button background was not changed (see Figure 16.24).

11. Save your changes and click the Close button at the bottom of the form. Leave the **Computer Inventory** database open if you are going to continue on to the next exercise. Otherwise, close the database.

2. Add Status Bar Instructions and Control Tips to a Field

The RAM field is set up to accept only specific entries —4, 8, 16, 32, 64, 128. In this exercise, you add instructions to the status bar for this field, then you add a ControlTip with the same message. If you did the first exercise, skip step 1. [L5, L6]

To add a status bar message to the RAM field, complete the following steps:

1. Find the **AC-1602** database file on your CD-ROM; send it to a new disk in drive A:. Right-click on the file name, choose Properties, and turn off read-only status. Right-click on the file name again, choose Rename, and call the file **Computer Inventory**. Open the database.

2. Click the Edit Hardware Information button on the main switchboard, then click the View button to switch to Design view.

3. Right-click the field text control box for the RAM field and select Properties from the shortcut menu.

4. Click the Other tab. Type the following message into the Status Bar Text box:

   Enter either 4, 8, 16, 32, 64, or 128

5. Type the following message into the ControlTip Text box:

   Enter:

   4

   8

   16

   32

   64

   128

   Make sure you press [Shift]+[Enter] to start each new line.

6. Close the Properties box. Click the View button to switch to Form view.

7. Place the insertion point in the RAM field and check the status bar to make sure the status bar message is displayed.

8. Test the ControlTip by moving the pointer over the RAM field (see Figure 16.24).

9. Save your changes and click the Close button at the bottom of the form. Leave the **Computer Inventory** database open if you are going to continue on to the next exercise. Otherwise, close the database.

3. Adding Buttons to a Toolbar

When you are entering data using a form, you often need to go back and look at the table to see all the entries together. The Form Datasheet view does the same thing, and there is a button that can be added to a toolbar to make the Datasheet view one click away. In this exercise, you add a Datasheet view button and a Form view button so you can toggle back and forth between views. If you did the previous exercise, skip the first step. [L7]

To add the Datasheet view and Form view buttons to a toolbar:

1. Find the AC-1602 database file on your CD-ROM; send it to a new disk in drive A:. Right-click on the file name, choose <u>P</u>roperties, and turn off read-only status. Right-click on the file name again, choose Rena<u>m</u>e, and call the file **Computer Inventory**. Open the database.

2. Click the Edit Hardware Information button on the main switchboard. If the Utility 1 toolbar is not displayed on your screen, right-click on any toolbar and select <u>C</u>ustomize from the shortcut menu.

3. Select the Tool<u>b</u>ars tab, if necessary, then click the Utility 1 check box.

4. Click the <u>C</u>ommands tab. Highlight the View option in the Categories list box.

5. Scroll down the Commands list box until you can see the Datasheet View option. Click and drag the Datasheet View button to the right side of the Utility 1 toolbar.

6. Click and drag the Form View button to the right side of the Utility 1 toolbar. (*Note:* Make sure you drag the button called Form view, and not the Forms button.)

7. Click the Datasheet View button in the Utility 1 toolbar and drag it to the right about 1/8 of an inch. This should insert a separator in the toolbar.

8. Close the Customize dialog box.

9. Click the Datasheet view button. Now click the Form view button. Click in the RAM field, then move the pointer above the RAM field text box. Your form should look like Figure 16.24.

10. Close the form and the database. If you are using a lab machine, restore the Utility 1 toolbar to its original condition, with no buttons, and turn it off.

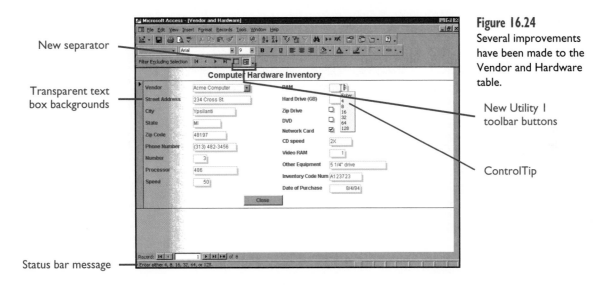

Figure 16.24
Several improvements have been made to the Vendor and Hardware table.

New separator

Transparent text box backgrounds

New Utility 1 toolbar buttons

ControlTip

Status bar message

Challenge

Challenge exercises expand on or are somewhat related to skills presented in the lessons. Each exercise provides a brief narrative introduction followed by instructions that are not as detailed as those in the Skill Drill section.

The database used for the Challenge section is a modified version of the one used in the Skill Drill section.

1. Adding Instructions to a Form

One of the things you did in this project was to add status bar instructions and ControlTips to an important field. There is another way to help the database user—add instructions directly to the form.

To add instructions to a form:

1. Find the AC-1603 database file on your CD-ROM, send it to drive A:, and remove the read-only status. Rename the file **Revised Computer Inventory** and open the file. Close the Main switchboard. Select the **Vendor and Hardware** form and open it in Design view.

2. Open the toolbox, if necessary, and add a label box to the right of the RAM field. The box should be about 5/8 inches wide and 1 1/4 inches tall.

3. Type the following text in the label box:

    RAM:

    4

    8

    16

    32

    64

    128

    256

4. Make the text the same color as the text in the controls.

5. Select the label box and add a border using the Line/Border Width button. Color the border the same blue as the text.

6. Adjust the size and shape of the box. Switch to Form view to see your changes (see Figure 16.25). Save your work and close the database, unless you plan to do the next exercise.

2. Hiding Controls on a Form

Some fields that you want to include on form printouts do not need to be displayed on the screen. You can hide fields that have been filled in automatically from a linked table. Hiding these fields can also keep inexperienced users from trying to change information that shouldn't be changed.

To hide controls on a form:

1. If you did not do the previous exercise, find the AC-1603 database file on your CD-ROM, send it to drive A:, and remove the read-only status. Rename the file **Revised Computer Inventory** and open the file. Close the Main switchboard. Select the **Vendor and Hardware** form and open it in Design view.

2. In the Vendor and Hardware form, when you select a Vendor from the drop-down menu, the Street Address, City, State, Zip Code, and Phone Number are filled in with data from the Vendors table. Use the Office Assistant to figure out how to hide those fields on the form (see Figure 16.25), but have them appear on a print-out. (*Note:* If you can't find help on this topic, try looking through the text control box properties for one of the fields.)

3. Save your work and close the database, unless you plan to do the next exercise.

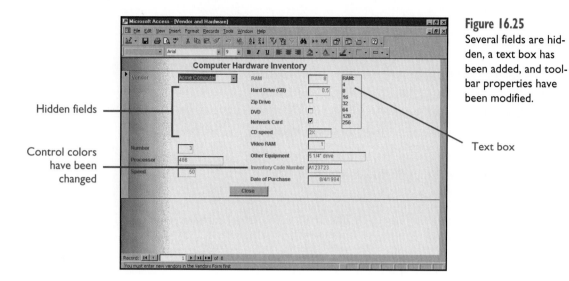

Figure 16.25
Several fields are hidden, a text box has been added, and toolbar properties have been modified.

Hidden fields

Control colors have been changed

Text box

3. Changing Toolbar Properties

Once you have set up the toolbars the way you want them, you can use the toolbar properties (yes, even toolbars have properties) to modify the way the toolbars work.

To change toolbar properties:

1. If you did not do the previous exercise, find the AC-1603 database file on your CD-ROM, send it to drive A:, and remove the read-only status. Rename the file **Revised Computer Inventory** and open the file. Close the Main switchboard. Select the Vendor and Hardware form and open it in Form view.

2. Activate the Customize dialog box. Click the Toolbars tab and select the Web toolbar. Click the Properties button.

3. In the Toolbar Properties dialog box, deselect the Allow Moving check box. Do the same for the Utility 1 dialog box. Close the Customize dialog box and try to move either of the utility toolbars. (*Note:* You can try some of the other options, if you want, but do not deselect the Allow Customizing option.)

4. Save your work and close the database.

Discovery Zone

Discovery Zone exercises help you gain advanced knowledge of project topics and application of skills. These exercises focus on enhancing your problem-solving skills. Numbered steps are not provided, but you are given hints, reminders, screen shots, and references to help you reach your goal for each exercise.

In these exercises you use a modified version of the census database you used in Lesson 1.

1. Creating a Custom Toolbar and Adding a Macro as a Button

There are times you will want to create a brand new toolbar. In fact, some regular database users create a set of toolbars, making available exactly the buttons they want. When you create a custom toolbar, it is stored with the database, not with the Access program, as was the case with the built-in utility toolbars. If you are going to create a database that gets a lot of use, custom toolbars can make the database easier to use. You can even put macros on the new toolbar.

In this exercise you use the `AC-1604` database, renamed `Creating a New Toolbar`.

Goal: Create a custom toolbar and add a macro to close the 1900 Alcona County Census form.

The toolbar should:

- be named `My Custom Toolbar`.
- contain one button—the macro called Close the 1900 Alcona County Census form.
- display both the macro icon and the name of the macro.
- have the button name changed to `Close the Form`.

Hint #1: Once the toolbar is created, you can drag the macro to the toolbar.

Hint #2: The Customize dialog box has to be open before you can change the name of the new button.

Hint #3: If you are stuck, remember that shortcut menus are often the answer.

2. Editing a Button on a Toolbar

When you create buttons from macros, all of the buttons look exactly alike. You can change the button design to a pre-set shape, or you can create your own icons for these buttons. (You can also simply name the buttons and leave the icons off entirely.) You either need to have completed the previous exercise, or you need to create a new toolbar and drag one of the existing macros onto it. Open the `AC-1604` database, if you didn't open it for the previous exercise, and rename it `Creating a New Toolbar`.

Goal: Create a button icon for the Close the Form button that looks like a red X.

The button should:

- look like a large red X.
- retain the Close the Form text.

Hint: Once again, think shortcut menu.

Your toolbar should look like Figure 16.26.

Figure 16.26
Your toolbar should
have a red X and the
button name displayed.

PinPoint Assessment

You have completed this project and its associated lessons, and have had an opportunity to assess your skills through the end-of-project questions and exercises. Now use the PinPoint software Evaluation Mode to further assess your comprehension of the specific exam activities you have just learned. You can also use the PinPoint Trainer Mode and the Show Me tutorials to practice these exam activities.

Managing Changing Data

Key terms introduced in this project include

- cascade delete
- cascade update
- update query

Objectives	Required Activity for MOUS	Exam Level
➤ Replace Data in a Table Using an Update Query	Create an action query (update, delete, insert)	Expert
➤ Replace Portions of Fields Using an Update Query	Create an action query (update, delete, insert)	Expert
➤ Update Tables Using a Calculated Expression	Create an action query (update, delete, insert)	Expert
➤ Update a Table Based on Values in Another Table	Create an action query (update, delete, insert)	Expert
➤ Update Linked Tables Automatically	Set Cascade Update and Cascade Delete options	Expert

Why Would I Do This?

When you work with data in a database, you are usually doing one of two things: adding new records (and deleting or archiving old ones), or modifying data that is already in the table. In the previous project, you looked at ways to improve data entry by refining forms. In this project, you learn how to update existing data.

An *update query* is a powerful type of action query that can be used to help you maintain your database by making a global update to records based on specified field criteria. It can be used to replace text fields or parts of text fields. This is useful in situations in which textual information is changed—when a new area code is created or a part number is changed. You can also use update queries to calculate changes in numeric fields. This feature is useful, for example, if you intend to raise prices by a certain percentage for an entire line of products.

In some cases, you may have a table that has new values for many individual records in another table. In Lesson 4, you learn how to use an update query to update one table based on the contents of another.

Finally, when you have tables that are joined, you have the option of causing changes in one table to be automatically made in related tables. Changes in customer identification numbers in one table can be automatically updated in a table of customer purchases, or those purchases could be automatically deleted if the customer's name is deleted.

Lesson 1: Replacing Data in a Table Using an Update Query

If you need to change the entire contents of a text field, such as a company's name that occurs in many records, you can use an update query, which enables you to set a condition that, when matched, cause changes to be made in the specified field.

When you run an update query it makes permanent changes to the records in your database. Unlike other queries, action queries do not display a dynaset of the results of the query. Therefore, it is usually a good idea to make a backup copy of your table prior to using an update query. In case you make an error, it is easier to recover when you have preserved a copy of the table prior to the changes. In the examples used in this project, however, you will not make backup copies of the tables to save space on your disk.

In this example, a company that provides industrial cleaning supplies has a database that tracks its customers and their orders. We know that one of their customers, AMIX Corp., has spun off its Michigan offices into a new company named Michlx. All the company names for AMIX Corp. contacts in Michigan need to be changed.

To Replace Data in a Table Using an Update Query

❶ Make a copy of the AC-1701 **database file from the CD-ROM. Right-click the filename; select P‌roperties from the shortcut menu, and remove the read-only status. Use the shortcut menu to rename the file** Cleaning Supplies**, and then open the database.**
The Cleaning Supplies database should now be open to the Tables area (see Figure 17.1). If it is not, click the tables object button.

❷ Click the Queries object button, and then click the New button on the Database toolbar.
The New Query dialog box displays.

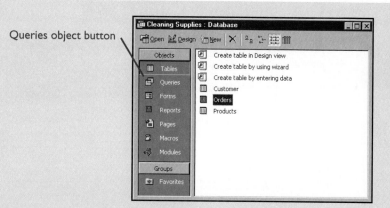

Queries object button

Figure 17.1
The Database window
displays the Tables
area of the Cleaning
Supplies database.

3 **In the list box, select Design view, and then click OK.**
The Show Table dialog box displays on top of the Query Design view.

4 **Click the Customer table name and then click <u>A</u>dd. Click the <u>C</u>lose
button to close the Show Table dialog box.**
The Customer table is added to the query Design view. The query Design view
contains the query design grid and one table (see Figure 17.2).

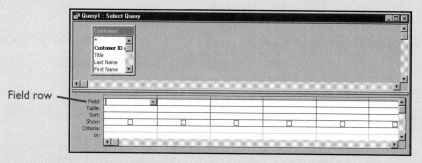

Field row

Figure 17.2
The query Design view
is shown with the
Customer table added.

5 **Add the Last Name, Company, and State fields (in that order) to the
Field row of the query design grid.**
The Last Name, Company, and State fields appear in the first three columns of
the query design. You now want to set up the query to find all the companies
named AMIX Corp. in Michigan.

6 **Enter the company name AMIX Corp. in the Criteria box in the
Company column and press ⏎Enter.**
Remember to include the period following the abbreviation for corporation.

7 **Enter MI in the Criteria box in the State column and press ⏎Enter.**
The criteria for company and state should identify all the company's contacts in
Michigan. Each of the entries are surrounded by quotation marks when you press
⏎Enter (see Figure 17.3).

8 **Click the View button to see if you have correctly identified the two
Michigan contacts.**
You only included three of the fields in this query for simplicity. The two
Michigan contacts are shown (see Figure 17.4). It is recommended that you cre-
ate a select query first so you can verify the results and check the number of
records that will be affected by the change.

continues ▶

To Replace Data in a Table Using an Update Query (continued)

Figure 17.3
The criteria for finding the AMIX Corporation's Michigan contacts were entered.

Criteria to identify data to be updated

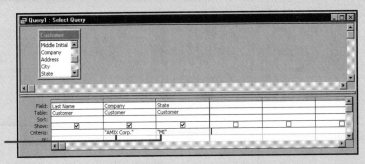

Figure 17.4
The two Michigan contacts are shown.

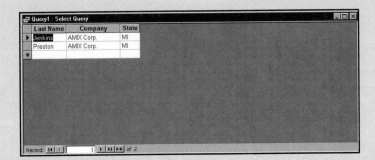

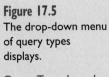

⑨ Click the View button again to return to the query Design view.

⑩ Click the down arrow on the Query Type button.
A drop-down menu displays (see Figure 17.5).

Figure 17.5
The drop-down menu of query types displays.

Query Type drop-down menu

The Update Query option

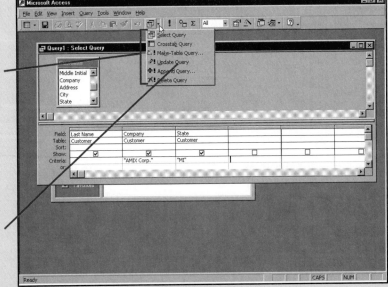

⑪ Select the Update Query option.
Notice that the Sort and Show rows were replaced by the Update To row in the query Design grid.

12 **Type the new regional company name, `MichIx`, in the Update To box of the Company column and press ⏎Enter.**

The new company name is placed in the Update To box in the Company column (see Figure 17.6).

The Update
To row

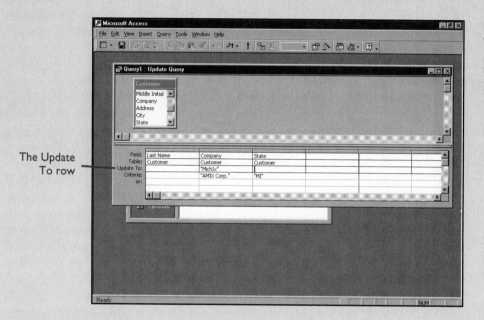

Figure 17.6
The new company name appears in the Update To box.

You are now ready to run the update query to change the AMIX Corp. records in Michigan to Michlx.

13 **Click the Run button on the toolbar.**

A warning message displays, advising that you are about to update two rows. This agrees with the number of records displayed when you viewed it as a select query. Once you click <u>Y</u>es, the change will be irreversible. The Undo button will not work following this step.

14 **Click <u>Y</u>es to update the records.**

The company names are changed but no dynaset is displayed. To verify that the change has been made, you need to check the table.

15 **Close the query and save it with the name `Update Company Name`.**

The Database window displays with the new query listed. Notice that the icon for the update query is different from the normal select query icon.

16 **Click the Tables object button and open the Customer table.**

Scroll through the records to confirm that the two customer contacts in Michigan have had their company name changed from AMIX Corp. to Michlx (see Figure 17.7).

17 **Close the table.**

Leave the `Cleaning Supplies` database open for use in the next lesson.

continues ▶

To Replace Data in a Table Using an Update Query (continued)

Figure 17.7
The new company name appears in the appropriate records.

These names were updated

This name was not updated

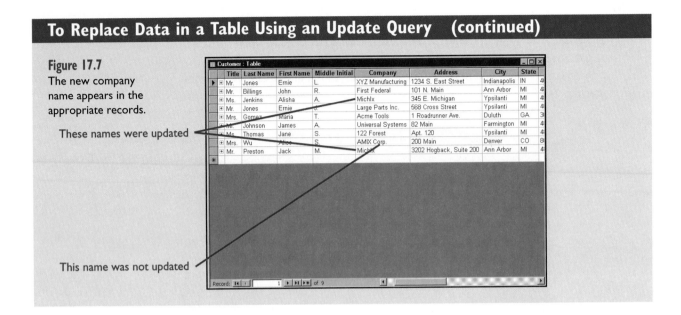

	Title	Last Name	First Name	Middle Initial	Company	Address	City	State	
Mr.	Jones	Ernie	L.	XYZ Manufacturing	1234 S. East Street	Indianapolis	IN	4
Mr.	Billings	John	R.	First Federal	101 N. Main	Ann Arbor	MI	4
Ms.	Jenkins	Alisha	A.	Michlx	345 E. Michigan	Ypsilanti	MI	4
Mr.	Jones	Ernie	J.	Large Parts Inc.	568 Cross Street	Ypsilanti	MI	4
Mrs.	Gomez	Maria	T.	Acme Tools	1 Roadrunner Ave.	Duluth	GA	3
Mr.	Johnson	James	A.	Universal Systems	82 Main	Farmington	MI	4
Ms.	Thomas	Jane	S.	122 Forest	Apt. 120	Ypsilanti	MI	4
Mrs.	Wu	Alice	S.	AMIX Corp.	200 Main	Denver	CO	8
Mr.	Preston	Jack	M.	Michlx	3202 Hogback, Suite 200	Ann Arbor	MI	4

Customer : Table

Record: 1 of 9

 Inside Stuff: **Fields Automatically Removed from Queries**
If you were to go back to Design view to examine the query, you would find that the Last Name field was removed. The field was dropped automatically because it was not used in the query.

 Expert

Lesson 2: Replacing Portions of Fields Using an Update Query

Some updates are based on a portion of a field. When the telephone company creates a new area code, it assigns some of the exchanges from the old area to the new area code. To automatically update your database, you may need to determine whether part of the field matches a criterion and then change only part of the data in each field.

In this lesson, you learn how to use expressions for selecting the left, middle, and right portions of a string of text characters. You also learn how to use these expressions in an update query.

To Replace Portions of Fields Using an Update Query

❶ **In the** `Cleaning Supplies` **database, click the Queries object button and click New.**
The New Query dialog box displays.

❷ **In the list box, select Design View, and then click OK.**
The Show Table dialog box displays.

❸ **Add the Customer Table to the query Design view and close the Show Table dialog box.**
The Customer table is added to the query design.

4 **Add the Last Name, Company, City, and Phone fields to the query design grid.**

The query design grid now has four fields (see Figure 17.8).

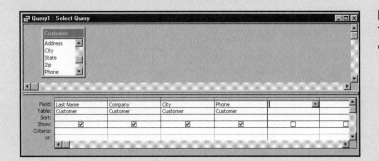

Figure 17.8
The query design grid displays four fields.

5 **Type the following expression in the Criteria box for the Phone field:**

`Left([Phone],9)="(313) 665"`

The Left expression extracts the characters at the left end of a string of text. In this example, you want to identify all phone numbers in the 313 area code that use the 665 exchange. You check for the first nine characters at the left end of the phone field. Notice that you count the parentheses and the space.

6 **Click the View button to switch to the Datasheet view to confirm that the criteria found the two records that match.**

The Datasheet view should show the two matching records (see Figure 17.9). If it does not show any records, you have made an error in entering the expression. Make sure you used the proper brackets and a space after the area code.

These records
match the criterion

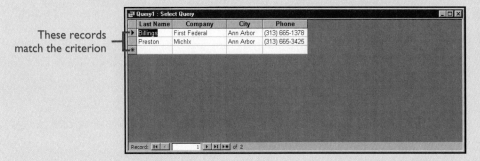

Figure 17.9
The query has found the records that match the phone number criteria.

7 **Click the View button.**

The program returns to Design view. Now, you change the query type and add another expression.

8 **Click the down arrow on the Query Type button on the toolbar and select Update Query from the drop-down menu.**

To Replace Portions of Fields Using an Update Query (continued)

9 **Enter the following expression in the Update To box of the Phone field:**

`"(311)"+Right([Phone],9)`

The purpose of this expression is to create a new phone number that begins with the new area code and the old exchange and then attaches the nine characters from the right end of the phone number (see Figure 17.10). (*Note:* The Phone field column was widened, so that you can see the full expression.)

Figure 17.10
The criteria and update expressions for replacing the area code for the 665 exchange are entered.

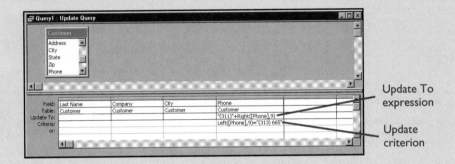

Update To expression

Update criterion

 Exam Note: **Working with Input Masks**

The Left and Right expressions use character counts based on the actual characters stored in the table. If the table was designed to use an input mask, the character count will be off. In the example in this lesson, the data was entered into the table with the parentheses, spaces, and dashes, so they were counted. The phone numbers in the Fax Phone field were entered using an input mask and do not contain the extra characters.

---

 10 **Click the Run button on the toolbar.**

A warning message displays, notifying you that you are about to make an irreversible change to two records. If it says that you are about to change more than two records, click <u>N</u>o and look for a problem.

11 **Click <u>Y</u>es to update the records.**

The phone numbers change. Make sure you have made recent backups of your tables before you use this procedure on important tables.

 Exam Note: **Use the Run Button**

An update query is not actually done until you click the Run button. Unlike a select query, clicking the View button does not run the query or change the records. Also, unlike a select query, a dynaset is not displayed when you click the Run button.

---

12 **Close the query and save it as `Update Area Code`.**

13 **Click the Tables object button and open the Customer table.**

Scroll through the records to confirm that the two phone numbers that were formerly (313) 665, are now (311) 665 (see Figure 17.11).

14 **Close the table.**

Leave the `Cleaning Supplies` database open for use in the next lesson.

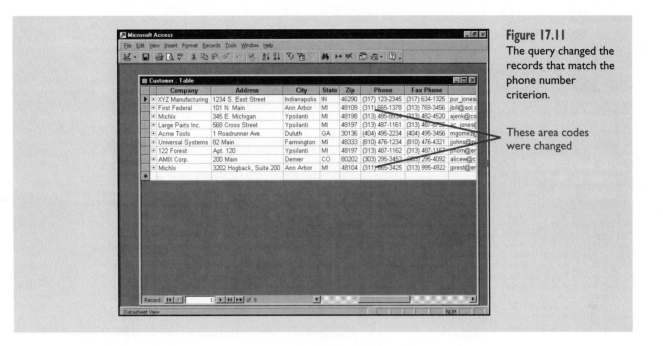

Figure 17.11
The query changed the records that match the phone number criterion.

These area codes were changed

 Inside Stuff: **The Mid Expression**

A third expression is similar to Right and Left. The Mid expression selects characters from inside the string of characters. To select the exchange numbers 665 from a phone number in this lesson, you would use the expression Mid([Phone],7,3). It would start at the seventh character and select three characters.

Lesson 3: Updating Tables Using a Calculated Expression

In the first two lessons, you revised data by using the update query to replace all or part of the text in a field. The update query can also be used to perform calculations on numeric fields through the use of algebra-like expressions.

In this lesson, you use a calculation to increase the price of goods by 10 percent as a late payment penalty. You also learn how to use more than one criterion to determine whether a bill is unpaid and overdue.

To Update Tables Using a Calculated Expression

1 In the `Cleaning Supplies` database, open the `Orders` table and look at the **Late Payment Factor** field.

Notice that all the factors are 1.0.

2 Close the Orders table. Click the Queries object button and click **N**ew. Select Design view, and then click OK.

The Show Table dialog box displays.

3 Select the Orders table and click the **A**dd button. Close the Show Table dialog box.

The Orders table is added to the query Design view.

continues ▶

To Update Tables Using a Calculated Expression (continued)

④ **Add the Order #, Date of Purchase, Date of Payment, and Late Payment Factor fields to the query design grid, in that order.**
The query design grid displays four fields (see Figure 17.12).

Figure 17.12
The query design grid shows the four selected fields.

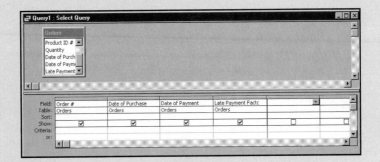

⑤ **Type the following expression in the Criteria box for the Date of Payment field: Is Null**
If a field has no entry, it is called a null value. This is not the same as a space or zero.

 ⑥ **Click the View button to switch to Datasheet view.**
In Datasheet view, you can confirm that the query found the records without a date for the Date of Payment field. The Datasheet view should show the thirteen matching records (see Figure 17.13).

Figure 17.13
The query found the unpaid bills.

Unpaid orders

Number of records that meet the Is Null criterion

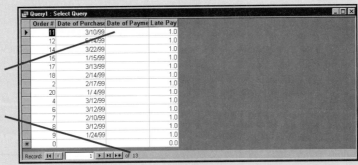

 ⑦ **Click the View button to return to Design view.**

⑧ **Type the following expression in the Criteria box for the Date of Purchase field: <2/1/99**
The computer treats dates as though they were sequential numbers that increase with time. The expression you just entered selects dates before February 1, 1999.

If two criteria are on the same line in the query design grid, they both must be met. In this case, the query finds records of purchases that have not been paid for and were made before 2/1/99.

9 **Click the View button to switch to Datasheet view.**
You can now confirm that the query found the records that have no date for the Date of Payment field and a purchase date before 2/1/99. The Datasheet view should show the three matching records with order numbers of 15, 20, and 9. (see Figure 17.14).

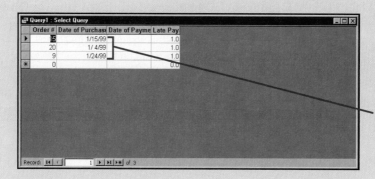

Figure 17.14
The bills are shown for purchases made before 2/1/99 that have not been paid.

These dates meet both conditions

10 **Click the View button to return to Design view.**

 Exam Note: **Identifying a Date**
Notice that the program has added # symbols around the date. If you ever have problems with a complex criterion where the program has not correctly identified a date you entered, you may need to enclose the date with # symbols. If this step does not work, make certain that you have entered the date criterion in a Date/Time data type field.

11 **Click the down arrow on the Query Type button and select Update Query from the drop-down menu.**

12 **Enter the following expression in the Update To box of the Late Payment Factor field:** [Late Payment Factor]*1.1
The purpose of this expression is to increase the price of the purchases that have not been paid on time by 10 percent (see Figure 17.15). The column width for the Late Payment Factor field has been widened to show the whole expression.

Pound symbols surround the date

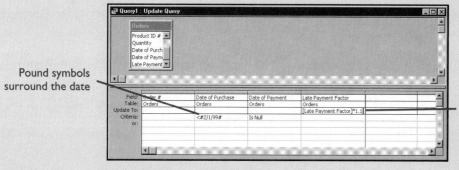

Figure 17.15
The Criteria and Update expressions for increasing the late payment factor are shown.

Calculated expression

13 **Click the Run button on the toolbar.**
A warning message displays, notifying you that you are about to update three rows. Make sure you have made recent backups of your tables before you use this procedure on important tables.

continues ▶

To Update Tables with a Calculated Expression   (continued)

⑭ Click Yes to update the records.
The Late Payment Factor values change.

⑮ Close the query and save it as Update for Late Payments.

 Exam Note: Running a Calculated Update Query
Do not run the update query more than once. It makes the calculation each time you run it. In this example, it increases the Late Payment Factor by 10 percent each time you run it.

⑯ Click the Tables object button and open the Orders table. Check to make sure the Late Payment Factor has been changed to 1.1 for three records.

⑰ Close the table and close the database.

 Inside Stuff: Documenting Data Prior to Running Update Queries
When you are using complex expressions in an update query it is easy to make a mistake. For this reason, it is important to first create the query as a Select query so you can view the results and see how many records will be affected. Because an update query does not produce the usual dynaset, you may also want to print the select query results so you have a permanent record of the data that will be changed when the update query is run.

 ## Lesson 4: Updating a Table Based on Values in Another Table

In some cases, it is convenient to change several values in one table and then apply them to another table. In this lesson, you learn how to update the suggested sale price on a table that lists the stock on hand in a warehouse.

To Update a Table Based on Values in Another Table

❶ Make a copy of the AC-1702 database file from the CD-ROM. Right-click the filename; select Properties from the shortcut menu, and remove the read-only status. Use the shortcut menu to rename the file Auto Parts, and then open the database.
The Database window should now be open to the Tables area (see Figure 17.16). If it is not, click the Tables object button.

❷ Select the Stock on Hand table and click Open.
Notice the field at the far right that indicates whether a particular lot of parts has been sold.

❸ Close the table. Click the Queries object button and click New.
The New Query dialog box displays.

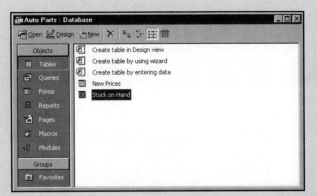

Figure 17.16
The tables in the Auto Parts database are displayed.

4 **Select Design View and click OK.**
The query Design view appears with the Show Table dialog box open in front of it.

5 **Add both tables to the query design and close the Show table dialog box.**
The query Design view displays the two tables joined by the Code field (see Figure 17.17).

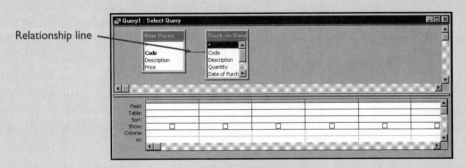

Relationship line

Figure 17.17
The query Design view displays two tables joined by the Code field.

6 **Scroll down the list of fields in the Stock on Hand table. Add the** **Suggested Price** and **Sold** **fields from the field list box to the query design grid.**
The query design shows the Suggested Price and Sold fields.

7 **Click the Query Type button on the toolbar and click** **U**pdate Query.
A row is added to the query design grid for update expressions.

8 **Enter the following expression in the Update To box in the Suggested Price column:**
[New Prices].[Price]
The first part of the expression identifies the table, and the second part identifies the field in that table. Notice the names are enclosed in square brackets and separated by a period.

This update replaces the values in the Stock on Hand table with those found in the New Prices table.

continues ▶

To Update a Table Based on Values in Another Table (continued)

9 **Type the following text in the Criteria box in the Sold column:**

No

This condition restricts the price changes to those items not yet sold (see Figure 17.18).

Figure 17.18
The criteria for changing the prices on the unsold inventory and the location of the price updates are added.

Update expression

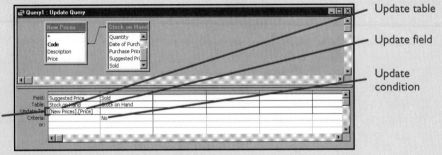

Update table
Update field
Update condition

10 **Close the query and name it** Update Prices.

11 **Click the Tables object button of the database. Open the** Stock on Hand **table.**

Notice that the first lot of 45 axles has already been sold at $300, and they are another 100 axles available for sale at $300. Also look at the prices for the other items available for sale.

12 **Close the Stock on Hand table and open the** New Prices **table.**

Notice that the new price for an axle is $285 for axles still in stock.

13 **Close the New Prices table and click the Queries object button. Select the** Update Prices **query, if necessary.**

14 **Click O̲pen.**

This type of query is an Action query that acts like a program. When you open it, it performs its function. In this case, you see a message box that asks whether you want to run the query (see Figure 17.19).

Figure 17.19
The message box cautions you that you are about to run an action query.

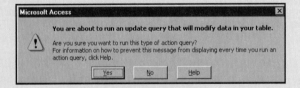

15 **Click Y̲es to continue.**

Another message appears, telling you that you are about to make permanent changes to five rows of the table (see Figure 17.20). There were six rows in the table, but one of them did not meet the criteria you placed in the Sold column. This is an indication the query is working properly.

16 **Click Y̲es to update the records.**

The records are updated, but nothing appears to happen on the screen.

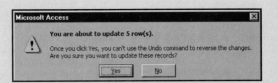

Figure 17.20
The message box informs you that you are about to make irreversible changes.

 Inside Stuff: **Back Up Your Work Before Running an Update Query**

It is easy to make a mistake when you are designing an update query, but very difficult to fix the results of a mistake. You can make a copy of the table before you attempt an update. To do this, click the Table object button; select the table you want to update, and use the Copy and Paste buttons from the menu bar to create a copy of the original table. The program enables you to give the backup table a new name. This procedure should be performed before you try to update an important table.

⑰ **Click the Tables object button and open the Stock on Hand table.**

Notice that the suggested price for the stock has changed, except for the first record that was marked as already sold (see Figure 17.21).

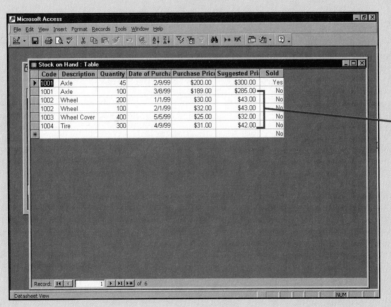

Figure 17.21
The Stock on Hand table is shown after the prices were changed.

Prices have been changed

⑱ **Close the table and the database.**

Lesson 5: Updating Linked Tables Automatically

If two tables are linked, it is important to protect the linking fields from unexpected changes. If two companies merge and one of the companies has to change its parts codes to match those of the other system, it is important to update the related customer records.

In this lesson, you learn how to set the relationship between a primary key and a related field in another table, set referential integrity, and select automatic update options such as ***cascade update*** and ***cascade delete***. An automatic update is an alternative method of updating tables to the one you learned in Lesson 4. It is easier to use, but you also must always be careful when dealing with automatic updates.

To Update Linked Tables Automatically

1 **Make a copy of the AC-1703 database file from the CD-ROM. Right-click the filename; select Properties from the shortcut menu, and remove the read-only status. Use the shortcut menu to rename the file Auto Parts 2, and then open the database.**
The Database window should now be open to the Tables area. If it is not, click the Tables object button. This is the same database you used in Lesson 4.

2 **Click the Relationships button on the toolbar.**
An empty window titled Relationships displays.

3 **Click the Show Table button on the toolbar.**
The Show Table dialog box displays the names of the two tables: New Prices and Stock on Hand.

4 **Add both tables to the Relationship window.**
You may need to move the Show Table dialog box to see the tables as they are added to the Relationships window.

5 **Click the Close button to close the Show Table dialog box.**
The Relationships window displays the two tables (see Figure 17.22). Notice that the Code field in the New Prices table displays in bold-faced type to indicate that it is the primary key field for that table.

Figure 17.22
The Relationships window displays the two tables in the Auto Parts 2 database.

Primary key field

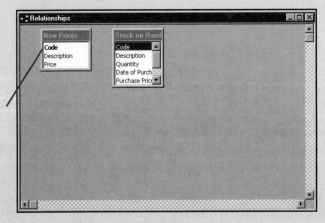

6 **Click and drag the Code field name from the New Prices table to the Code field in the Stock on Hand table.**
The Edit Relationships dialog box opens so you can define the relationship (see Figure 17.23). A one-to-many relationship has been identified automatically.

7 **Click the Enforce Referential Integrity check box.**
Two more options that were previously dimmed now become available.

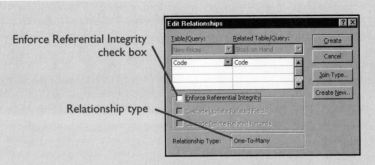

Figure 17.23
The Edit Relationships dialog box identifies the relationship as one-to-many.

8 **Click both the Cascade Update Related Fields and the Cascade Delete Related Records check boxes.**

This enables you to perform automatic updates and deletions of the records in the Stock on Hand table if changes are made to the code field in the New Prices table (see Figure 17.24).

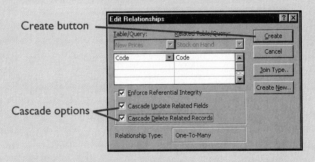

Figure 17.24
The Edit Relationships dialog box is set for automatic updating.

9 **Click the Create button to create the relationship, and then close the Relationships window and save the changes to the layout.**

10 **Open the New Prices table.**

11 **Change the code for axles from 1001 to 1007 and close the table.**

Because of the relationship you created, the records in the Stock on Hand table should now show that the new code for axles is 1007.

12 **Open the Stock on Hand table.**

The code for axles was automatically changed (see Figure 17.25). Notice that the axles are listed at the end of the table. This is because the Code field was indexed and the table was automatically sorted.

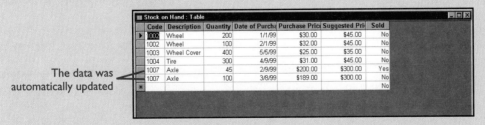

Figure 17.25
The code for axles was updated.

continues ▶

To Update Linked Tables Automatically   (continued)

13 **Close the Stock on Hand table and open the New Prices table. Click the record selector for the first row to select the record for Wheel.**
The first row is selected (see Figure 17.26).

Figure 17.26
The first row of the New Prices table is selected.

Record selector

14 **Press Del to delete this record.**
A message box displays to inform you this record will be deleted, as well as an unspecified number of records in related tables (see Figure 17.27).

Figure 17.27
A message box warns you when the cascade delete feature is about to delete records in related tables.

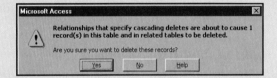

15 **Click Yes to delete the records.**
16 **Close the New Prices table and open the Stock on Hand table.**
Notice that both records that had the code 1002 for Wheels were deleted from this table.

17 **Close the table and the database.**
Close Access unless you are going to proceed to the exercises.

Summary

In this project, you learned several methods that you can use to automatically update existing data in an Access table. You replaced whole fields and parts of fields using the update query. You used the update query to calculate a change in the values in a table, and to update a table based on values in another table. Finally, you learned to use the cascade update and cascade delete features to modify and delete records in a related table when changes are made to data in the primary or parent table.

You can learn more about update queries by looking through the available help on that topic using the Office Assistant. Help also has useful information about the cascade update and cascade delete features. Read this information before using these features on your databases.

Checking Concepts and Terms

True/False

For each of the following statements, check *T* or *F* to indicate whether the statement is true or false.

__T __F **1.** In an update query you can use only two fields: the one you want to update and one other field for a single criterion. [L3]

__T __F **2.** If you make a mistake in the update query design and update the wrong fields, you can use Edit and Undo from the menu to undo the mistake. [L1]

__T__F **3.** If two tables are related using Cascade Delete Related Records as a condition of the join, deleting a record in the primary or parent table causes related records in the secondary or child table to be deleted. [L5]

__T __F **4.** When you run a calculation in an update query, running it a second time has no effect. [L3]

__T __F **5.** When you are counting the number of characters you want to look at using a Left or Right expression, it is important to know whether an input mask is being used in that field. [L3]

Multiple Choice

Circle the letter of the correct answer for each of the following questions.

1. An update query can be used to _____. [Intro]
   a. replace data in a text field
   b. make calculations in a numeric field
   c. change data in a field based on data in another table
   d. all of the above

2. To select the first five characters in the Name field, use the following expression: [L2]
   a. Left[(Name), 5]
   b. Left([Name],5)
   c. Right([Name],5)
   d. First([Name],5)

3. To update a field based on the Name field in the Customer table, which expression would you use? [L4]
   a. [Name].[Customer]
   b. (Customer)+(Name)
   c. [Customer].[Name]
   d. Left[Customer]+Right[Name]

4. If you want to increase all the prices in the Price field by 10 percent, which expression could you use? [L3]
   a. [Price] + 10%
   b. [Price]*.1
   c. [Price]*1.1
   d. [Price]/.1

5. Null is the same as _____. [L3]
   a. a blank field
   b. the number 0
   c. a space
   d. all of the above

Screen ID

Label each element of the Access screen shown in Figures 17.28

Figure 17.28

A. Empty field criterion

B. Instructs the program what to update

C. Query Type button

D. Calculation expression

E. Date criterion

F. Conditions are placed in this row

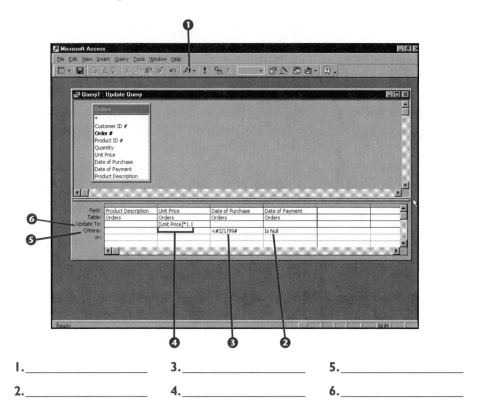

1._____ 3._____ 5._____

2._____ 4._____ 6._____

Skill Drill

Skill Drill exercises reinforce project skills. Each skill reinforced is the same, or nearly the same, as a skill presented in the project. Each exercise includes a brief narrative introduction, followed by detailed instructions in a step-by-step format.

In this exercise, you work with a CD collection database. It consists of two tables—a table of CDs and a table of CD labels.

1. Updating a Table with a New Company Label

You find out that the full name of the RCA label is RCA Victor. In this exercise, you use a simple update query to change the label name. You also change the name in the Label table so you can create a relationship between the two tables. It is usually a good idea to run an update query first as a select query to determine how many records will be affected. In this exercise, however, you are told how many records will be changed

To update a table with a new company label:

1. Make a copy of the **AC-1704** database file from the CD-ROM. Right-click the filename; select Properties from the shortcut menu, and remove the read-only status. Use the shortcut menu to rename the file **CD Collection**, and then open the database.

2. Click the Queries object button, and click New.

3. Choose Design view; add the CD Collection, and close the Show Table dialog box.

4. Add the Label field to the query design grid.

5. Use the Query Type button and select Update Query.

6. Type **RCA** in the Criteria box and **RCA Victor** in the Update To box.

7. Click the Run button on the toolbar to run the query. This action should change 24 rows.

8. Close the query and save it as `RCA Victor`.

9. Click the Tables object button and open the CD Collection table. Scroll down through the Label field to make sure your changes were made. Close the table. (*Hint:* if you sort on the Label field it will be easier to find all affected records.)

10. Open the Label table and change RCA to `RCA Victor`. (This was not changed automatically.) Now when you relate the two tables, you can establish referential integrity. Close the table.

11. Leave the `CD Collection` database open if you intend to do the next exercise.

2. Identifying Multiple Disk Sets by Analyzing the Serial Number

The serial numbers for certain CD labels identify multiple CD sets. In this exercise, you add a field and text to that field for records from a record company that begin with a specific prefix.

To identify multiple disk sets by analyzing the serial number:

1. Skip this step if you did the previous exercise. Make a copy of the `AC-1704` database file from the CD-ROM. Right-click the filename; select Properties from the shortcut menu, and remove the read-only status. Use the shortcut menu to rename the file `CD Collection`, and then open the database.

2. Open the `CD Collection` table in Design view.

3. Add a new field called `Multiple Disks`; select the Yes/No data type; close the table, and save your changes.

4. Click the Queries object button and click New.

5. Choose Design view. Add the CD Collection to the query design and close the Show Table dialog box.

6. Add the Label, Serial number, and Multiple Disks fields to the query design grid.

7. Use the Query Type button and select Update Query.

8. Type `Epic` in the Criteria box for the Label field.

9. In the Criteria box for the Serial number field type `Left([Serial number],3)=E2K`.

10. Type `Yes` in the Multiple Disk Update To box.

11. Click the Run button on the toolbar to run the query. One row should change.

12. Close the query and save it as `Multiple Disk Update`.

13. Click the Tables object button and open the CD Collection table. Scroll down to see what happened. Notice that typing Yes in the Update To box of a Yes/No field places a check mark in the check box for that field. Close the table.

14. Leave the `CD Collection` database open if you intend to do the next exercise.

3. Creating a Cascade Update

The table of Label names should be related to the CD Collection table. That way, any changes you make to the label name in the Label table can be automatically updated in all the related records in the CD Collection table.

To create a cascade update:

1. Skip this step if you did the previous exercise. Make a copy of the `AC-1704` database file from the CD-ROM. Right-click the filename; select Properties from the shortcut menu, and remove the read-only status. Use the shortcut menu to rename the file `CD Collection`, and then open the database.

2. Click the Relationships button on the toolbar.

3. Click the Add button to add the CD Collection table.

4. Select the Label table and click the Add button. Click the Close button to close the Show Table dialog box.

5. Drag the primary key in the Label table (the Label field) to the Label field in the CD Collection table.

6. In the Edit Relationships dialog box, select Enforce Referential Integrity and click the Cascade Update Related Fields check box.

7. Click the Create button to create the relationship, and then close the Relationships window. Choose Yes to save the relationship.

8. Open the **CD Collection** table and click anywhere in the label field. Click the Sort Ascending button to sort the labels. Scroll down to see the entries titled MHS.

9. Close the CD Collection table and save your changes. Open the **Label** table.

10. Scroll down until you find the MHS record. Highlight MHS and type **Musical Heritage Society**. Close the Label table.

11. Open the **CD Collection** table. Scroll down to the previous location of the MHS entries. Notice that all of them were changed to Musical Heritage Society.

12. Close the table and close the database.

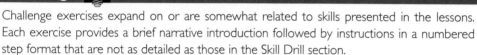

Challenge

Challenge exercises expand on or are somewhat related to skills presented in the lessons. Each exercise provides a brief narrative introduction followed by instructions in a numbered step format that are not as detailed as those in the Skill Drill section.

You use three databases in the Challenge section. The first exercise is based on the same database you used in the Skill Drill section. The second database is a company personnel file, and the third database uses U.S. motor vehicle statistics.

1. Adding Text to Fields Using an Update Query

In Lesson 3, you learned how to update a numeric field by using a mathematical expression (in that case, multiplying the value in a field by 1.1). You can also update a text field by adding text to it. While looking over your CD Collection table, you discovered that you forgot to use the proper prefix in the serial numbers for about half of the Deutsche Grammophon CDs. The serial numbers are all supposed to begin with the letter D, followed by a space. In this exercise, you create an update query that identifies the mislabeled serial numbers and then you add the correct prefix.

To add text to fields using an update query:

1. Copy the **AC-1705** database file from the CD-ROM, remove the read-only status, re-name the file **CD Collection 2**, and open the database.

2. Look at the serial numbers for the Deutsche Grammophon CDs. Notice that all the incorrect entries begin with the number 4.

3. Create a new query in Design view, and base it on the CD Collection table.

4. Add the Label and Serial number fields to the query design grid.

5. Change the query to Update Query. Enter **Deutsche Grammophon** in the first Criteria box for the Label field. Be careful about the spelling!

6. Type **Left([Serial number],1)=4** in the first Criteria box for the Serial number field.

7. Type **"D "+[Serial number]** (including the quotation marks and the space after the letter D) in the Update To box for the Serial number field. This adds the letter D and a space to the beginning of the existing serial number.

8. Run the query to update the six incorrect serial numbers. Save your changes as **DG Update**.

9. Check the CD Collection table to make sure your query worked. When you are done, close the table and close the database.

2. Updating Salaries Based on Department

The Online Products Company has been through some rough times, but a new company name and focus have made them profitable again. It is time to calculate the raises, and the boss decides that everyone deserves a 5 percent raise. The Marketing department reminds the boss that they were the only group that made concessions in the previous two years, and convinces her that they deserve a 10 percent raise. The boss agrees. In this exercise, you create an update query to calculate the new salaries. If you have done all of the exercises in this project, you should use a new floppy disk for this exercise so you do not run out of space.

To update salaries based on department:

1. Copy the `AC-1706` database file from the CD-ROM; remove the read-only status; rename the file `Online Products`, and open the database.

2. Look in Help to figure out how to give the Marketing people 10 percent raises, while giving the others a 5 percent raise. Look up the IIf function and use it in the Update To row. This is the Immediate If function, which is a conditional if that provides one result if a condition is true, and a second result if the same condition is false.

3. Create a select query to test the calculated field you create. Run the query to test the accuracy of your expression.

4. Once you know the expression is correct, change the query type and copy the expression to the Update To row. *Hint:* You do not need to enter anything into the Criteria row.

5. Run the query and save it as `Salary Update`.

6. Verify that the records were updated in the table.

7. When you are done, close the table and close the database.

3. Creating a Calculated Field to Update a Table Field in Another Table

The database you work with in the next exercise shows the number of privately and publicly owned cars and trucks in the 50 U.S. states and the District of Columbia. One table contains the raw data from the U.S. Department of Transportation; the second table contains projected increases of vehicles by location. (These numbers are not from the D.O.T.; they were estimated for this exercise only.) In this exercise, you use the Expression Builder to create a formula to update a new field.

To create a calculated field to update a table field in another table:

1. Copy the `AC-1707` database file from the CD-ROM, remove the read-only status, rename the file `Motor Vehicles by State`, and open the database. Look through both tables to get a feel for the data.

2. Create a relationship between the Location fields in both tables and enforce referential integrity.

3. Add a Number field to the Projected Increases table called `Cars in 10 Years`.

4. Create a new query in Design view. Add both the Projected Increases table and the Vehicles table.

5. Add the Cars in 10 Years field to the query design grid from the Projected Increases table. Change the query type to an update query.

6. Click in the Update To box and click the Build button on the toolbar. Open the Vehicles folder in the Tables folder. Double-click Cars Privately Owned to move it to the Build window.

7. Click the Plus button, then double-click the Cars Privately Owned field again.

8. Click the multiplication (*) symbol. Open the `Projected Increases` folder in the Tables folder, and then double-click the 10 Year Projected Increase field. The last three steps added the current number of vehicles and the projected percentage increase multiplied by the same number.

9. Run the query, and then save it as `Projected Number of Cars`.

10. Check the Projected Increases table to make sure your update was successful. (Alabama should have 1,833,647 cars and Alaska should have 249,124 cars.) Close the database.

Discovery Zone

Discovery Zone exercises help you gain advanced knowledge of project topics and application of skills. These exercises focus on enhancing your problem-solving skills. Numbered steps are not provided, but you are given hints, reminders, screen shots, and references to help you reach your goal for each exercise.

In both of these exercises you use a PC Training database. This database contains two tables. The first contains information about each employee, including whether or not the employee has completed training in each of six Office applications. The other table is used for tracking software training and identifying the company's Microsoft Office experts.

1. Creating Update Queries to Update a Second Table

The Human Resources department tracks employee training, so that they can plan for upcoming workshops and seminars. They keep a list of employees, uniquely identified by their Social Security numbers. They track which type of computer each employee uses, and whether the employee has completed the company's rigorous training program for six Office applications. As employees complete the training for an application, the trainer enters a 1 into that column.

A second table needs to be updated every month. This table provides the information for a training chart that is sent to each supervisor in the company. It contains a list of employees and a column for each application. If the employee has completed the training, the word **completed** appears in that column. You are assigned the job of figuring out a way to update this table. You use the `AC-1708` file, renamed `Software Training`.

Goal: Create a way to update each of the six software application columns.

■ You should create a relationship between the Social Security Number fields and enforce referential integrity.

■ You may need more than one query to complete this assignment.

■ Each query should be saved and named, so that it can be re-run each month.

Hint #1: After you have successfully tested one query, you can make copies and then modify each copy.

Hint #2: When you modify a copy of a query, make sure you modify all necessary fields. Rather than deleting and replacing fields, try using the drop-down menu in the Field text box.

2. Updating a Field Based on Several Other Fields

The company sends employees to take Microsoft certification tests when they have completed the training on an application, and gives bonuses for each test passed. The company also has an internal certification program; when an employee completes training for all six applications, he or she is certified as a Company Office Expert and given a raise in pay to go along with the added responsibility of helping other users who have software problems. (To become a Company Office Expert, Macintosh users need to take Windows training for several of the programs.) Use the AC-1708 file, renamed Software Training.

Goal: Create a query that puts a check in the Office Expert field check box when an employee has completed training in all six applications.

Remember that the employee must have completed training for all six applications. Call the new query Office Expert Update.

The Microsoft Software Level table should look like Figure 17.29. If you did not do the first Discovery Zone exercise, then the word "Completed" will not show in the results, only the checkmarks in the Office Expert field will show.

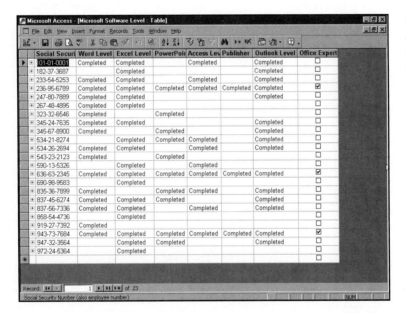

Figure 17.29
After running the query, boxes are marked completed for the training that each employee has finished.

Social Securi	Word Level	Excel Level	PowerPoir	Access Lev	Publisher	Outlook Level	Office Expert
101-01-0001	Completed	Completed		Completed		Completed	☐
182-37-3687		Completed				Completed	☐
233-54-5253	Completed	Completed		Completed		Completed	☐
236-95-6789	Completed	Completed	Completed	Completed	Completed	Completed	☑
247-80-7889	Completed	Completed				Completed	☐
267-48-4895	Completed	Completed					☐
323-32-6546	Completed		Completed				☐
345-24-7635	Completed	Completed				Completed	☐
345-67-8900	Completed		Completed			Completed	☐
534-21-8274		Completed	Completed	Completed		Completed	☐
534-26-2694	Completed	Completed		Completed		Completed	☐
543-23-2123	Completed		Completed				☐
590-13-5326		Completed		Completed			☐
636-63-2345	Completed	Completed	Completed	Completed	Completed	Completed	☑
690-98-9583		Completed					☐
835-36-7899	Completed		Completed	Completed		Completed	☐
837-45-6274	Completed	Completed	Completed			Completed	☐
837-56-7336	Completed	Completed		Completed		Completed	☐
858-54-4736		Completed					☐
919-27-7392	Completed						☐
943-73-7684	Completed	Completed	Completed	Completed	Completed	Completed	☑
947-32-3564		Completed	Completed			Completed	☐
972-24-5364		Completed					☐

Record: 1 of 23

Social Security Number (also employee number)

PinPoint Assessment

You have completed this project and its associated lessons, and have had an opportunity to assess your skills through the end-of-project questions and exercises. Now use the PinPoint software Evaluation Mode to further assess your comprehension of the specific exam activities you have just learned. You can also use the PinPoint Trainer Mode and the Show Me tutorials to practice these exam activities.

Using Access Tools

Key terms introduced in this project include

- AutoCorrect
- Name AutoCorrect
- Office Links
- Performance Analyzer
- Table Analyzer

Objectives	Required Activity for MOUS	Exam Level
➤ Customize Data Entry Using AutoCorrect		
➤ Analyze a Table	Use AddIns	Expert
➤ Analyze Database Performance	Use AddIns	Expert
➤ Update the Database Using Name AutoCorrect		
➤ Use Office Links to Analyze Data with Excel	Export database records to Excel	Expert

Why Would I Do This?

Access provides a full range of tools to help you edit data, analyze components of your database, and connect to other Microsoft Office applications. These tools help you, the database designer, to control and modify your database to best suit your needs. You have already used some of the Access tools. For example, in Project 9, "Managing Data Using Small, Related Tables," you printed the table relationships to help you analyze your database. In Project 13, "Managing Your Databases," you compacted and repaired files and the Access program itself. There is also a full set of security tools that you will use in Project 21, "Sharing a Database with Others."

Access includes an **AutoCorrect** tool, which corrects common mistakes and expands a few letters into short phrases. You may be familiar with this tool from Microsoft Word, Excel, or PowerPoint. Although the need for this tool is not as obvious in a database as it is in other applications, there are certain situations where it can be very useful.

In addition to the Documenter, which you used in Project 15, "Designing a Complex Database," Access provides two other very powerful analysis tools, one for tables only and two for any database object. With the **Table Analyzer**, an Access wizard will help you determine if there is redundant data in the database. If there is, it will suggest ways of splitting up the table into smaller, more efficient, related tables. The **Performance Analyzer** is a wizard that makes recommendations about the structures of various database components.

Access 2000 has, for the first time, included a feature that automatically updates dependent parts of the database when an object or field is renamed. In the past, when you renamed a field in a table, you had to go through all of the other database objects and update the new name. The **Name AutoCorrect** feature automatically updates new field names in other objects, such as forms and reports, and in calculated fields that contain the new field name. This feature automatically updates changes in object names, as well as fields.

Finally, Access offers **Office Links** to help you use the capabilities of other Microsoft applications to analyze and report your data. You can send data to Excel for further analysis or advanced graphing. You can also send information to Word if you need a quick, attractive report.

Lesson 1: Customizing Data Entry Using AutoCorrect

Combo and list boxes offer an excellent way to create shortcuts for many data entry tasks. An alternative method for creating data entry shortcuts is to use the AutoCorrect feature in Access. The AutoCorrect feature is available in other Microsoft Office applications, such as Word, Excel, and PowerPoint. An advantage of using AutoCorrect rather than list or combo boxes is that the AutoCorrect feature works in every field in which you are entering data—AutoCorrect entries will also work in other Microsoft applications even though you created them in Access. AutoCorrect also works when you are adding a word or phrase that is only part of a field.

To Customize Data Entry Using AutoCorrect

❶ **Make a copy of the AC-1801 database file from the CD-ROM. Right-click on the file name, select Properties from the shortcut menu, and remove the read-only status. Use the shortcut menu to rename the file Books of Stories, then open the database.**
Make sure you use a disk that has enough room on it.

2 **Click the Forms object button, if necessary. Double-click the Book Information Data Input form.**

3 **Use the Next Record navigation button to move to record 8.**

This record has a publisher (Doubleday, Page) that is not in the combo box for the Publisher field (see Figure 18.1). You can add this publisher as a new entry to the combo box, or you can use the AutoCorrect feature to see how it works.

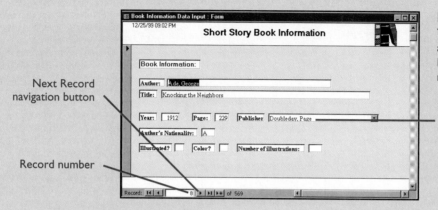

Figure 18.1
This record contains an entry in the Publisher field that is not in the combo box.

Publisher name that is not in the combo box

Next Record navigation button

Record number

4 **Choose Tools, AutoCorrect from the menu.**

The AutoCorrect dialog box is displayed (see Figure 18.2). Notice that there is an option to correct two capital letters at the beginning of a word. There are also options to capitalize the first letter of sentences, capitalize the days of the week, and adjust for accidental use of Caps Lock. The feature you will want to use is Replace text as you type, so make sure that check box is selected.

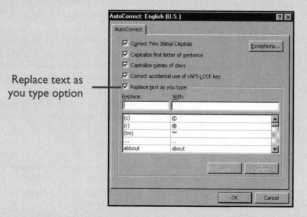

Figure 18.2
The AutoCorrect dialog box gives you five options.

Replace text as you type option

If You Have Problems...

If you take your database to a different computer and try your new AutoCorrect entry, it will not work. AutoCorrect entries are stored on the computer, not attached to your database file. This makes them very handy on machines that you use regularly, but are not of much use if you use several different computers.

continues ▶

To Customize Data Entry Using AutoCorrect   (continued)

5 **Type dp in the Replace text box.**
This is an abbreviation that will be easy to remember.

6 **Type Doubleday, Page in the With text box.**
Make sure you type the text exactly as shown, including the capital letters and the comma (see Figure 18.3).

Figure 18.3
In the With text box, type exactly what you want to appear in the field.

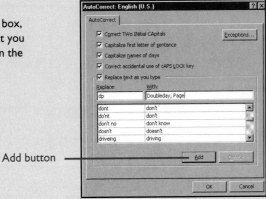

Add button

7 **Click the Add button, then click OK.**
The shortcut has now been added to the AutoCorrect list.

 8 **Click the New Record button.**

9 **Click in the Publisher field, type dp, then press ⏎Enter.**
Notice that the dp has been replaced by Doubleday, Page exactly as you typed it into the AutoCorrect list (see Figure 18.4). This entry is now stored in a common location for all of the Microsoft applications.

Figure 18.4
The AutoCorrect entry expands when you move to the next field.

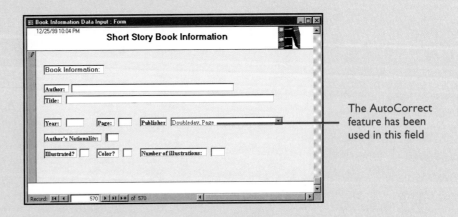

The AutoCorrect feature has been used in this field

 Inside Stuff: How to Activate an AutoCorrect Entry
In the above example, you pressed ⏎Enter to activate the AutoCorrect entry. You can also do this by pressing Spacebar, Tab⇆, or a punctuation mark.

Launch Microsoft Word.

 Choose Tools, AutoCorrect from the menu and scroll down to see if dp is there.

Notice that it does, in fact, show up in the Microsoft Word AutoCorrect list. It will also appear in PowerPoint and Excel. This is because the AutoCorrect list is stored on the computer's hard drive as a shared file available to all Microsoft Office products. This can be a great timesaver for you.

 Inside Stuff: **The AutoCorrect Feature in Other Microsoft Applications**

While you are in Word, take a look at the tabs at the top of the AutoCorrect dialog box. There are several options available for advanced features. Access only has the AutoCorrect tab, as does Excel and PowerPoint.

 Close the AutoCorrect dialog box in Word. Type dp and then press ⟨Spacebar⟩**.**

The abbreviation is expanded into the publisher's name exactly as it did in your Access form.

 Inside Stuff: **Removing an AutoCorrect Entry**

If you are using a computer in a lab, you need to remove the AutoCorrect entry you just added. To do this, return to the AutoCorrect window, scroll down and select the entry you just added, and press ⟨Del⟩.

 Close Word, but don't save your changes.

 Close the Book Information Data Input form, then close the Books of Stories database.

 Exam Note: **Setting AutoCorrect Exceptions**

There will be times when you want to use one of the AutoCorrect options, but want to make exceptions in certain cases. For example, you might often type terms like CD or PC. If you were using the Correct TWo INitial CApitals option, the second letter of each would be automatically changed to lower case. To fix this problem, click the Exceptions button in the AutoCorrect dialog box. Click the INitial CApitals tab, and then type in your exceptions.

Lesson 2: Analyzing a Table

Access provides three analysis tools to help you fine-tune your database—a Table Analyzer, a Performance Analyzer, and a Documenter. These tools help you in different ways. The Table Analyzer contains a wizard that looks at a table, determines which fields contain duplicated information, then determines how you might want to break the large table into smaller, more efficient linked tables. If you are not interested in having the Access program determine which fields to break out of the original table, you can identify the fields yourself.

In this lesson, you analyze the table in a database of a television viewing log. This comes from a small study by a local cable company of the number of hours each person watches one of five major channels.

To Analyze a Table

1 **Make a copy of the `AC-1802` database file from the CD-ROM. Right-click on the file name, select Properties from the shortcut menu, and remove the read-only status. Use the shortcut menu to rename the file `TV Viewing Habits`, and then open the database.**
It does not matter where you are—the analyzers work from anywhere in the database.

2 **Choose Tools, Analyze from the menu, and then select Table.**
This wizard has two introductory screens that are optional. Compare your screen to Figure 18.5. (If your screen does not match the figure below, read the introductory screens and click the Next button until you reach this screen.) This dialog box displays all of the tables in the database. It also enables you to turn on the introductory screens that describe the process in detail. Turn those on if you are interested, then click Back to view them.

 If You Have Problems...
The Table Analyzer wizard is not installed by default. If you are using a computer that has not had that option installed, follow the directions on the screen to install it using the Office CD-ROM, or ask your lab manager for further instructions.

Figure 18.5
The first Table Analyzer Wizard dialog box enables you to choose a table to analyze.

Turn the introductory screens on and off here

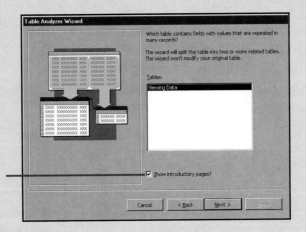

3 **The Viewing Data table is already selected, so click Next.**
The second Table Analyzer Wizard dialog box sets the program's level of control over the process.

4 **Select Yes, let the Wizard decide option, and then click Next.**
Access decides which fields have sufficient duplication to warrant a separate table. It sets up the structure of the resulting tables, and shows you the links it will create. If the potential tables are off the screen, click in the title bars and drag the table lists until you can see them all. Notice that some of the changes make sense, while others, such as separating the First Name and Last Name fields, make no sense at all (see Figure 18.6).

Several fields have been separated from the original table. Because the tables need to be linked, Access has created key fields called Generated Unique ID for each of the new tables. A lookup field has also been included for each of the new tables.

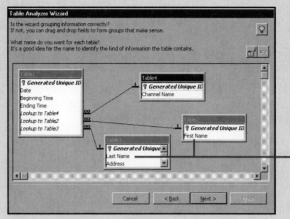

Figure 18.6
The third Table Analyzer Wizard dialog box shows how the tables could be broken up and how they will be linked.

The First Name field should be with the Last Name field

5 **Click the First Name field in Table2 and drag it down to Table3.**
Because the First Name field was the only original field in Table2, that table is removed, and the lookup field referring to it has also been removed (see Figure 18.7).

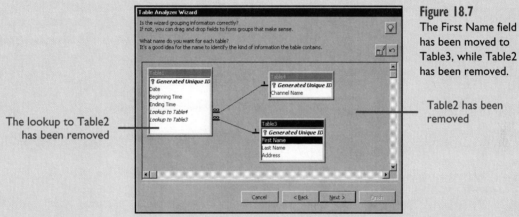

The lookup to Table2 has been removed

Figure 18.7
The First Name field has been moved to Table3, while Table2 has been removed.

Table2 has been removed

It is now a good idea to rename the tables. Make sure you use descriptive names.

6 **Double-click the title bar for Table1. Type `Dates and Times` in the Table Name box. Repeat this process until all three tables have been renamed, using `Channels` for the table containing the Channel Name field, and `Viewer Information` for the other table.**
Your Table Analyzer Wizard dialog box should look like Figure 18.8.

7 **Click Next.**
The next Table Analyzer Wizard dialog box is displayed. This dialog box asks if you are satisfied with the primary key field chosen by the program. If not, you are told how to assign another field as the primary key.

continues ▶

To Analyze a Table (continued)

Figure 18.8
All three tables have been renamed.

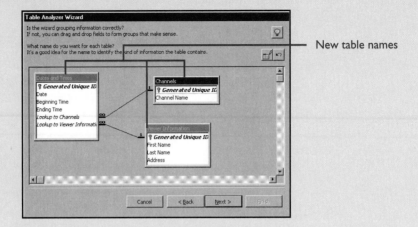

New table names

⑧ **Click Next.**

After a brief delay, the next Table Analyzer Wizard dialog box is displayed (see Figure 18.9). The purpose of this dialog box is to identify identical items, one or more of which might have been misspelled or entered differently. If you want to change an incorrect entry, choose a correction from the drop-down list in the Correction column, or type a new entry. The data in this dialog box is often incorrectly identified as being a problem, although at times it does catch errors. There are no changes to be made to this list.

Figure 18.9
The next Table Analyzer Wizard dialog box looks for typos or inconsistent duplicate entries.

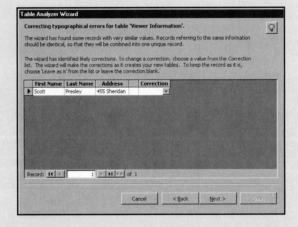

⑨ **Click Next.**

A warning dialog box appears asking if you are sure you want to move on (see Figure 18.10).

Figure 18.10
The program warns you that you have made no changes, even though changes were suggested.

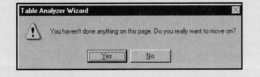

⑩ **Click Yes.**

Possible errors are displayed for a second table.

⓫ Click Next, then click Yes to move on.

The next Table Analyzer Wizard dialog box is displayed. This dialog box asks if you want to create a query that will look like your original table.

 Inside Stuff: Creating a Query to Look Like Your Original Table

It is usually a good idea to create this query. Not only will you appear to be working from your original table, Access will also make the links to make sure all forms and reports can still find the necessary information.

⓬ Make sure the Yes, create the query option is selected, turn off the Help option, then click Finish.

After a brief delay, the program shows the results of the query, which has the same information as the original table.

⓭ Click OK to close the Table Analyzer Wizard, then close the query. Move to the Tables object button, if necessary, and open the Dates and Times table.

Notice that the Channels are shown in a column called Lookup to Channels (see Figure 18.11). It is now a lookup field, taking its information from the Channels table. The same holds true for the Viewer Information table. In this case, the column widths have been adjusted so you can see the results more clearly.

Lookups to other tables

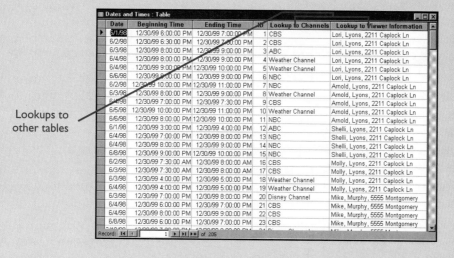

Figure 18.11
The Dates and Times table is now joined to two other tables.

⓮ Click the Save button to save your changes. Close the table and the database.

Leave Access open for the next lesson.

Lesson 3: Analyzing Database Performance

In the previous lesson, you learned how to use an analysis tool to analyze a table. Access also offers a tool to analyze the performance of a database. This analysis is not restricted to tables, but will work on all database objects. It is always a good idea to back up your database before you run any of the analyzers.

In this lesson, you analyze all of the database objects in a database and correct two of the problems found.

To Analyze Database Performance

❶ Make a copy of the AC-1803 database file from the CD-ROM. Right-click on the file name, select Properties from the shortcut menu, and remove the read-only status. Use the shortcut menu to rename the file Checking Performance, and then open the database.

The Database window should now be open to the Tables area, although it does not matter what area you are in. The analyzers work from anywhere in the database.

❷ Choose Tools, Analyze from the menu, then select Performance. Install the wizard, if necessary.

The first Performance Analyzer dialog box is displayed (see Figure 18.12). This dialog box has several tabs that enable you to choose the database object type you want to work on.

Figure 18.12
The first Performance Analyzer dialog box enables you to choose a table to analyze.

Table check box

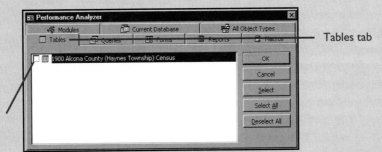

Tables tab

❸ Click the check box for the only table in the database and click OK.

The Performance Analyzer looks at the table, and has no suggestions to improve it (see Figure 18.13).

Figure 18.13
The Performance Analyzer found no problems with the table.

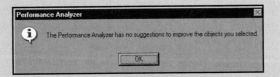

❹ Click OK, then once again choose Tools, Analyze, Performance from the menu.

The first Performance analyzer dialog box is again displayed.

❺ Choose the All Object Types tab, and then click Select All.

All of the objects in the database are shown, and all of them have been selected (see Figure 18.14).

❻ Click OK.

The Performance Analyzer now analyzes each object in the database. This procedure can take a long time in a complex database, particularly if you are using a slow machine or are operating on a network version of the software.

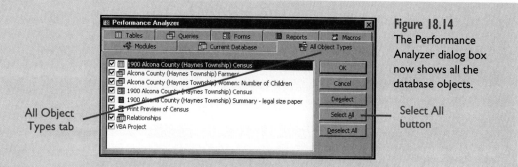

All Object Types tab

Select All button

Figure 18.14
The Performance Analyzer dialog box now shows all the database objects.

The Recommendations, Suggestions, and Ideas are shown, along with the database object they refer to. The Analysis Notes at the bottom of the dialog box further describe the Analysis Results for the first item on the list (see Figure 18.15). When any other object listed in the Analysis Results is selected, the Analysis Notes will change to describe the highlighted item. In this case, the only items you will act on are the two that are shown as Recommendations.

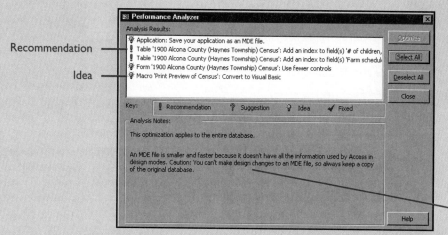

Recommendation

Idea

Figure 18.15
The Performance analyzer gives Recommendations, Suggestions, and Ideas on how to improve database performance.

Description of selected (or first) option

 Exam Note: Accepting Performance Analyzer Recommendations

Some of the Recommendations, Suggestions, and Ideas make great sense, while others seem to make no sense at all. Be careful when you make changes based on the analyzers, particularly those you are not sure of. Back up your database before you run the Performance Analyzer.

---

7 **Select the second item in the list.**

This item recommends that an index be added to fields in the table to improve the operations of one of the queries. (Read the details in the Analysis Notes area.)

8 **Click the Optimize button in the dialog box.**

This tells the computer to accept the Performance Analyzer recommendation.

9 **Select the third item in the list.**

This item also recommends that an index be added to fields in the table, this time to improve the operation of a second query.

continues ▶

To Analyze Database Performance (continued)

⑩ **Click the <u>O</u>ptimize button.**
Check marks indicate that optimization has been performed on two of the items (see Figure 18.16).

Figure 18.16
Two of the recom-
mendations have been
performed.

Optimized items

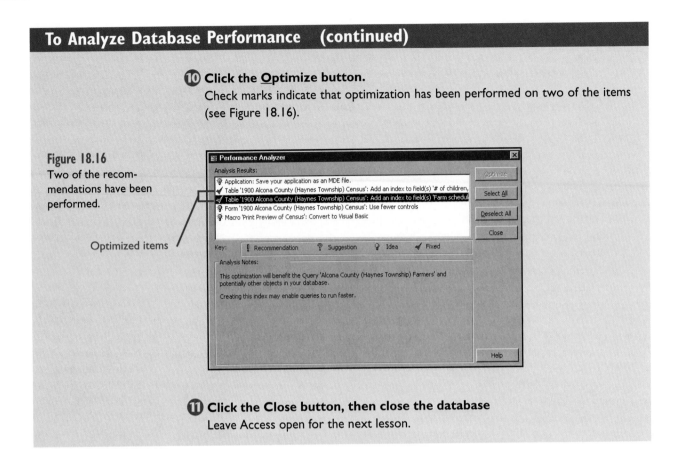

⑪ **Click the Close button, then close the database**
Leave Access open for the next lesson.

Lesson 4: Updating the Database Using Name AutoCorrect

Databases tend to constantly evolve. Object names and field names are often changed, which has led to problems in the past. A change in a field name meant that the database designer had to change all references to that field in every query, form, report, or other object that depended on it. If the field was numeric, any formulas or expressions that used it also had to be changed. The same held true with object names. Access 2000 has now included a Name AutoCorrect feature that automatically updates the database every time a name change occurs.

In this lesson, you work with a database that contains statistics about publicly and privately owned cars and trucks in the United States.

To Update a Database Using Name AutoCorrect

① **Make a copy of the AC-1804 database file from the CD-ROM. Right-click on the file name, select <u>P</u>roperties from the shortcut menu, and remove the read-only status. Use the shortcut menu to rename the file Using Name AutoCorrect, and then open the database.**
Make sure you use a disk that has enough room on it.

② **Click the Queries object button, if necessary. Select the Total Cars and Trucks query and click the Design button.**

The query is opened in Design view (see Figure 18.17). Notice that the fourth field is an expression (as is the seventh field, which is off the screen). The fields in the second and third columns are added together to get a total of cars by state. It is difficult to read the expression in the narrow column.

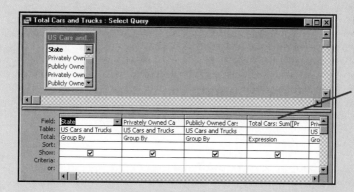

Figure 18.17
The query is open in Design view.

Expression

③ **Right-click in the Field box of the fourth column and select Zoom from the shortcut menu.**

The expression is now easy to read (see Figure 18.18). Look at the field names in the expression—they match the field names in the second and third columns of the query design grid.

Figure 18.18
The Zoom button makes a long expression easy to read.

④ **Click OK, then close the query.**

Do not save changes if prompted.

⑤ **Click the Tables object button. Click the Design button to open the US Cars and Trucks table in Design view.**

⑥ **Change the name of the second field to Private Cars, the third field to Public Cars, the fourth field to Private Trucks, and the fifth field to Public Trucks.**

Your table Design window should look like Figure 18.19.

⑦ **Close the table and save your changes. Click the Queries object button and open the Total Cars and Trucks query in Design view.**

Notice that the field names have been changed in the second and third columns.

continues ▶

To Update a Database Using Name AutoCorrect   (continued)

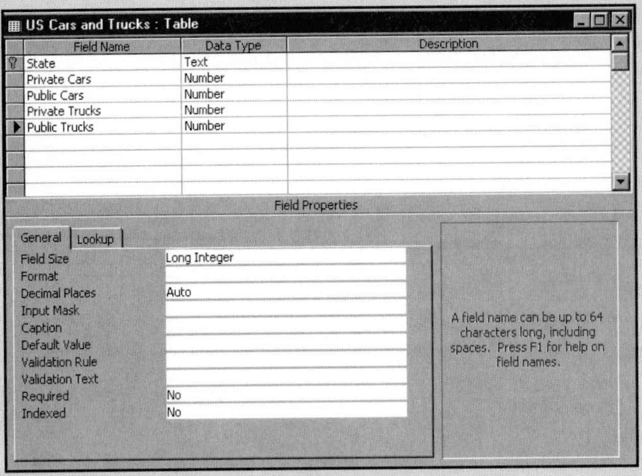

Figure 18.19
Four of the five field names have been changed.

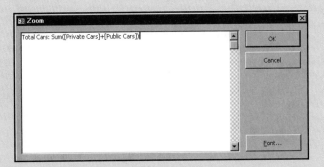

8 **Right-click in the Field box of the fourth column and select Zoom from the shortcut menu.**
The field names in the expression have also been changed (see Figure 18.20).

Figure 18.20
The field names in the expression have been automatically changed to match the new field names in the table.

9 **Close the Zoom dialog box and the query.**
Do not save changes if prompted.

10 **Click the Forms object button, and then open the Total Cars and Trucks form.**
Notice that the numbers are correct, but the field labels have not changed (see Figure 18.21). If you want to change the labels, you need to do that in Design view.

Figure 18.21
The Name AutoCorrect feature does not change the text used in labels in forms and reports.

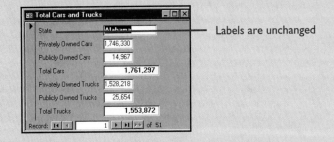

Labels are unchanged

11 **Close the form, then close the database.**
Leave Access open for the next lesson.

Exam Note: **The Name AutoCorrect Feature and Older Versions of Access**

If you are using a database created in Access 97, the above procedure will not work automatically. Once you have converted the database to Access 2000, choose Tools, Options from the menu. Click the General tab and click the check boxes for the Track name AutoCorrect info and the Perform name AutoCorrect options in the Name AutoCorrect area.

If your database was created on an even earlier version of Access and then upgraded as new versions came out, you may have problems getting this feature to work. Try turning on the Name AutoCorrect feature, then change one of the field names in a table. If it does not work, you will need to make these changes manually. If it is a simple database, you can export the data to Excel, create a new database, and import the data. You will need to recreate the other database objects.

Lesson 5: Using Office Links to Analyze Data with Excel

In many cases you will want to perform calculations using the fields in your database. While Access has many capabilities, such as calculated fields and summaries on reports, it is usually far easier to perform calculations in an Excel spreadsheet. You can send the contents of a table to Excel, but in many cases it is better to send a query that contains only the data you want to use. You can also send data to Excel from forms and reports.

In this lesson, you use a modified query from the census database you used in Lesson 3. The query is a summary of women who have had children, as reported in the 1900 census. It contains only three fields—the mother's birthplace, the number of children each woman had, and the number of children still living. The data will be transferred to Excel for analysis. This lesson requires that you have Microsoft Excel available.

To Use Office Links to Analyze Data with Excel

1 **Make a copy of the AC-1805 database file from the CD-ROM. Right click on the file name, select Properties from the shortcut menu, and remove the read-only status. Use the shortcut menu to rename the file Analyze with Excel, and then open the database.**
Make sure you use a disk that has enough room on it.

2 **Click the Queries object button if necessary. Select and Open the Haynes Township Women—Number of Children query.**
Notice that the query contains only three of the 38 fields in the 1900 Alcona County (Haynes Township) Census table (see Figure 18.22).

3 **Choose Tools, Office Links from the menu, and then select Analyze It with MS Excel.**

You can also click the OfficeLinks button on the Database toolbar and select Analyze It with MS Excel from the drop-down list. The program opens Excel and transfers the data from the query to the Excel program. This is now an Excel file, and can be edited, modified, and saved in the same way you would work on any other Excel file (see Figure 18.23). The file is given the same name as the database object from which it is derived.

continues ▶

To Use Office Links to Analyze Data with Excel (continued)

Figure 18.22
The query contains only three fields.

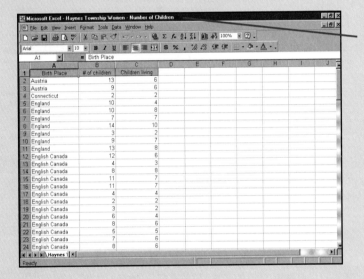

The spreadsheet name is the same as the query name

Figure 18.23
The Analyze It With MS Excel option creates a new Excel file and transfers data from Access.

 Inside Stuff: **Interactivity Between Excel and Access**
The Excel file created in this way is not linked to the original database source. Updates that you make to the data in Access will not be transferred to the new Excel file, and changes you make to the Excel spreadsheet will not be reflected in the Access database.

4 **Click in cell A1, scroll down to the bottom of the data, hold down**
↑Shift), and click in cell C133.
All of the data is selected.

5 **Choose Data, Subtotals from the menu to display the Subtotals dialog box. Click the check box for the number of children in the Add subtotal to scroll box.**
Excel now calculates subtotals for number of children and Children living. Your Subtotal dialog box should look like Figure 18.24.

6 **Click OK, then return to the top of the worksheet. Click the line on the right side of the column selector for the first column (the one labeled A), and widen the column by about 1/2 inch.**

Figure 18.24
The Subtotals dialog box has been set to group on Birth Place and add up the other two fields.

7 **Click the second level box at the top of the column at the very left side of the window. Click in cell A1 to turn off the highlighting.**
The worksheet displays only the group totals and grand total (see Figure 18.25). Notice how much easier it is to do sophisticated data analysis in Excel.

Second level selector

Grand totals

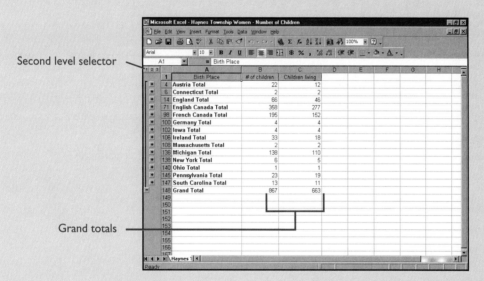

Figure 18.25
The group subtotals and grand total are displayed.

8 **Close Excel and save your changes. If the program asks you to save it in the most recent format, click Yes.**

9 **Close the query and close the database.**
Close Access unless you are going to proceed to the exercises.

Exam Note: **Exporting Selected Records to Excel**
You do not have to export all of the records in a table or query. To export a subset of the records, select the records you want to export, and then choose File, Export from the menu. Click the Save formatted check box, give the file a name and location, and choose a file type from the Save as type drop-down menu. Finally, click the drop-down arrow on the Save All button and select Save Selection from the list.

Summary

In this project you used some of the tools and utilities available to you in Access. These include an AutoCorrect feature, which is used in other Microsoft Office applications. You also used two of the analysis tools to analyze a table and optimize database performance. You used the Name AutoCorrect feature to update a changed field name in database objects and expressions. Finally, you used the Office Links tool to analyze Excel data from a database query.

You can learn more about the Access analyzer tools by going to the help index and typing in `analyzer`. These analysis tools will become more and more important to you as you create more complex databases.

Checking Concepts and Terms ✓

True/False

For each of the following statements, check *T* or *F* to indicate whether the statement is true or false.

__T __F **1.** An AutoCorrect shortcut added in Access will also be available in Excel. [L2]

__T __F **2.** You can run the Analyze tools from anywhere in the database. [L3]

__T __F **3.** Choose <u>O</u>ptimize to accept a Performance Analyzer recommendation. [L4]

__T __F **4.** The three analysis tools are the Table Analyzer, the Performance Analyzer, and the Office Links. [L3]

__T __F **5.** The Name AutoCorrect feature works well with databases created in any version of Access. [L2]

Multiple Choice

Circle the letter of the correct answer for each of the following questions.

1. It is usually a good idea to accept a Performance Analyzer recommendation to index a field if you ever plan to _____ on that field. [L4]

a. run a Spelling check

b. do a Performance Analysis

c. sort

d. create a Crosstab

2. When you send a query to Excel using Office Links: [L6]

a. the spreadsheet is not linked to the source database and won't be updated as you update information in the database

b. the file is automatically updated as you update the database

c. you can change information in the spreadsheet and the changes will also be made in the database

d. the query will look at the spreadsheet and import the information to your database

3. The Performance Analyzer offers: [L4]

a. recommendations

b. suggestions

c. ideas

d. all of the above

4. The Table Analyzer: [L3]

   a. optimizes field names

   b. makes sure tables interact properly with queries, forms, and records

   c. provides a description of each field, data type, and relationship

   d. determines whether a table should be broken down into two or more smaller tables

5. An advantage of using the AutoCorrect feature instead of combo boxes or list boxes is that the AutoCorrect feature can be used: [L2]

   a. in any field, rather than just one field

   b. by other Microsoft applications

   c. to enter only a part of a field

   d. all of the above

Skill Drill

Skill Drill exercises reinforce project skills. Each skill reinforced is the same, or nearly the same, as a skill presented in the project. Each exercise includes a brief narrative introduction, followed by detailed instructions in a step-by-step format.

1. Using the Table Analyzer

The Table Analyzer can help you make your tables more efficient and easier to extract information from. In this exercise, you work with a table of Alaskan geographical locations that was not set up using good design techniques.

To use the Table Analyzer:

1. Make a copy of the AC-1806 database file from the CD-ROM. Right-click on the file name, select Properties from the shortcut menu, and remove the read-only status. Use the shortcut menu to rename the file **Alaska Locations**, then open the database.

2. Select Tools, Analyze, Table from the menu.

3. Skip the two introduction screens, if necessary, by clicking Next twice. Select the Geography table.

4. Let the wizard decide how to break up the table. Accept the three tables as they are shown.

5. Rename Table1 as **Location**.

6. Rename Table2 as **Borough**.

7. Rename Table3 as **Type**.

8. Click Next, then click Next three times to accept the primary key fields and skip the typographical error screen. Click Yes when asked if you really want to move to the next screen.

9. Choose to create a query to match the original table, deselect the help check box, then click Finish.

10. Close the query and close the database.

2. Analyzing Database Performance

The database used for this exercise contains tables, queries, forms, and reports. To see how they work together, and what might be done to improve operation, it is a good idea to run the Performance Analyzer. Remember, before you do this to an important database make a backup copy.

To analyze database performance:

1. Copy AC-1807, remove the read only status, and rename the file **New CD Collection**.

2. Select Tools, Analyze, Performance from the menu.

3. Click the All Object Types tab from the Performance Analyzer dialog box.

4. Click the Select All button to select all of the database objects.

5. Click OK to run the Performance Analyzer.

6. Select the second item in the list (the recommendation to add an index to the Label field).

7. Click the Optimize button.

8. Click the Close button to close the Performance Analyzer dialog box. Close the database.

3. Using Office Links Feature to Analyze Data

Excel is an excellent program to analyze Access tables or queries that contain a lot of numerical fields. In this exercise, you will use a database about Arizona tornadoes to look at casualties by county.

To use the Office Links feature to analyze data:

1. Copy AC-1808, remove the read only status, and rename the file **Updated Arizona Tornadoes**.

2. Open the database, then click the Queries object button.

3. Highlight the Arizona Counties with Tornado Casualties query and click the Design button. Notice that this query displays only those counties in which a tornado-related injury or fatality has occurred in the 45 years of the study.

4. Click the View button to switch to Datasheet view.

5. Select Tools, Office Links, Analyze It with MS Excel.

6. Click in cell A1, hold down Shift, and click in cell C21.

7. Select Data, Subtotals from the menu.

8. Click the check box next to the Killed field so that the subtotals will show all of the casualties, then click OK.

9. Widen column A by about 1/2 inch.

10. Click the second level button to view just the group totals and grand total.

11. Click the Print button to print out the page.

12. Close Excel and save your changes in the latest Excel format.

13. Close the query and close the database.

Challenge 💡

Challenge exercises expand on or are somewhat related to skills presented in the lessons. Each exercise provides a brief narrative introduction followed by instructions in a numbered step format that are not as detailed as those in the Skill Drill section.

In these Challenge exercises, you use two familiar databases and create a new one.

1. Checking the Spelling

There are several tools available in Access that you have not used yet. One of them is a spelling checker that is also available in many other Office applications. The CD Collection database you used in Exercise 2 of the Skill Drill section is ideal for trying out the spelling checker. In this exercise, you check the spelling of the CD Title field.

To check your spelling:

1. Copy AC-1807, remove the read only status, and rename the file **CD Collection Spelling Check**.

2. Open the database, open the **CD Collection** table, then select the CD Title column.

3. Click the Spelling button to begin the spelling check.

4. Change Gratest to **Greatest**.

5. Click Ignore for Antal, Dorati, and Kodaly.

6. Click Ignore All when you reach Bartok, because this name appears several times in the field.

7. Ignore Bacchanales and Royale. The next unrecognized word is Oout, which is misspelled twice.

8. Click Change All to change both misspellings at once.

9. Click the Close button to close the Spelling dialog box.

10. Close the table and close the database.

2. Using the Documenter to Get Detailed Information about an Object

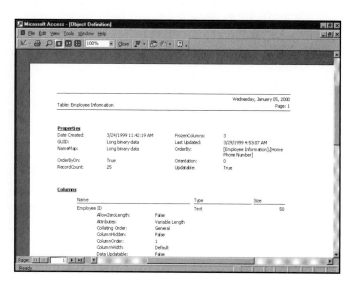

The Documenter is another tool provided by Access to help you design and manage your database. The Documenter provides you with the design characteristics of an object in a database. It can also be used to display the design characteristics of all of the objects in the database. You can also specify the level of detail you want to see. In this exercise, you use the Documenter on one object, but with all of the details turned on.

To use the Documenter to get detailed information about an object:

1. Copy AC-1809, remove the read only status, and rename the file Working with the Documenter.
2. Choose Tools, Analyze, Documenter from the menu. Click several of the tabs to see the various objects in the database. When you are through, click the All Object Types tab.
3. Select only the Employee Information table. In the Options area, include Properties and Relationships for the table.
4. Include Names, Data Types, Sizes, and Properties for the fields.
5. Include Names, Fields, and Properties for the indexes.
6. Run the Documenter (this may take a while). Look through the documenter report. The first page of your report should look like Figure 18.26.
7. Find the page that displays the details about the relationships. Print only that page.
8. Close the Print Preview window, then close the database.

Figure 18.26
The Documenter creates a report that shows the design characteristics of selected objects.

3. Change the Default Field Settings

The common uses for Access databases depend on whether the database is designed for use at home, in an educational setting, or in the business world. The default field settings can be changed to accommodate the way you most often use a database.

In this exercise, use the available help to figure out how to change several of the field defaults.

To change the default field settings:

1. Create a new database and accept the default name. The name of this database is unimportant—you will want to delete it when you are through with this exercise.

2. Change the default field size to 25, change the default number type to Single, and change the default field type to number. (*Note:* If you are doing these exercises in a lab setting, check with the lab manager before making these changes.)

3. Create a new table to make sure your changes took effect. Do not save the table.

4. Change the default field size back to 50, the default number type to long integer, and the default field type to text. Create a new table to make sure the default settings were properly restored. Do not save the table.

5. Close the database and close Access. Use the Windows Explorer to delete the database you just created.

Discovery Zone

Discovery Zone exercises help you gain advanced knowledge of project topics and application of skills. These exercises focus on enhancing your problem-solving skills. Numbered steps are not provided, but you are given hints, reminders, screen shots, and references to help you reach your goal for each exercise.

In these exercises you use a database containing a table of business contacts. In the first exercise, you set up a mail merge with a Word document. In the second exercise, you change the look of the Access screen.

1. Creating a Mail Merge Document Based on an Access Table

You may have learned how to create a mail merge document in Word, but there is a very effective way to create the same type of document using Access. Because you will probably have your mailing list in Access anyway, this is the preferred way to create mail merge documents in many situations.

Use the **AC-1810** file and save it as **Using Mail Merge**. Open up the **Contacts** table and select the Merge It with MS Word office link. You may be able to figure out how to create the document just by looking at the screen, especially if you already know how to use mail merge in Word. If not, use the help menu.

Goal: Create a new mail merge document based on an Access table.

(*Note:* Field names are displayed below as <Field Name>). The document should have:

■ the current date in the first line, followed by a blank line.

■ the customer's <First Name> and <Last Name> in the next line.

■ the <Address> in the next line.

■ the <City> followed by a comma and a space, followed by the <State>, followed by the <ZIP> in the next line.

■ a blank line, followed by a line that reads **Dear** <First Name>:

■ another blank line, followed by a paragraph that reads:

How are things in <City>? I'm just dropping you a line to let you know about our annual mid-winter sale!

Your mail merge document should look like Figure 18.27.

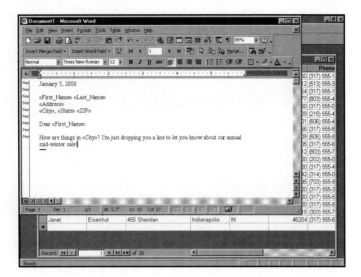

Figure 18.27
The mail merge document draws its data from an Access table.

View the mail merge document with the actual data from the Access table. Print only the fifth record. Close Word and save the document as `Customer Contact Letter`. Close the Contacts table, and leave the database open for the next exercise.

2. Changing the Look of the Access Screen

You may be able to make the Access datasheet window more visually appealing, although always remember that what is appealing to one person may be unsettling to another. If you did not do the first Discovery Zone exercise, use the `AC-1810` file and save it as `Using Mail Merge`.

Goal: Change the look of the Access window.

Your new Access screen should:

- use a dark blue font instead of the default black font.
- have aqua gridlines instead of the default silver gridlines.
- use the Times New Roman font instead of the default Arial font.
- use a 12 point font instead of the default 10 point font.
- have a default column width of 1.5 inches instead of the default 1 inch column width.
- use a sunken cell effect instead of the default flat effect.

(*Hint:* If you made your changes with a table or query open to Datasheet view, you will have to close and reopen it to see the effects of your changes.)

Test your new-look screen, which should look like Figure 18.28. If you like it, and you are using a one-person machine, you can leave it. Try other combinations. If you are using a multi-user machine, change the settings back to the defaults when you are through.

Figure 18.28
The look of the
datasheet has been
substantially changed.

PinPoint Assessment

You have completed this project and its associated lessons, and have had an opportunity to assess your skills through the end-of-project questions and exercises. Now use the PinPoint software Evaluation Mode to further assess your comprehension of the specific exam activities you have just learned. You can also use the PinPoint Trainer Mode and the Show Me tutorials to practice these exam activities.

Project 19

Analyzing and Reporting Data

Key terms introduced in this project include

- crosstab
- PivotTable
- subreport

Objectives	Required Activity for MOUS	Exam Level
➤ Use the Totals Tool in a Query	Create a totals query	Expert
➤ Create Crosstab Queries Based on Multiple Tables		
➤ Add a Subform to an Existing Form	Use the Subform control and synchronize forms	Expert
➤ Insert Subreports into Reports Using the Subform/Subreport Wizard	Use the Subreport control and synchronize reports	Expert
➤ Create Charts as Forms Using the Chart Wizard	Present information as a chart (MS Graph)	Expert

Why Would I Do This?

The best database is of little use unless its data can be turned into information that can be communicated to others. You need to be able to summarize data in different ways depending on the type of information and the audience for whom it is intended.

If you need a quick analysis of one field in relation to another field, you can perform a quick calculation using a query and the Totals tool. If you need to analyze more than two fields, a crosstab query and its report are very useful.

A **crosstab** is a very powerful query used to produce a table that counts, averages, or sums data by the groupings that you specify. For example, if you sent out a survey with ten questions, you would enter each person's responses in a single record. If you got 1,000 responses, you would have 1,000 records, each with a numeric response (e.g., a 1 to 5 rating scale) to the ten questions. Counting the number of times each response was given for each question would take a long time. A crosstab query can give you a table of responses in seconds. You can even set criteria and add calculations to the crosstab query.

Subforms and **subreports** are tools used to summarize and present data taken from related tables. You created forms and subforms using a wizard in Project 10, "Adding Useful Features to Your Forms," but you can also modify an existing form by adding a subform. You can also create reports that display data from related tables in a report/subreport format. Just like a main form/subform, a subreport is a report that is placed within another main report. The subreport displays the data from another table that is related to each record in the main part of the report. These data presentation tools are very effective when tables are related in a one-to-many relationship.

Sometimes data that can be presented in text form can be more effectively displayed as a chart. Access provides a charting tool that enables you to chart data from tables.

 ## Lesson 1: Using the Totals Tool in a Query

In many cases you will want to use your database to retrieve simple summary information; that is, grouped data in one field and a calculation based on a second, related field. Access enables you to do this easily using a query and the Totals tool. You were introduced to the Totals tool Project 4, "Querying Your Database."

In this example, you create a query based on two tables that store the product name and the number of units sold for each product. The database you will be using for this project is a shortened database of information about the customers, products, and orders received by a small cleaning supply company during the second half of 1999.

To Use the Totals Tool in a Query

❶ Copy the AC-1901 database file from the CD-ROM to your disk, remove the read-only status, rename the copy Data Analysis, and open the database.
The Database window should now be open to the Tables area.

❷ Click the Queries object button, if necessary, then click the New button.
The New Query dialog box is displayed.

❸ Click Design view, then click OK.
The Show Table dialog box lists four tables (see Figure 19.01).

Figure 19.1
The Show Table dialog
box displays the
database tables.

❹ Add the Products table and Orders table to the query, then close the Show Table dialog box.
The query Design window shows the Products and Orders tables, and displays the one-to-many relationship between the Product ID number fields (see Figure 19.2).

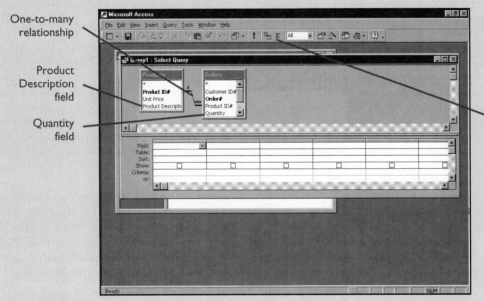

One-to-many
relationship

Product
Description
field

Quantity
field

Totals button

Figure 19.2
The Customers and
Orders tables have
been added to the
query Design window.

❺ Double-click the Product Description field in the Products field list.
The Product Description field is added to the Field row.

❻ Double-click the Quantity field in the Orders field list.
The Quantity field is added to the Field row.

❼ Click the Totals button on the toolbar.
A new Total row is added to the query design grid (see Figure 19.3).

❽ Click the Total box in the Quantity column in the query design grid. Click the down arrow and select Sum from the drop-down list.
The design grid now shows you that when the query is run, you will see the sums in the Quantity column displayed by Product Description (see Figure 19.4).

continues ▶

To Use the Totals Tool in a Query (continued)

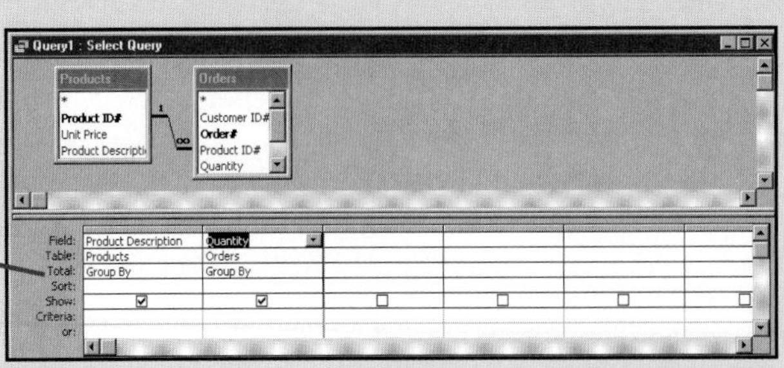

Figure 19.3
The query design grid now includes a Total row.

Total row

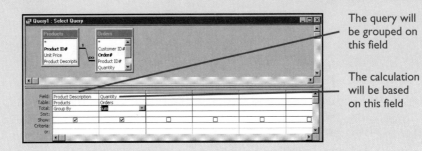

Figure 19.4
The resulting query displays the total number of orders by product description.

The query will be grouped on this field

The calculation will be based on this field

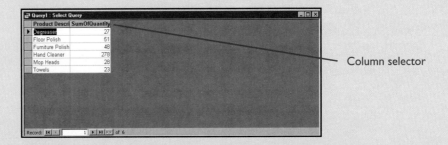

⑨ Click the Run button to run the query.
The query looks in the Products table to get the description of the product based on the Product ID number field, then sums the total number of units ordered for each product (see Figure 19.5).

Figure 19.5
The query has used the Totals tool to calculate grouped data.

Column selector

⑩ Click the column selector for the SumOfQuantity column to select the column, then click the Sort Descending button on the toolbar.
The quantities are now sorted from the highest to the lowest number of products ordered (see Figure 19.6).

Figure 19.6
The quantities are now sorted in descending order.

⑪ Close the query window and save the query as Sales by Product.
Keep the Data Analysis database open for the next lesson.

Lesson 2: Creating Crosstab Queries Based on Multiple Tables

A crosstab query produces a dynaset where the contents of one field provide the column headings and the contents of another field are used as row headings. A third value is used in the cells that intersect the rows and columns. The intersection cell is used to calculate the sum, average, count or other type of total based on values that match both the row and column fields.

In this example, you create a crosstab query based on three tables that show customer information and orders placed by those customers for various types of cleaning supplies. The crosstab query calculates the total quantity of each item sold to each customer.

To Create a Crosstab Query Based on Multiple Tables

1 **In the `Data Analysis` database, click the Queries object button, then click the _N_ew button.**
The New Query dialog box is displayed.

2 **Click Design View, then click OK.**

 Exam Note: Using the Crosstab Query Wizard
You can also use the Crosstab Query Wizard to create a crosstab query, and you will use it in the Challenge exercises. The Design View option also enables you to create crosstab queries, but gives you more control over the process and also lets you see how the process works—important information when you need to create or modify more complex crosstab queries.

3 **Add the Customers, Orders and Products tables to the query Design window, then close the Show Table dialog box.**
The Customers, Orders, and Products tables are added to the query Design window. Notice that all three tables are related.

4 **Click the Query Type button and select the Crosstab Query option.**
Notice that the design grid now has two new rows named Total and Crosstab (see Figure 19.7). The Show row has been automatically removed because all of the fields used in a crosstab query must be displayed.

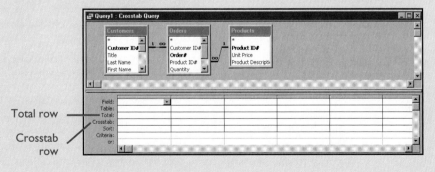
Total row
Crosstab row

Figure 19.7
The Crosstab Query table includes Crosstab and Total rows in the design grid.

continues ▶

To Create a Crosstab Query Based on Multiple Tables   (continued)

⑤ Scroll down the list of fields in the Customers table to the Company field. Add the Company field to the first column of the query table.
The first column shows the Company field and fills in the next two boxes with the table name and the default setting of Group By in the Total box.

The company names will be used as row headings on the left side of the Crosstab dynaset that is produced.

⑥ Click the Crosstab box in the Company column then click the down arrow at the right side of the box to reveal a menu of choices.
A menu of options for the Crosstab box is displayed (see Figure 19.8).

Figure 19.8
The Crosstab drop-down list gives you several options.

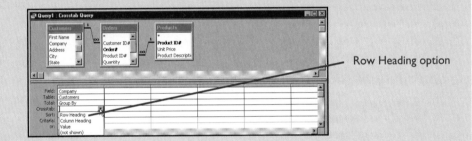

Row Heading option

⑦ Click the Row Heading option.

⑧ In the Products table, double-click the Product Description field to add it to the query design grid.
The Product Description field is added to the second column in the query design grid. The name of each type of product will be used as the column headings in the resulting Crosstab dynaset.

⑨ Click the Crosstab box in the Product Description column and the down arrow in that box. Select Column Heading from the list of options.

⑩ Double-click the Quantity field from the Orders table to place it in the third column.
You want to know the quantity of each type of product sold to each customer and display it in the cells of the resulting Crosstab dynaset.

⑪ Click the Crosstab box in the Quantity column and click the down arrow in that box. Select Value from the list of options.
This specifies that the program will calculate a numeric result to be placed in the table. The last step in creating the crosstab is to change the Total box from Group By to a mathematical operation.

 Exam Note: **Minimum Requirements for a Crosstab Query**
When you create a crosstab query you must have at least one field identified as a column heading, one field identified as a value, and at least one field identified as a row heading. The order of these three fields is irrelevant.

You can have more than one row heading, which will create subheads in the rows, but the main row head field needs to be to the left of the subhead field.

---

12 **Click the Total box in the Quantity column, then click the down arrow. Select Sum from the drop-down list.**
Your design grid should look like Figure 19.9.

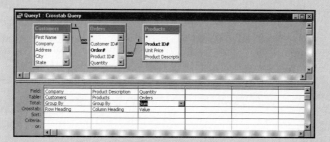

Figure 19.9
The crosstab query setup is complete, with a row heading, a column heading, and a value field selected.

13 **Click the Run button on the toolbar.**
The crosstab query is displayed in Datasheet view (see Figure 19.10).

The crosstab query has added up all of the sales of each product by company. There are nine companies in the Customers table, but only eight are listed here. That is because one of the customers did not place an order.

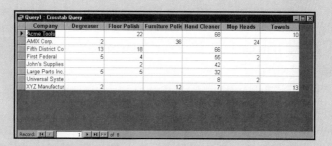

Figure 19.10
The crosstab query Datasheet view displays total unit sales by company and product.

14 **Close the query and save it with the name `Products Sold Listed by Customer`. Leave the `Data Analysis` database open for the next lesson.**

Lesson 3: Adding a Subform to an Existing Form

It is often useful to be able to review the data in linked tables simultaneously. Using the form/subform approach, you can create an individualized statement that shows all of the orders placed by one customer on a single form. The subform is a form placed within another main form. The subform shows the data from another table that are related to the selected record in the main form. This provides a reporting tool that could be used to communicate with customers, or it could be used by sales representatives to track sales by customer.

In Project 10, "Adding Useful Features to Your Forms," you learned how to create a form/subform using the Form Wizard. In this lesson, you take an existing form, open it in Design view, and add another existing form to it. You also modify the new form so that you can print a copy of it as a report of a customer's orders. You place a form based on a customer orders table (the subform) within another form based on a table of general customer information.

To Add a Subform to an Existing Form

1 **In the Data Analysis database, click the Forms object button, click the Company Information form, then click the Design button.**
The Company Information form opens in Design view.

The first step in adding a subform to an existing form is to open the form that is based on the table that has the primary key field on the "one" side of the one-to-many relationship. This is the main part of the form. In this case, the Company Information table contains the primary key field, Customer ID number.

 Exam Note: **The Primary Key Field in the Main Form**
The table on which the main form is based contains the primary key field that is used to link the related records in the underlying table used for the subform. A relationship between these tables should be established prior to creating a main form or subform. It is not necessary, however, to display the primary key field in the form. This relationship is what synchronizes the subform to display only the records related to the one record displayed in the main form. For more information on synchronizing a main form and a subform read the Help topic "How Microsoft Access links main forms and subforms."

 2 **Maximize the Design window. Click the Toolbox button on the toolbar if the Toolbox is not already displayed on the screen.**

 3 **If necessary, click the Controls Wizard button on the Toolbox to activate the form wizards.**

 4 **Click the Subform/Subreport button on the Toolbox. Click and drag a 2 by 6 inch rectangle that fills the lower portion of the currently open form.**
When you draw the rectangle, it appears as a thin line. This marks the boundary of the subform (see Figure 19.11).

Figure 19.11
The Company Information form displays the designated area for the subform.

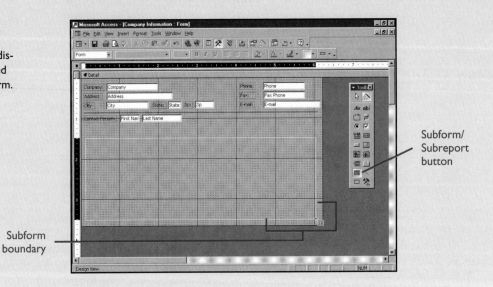

Subform/ Subreport button

Subform boundary

5 **Release the mouse button.**

When you release the mouse button, the Subform/Subreport Wizard is activated. After a short delay the first SubForm Wizard dialog box is displayed. This dialog box asks whether you want to draw the data from a table or query, or use an existing form.

6 **Select the** `Use an existing form` **option, then select the Orders form, if necessary.**

The dialog box should look like Figure 19.12.

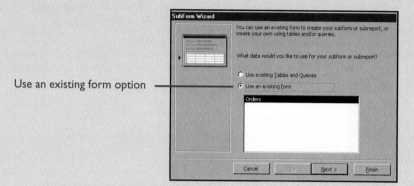

Use an existing form option —————

Figure 19.12
The first SubForm Wizard dialog box asks for a data source.

7 **Click Next.**

The second SubForm Wizard dialog box is displayed (see Figure 19.13). It identifies the field that links the two tables and gives you the option of linking the two forms using that field, of leaving the two forms unlinked, or of defining your own link.

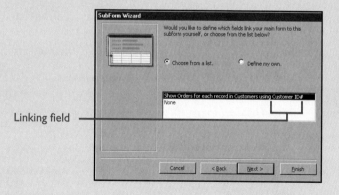

Linking field —————

Figure 19.13
The second SubForm Wizard dialog box enables you to identify the field you want to link between the main form and the subform.

8 **Accept the default settings to use the Customer ID# field as the link. Click Next.**

The final SubForm Wizard asks for a name for the subform.

9 **Click the Finish button to accept the default name, Orders.**

The Wizard finishes the design and returns you to the design of the Company Information form.

continues ▶

To Add a Subform to an Existing Form   (continued)

 ⑩ Click the View button to switch to Form view.
The Company Information form is shown with the subform Orders embedded in it. The subform used in this example is a tabular form (see Figure 19.14).

Figure 19.14
The Company Information form is shown with the Orders form embedded in it.

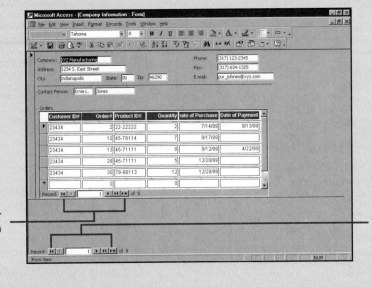

Navigation buttons for the Orders subform

Navigation buttons for the Company Information main form

 Inside Stuff: Formatting the Subform
If you don't like the way the subform looks, you can move back to Design view and adjust the size of the subform by clicking anywhere in the subform and using the sizing handles. You can also resize column widths and change character formatting, just like you would do with the main form.

 ⑪ Click the Next Record navigation button for the Company Information form.
Notice that the Orders form only shows the records that match the customer in the Company Information form.

⑫ Continue to click the Next Record button for the Company Information form until you get to the seventh record.
Notice that the Orders subform remains empty, because there are no related records for that company.

⑬ Close the form and save the changes. Leave the `Data Analysis` database open for the next lesson.

 Exam Note: Creating a Separate Subform
When you use the Form Wizard to create a form with a subform, the subform is saved separately. When you use the above procedure to add a subform to an existing form, the subform is embedded in the main form and no separate form is created.

Lesson 4: Inserting Subreports into Reports Using the Subform/Subreport Wizard

It is also possible to combine two reports that are based on joined tables. In this lesson, you learn how to combine a report that shows the customer information from the Customers table, with the individual orders by that customer shown in a tabular format report.

First, you will preview the two reports that will be joined. These reports are already provided, for your convenience. The Customers report is based on the Customers table and was created with a columnar AutoReport and then modified by rearranging the fields. The Orders report is based on the Orders table and was created with a tabular AutoReport.

To Preview the Two Reports

❶ **In the `Data Analysis` database, click the Reports object button. Double-click the `Customers` report.**
The preview of the Customers report is displayed. This will be the main report.

❷ **Maximize the report window, if necessary. Scroll around to view the report, and use the navigation buttons to examine more than one page.**
Information about each company is displayed (see Figure 19.15).

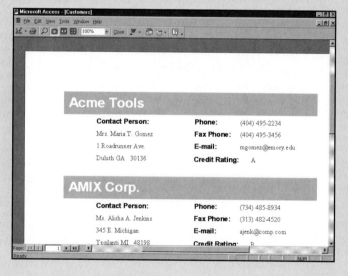

Figure 19.15
The Customers report will be the main report.

❸ **Close the Customers report.**

❹ **Double-click the `Orders` report.**
The preview of the Orders report is displayed. Scroll around to see the makeup of this report.

❺ **Close the Orders report.**

In the next section, you learn how to make the Orders report a subreport of the Customers report.

To Combine the Reports

1 **Click the Customers report to select it, then click Design. Click the Toolbox button to open the Toolbox, if necessary.**

The Customers report opens in Design view (see Figure 19.16).

Figure 19.16
The Design view of the Customers report shows the report layout.

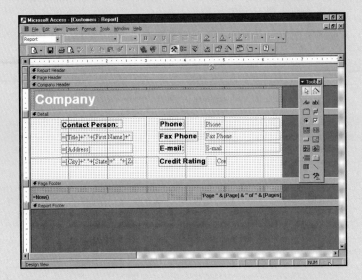

2 **Maximize the report Design window, if necessary.**

To make room for the subreport, you first expand the Details area of the report.

3 **Position the mouse pointer at the top of the Page Footer section divider. When the pointer is shaped like a double-headed arrow, click and drag down until the detail section is approximately 3 inches high, as shown in Figure 19.17.**

Use the vertical ruler to help determine how large to make the area. The subreport will be added to the detail section of the Customers report.

Figure 19.17
The detail area is expanded so there is room to insert the subreport.

Mouse pointer

3 inch mark

4 **Click the Subform/Subreport button in the Toolbox and draw a rectangle in the empty portion of the report design.**

Click and hold down the mouse button to draw a rectangle to indicate the location of the subreport (see Figure 19.18).

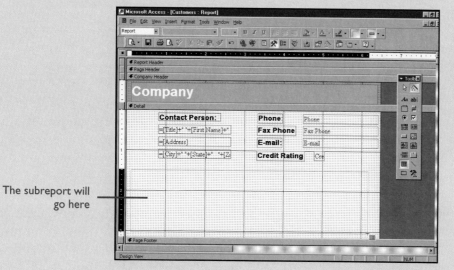

The subreport will go here

Figure 19.18
The area for the subreport in the Customers report is drawn.

When you release the mouse button, the first Subform/Subreport Wizard dialog box is displayed.

5 **Select the Use an existing report or form option and make sure the Orders report is selected.**

The first Wizard dialog box enables you to select an existing report or form, or to create a new report from a table or query. Make sure you choose the Orders report, not the Orders form.

6 **Click Next.**

The second Wizard dialog box is displayed. If the reports you have selected are based on tables that are joined in a one-to-many relationship, you see a choice that links the reports in the same way.

7 **Select the Choose from a list option, if necessary. Select the first link, entitled Show Orders for each record in Customers using Customer ID#. Click Next.**

Both of these options should be the defaults. The final Wizard dialog box asks for a name for the subreport.

8 **Accept the default name Orders and click Finish.**

The Wizard places the subreport in the report design detail section. Notice that the size of the subreport does not match the rectangle you drew (see Figure 19.19). The title of the subreport may overlap the bottom row of fields in the Customer table.

continues ▶

To Combine the Reports (continued)

Figure 19.19
The Orders table has been inserted as a sub-report in the Customers table.

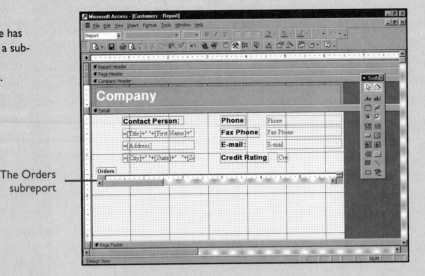

The Orders subreport

If You Have Problems...

If the Orders subreport overlaps the bottom fields in the Customers report, you will want to move it down. Click on the subreport. Move to the top of the subreport until the pointer changes into a hand, then click and drag the subreport to its desired location.

 9 **Click the Print Preview button on the toolbar to preview the report. Maximize the window, if necessary.**

Notice that the list of orders is restricted to those that match the customer information above. Also, there is an extra "Orders" title that the program automatically included (see Figure 19.20).

Figure 19.20
A preview of the final report shows orders for one customer.

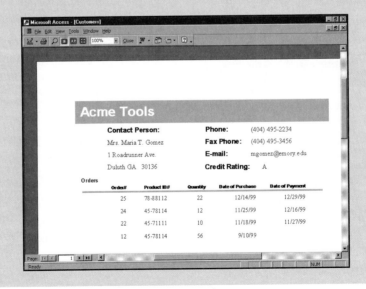

⑩ Use the navigation buttons to scroll through the report. Click any-where on the report to see a full-page view.

Notice that the report only shows one company per page, except for First Federal, which shows Jane's Cleaning at the bottom of the page. To ensure that one company is printed per page you can change a property for the Detail Section.

⑪ Click the View button to return to the Design view of the report

⑫ Right-click the Detail Section divider and choose <u>P</u>roperties from the shortcut menu.

The Section: Detail property box is displayed.

⑬ Click the Format tab and click in the Force New Page box.

A list arrow is displayed in the Force New Page box.

⑭ Click the list arrow and choose After Section from the list of options (see Figure 19.21).

To ensure that each company's records print on a separate page, you can choose to force a new page before or after a section, or both.

Detail Property box is opened

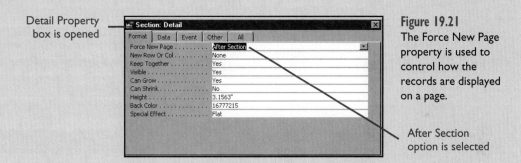

Figure 19.21
The Force New Page property is used to control how the records are displayed on a page.

After Section option is selected

⑮ Close the property box. Click the Print Preview button to return to the report. Scroll through the report to verify that Jane's Cleaning is now on its own page.

⑯ Close the report and save the changes.

Leave the Data Analysis database open for use in the next lesson.

 Exam Note: Reports That are Too Wide

One problem is consistently encountered when creating reports—the report is too wide for the page settings. This can cause many problems, including one field being printed on a page by itself, or a blank page printed for every page with data on it.

When you get a message telling you that your report does not fit, check the margins by choosing <u>F</u>ile, Page Set<u>u</u>p from the menu (you may be able to fix the problem by decreasing the left and right margins). Figure out the maximum width of your report, then use the ruler to move all of the fields and lines so that the report width is slightly less than the allowed page width. Finally, grab the right edge of the report area and drag it to the left until it is narrower the maximum page width.

Lesson 5: Creating Charts as Forms Using the Chart Wizard

Some types of information are best presented using charts instead of numbers. Access has a built-in Chart wizard that uses an application called Microsoft Graph 2000 to help you create a chart. You can create most of the common chart types, including column charts, pie charts, and bar charts. You can create a chart as a form or as a report. Charts created as forms are easier to work with and edit than those created as reports.

In this lesson, you create a chart as a form using the Chart Wizard. Then you do some minor editing to the chart using the Microsoft Graph 2000 program.

To Create a Chart as a Form Using the Chart Wizard

1 In the `Data Analysis` database, click on the Form object button, if necessary, then click **N**ew.
The New Form dialog box is displayed.

2 Select the Chart Wizard. Select the Sales by Product query from the drop-down list, then click OK.
The first Chart Wizard dialog box is displayed, asking which fields contain the data you want to chart. This is the query you created in Lesson 1.

> **X** *If You Have Problems...*
> If Microsoft Graph 2000 has not been installed on your machine, you need to get the original installation disks to install this feature, or install it from your network.

3 Add both the Product Description and SumOfQuantity fields to the Fields for Chart box. Then click **N**ext.
The second Chart Wizard dialog box is displayed, asking what type of chart you want to use (see Figure 19.22). When you click a chart type, a description of that type appears in a box on the right-hand side of the dialog box.

Figure 19.22
The second Chart Wizard dialog box asks you to choose a chart type.

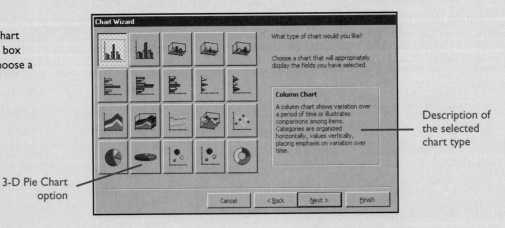

3-D Pie Chart option

Description of the selected chart type

4 Select the 3-D Pie Chart, the second example in the last row, then click **N**ext.
The third Chart Wizard dialog box is displayed, showing the Sum of Quantity field at the bottom (see Figure 19.23). No changes are made in this dialog box.

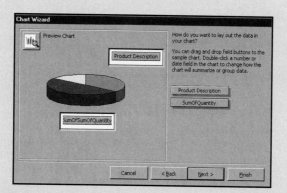

Figure 19.23
The third Chart Wizard dialog box shows the chart layout.

⑤ Click Next.
The fourth Chart Wizard dialog box is displayed.

⑥ Accept Sales by Product as the chart title. Select Yes, display a legend, then click Finish.
Because this is a pie chart, a legend is useful to identify the different parts of the pie.

The final report is shown in Preview mode. There are some problems with the chart. Particularly, the legend is too large for the display area (see Figure 19.24). The chart needs to be enlarged.

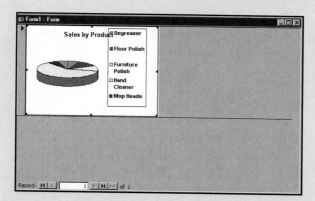

Figure 19.24
The chart area is too small to accommodate the legend and the pie chart.

⑦ Click the View button in the toolbar.
The Design view of the chart is displayed. First you need to enlarge the white background area for the chart.

⑧ Click the white background area of the chart to select it. Click and drag the sizing handle in the lower right corner down to the 3.5 inch mark on the vertical ruler and right to the 5 inch mark on the horizontal ruler
Use the vertical and horizontal rulers to help judge the size of the chart display area (see Figure 19.25).

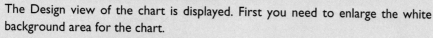

continues ▶

To Create a Chart as a Form Using the Chart Wizard   (continued)

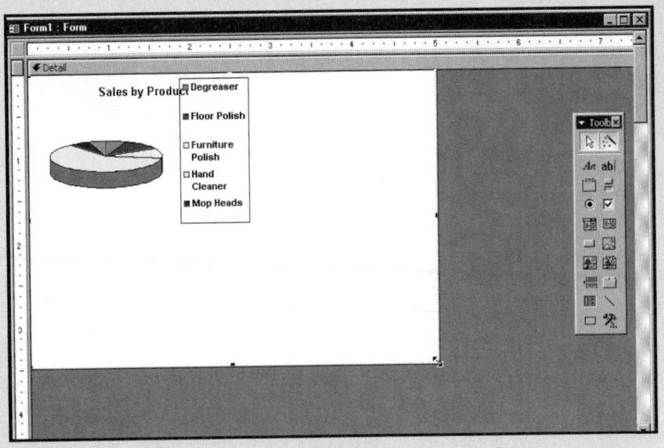

Figure 19.25
Use a sizing handle to expand the background area for the chart.

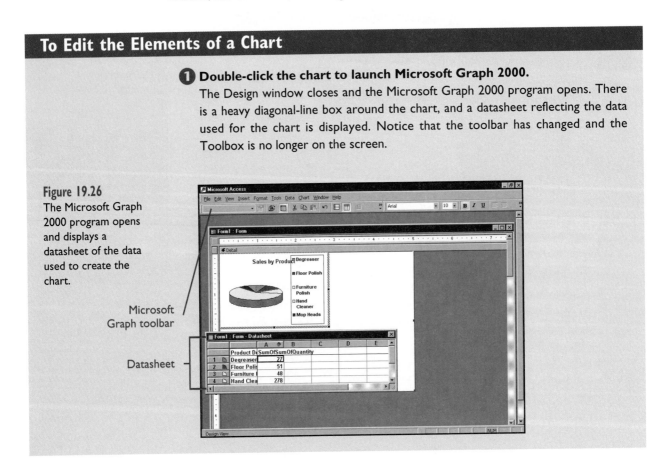

Leave the chart open for the next section of this lesson.

To edit the chart elements, such as the legend, the font, and font size, or the color selections, you need to use the Microsoft Graph program. When you double-click on the chart, the graphing program automatically activates. If you click outside of the chart, the graphing program closes and the design view of the chart returns. Next you move the legend to a new location, add data labels, and change the color of one of the pie pieces.

To Edit the Elements of a Chart

① **Double-click the chart to launch Microsoft Graph 2000.**
The Design window closes and the Microsoft Graph 2000 program opens. There is a heavy diagonal-line box around the chart, and a datasheet reflecting the data used for the chart is displayed. Notice that the toolbar has changed and the Toolbox is no longer on the screen.

Figure 19.26
The Microsoft Graph 2000 program opens and displays a datasheet of the data used to create the chart.

Microsoft Graph toolbar

Datasheet

***Exam Note:*   Using the Report Chart Wizard**
If you create a chart as a report rather than a form, everything is the same up to this point in the procedure. When you go to the Microsoft Graph 2000 program in a report chart, however, the datasheet and graph that are displayed contain sample data rather than the real data that was used to create the report. Editing a chart created as a report is more challenging because you don't see the real information, and are working blind as far as the effect it is having on your chart.

2 Close the datasheet. Move the pointer to the lower right corner of the chart area; click and drag down and to the right so that the chart fits in the display area.
Your chart should look like Figure 19.27.

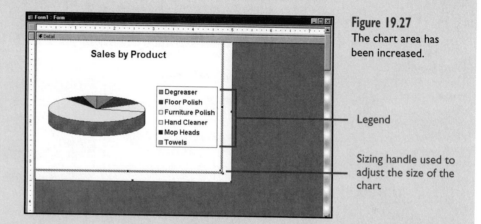

Figure 19.27
The chart area has been increased.

Legend

Sizing handle used to adjust the size of the chart

 If You Have Problems...
If you click off of the chart, the program returns to the Design view of the chart and closes the Microsoft Graph 2000 program. If the heavy line around the chart disappears, double-click on the chart and try again. Another way to tell you have left the Graph program is if the Design view toolbar or Toolbox reappears on the screen.

3 Right-click the legend to select it and choose F*o*rmat Legend from the shortcut menu.
The Format Legend dialog box opens. This can be used to change the patterns, font, and location of the legend (see Figure 19.28).

4 Click the Placement tab and choose *B*ottom as the location for the legend, then click OK.
The legend is moved to the bottom of the chart and the chart is resized to fill the remaining space (see Figure 19.29).

5 Right-click on the pie and choose F*o*rmat Data Series from the shortcut menu.
The Format Data Series dialog box opens. With this dialog box you can change colors, add data labels, or rotate the pie.

continues ▶

To Edit the Elements of a Chart   (continued)

Figure 19.28
The Format Legend
dialog box is used to
change characteristics
of the chart legend.

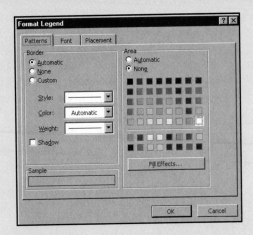

Figure 19.29
The legend is
relocated and the pie
chart fills the
remaining space.

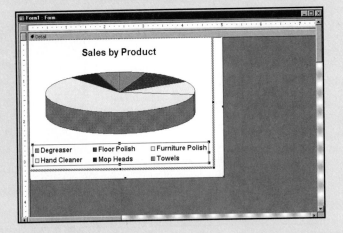

❻ **Click the Data Labels tab and choose Show value. Deselect Show
leader lines, and select Show legend key next to label (see Figure
19.30).**
The chart will show the value next to each slice and use a label key to help identify each number with the color of the related pie slice.

Figure 19.30
The Format Data
Series dialog box of-
fers several options
for displaying data la-
bels on a chart.

Data labels
options

Legend key option selected

Deselect leader lines

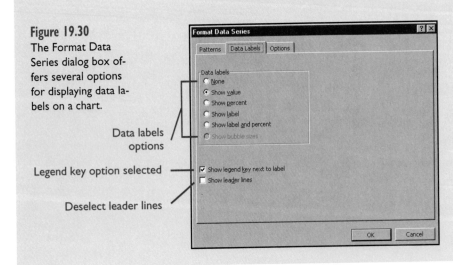

7 **Click the Options tab and change the <u>A</u>ngle of first slice box to 180 degrees (see Figure 19.31).**

The preview window enables you to see the effect of the change. Moving the largest slice to the other side of the pie helps to display the details of the smaller pieces more clearly.

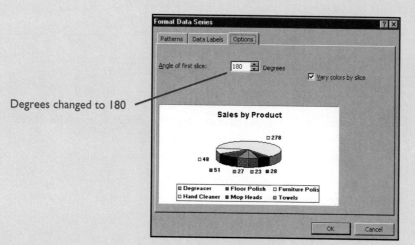

Degrees changed to 180

Figure 19.31
The pie is rotated using the Options page of the Format Data Series dialog box.

8 **Click OK.**

The dialog box closes and you can see the effect of your changes on the chart. Next you decide the colors used for the Floor Polish and the Mop Heads are too similar and you want to use a different color for one of these pieces.

9 **Click the Floor Polish pie piece to select it.**

The sizing handles move from the pie as a whole to the specific piece you selected. Notice the ScreenTip that identifies the pie slice you have selected (see Figure 19.32).

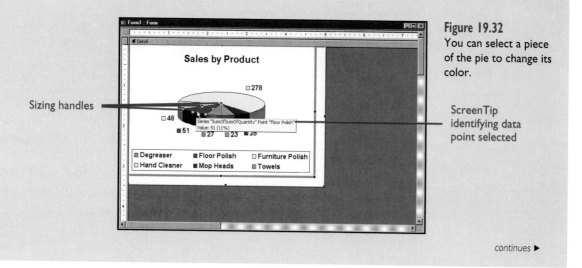

Sizing handles

Figure 19.32
You can select a piece of the pie to change its color.

ScreenTip identifying data point selected

continues ▶

To Edit the Elements of a Chart   (continued)

 Exam Note: **Selecting One Data Point**
To select one data point, you click once to select all the data points, then you click a second time to select the particular data point you want to change. Do not double-click, because that action will automatically open the related dialog box for the entire element that you clicked, in this case the whole pie.

10 **Right-click the selected pie piece and choose F_ormat Data Point from the shortcut menu.**
The Format Data Point dialog box opens.

11 **Click the Patterns tab and choose the fifth color in the second row, then click OK.**
The dialog box closes and the Floor Polish color is changed.

12 **Click in the open gray area of the Form window.**
The Microsoft Graph 2000 program closes and the Design view is displayed.

 13 **Click the View button.**
The final chart is displayed as shown in Figure 19.33.

Figure 19.33
The chart showing the sales by product is completed.

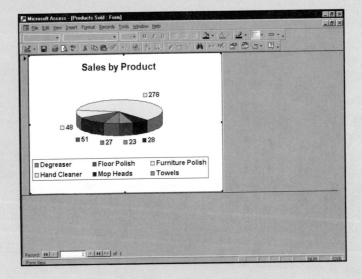

14 **Close the chart and save it with the name Products Sold. Close the database.**
If you have completed your session on the computer, exit Access and shut down Windows before you turn off the computer. Otherwise, continue with the following exercises.

Inside Stuff: Creating Charts in Excel
You can also create charts using Excel. If you are familiar with the Excel program, you might find it easier to export your data to Excel and use the Excel charting tools to graph your data. The Microsoft Graph 2000 program that you use in Access uses most of the same tools and techniques that are used in the Excel program. The Excel program is somewhat more flexible, however. For example a chart created in Excel can be sized to fill an entire page.

Summary

In this project you worked with several data analysis and reporting tools using queries, forms, and reports. You added totals to a select query, and summarized data using a crosstab query. You also embedded a subform in a main form, and a subreport in an existing report. Finally, you created a chart.

Crosstab queries are very powerful data analysis tools. You can learn more about using crosstab queries by reading the available Help topics on this type of query.

Checking Concepts and Terms

True/False

For each of the following statements, check T or F to indicate whether the statement is true or false.

__T __F   **1.** The Totals query feature needs to be based on a minimum of three fields. [L1]

__T __F   **2.** The design for a crosstab query must have at least one row header, column header, and value. [L2]

__T __F   **3.** In a crosstab query design, the field that has been chosen to provide the values in the cells must have its Totals box changed to "Group By." [L2]

__T __F   **4.** If the records in a subform are going to be linked to the records in the main form, the tables on which they are based must be joined in a one-to-many relationship. [L3]

__T __F   **5.** When you edit a chart created as a form in Access, the data displayed in the Microsoft Graph program is the data that is being charted. [L5]

Multiple Choice

Circle the letter of the correct answer for each of the following questions.

1. If a form and its subform are based on tables that are joined in a one-to-many relationship, _____. [L3]

   a. the records shown in the subform are limited to those that match the record shown in the main form

   b. both parts of the form use the same navigation buttons

   c. both tables use the same field as a primary key

   d. the many side of the relationship is used for the main part of the form.

2. To add a subreport to a report, you can _____. [L4]

   a. choose from a list of existing reports

   b. create a report based on a table

   c. create a report based on a query

   d. all of the above

3. Charts can be created in Access as a type of _____. [L5]

   a. table

   b. query

   c. form

   d. macro

4. The SubForm/Subreport Wizard found in the Toolbox can be used to _____. [L3,L4]

   a. create the main part of the form

   b. create both reports with subreports and forms with subforms

   c. add a subform from an existing report

   d. all of the above

5. In a crosstab query, the data that appears in the intersection of the columns and rows is known as the _____. [L2]

   a. value field

   b. quantity field

   c. amount field

   d. count field

Screen ID

Label each element of the Access screen shown in Figure 19.34

Figure 19.34

A. Field used for row headings

B. Column label

C. Crosstab query icon

D. Field used in the inter-section of rows and columns

E. Identifies each fields function in the query

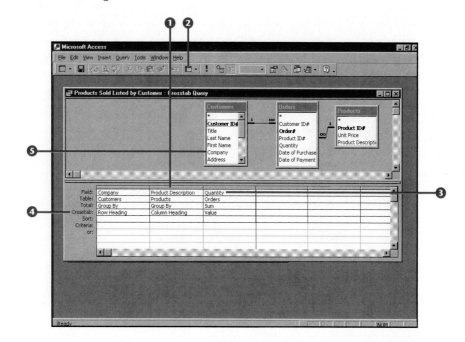

1._____ 3._____ 5._____

2._____ 4._____

Skill Drill

Skill Drill exercises reinforce project skills. Each skill reinforced is the same, or nearly the same, as a skill presented in the project. Each exercise includes a brief narrative introduction, followed by detailed instructions in a step-by-step format.

In the these exercises, you will be using a transcription of the 1880 Alcona County, Michigan federal census. Some of the entries have been standardized for such things as spelling and occupation names. You will notice that this database has a field (Place) with repetitive data. When this database was designed, it was felt that all of the fields should be in one table because of the nature of the data.

1. Creating a Crosstab Query

A glance through the Alcona County data will show you that there were a number of different occupations in the county in 1880. A crosstab query will enable you to find out how many people are listed in each job category, and display them by gender. (*Note:* At School was an occupation, as was At Home for people who were out of school but not yet married.)

To create a crosstab query:

1. Copy the **AC-1902** database file from the CD-ROM to drive A. Right-click the filename; select Properties from the shortcut menu, and remove the read-only status. Use the shortcut menu to rename the file **1880 Alcona Census**, and then open the database.

2. Click the Queries object button, if necessary, then click New. Choose Design View from the New Query dialog box, then click OK.

3. Add the 1880 Alcona County Census table to the query Design window and close the Show Table dialog box.

4. Add the Occupation field to the first column in the design grid, then add the Sex and ID fields to the second and third columns.

5. Click the Query Type button in the toolbar and select the Crosstab Query option.

6. Click in the Crosstab box for the Occupation field and select Row Heading from the drop-down list. Use the same procedure to select Column Heading for the Sex field and Value for the ID field.

7. Click in the Total box for the ID field and select Count from the drop-down list. It does not matter which field you choose to be counted, as long as there are entries in it for every record. The primary key field is often used for this type of situation.

8. Click the Run button. Notice that the first column shows that 393 females and 367 males have no occupation listed. (These are usually small children, but not always.)

9. Scroll down the list to see the different occupations for men and women in this county in 1880. When you are through, close the query and name it **Occupations**. Leave the database open if you plan to do the next exercise.

2. Creating a Chart

In this exercise you create a chart to show the average age by location in the county. This is the type of data that is can be represented by a chart.

To create a chart:

1. If you did the first exercise, skip this step. Copy the **AC-1902** database file from the CD-ROM to drive A. Right-click the filename; select Properties from the shortcut menu, and remove the read-only status. Use the shortcut menu to rename the file **1880 Alcona Census**, and then open the database.

2. Click the Forms object button and click the New button. Select the Chart Wizard, choose the 1880 Alcona County Census from the drop-down list, and click OK.

3. Add the Place and Age fields to the Fields for Chart box and click Next.

4. Select the Column chart type and click Next.

5. Double-click the SumOfAge button near the upper-left corner of the Chart Wizard dialog box. Choose Avg from the list and click OK.

6. Click Next. Choose not to display a legend, then click Finish.

7. Click the View button to switch to Design view. Maximize the window.

8. Click to select the chart area and drag down and to the right until the chart area is about 5 inches wide and about 3 inches high. Use the rulers to help you, and adjust the size as necessary.

9. Double-click on the chart. Grab the handle in the lower-right corner and drag down and to the right until the chart almost fills the chart area. You may have to move or close the datasheet to do this.

10. Click on one of the columns, then click a second time to select that individual data point. Right-click the selected column and choose Format Data Point from the shortcut menu. Choose a color of your choice and click OK. Repeat for each column until they are each a different color.

11. Click in an empty area of the form to close the Microsoft Graph program, then click the View button to go to the form view. Your chart should look similar to the one in Figure 19.35.

12. When you are through, close the form and save it as **Average Age Chart**. Close the database.

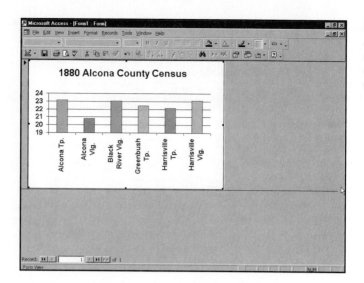

Figure 19.35
An Access chart
shows the average age
of residents by loca-
tion.

3. Adding a Subreport to an Existing Report

In this exercise you will create a report with a subreport using two existing reports. The database you will be using will be the short story database you used earlier in this book. You will open a report on the information about each book, then add a subreport showing each story in the book, along with the author and year published information. The file size of this database is 756 KB, and will not fit on the same disk with the previous two files. Therefore, if you are using diskettes, you should start with an empty one for this exercise.

To add a subreport to an existing report:

1. Copy the **AC-1903** database file from the CD-ROM to a new disk. Right-click on the file name, select Properties from the shortcut menu, and remove the read-only status. Use the shortcut menu to rename the file **Short Story Collections**, then open the database.

2. Click the Reports object button and select the Book Information report.

3. Click the Design button and maximize the screen.

4. Click and drag the Page Footer bar and down an inch or so, to make room in the Detail area for the subreport.

5. Click the Subform/Subreport button in the Toolbox and draw a box for the subreport about 1/2 inch under the beginning of the Year of Publication label. Drag the box to the right to about the 6 1/4 inch mark and make it about 1/2 inch deep.

6. Choose to use the existing Short Stories report as the subreport. Click Next.

7. Choose to link to each record in Book Information using the Book Title field.

8. Change the subreport label to read **Short stories in this book:**.

9. Click the View button on the toolbar to see your report/subreport. It should look like Figure 19.36. If you need to, return to Design view and modify the report design.

   (*Hint:* If the report has blank pages on every other page, you may need to reduce the size of the subreport by dragging the subreport scrollbar away from the right-edge of the report design grid. Then drag the edge of the grid to the left so it does not exceed the 6 1/2 inch mark on the horizontal ruler.)

10. Save any changes and print the first page of the report, then close the database.

Figure 19.36
The short stories included in each book are listed below the book information.

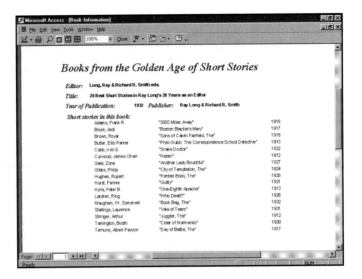

Challenge

Challenge exercises expand on or are somewhat related to skills presented in the lessons. Each exercise provides a brief narrative introduction followed by instructions in a numbered step format that are not as detailed as those in the Skill Drill section.

You use two databases in the Challenge section. The first is the consulting database you created in Project 15, " Designing a Complex Database." The second is a five-year database of U.S. tornadoes.

1. Adding Conditions to the Totals Feature in a Query

In this exercise, you create a query based on another query. You then show the costs of each project for a one week period using the criteria based on a field that is not displayed.

To add conditions to the total feature in a query:

1. Make a copy of the AC-1904 database file, remove the read-only status, rename the file **Consulting Projects**, then open the database.

2. Create a new query in Design view. Add the Cost to Client query, then add the Project Name, Cost, and Date fields to the design grid. *Hint*: Click the Queries Tab in the Show Table box to find the Cost to Client Query.

3. Add the Total row. Group on the Project Name field and create a Sum on the Cost field.

4. In the Total row of the Date column, select the Where option. This turns off the Show check box. Type **Between 4/3/00 and 4/7/00** in the Criteria box.

5. Run the query. The totals are for one week only.

6. Close the query and save it as **One Week Costs**. Close the database.

2. Create a Crosstab Query with Two Levels of Row Headers

You can group data in a crosstab query using the row header and column header. Sometimes you need to create a subgroup on a main group. You can do this in a crosstab query by adding a second row header, but you can't subgroup on the column header. In this exercise you use a database of five years of U.S. tornado data and create a query using the Crosstab Query Wizard. You will display the F-scales (intensity levels) of the tornadoes grouped on the county and subgrouped on the year. Because of the size of the database used in this exercise, you should copy the file to an empty floppy disk.

To create a crosstab query with two level of row headers:

I. Make a copy of the **AC-1905** database file, remove the read-only status, rename the file **Five Year Tornado Data**, then open the database.

2. Create a new query using the Crosstab Query Wizard. Click the Queries option button and select the List of 1991-95 US Tornadoes query in the first Wizard dialog box.

3. Add the County Name field, then add the Year field as Row Headings in the second Wizard dialog box.

4. Add the FScale field as the Column Heading in the third Wizard dialog box.

5. Select the Count function for the State Name field as the calculation in the fourth Wizard dialog box. Deselect the row sums.

6. Call the query **F-Scales by County and Year**.

7. Switch to Design view and add the State Name field again. Select Where in the Total row of the new field, then type **Texas** into the Criteria box under the State Name field. This will limit the crosstab to Texas tornadoes. View the query.

8. Save the modified query as **F-Scales by County and Year in Texas**. Close the query. Leave the database open if you intend to do the next exercise.

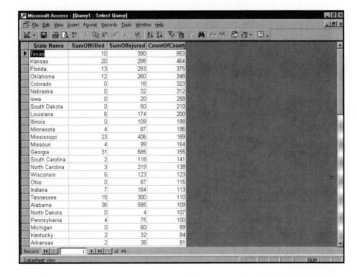

Figure 19.37

3. Create a Query That Displays More Than One Function

You can create a query that displays more than one function. In this exercise, you work with the Five Year Tornado Data database.

To create a query that displays more than one function:

1. If you did the last exercise, open the **Five Year Tornado Data** database used in the previous exercise. Or, if necessary, make a copy of the **AC-1905** database file, remove the read-only status, rename the file **Five Year Tornado Data**, then open the database.

2. Create a new query. Include the State Names and 1991-1995 US Tornadoes tables.

3. Include the State Name, Killed, Injured, and CountyID fields.

4. Use the Totals function to display the state-by-state statistics for the total number of people killed and injured, and the number of tornadoes. *Hint:* Use the Count function on the CountyID field to count the number of tornadoes.

5. Sort on the counting field in descending order.

6. Save the query and name it **Summary Statistics by State**. Run the query. Texas should display at the top of the list with 953 tornadoes in the Count of County field.

7. Close the query and close the database.

Discovery Zone

Discovery Zone exercises help you gain advanced knowledge of project topics and application of skills. These exercises focus on enhancing your problem-solving skills. Numbered steps are not provided, but you are given hints, reminders, screen shots, and references to help you reach your goal for each exercise.

Both of these exercises use the five year tornado database that was used in the Challenge exercises. Each exercise is independent. If you want, you can use the file you worked with in the Challenge 2 and 3 exercise. Otherwise, make a copy of the **AC-1905** database file, remove the read-only status, rename the file **Five Year Tornado Data2**.

1. Create a PivotTable Form

A **PivotTable** is an interactive form that is similar to a crosstab query. You can group data in rows and columns and have data calculated for the intersection of the rows and columns. Use Help and read the topics about creating a PivotTable. Access uses the Excel PivotTable program to create a PivotTable form. Excel opens so you can create and edit the PivotTable, and then it closes when you are done so you can view the results as a form in Access. You can change the height or width of the form in the form Design view in Access. Anything else that you might want to change has to be done in Excel.

Goal: Create a PivotTable form in Access for the tornado database.

The PivotTable should:

- use the List of 1991-1995 US Tornadoes query
- use the State field as the page
- use the Year field as the row header
- use the FScale field as the column header
- use the killed and injured fields for the data area

Hint #1: After the PivotTable Wizard opens, choose all of the fields you will be using, then click OK. Choose Layout and place the fields in the locations as specified above.

Hint #2: Use the Design view of the form to increase the width of the PivotTable object so you can see the grand total column. You may need to move the object to the left so it does not exceed the 6.5 inch mark on the grid.

After the form is created, use the Edit PivotTable Object button to return to Excel. Click the Refresh Data button on the PivotTable toolbar and select Alabama using the list arrow for the State Name field. The table will recalculate the data for the selected state.

Save the form as **Alabama PivotTable**.

Your PivotTable should look like Figure 19.38.

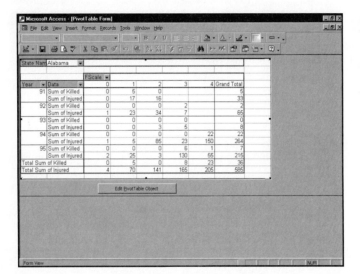

Figure 19.38
The PivotTable includes a row, column and page grouping, and summary for two fields.

2. Using Access Data to Create an Excel Chart

In addition to creating a chart in Access, you can also export data to Excel and create the chart in that environment. If you are already familiar with using Excel, you might find this to be a preferable option. Creating a chart in Excel simply requires that you find the Chart Wizard button and follow instructions. In this exercise, you create a query to count the number of tornadoes at each F-Scale level and send the data to Excel for charting. (*Note:* You must have Excel available to complete this exercise.)

If necessary, open the Five Year Tornado Data file, or make a copy of the **AC-1905** database file, remove the read-only status, rename the file **Five Year Tornado Data2**, then open the database.

Goal: Create a chart in Excel based on a query created in Access.

For this exercise you should:

- create an Access query that has two columns; one with the different F-Scale levels and one with the total number of tornadoes at each level.
- send the data to Excel.
- change the F-Scale column numbers to text.
- select the data and then use the Excel Chart Wizard to create a chart (you may need to use the Excel help).
- use **Number of Tornadoes by F-Scale** as the chart title. The x-axis label should read **F-Scale**.
- name the query **F-Scale Totals** and the Excel spreadsheet **F-Scale Chart**.
- add data labels to the columns.

■ remove the gray background from the plot area.

Hint #1: An easy way to change a number to text in Excel is to put an apostrophe (') before the number.

Hint #2: If you want to change something on an Excel chart, double-click on it.

Your finished chart should look like Figure 19.39.

Figure 19.39
The Excel chart displays the total number of tornadoes recorded for each F-Scale rating.

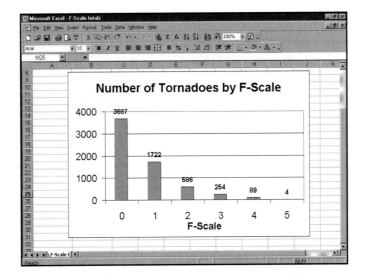

PinPoint Assessment

You have completed this project and its associated lessons, and have had an opportunity to assess your skills through the end-of-project questions and exercises. Now use the PinPoint software Evaluation Mode to further assess your comprehension of the specific exam activities you have just learned. You can also use the PinPoint Trainer Mode and the Show Me tutorials to practice these exam activities.

Filtering Data in a Linked Table Using Parameters and Form Filters

Key terms introduced in this project include

- excluding operators
- Filter by Form
- Filter by Selection
- parameter query
- SQL

Objectives	Required Activity for MOUS	Exam Level
➤ Use Data in Another Database	Import data to a new table	Core
	Link to existing data	Expert
➤ Select Records Using Filter by Selection	Apply and remove filters (filter by form and filter by selection)	Core
	Apply Filters (filter by form and filter by selection) in a query's recordset	Expert
➤ Select Records Using Filter by Form	Apply and remove filters (filter by form and filter by selection)	Core
	Apply Filters (filter by form and filter by selection) in a query's recordset	Expert
➤ Use Parameters as Matching Criteria in a Query	Create a parameter query	Expert
➤ Use Parameters with Comparison Operators in a Query	Create a parameter query	Expert
➤ Use Parameters with Wildcards as Criteria in a Query	Create a parameter query	Expert

Why Would I Do This?

Sometimes you will want to use information that is contained in another database. You may be able to import the table to your database and use it, or you may prefer to just link to the table and use it without importing the data. Importing the data makes it part of your database, and is generally done when you want control over the data, or the table is relatively small. Linking to a table is useful when the database is particularly large or is restricted in some manner that would prevent you from importing it.

Once you have gathered the data you want to use, you can extract and examine the data for a variety of purposes. You seldom need to look at all of the records at any one time. You already know how to use criteria in a query to restrict the data that is displayed. There are also quick methods, using both queries and forms, to view the desired subset of data (dynaset) that you need to see.

In this project, you learn how to import a table from another database, and then link to a large database table. You learn to create queries that enable you to control the output each time the query is run. A *parameter query* asks you for input whenever the query is used, and uses your input as the criteria for the query. In this way, you can use the same query structure repeatedly and vary the criteria without having to go to the design of the query to make changes. If you base a report on a query that uses a parameter, you can control the output of the report by entering a value in the parameter value box that displays when the report is run.

You also learn how to use two of the most powerful data-searching features of Access—*Filter by Selection* and *Filter by Form*. The Filter by Selection feature enables you to scroll through a form and select the desired entry in a field. When you click on the Filter by Selection button, all records that match the entry in the field are displayed. The Filter by Form feature can be used in the Datasheet view of a table or in Form view. It enables you to type in desired field entries in one or more fields at a time.

When you have completed this project, you will have created a parameter query to limit records displayed, and used a form to filter data.

 ## Lesson 1: Using Data in Another Database

In this lesson, you open a database that contains a table that lists the names of the counties in all of the states in the United States. Then you import a table that is a list of the state names along with an identifying number. You then link to a large table of tornado data in another database that resides on the CD-ROM that came with your book. The tornado database contains over 38,000 records of all of the reported tornadoes that occurred in the United States from 1950 to 1995. This database was originally extracted from a government database over the Internet. It does not list the states or counties by name, but rather assigns a number to these fields. Later in this project you will use this information in combination with the other two tables to extract useful information about the number and effect of tornadoes in the United States. To use the three tables together you create a relationship using the Relationships window.

To Use Data in Another Database

 1 **Locate the student data file AC-2001 on the CD-ROM and make a copy of it. Remove the read-only property and then rename the copy** Tornado Analysis. **Open the** Tornado Analysis **database.**
The Database window displays the Tables area that lists a table for County Names.

2 **Choose File, Get External Data, Import from the menu.**
The Import dialog box opens showing the available databases. This is similar to the Open or Save As dialog boxes. First you locate the file, then you import it.

3 **In the Look in drop-down list box, locate the CD-ROM if necessary. Select AC-2002 from the list of files available for this Project, and then click Import.**
The Import Objects dialog box displays and shows the State Names table.

4 **Select the State names table and click OK.**
The States Names table is imported and displays on the table list in the Tornado Analysis database (see Figure 20.1).

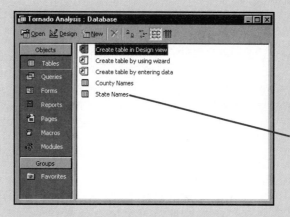

Figure 20.1
The Database window displays the County Names table and the imported States Names table.

Imported table

5 **Choose File, Get External Data, Link Tables from the menu.**
The Link dialog box opens. This works just like the Import dialog box.

6 **Locate the 45 Year Tornado Records database in the folder for this project.**
Figure 20.2 shows the Link dialog box with the 45 Year Tornado Records database selected.

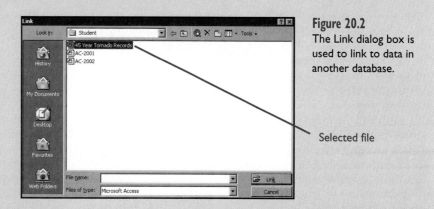

Figure 20.2
The Link dialog box is used to link to data in another database.

Selected file

7 **Click the Link button and choose the Tornadoes table from the Link Tables dialog box. Click OK.**
Figure 20.3 shows the Tornadoes table listed in the table area with an arrow next to it to indicate that this is a linked table.

continues ▶

To Use Data in Another Database (continued)

Figure 20.3
The Tornadoes table is shown as a linked table.

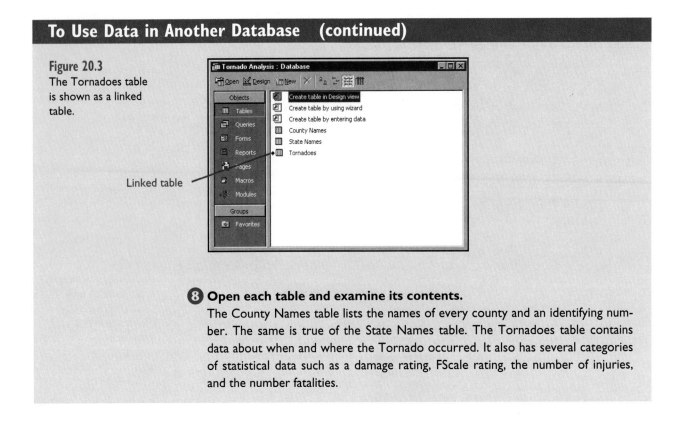

Linked table

8 **Open each table and examine its contents.**
The County Names table lists the names of every county and an identifying number. The same is true of the State Names table. The Tornadoes table contains data about when and where the Tornado occurred. It also has several categories of statistical data such as a damage rating, FScale rating, the number of injuries, and the number fatalities.

Before you can use these tables to extract meaningful data they must first be related.

You use the State field and the CountyID field to create one-to-many relationships with the Tornadoes table. Both of these fields are the primary key in the one side of the relationship. The Tornado table does not have a primary key designated, although there is an ID field that uniquely identifies each tornado.

To Create a One-to-Many Relationship

1 **Make sure all of the tables are closed. Click the Relationship button. If necessary, click the Show Table button to display the Show Table dialog box.**
The Relationships window opens and the Show table dialog box is displayed as shown in Figure 20.4.

Figure 20.4
The Show Table dialog box is used to select tables or queries that you want to include in the Relationships window.

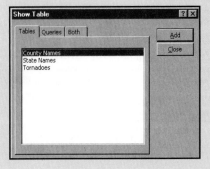

2 **Double-click on each of the three table names to add them to the Relationships window, then close the Show Table dialog box.**

> **X** *If You Have Problems...*
>
> When you double-click on a table name it is added to the window. The Show Table dialog box may temporarily hide a table field list. Every time you double-click on a table name it will be added to the Relationships window. If a table field list is displayed more than once, select one of the copies and press Del to remove the extra copy.

3 **Click and drag the lower edge of the Tornadoes field list box until you can see all of the fields. Drag the right edge of the box to display the names as shown in Figure 20.5.**

4 **Click and drag the Tornadoes field list box to the center of the window and drag the State Names field list box to the right as shown in Figure 20.5.**

This step is not necessary, but it makes it easier to see the relationships when the join lines are added.

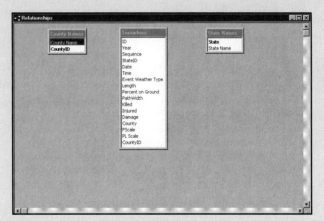

Figure 20.5
The Tornado field list is expanded and placed in the center of the window between the other two tables.

5 **Click CountyID from the County Names table and drag it to the CountyID field in the Tornadoes table.**

The Edit Relationships dialog box opens as shown in Figure 20.6. Notice that the Enforce Referential Integrity option is dimmed. You cannot choose this option when using a Linked table in a relationship.

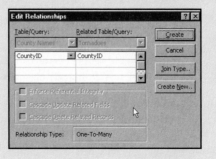

Figure 20.6
The relationship is created using the Edit Relationships dialog box.

continues ▶

To Create a One-to-Many Relationship   (continued)

6 **Click Create. Click State from the State Names table and drag it to the StateID field in the Tornadoes table. Click Create in the Edit Relationships dialog box.**
The Relationships window now shows a join line between the County Names and the Tornadoes field lists, and between the State Names and the Tornadoes field lists (see Figure 20.7).

Figure 20.7
The relationship between the tables is defined.

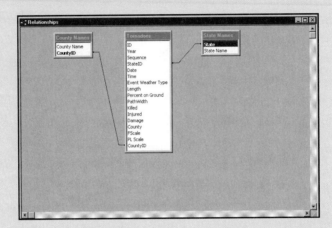

7 **Click the Close button to close the Relationships window. Choose Yes when prompted to save the changes to the layout of the window.**

8 **Leave the** Tornado Analysis **database open for the next lesson.**

 **Lesson 2: Selecting Records Using Filter by Selection**

A quick method that can be used to examine data in a table is to select an entry in one of the fields and click the Filter by Selection button. A matching filter is immediately applied to the table and only those records that have the same value in that field are shown. Filters can be applied to either tables or queries in the Datasheet view

In this lesson, you create a query and then use the Filter by Selection feature to display the records for one year.

To Select Records Using Filter by Selection

1 **Click the Queries object button. Double-click the Create query by using a wizard shortcut.**
The Simple Query Wizard dialog box opens. Using the Simple Query Wizard is another way to quickly create a query.

2 **Choose the State Names table from the Tables/Queries drop-down list box and add the State Name field to the Selected Fields box.**

3 **Choose the County Names table and add the County Name field to the Selected Fields box.**

④ Choose the Tornadoes table and add the Year, Date, Time, Killed, and Injured fields to the Selected Fields box.

The Simple Query Wizard dialog box now displays the list of fields for this query (see Figure 20.8).

Select table here —

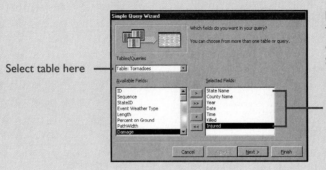

Figure 20.8
The fields you want to display are listed in the Simple Query Wizard.

Fields selected for the query

⑤ Click Finish. The query is automatically named after the first field, State Names Query.

The query now displays the list of tornadoes.

 Inside Stuff: **Why Fewer Records Display in the Query**
The State Names query only displays 37,957 records out of the 38,486 records in the Tornadoes table. This discrepancy because of the fact that all of the state and county identification numbers do not have matching records in the State Names and County Names tables. Some counties have merged with others or changed their names since 1950 when these records begin.

⑥ Maximize the query window, if necessary. Click on 51 in the year field.

In this datasheet, the tornadoes are displayed by State. You would like to see all the tornadoes in 1951 for all the states.

⑦ Click the Filter by Selection button.

A filter is applied that limits the display to tornadoes that occurred in 1951 as shown in Figure 20.9. Notice that there were 267 such tornadoes. Also notice that FLTR appears in the status bar to indicate that a filter has been applied to the data.

⑧ Click the Remove Filter button. Leave the State Names Query open for use in the next lesson.

The filter is removed and all 37,957 records are displayed again.

continues ▶

To Select Records Using Filter by Selection (continued)

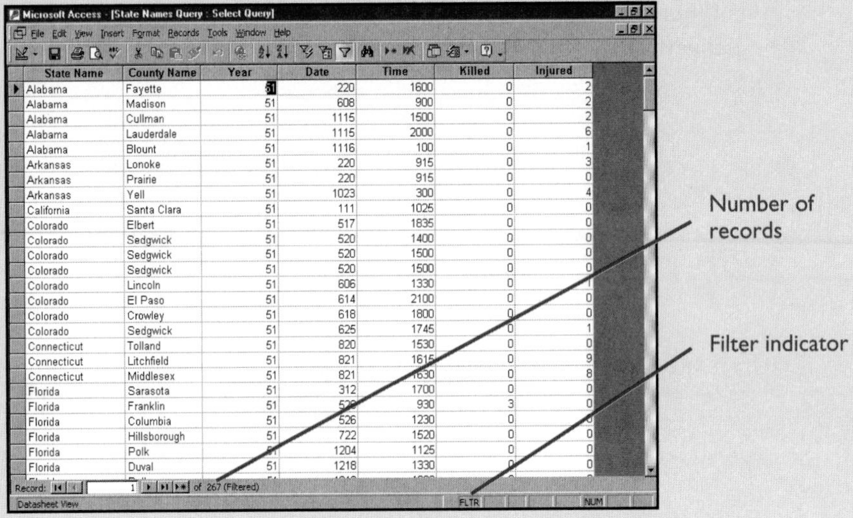

Figure 20.9
The Filter by Selection window can be used to select the data you want to view.

Number of records

Filter indicator

Core Expert **Lesson 3: Selecting Records Using Filter by Form**

Another quick method that can be used to examine data displayed in tables, queries, and forms is to use a form filter. A form filter provides more options than using Filter by Selection. Although it is not as flexible as a query, and is generally not saved, the form filter technique can give you a quick and easy way of limiting data.

In the following steps you apply additional criteria in more than one field of the State Names Query to filter the records shown. The following example is used to identify the tornadoes that occurred in Texas in 1953.

To Select Records Using Filter by Form

 1 **In the State Names Query, click the Filter by Form button. Click in the State Name field, type Texas, and then press ↵Enter).**
Notice that quotation marks are automatically added to the name. This is typical of a criterion for a text field.

2 **Enter 53 in the Year field.**
This field is a number data type and quotations are not used. These two criteria will be used to filter the records to display those that match (see Figure 20.10).

Figure 20.10
The filter by form feature may be used to enter multiple filtering criteria.

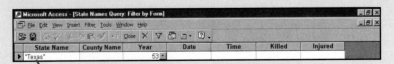

The program adds quotation marks to criteria in text fields

 3 **Click the Apply Filter button.**
A list of the thirty-three tornadoes that occurred in Texas that year displays.

④ Click the Remove Filter button.

All the records are displayed. Leave the `State Names Query` open for use in the next section.

 Inside Stuff: **Apply/Remove Filter Button**

The Apply/Remove Filter button is a toggle button that adds or removes a filter depending on the current state of the data that is being displayed. The ScreenTip that displays when you point to the button changes name to indicate that you are about to apply or remove a filter. When a filter has been applied, the button appears depressed, or selected.

You can fill in several fields in the form filter. Records will have to match all of the entries to be displayed. In some cases, you may want to see all the records that meet two different sets of criteria.

Next, you filter the records to see the tornadoes that occurred in 1953 in Texas or Oklahoma.

To Filter Using Two Sets of Criteria

❶ Click the Filter by Form button to reveal the design of the filter.

Notice that the previous set of conditions were not deleted and they still specify the Texas tornadoes from 1953.

❷ Click the Or tab at the bottom of the window.

A second form displays in which you can enter a new set of criteria.

❸ Enter `Oklahoma` in the State field and `53` in the Year field.

A second set of conditions may be used. A third option is also added—note the second Or tab (see Figure 20.11).

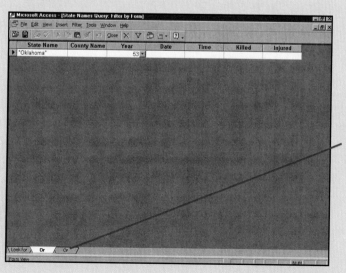

Figure 20.11
A second set of criteria for tornadoes in Oklahoma in 1953 is added.

Additional sets of criteria may be added

continues ▶

To Filter Using Two Sets of Criteria (continued)

 4 **Click the Apply Filter button.**
The eighty-nine tornadoes that meet one set of criteria or the other set are displayed.

 5 **Click the Filter by Form button. Click the Clear Grid button.**
The Clear Grid button removes all the criteria from the Filter by Form grid.

 6 **Click the Apply Filter button.**
The empty criteria are applied. This is the method used to erase the criteria. Notice the Apply Filter button is dim, indicating that no filter criteria exist.

> 🖎 *Exam Note:* **Storing Filter Conditions**
> If you create a filter, it is stored with the database object if you save the changes. When the table, query, or form is open, you can tell if a filter condition exists by looking at the Apply Filter button. If it is dim, no filter condition exists. If it is active, a filter condition exists that may be applied by clicking the button. The name of the Remove Filter button may be misleading. It does not erase the filter conditions, it just removes the application of the filter.

---

7 **Close the query and save the changes. Leave the** `Tornado Analysis` **database open for use in the next lesson.**

Expert ## Lesson 4: Using Parameters as Matching Criteria in a Query

Form filters are helpful when you want to take a quick look at your data based on a particular filter, but there are many more things that you can do to filter data using queries. One of the most useful features in a query is the use of parameters. Parameters can make your queries more flexible, especially when you need to use the same query structure, but vary the data displayed by repeatedly changing the criteria for one or more fields.

In this lesson, you learn how to enter a prompting message in the criteria box instead of a value. When the query is run, a dialog box that displays your message will open and allow the user to enter a value. This method enables the user to enter a different value each time the query is run.

To Use a Parameter as a Matching Criteria in a Query

1 **Right-click on the State Names Query in the Database window and choose** <u>C</u>**opy from the shortcut menu.**

2 **Right-click on an empty part of the queries window and select** <u>P</u>**aste from the shortcut menu. Enter** `Times` **as the new query name and click OK.**

3 **Repeat the previous step to create another copy of the State Names query, but name it** `County`**.**

4 **Select the State Names query and click the** <u>D</u>**esign button.**
The State Names query opens in Design view.

5 **Enter the following in the criteria box under State Names:** [Please enter a State Name:]

Be sure to use square brackets, not parentheses (see Figure 20.12).

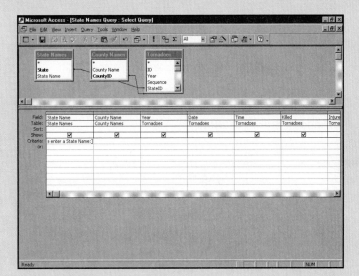

Figure 20.12
Messages enclosed in square brackets can be used instead of entering a single criterion.

 Exam Note: **Contents of a Parameter**

If you enclose a phrase inside square brackets in a query design, the program prompts you to enter a value to be used in place of the phrase, unless the word or phrase in the brackets is a field name. If a field name is placed within the brackets, the current value of the field is used.

---

6 **Click the Run button.**

A message box displays the words you typed between the square brackets in the criteria box for the State Names field (see Figure 20.13).

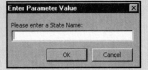

Figure 20.13
A parameter query enables the user to enter the criteria when the query is run.

7 **Type** Ohio **and click OK.**

The 731 tornadoes that occurred in Ohio are displayed.

8 **Press** (Shift) + (F9), **type** Indiana **and press** (Enter).

The key combination of (Shift)+(F9) reopens the message box so you can enter a new value for the query. There are 1035 records displayed for Indiana.

9 **Close the query and save the changes. Leave the** Tornado Analysis **database open for use in the next lesson.**

Lesson 5: Using Parameters with Comparison Operators in a Query

Parameters can be used in place of values for criteria that are specified to determine ranges. By using a parameter, the user can control the range of dates, or upper and lower limits each time the query is run. For example, rather than entering "Between 01/01/00 And 03/31/00" as a criterion, you can create a parameter value box that requests the user to enter a beginning date and an ending date. Then the query can be used for a variety of different time periods without changing the query design.

In this lesson, you learn to use parameters in criteria that select a range of times. You also learn to use the Zoom property when working with long criteria. Continue using the Tornado Analysis database.

To Use Parameters with Comparison Operators in a Query

➊ **Select the Times query and click the <u>D</u>esign button.**

➋ **Right-click on the Criteria box in the Time field. Select <u>Z</u>oom from the shortcut menu.**
The Zoom dialog box opens. It can be used to enter and edit long criteria that would not be easily viewed in the criteria box.

➌ **Enter the following expression:**
Between [Enter the starting time:] and [Enter the ending time:]

The user will be able to enter starting and ending times when the query is run (see Figure 20.14).

Figure 20.14
Long criteria may be entered using the Zoom dialog box.

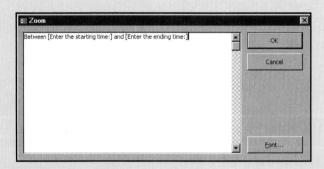

➍ **Click OK, then click the Run button.**
The Enter Parameter Value dialog box appears.

➎ **Type 0000 and click OK.**
The data is stored using a 24-hour time format starting at midnight. All times are given in local time. The second window opens with the second message.

➏ **Type 0100 and click OK.**
The 713 tornadoes that occurred between midnight (0) and one a.m. (100) are displayed. Scroll down the records. Notice that 0 and 100 are included. The Between operator includes values entered to define the range.

➐ **Close the query and save the changes. Leave the Tornado Analysis database open.**

Inside Stuff: **Comparison Operators**

You can use a variety of comparison operators in filters or parameter queries such as Equal, =; Greater Than, >; Less Than, <; Less Than or Equal, <=; Greater Than or Equal, >=; and Not Equal, <>. Operators like <> are called *excluding operators* because they are used to exclude the records that meet the criteria rather than include them.

 Exam Note: **Working with Empty Fields**

There are times when you want to exclude records that have empty fields. For example, if you do a calculation in a query in which you divide one field by the other, it is important that you do not try to divide by an empty field because it will result in an error message. An empty field is a Null value. You can use a criterion of Is Not Null to make sure that no records with an empty field are included. You can use the Is Null operator to select empty fields.

Lesson 6: Using Parameters with Wildcards as Criteria in a Query

An asterisk can be used in place of text to complete an entry in a text field if the Like operator is used with the parameter criteria. The Like operator allows a match between a partial entry and the value in a field.

In this lesson you use wildcards to locate counties when you only know part of the correct name.

To Use Parameters with Wildcards as Criteria in a Query

1 **In the** `Tornado Analysis` **database, select the County query and click the** **D**esign button.

2 **Right-click on the Criteria box in the County Name field and select** **Z**oom from the shortcut menu.

3 **Type the following operator and message:**

`Like [Enter county name, may be completed with *:]`

The Like operator enables the use of asterisks. Remember to use square brackets as shown in Figure 20.15.

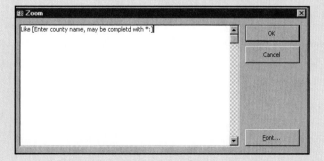

Figure 20.15
A parameter criteria written with the Like operator enables the user to use a wildcard.

continues ▶

To Use Parameters with Wildcards as Criteria in a Query (continued)

4 Click OK, then click the Run button.
The Enter Parameter Value dialog box appears.

5 Type Tus* and click OK.
All the county names that begin with Tus are displayed.

6 Scroll down the list of county names to display the two other counties whose names start with Tus.
It is important to inspect the records to see if there are unintended matches included in the records. Your results should show 41 records in three states and three different county names.

7 Click the list arrow next to the View button and select SQL View from the drop-down list.
The SQL View is displayed. *SQL,* pronounced "sequel," is an acronym for Structured Query Language. This view displays the SQL statement that is written by the Microsoft Access program for each query that you design.

8 Close the query and save the change. Close the database.

Inside Stuff: **Standard Query Language (SQL)**
SQL has been standardized by the American National Standards Institute (ANSI) and is promoted for use with relational databases. SQL statements written by the Microsoft Access program facilitate its capability to communicate with other database programs. If you know how to write SQL statements, you could design or modify queries using the SQL View.

Summary

You do not have to import a large table into your database to analyze it. It is possible to link to a large table and incorporate it into the relationships, queries, and other database objects.

The Filter by Selection option is used for simple matching criteria based on the currently selected field. The Filter by Form option has more options and can be used to filter on several fields in more than one combination.

Specific criteria can be replaced by prompting phrases enclosed between square brackets. A query that uses this feature to input a criterion is known as a parameter query. It enables the user to specify a different criteria value each time the query is run.

Checking Concepts and Terms ✓

True/False

For each of the following statements, check *T* or *F* to indicate whether the statement is true or false.

__T __F **1.** If you enclose a phrase inside square brackets in a query design, the program prompts you to enter a value, unless the word or phrase in the brackets is a field name. [L4]

__T __F **2.** Using parameters enables user input to restrict the output of a report. [L4]

__T __F **3.** If the Apply Filter button is gray (or dim), there are no filter conditions to be applied. [L3]

__T __F **4.** If you click the Remove Filter button, the filter is erased and you have to create it again if you need it in the future. [L3]

__T __F **5.** A wildcard can be used to replace numbers, not text. [L6]

Multiple Choice

Circle the letter of the correct answer for each of the following questions.

1. Which of the following expressions correctly uses a parameter to prompt the user for input? (Assume that Company and Product are field names.) [L4]

a. (Enter the Company Name)

b. [Enter the Product Name]

c. [Company]

d. [Product]

2. If you had a database of books that had been loaned out from a library and wanted to show all the books by a certain popular author that had been loaned out during a particular month, you would _____. [L2]

a. place the insertion point in the author field and use filter by selection

b. place the insertion point in the date field and use filter by selection

c. scroll through the records using the navigation buttons and place a bookmark in each record that met the criteria

d. use the Filter by Form button and put the author's name in the author field and a logical criteria such as, Between 1/1/97 and 1/31/97, in the date field

3. To permanently remove a filter _____. [L3]

a. create a new empty filter and apply it to the form or query, then save the changes

b. click the delete button on the keyboard

c. right-click on the filter and click delete from the shortcut menu

d. click the Remove Filter button

4. If you link to a table rather than import it, you cannot _____. [L1]

a. use it to create a query

b. use it in a relationship

c. change the data in the table

d. use its data in a report

5. An advantage of using a parameter query is _____. [L4]

a. users can control the output of the query by entering a value in the Parameter Value dialog box

b. you can use the same query structure repeatedly without having to open up the design of the query and make changes

c. a form or report can be based on a parameter query

d. all of the above are advantages

Screen ID

Label each element of the Access screen shown in Figures 20.16.

Figure 20.16

A. Number of records that meet the criteria

B. Filter by Selection

C. Filter indicator

D. Filter by Form

E. Remove Filter

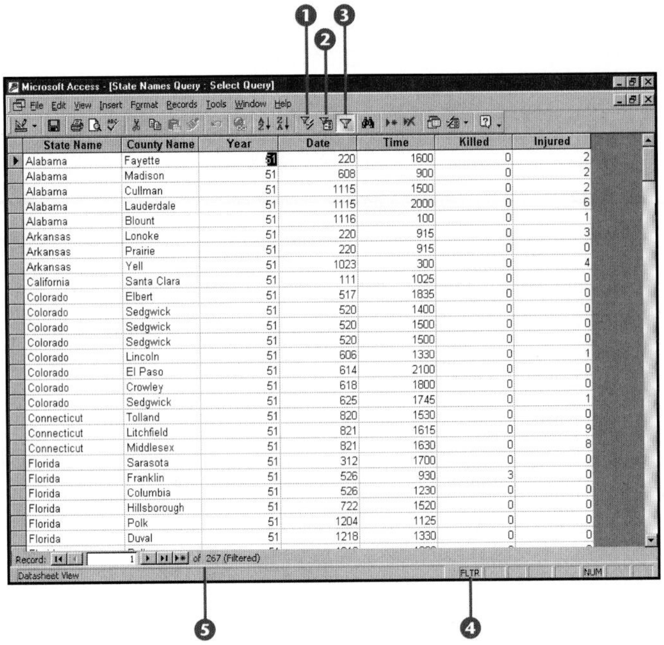

1. _____ 3. _____ 5. _____

2. _____ 4. _____

Skill Drill

Skill Drill exercises reinforce project skills. Each skill reinforced is the same, or nearly the same, as a skill presented in the project. Each exercise includes a brief narrative introduction, followed by detailed instructions in a step-by-step format.

All of the Skill Drill exercises use the same database. Before you begin, copy the file **AC-2003** from the CD-ROM to your floppy disk, remove the read-only property, and rename it **Library**. Each exercise is independent and does not require the completion of a previous exercise.

1. Using Filter by Selection and Filter by Form

Practice what you have learned on a different database. Open the **Library** database. Use the Filter by Selection feature to display only books published in 1992. Then use the Filter by Form feature to display the books that have been borrowed in 1997.

To use Filter by Selection and Filter by Form:

1. Open the **Library** database and open the **Books** table.

2. In the Publication Dates field click on one of the 1992 dates.

3. Click the Filter by Selection button.

   The four books published in 1992 are displayed.

4. Click the Print button to print the table.

5. Click the Remove Filter button and close the table.

6. Open the Borrow table.

7. Click the Filter by Form button.

8. Enter the following condition in the Borrow Date box:

   Between 1/1/00 and 12/31/00

9. Click the Apply Filter button.

10. Click the Print button to print the three books listed.

11. Click on the Remove Filter button to disable the filter.

12. Close the table but do not save the changes. If you intend to do the next exercise leave the database open.

2. Using a Parameter with the Like Operator for Partial Matches

Create a query that uses the Like operator with a parameter to be able to enter the first few letters of a selection and produce matches.

To use a parameter with the Like Operator for partial matches:

1. Open the **Library** database, if necessary, and open the query **Mysteries** in the Design view.

2. In the Type of Book column, replace the "Mystery" criteria with the following:

   `[Enter the type of book:]`

3. Click the Run button to look at the Datasheet view. When the Enter Parameter Value dialog box appears, type any one of the following and click OK.

   `Mystery, Fiction, Classic, Non-Fiction, Science Fiction, or Humor`

4. Return to the Design view. Add the conditional word `Like` to the criteria. The new criteria should be:

   `Like [Enter the type of book:]`

5. Run the query again. Enter an asterisk to see all of the titles.

6. Press **⬆Shift**+**F9** to bring up the Enter Parameter Value message box. Enter `Mys*` and press **⏎Enter**.

7. Asterisks can be used to replace parts of fields you are trying to match when you use the Like operator; for example, Mys* would find any book type starting with "Mys".

8. Close the query and save the changes. Leave the database open if you intend to complete the next exercise.

3. Using the Between Operator with Two Parameters

In the following exercise you use the Between operator with two parameters to determine which books were borrowed between any two dates.

To use the Between operator with two parameters:

1. Open the **Library** database, if necessary.

2. Click the Queries tab and select the Borrowed Books query. Open it in Design view.

3. Enter the following criterion in the criteria box of the Borrower Date field:

   `Between [From:] and [To:]`

4. Click the Run button. Enter `5/1/00` in the From: box and click OK. Enter `8/31/00` in the To: box to see which books were borrowed during the summer.

5. Print the list (one book).

6. Close the query and save the changes. Close the database.

Challenge

Challenge exercises expand on or are somewhat related to skills presented in the lessons. Each exercise provides a brief narrative introduction followed by instructions in a numbered step format that are not as detailed as those in the Skill Drill section.

Use the Tornado Analysis database that you created during this project for all of the following Challenge exercises.

I. Using a Parameter to Provide User Input in a Calculation

In this exercise, you create a parameter message box that allows the user to enter a conversion factor to display the measurement in miles, meters, or kilometers. When working with large tables, it is valuable to be able to remove records that have no entry in a particular field. The path length was not recorded in many cases and there is no reason to display records in the Path Length query that do not have an entry. Some of the records have a path length of zero so it is necessary to distinguish between an empty field and one that contains a zero. After you create the calculated parameter message box, you then enter criterion to remove empty records.

To use a parameter to provide user input in a calculation:

1. Open the `Tornado Analysis` database and click the Queries button.

2. Double-click the Create query by using the Wizard shortcut.

3. Choose the State Names table and select the State Name field. Choose the County Names table and select the County Name field. Choose the Tornadoes table and select the Year, Date, and Length from the Tornadoes table. Click Next.

4. Click Next to accept the Detail setting. Enter `Path Length` as the title. Click Finish to create the query.

5. Change to the Design view of the Path Length query. Right-click in the first empty Field box and choose Zoom from the shortcut menu.

6. Enter the following calculation:

   `Length (other units):[Length]*[Enter length conversion factor:]`

7. Click OK and then click the Run button.

8. Enter `.0001894` to convert the path length to miles. Click OK. If necessary, scroll the window to view the new, calculated field. Notice that many of the records do not have a length recorded; therefore, the calculated field is also empty.

9. Click the View button to return to Design view. Enter the following criterion for the Length field:

   `Is Not Null`

10. This removes any fields where a value has not been recorded.

11. Click the Run button. Enter `.0003048` to convert the lengths to kilometers. Notice that the number of records displayed is reduced to 25,303. The records with empty fields are not displayed.

12. Close the query and save the change. Leave the database open if you intend to do the next exercise.

2. Using the Like Operator with Two Asterisks to Match Any Part of the Field

When you use the Like operator with a parameter, you can finish the entry using a single asterisk. This method may require some user training and does not work if you are looking for part of a name that is not at the beginning of the name.

To use the Like operator with two asterisks to match any part of the field:

1. Right-click on the County query and select Copy from the shortcut menu. Right-click on the empty white area and select Paste from the shortcut menu.

2. Enter `Find Partial County Names` and click OK.

3. Open the `Find Partial County Names` query in the Design view.

4. Right-click the existing criteria in the County Name field and select Zoom from the shortcut menu.

5. Replace the existing criterion with the following:

```
Like"*"+[Enter partial county name:]+"*"
```

6. Click OK then click the Run button.

7. Enter **town** in the dialog box and click OK. Tornadoes in Towner county and Georgetown county are displayed.

8. Print the list of 15 tornadoes in these two counties.

9. Close the query and save the changes. Leave the database open if you intend to do the next exercise.

3. Using the Filter Shortcut Menu to Filter by Exclusion and to Create a Compound Filter

In this exercise you first create a filter using the shortcut menu to view everything except the records that match the selection. You can also combine filter conditions with the "And" operator. You use the shortcut menu again to exclude all the Tornadoes from Texas and Florida.

To use the Filter Shortcut menu to filter by exclusion and to create a compound filter:

1. Copy the State Names Query and rename the copy **Tornado Information**. Open the Design view and remove the parameter from the State Name field. Switch to the Datasheet view of the query.

2. Right-click on Alabama in one of the records. Choose Filter Excluding Selection. None of the Alabama records are displayed.

3. Click the Filter by Form button. Notice that the not equal operator, <>, was automatically applied to the selected field value.

4. Close the Filter by Form view. Click the Remove Filter button.

5. Right-click on one of the state names. Click in the Filter For box.

6. Enter the following criterion:

```
Not "Texas" and Not "Florida"
```

7. Drag the scrollbar down the list to confirm that no tornadoes from Texas or Florida are listed.

8. Click the Filter by Form, clear the grid, and apply the empty filter.

9. Close the query and save the changes. Leave the database open if you intend to do the Discovery Zone exercises.

Discovery Zone

Discovery Zone exercises help you gain advanced knowledge of project topics and/or application of skills. These exercises focus on enhancing your problem-solving skills. Numbered steps are not provided, but you are given hints, reminders, screen shots, and/or references to help you reach your goal for each exercise.

In these exercises you use the Tornado Analysis database that you created in the project.

1. Using the Concatenation Operator

Sometimes it is useful to combine two fields together. This type of operation is called concatenation. It is possible to use this operator with parameters to create a calculated field that combines two other fields. The symbol used for concatenation is the ampersand, &.

Goal: Use the concatenation operator in a calculated field to combine the Date and Year fields.

To produce a calculated field that uses two parameters, Date and Year, and concatenates them into a single field:

- Open the `Tornado Analysis` database, if necessary, and open the `Tornado Information` query in Design view.

- Create a calculated field that contains the Date and Year field names within square brackets, separated by an ampersand.

- Run the query. The new column should display the date information (day and month in this case) and year in one field. An example of a date on May 13, 1992, would be 51392.

- Close the query and save the changes.

2. To Filter a Database to Answer Specific Questions

Use the skills that you have learned about filters and queries to answer the following questions about the tornadoes that occurred in the United States and its territories during the period from 1950 to 1995.

Ultimately, you will need to decide what combination of filters and queries to use to determine answers to questions regarding a table of data.

Goal: Create queries and use appropriate filters to answer a set of questions.

Create a new query named `Questions` that contains the State Name and County name fields plus whichever fields you deem appropriate from the Tornadoes table to answer the following questions:

- How many tornadoes have killed more than 20 people?

- How many tornadoes have occurred in the county where you live? How many of them killed someone?

- How many tornadoes have occurred in Texas in 1955?

- How many tornadoes have occurred in Michigan in 1953?

- How many tornadoes have occurred in Oklahoma in 1993?

- How many tornadoes have occurred in Florida in 1990?

Close the query and save the changes. Close the database.

PinPoint Assessment

You have completed this project and its associated lessons, and have had an opportunity to assess your skills through the end-of-project questions and exercises. Now use the PinPoint software Evaluation Mode to further assess your comprehension of the specific exam activities you have just learned. You can also use the PinPoint Trainer Mode and the Show Me tutorials to practice these exam activities.

Sharing a Database with Others

Key terms introduced in this project include

- share-level security
- encryption
- password
- user-level security
- startup parameters

Objectives	Required Activity for MOUS	Exam Level
➤ Assign a Password to Your Database	Set and modify a database password	Expert
➤ Change or Remove a Database Password	Set and modify a database password	Expert
➤ Encrypt a Database	Encrypt and decrypt a database	Expert
➤ How to Decrypt a Database	Encrypt and decrypt a database	Expert
➤ Set Startup Parameters	Set startup options	Expert
➤ Set Access Defaults	Set startup options	Expert

Why Would I Do This?

Many features of Access are designed to enable users to share data and to gain access to data used by others. Problems can arise from sharing data with others, however. Someone may make changes to the tables, forms, reports, or queries you have created, or he or she may enter data into the tables in a non-standard format. In some cases, your database may contain sensitive information that is not for general distribution, or proprietary information that is valuable to the company. In this lesson, you learn some techniques that provide some protection from accidental changes. You also learn useful safeguards to protect your database from intentional damage or theft.

Many people who need to use databases do not have the need or the time to learn how to use Access. It is possible to customize a database so that these users are guided through the functions they need to use. You can do this by setting startup and default parameters that will lead these users to custom menus that open forms with customized toolbars.

 ## Lesson 1: Assigning a Password to Your Database

Adding security to your database is like putting a new lock on a door. It provides a measure of protection from some intruders, but putting a lock on a door also has several drawbacks:

- It slows you down every time you want to pass through the door.
- Other people who need to pass through the door must ask you for the key.
- If you give a duplicate key to someone, you do not know what he or she will do with it.
- There are people who have master keys to that type of lock.
- There are people who understand how the lock works and know how to pick it.
- If you lose the only key, it can be very inconvenient.

In spite of these disadvantages, most of us still use locks on our doors. Similarly, you may also want to add a measure of security to your database.

In this lesson, you learn how to require a **_password_** to open a database. Passwords are a mix of letters, numbers, and symbols that are used to identify an authorized user. Using a password to protect a database is called **_share-level security_**.

Use an empty, formatted disk to start this project if you are using a floppy disk to store your files.

To Assign a Password to Your Database

1 Make a copy of the `AC-2101` database file from the **CD-ROM. Right-click the filename; select Properties from the shortcut menu, and remove the Read-only property. Use the shortcut menu to rename the file** `Prices`.

2 Launch Access, if necessary, and choose to open an existing database. Locate the Prices database but do not open it.

3 Click the `Prices` database to select it, if necessary. Click the drop-down arrow on the Open button.
The drop-down list displays several options. Opening the database in Exclusive mode prevents any other users from accessing the database while you are making changes. It is required for the following procedure even if you are not using Access in a network environment (see Figure 21.1).

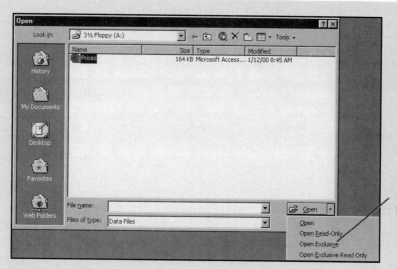

Figure 21.1
Use the Open Exclusive option to open the Prices database for exclusive use.

The database must be in use by only one person

④ Click Open Exclusive.
The Prices database opens.

⑤ Choose Tools, Security from the menu, then select Set Database Password.
The Set Database Password dialog box appears (see Figure 21.2)

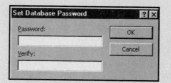

Figure 21.2
The Set Database Password dialog box enables you to set a new password.

⑥ Type ABCabc! in the Password text box.
You will see asterisks in the Password box instead of the letters you typed. This prevents someone from looking over your shoulder and seeing your password. If you are not sure what you typed, press *Backspace* and try again carefully.

⑦ Press Tab↹ and type the same password in the Verify box. Asterisks will be displayed instead of the letters that you type. Click OK.
Be sure to use the same case (uppercase or lowercase) that you typed in the Password text box. The Set Database Password dialog box closes and the Database window reappears.

⑧ Close the Prices database and then open it as you would normally.
You do not have to select the Exclusive option this time. The Password Required dialog box appears (see Figure 21.3).

Figure 21.3
The Password Required dialog box is shown before the password has been entered.

continues ▶

To Assign a Password to Your Database   (continued)

9 **Carefully type the password and click OK.**
The database opens if you correctly matched the password. If you did not match the password exactly, including the proper upper- and lowercase characters, you see a warning box and then return to the Password Required dialog box to try again.

10 **Close the database. Leave Access open for the next lesson.**

 Inside Stuff: **Guidelines for Choosing Passwords**
Passwords in Access can be very simple and short, or complex and up to 14 characters in length. To get the best security out of your password, do not use a date or a word that would be listed in a dictionary. Do not use passwords others might be able to guess, such as a family member's name, your social security number, or a commonly used phone number. Make the password at least six characters long and include a character that is not a letter. If you do want to use an easily recalled word or date, insert an extra symbol. In the example in this lesson, the password included an exclamation mark for this purpose.

 ## Lesson 2: Changing or Removing a Database Password

Once you have added a password to your database you may need to change or remove it.

In this lesson, you learn how to change or remove the database password.

To Change or Remove a Database Password

1 **Choose File, Open. Select the Prices database on drive A: then click the drop-down arrow next to the Open button and choose Open Exclusive.**
The Password Required dialog box appears.

2 **Enter the password you created in Lesson 1, then click OK.**

3 **Choose Tools, Security from the menu bar; then choose Unset Database Password.**
The Unset Database Password dialog box appears

4 **Type the original password you created in Lesson 1 and click OK.**
The database can now be opened without a password.

5 **Close the database. Leave Access open for the next lesson.**

 Inside Stuff: **When to Use the Open Exclusive Option**
It is not necessary to use the Open Exclusive option if you are not changing the password.

Lesson 3: Encrypting a Database

Even though the database program is protected by a password, it is possible to view the data by opening the database with a word processing program. Most of the screen of the word processing program is filled with unrecognizable characters, but some of the data in the tables is still readable. If you use the **encryption** feature the file will be stored as a code that is not easily read.

In this section, you copy a database to your floppy disk and confirm that it is password protected.

To Confirm That a Database is Password Protected

1 **Make a copy of the** AC-2102 **database file from the CD-ROM. Right-click the filename; select** P**roperties from the shortcut menu, and remove the** R**ead-only property. Use the shortcut menu to rename the file** Performance Evaluation.

2 **Select the** Performance Evaluation **file and click the** O**pen button.**
The Password dialog window opens. You do not know the correct password for this database. Try a password to see what happens.

3 **Enter a code of your choice. Click OK.**
An error message displays when the program detects the incorrect password.

4 **Click OK. Click the Cancel button. Leave Access open.**
You were not successful in opening the password-protected database.

It is still possible to read some of the text in a database by using a word processing program.

In this section, you use the Word program to view the database code and search for embedded text.

To View Embedded Text in a Database Using a Word Processing Program

1 **Launch Word. Click the Open button. In the Files of** t**ype drop-down list, select All Files, and locate the** Performance Evaluation **file on your floppy disk. Select the file and click the** O**pen button.**

2 **Click the** P**lain Text option button and click OK.**
The computer codes that Access uses to manage the database do not translate into meaningful text. However, the contents of the text fields may be read. The problem is to find useful information in hundreds of pages of symbols (see Figure 21.4). The symbols that are displayed may vary from one computer to another. The code is shown in N**ormal view.

3 **Choose** E**dit,** F**ind from the menu.**
Because the topic of this database is performance evaluations, you can search for words that are likely to be used.

continues ▶

To View Embedded Text in a Database Using a Word Processing Program (continued)

Figure 21.4
Most of the code in the database file is meaningless when viewed in Word.

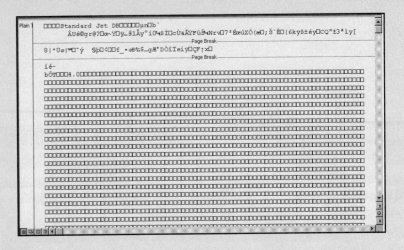

④ **Type** expectations **in the Fin_d what box. Click the _Find Next button. Click Cancel to close the Find and Replace dialog box.**

Social security numbers and performance evaluations are easily recognizable (see Figure 21.5). Clearly, password protection is useful but not sufficient by itself to keep someone from reading the contents of text fields.

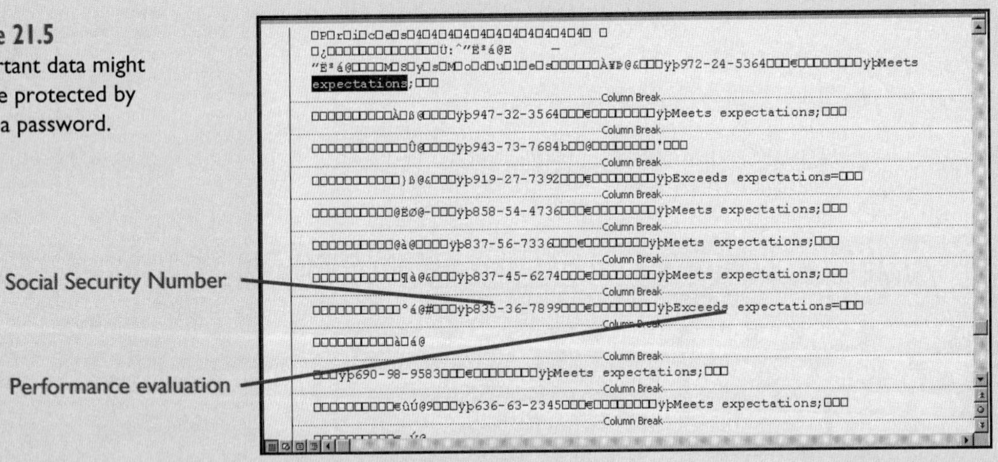

Figure 21.5
Important data might not be protected by using a password.

Social Security Number

Performance evaluation

⑤ **Close the document. Leave Word open.**

Access has an encryption feature that encodes the contents of the fields.

In the next section, you encrypt the database.

To Encrypt a Database

1 Switch to Access. Choose Tools, Security, Encrypt/Decrypt Database.
The Encrypt/Decrypt Database dialog box opens.

2 Change the Look in box to display the files on the floppy disk in drive A:. Select Performance Evaluation and click OK.
The Password Required dialog window opens. Because this database is password protected, you cannot make changes to it without the password. The password is provided in the next step.

3 Type jmp and click OK.
The Encrypt Database As window opens.

4 Enter Encrypted Evaluations in the File name text box and click Save.
The database is encrypted and saved under the new name.

5 Switch back to Word. Follow the procedure described above to open the Encrypted Evaluations database in Word and search for Expectations.
This time the search is unsuccessful. The text has been encoded and is no longer readable by this method.

6 Close the file and close Word. Leave Access open for the next lesson.

 Inside Stuff: User-level Security
The share-level security measures mentioned in these lessons are useful in providing a first line of defense. Access provides a more sophisticated level of security that is particularly useful in a network environment. It is called **user-level security**. Do not attempt to make changes to user-level security on a network without the permission and cooperation of the network administrator. You could end up reinstalling Access or locking yourself and others out of a database. You learn more about user-level security in the Discovery Zone exercises at the end of this project.

 Exam Note: How to Decrypt a Database
Make sure the database is closed and not in use by anyone else. Select Tools, Security, Encrypt/Decrypt Database. Select the encrypted database and click OK. Enter the password, then provide a name for the decrypted database.

Lesson 4: Setting Startup Parameters

It is possible to control the way the database appears when it is opened. You can decide which toolbars are available to the user, and you can open a switchboard form automatically. These options are called **startup parameters**.

In this lesson, you learn how to open the switchboard automatically whenever the database is opened. You can also disable several features that are very useful while the database is being designed but that are not necessary while someone else is using it.

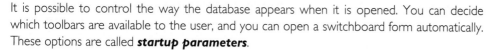

To Set Startup Parameters

❶ Make a copy of the `AC-2103` **database file from the CD-ROM. Right-click the filename; select** <u>P</u>**roperties from the shortcut menu, and remove the** <u>R</u>**ead-only property. Use the shortcut menu to rename the file** `Customer with Switchboard`**.**

❷ Open the Customer with Switchboard database. Choose <u>T</u>**ools, Start**<u>u</u>**p from the menu.**

The Startup dialog box appears (see Figure 21.6).

Figure 21.6
The Startup dialog box allows the designer to control the toolbars and menus to simplify them or to restrict the user's ability to change the design.

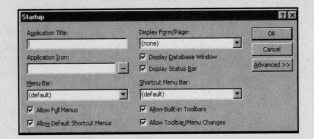

❸ In the Display <u>F</u>**orm/Page drop-down list, select Switchboard.**

The Switchboard form opens automatically when the database is opened.

❹ Click Display <u>D</u>**atabase Window to deselect it.**

When you close the switchboard form, the Database window will not be available to the user so he or she cannot get into the design of the database.

❺ Check the Display Status <u>B</u>**ar check box to make sure it is selected.**

This option could remove the status bar from the bottom of the screen to increase the available window space and simplify the screen. Leave it turned on in this example.

❻ Click A<u>l</u>**low Built-in Toolbars to deselect it.**

This option removes the toolbar from the top of the screen to increase the available window space and simplify the screen.

❼ Click Allow Toolbar/Menu Changes to deselect it.

This prevents a user from adding the toolbars back to the screen.

❽ Click Allow F<u>u</u>**ll Menus to deselect it.**

This changes the menu options from a full list of editing choices to a short list of choices that are appropriate to using the database rather than designing it.

❾ Click Allo<u>w</u> **Default Shortcut Menus to deselect it.**

This disables the shortcut menus options that are normally available by clicking with the right mouse button. Check to make sure that your dialog box looks like Figure 21.7.

 Inside Stuff: **Other Startup Options**

The Startup dialog box can also help you design your own menu bars and shortcut menus. You can also use this dialog box to create a special icon on the desktop that will run this version of the database. Do not use these options at this time.

Items without check marks will
not be displayed

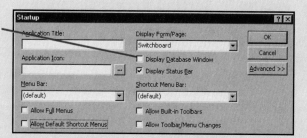

Figure 21.7
The Startup dialog box
displays the new
settings.

⑩ Click OK to close the Startup dialog box. Close the database.
The next time the Customer with Switchboard database is opened, the startup
parameters will be used and the switchboard will open automatically.

⑪ Open the Customer with Switchboard database again.
The Switchboard form opens automatically. Notice that there are several differences. The menus have fewer choices, the right mouse button does not produce
a shortcut menu, and the toolbar is not available (see Figure 21.8).

The menu has
fewer choices

The toolbars
are not
available

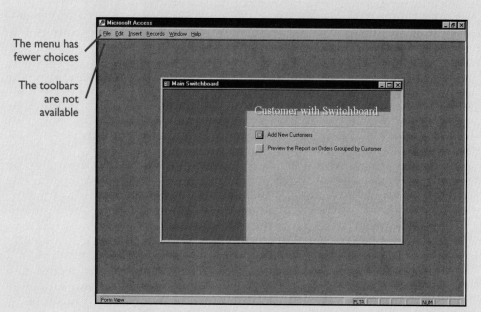

Figure 21.8
The Switchboard form
can be displayed with
fewer user options
available on the Access
menus, and the
toolbars are turned
off.

⑫ Close the Switchboard form.
The settings from the startup will stay in effect until Access is closed.

⑬ Close Access.
When you start Access again, the normal toolbars and menus will be displayed.

 Exam Note: **How to Override the Startup Parameters**
If you choose to suppress the display of the toolbar and menu options used for design, you do not have a way to change the startup parameters. To open the database and by-pass the startup parameters, hold down ⊕Shift when you open the
database.

Lesson 5: Setting Access Defaults

Startups control the environment of a single database, while Access defaults control the environment for any Access database that is opened from your installed copy of Access.

In this lesson, you learn how to change some of the defaults that Access uses.

To Set Access Defaults

① **Launch Access and open the Prices database from your floppy disk.**
The Prices database opens. The normal menus and toolbars are visible.

② **Choose Tools, Options from the menu.**
The Options dialog box appears.

③ **Click the Keyboard tab.**
The default settings are displayed for movement of the cursor are displayed after ⏎Enter is pressed or when the arrow keys are used (see Figure 21.9).

Figure 21.9
The Options dialog box can be used to set defaults for the Access program.

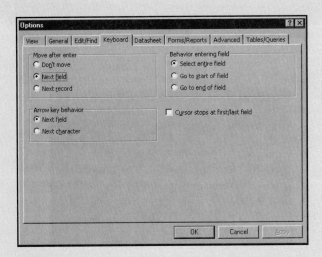

The default setting for movement of the cursor after ⏎Enter is pressed is to move it to the next field to the right in the current record. If you are entering or changing the data in one field, it would be more convenient to automatically move to the next record.

④ **Click on Next record in the Move after Enter area.**

⑤ **Click the Apply button.**
The cursor moves down the column of data each time you press ⏎Enter when you are in a datasheet view. If you are in a form, the view will page from one record to the next and remain in the same field when you press ⏎Enter.

⑥ **Click the Datasheet tab.**
The default options for the appearance of the datasheet are displayed (see Figure 21.10).

Changes on this form affect the appearance of any datasheet opened in Access.

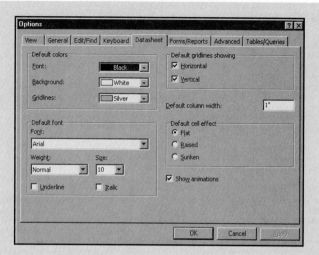

Figure 21.10
The default values for the Datasheet view are displayed.

⑦ **Change the default colors to White, Gray, and Aqua for the Font, Background, and Gridlines options, respectively. Click the Vertical option in the Default Gridlines Showing section to deselect it.**
The Options Datasheet dialog box should look like Figure 21.11.

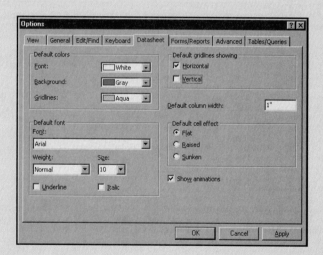

Figure 21.11
The Options Datasheet dialog box displays the new settings.

⑧ **Click OK to close the Options dialog box.**
These new settings are applied upon closing this dialog box.

⑨ **Open the Stock on Hand table in Datasheet view.**
The new default colors and gridlines settings are displayed (see Figure 21.12).

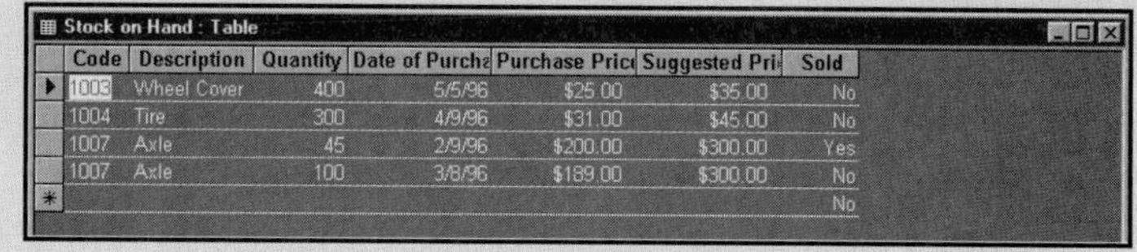

Figure 21.12
The Customer table in Datasheet view displays the new default settings.

continues ▶

To Set Access Defaults   (continued)

10 **Press ⏎Enter several times.**

Notice how the cursor moves down the column, from one record to the next, rather than across the fields.

11 **Close the table.**

12 **Choose Tools, Options from the menu.**

If you share your computer with others, it is important that you return the settings to their original values.

13 **Click on the Datasheet tab. Change the default colors back to Black, White, and Silver for the Font, Background, and Gridlines options, respectively. Click the Vertical Default Gridlines check box to select it.**

14 **Click on the Keyboard tab. Change the Move After Enter option to Next field.**

15 **Click on OK to make the changes and restore the original settings.**

16 **Close the table and close the database. Close Access.**

Inside Stuff: **Default Settings Affect Other Databases**

Use caution when changing the default Access settings, because they will affect all of your Access databases. If you share your computer with others in a laboratory setting, it would be discourteous to personalize the program without the consent of others who may not know how to change it back. Also, if you are using a copy of Access that is installed on a network server, the defaults will affect anyone else in your workgroup who uses the program. In the previous lesson, we only changed defaults that affected appearance. You could change operational defaults that could affect the function of the program, and you may not remember the original settings. Use this feature with care.

Summary

You can make it more difficult for unauthorized people to view your data by adding a password and encrypting the database.

If you are designing a database for use by others, you can restrict the use of editing features and change default settings for color and movement of the cursor.

Checking Concepts and Terms ✓

True/False

For each of the following, check *T* or *F* to indicate whether the statement is true or false.

__T __F   **1.** To add a password to a database, the first step is to open it by double-clicking on its name or icon. [L1]

__T __F   **2.** To remove the password from a database, you must open the database. This implies that you know what the password is. [L2]

__T __F **3.** Encrypting a database prevents someone from reading data in the database by using a word processing program. [L3]

__T __F **4.** The best passwords are the ones you do not forget. Keep it simple—use something short such as your birth date. [L1]

__T __F **5.** Startup parameters may be used to disable certain toolbar and menu items that are normally used to edit the design of the database. [L4]

Multiple Choice

Circle the letter of the correct answer for each of the following questions.

1. Startup parameters _____. [L4]

  a. are set with all of the databases closed

  b. affect all databases opened by that installation of Access

  c. are set after a database has been opened and only affect that database

  d. are used to flash warning messages on the screen if there is too much traffic on the network

2. A good password should have the following characteristics to make it hard to guess. [L1]

  a. It should be an easy to remember date.

  b. It should be an obscure word from the dictionary.

  c. It should include a symbol that is not a normal letter or number.

  d. It should be the same for all of your accounts.

3. If you have set the startup parameters so that they do not allow full menus, the Tools option does not appear. How do you change the startup parameters? [L4]

  a. Reinstall Access.

  b. Copy all of the data, forms, queries, and reports into a new database.

  c. Hold down Ctrl when you start Access.

  d. Close and re-open Access. Hold down ⬆Shift when you open the database.

4. A setting that applies to all of the databases opened in Access is called which of the following? [L4]

  a. Default setting

  b. Startup setting

  c. Response setting

  d. Backup setting

5. When you want to add or remove a password, the database must be opened in which of the following modes? [L2]

  a. Password mode

  b. Exclusive mode

  c. Read-only mode

  d. Archive mode

Skill Drill

Skill Drill exercises reinforce project skills. Each skill reinforced is the same, or nearly the same, as a skill presented in the project. Each exercise includes a brief narrative introduction, followed by detailed instructions in a step-by-step format.

1. Adding a Password to a Database

In the following exercise, you will add a password to protect a database named Books.

To add a password to a database:

1. Make a copy of the `AC-2104` database file from the CD-ROM. Right-click the filename; select Properties from the shortcut menu, and remove the Read-only property. Use the shortcut menu to rename the file `Books`.

2. Launch Access, if necessary, and choose to open an existing database. Locate the Books database but do not open it.

3. Select the `Books` file, click the drop-down arrow on the Open button and open the Books database in Exclusive mode.

4. Choose Tools, Security, Set Database Password from the menu.

5. Type the password `Books`.

6. Verify the password by typing it again. Make sure to capitalize the first letter as shown.

7. Close the database and then reopen it. Try typing in the password as `books` to see if capitalization makes a difference. If that does not work, try `Books`.

8. Close the database.

2. Removing a Password from a Database

In this exercise, you remove a password from the Books database.

To remove a password from a database:

1. Make a copy of the `AC-2105` database file from the CD-ROM. Right-click the filename; select Properties from the shortcut menu, and remove the Read-only property. Use the shortcut menu to rename the file `Club`.

2. Open the `Club` database in Exclusive mode. Use the Password `Club`.

3. Choose Tools, Security, Unset Database Password from the menu.

4. Enter the password `Club`. Click OK.

5. Close the database and then reopen it. Confirm that the password is no longer required. Close the database.

3. Opening a Switchboard Automatically Whenever the Database is Opened

In this exercise you set the startup parameters of a database to open a switchboard whenever the database is opened. In this way, you can create a database that a novice can use successfully without having to master the details of the Access program.

To open a switchboard automatically whenever the database is opened:

1. Make a copy of the `AC-2106` database file from the CD-ROM. Right-click the filename; select Properties from the shortcut menu, and remove the Read-only property. Use the shortcut menu to rename the file `Books with Switchboard`.

2. Open the database and open the Startup parameters dialog box from the Tools menu.

3. Choose the Switchboard form as the display form opened upon startup.

4. Click OK to close the Startup window. Close the database

5. Open the `Books with Switchboard` database. The switchboard should appear automatically. Test both buttons.

6. Close the form, report preview, and the database but leave Access open if you plan to do the next exercises.

Challenge

Challenge exercises expand on or are somewhat related to skills presented in the lessons. Each exercise provides a brief narrative introduction followed by instructions in a numbered step or bullet list format that are not as detailed as those in the Skill Drill section.

Before starting these exercises, insert an empty, formatted floppy disk in drive A:. In the following exercises, you use a file that is similar to the one that was created in the first project.

1. Prevent Change to Data in One Field

There are various levels of security. In many cases, you just want to prevent accidental changes made by a well-meaning person. In such cases, it is sufficient to change the property of a field in a form to prevent accidental entries.

In the following exercise, a form named Update General Employee Information is used to make changes to non-sensitive data when people move or change their names. The Employee ID is displayed in this form but you do not want a part-time employee to accidentally change the employee number. A simple way to do that is to change the property of the field in that form.

Use an empty, formatted disk for the remaining exercises.

To prevent changes to data in one field:

1. Make a copy of the **AC-2107** database file from the CD-ROM. Right-click the filename; select Properties from the shortcut menu, and remove the Read-only property. Use the shortcut menu to rename the file **Projects**.

2. Open the Projects database. Click the Forms button and select Update General Employee Information.

3. Open the form in the Design view.

4. Right-click on the Employee ID text box (not the label box) and select Properties from the shortcut menu.

5. Click the Data tab. Change the Locked option from No to Yes. Close the Properties window.

6. Save the changes and switch to the Form view. Try to change the Employee ID number. It is not changeable and cannot be changed. Close the form.

7. Open the Employee Information table. Attempt to edit one of the Employee ID numbers. You can still edit the table—locking the field in the form simply prevents accidents. Press Esc to restore the Employee ID number. Close the table.

8. Leave the database open if you plan to do the next exercise and skip the first two steps.

2. Hide and Unhide Columns in a Table

Some information is not sensitive enough to warrant too much effort at concealment but it would be better if it is not displayed to everyone who looks at the table. An option that works well in this case is to hide the column or columns. Users who are not particularly familiar with Access will not think to look for hidden columns.

If you did not do the previous challenge exercise, perform steps one and two and open the Projects database before you start this exercise.

To hide and unhide columns in a table:

1. Make a copy of the `AC-2107` database file from the CD-ROM. Right-click the filename; select Properties from the shortcut menu, and remove the Read-only property. Use the shortcut menu to rename the file `Projects`.

2. Select the `Employee Information` table and open it in Datasheet view. Maximize the window.

3. Scroll across to the right to display the Emergency Contact Number, Contact Person, and Relationship to Employee fields.

4. Choose Format, Unhide Columns. (*Note:* It is easier to use the Unhide option to hide columns than it is to select and hide them.)

5. Deselect the Emergency Contact Number, Contact Person, and Relationship to Employee fields and click Close. The columns are not displayed.

6. Use this procedure to unhide the Emergency Contact Number.

7. Close the table and save the changes. If you plan to do the next exercise, keep the database open and skip the first two steps.

3. Hide a Table, a Relationship, and a Form in a Database

It is also possible to hide database objects. This is a two-part process in which you first designate the object to be hidden, such as a table or form, and then change one of the Access options that displays hidden objects.

To hide a table, a relationship, and a form in a database:

1. Make a copy of the `AC-2107` database file from the CD-ROM. Right-click the filename; select Properties from the shortcut menu, and remove the Read-only property. Use the shortcut menu to rename the file `Projects`.

2. Click the Tables button and locate the Private table.

3. Right-click on the Private table and select Properties from the shortcut menu.

4. Click the Hidden attribute to turn it on to hide the table. Click OK. The icon for the Private table is hidden.

5. Locate the form, `Update Sensitive Information`. Repeat the previous two steps to turn on its Hidden attribute.

6. To unhide database objects, choose Tools, Options, and click the View tab, if necessary. Click the check box next to Hidden objects to select it.

7. Click OK to apply and close the window. The icons for the table and form display but are dimmed.

8. Right-click on the Update Sensitive Information form and deselect its Hidden property. Leave the Hidden property selected for the Private table.

9. Set the option back to its original setting where it does not display hidden objects. The Update Sensitive Information form is visible but the Private table is not. (Normally you would hide both but one is restored to demonstrate that you know how to unhide a database object.) Close the database.

Discovery Zone

Discovery Zone exercises help you gain advanced knowledge of project topics and application of skills. These exercises focus on enhancing your problem-solving skills. Numbered steps are not provided, but you are given hints, reminders, screen shots, and references to help you reach your goal for each exercise.

You started this book by gathering information needed to design a database. In that scenario, you were the expert. In the following exercises, you learn how to provide a network administrator with the information he or she needs to design a user-level security system for your Access databases. Network administrators are familiar with setting up user-level security and you need to work with your network administrator to set up a similar system in Access.

1. Print Out Help Pages on Workgroups

A workgroup has an administrator who decides what groups exist in the workgroup and what those groups are allowed to do. He or she may then decide who is a member in each group.

There is plenty of information available from the Office Assistant about workgroups.

Goal: Print several reference pages concerning workgroups.

To print out some of the help pages that are most useful:

- Choose Help, Microsoft Access Help from the menu. Click the Office Assistant and search for the phrase, User-level security. Choose Protect a Microsoft Access database and its tables, queries, forms, reports, and macros with user-level security from the resulting list of topics.
- Click the Work with workgroup information files hyperlink.
- Click the Printer icon. The Print window opens. Click the check box labeled Print all linked documents. Click OK. The program will print a document for each of the links on this page—about 11 pages.

The next step is to learn something about user and group accounts.

There are some terms used that are very similar and often confused with one another. There is a high-level administrative group named Admins. Unfortunately, the program uses a very similar name, Admin, for an unknown user. Another opportunity for confusion is that there is a group named Users, but the help messages often refer to two or more people as users.

Goal: Print several reference pages concerning user and group accounts.

To print out some of the help pages that are most useful:

- Confirm that you are on the help page titled, Work with a workgroup information file. Click the Back button at the top of the Help screen to return to the Protect a Microsoft Access database and its tables, queries, forms, reports, and macros with user-level security. Click on the Work with user and group accounts hyperlink.
- Click the Printer icon. The Print window opens. Click the check box labeled Print all linked documents. Click OK. The program will print a document for each of the links on this page—about 13 pages.
- Take some time to read these pages. Do not be surprised if you find them confusing, the following exercise will help you organize the material.
- Close Help.

- This is a difficult subject to learn from these pages. Do not attempt to apply what you learn in these pages to a computer that is used on a network without consulting with the network administrator. You can easily make a mistake that would result in locking people out of databases and causing a great deal of trouble. Even if you are working on your own computer that is not attached to a network, you could end up reinstalling Access and permanently locking yourself out of databases.

2. Planning to Implement User-level Security

This time, you are on the user end of the interview. It is your job to describe what the workgroups, user groups, memberships, and permissions should be. Prepare a planning sheet that you can give to the network administrator.

Goal: Fill out a planning sheet that describes the workgroup, user groups, memberships, and permissions that you plan to use.

To prepare for implementing user-level security:

- Launch Word and open the file, **AC-2108** from the CD-ROM. Save the form on your floppy disk using the name **Security Plan**.

- Choose a name for the workgroup and identify who will have the authority to administer it. Enter your name and make up a name for the network administrator.

- Fill in the appropriate boxes on the form to describe three user groups—Full Permissions, Enter Data, Read-only. The Enter Data group has permission to enter data into all of the tables except the Private table. The Read-only group may look at any form or report but no tables or queries.

- Fill in the appropriate boxes on the form to describe four users; Juan, Sally, Shaleen, and Bill.

- Assign the four people to the three groups.

- Print the form.

PinPoint Assessment

You have completed this project and its associated lessons, and have had an opportunity to assess your skills through the end-of-project questions and exercises. Now use the PinPoint software Evaluation Mode to further assess your comprehension of the specific exam activities you have just learned. You can also use the PinPoint Trainer Mode and the Show Me tutorials to practice these exam activities.

Appendix A

Using the MOUS PinPoint 2000 Training and Testing Software

Objectives

➤ Install and Start the PinPoint Launcher

➤ Start and Run PinPoint Trainers and Evaluation

➤ View Trainer and Evaluation Results

➤ Recover from a Crash

➤ Remove PinPoint from Your Computer

Introduction to PinPoint 2000

PinPoint 2000 is a software product that provides interactive training and testing in Microsoft Office 2000 programs. It is designed to supplement the projects in this book and will aid you in preparing for the MOUS certification exams. PinPoint 2000 is included on the CD-ROM in the back of this text. PinPoint 2000 Trainers and Evaluations currently run under Windows 95, Windows 98 and Windows NT 4.

The MOUS PinPoint software consists of Trainers and Evaluations. Trainers are used to hone your Office user skills. Evaluations are used to evaluate your performance of those skills.

PinPoint 2000 requires a full custom installation of Office 2000 to your computer. A full custom installation is an option you select at the time you install Microsoft Office 2000, and means that all components of the software are installed.

The PinPoint 2000 Launcher

Your PinPoint 2000 CD contains a selection of PinPoint 2000 Trainers and Evaluations that cover many of the skills that you may need for using Word 2000, Excel 2000, PowerPoint 2000 and Access 2000.

Concurrency

PinPoint 2000 Trainers and Evaluations are considered "concurrent." This means that a Trainer (or Evaluation) is run simultaneously with the Office 2000 application you are learning or being tested in. For example, when you run a Pinpoint Excel 2000 Trainer, the Microsoft Excel 2000 application is automatically started and runs at the same time. By working directly in the Office 2000 application, you master the real application, rather than just practice on a simulation of the application.

Today's more advanced applications (like those in Office 2000) often allow more than one way to perform a given task. Concurrency with the real application gives you the freedom to choose the method that you like or that you already know. This gives you the optimal training and testing environment.

Trainer/Evaluation Pairs

Trainers and Evaluations come in pairs. For example, there is a Trainer/Evaluation pair for Word 2000 called "Expert Creating a Newsletter." This means that there is both a Trainer and an Evaluation for "Expert Creating a Newsletter."

Pinpoint Word 2000, Excel 2000, PowerPoint 2000, and Access 2000 all have such sets of Trainers and Evaluations.

Tasks

Each Trainer/Evaluation pair, or *module*, is a set of tasks grouped according to level (Core or Expert) and skill set.

Trainers

If you need help to complete the task you can click the Show Me button and activate the Show Me feature The Show Me will run a demonstration of how to perform a similar task.

After you attempt the task, the program checks your work and tells you if you performed the task correctly or incorrectly. In either case you have three choices:

- Retry the task.
- Have the Trainer demonstrate with the task's Show Me an efficient method of completing the task.
- Move on to the next task.

After you have completed all of the tasks in the module, you can study your performance by looking at the report that appears when you click the Report tab on the Launcher. Reports are covered in Lesson 7.

You may take a Trainer as many times as you like. As you do so, the Launcher keeps track of how you perform, even over different days, so that when you run a Trainer another time, the Trainer is set up to run only those tasks that were performed incorrectly on all of your previous run(s).

Evaluations

Since an Evaluation is really a test, it does not give you immediate feedback. You also cannot go back to a previous task or watch a demonstration of how to do the current task. You simply move from task to task until you have attempted all of the tasks in the Evaluation.

When you have finished, you can look at the report in the Reports section to see how you performed.

You can take an Evaluation as many times as you like. While you do so, the Launcher program keeps a record of how you have performed. As a result, if you take a Trainer after the corresponding Evaluation has been taken, the Trainer will set up to run only those tasks that were performed incorrectly on the Evaluation.

System Requirements

Table A.1 shows the system requirements to run PinPoint 2000 software on your computer.

Table A.1   PinPoint 2000 System Requirements

Component	Requirement
CPU	Minimum: Pentium
	Recommended: 166 MHz Pentium or better
Operating System	Windows 95, Windows 98 or WindowsNT 4.0 sp5
Installed Applications	Full Custom Installation of Office 2000*
	Printer
RAM	Minimum: 16 MB
	Recommended: 32 MB or higher

*Office 2000 must be installed before installing PinPoint 2000. If a Full Custom Installation of Office 2000 has not been performed, some tasks will not be available, because the components required for those tasks will not have been installed. The tasks will not be counted as right or wrong but recorded as N/A.

Table A.1 PinPoint 2000 System Requirements (continued)

Component	Requirement
Hard Drive Space	Minimum: Installing PinPoint 2000 software requires about 4 MB of hard drive space.
	Recommended: For efficient operation, however, you should make sure you have at least 100 MB of unused drive space after installing PinPoint 2000.
CD-ROM Drive	4X speed or faster
Video	Minimum: Color VGA video display running at 640x480 resolution with 16 colors.
	Recommended: Color VGA video display running at 800x600 (or higher) resolution with 16 colors.
	Note for Gateway computer users: If running a P5 90 (or less) Gateway computer, obtain the latest ATI "Mach 64" video driver from Gateway. This can be downloaded from Gateway's web site.

Running PinPoint 2000

Now that you know what PinPoint 2000 is and what is required to use it, you now see how to install and use the Launcher, and start and run Trainers and Evaluations. You also see how to view Trainer and Evaluation reports. Lastly, you find out how to recover from a crash of PinPoint 2000, should one occur.

Lesson 1: Installing the Launcher on Your Computer

To run the PinPoint 2000 Trainers or Evaluations, you must first install the Launcher program.

To Install the Launcher

1 Start Windows on your computer.

2 Be sure that Office 2000 has already been installed to your computer with a **Full Custom Install**. If this is not the case, perform this installation before you continue with step 3.

3 Insert the **PinPoint 2000 CD** into your **CD-ROM** drive.

4 From the Start menu, select Run.

5 In the Run dialog box, enter the path to the **SETUP.EXE** file found in the root directory of the CD. For example, if your CD-ROM drive has been assigned the letter **D**, you would enter **D:\setup.exe** as shown in **Figure A.1**.
Note: If your CD-ROM drive has been assigned a letter different from D, use that letter to begin the path in this dialog box. For example, if your CD-ROM drive has been assigned the drive letter E, enter E:\setup.exe in this dialog box.

6 Click OK.

7 When the **Setup Type** screen appears, select **Normal Single-User Installation**.

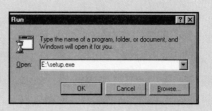

Figure A.1

❽ Click Next to continue.

You are given a choice concerning the location of the PinPoint 2000 folder

The recommended location of the PinPoint 2000 folder is shown as the default. (*Note:* Two files that initially take up only 109 KB will be placed in this folder.)

If you prefer to use a different path or name for the `PinPoint 2000` folder click the Browse button and navigate to the location you prefer, or rename the folder.

❾ Click Next to continue.

After the installation is complete, the PinPoint 2000 program group window appears.

❿ Close the PinPoint 2000 program group window.

If the installation has occurred correctly, the following changes have been made to your computer:

- A PinPoint 2000 shortcut icon has been installed that will enable you to run the Launcher program via the Start menu.

- A new folder called PinPoint 2000 has been created on the hard drive of your computer (see Figure A.2).

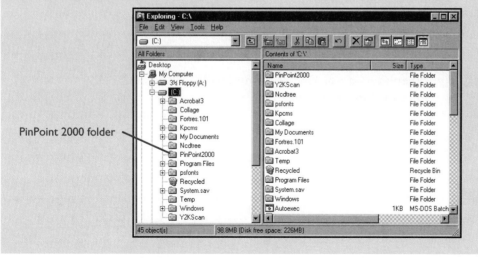

Figure A.2

PinPoint 2000 folder

The PinPoint 2000 folder contains:

- An empty database file, CC_Admin.mdb. As you run Trainers and Evaluations, this file records your performance.

- A small file, Uninst.isu, that is used for removing PinPoint 2000 from your computer.

Note: If your computer is configured so that file extensions are turned off, the CC_Admin.mdb file will appear without the .mdb extension.

Some files necessary for database access have been added to the Windows\System folder.

Lesson 2: Preparing to Run the PinPoint 2000 Launcher

Before running the PinPoint 2000 Launcher, it is necessary to initialize each of the Microsoft applications (Word 2000, Excel 2000, PowerPoint 2000, and Access 2000) at least one time. If you have already used each of these applications, you can ignore this section.

Initializing these applications enables PinPoint training and testing to run in a more stable environment. You will need to provide user information in the first application that you run.

Preparing to Run PinPoint 2000

1. **Start Microsoft Word 2000.**
2. **When the User Name dialog box appears type your Name and Initials.**
3. **Click OK to confirm.**
4. **When the Word window is completely set up and ready for use, you can close the application.**
5. **Start Microsoft Excel 2000.**
6. **When the Excel window is completely set up and ready for use, you can close the application.**
7. **Start Microsoft PowerPoint 2000.**
8. **When the PowerPoint window is completely set up and ready for use, you may close the application.**
9. **Start Microsoft Access 2000.**
10. **When the Access window is completely set up and ready for use, you can close the application.**

You are ready to run the Launcher program and begin Trainers and Evaluations.

Lesson 3: Starting the PinPoint 2000 Launcher

The Launcher program enables you to run Trainers and Evaluations. It also gives you a performance report after you have taken a Trainer or Evaluation.

To Start the PinPoint 2000 Launcher

1 **Select Start, Programs, PinPoint 2000, PinPoint 2000 (see Figure A.3).**

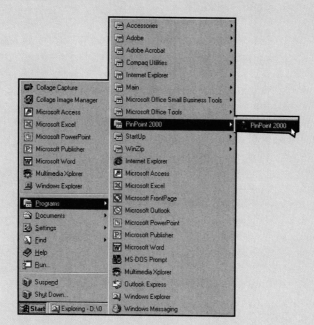

Figure A.3

2 **Enter a user name and password (see Figure A.4).**

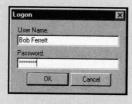

Figure A.4

The user name and password can consist of any characters, as long as neither of them exceeds 50 characters. They are NOT case sensitive: It doesn't matter if you use upper- or lowercase letters.

If more than one person will be running PinPoint 2000 from your computer, each person must enter a different user name. However, passwords can be the same.

3 **Click OK in the Logon dialog box.**
If you are logging on for the first time, you need to enter some information in the User Information dialog box.

4 **Enter the requested information and click OK.**
The PinPoint 2000 Launcher screen appears (see Figure A.5).

continues ▶

To Start the PinPoint 2000 Launcher   (continued)

Figure A.5

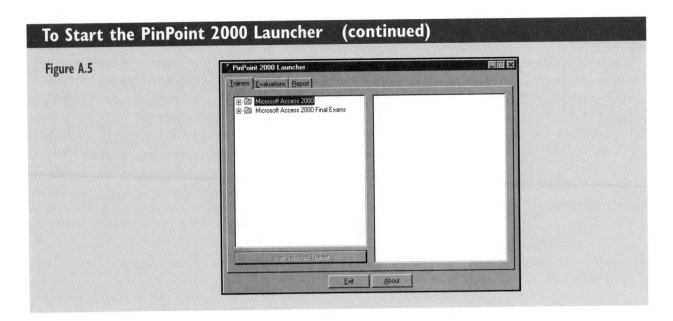

You are now ready to run PinPoint Trainers and Evaluations.

Lesson 4: Starting PinPoint 2000 Trainers and Evaluations

To Start Trainers and Evaluations

1 From the PinPoint Launcher, click the Trainers tab if you want to start a Trainer, or the Evaluations tab if you want to start an Evaluation (see Figure A.6).

Figure A.6

Trainer tab

Evaluation tab

Report tab

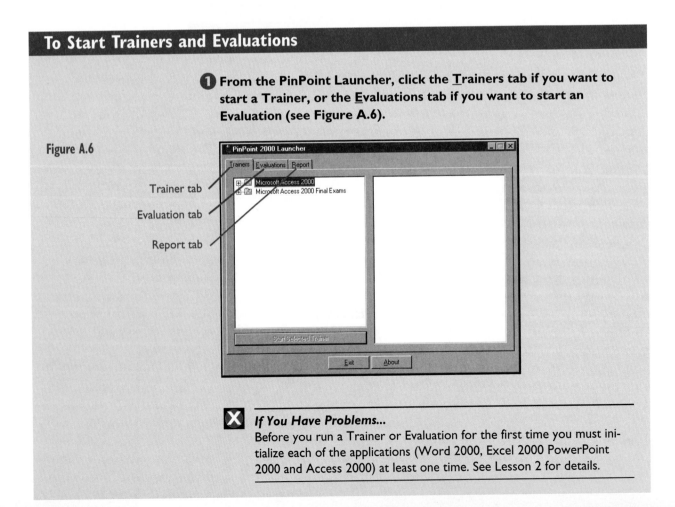

X **If You Have Problems...**
Before you run a Trainer or Evaluation for the first time you must initialize each of the applications (Word 2000, Excel 2000 PowerPoint 2000 and Access 2000) at least one time. See Lesson 2 for details.

② **Click the plus sign (+) to open an application's modules and exams. The plus sign becomes a minus sign (–), as shown in Figure A.7.**

Click here to open
and close the modules
and exams

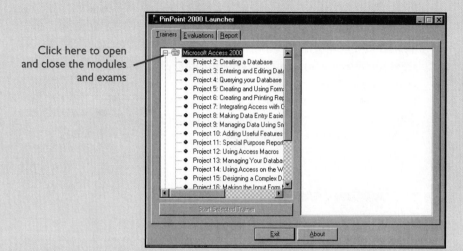

Figure A.7

③ **Select the module or exam that you want to run.**

The individual tasks that are part of the Trainer or Evaluation appear in the pane on the right.

④ **If you are running a Trainer without an Evaluation, you can select or deselect individual training tasks by clicking on the box beside the task name (see Figure A.8).**

The tasks that are deselected will not run during the Trainer. This enables you to adjust your training to include only those tasks that you do not already know how to do.

When running an Evaluation, however, you cannot deselect individual tasks. All tasks will run.

Select or deselect
tasks here

Start Selected
Trainer button

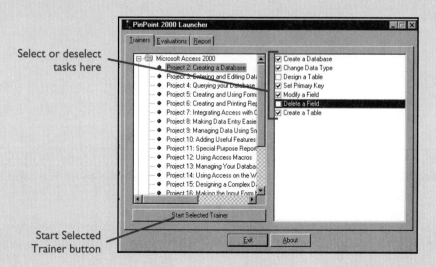

Figure A.8

continues ▶

To Start Trainers and Evaluations (continued)

5 Click Start Selected Trainer **button if you are starting a Trainer.**
Click the Start Selected Evaluation **button if you are starting an**
Evaluation.

6 **When you start the Trainer, you might encounter a warning mes-**
sage instructing you to change your computer's Taskbar settings
(see Figure A.9).

If this message appears, follow its instructions before proceeding. Changing
your taskbar settings in this way is necessary for proper functioning of a
PinPoint Trainer. You can carry out the instructions given without canceling
the box.

Figure A.9

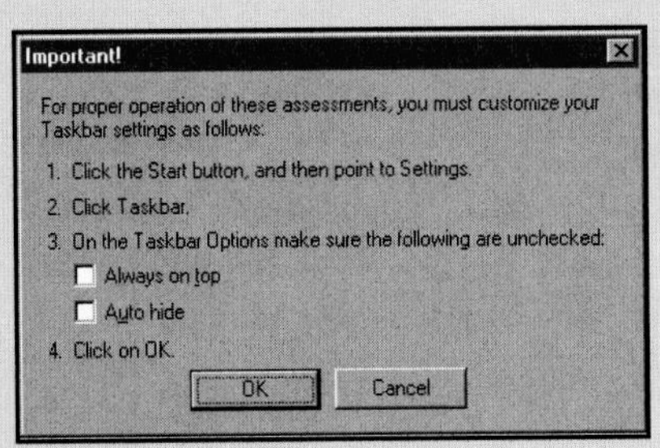

The PinPoint 2000 Launcher dialog box with your name and module selection
appears (see Figure A.10).

Figure A.10

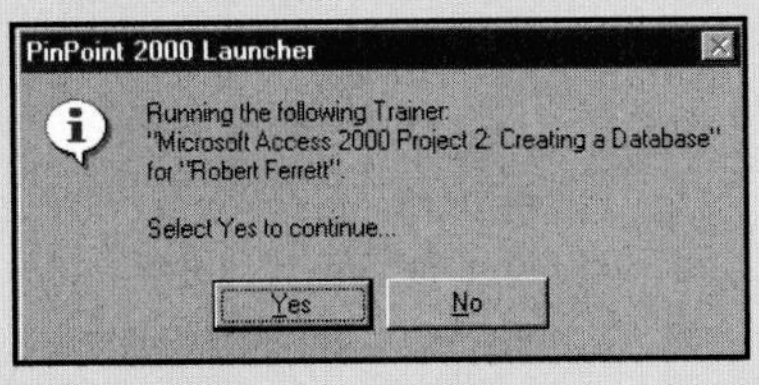

7 **Click Yes to continue.**
The Trainer or Evaluation starts.

Proceed to the next two sections to see how to run Trainers and Evaluations.

Lesson 5: Running a Trainer

This lesson shows you how to run a Trainer. It also details how to handle some of the situations you might encounter during a Trainer.

To Run a Trainer

1 **Once your name and the selected module are displayed, click OK to**
begin the Trainer.
The PinPoint 2000 launcher dialog box appears before a Trainer runs (see
Figure A.11).

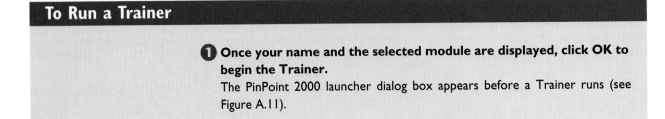

Figure A.11

3 Click Yes to continue.

The first thing you see is an introduction to how all PinPoint 2000 Trainers work. If you want to see the demonstration of how a PinPoint Trainer works and how to use the PinPoint 2000 controls, press any key or click the mouse to continue.

4 Skip through the introduction for now and go directly to a task.

After initializing, the Trainer opens the first selected task.

> **Inside Stuff: Exiting the Introduction**
>
> You can exit the introduction at any time by pressing Esc and moving straight to the training.

The task instructions display in a moveable instruction box that hovers over the application (see Figure A.12).

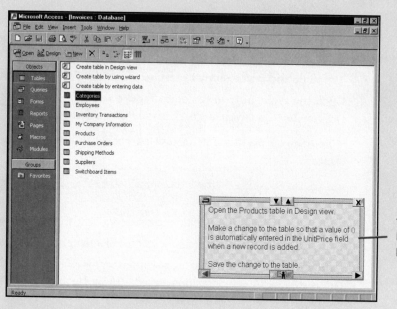

Figure A.12

The instruction box can be moved to different parts of the screen

> **If You Have Problems...**
>
> If the instruction box is blocking your view of something, you can drag it to another part of the screen. To instantly move the box to the other side of the screen, right-click the instruction box.

Notice the PinPoint control buttons that appear on the perimeter of the instruction box. Use these buttons to interact with the Trainer according to your needs (see Figure A.13).

continues ▶

To Run a Trainer   (continued)

Figure A.13

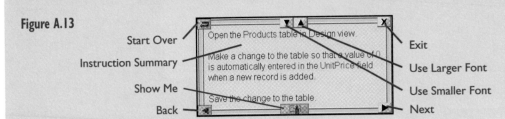

Start Over

Instruction Summary

Show Me

Back

Exit

Use Larger Font

Use Smaller Font

Next

The features of the instruction box in Figure A.13 and their descriptions are listed here:

- The Instruction Summary displays the task to be completed. Instructions remain visible during the task.
- The Start Over button starts the current task again.
- The Back button returns you to the previous task.
- The Show Me button gives you a step-by-step demonstration using a similar example.
- The Use Larger Font and Use Smaller Font buttons enlarge or reduce the size of the box and text.
- The Quit button ends the current training session and returns you to the Launcher.
- The Next button checks a finished task for correct performance and moves you to the next task.

5 **Try to do the task exactly as instructed in the PinPoint instruction box.**

6 **Click the Next button (refer to Figure A.13).**
PinPoint 2000 gives you feedback in the Results dialog box.

Whether you performed the task correctly or not, you now have three choices:

- Click the Show Me button to display a step-by-step demonstration using a similar example.
- Click the Try Task Again button to set up the task so you can attempt it again.
- Click the Next Task button to move on and attempt the next task.

If you click the Show Me button, a demonstration of how to perform a similar task is given. This demonstration, called a Show Me, begins with a summary of the steps required to perform the task.

7 **Press any key or click the mouse to advance the next Show Me box.**
Usually the key concept behind the particular skill is explained during the Show Me.

After the instruction summary (and possibly a key concept), each of the instructions in the summary is explained and demonstrated in detail.

 Inside Stuff: **Exiting Show Me Demonstrations**
If you want to exit from the Show Me demonstration at any point, press Esc to return to the PinPoint task.

During the Show Me demonstration, the mouse pointer moves and text is entered automatically when appropriate to the demonstration, but whenever the description or action is completed the demonstration halts until the user prompts it to continue with either a mouse click or a key stroke.

After the demonstration is complete, you can perform the task yourself.

❽ Continue through the PinPoint Trainer at your own pace, attempting each task and watching Show Me demonstrations when you need help.

When you have finished with the training session, the Trainers screen of the Launcher is visible again. You can see a report of your performance by clicking the Report tab in the Launcher (viewing reports is covered in Lesson 7).

 Inside Stuff: **Exiting Trainers**

You are free to exit from the training at any time by clicking the Exit button (refer to Figure A.13). When you attempt to exit a Trainer before it is finished, you are asked to confirm this decision (see Figure A.14).

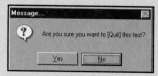

Figure A.14

If you want to exit from the trainer at this point, click Yes.

Lesson 6: Running an Evaluation

This lesson shows you how to run an Evaluation. It also details how to handle some of the situations you might encounter during an Evaluation.

To Run an Evaluation

❶ When you start the Evaluation, you might encounter a warning message instructing you to change your computer's Taskbar settings (refer to Figure A.9).

If this message appears, follow its instructions before proceeding. Changing your taskbar settings in this way is necessary for proper functioning of a PinPoint Trainer. You can carry out the instructions given without canceling the box.

❷ After you have carried out the steps listed, click OK to continue.

The Pinpoint 2000 Launcher dialog box appears before an Evaluation runs (refer to Figure A.11).

❸ Click Yes to continue.

The first thing you see is an introduction to how all PinPoint 2000 Evaluations work. If you want to see the demonstration of how an Evaluation works and how to use the PinPoint 2000 controls, press any key or click the mouse to continue past each screen. If you do not need to see the demonstration, press Esc to go straight to the testing.

continues ▶

To Run an Evaluation (continued)

Like a Trainer, an Evaluation presents you with a task to perform. In an Evaluation, however, the Start Over, Back, and Show Me buttons are all disabled. Therefore, you cannot restart a task, return to a previous task, or run a Show Me demonstration of how to perform the task.

4 After attempting a task, click the Next button to continue to the next task.

Normally, you would attempt all of the tasks in the Evaluation. But if you need to finish early and click the Exit button before you have attempted all of the tasks, the message box in Figure A.14 will display. Click the Yes button if you want to exit the Evaluation and go back to the Launcher program.

5 You can view a report of your performance by clicking the Report tab in the Launcher.

See the next section for details about viewing reports.

Inside Stuff: **What to Avoid While Running Trainers and Evaluations**
Keep the following in mind for PinPoint 2000 Trainers and Evaluations to run properly:

- Only perform actions that the PinPoint task instructions ask you to perform.

- Do not exit from the Microsoft Office 2000 application in which you are training or testing unless you are told to do so.

- Do not close the example document (the document that PinPoint opens for you when you begin a task) unless you are told to do so.

- Do not run other programs (such as email, Internet browsers, virus shields, system monitors, and so on) at the same time as running PinPoint, unless you are asked to do so.

- Do not change views in one of the Office 2000 applications unless you are asked to do so.

- Do not change the way your Windows operating system or Office 2000 applications are configured by default.

- Do not turn off your computer in the middle of a PinPoint Trainer or Evaluation. Instead, first exit from the Trainer or Evaluation, and then turn off your computer.

Lesson 7: Viewing Reports in the Launcher

After you have taken at least one PinPoint 2000 Trainer or Evaluation, you can view detailed reports at any time concerning your performance on any of the modules that you have taken.

To View Reports in the Launcher

1 **If the Launcher is not running, click Start, Programs, PinPoint 2000, PinPoint 2000 to run it. Then log on.**

2 **Click the Report tab.**
The Report screen appears (see Figure A.15).

Click the Report tab to view a detailed report of your performance

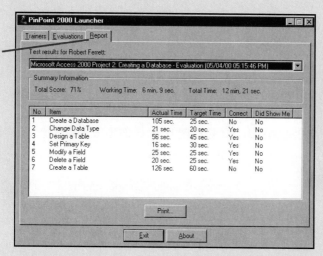

Figure A.15

The very last Trainer or Evaluation that you ran displays onscreen. The information displayed in the Report screen is as follows:

■ *Total Score*—The percentage of the correctly performed tasks out of the total number of tasks set to run.

■ *Working Time*—The total time you actually spent working on all of the tasks in the Trainer or Evaluation.

■ *Total Time*—The total time you spent running the entire Trainer or Evaluation.

■ *Item*—The name of the task.

■ *Actual Time*—The time you took to perform the task.

■ *Target Time*—A reasonable amount of time required to perform the task by an efficient method.

■ *Correct*—Displays Yes if you performed the task correctly; No if you did not.

■ *Did Show-Me*—Displays Yes if you ran a Show Me demonstration for that task; No if you did not.

Note: A blank or dotted line running through the task line, or N/A, indicate that the task was not taken.

3 **If you want to print a report, click the Print button.**

4 **If you want to see a report for a Trainer or Evaluation that you took previously, select it from the Test results for <*your name*> drop-down list.**
The reports are listed in the order in which they were taken.

Note: You will see only your own reports on the Reports screen and not the reports for anyone else using PinPoint on your computer.

Inside Stuff: User History

An important feature of the PinPoint 2000 Launcher is its capability to keep track of your history of running Trainers and Evaluations. The Launcher uses your history to reconfigure a Trainer each successive time you run it. To "re-configure" means to change the tasks that will run.

The Launcher does not reconfigure an Evaluation the same way it does a Trainer. No matter which tasks you have performed correctly in the past (on either a Trainer or Evaluation), all tasks are automatically selected to be run when you attempt to take an Evaluation.

Lesson 8: Recovering from a Crash During a Trainer or Evaluation

If your computer crashes while you are running a Trainer or Evaluation, all the work you have already done is not wasted. You do not need to start the Trainer or Evaluation over again from the beginning. To recover from a crash during a Trainer or Evaluation, follow these simple instructions.

To Recover from a Crash

1 **Reboot your computer.**

2 **Start the Launcher again and log on as usual.**

3 **When a message like the one in Figure A.16 appears, close the Office application you were working on (if it's still running in the background) by clicking the Close button in the top right corner of the application window.**

Figure A.16

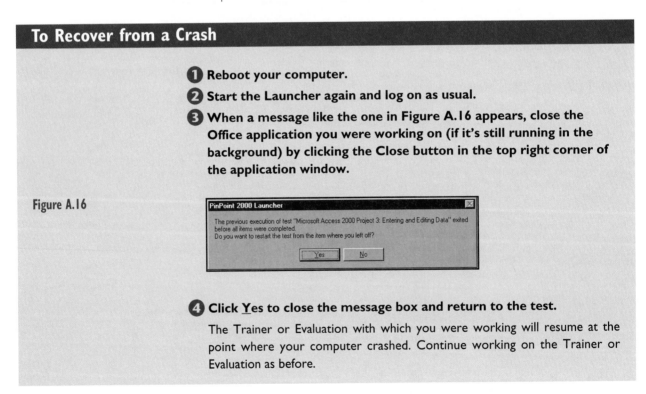

4 **Click Yes to close the message box and return to the test.**

The Trainer or Evaluation with which you were working will resume at the point where your computer crashed. Continue working on the Trainer or Evaluation as before.

Lesson 9: Removing PinPoint 2000

When you have finished training and testing with PinPoint 2000, you may want to remove the Launcher program from your computer. PinPoint 2000 can be removed using the procedure for removing most other applications from your computer.

To Remove PinPoint 2000

1 **From the Start menu, select Settings, Control Panel.**

2 **Double-click the Add/Remove Programs icon.**
The Add/Remove Programs Properties dialog box displays.

3 **Select PinPoint 2000.**

4 **Click the Add/Remove button.**

5 **Confirm the removal of PinPoint 2000 by clicking Yes in the dialog box.**

6 **If the Remove Shared File? dialog box appears, click the Yes To All button (see Figure A.17).**

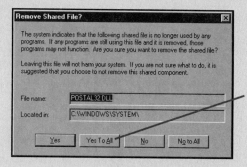

Figure A.17

Click here to uninstall PinPoint 2000

7 **When the Remove Programs From Your Computer dialog box reports `Uninstall successfully completed`, click OK.**

8 **Click OK in the Add/Remove Programs Properties dialog box.**

9 **Close the Control Panel window.**
PinPoint 2000 has now been completely removed from your computer.

Summary

PinPoint 2000 is a very valuable tool for preparing yourself for a MOUS Exam. You've learned how to install and start the PinPoint Launcher. You can now run Trainers and Evaluations, and view a report of their results. You also know what to avoid while running Trainers and Evaluations. You've seen how to recover if PinPoint crashes. And finally, you've learned how to uninstall PinPoint when you no longer need it. You are now

Preparing for MOUS Certification

This appendix gives you information that you need regarding the certification exams—how to register, what is covered in the tests, how the tests are administered, and so on. Because this information may change, be sure to visit www.mous.net for the latest updates.

What This Book Offers

This text is certified for both levels of certification:

- Core—You are able to manage a wide range of real world tasks efficiently.
- Expert—In addition to the everyday tasks at the Core level, you are able to handle complex assignments and have a thorough understanding of a program's advanced features.

In addition to the Core and Expert levels, Microsoft now offers a Master certification, which indicates that you have a comprehensive understanding of Microsoft Office 2000 and many of its advanced features. A Master certification requires students to successfully pass all five of the required exams: Word, Excel, PowerPoint, Access and Outlook.

Each exam includes a list of tasks you may be asked to perform. The lessons in this book identify these required tasks with an icon in the margin. You can also review the MOUS Skill Guide in the front of this book to become familiar with these required tasks.

In addition to these icons, this book contains various study aids that not only help you pass the test, but also teach you how the software functions. You can use this book in a class-room or lab setting, or you can work through each project on your own using the PinPoint CD-ROM. You don't have to move through the book from front to back as each project stands on its own. Each project is broken down into lessons, which are then broken down into step-by-step instructions.

The PinPoint CD-ROM includes Project Review Tests for each MOUS Exam skill set. The coverage has two parts: a Task and a Show Me. The Task requires you to do something, (for example, format a document) and the Show Me demonstrates how to perform that task. In addition, each PinPoint has a practice test that mirrors the actual MOUS exams.

Follow the steps within each of the lessons, and use the PinPoint software as an evaluation of your comprehension. If you get stuck, be sure to use the Show Me demonstration.

Registering for and Taking the Exam

All MOUS exams are administered by a MOUS Authorized Testing Center (ATC). Most MOUS ATCs require pre-registration. To pre-register contact a local ATC directly. You can find a center near you by visiting the MOUS Web site at www.mous.net. Some ATCs accept walk-in examination candidates, allowing on-the-spot registration and examination. Be sure to check with a specific ACT to make certain of their registration policy.

The exam is not written and there are no multiple choice or true-false questions. You perform the required tasks on a computer running the live Microsoft application. A typical exam takes 45 to 60 minutes to complete. You must work through each task in the exam as quickly as you can.

All examination data is encrypted, and the examination process is closely monitored so your test scores are completely confidential. Examination results are provided only to the candidate and to Microsoft.

The Day of the Exam

Bring the following items with you to the testing center on exam day:

- Picture ID—driver's license or passport
- Your MOUS identification number (if you have take a previous MOUS certification exam)
- ATC Student ID, if applicable

At the exam center, you can expect to first complete the candidate information section, which provides the information necessary to complete your MOUS certificate.

After confirming your ID, the administrator will seat you at the test computer, log you onto the test system, and open your test module. You are now ready to begin.

To start the test, click the "Start Test" button and you're ready to begin your certification exam.

The Exam Itself

Instructions are displayed in a separate window on the screen. You can close the instruction window by clicking on it. You can restore it by clicking "Instructions" on the test information bar at the bottom of the screen. Read the test instructions carefully. Once you have started, a box in the bottom right corner of the screen indicates the question on which you are currently working. (For example, "question 3 of 50".)

If anything abnormal happens during the exam, or if the application "crashes," stop immediately and contact the administrator. The administrator will restart the test from where you left off. You will not be penalized any time for this.

When you have completed your exam, the computer will calculate your score. The scoring process takes a short time, and you will be notified onscreen whether you passed or failed. You may then ask the administrator to give you a printed report.

If you complete the exam successfully, your MOUS certificate will be delivered within 2-3 weeks.

General Tips

Unlike earlier MOUS exams, the results of the Office 2000 MOUS exams are expressed as a value on a 1000-point scale, rather than a percentage.

Each activity or question on the Office 2000 MOUS exams is comprised of several individually scored subtasks. A candidates's score is derived from the number of subtasks successfully completed and the "weight" or difficulty assigned to each.

Pay close attention to how each question is worded. Answers must be precise, resolving the question exactly as asked.

You can use any combination of menus, toolbars and shortcut keys to complete each assigned task. Answers are scored based on the result, not the method you use or the time taken to complete each required task. Extra keystrokes or mouse clicks will not count against your score as long as you achieve the correct result within the time limit given.

Remember that the overall test is timed. While spending a lot of time on an individual answer will not adversely affect the scoring of that particular question, taking too long may not leave you with enough time to complete the entire test.

Answers are either right or wrong. You do not get credit for partial answers.

Important! Check to make sure you have entirely completed each question before clicking the NEXT TASK button. Once you press the NEXT TASK button, you will not be able to return to that question. A question will be scored as wrong if it is not completed properly before moving to the next question.

Save your Results Page that prints at the end of the exam. It is your confirmation that you passed the exam.

Take note of these cautions:

- DON'T leave dialog boxes, Help menus, toolbars, or menus open.
- DON'T leave tables, boxes, or cells "active or highlighted" unless instructed to do so.
- DON'T click the NEXT TASK button until you have "completely" answered the current question.

Lastly, be sure to visit the mous.net Web site for specific information on the Office 2000 exams, more testing tips, and to download a free demo of the exams.

Glossary

All key terms appearing in this book (in bold italic) are listed alphabetically in this Glossary for easy reference. If you want to learn more about a feature or concept, turn to the page reference shown after its definition. You can also use the Index to find the term's other significant occurrences.

actions   Access-defined functions that perform a database task in a macro. [pg. 298]

archive table   A table designed to hold inactive or completed records to remove them from an actively used table. [pg. 324]

arguments   Values needed for a macro to perform its function. [pg. 298]

AutoCorrect   A tool that enables you to enter shortcuts for longer words or phrases, or to correct common typos. [pg. 458]

AutoForm   A form that is created automatically by Access that includes all the fields in a table. [pg. 102]

AutoReport   A report created automatically by Access that includes all the fields in a table. [pg. 128]

bitmap format   A format where images are stored by recording individual bits of information for each tiny portion of the screen. [pg. 285]

browser   A program that enables you to view Web pages on the Internet. Examples are Internet Explorer and Netscape Navigator. [pg. 161]

calculated field   A field that displays the result of an expression rather than displaying stored values. [pg. 86]

cascade   A table relationships option that enables you to change one field, which then automatically changes related fields in other tables. [pg. 208]

cascade delete   To delete related data in a second table by deleting a record in the first table. The tables must be joined. [pg. 446]

cascade update   To change data in a second table by making a data change in the first table. The tables must be joined. [pg. 446]

clipboard   A temporary storage location for whatever you have copied or cut from your document. [pg. 54]

column selector   The thin gray line above the field name in Query Design view. When you click the column selector, the whole column is selected. [pg. 77]

combo box   A combination of a text box and a list box; also another name for a lookup drop-down box. [pg. 205]

compact   To reduce the size of a file. [pg. 329]

comparison operators   Used to compare values to see if a field contains values that are greater than, equal to, or less than another value. You can also use comparison operators to search for values that are between two other values. [pg. 83]

control   Any object on a form or report, such as a text box, label, line, checkbox, or option button. [pg. 107]

ControlTip   A pop-up tip that can be added to a control; similar to a ScreenTip. [pg. 416]

criteria   A test or set of conditions that limits the records included in a query. [pg. 79]

criterion   A single condition in a query that limits the records. [pg. 79]

crosstab   A query used for summarizing data from large databases that summarizes the relationship between two (or more) fields. [pg. 482]

current record indicator   An arrow in the record selector that shows which record is currently active. [pg. 50]

data access page   A special type of Web page that has been designed for viewing and working with data from the Internet. [pg. 161]

data type   A definition of the kind of data that can be entered into a field. [pg. 27]

database   A program that allows you to store, retrieve, analyze, and print large amounts of information. [pg. 2]

Database window   A window that displays a list of the table, query, form, report, macro, and module objects that comprise a database. [pg. 5]

Datasheet view   The row-and-column view you use when you enter or edit records in a table. [pg. 24]

default value   A value that automatically appears in a field of a new record. [pg. 194]

delimiter   A character that separates fields in a text file. Common delimiters are tabs, commas, semicolons, and spaces. [pg. 170]

design grid   Used to define the conditions of a query. You can specify fields, sort order, and criteria to be used to search your database. [pg. 72]

Design view   The view in which the elements of an object can be created, included, modified, or controlled. In the Design view of a table you see columns for the field name, data type, and description, as well as properties specified for each field. [pg. 24]

dynaset   A subset of records created as a result of a query. [pg. 70]

encryption   Use of an encoding method to prevent unauthorized use. [pg. 537]

enforce reference integrity   A choice in a table relationship that prevents orphan (unmatched) records in the many tables. [pg. 208]

equi-join   Another name for an **inner join**. [pg. 381]

excluding operators   Operators used in a query to exclude records that meet the criterion. [pg. 525]

expand indicator   A plus or minus symbol to the left of a field to indicate that related information from another table is attached to that record. [pg. 211]

expression   A combination of field names and operators that produces a result, such as performing calculations, displaying built-in functions, or setting limits. You can include expressions in reports and other Access objects, such as macros. [pg. 83]

Expression Builder   A program that helps the user create formulas for many Access uses. [pg. 184]

field   A single category of data or information; the column headings in a database table. [pg. 2]

field label   See **label**

field list   A list of the fields from a table. [pg. 72]

field text box   A placeholder for the contents of a field in a database. Field text boxes show the actual data that has been entered into a table. [pg. 109]

fifth normal form   There are no duplicate non-key fields. [pg. 385]

Filter by Form   A searching feature that enables you to type the desired value(s) into one or more fields on a blank form and then find all of the other records that match those values. [pg. 514]

Filter by Selection   A searching feature that enables you to select the desired value in a field and then find all of the other records that match that value. [pg. 514]

Find Duplicate Query Wizard   Creates a query that finds records with duplicate field values in a single table or query. [pg. 221]

Find Unmatched Query Wizard   Creates a query that finds records in one table that have no related records in another table. [pg. 221]

first normal form   The cells in the table must hold a single value; there are no repeating groups or arrays; all entries in the same column are of the same kind; each column has a unique name; the order of the columns is insignificant; no two rows are identical; and their order is insignificant. [pg. 385]

foreign key   The corresponding field in another table that is linked to the primary key; the field on the many side of a one-to-many relationship. [pg. 207]

form   A type of object you can use to enter, edit, and view records. Think of a form as a fill-in-the-blanks screen. [pg. 102]

form detail   The main part of a form, in which the records are displayed. [pg. 107]

form footer   An area at the bottom of a form containing controls such as labels, dates, or page numbers. [pg. 107]

form header   An area at the top of a form containing controls such as labels, dates, or graphics. [pg. 107]

format   The way data is displayed. [pg. 176]

Format Painter   A tool that enables you to copy the formatting of a control and paste the format onto another control. [pg. 407]

fourth normal form   There are no one-to-many relationships between the primary key field and another non-key field in the same table. [pg. 385]

FTP   File Transfer Protocol—A method for transferring files between computers over a network or the Internet. [pg. 369]

HTML   The standard programming language used for writing documents that can be viewed on the Internet by many different browsers. The acronym stands for Hypertext Markup Language. [pg. 357]

hyperlink   A connection between one document and another document stored on the user's personal computer, local area network (LAN), or the World Wide Web. [pg. 348]

index   A location guide built by Access for all primary key fields that helps speed up searching and sorting for those fields. Indexes can also be created for other fields, as long as they are not OLE or Memo fields. [pg. 31]

indexed field   A field for which Access builds a location guide; an index speeds up sorting or searching on a field. [pg. 189]

inner join   Only the records that match from both tables; also known as an **equi-join**. [pg. 381]

input mask   A data entry structure that forces data entry into a selected format. [pg. 181]

Internet   The worldwide computer communication network that is based on open standards for operating systems and communication. [pg. 348]

intersection table   A table that is used as an intermediary between two other tables to make a many-to-many relationship possible by creating two one-to-many relationships. It contains the key fields from both tables as foreign keys. [pg. 382]

intranet   A communication network within a company that uses the same software and standards as the Internet. [pg. 348]

join   The manner in which the common fields between two tables are associated. [pg. 379]

label   The field name attached to a field text box in a form or report. It can also be a description placed in a label box on a form or report. In either case a label is not bound to a table. [pg. 108]

LAN   local area network—A network consisting of a group of personal computers or workstations that are connected through a computer that coordinates their communications with each other and the outside world. [pg. 348]

landscape orientation   Horizontal orientation of a printed page. [pg. 129]

launch   To run a Microsoft Office program. [pg. 4]

left outer join   All of the records in the table at the left plus the matching records in the table on the right. In a one-to-many relationship, it is assumed that the "one" table is on the left. [pg. 381]

list box   A data entry list that looks up valid entries from a table, query, or source list, and does not allow the user to type in new data. [pg. 238]

macro   Pre-defined command that can be used to automate a wide range of tasks in a database such as opening and closing forms or reports, printing information, or finding records. [pg. 298]

Macro Builder   A tool that makes the macro creation process easier. [pg. 422]

mail merge   A word processing feature that allows you to customize documents using information from a database table. [pg. 153]

many-to-many   A type of relationship where a record in one table may be related to more than one record in a second table and a record in the second table may be related to more than one record in the first table. [pg. 382]

MDE file   A file saved in a protected format so that the user can use the database, but not change any forms, reports, or Visual Basic code. [pg. 345]

Name AutoCorrect   A feature that automatically updates related parts of the database when an object or field is renamed. [pg. 458]

normalize   Applying design rules to table structure. [pg. 384]

Null value   A field with no data entered into it. It is not the same as an entry of zero. [pg. 90]

object   A general term for the components of an Access database, including tables, queries, forms, reports, pages, macros, and modules. [pg. 2]

Object Linking and Embedding (OLE)   A set of standards that enables you to insert objects, such as pictures or spreadsheets, from one document created with one application into documents created with another application. [pg. 27]

Office Assistant   The Help feature that answers questions. [pg. 11]

Office Clipboard   Similar to the Windows clipboard, but it can hold up to 12 items from any of the Office programs. [pg. 56]

Office Links   A set of tools that enables you to create a mail merge, report data using Word, and analyze data using Excel. [pg. 458]

one-to-many   A type of relationship where a record in one table may be related to more than one record in a second table. [pg. 206]

parameter query   A query that uses a message box to ask the user for input whenever the query is run. The parameter, or value, entered by the user acts as a criterion that limits the records displayed. [pg. 514]

password   A word or other string of characters that is required in order to gain full or partial access to a multi-user computer system or its data resources. [pg. 534]

pencil icon   An icon that looks like a pencil. It is displayed in the record selector when you are editing a record in Datasheet view indicating that the current changes have not yet been saved. [pg. 52]

Performance Analyzer   A tool that looks at database objects and gives recommendations, suggestions, and ideas for improving their performance. [pg. 458]

PivotTable   An interactive form that is similar to a crosstab query, showing the relationship between fields in a spreadsheet-like format. [pg. 510]

placeholder   A character used to reserve a spot for a character in an input mask. [pg. 182]

portrait orientation   Vertical orientation of a printed page. This is by far the most common page orientation. [pg. 129]

primary key   A field that contains a unique value for each record and is used to identify the record. [pg. 31]

properties   The characteristics of a screen element. For example, a number has such properties as number of decimal places, format, font size, and others. Also, the characteristics of a file. [pg. 4]

query   One of the objects in a database, queries are used to sort, search, and limit the data to just those records that you need to examine. [pg. 5]

read-only   A database file that has been opened but cannot be changed. This occurs when you open a database file on a CD-ROM. [pg. 2]

record   A group of data pertaining to one event, transaction, or person. The categories of information in a record are called fields. [pg. 2]

record selector   The gray area to the left of a record. It indicates whether the record is selected or being edited. Clicking on it selects the whole record. [pg. 49]

referential integrity   A matching field is required to exist in the joined table. [pg. 384]

relationship   The connection between two tables. [pg. 31]

report   Database objects that are designed to print and/or summarize selected fields. [pg. 128]

right outer join   All of the records in the table at the right plus the matching records in the table on the left. In a one-to-many relationship, it is assumed that the "many" table is on the right. [pg. 381]

row selector   The gray area to the left of a field in Design view. Clicking a box in this area selects the entire row. [pg. 32]

sans serif   A typeface without serifs. [pg. 268]

ScreenTip   The name of a button that pops up when you hold the pointer over the button. [pg. 9]

second normal form   The table is in first normal form and all the non-key fields in the table relate to the primary key, which is made of a combination of two or more fields. [pg. 385]

Section Bar   A bar at the top of a section in the Design view of a report. [pg. 294]

select query   Lists data that meets conditions set by the user. [pg. 72]

selection handles   Small squares that appear at the corners and on the edges of a box that can be used to change the size of the box. [pg. 111]

serif   A horizontal line finishing off the main strokes of a letter, as at the top and bottom of the letter "M." [pg. 268]

share level security   A password is required to open the database. [pg. 534]

SQL   Pronounced "Sequel," SQL is an acronym for Structured Query Language. It is a programming language that has been standardized by the American National Standards Institute (ANSI) and is promoted for use with relational databases. SQL statements written by the Microsoft Access program facilitate its ability to communicate with other database programs. [pg. 526]

startup parameters   The settings used to control the way a database is opened and what features are available to the user. [pg. 539]

static HTML pages   Web pages that are not interactive. [pg. 357]

subdatasheet   A secondary datasheet in a table that shows related information from another (related) table. [pg. 211]

subform   A form within a form. A subform shows the "many" records related to the selected record in the primary form. [pg. 234]

subreport   A report placed within another (main) report showing data from another table that is related to the selected record from the main part of the report. [pg. 482]

switchboard   A special purpose form that contains buttons that are used to open forms for data input, editing, or review as well as reports, tables, or other database objects. [pg. 298]

tab order   The order in which the insertion point jumps from field to field on a form. [pg. 113]

table   One of the objects in an Access database, tables store data in row-and-column format and are the foundation of the database. [pg. 2]

Table Analyzer   A tool that looks for duplications in fields and splits tables to make them more efficient. [pg. 458]

text qualifier   Single or double quotation marks that surround text entries in a delimited text file. [pg. 326]

third normal form   The table is in second normal form and has no transitive dependencies. [pg. 385]

unbound object   An object not connected to an underlying table. [pg. 273]

update query   A type of action query that enables you to replace all or part of a field, or alter the contents of a numeric field by performing calculations. [pg. 432]

URL   A type of Internet address. The acronym stands for Uniform Resource Locator. [pg. 349]

user-level security   A way of controlling access to a database by individual user. This is a more sophisticated security procedure for a network than share-level security. [pg. 539]

validation rule   An expression that Access uses to check the data entered into a field. [pg. 184]

validation text   The text that is displayed when data that doesn't match a validation rule is entered into a field. [pg. 184]

Web browser   A software application used to view and interact with sites on the World Wide Web. Two popular browsers are Netscape Navigator and Microsoft Internet Explorer. [pg. 348]

What's This?   The Help feature that describes parts of the screen. When you click on a screen feature with the What's This? pointer (a question mark), a window opens which describes that screen feature. [pg. 11]

wildcard   A symbol that is used to help search for unspecified data. There are several different wildcards that can be used in a search. [pg. 85]

World Wide Web   A graphical interface that links sites on the Internet and enables a user to easily jump from one site to another. [pg. 348]

Index

A

Access. *See also* databases
  closing, 15
  files, 8
  new features, 19
  saving as, 328-329
  tools, 66-67
  windows, 8-9
actions, 298
Add mode, 310
Address Book
  closing, 6
  Database window, 8-9
  opening, 4-6
  tables
    closing, 8
    opening, 6-7
Align Left command (Format menu), 138
aligning text, 411-413
Analyze It With Excel option, 472
analyzing
  databases, 465-467, 475
  Excel, Office links, 471-473, 476
  serial numbers, 451
  tables, 461-465, 475
And operator, 83
ANSI (American National Standards Institute), 525
Answer Wizard, 12, 329
appending records, creating queries, 335-336, 343
applications
  Excel. *See* Excel
  Word. *See* Word
Archive Setup Query, modifying, 333-334, 343
archive tables
  records
    appending, 335-336, 343
    deleting, 333-334, 343
  queries, creating, 331-333, 343
arguments, 298
assigning passwords, 534-536, 546
asterisks (*), 99

B

attaching macros to forms, 422
AutoCorrect, 67
  customizing, 458-461
  deleting, 461
  exceptions, configuring, 461
  Name AutoCorrect, 468-471
AutoForm, 102, 391
  creating, 102, 104, 119
  tab order, modifying, 249-250, 260
automatically filling fields, 243-245
AutoReport, 128, 491
AutoReport Wizard, 131
average function, 292-293

background colors, 404-406, 425-426
backing up
  Export feature, 324-326, 328
  saving. *See* saving
Between operator, 529
bitmaps, 285
border colors, 404-406
boxes
  combo, 205, 241-242
  list, creating, 238-240
  text, resizing Computer Type, 240
breaks
  forms, 122
  grouped records, 280-282
browsers, Web
  databases, interacting, 164-165, 169-170
  viewing HTML, 348, 360-362
buttons
  adding, 419-420
  colors, 404-406
  deleting, 420
  editing, 430
  macros
    adding as, 429
    executing, 305-308
  Run, 438
  switchboard, executing queries, 337-338

C

calculated controls, 262
calculated fields
  headers/footers, 282-283, 285, 291
  reports, creating, 271-276
calculating
  expressions, 439-442
  fields
    creating, 453-454
    Office links, 471-473, 476
    queries, 86-88, 98
  grouped data, 484
  null values, 90
  queries, 96
  reports, adding, 137
  Total function, 90-92
  update queries, 442
  user input parameters, 530
CanGrow property, 294
captions, 99
cascade deleting, 208, 446-448
cascade updates, 208, 452
charts
  editing, 498-502
  Excel, creating, 502, 511
  forms, creating as, 496-498, 506
checking spelling, 476
Choose Builder dialog box, 303, 422
Clipboard, 54-56. *See also* copying
Clippit. *See* Office Assistant
Close command (File menu), 18
closing
  Access, 15
  Address Book, 6, 8
  confirmation dialog boxes, 338
  databases, 15, 18
  files, 6-8
  forms, 107, 298-299
Color dialog box, 412
colors
  control backgrounds, 425-426
  fields, 413
  modifying, 404-406, 411-413

Column Width command (Format menu), 58

columns

freezing, 65

hiding, 56-58, 547-548

Lookup, creating, 191-194, 198-200

resizing, 56-57

selectors, 77

unhiding, 547-548

combining reports, 492

combo boxes, 205

entries, searching, 241-242

forms, adding, 260

Command Button Wizard, 319

command buttons, 319

commands

Edit menu

Find, 105, 537

Primary Key, 32

Replace, 66

Select Record, 55

Undo, 38, 53, 105

File menu

Close, 18

Export, 340, 358, 473

Get External Data, 158, 514

Import, 158

New, 26

Open, 18

Page Setup, 129, 255

Print, 94, 130, 168, 257

Print Relationships, 392

Save, 107

Save As, 4, 31, 80

Format menu

Align Left, 138

Cells, 167

Column Width, 58

Hide Columns, 57-58

Size To Tallest, 138

Size To Widest, 138

Unhide Columns, 57

Insert menu (Subdatasheet), 212

New menu (Form Wizard), 243

Tools menu

Analyze, 462

AutoCorrect, 459

Database Utilities, 313

Office Links, 472

Options, 9, 415, 542

Replication, 329

Security, 536

Startup, 540

View menu

Clipboard, 56

Header/Footer, 114

Options, 3

Table Design, 37

Toolbars, 37, 156

Windows menu (Tile Vertically), 337

compacting files, 329-330, 342

comparison operators, 83-84, 524-525

compound filters, creating, 531

Computer Type text box, resizing, 240

concatenation operators, 531-532

conditional formats, 179-181

conditions

macros, configuring, 321

queries, adding, 508

configuring

AutoCorrect, 461

calculated fields, 271-276, 453-454

cascade updates, 452

charts

as forms, 496-498, 506

Excel, 502, 511

colors, 404-406

columns, 56-58

compound filters, 531

conditional formats, 179-181

crosstab queries

multiple tables, 485-486, 505-506

row headers, 509

databases, 24-26, 42-43, 176-178, 197

Database Wizard, 45

deleting redundant fields, 384-387

documenting design, 392

Format Painter, 407-408

output, 372-374

separating fields, 374-378

testing, 388-392

defaults, 542, 544

forms, 234-237, 421

labels (reports), 149

list boxes, 238-240

macros

closing forms, 298-299

conditions, 321

Macro window, 317-318

opening forms, 302-305

opening switchboard forms, 314-315

printing macros, 299-301

mailing labels, 266-271, 289

margins, 255

multiple controls, 409-411

multiple-page HTML documents, 368

one-to-many relationships, 516-517

PivotTable forms, 510

primary keys, 31-32

printing mailing labels, 271

queries, 212-214, 228-229, 388-390

appending records, 335-336, 343

archive tables, 331-333, 343

tables, 464

testing forms, 390-392

replicas, 329

reports, 399-400

numbers, 146

Report Wizards, 130-133, 145

startup parameters, 539-541

subforms, 251-254, 261, 490

summary reports, 398

summary-only reports, 293

switchboards, 308-313, 318, 321

tables

Design view, 26-30

existing databases, 44

mail merge documents, 478

saving, 31-32

storing repetitive data, 204-205

Table Wizard, 44

text

aligning, 411-413

tables, 66

update queries, 454-455

confirmation dialog boxes, closing, 338

Consulting databases, troubleshooting, 387

Contacts table, 7

Control Wizard, 305

controls, 107

calculated, adding, 262

colors, 425-426

ControlTips, adding, 416-418

forms, hiding, 428

multiple, formatting, 409-411

ControlTips

adding, 416-418

fields, adding to, 426

text, moving, 417

Convert/Open Database window, 152

converting databases

Access 97, 328-329

previous versions, 153

copying

databases, 2-4, 407-408

fields, 55, 186

queries, 91

records, 54-56

reports, 140

status bars, 415

text (ControlTips), 417

correcting. See AutoCorrect

counting fields, 92

criteria

editing, 390

entering, 79

multiple

applying, 439-442

filtering, 521

queries, 79-83, 96, 522-523
validation, 184-187
wildcards, 85, 525-526
crosstab queries, 482
multiple tables, 485-486, 505-506
row headers, 509
current record indicator, 50
Customers and Orders tables, 483
Customize dialog box, 418-420
customizing
AutoCorrect, 458-461
ControlTips, adding, 416-418
forms, 121
reports, 134-139, 145-147
groups, 148-149
saving, 139-140
text defaults, 199
toolbars, 418-421, 429

D

data access pages
creating, 169, 172
queries, creating, 173
saving, 162-163, 167
data entry, AutoCorrect, 458-461
data points, selecting, 502
data types, 27
editing, 43
optimizing, 201-202
selecting, 36
Database to Compact From dialog box, 330
Database Utilities command (Tools menu), 313
Database window, 5, 176
Database Wizard, 26, 45
databases
Access 97, saving as, 328-329
Address Book. See Address Book
AutoCorrect, 459-461
browsers, interacting, 164-165, 169-170
captions, adding, 99
cascade updates, creating, 452
CD-ROMs, opening, 18
charts
creating as forms, 496-498, 506
editing, 498-502
closing, 6, 15
colors, 404-406, 411-413
conditional formats, 179-181
configuring
deleting redundant fields, 384-387
output, 372-374
separating fields, 374-378
Consulting, troubleshooting, 387
controls, 425-426

ControlTips, adding, 416-418
copying, 2-4
creating, 24-26, 42-43, 45
decrypting, 539
defaults
configuring, 542, 544
entering, 194-195
design, modifying, 396-397
desktop shortcuts, creating, 66
Documenter tool, 477
embedded text, viewing, 537-538
encrypting, 537-539
Excel, exporting, 340
Export feature, 324-326, 328
fields
defaults, 477
entering dates, 245-247
filling, 243-245
replacing data, 436-438
requiring entries, 188-189
restricting entries, 184-187
security, 547
updating, 455
files, compacting, 329-330, 342
filtering, 532
footers
hyperlinks, 262
page numbers, 261
formatting, 176-178, 197
forms
adding combo boxes, 260
adding dates/time, 247-248
adding hyperlinks (Excel), 354-355
adding hyperlinks from, 348-354, 365
adding images, 263
attaching macros, 422
creating macros, 298-299, 302-305
executing macros, 305-308
hiding controls, 428
instructions, 427-428
printing, 254-257
subforms, 487-490
testing subforms, 398-399
indexes
multiple fields, 200
preventing multiple entries, 189-190
input masks, 181-183, 198
linking, 514-517
list boxes, creating, 238-240
macros, adding as buttons, 429
menus, 18
moving (Format Painter), 407-408
multiple controls, formatting, 409-411
multiple tables (crosstab queries), 485-486, 505-506
Name AutoCorrect feature, 468-471

naming, 26, 160
normalization, 402
objects
closing, 8
creating MDE files, 345
exporting, 345
opening, 6-7
saving as static HTML pages, 357-360
Office links, analyzing Excel, 471-473, 476
opening, 4-6, 156, 172
optimizing, 231
passwords
assigning, 534, 536, 546
deleting, 546
modifying, 536
performance, analyzing, 465-467, 475
PivotTable forms, creating, 510
queries
adding conditions, 508
archive tables, 331-333, 343
asterisks (*), 99
calculated fields, 86-88, 98
calculating, 96
comparison operators, 83-84
creating, 70-72, 95, 97
criteria, 79-83, 96
limiting records, 97
linking form letters, 401
modifying fields, 88-89
modifying properties, 92-94
saving, 75-76
searching date ranges, 98
selecting fields, 73-75
Total function, 90-92
Totals tool, 482-484
wildcards, 85-86
records, 52. See also records
Filter by Form, 520-522, 528
Filter by Selection, 518-520
renaming, 2-4
replicas, creating, 329
reports
combining, 492
creating macros, 299-301
publishing to Word, 346
restoring, 328
rules, 385
security, 377
shortcuts, 21
startup parameters, 539-541
status bar instructions, adding, 413-415, 426
subdatasheets
adding data, 231-232
viewing, 211

subforms
  adding records, 254
  creating, 251-253, 261
subreports, inserting, 491-495, 507
switchboards
  creating, 308-313, 318
  opening, 546
tab order, 249-250, 260
tables
  adding, 44, 228-229
  analyzing, 461-465, 475
  calculated expressions, 439-442
  copying to documents, 173
  defining relationships, 206-209
  deleting fields, 39-40, 43
  Design view, 26-30
  documenting design, 392
  editing fields, 35-36
  editing relationships, 230
  fields, 33-34, 43
  filling data, 216-217
  hiding columns, 547-548
  importing, 158-160, 168, 514-517
  linking to documents, 155-157, 161
  mail merge documents, 478
  many-to-many relationships, 382-384
  merging documents, 156-157, 161
  moving fields, 37-39, 43
  one-to-many relationships, 229-230
  pasting from Excel, 173
  printing relationships, 209-210, 212
  queries, 212-214
  referential integrity, 229
  relating relationships, 378-381
  replacing data, 432-436
  saving, 31-32
  searching duplicate records, 221-224
  storing repetitive data, 204-205
  Table Wizard, 44
  unhiding columns, 547-548
  update queries, 454-455
  updating, 219-221, 446-448, 450-451
  values, 442-445
testing, 388-392
text, aligning, 411-413
toolbars
  adding buttons, 426-427
  customizing, 418-421, 429
  editing buttons, 430
  properties, 429
tracking, 42-43
troubleshooting, 329-330, 342
versions, converting from, 153

Web pages
  creating, 169, 172
  queries, 173
  saving as, 162-163, 167
  zooming, 469
Datasheet view, 9, 24, 29
  modifying, 37-39
  queries. See queries
  tables, creating, 44
dates
  fields, entering, 245-247
  querying, 441
  ranges, searching, 98
decrypting databases, 539
defaults
  configuring, 542, 544
  fields, 477
  text, formatting, 199
  values, entering, 194-195
defining
  output, 372-374
  primary keys, 32
  relationships, 206-209, 518
deleting
  archived records, 333-334, 343
  AutoCorrect, 461
  buttons, 420
  data, 219-221
  duplicate fields, 280
  fields
    redundant fields, 384-387
    tables, 39-40, 43
  passwords, 546
  records, 55, 65
  tables, 446-448, 463
delimiters, 173, 326
design grids, 72
Design view, 24
  fields, 30
  forms, creating, 107-108, 120
  modifying, 37-39
  reports, modifying, 134-139, 147
  tables
    creating, 26-30
    fields, 30
desktop shortcuts, creating, 21, 66
disks
  multiple disk sets, searching, 451
  Display Database window, 540
  dividing
  tables, 378-381
Documenter, 477
documenting database designs, 392
drop-down lists, adding, 123-124
duplicate fields, deleting, 280

duplicate records, searching for, 221-224
dynasets, 70

E
Edit menu commands
  Find, 105, 537
  Primary Key, 32
  Replace, 66
  Select Record, 55
  Undo, 38, 53, 105
Edit Relationships dialog box, 207, 379, 446-447, 517
Edit Relationships window, 384
Edit Switchboard Item dialog box, 310
editing
  buttons, 430
  charts, 498-502
  criteria, 390
  data types, 43
  fields, 35-36, 53
  forms, 104-105, 120
  labels, 269, 289
  records, 52-53, 64
  reports
    renaming, 135
    tables
    relationships, 230
embedded text, viewing, 537-538
empty fields, 525
encrypting databases, 537-539
enforcing referential integrity, 207, 227-230
Enter Parameter Value dialog box, 524
entering
  AutoCorrect, 458-461
  criteria, 79
  data
    adding tables, 44
    headers/footers, 121
    updating tables, 219-221
  dates (fields), 245-247
  default values, 194-195
  fields
    preventing multiple entries, 189-190
    requiring, 188-189
    restricting, 184-187
  forms, 104-105, 120
  list selections, 240
equal signs (=), 87
equi-joins, 381
exams, 569-571
Excel
  charts, creating, 502, 511
  databases, exporting, 340
  Office links, analyzing with, 471-473, 476

queries. *See* queries
records, exporting, 473
tables (Access)
 importing, 158-160, 168
 moving, 161
exceptions (AutoCorrect),
configuring, 461
excluding operators, 525
executing
calculated update queries, 442
macros
 forms, 305-308
 queries, 337-338
 switchboard items, 311-313
queries, 75
exiting. *See closing*
expand indicators, 211
Export dialog box, 358
Export Table Orders To dialog
box, 339
Export Text Wizard dialog box, 325
exporting
databases
 Excel, 340
 objects, 345
records (Excel), 473
saving data, 324-328
tables (RTF), 344
Expression Builder, 187
Expression Builder dialog box, 185, 246
expressions
applying, 285
calculated, updating tables, 439-442
Mid, 439
queries, 83-84
reports, 137
wildcards, 85
zooming, 469

F

Field Properties dialog box, 89
fields
adding, 30
calculated
 creating, 453-454
 creating in reports, 271-276
 headers/footers, 282-283, 285, 291
 calculating
 queries, 86-88, 98
captions, adding, 99
colors, adding, 413
conditional formats, 179-181
ControlTips, adding, 426
copying, 55, 186
counting, 92
data types, editing, 43

dates, entering, 245-247
defaults, modifying, 477
Design view, 30
duplicate
 deleting, 280
 editing, 53
 emergency contact list reports
 selecting, 395-396
empty, 525
entries
 requiring, 188-189
 restricting, 184-187
foreign keys, modifying, 221
formatting, 176-178, 197
forms, adding, 109-111
grouping, 92
ID (row selectors), 32
indexes
 multiple entries, 200
 preventing multiple entries, 189-190
labels, 109
Like operator, 530-531
lists, 72, 99
lookup columns, adding, 198-200
multiple
 grouping, 294
 sorting, 62, 79
naming, 35
primary keys, 488
 adding to existing tables, 45
 creating, 31-32, 45
 indexes, 31
properties
 adding, 234-237
 modifying, 88-89
queries
 filling, 243-245
 selecting, 73-75
redundant, deleting, 384-387
reports
 adding, 138, 373
 selecting, 132
selecting, 396-397
status bar instructions, adding, 426
tables
 adding, 33-34, 43
 deleting, 39-40, 43
 editing, 35-36
 moving, 37-39, 43
text
 adding, 452
 input masks, 198
 limiting records, 97
 viewing, 294
text boxes, 109
Total function, 90-92

troubleshooting, 109
update queries, 432-438
updating, 455
File menu commands, 9
Close, 18
Export, 340, 358, 473
Get External Data, 158, 514
Import, 158
Link Tables, 515
New, 26
Open, 18
Page Setup, 129, 255
Print, 94, 130, 168, 257
Print Relationships, 392
Save, 107
Save As, 4, 31, 80
File New Database dialog box, 25
File Transfer Protocol (FTP), 369
files, 2. *See also* **databases**
CD-ROMs, opening, 18
closing, 6, 15
compacting, 329-330, 342
copying, 2-4
HTML, uploading, 369
hyperlinks
 adding, 348-354, 365
 Excel, 354-355
MDE, creating, 345
menus, 18
modifying, 153
objects
 closing, 8
 opening, 6-7
opening, 2, 4-6
RTF (Rich Text Format), exporting
 tables, 344
selecting, 153
text
 creating from tables, 342
 creating queries from, 344
 naming, 326-327
 saving data into, 324-326, 328
filling
fields (queries), 243-245
tables, 216-217
Filter by Exclusion, 531
Filter by Form, 514, 520-522, 528
Filter by Selection, 514, 518-520
filtering, 531
databases, 532
multiple criteria, 521
Find and Replace dialog box, 58-59
Find command (Edit menu), 105, 537
Find Duplicates Query Wizard, 221
finding. *See searching*
First Normal Form, 385

floppy disks, compacting files, 331

fonts, 268

colors, 405

Formatting toolbar, 116

mailing labels, 271

troubleshooting, 156

footers

calculated fields, adding, 282-285, 291

forms, 107, 121

hyperlinks, 262

numbering, 261

reports, 137

Force New Page property, 495

foreign keys, 207, 214

modifying, 221

tables, 216-217

Form Design view, 234-237

form letters, linking queries, 401

Form view, 107, 413-415, 426

Form Wizard, 102, 107

adding records, 254

creating, 251-253, 261

Form Wizard dialog box, 243-244, 251

Format Data Point dialog box, 502

Format Data Series dialog box, 499-501

Format Legend dialog box, 499-500

Format menu commands

Align Left, 138

Cells, 167

Column Width, 58

Hide Columns, 57-58

Size To Tallest, 138

Size To Widest, 138

Unhide Columns, 57

Format Painter, 407-408

Format Property dialog box, 180

formatting

AutoCorrect exceptions, 461

calculated fields, 453-454, 271-276

cascade updates, 452

charts

as forms, 496-498, 506

Excel, 502, 511

colors, 404-406

column widths, 56-58

compound filters, 531

conditional formats, 179-181

crosstab queries

multiple tables, 485-486, 505-506

row headers, 509

data, creating consistent formats, 176-178, 197

databases, 24-26, 42-43

Database Wizard, 45

documenting design, 392

Format Painter, 407-408

output, 372-374

separating fields, 374-378

testing, 388-392

defaults, 199, 542, 544

forms, 234-237

AutoForm, 102, 104, 119

Design view, 107-108, 120

properties, 421

hyperlinks, 351

input masks, 201

labels (reports), 149

list boxes, 238-240

Lookup columns, 191-194, 198-200

macros

Macro window, 317-318

opening switchboard forms, 314-315

mailing labels, 266-271, 289

multiple controls, 409-411

multiple-page HTML documents, 368

multiple queries, viewing functions, 510

one-to-many relationships, 516-517

PivotTable forms, 510

primary keys, 31-32

queries, 212-214, 228-229, 388-390

appending records, 335-336, 343

archive tables, 331-333, 343

saving as HTML, 366

tables, 464

testing forms, 390-392

replicas, 329

reports, 399-400, 495

numbers, 146

Report Wizards, 130-133, 145

startup parameters, 539-541

subforms, 251-254, 261, 490

summary reports, 398

summary-only reports, 293

switchboards, 308-313, 318

blank forms, 321

tables, 193

Design view, 26-30

existing databases, 44

mail merge documents, 478

one-to-many relationships, 229-230

saving, 31-32

saving as HTML, 366

storing repetitive data, 204-205

Table Wizard, 44

tables, 237

text, 66

alignment, 411-413

update queries, 454-455

forms, 102

AutoForms, creating, 102, 104, 119

breaks, inserting, 122

calculated controls, adding, 262

charts, creating as, 496-498, 506

closing, 107, 298-299

combo boxes

adding, 260

inserting, 124

controls, hiding, 428

creating (Design view), 107-108, 120

customizing, 121

data, importing from multiple tables, 263

dates/time

adding, 247-248

drop-down lists

adding, 123-124

editing, 104-105, 120

entering data, 104-105, 120

fields, adding, 109-111

footers, adding hyperlinks, 262

formatting, 234-237

Forts Normal Form, 385

headers, adding, 114-117, 121

hiding, 548

hyperlinks

adding from, 348-354, 365

Excel, 354-355

images

adding, 263

instructions

adding, 427-428

labels

adding, 114-117

letters (Word)

copying tables, 173

linking tables, 155-157, 161

merging tables, 156-157, 161

Macro Builder, viewing, 317-318

macros

attaching, 422

executing, 305-308

modifying, 111

moving, 111-113

opening, 106

PC Training Data Entry, 237

PivotTable, creating, 510

printing, 117, 122, 254-257

properties, configuring, 421

queries, testing, 390-392

resizing, 111-113

saving, 106

sections, 107

selection handles, 111

Software Training Data Entry, 235

subforms

adding, 487-490

adding records, 254

creating, 251-253, 261

testing, 398-399

switchboard, 314-315, 541
tabs, 124-125
    order, 249-250, 260
Web pages
    creating, 169, 172
    saving as, 162-163, 167
formulas, troubleshooting, 88
freezing columns, 65
FTP (File Transfer Protocol), 369
functions
    average, 292-293
    Help, 19
    multiple, creating queries, 510
    reports, adding, 137
    Total, 90-92

G

Get External Data command (File
    menu), 158, 514
graphics
    backgrounds, inserting, 285-286
    forms, adding, 263
grids, 72
grouped data
    calculating, 484
    crosstab queries, 509
    fields, 92
    headers/footers, 282-283, 285, 291
    multiple fields, 294
    records, 277-280, 290-292
    reports
        modifying, 148-149
        starting, 280-282

H

Header/Footer command (View
    menu), 114
headers
    calculated fields, adding, 282-283,
        285, 291
    forms, 107
        adding, 114-117
        entering data, 121
    labels
        adding, 140-142
        formatting, 149
    rows, creating crosstab queries, 509
Help, 11-13, 19
    function keys, 19
    indexes, 20
    Internet, 21
    printing, 549
    What's This? feature, 14
Hide Columns command (Format
    menu), 57-58

hiding
    columns, 56-58, 547-548
    controls, 428
    forms, 548
    relationships, 548
    tables, 548
HTML (Hypertext Markup Language),
    357
    multiple-page documents, creating, 368
    queries, saving as, 366
    static pages, saving database objects, 357-
        360
    tables, saving as, 366
    viewing, 360-362
hyperlinks
    adding from forms, 348-354, 365
    Excel, 354-355
    footers, adding, 262
    formatting, 351
    PowerPoint, adding, 367
    text, 350
    URLs (Uniform Resource Locators),
        adding, 367
    Word, 365

I-J-K

ID fields (row selectors), 32
images
    backgrounds, inserting, 285-286
    forms, adding, 263
importing
    form data, 263
    tables, 514-517
        dBASE III, 173
        Excel, 158-160, 168
        text, 173
indexes
    fields
        multiple entries, 200
        preventing multiple entries, 189-190
    Help, 13, 20
    primary keys, 31
inner joins, 381
input parameters, calculating, 530
input masks, 181-183, 198
    applying, 438
    creating, 201
inserting
    breaks, 122
    buttons, 419-420, 426-427
    calculated controls, 262
    calculated fields (queries), 86-88, 98
    calculations (reports), 137
    captions (queries), 99
    combo boxes, 124, 260
    conditions (queries), 508

ControlTips, 416-418
criteria, 80. See also expressions
data (subdatasheets), 231-232
dates/time
    forms, 247-248
    fields, 30
    forms, 109-111
    reports, 138, 373
    tables, 33-34, 43
functions (reports), 137
graphics, background, 285-286
headers, 114-117
hyperlinks
    Excel, 354-355
    footers, 262
    from forms, 348-354, 365
    PowerPoint, 367
    URLs (Uniform Resource Locators), 367
images, 263
instructions, 427-428
labels
    forms, 114-117
    reports, 140-142
lookup columns, 198-200
macros
    as buttons, 429
    page numbers
    footers, 261
primary key fields, 45
records, 65, 254
status bar instructions (Form view),
    413-415, 426
subforms, 487-490
subreports, 491-495, 507
tables, 209, 228-229
text (fields), 452
installing
    PinPoint 2000 software, 554-556
    Table Analyzer wizard, 462
    wizards, 5
instructions (forms), adding, 427-428
interactive forms
    PivotTables, 510
    tables, 164-165, 169-170
    Web pages
        creating, 169, 172
        queries, creating, 173
        saving as, 162-163, 167
interfaces
    Access, 8-9
    modifying, 479-480
Internet, 348. See also World Wide
    Web
    Help, 21
    uploading files, 369
intersection tables, 382

intranets, 348
joins, 216-217, 377-381
keyboard shortcuts, 6, 411
   databases, creating, 26
   desktop shortcuts, creating, 21, 66
   fields, adding, 30
   Print command, 130
   records, navigating, 52
   tables, saving, 32
keys
   foreign, 207, 214
      filling data, 216-217
      modifying, 221
   Help function, 19
   primary
      creating, 31-32, 45
      defining, 32
      indexes, 31
      sorting records, 60-62
   symbols, 32

L

Label Wizard, 149, 266-271, 289
labels, 108
   fields, 109
   forms, adding, 114-117
   mailing
      configuring printing, 271
      creating, 266-271, 289
      sizing fonts, 271
   moving, 113
   reports
      adding, 140-142
      formatting, 149
LAN (local area network), 348
landscape orientation, 129
left outer joins, 381
legends, 497, 500
Like operator
   fields, matching, 530-531
   parameters, partial matches, 529
limiting records, 97
linking
   databases, 514-517
   Office, analyzing Excel data, 471-473, 476
   queries (form letters), 401
   tables, 378-381
      automatically, 446-448
      documents (Word), 155-157, 161
      many-t-many relationships, 382-384
lists
   drop-down, 123-124
   fields, 72, 99

Lookup columns, creating, 191-194, 198-200
   selections, entering, 240
lists boxes, creating, 238-240
Lookup columns, creating, 191-194, 198-200
Lookup Wizard, 27, 191-194, 198-200, 205, 241-242

M

Macro Builder forms
   attaching macros, 422
   viewing, 317-318
macros, 298
   as buttons, adding, 429
   closing forms, 298-299
   conditions, configuring, 321
   creating
      Macro Window, 317-318
      opening forms, 302-305
   existing, 319
   executing
      forms, 305-308
      queries, 337-338
   Macro Builder, attaching to forms, 422
   printing reports, 299-301
   switchboards
      opening, 314-315
      executing, 311-313
mail merge
   memos, printing, 168, 171
   queries, 158
   tables, 156-157, 161
mailing labels
   creating, 266-271, 289
   fonts, sizing, 271
   printing, configuring, 271
Make Table dialog box, 332
Make Table query dialog box, 334
many-to-many relationships, 382-384
margins
   configuring, 255
   reports, 145
matching
   criteria (queries), 79-83, 96, 522-523
   fields (Like operator), 530-531
MDE files (database objects), creating, 345
menus, 18
merging (Word documents), 156-157, 161, 163
messages
   prompting, 522-523
   status bars, adding ControlTips, 416-418
Microsoft Web page, 21

Mid expressions, 439
MOUS certification, 569-571
moving
   databases
      Format Painter, 407-408
      objects, 345
   fields, 37-39, 43
   forms, 111-113
   label boxes, 113
   records, 50-51, 54-56, 473
   reports, 140
   status bars, 415
   tables, 167, 377
   ControlTips, 417
   properties, 113, 411-413
multi-tiered switchboards, 320

N

Name AutoCorrect, 468-471
naming
   databases, 3, 26, 160
   documents, 160
   fields, 35
   files, 153
   forms, 106
   reports, 135, 139-140
   tables, 31, 463
   text files, 326-327
navigating
   Access windows, 8-9
   records, 50-52
   subdatasheets, 211
negative values, conditional formats, 179-181
New command (File menu), 26
new features, 19
New Form dialog box, 102, 107, 243, 251, 496
New menu commands (Form Wizard), 243
New Query dialog box, 71, 81, 212, 222, 331, 432, 482
New Report dialog box, 130-133, 145, 267
New Table dialog box, 27-28
normalization, 384, 402
null values, 189
   calculating, 90
   conditional formats, 179-181
numbering footers, 261
numbers
   reports, 146
   serial, analyzing, 451

O

Object Linking and Embedding (OLE), 27

objects
closing, 8
databases
exporting, 345
saving as static HTML pages, 357-360
Name AutoCorrect feature, 468-471
opening, 6-7
unbound, 273

Office links, 458, 471-473, 476
Office Assistant, 11-14, 19-20
Office Clipboard, 56
Office Find Files dialog box, 330
OLE (Object Linking and Embedding), 27
one-to-many relationships, 206, 514, 516-517. *See also* relationships
creating, 229-230
tables, 378-381
one-to-one relationships, 378-381
online. *See Internet*
Open command (File menu), 18
Open dialog box, 2, 4, 7, 18, 176
Open Exclusive option, 536
opening
Address Book, 4-6
AutoCorrect, 460
databases, 156, 172
CD-ROMs, 18
menus, 18
shortcuts, 6
File menu, 9
files, 2, 4-7
forms, 106, 302-305
Properties dialog box, 94
queries, 91
switchboards, 314-315, 546
tables (Address Book), 6-7
Zoom dialog box, 87
operators
And, 83
Between, 529
Between...And, 98
comparison
parameters, 524-525
queries, 83-84
concatenation, 531-532
excluding, 525
Like
matching fields, 530-531
partial matches, 529
Or, 83

optimizing
data types, 201-202
databases, 231, 465-467, 475
options
Analyze It With Excel, 472
Open Exclusive, 536
startup parameters
configuring, 539-541
Options command (Tools menu), 9, 415, 542
Options command (View menu), 3
Options Datasheet dialog box, 543
Options dialog box, 415, 542
Or operators, 83
orders (tabs), modifying, 249-250, 260
output
configuring, 372-378
reports, 134-135
tables , 128-130, 144

P

Page Setup dialog box, 129, 255
Page Wizard, 161-162, 169
palettes. *See colors*
partial matches (Like operators), 529
passwords
assigning, 534, 536, 546
deleting, 546
modifying, 536
selecting, 536
Paste As dialog box, 91, 335
pasting
fields, 186
records, 54-56
status bars, 415
tables, 173, 377
text, 417
PC Training Data Entry form, 237
Performance Analyzer, 458, 465-467, 475
PinPoint 2000, 552-554
concurrency with Office applications, 552
crashes, 566
Evaluations, 553
running, 563-564
starting, 558-560
Trainer/Evaluation pairs, 552
installing, 554-556
Launcher, 552
reports, 563-566
starting
PinPoint, 556-558
Trainers/Evaluations, 558-560
system requirements, 553-554

Trainers, 552-553
running, 560-564
starting, 558-560
Trainer/Evaluation pairs, 552
uninstalling, 566-567
PivotTable forms, creating, 510
placeholders, 182
planning databases
output, 372-374
separating fields, 374-378
portrait orientation, 130
positive vales (conditional formats), 179-181
PowerPoint
hyperlinks, adding, 367
multiple entries, 189-190
preferences
AutoCorrect, 458-461
ControlTips, 416-418
reports, 134, 136-140, 145, 147
toolbars, 418-421, 429
previewing
charts, 497
printing, 129, 255
reports, 135
previous versions. *See versions*
Primary Key command (Edit menu), 32
primary keys
creating, 31-32
defining, 32
existing tables, adding to, 45
fields, 488
indexes, 31
multiple fields, creating, 45
records, sorting, 60-62
Print dialog box, 94, 130, 157, 257
printing
forms, 117, 122, 254-257
Help, 549
mail merge, 168, 171
mailing labels, configuring, 271
previewing, 129, 255
queries, 94
records, 117
relationships, 209-212, 392
reports, 134-135, 299-301
tables, 128-130, 144
documenting databases, 392
relationships, 228
prompting messages, viewing, 522-523
Properties dialog box, 4, 94, 147, 285, 417, 423
protecting database objects (MDE files), 345
publishing
reports (Word), 346
forms (headers/footers), 121

Q

qualifiers (text), 326
queries, 6
    archive tables, creating, 331-333, 343
    Between...And operators, searching date
        ranges, 98
    calculated fields, 86-88, 98
    calculating, 96
    captions, adding, 99
    combo boxes, searching, 241-242
    comparison operators, 83-84
    copying, 91
    creating, 70-72, 95, 97, 212-214, 388-392
    criteria, 79-83, 96
    crosstabs. *See* crosstab queries
    data access pages, creating, 173
    dates, 441
    Excel, analyzing data, 471-473, 476
    executing, 75
    field lists, 99
    fields
        filling, 243-245
        modifying, 88-89
        selecting, 73-75
    filling data, 216-217
    form letters, linking, 401
    HTML (Hypertext Markup Language),
        saving as, 366
    macros, executing, 337-338
    mail merge, 158
    modifying, 77-78, 359
    multiple, creating queries, 510
    opening, 91
    parameters, 514
        comparison operators, 524-525
        matching criteria, 522-523
        wildcards, 525-526
    printing, 94, 128-130, 144
    properties, 92-94, 99
    records
        appending, 335-336, 343
        limiting, 97
    sorting, 77-78
    tables
        creating, 228-229, 464
        updating, 219-221
    text files, creating from, 344
    Totals tool, 482-484, 508
    troubleshooting, 81, 333, 343
    update, 432
        adding text to fields, 452
        executing, 442
        replacing data in fields, 432-438
        saving data, 444
        troubleshooting, 442
    wildcards, 85-86
Query Design view, 84

Query dialog box, 332
Query Properties dialog box, 92
Query Wizard, 71

R

ranges (dates), searching, 98
read-only mode (macros), 302-305
records
    adding, 48-50, 55, 64, 280-282
    AutoCorrect, 459-461
    copying/pasting, 54-56
    criteria (queries), 79-83, 96
    deleting, 55, 65
    editing, 52-53, 64
    Excel, exporting, 473
    existing tables, searching, 221-224
    Filter by Form, 520-522, 528
    Filter by Selection, 518-520
    grouping, 277-280, 290
    inserting, 65
    limiting, 97
    navigating, 50-52
    printing, 117
    queries, appending, 335-336, 343
    replacing, 65-66
    Report Wizard, grouping, 292
    saving, 53
    searching, 58-60, 65-66, 85
    sorting, 60-62, 162, 220, 277-280, 290
    tables
        deleting, 333-334, 343
        printing, 128-130, 144
    unmatched, searching, 227-228
redundant fields, deleting, 384-387
referential integrity
    enforcing, 207, 227-230
    tables, 229, 384
relationships, 228-229, 378-381
    editing, 230
    hiding, 548
    many-to-many relationships, 382-384
    one-to-many, 229-230, 514-517
    printing, 392
    reports, updating, 211
    tables, 31
        defining, 206-209, 518
        many-to-many, 382-384
        printing, 209-210, 212, 228
        relating, 378-381
    unmatched records, searching, 227-228
removing. *See* deleting
renaming, *See* naming
replacing
    records, 65-66
    text, 459
    update queries, 432-438

Replication command (Tools
    menu), 329
Report Chart Wizard, 499
Report Wizard, 130-133, 145, 292
reports, 128
    AutoReport Wizard, 131
    calculated fields, creating, 271-276
    combining, 492
    copying, 140
    creating, 399-400
    emergency contact lists, selecting fields,
        395-396
    expressions, 137
    fields
        adding, 138, 373
        selecting, 132
    footers, 137
    formatting, 495
    graphic backgrounds, 285-286
    groups
        modifying, 148-149
        starting, 280-282
    labels
        adding, 140-142
        creating, 266-271, 289
        formatting, 149
    margins, 145
    modifying, 134, 136-139, 145, 147
    numbers, formatting, 146
    previewing, 135
    printing, 134-135, 299-301
    records, grouping, 277-280, 290
    relationships, updating, 211
    renaming, 135, 139-140
    Report Wizards, 130-133, 145
    subreports, inserting, 491-495, 507
    summary, 145-146, 398
    summary-only, 293
    wizards, 136
    Word, publishing, 346
Required Property dialog box, 188
resizing
    charts, 497
    columns, 56-57
    Computer Type text box, 240
    forms, 111-113
restoring databases, 328
restricting entries (fields), 184-187
results (queries), 93
right outer joins, 381
rows
    headers, creating crosstab queries, 509
    selectors, 32
RTF (rich text format), 344

rules
databases, 385
validation, 184
Run button, 438

S

salaries, updating, 453
sans serifs, 268
Save As command (File menu), 4,
31, 80
Save As Data Access Page dialog
box, 163
Save As dialog box, 31, 75, 106, 140
Save command (File menu), 107
saving
data
Export feature, 324-326, 328
update queries, 444
databases
objects as static HTML pages, 357-360
as Access 97, 328-329
forms, 106
queries, 75-76
as HTML, 366
records, 53
repetitive data in tables, 204-205
reports, renaming, 139-140
tables, 31-32
as HTML, 366
keyboard shortcuts, 32
Web pages, 162-163, 167
screens. See interfaces
searching
combo boxes, 241-242
dates, 441
Between...And operator, 98
Help, 11. *See also* Office Assistant
multiple disk sets, 451
records, 58-60, 65-66, 85
tables, 221-224
text fields, 97
unmatched records, 227-228
section bars, 294
sections
forms, 107
headers/footers, adding, 114
security
databases, 377
assigning passwords, 534, 536, 546
deleting passwords, 546
encrypting, 537-539
MDE files, 345
modifying passwords, 536
single fields, 547
user-level, 539, 550
Security command (Tools menu), 536

select queries, 75
Select Query window, 72, 213
Select Record command (Edit
menu), 55
selecting
columns, 77
data points, 502
data types, 36
fields, 396-397
emergency contact list reports, 395-396
queries, 73-75
reports, 132
files, 153
lists, entering, 240
multiple controls (shortcuts), 411
passwords, 536
records
Filter by Form, 520-522, 528
Filter by Selection, 518-520
selection handles (forms), 111
selectors, row, 32
separating
fields, 374-378
serial numbers
analyzing, 451
serifs, 268
Set Database Password dialog box, 535
share-level security, 534
databases
desktops, 21
opening, 6
multiple controls, 411
shortcuts, 6, 411
databases, creating, 26
desktop, creating, 21, 66
fields, adding, 30
Print command, 130
records, navigating, 52
tables, saving, 32
Show Table dialog box, 71-72, 81, 84,
206, 213, 331, 433, 482-483, 516
simple queries, creating, 95, 97
Simple Query Wizard dialog box, 518
single fields (security), 547
Size To Tallest command (Format
menu), 138
Size To Widest command (Format
menu), 138
sizing
charts, 497
fonts (mailing labels), 271
sorting
multiple fields, 62, 79
queries, 77-78
records, 60-62, 162, 220, 277-280, 290
Sorting and Grouping dialog box, 278
spell checker, 66, 476

spreadsheets. See Excel
SQL (Structured Query Language),
526
standards, database, 385
starting
AutoCorrect, 460
groups (reports), 280-282
mail merge (Word), 163
PinPoint, 556-560
Properties dialog box, 94
queries, 70-72, 91
switchboard forms, creating macros,
314-315
Zoom dialog box, 87
Startup command (Tools menu), 540
startup parameters, configuring,
539-541
static HTML pages
database objects, saving as, 357-360
status bars, 9
ControlTips, adding, 416-418
instructions
adding, 413-415, 426
fields, 426
moving, 415
Structured Query Language
(SQL), 526
subdatasheets
adding data, 231-232
viewing, 209-212
Subform Wizard dialog box, 488
Subform/Subreport Wizard
subreports, inserting, 491-495, 507
subforms, creating, 251-253, 261
formatting, 490
forms
adding, 487-490
testing, 398-399
records, adding, 254
Subtotals dialog box, 473
summarizing
reports, 145-146
design, 398
summary-only reports, 293
queries (Total function), 90-92
Summary Options dialog box, 146
summary-only reports, 293
Switchboard Manager, 308-313, 318
switchboards, 298, 541
blank forms, creating, 321
creating, 308-313, 318
forms, opening, 314-315
macros, executing queries, 337-338
modifying, 313
multi-tiered, 320
opening, 546
symbols, key, 32

T

Tab Order dialog box, 249-250. *See also* **tabs**
Table Analyzer, 458
Table Design view, 37, 176
Table Wizard, 44
tables
  analyzing, 461-465, 475
  archives
    appending records, 335-336, 343
    creating, 331-333, 343
    deleting, 333-334, 343
  browsers, interacting, 164-165, 169-170
  calculated expressions, updating, 439-442
  closing, 8
  columns
    hiding, 547-548
    modifying, 56-58
    unhiding, 547-548
  combo boxes, searching, 241-242
  Contacts, 7
  Customer and Orders, 483
  dBASE III, importing, 173
  deleting, 463
  Design view, creating, 26-30
  dividing, 378-381
  documents (Word)
    copying, 173
    linking, 155-157, 161
    merging, 156-157, 161
  Excel
    exporting, 340
    importing, 158-160, 168
    moving, 161
  existing databases
    adding to, 44
    Table Wizard, 44
  fields
    adding, 33-34, 43
    deleting, 39-40, 43
    editing, 35-36
    moving, 37-39, 43
    separating, 374-378
  filling data, 216-217
  formatting, 193, 237
  hiding, 548
  HTML (Hypertext Markup Language), 366
  importing, 514-517
  intersection, 382
  joining, 377, 379
  linking, 378-384
  mail merge documents, creating, 478
  multiple
    creating crosstab queries, 485-486,
      505-506
    creating update queries, 454-455
    importing form data, 263

  naming, 31
  opening, 6-7
  pasting, 377
  primary key fields, adding, 45
  printing, 128-130, 144, 392
  queries
    creating, 212-214, 228-229, 464
    updating, 219-221
  records, 54. *See also* records
  referential integrity, 229, 384
  relating, 228-229
  relationships, 31
    defining, 206-209, 518
    editing, 230
    many-to-many, 382-384
    one-to-many, 229-230
    printing, 209-212, 228
    relating, 378-381
  renaming, 463
  RTF (Rich Text Format), exporting, 344
  saving, 31-32
  storing repetitive data, 204-205
  subdatasheets, creating, 212
  text
    creating, 342
    formatting, 66
  update queries, replacing data, 432-436
  updating, 450-451
    creating calculated fields, 453-454
    linking automatically, 446-448
  values, updating, 442-445
tabs
  forms, 124-125
  order, 113, 249-250, 260
testing
  databases, 388-392
  subforms, 398-399
text
  boxes
    fields, 109
    moving, 113
    resizing Computer Type, 240
  colors, 404-406
  ControlTips, moving, 417
  defaults, formatting, 199
  embedded, viewing, 537-538
  fields
    adding, 452
    formatting, 197
    input masks, 198
    limiting records, 97
    update queries, 432-438
    viewing, 294
  files
    creating from tables, 342
    creating queries from, 344
    naming, 326-327

  hyperlinks, 350
  naming, 160
  qualifiers, 326
  replacing, 459
  saving data into, 324-326, 328
  tables
    formatting, 66
    importing, 173
  validation, 184
  Word
    copying tables, 173
    linking to tables, 155-157, 161
    merging tables, 156-157, 161
Text Box tool, 273
Tile Vertically command (Window menu), 337
title bars, 9
toolbars
  buttons
    adding, 419-420, 426-427
    deleting, 420
    editing, 430
  Clipboard, 56
  customizing, 418-421, 429
  Formatting, 116
  Mail Merge, 156
  properties, 429
  resetting, 421
  Table Design, 37
  Utility 1, 419
  Web, 352
Toolbars command (View menu), 37, 156
tools
  Access, 66-67
  AutoCorrect, 458
  Documenter, 477
  Macro Builder, 422
  Performance Analyzer, 465-467, 475
  spell checker, 476
  Table Analyzer, 461-465, 475
  Text Box, 273
  Total function, 90-92
  Totals, 482-484, 508
Tools menu commands
  Analyze, 462
  AutoCorrect, 459
  Database Utilities, 313
  Office Links, 472
  Options, 9, 415, 542
  Replication, 329
  Security, 536
  Startup, 540
Total function, 90-92
Totals tool (queries), 482-484, 508
tracking databases, 42-43
Trainers. *See* **PinPoint 2000**

troubleshooting, 11-13, 19
    Consulting database, 387
    data access pages, 169, 172
    databases, 329-330, 342
    fields, 109
    fonts, 156
    Format Painter, 408
    formulas, 88
    function keys (Help), 19
    queries, 81, 333, 343
    Table Analyzer wizard, 462
    update queries, 442
    What's This? feature, 14

U

unbound objects, 273
Undo command (Edit menu), 38, 53, 105
unhiding columns, 57-58
Uniform Resource Locators. See URLs
unmatched records, searching, 227-228
Unset Database Password dialog boxes, 536
update queries, 432
    executing, 442
    fields, replacing data, 436-438
    saving data, 444
    tables
        creating, 454-455
        replacing data, 432-436
    text, adding to fields, 452
    troubleshooting, 442
updating
    cascade updates, creating, 452
    fields, 455
    Name AutoCorrect feature, 468-471
    relationships reports, 211
    salaries, 453
    tables, 450-451
        calculated expressions, 439-442
        creating calculated fields, 453-454
        linking automatically, 446-448
        pasting cells (Excel), 173
        queries, 219-221
        values, 442-445
uploading HTML files, 369
URLs (Uniform Resource Locators), 349, 367
user input parameters, 530
user-level security, 539, 550
utilities
    Access, 66-67
    Documenter, 477
    Macro Builder, 422

    Performance Analyzer, 465-467, 475
    spell checker, 476
    Table Analyzer, 461-465, 475
    Totals, 482-484, 508
Utility I toolbar, 419

V

validation criteria, 184-187
VBA (Visual Basic for Applications), 345
versions
    Access 97, saving as, 328-329
    converting, 153
    Name AutoCorrect feature, 470
    opening, 156, 172
View menu commands
    Clipboard, 56
    Header/Footer, 114
    Options, 3
    Table Design, 37
    Toolbars, 37, 156
viewing
    embedded text, 537-538
    expressions, 469
    forms (Macro Builder), 317-318
    functions (multiple queries), 510
    HTML (Hypertext Markup Language), 360-362
    prompting messages, 522-523
    subdatasheets, 209-212
    text fields (CanGrow property), 294
    Web toolbar, 353
views
    Datasheet, 9, 24, 29
        creating tables, 44
        modifying, 37-39
    Design, 24
        creating forms, 107-108, 120
        creating tables, 26-30
        modifying, 37-39
        modifying reports, 134, 136-139, 147
    Form, 107, 234-237, 413-415, 426
    modifying, 37-39
    Query Design, 84
    Table Design, 176

W-Z

Web toolbar, 352
What's This? feature, 13-14. *See also* Office Assistant
white space
    configuring, 255
    reports, 145
width (columns), 56-58
wildcards, 85-86, 525-526

wizards
    adding, 5
    Answer, 12, 329
    AutoForm, 102, 104, 119
    AutoReport, 131
    charts, 496-498, 506
    Command Button, 319
    Control, 305
    Crosstab Query, 485
    Database, 26, 45
    Find Duplicates Query, 221
    Find Unmatched Query, 221
    Form, 102, 107
        adding records, 254
        creating subforms, 251-253, 261
    Import, 173
    Import Spreadsheet, 159
    Input Masks, 181
    Label, 149, 266-271, 289
    Lookup, 27, 191-194, 198-200, 241-242
    Microsoft Word Mail Merge, 154
    Page, 161-162, 169
    Performance Analyzer, 458
    Query, 71
    Report, 130-133, 136, 145, 292
    Report Chart, 499
    Simple Query, 518
    Subform/Subreport, 491-495, 507
    Table, 44
    Table Analyzer, 458, 461-465, 475
Word
    embedded text, viewing, 537-538
    forms, linking, 365
    mail merge, starting, 163
    reports, publishing, 346
    tables (Access)
        copying, 173
        linking, 155-157, 161
        merging, 156-157, 161
worksheets. *See* Excel
World Wide Web, 348
    browsers, 164-165, 169-170, 348
    HTML
        uploading, 369
        viewing, 360-362
    queries
        creating, 173
        saving as, 162-163, 167
    Web pages
        creating, 169, 172
        Microsoft Help, 21

Zoom dialog box, 86-87, 524
Zoom property, 390, 469

SINGLE PC LICENSE AGREEMENT AND LIMITED WARRANTY

READ THIS LICENSE CAREFULLY BEFORE USING THIS PACKAGE. BY USING THIS PACKAGE, YOU ARE AGREE-ING TO THE TERMS AND CONDITIONS OF THIS LICENSE. IF YOU DO NOT AGREE, DO NOT USE THE PACKAGE. PROMPTLY RETURN THE UNUSED PACKAGE AND ALL ACCOMPANYING ITEMS TO THE PLACE YOU OBTAINED. *THESE TERMS APPLY TO ALL LICENSED SOFTWARE ON THE DISK EXCEPT THAT THE TERMS FOR USE OF ANY SHARE-WARE OR FREEWARE ON THE DISKETTES ARE AS SET FORTH IN THE ELECTRONIC LICENSE LOCATED ON THE DISK:*

1. GRANT OF LICENSE and OWNERSHIP: The enclosed computer programs and data ("Software") are licensed, not sold, to you by Prentice-Hall, Inc. ("We" or the "Company") and in consideration of your purchase or adoption of the accompanying Company textbooks and/or other materials, and your agreement to these terms. We reserve any rights not granted to you. You own only the disk(s) but we and/or our licensors own the Software itself. This license allows you to use and display your copy of the Software on a single computer (i.e., with a single CPU) at a single location for academic use only, so long as you comply with the terms of this Agreement. You may make one copy for back up, or transfer your copy to another CPU, provided that the Software is usable on only one computer.

2. RESTRICTIONS: You may not transfer or distribute the Software or documentation to anyone else. Except for backup, you may not copy the documentation or the Software. You may not network the Software or otherwise use it on more than one computer or computer terminal at the same time. You may not reverse engineer, disassemble, decompile, modify, adapt, translate, or create derivative works based on the Software or the Documentation. You may be held legally responsible for any copying or copyright infringement which is caused by your failure to abide by the terms of these restrictions.

3. TERMINATION: This license is effective until terminated. This license will terminate automatically without notice from the Company if you fail to comply with any provisions or limitations of this license. Upon termination, you shall destroy the Documentation and all copies of the Software. All provisions of this Agreement as to limitation and disclaimer of warranties, limitation of liability, remedies or damages, and our ownership rights shall survive termination.

4. LIMITED WARRANTY AND DISCLAIMER OF WARRANTY: Company warrants that for a period of 60 days from the date you purchase this SOFTWARE (or purchase or adopt the accompanying textbook), the Software, when properly installed and used in accordance with the Documentation, will operate in substantial conformity with the description of the Software set forth in the Documentation, and that for a period of 30 days the disk(s) on which the Software is delivered shall be free from defects in materials and workmanship under normal use. The Company does not warrant that the Software will meet your requirements or that the operation of the Software will be uninterrupted or error-free. Your only remedy and the Company's only obligation under these limited warranties is, at the Company's option, return of the disk for a refund of any amounts paid for it by you or replacement of the disk. THIS LIMITED WARRANTY IS THE ONLY WARRANTY PROVIDED BY THE COMPANY AND ITS LICEN-SORS, AND THE COMPANY AND ITS LICENSORS DISCLAIM ALL OTHER WARRANTIES, EXPRESS OR IMPLIED, INCLUDING WITHOUT LIMITATION, THE IMPLIED WARRANTIES OF MERCHANTABILITY AND FITNESS FOR A PARTICU-LAR PURPOSE. THE COMPANY DOES NOT WARRANT, GUARANTEE OR MAKE ANY REPRESENTATION REGARDING THE ACCURACY, RELIABILITY, CURRENTNESS, USE, OR RESULTS OF USE, OF THE SOFTWARE.

5. LIMITATION OF REMEDIES AND DAMAGES: IN NO EVENT, SHALL THE COMPANY OR ITS EMPLOYEES, AGENTS, LICENSORS, OR CONTRACTORS BE LIABLE FOR ANY INCIDENTAL, INDIRECT, SPECIAL, OR CONSEQUENTIAL DAM-AGES ARISING OUT OF OR IN CONNECTION WITH THIS LICENSE OR THE SOFTWARE, INCLUDING FOR LOSS OF USE, LOSS OF DATA, LOSS OF INCOME OR PROFIT, OR OTHER LOSSES, SUSTAINED AS A RESULT OF INJURY TO ANY PER-SON, OR LOSS OF OR DAMAGE TO PROPERTY, OR CLAIMS OF THIRD PARTIES, EVEN IF THE COMPANY OR AN AUTHORIZED REPRESENTATIVE OF THE COMPANY HAS BEEN ADVISED OF THE POSSIBILITY OF SUCH DAMAGES. IN NO EVENT SHALL THE LIABILITY OF THE COMPANY FOR DAMAGES WITH RESPECT TO THE SOFTWARE EXCEED THE AMOUNTS ACTUALLY PAID BY YOU, IF ANY, FOR THE SOFTWARE OR THE ACCOMPANYING TEXTBOOK. BECAUSE SOME JURISDICTIONS DO NOT ALLOW THE LIMITATION OF LIABILITY IN CERTAIN CIRCUMSTANCES, THE ABOVE LIM-ITATIONS MAY NOT ALWAYS APPLY TO YOU.

6. GENERAL: THIS AGREEMENT SHALL BE CONSTRUED IN ACCORDANCE WITH THE LAWS OF THE UNITED STATES OF AMERICA AND THE STATE OF NEW YORK, APPLICABLE TO CONTRACTS MADE IN NEW YORK, AND SHALL BENE-FIT THE COMPANY, ITS AFFILIATES AND ASSIGNEES. HIS AGREEMENT IS THE COMPLETE AND EXCLUSIVE STATEMENT OF THE AGREEMENT BETWEEN YOU AND THE COMPANY AND SUPERSEDES ALL PROPOSALS OR PRIOR AGREEMENTS, ORAL, OR WRITTEN, AND ANY OTHER COMMUNICATIONS BETWEEN YOU AND THE COMPANY OR ANY REPRESEN-TATIVE OF THE COMPANY RELATING TO THE SUBJECT MATTER OF THIS AGREEMENT. If you are a U.S. Government user, this Software is licensed with "restricted rights" as set forth in subparagraphs (a)-(d) of the Commercial Computer-Restricted Rights clause at FAR 52.227-19 or in subparagraphs (c)(1)(ii) of the Rights in Technical Data and Computer Software clause at DFARS 252.227-7013, and similar clauses, as applicable.

Should you have any questions concerning this agreement or if you wish to contact the Company for any reason, please contact in writing:

Director, New Media

Prentice Hall

1 Lake Street

Upper Saddle River, New Jersey 07458